Troubleshooting the PC

Patrick E. Regan
Intel Corporation

Prentice Hall
Upper Saddle River, New Jersey   Columbus, Ohio

Library of Congress Cataloging-in-Publication Data

Regan, Patrick E.
  Troubleshooting the PC / Patrick Regan.
    p. cm.
  Includes index.
  ISBN 0-13-095796-8
    1. Microcomputers—Maintenance and repair. I. Title.
TK7887.R44 2000   99-15344
004.165—dc21   CIP

Publisher: Charles E. Stewart, Jr.
Associate Editor: Kate Linsner
Production Editor: Alexandrina Benedicto Wolf
Cover photo: The Stock Market
Cover Design Coordinator: Karrie Converse-Jones
Production Coordination: Clarinda Publication Services
Cover Designer: Janoski Advertising Design
Production Manager: Deidra M. Schwartz
Marketing Manager: Ben Leonard

This book was set in Times Roman by The Clarinda Company and was printed
and bound by The Banta Company. The cover was printed by Phoenix Color Corp.

Box shots reprinted with permission from Microsoft Corporation.
This publication includes images from CorelDRAW.

© 2000 by Prentice-Hall, Inc.
Pearson Education
Upper Saddle River, New Jersey 07458

Printed in the United States of America

10 9 8 7 6 5 4 3 2 1

ISBN: 0-13-095796-8

Prentice-Hall International (UK) Limited, *London*
Prentice-Hall of Australia Pty. Limited, *Sydney*
Prentice-Hall Canada Inc., *Toronto*
Prentice-Hall Hispanoamericana, S. A., *Mexico*
Prentice-Hall of India Private Limited, *New Delhi*
Prentice-Hall of Japan, Inc., *Tokyo*
Prentice-Hall (Singapore) Pte. Ltd., *Singapore*
Editora Prentice-Hall do Brasil, Ltda., *Rio de Janeiro*

Dedicated to my father, who always was there when I needed him.

Preface

Computers are a fast-paced technology that requires constant learning. People who learn how to fix computers must become familiar with new and old technology to become effective technicians.

This book is intended for the basic computer user who wants to be a successful PC technician and who may desire to pass the A+ PC technician exam. For more information on the A+ test, see Appendix A. It is assumed that users of this book are familiar with the computer, know how to use the computer, have a general understanding of Windows 3.XX or Windows 95/98, and have basic word-processing and spreadsheets skills.

Each of the chapters usually begins with basic concepts and ends with a troubleshooting section that includes questions to check understanding, emphasize troubleshooting skills, and prepare the reader to take the A+ test. Each chapter also includes hands-on exercises to reinforce basic skills and troubleshooting practices.

When planning a computer curriculum, it is often difficult for a group of computer professionals to agree on the order of topics. In this book, the basic hardware components (microprocessor, motherboard, RAM, and drives) are covered first, followed by the add-on peripherals. The book ends with the operating systems. Depending on their experience, instructors may choose a different order.

As you go through the book, you will notice that a lot of information is repeated. This allows the chapters to be taught out of order and helps to complete the overall picture. In addition, I have found that the best way to teach this material is to repeat the information several times and combine it with hands-on exercises.

I have included important web sites that are necessary to become a successful computer technician. However, I also left out many web sites so that students could learn how to find information on the Internet. Therefore, some of the hands-on exercises include finding patches, drivers, jumper settings, and technical information on the Internet.

Brief Contents

Contents

1 A PC Overview

INTRODUCTION

Before you can do any troubleshooting, you must learn the components of the personal computer, or PC. These include the case, monitor, and keyboard. In addition, you must be familiar with the operating system and application software and have a basic understanding of how they interact with hardware. This chapter introduces you to the primary basic components of the computer, the most common operating systems, and the application software packages used today.

OBJECTIVES

1. Explain the difference between a personal computer, minicomputer, and mainframe computer.
2. Explain the difference between hardware and software.

1

3. Explain the importance of data.
4. Identify the major PC components.
5. Identify the purpose of all the major PC components.
6. Given the size and density of a floppy disk, state its capacity.
7. List the purpose and function of the operating system.
8. Compare and differentiate the common PC operating systems.
9. Explain the difference between an operating system and an operating environment.
10. Explain the difference between the de jure standard and the de facto standard.
11. Explain how software interacts with hardware.

1.1 COMPUTERS

A **computer** is a machine composed of electronic devices used to process data. **Data** are the raw facts, numbers, letters, or symbols that the computer processes into meaningful information. Examples of data include a letter to a company or a client, a report for your boss, a budget proposal for a large project, or an address book of your friends' and business associates' addresses. Whatever the data, once it is saved (or written to disk), it can be retrieved at any time, printed on paper, or sent to someone else over the telephone lines.

Computers can be classified into four main groups: personal computers, minicomputers, mainframe computers, and supercomputers. This book focuses on the first type, the personal computer, sometimes known as the **PC.** It is based on the Intel microprocessor (the microprocessor is the "brain" of the computer).

A **personal computer** is a computer that is meant to be used by one person. It usually consists of a case that contains the essential electronic and mechanical parts of the computer, a monitor so that you can output (display) data, and a keyboard so that you can input (insert) data.

Personal computers can be divided into desktop models and portable computers. (See fig. 1.1.) Desktop computers are small enough to fit on a desk but are too big to carry with you. Portable computers (including laptops, notebooks, and subnotebooks) are fully functional computers that can be carried with you. Desktop computers tend to be more powerful and more flexible than portable computers.

Minicomputers, mainframe computers, and supercomputers use a single central computer. These computers, which are much more powerful than any single PC, are designed for many people to use at the same time through dumb terminals. A dumb terminal has a keyboard and a monitor that allows the user to input and view data, but it does not have a microprocessor or RAM (a type of memory) to process data. Therefore, while a PC does its own processing, dumb terminals rely on a central computer to perform tasks. These computers are considered noninteractive because they usually run in batch mode, where tasks are submitted as individual jobs by the users.

As personal computers became popular and more powerful, people wanted to connect personal computers together to form a network. A network can share data files, application

FIGURE 1.1 Personal computers (desktop PC and notebook PC)

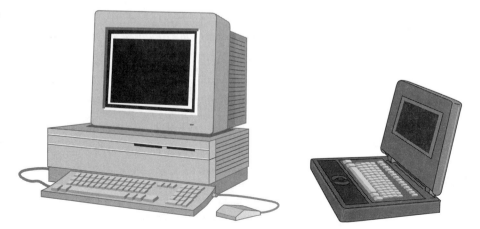

programs, and expensive printers, as well as provide communication capabilities such as connecting to the Internet.

When discussing computers in detail, you must break the computer into three major elements. They are:

1. Hardware
2. Software
3. User

Hardware is defined as the physical components that make up the personal computer. If you can touch and carry an item, the item is hardware. The major hardware components consist of the system unit (usually containing a motherboard, RAM chips, expansion cards, floppy drives, and a hard drive), the monitor, and the keyboard.

Software, also known as a program or an application, is a series of instructions that are loaded into the computer's memory. These instructions tell the computer what to do and when to do it. It controls the hardware and manipulates data.

When you buy a software package, the instructions are written on a floppy disk or a compact disk (CD-ROM). Although the instructions are written on the disk, the disk is considered to be a hardware item because it is something that you can touch and carry. The instructions themselves represent software.

The **user** is the computer operator who tells the computer what to do. Typically, the user gives a command or performs an action and the commands or actions are interpreted by the computer to perform the specified task. Some of the commands and tasks may start another program, delete a file from your hard drive, print a document, or e-mail a message using your modem.

Since data represent hours of work that may consist of irreplaceable information, it is the most valuable element to the user. Therefore, all efforts must be made to protect it. This includes ensuring that the hardware is working properly; that the user is developing good work habits that will enhance data protection; and that the user is making extra copies of the important data, also known as **backing up** the data.

1.2 PC HISTORY

The first personal computer, was introduced in 1975 by a company called MITS. Their computer, the Altair, included an Intel 8080 microprocessor, a power supply, a number of lights, and 256 bytes of memory. If you don't understand what some of these items are, don't worry, because they will all be explained to you. For now, let us say that by today's standard, this computer would be nothing more than a "toy with lights."

IBM's first attempt at the personal computer market was a computer that had 16 kilobytes (abbreviated KB or K) of memory, a display (to view the software and data), and a tape drive (to store the software and data). Unfortunately for IBM, it never became successful because of its $9,000 price tag in 1975.

In 1976, Apple introduced the Apple I computer, which consisted of a circuit board screwed into a piece of plywood. The following year, Apple introduced the now-classic Apple II computer, which represented the first affordable personal computer. Its general design was used in later designs of other personal computers.

In 1981, IBM introduced the original **IBM PC** (model 5150), which quickly became the personal computer standard. It contained an Intel 8088 microprocessor, 16 KB of RAM, a 63.5-watt power supply, a monochrome monitor, and one 320 KB or 360 KB disk drive. One of the popular features of the IBM PC was that it was expandable. With this feature, you could upgrade to new technology as it became available without replacing the whole computer.

Since technology has changed so rapidly through the years, today the IBM PC is an extremely outdated machine. Today's average personal computer would have at least a Pentium II microprocessor, 64 MB (megabytes) of RAM, a 4 GB (4-gigabyte) hard drive, one 1.44 MB floppy disk drive, a 220-watt power supply, a color Super VGA monitor, a sound card, and a CD-ROM drive. Again, if you don't understand these terms, don't worry; they will be explained throughout the book.

1.3 PARTS OF THE COMPUTER

The computer is divided into three main parts: the case, the monitor, and the keyboard. Most of what makes up the computer is located in the case, such as the microprocessor, motherboard, RAM, floppy disk drives, and hard drive. The case is designed to protect these components. In addition, other **peripherals** (external devices attached to the computer) may be added. Peripherals include printers, external disk drives, monitors, keyboards, mice, and external modems. (See table 1.1.)

TABLE 1.1   PC components

Component	Purpose
Case	The case is the box that most of the computer components rest in, and it is designed to protect these components. It contains the power supply (supplies dc power to the rest of the computer), motherboard, floppy drives, hard drive, expansion cards (including the sound card), CD-ROM drive, and RAM. (See chapter 9.)
Floppy drive	Floppy drives enable you to read and write data to and from floppy disks, small, thin plastic disks used for long-term storage of files. The storage capacity of a disk is very limited, but the disk can easily be taken to another computer. (See chapter 11.)
Hard drive	The hard drive (sometimes called a hard disk or fixed disk) is the principal device for storing programs and data. It usually has a large capacity and is much quicker than the floppy disk drive. Generally, it is not removed from the computer. (See chapter 10.)
Keyboard	The keyboard is a device similar to a typewriter by which the user inputs instructions and data into the computer. The keyboard is the main input device. (See chapter 16.)
Monitor	The monitor is a device similar to a television. The monitor is the computer's main output device. It is also called a display or video. (See chapter 15.)
Motherboard and microprocessor	The motherboard is the circuit board, which is the central core of the computer. (See chapter 7.) On the motherboard, there is a microprocessor (also known as a CPU). The microprocessor does most of the computer's work. (See chapter 5.) The motherboard is expandable using expansion cards. (See chapter 8.)
RAM (random access memory)	The RAM chips are integrated chips used for short-term memory. RAM holds program instructions and data, which the microprocessor directly accesses. RAM chips are volatile, meaning they immediately lose their data when the computer is shut off. (See chapter 6.)
ROM (read-only memory)	The ROM chips contain encoded progam instructions and data that the microprocessor accesses directly. Unlike RAM, ROM instructions are permanent and generally cannot be changed or erased. (See chapter 7.)
Printer	The printer is a common output device used with computers. This device produces images of text and graphics on paper. Some printers can also produce color images. (See chapter 19.)
Modem	Modem stands for modulator/demodulator. This device is communication hardware that enables transmission of data through telephone lines. (See chapter 18.)
Pointing devices (mice and trackballs)	Mice and trackballs are devices that can move the cursor back and forth on the screen (assuming the software supports pointing devices). Using these devices is easy and sometimes quicker than using the keyboard, which can improve productivity. Note: Pointing devices are enhancements to a keyboard, not replacements. (See chapter 16.)
CD-ROM drive	Compact disks (CDs) store large quantities of data that are accessed using a CD-ROM drive. CDs are similar to hard drives and floppy disks; however, most CDs are designed to provide read-only data. (See chapter 12.)
Sound card	The sound card adds music, speech, and sound effects to the PC. (See chapter 17.)

1.3.1 MOTHERBOARDS AND MICROPROCESSORS

The computer is built around an integrated chip called the **microprocessor.** The microprocessor is sometimes referred to as the **central processing unit (CPU).** (See fig. 1.2.) It is considered the "brain" of the computer since all the instructions it performs are mathematical calculations and logical comparisons. IBM and IBM-compatible computers use Intel, Cyrix, and AMD microprocessors, while Apple computers use Motorola microprocessors.

The Intel microprocessors found in the IBM and IBM-compatible computers are the 8088, 8086, 80286, 80386DX, 80386SX, 80486DX, 80486SX, Pentium, Pentium Pro, and Pentium II. Computers that use the 8088 or 8086 microprocessors are known as XT computers. The XT stands for *extended technology.* Computers with 80286 microprocessors are known as AT computers, which stands for *advanced technology.* The term XT was derived from the IBM XT (model 5160), and the term AT was derived from the IBM AT.

The speed of the microprocessor is usually expressed in megahertz (MHz). One megahertz is equal to 1 million cycles per second. During each cycle, a circuit will react in a predictable way. These reactions make the computer do what it does.

The microprocessor is the central component of the computer. It is plugged into a large circuit board called the **motherboard** or **system board.** The motherboard allows the microprocessor to branch out and communicate with all the other computer components; it can be considered the nervous system of the PC. Daughter boards, commonly called **expansion cards,** are used to expand the motherboard.

1.3.2 MEMORY

RAM, or **random access memory,** is the computer's short-term or temporary memory. Program instructions and data are stored on the RAM chips, which the microprocessor accesses directly. The more RAM you have, the more instructions and data you can load. The amount of RAM greatly affects the performance of the PC. Unfortunately, if power is discontinued to the RAM, such as what occurs when you shut off your PC, the contents of the RAM disappear. This is why we use disks (floppy disks and hard disks) for long-term storage.

FIGURE 1.2   Motherboard with CPU and RAM

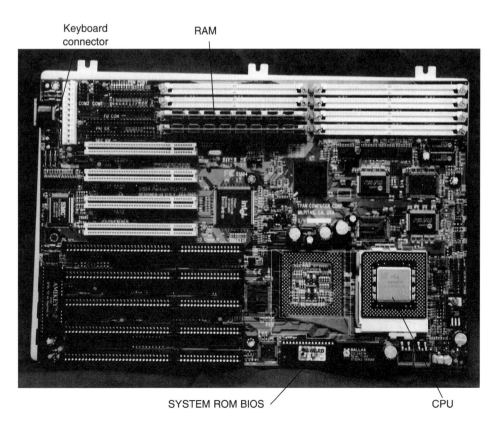

Keyboard connector   RAM

SYSTEM ROM BIOS   CPU

TABLE 1.2   Floppy disk capacity

Size	DS/DD	DS/HD	DS/ED
5¼-inch	360 KB	1.2 MB	
3½-inch	720 KB	1.44 MB	2.88 MB

Another type of memory used in the PC is **ROM,** or **read-only memory.** ROM contains instructions and data that the microprocessor accesses directly. It differs from RAM in that ROM instructions are permanent and cannot be changed or erased by normal means. The instructions in ROM chips can be thought of as the instincts of the computer. Instructions that control much of the computer's input/output functions, such as communicating with disks, RAM, and the monitor, are stored in the ROM chips and are known as the **BIOS (basic input/output system).**

1.3.3   HARD DRIVES AND FLOPPY DISK DRIVES

Disks are half-electronic, half-mechanical devices that store magnetic fields on rotating platters. The magnetic fields represent the data. Disks are usually classified as hard disks or floppy disks. Floppy disks do not hold as much information as hard disks, but they can be easily transported from one computer to another. Hard disks, on the other hand, are much faster than floppy disks and have a greater storage capacity.

Floppy disks come in two sizes, 5¼ inches and 3½ inches in diameter. (See fig. 1.3.) There are three different densities for floppy disks: double density (DD), high density (HD), and extra density (ED). The 5¼-inch disks come in only DD or HD, while the 3½-inch disks can come in any of the the three densities. All the floppy disks today are double-sided (DS), which means that the disk drive reads both sides of the floppy disk. (See table 1.2.) Today the most common disks are DS/HD 3½-inch disks, which can hold 1.44 MB of data. (The 3½-inch DS/ED disks, which can hold 2.88 MB of data, were never widely accepted. Although they hold more than the 1.44 MB disks, their size is still too limiting for today's large files.)

1.3.4   MONITORS

The **monitor** is the standard output device, similar to a television. Monitors are characterized by their size and resolution. The size of a monitor is measured diagonally across the screen. Typical monitors range from 14 inches to 21 inches.

The **resolution** of a computer monitor is determined by the number of **pixels** (picture elements) or dots going across the screen and the number of pixels or dots going down the screen. A typical resolution for a standard VGA monitor is 640 pixels across the screen and 480 pixels down, giving it a resolution of 640 × 480. At this resolution, the standard VGA displays 16 colors at one time. A Super VGA monitor has a higher resolution, such as 800 × 600 or 1024 × 768, and can use up to 16 million colors or more on the screen at the same time, allowing for photographic-quality screen output.

FIGURE 1.3   Floppy disks (5¼-inch and 3½-inch)

1.3.5 KEYBOARDS

The **keyboard** is the primary input device. It is used to input or enter letters, numbers, symbols, punctuation, and commands into the computer. It includes the same keys as a typewriter. Most keyboards include a numeric keypad, cursor movement keys, and 12 function keys. Today, most keyboards are 101-, 102-, or 104-key keyboards. Of course, the name is derived from the number of keys on the keyboard.

1.3.6 PRINTERS

The **printer** is an output device that allows the user to take information from the computer and print it on paper. Just as there are many types of computers and monitors, there are many different types of printers. Most printers connect directly to the computer through the parallel port, a special connector located at the back of the computer. (See table 4.1.) The port is a device that can communicate eight bits at a time. (A bit is a binary digit based on 0's and 1's. Eight bits are equal to one byte of data, which represents a single character.)

Printers can be divided into impact and nonimpact printers. Impact printers have movable parts that strike an ink ribbon against a sheet of paper. Impact printers include daisy wheel/ball printers and dot-matrix printers. (See fig. 1.4.) Their disadvantages are that they are slow and noisy, and their output is not considered to be high quality or "letter-perfect," except for the wheel/ball printers. In addition, the availability of dot-matrix printers is limited since they are not as popular as they used to be.

Instead of striking the paper, nonimpact printers use other methods to print. Nonimpact printers include inkjet printers, laser printers, and thermal printers. The inkjet and laser printers are the most commonly used.

Inkjet printers spray ink though a small hole. They are superior to dot-matrix printers in that they have better print quality and are much quieter. Today an inkjet printer costs about the same as a dot-matrix printer and they both operate at the same speed. (See fig. 1.5.)

The best-looking print comes from a laser printer. (See fig. 1.6.) The printer works similar to a photocopy machine using fine toner powder to transfer images to paper. By heating (fusing) the toner, it becomes permanent on the paper. The laser printer is of extremely high quality with a wide range of fonts and graphics. It is also quiet and fast. Of course, it is more expensive than other types of printers. The most popular laser printers are produced by Hewlett-Packard.

FIGURE 1.4   Dot-matrix printer

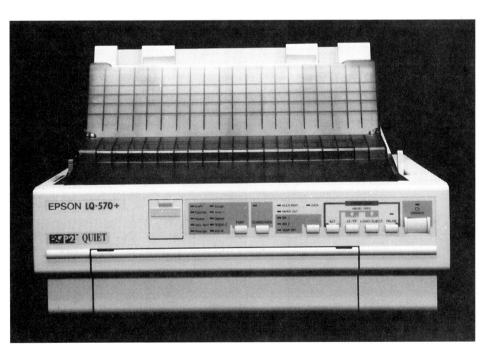

FIGURE 1.5   Inkjet printer

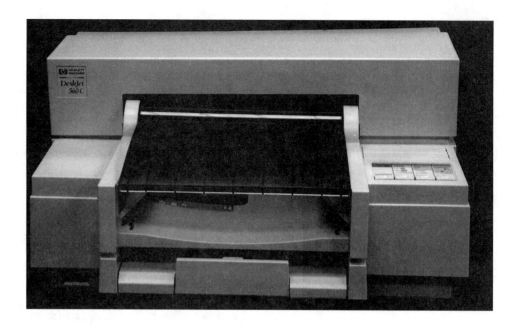

1.3.7   SERIAL DEVICES

Serial devices are devices that can communicate one bit at a time. They are often connected to a serial port. (See table 4.1.) The most popular serial device is the pointing device, such as a mouse or trackball. (See fig. 1.7.) A **mouse** is a small device that fits in your hand. A ball is located on the bottom of the device. When you run the ball along a surface, you are able to easily move an arrow (mouse pointer) on the screen. With this arrow, you can perform certain actions quickly and more precisely than with the keyboard. This includes line drawing, deleting words, or running applications. The **trackball** is similar to a mouse except that the ball is on the top of the device. You use your fingers to roll the ball. As the ball moves, the mouse pointer moves.

FIGURE 1.6   Laser printer

FIGURE 1.7 Mouse and track-ball

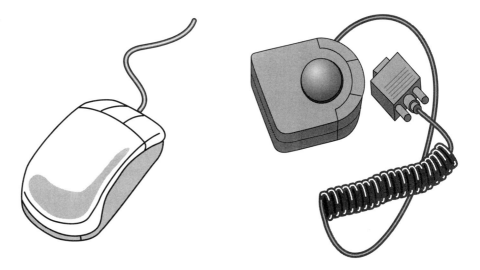

As computers became more popular, connectivity was added to the PC so that it could communicate with other computers. One of the more common peripherals used to enable PCs to communicate with other PCs is the **modem,** which actually stands for modulator/demodulator. It allows users to "talk" to other computers through a telephone line. By using a modem, you can connect to the Internet, call up bulletin boards (BBS), and use other telephone services. You can access online encyclopedias and informational databases, make airline reservations, and do shopping and banking. Today, most modems also have fax (facsimile transmission) capabilities.

1.3.8 MULTIMEDIA PERIPHERALS

A computer system that combines text, graphics, animation, and sound is known as a **multimedia system.** A **sound card** is used to add digitized sound to the PC. A video-interface card allows you to take a television signal and display it on your computer screen. To add pictures into your documents, you can create them with a draw or paint program or scan them in with a **scanner.**

The **compact disk (CD)** is one of the newer additions to the PC. (See fig. 1.8.) Information is stored on the compact disk using laser light. This newer technology allows a single disk to hold enormous amounts of information (for instance, 650 MB of data, or approximately the equivalent of 450 floppy disks). A PC's CD-ROM drive can read CD-ROM data disks, music CDs, and photo CDs. Though most CDs are designed to be read-only (CD-ROM), there may come a day when rewritable compact disks completely replace hard disks and floppy disks.

FIGURE 1.8 Compact disk

1.4 SOFTWARE

As you have seen with hardware, the computer has many parts, and each component is designed for a particular function. Software is very similar. It can be divided into two primary categories—application software and system software.

Software is designed by programmers. A programmer or group of programmers writes the instructions using a programming language resembling English. Some of these languages include BASIC language, C language, and assembly language. Since the computer cannot understand English, it must first translate the English commands into machine language (commands understood by the CPU) written in binary code, consisting of combinations of the numbers 1 and 0. (This corresponds to the bipolar, or on/off, state of electrical components, where "on" equals 1 and "off" equals 0.) Translating the commands into binary code is called compiling a program, which is completed by system software known as a compiler.

1.4.1 APPLICATION SOFTWARE

Application software allows a user to input, process, and output data to create usable information. It is this type of software that allows the user to create a letter, report, budget, chart, graph, or database.

The most common application software is the **word processor.** (See fig. 1.9.) Word processing software allows you to type a document, much like a typewriter. Additional features include a spell checker, a grammar checker, a find-and-replace function, and the ability to move text. The most popular word processing programs include Microsoft Word and Corel WordPerfect.

Another type of application software is **spreadsheet** software. Most people think of spreadsheets as tables of numbers or financial models. If the spreadsheet is created using formulas and a value is changed, the entire spreadsheet is automatically recalculated. Today spreadsheets do a lot more than "number crunching." They sort numbers, create graphs, and perform data analysis. The two most popular spreadsheet programs are Microsoft Excel and Lotus 1-2-3.

Database application software allows users to work with files of related data. An address book or employee records are examples of database files. The data can be organized and quickly retrieved. The most popular database application is Microsoft Access.

There are many other types of application software. Graphics programs allow you to create graphs and pictures. **Desktop publishing programs** allow you to combine graphics and text to create newsletters and reports. **Draw** and **paint programs** allow you to become an artist using the mouse or other input devices instead of a pencil, pen, or brush.

Finally, there are computer games and educational software packages. Unlike early games and text-based tutorials, these packages are complex, sophisticated software consisting of exciting graphics, sound, and animation.

FIGURE 1.9   Word processor

1.4.2 OPERATING SYSTEM SOFTWARE

Although application software is the best-known software, it is not the only type of software. The **system software** directs the entire system. Operating systems and compilers make up most of the system software. The only system software that this book will discuss in detail is that of the operating system.

The **operating system (OS)** is the computer's most important software. It coordinates the actions of the hardware, the software, and the user so that they can work as one. Table 1.3 shows today's common operating systems.

The operating system is essential to the computer. During **boot-up,** the operating system is loaded (copied) from the boot disk (typically the hard disk) to RAM. It provides an interface to the user so that he or she can start other programs by entering a command at the keyboard or by using the mouse to perform an action. Of course, depending on the actions of the user and the instructions specified in the software, the operating system directs the computer's hardware. When you save a file to a disk, the OS automatically records the location so that you can find and access the file in the future and so that the operating system will not accidentally write over it with another file.

Operating systems have one of two types of interface, command-driven or icon-driven. The command-driven operating systems, such as DOS and UNIX, require that you type in commands from the keyboard. With the command-driven interface, you must know the correct spelling, syntax, parameters, and punctuation for each command. If you have one character that is wrong or out of place, you will receive an error message or an incorrect response. Mastering a command-driven OS requires memorization of the correct way to type each command.

The other type of interface is icon-driven. Icon-driven operating systems (such as Windows 95, Windows 98, and Windows NT) are known as "graphical interfaces" because they use small pictures known as icons to represent a function or application. The programs are started by using a mouse or trackball to move an arrow to an icon and then pressing a button on the mouse. Since the operating system uses icons, it requires a much smaller learning curve than a command-driven system. Operating systems that use icons are known to have a **graphical user interface (GUI).** Most people like the look and feel of an icon-driven operating system and consider it user-friendly. **User-friendly** is a term indicating that computer equipment or software is easy to understand and operate. Today most operating systems use a graphical interface.

Another characteristic of an operating system is that of single tasking versus multitasking. Single tasking allows one application to work at one time, while multitasking allows more than one application to work at one time. Depending upon the application programs

TABLE 1.3 Operating systems

Operating System	Interface	Comments
DOS	Command-driven	First PC operating system, which still exists on many PCs
UNIX	Command-driven	PC operating system usually associated with local area networks (LANs) and the Internet
OS/2	Icon-driven	IBM's graphical user interface
Microsoft Windows 95, Microsoft Windows 98	Icon-driven	Microsoft's replacements for DOS and the Windows 3.XX operating environment
Microsoft Windows NT	Icon-driven	Microsoft's newest graphical user interface OS
System 6, System 7, System 8	Icon-driven	Macintosh's operating systems

FIGURE 1.10   DOS
(a command-driven operating system)

and the type of operating system, you can run two or more programs, share information, and switch back and forth between the different applications. Today's PC can process jobs in the background (i.e., printing or complicated calculations) while you work on something else (i.e., typing a report). When an operating system has a GUI, it is usually multitasking.

1.4.3   MS-DOS AND MICROSOFT WINDOWS 3.XX

A common operating system used today is **Microsoft DOS** (commonly known as MS-DOS or just DOS). DOS, which stands for disk operating system, was included with the original IBM PC and can still be found on many PCs. (See fig. 1.10.)

Some 286 computers (meaning those with the Intel 286 processor) and most 386 computers (those with the Intel 386 processor) that have DOS also have Microsoft Windows 3.XX. "XX" represents any of the version numbers released as improvements to Microsoft Windows 3.0. Although Windows 3.XX provides a GUI to DOS, Windows 3.XX cannot boot the computer. Instead, the computer is booted using DOS, and Windows is loaded on top of DOS. Therefore, Windows 3.XX is an **operating environment,** not an operating system. (See fig. 1.11.)

FIGURE 1.11   Windows 3.XX

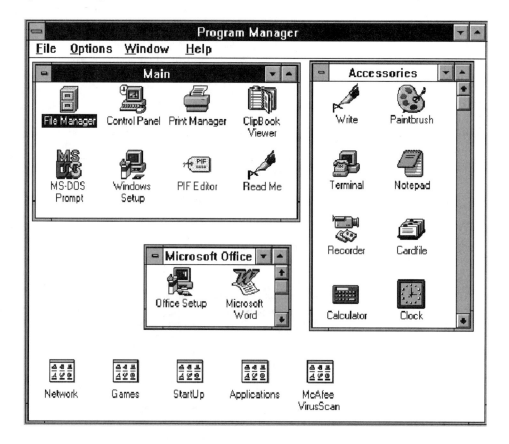

FIGURE 1.12   Windows 95

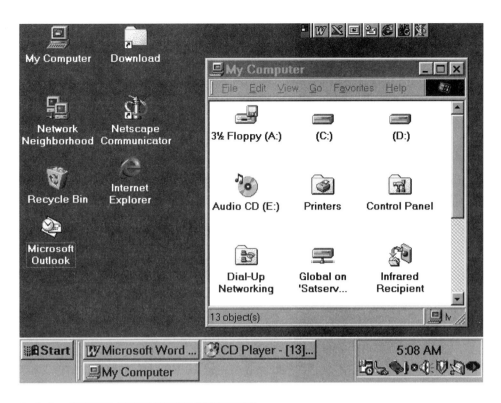

1.4.4   OTHER OPERATING SYSTEMS

Operating System/2 (OS/2) began as an effort by IBM and Microsoft to replace MS-DOS. It is an icon-driven, multitasking operating system requiring a 386 machine. Due to a fallout between the two companies, IBM owns OS/2 and Microsoft developed **Microsoft Windows NT. Microsoft Windows 95** and **Microsoft Windows 98** are the operating systems that eventually replaced DOS and Windows 3.XX. (See fig. 1.12.) OS/2, Windows 95, Windows 98, and Windows NT can run most Windows 3.XX applications and DOS applications.

1.5   SOFTWARE VERSIONS

Since the original IBM PC was introduced, IBM has produced many versions of the personal computer. Usually the major changes were based on the introduction of a new Intel microprocessor or other new technology.

Like hardware, software has to change to make use of the new technology. To signify these changes, software companies number their software with a version number. To display the version in DOS, you would enter the VER command at the DOS prompt. Windows 95, Windows 98, and Windows NT list the version number in the System icon/applet in the Control Panel. The version for Windows 3.XX and Windows applications can be shown when you select the About. . . option in the Help menu. By knowing the version number, it will help you determine the software's capabilities, determine when it is appropriate to purchase an upgrade, and find patches or other updates. You will also need to know the version number when talking to a manufacturer's technical support person.

When a software package releases a new version, its version number increases. If it increases by a whole number, it usually means major changes (updates) to the program. When it increases by .1, it indicates moderate changes. When it increases by only .01, it indicates minor changes. For example, WordPerfect 5.1 was a moderate update to WordPerfect 5.0 because pull-down menus and mouse control were added. Lotus 1-2-3 version 3.0 was a major change from Lotus 1-2-3 version 2.2 because graphical interfacing and 3-D graphing were added. More recently, Microsoft Windows NT 3.51, which included the older Windows 3.XX interface, was upgraded to Windows NT 4.0 when its Windows 3.XX interface was replaced with the Windows 95 interface. Table 1.4 lists all the DOS versions and the changes since the previous version.

TABLE 1.4 DOS versions

DOS Version	Significant Changes	Release Date
1.0	Original DOS version	8/81
1.1	Allowed use of 5¼-inch double-sided disks	5/82
2.0	Supported hard drives and multiple directories	3/83
3.0	Allowed use of high-capacity disks, RAM disks, volume names, and the ATTRIB command	8/84
3.1	Included support for networks	3/85
3.2	Supported 3½-inch double-density disk drives	3/86
3.3	Supported 3½-inch high-density disk drives	4/87
4.0	Introduced DOS Shell and MEM; accommodated larger files and disk capacity	6/88
4.01	Fixed bugs in DOS 4.0	8/88
5.0	Included enhanced memory management, task swapping, EDIT program, and improved DOS Shell	6/91
6.0	Improved memory management; added disk compression, virus checking, and other utilities	5/93
6.20	Improved Doublespace and fixed quirks introduced in 6.0; DOS 6.2 was to have represented the last DOS	8/93
6.21	Removed Doublespace because of a lawsuit	5/94
6.22	Substituted new utilities for those removed in version 6.21	5/94

Not all software companies use the version number scheme as depicted in table 1.4. To help simplify the system, many companies are now using the year to indicate the version. Microsoft Windows 95, Windows 98, Office 95, and Office 97 are good examples of this system. This is not always a perfect system since some companies introduce several versions within the same year or might not have made any significant changes from one year's version to the next year's version. For these situations, companies may assign or change a letter. For example, Windows 95 was introduced in 1995. After loading a service pack to fix some bugs within the operating system, the newer version was known as Windows 95a. Later, after fixing some minor problems and adding some new features, Windows 95b (OSR2) was introduced, followed by Windows 95b (OSR2.5).

1.6 STANDARDS

To overcome compatibility issues, hardware and software often follow **standards** (specifications that either are dictated by the computer industry or are the most common in the industry). Standards exist for operating systems, data formats, communication protocols, and electrical interfaces. If a product does not follow a widely used standard, it is usually not widely accepted in the computer market and often causes problems with your PC. As far as the user is concerned, standards help you determine what hardware and software to purchase, and they allow you to customize a system made of components from different manufacturers.

As new technology is introduced, manufacturers are usually rushing to get their product out so that it has a better chance of becoming the standard. Often, competing computer manufacturers introduce similar technology at the same time. Until one is designated as the

TABLE 1.5   Common standards committees

Committee	Description
American National Standards Institute (ANSI) http://www.ansi.org	ANSI is primarily concerned with software. ANSI has defined standards for a number of programming languages, including C language and the SCSI interface.
Comité Consultatif Internationale Télégraphique et Téléphonique (CCITT)	CCITT defines international standards, particularly communications protocols.
Institute of Electrical and Electronic Engineers (IEEE) http://www.ieee.org/	IEEE sets standards for most types of electrical interfaces, including RS-232C (serial communication interface) and network communications.
International Organization for Standardization (ISO) http://www.iso.ch/	ISO is an international standard for communications and information exchange.
Video Electronics Standards Association (VESA) http://www.vesa.org	An organization that standardized Super VGA video systems and other video specifications.

standard, other companies and customers are sometimes forced to take sides. Since it is sometimes difficult to determine what will emerge as the true standard because the technology sometimes needs to mature, it is best to wait to see what happens before making an expensive purchase.

There are two main types of standards. The first standard is called the de jure standard. The **de jure standard,** or the "by law" standard, is a standard that has been dictated by an appointed committee, such as the International Organization for Standardization (ISO). Some of the more common standard committees are shown in table 1.5. The other type of standard is the de facto standard. The **de facto standard,** or the "from the fact" standard, is a standard that has been accepted by the industry just because it is the most common. These standards are not recognized by a standards committee. For example, the de facto for microprocessors is those produced by Intel, while the de facto for sound cards is those produced by Creative Labs.

When a system or standard has an **open architecture,** it indicates that the specifications of the system or standard are public. This includes approved standards as well as privately designed architecture whose specifications are made public by the designers. The advantage of an open architecture is that anyone can design products based on the architecture and design add-on products for it. Of course, this also allows other manufacturers to duplicate the product.

The opposite of an open architecture is a **proprietary system.** A proprietary system is privately owned and controlled by a company that has not divulged specifications that would allow other companies to duplicate the product. Proprietary architectures often do not allow mixing and matching products from different manufacturers and may cause hardware and software compatibility problems.

1.7   SOFTWARE AND HARDWARE TOGETHER

When you turn on the computer, the microprocessor does a quick power check to make sure that the power supply can supply enough power to all the PC components. When the power check is complete, the microprocessor then goes to the instructions in the system ROM BIOS and starts executing them. The instructions tell the microprocessor to test and initialize the major PC components. Next, the microprocessor looks for other ROM BIOS chips so that it can get more instructions on how to initialize devices not specified in the system ROM BIOS.

FIGURE 1.13 The user interacting with the computer

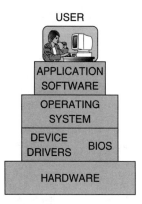

USER

APPLICATION SOFTWARE

OPERATING SYSTEM

DEVICE DRIVERS   BIOS

HARDWARE

Still following the instructions in the system ROM BIOS, the microprocessor starts looking for a boot device (typically, the A drive followed by the C drive). On the boot device, it will find additional instructions on how to boot, or load, the operating system into RAM.

While the operating system is loading, the operating system instructions tell the microprocessor to find and load (copy into RAM) drivers from the disk. The drivers contain instructions on initializing the hardware not specified in the ROM BIOS chips, and they specify how the OS is to interface with the hardware. In addition, the drivers load instructions for the operating system interface and configure the operating system environment.

The operating system waits until the user performs a task or enters a command. When the user performs a task, such as double-clicking on an icon or entering a command to start a program, the microprocessor receives signals from the input device (pointing device or keyboard) telling the microprocessor that it has a task to process. The microprocessor then processes instructions that are already in RAM to interpret the tasks or command and performs the designated function. Often, the instructions will tell the microprocessor to open additional files from disk and copy more instructions into RAM.

If you create a new document using a software program, the program tells the microprocessor to designate a memory area in RAM to hold the document. As the user inputs data into the document, the data are stored in the designated memory area. If the user decides to open a file that has already been created, the memory area is designated and the data is copied from a file on the disk into RAM. During this process, the microprocessor has to access instructions from RAM and the ROM BIOS on how to access certain hardware components. (See fig. 1.13.)

After the document has been created, the user may decide to save his or her document to the hard drive. Again, the mouse or keyboard is used to issue commands from the application software. The application software relays those commands to the operating system, which then tells the hardware to copy the document from RAM to the hard drive. If the user decides to perform a spell check or grammar check, change the appearance of text, or add a picture to the document, the necessary instructions are executed by the microprocessor. Additional instructions are often loaded from the disk into RAM. Since the microprocessor accesses the data and instructions that are in RAM, the amount of RAM determines the amount of instructions and data that the microprocessor can have open (ready to be accessed in RAM) at once.

SUMMARY

1. A computer is a machine composed of electronic devices used to process data.
2. Data are the raw facts, numbers, letters, or symbols that the computer processes into meaningful information.
3. A personal computer is a computer meant to be used by one person.
4. Software is a series of instructions that tell the computer what to do and when to do it.
5. The microprocessor is an integrated chip that the computer is built around. It is often thought of as the "brain" of the computer.
6. RAM, or random access memory, is the short-term memory for the computer. All data stored in RAM are lost when the computer is shut off.

7. ROM, or read-only memory, contains instructions and data that the microprocessor accesses directly. Different from RAM, ROM instructions are permanent and cannot be changed or erased by normal means.

8. Instructions that control much of the computer's input/output functions, such as communicating with disks, RAM, and the monitor, are kept in the ROM chips and are known as the BIOS (basic input/output system).

9. The computer display, commonly known as the monitor, is the PC's most commonly used output device.

10. The keyboard is the primary input device and is arranged much like a typewriter.

11. Application software lets a user input information to create or edit a document or report.

12. The operating system (OS) coordinates the actions of the hardware, software, and user.

13. DOS is a common command-driven operating system found on older PCs.

14. Windows 3.XX is not an operating system; rather, it is an operating environment that works on top of DOS.

15. Newer operating systems, such as Microsoft Windows 95, Microsoft Windows 98, and Microsoft Windows NT, have graphical user interfaces (GUIs).

16. Software, also known as a program or application, consists of programming language code that is converted to machine code by a programmer using system software called a compiler.

17. Much like hardware, software is frequently improved.

18. To overcome compatibility issues, hardware and software often follow standards, or dictated specifications.

19. The de jure standard, or the "by law" standard, is a standard that has been dictated by an appointed committee.

20. The de facto standard, or the "from the fact" standard, is a standard that has been accepted by the industry just because it is the most common.

QUESTIONS

1. Which of the following is designed to be used by one person?
   a. personal computer
   b. mainframe computer
   c. minicomputer
   d. mid-range computer
   e. supercomputer

2. You have a CD-ROM that contains the Microsoft Windows NT installation program. The instructions written on the disk are:
   a. hardware
   b. software
   c. RAM
   d. electrical signals

3. The screen display is made up of an arrangement of dots called:
   a. graphics
   b. resolution
   c. pixels
   d. VGA

4. Which component is the computer built around?
   a. the RAM
   b. the hard drive
   c. the monitor
   d. the microprocessor
   e. the BIOS

5. Which instructions control much of the computer's input/output functions, such as communicating with disks, RAM, and the monitor?
   a. BIOS
   b. microcode
   c. CMOS
   d. temporary

6. Which of the following is the primary input device?
   a. keyboard
   b. monitor
   c. printer
   d. mouse
   e. modem
   f. disk

7. Which of the following is the primary output device?
   a. keyboard
   b. monitor
   c. printer
   d. mouse
   e. modem
   f. disk

8. Which device allows you to communicate with another computer by using the phone lines?
   - a. keyboard
   - b. monitor
   - c. printer
   - d. mouse
   - e. modem
   - f. disk

9. Software that allows the user to input information to create or edit a document or report is:
   - a. operating system software
   - b. application software
   - c. a software utility
   - d. a software diagnostic package

10. The most common application software that allows the user to type letters and reports is a:
    - a. word processing package
    - b. spreadsheet package
    - c. database package
    - d. desktop publishing package

11. The PC's most important software, which coordinates the hardware, software, and the user, is:
    - a. utility software
    - b. device drivers software
    - c. operating system software
    - d. integrated software
    - e. none of the above

12. Which of the following operating systems is *not* icon-driven?
    - a. Microsoft Windows NT
    - b. OS/2
    - c. UNIX
    - d. System 7
    - e. Microsoft Windows 95

13. *True or false*—Microsoft Windows 3.11 is an icon-driven operating system.

14. Which standard is a standard because it the most commonly used?
    - a. de jure standard
    - b. de facto standard
    - c. your company standard
    - d. the one that you prefer

15. The microprocessor executes instructions kept in (choose two answers):
    - a. RAM
    - b. ROM
    - c. the hard drive
    - d. the keyboard
    - e. the monitor

16. Instructions to initialize and control hardware not specified in the BIOS are called:
    - a. ROM
    - b. drivers
    - c. utilities
    - d. compilers

2

The PC Technician

INTRODUCTION

As a computer technician, consultant, or support person, you are a detective in the PC world. When the computer fails for any reason, it is your job to find the problem and correct it quickly with a minimum loss of data. Finding the problem is not always the easiest thing to do. However, if you possess a working knowledge of the PC, combined with a little technique and a little patience, no problem will be too difficult to solve.

OBJECTIVES

1. List and describe the different computer problem classifications.
2. List and describe the steps in troubleshooting a problem.
3. List places to go to find additional help.
4. Research a topic on the Internet.
5. Given a scenario, determine if software piracy is occurring.
6. List the common tools needed to effectively troubleshoot and fix a PC.
7. Install and run a software diagnostic package.
8. Create a boot disk with the most common operating system files used to fix a computer.

2.1 COMPUTER PROBLEMS

When a computer has a problem, the user's first response is, "Oh no, not now!" I am sure that you will agree that there is no good time for a computer to break down. (See Fig. 2.1.) Of course, with some good maintenance, excellent backup procedures, and a little bit of knowledge, you can easily minimize computer failure and data loss.

2.1.1 BEFORE YOU TROUBLESHOOT

When encountering a computer problem, you should follow certain guidelines. First, your mind must be clear and rested. You must be able to concentrate on the problem. If not, you may overlook something that was obvious, such as the power cord not being plugged in.

Next, don't panic, don't get frustrated, and allow enough time to do the job right. If you panic, you may do something that will make the situation worse. If you start to get frustrated, take a break. You will be amazed at how five or ten minutes away from the problem will clear your mind and will allow you to look at the problem a little differently when you come back. Finally, make sure that you have enough time to properly analyze the problem, fix the problem, and properly test the system after the repair. Again, if you rush a job, you may make the problem worse or you may overlook something simple.

2.1.2 TYPES OF PROBLEMS

When troubleshooting the PC, you must keep an open mind about the cause of the problem. It could be a hardware failure, a compatibility problem, an improper configuration, a software glitch, an environmental factor, or a user error. (See table 2.1.) Some problems could be due to a faulty component, such as a hard drive, floppy drive, power supply, cable, or modem. In addition, problems can be caused by viruses, software that is not compatible with a screen saver, CMOS setup program settings, power management features, Control Panel settings, software drivers, hardware settings, power fluctuations, or electromagnetic interference.

2.1.3 GATHERING INFORMATION

You need to gather information before trying to fix the problem. First, make sure that you can duplicate the problem and that the user is not part of the problem. Also determine if the problem is always repeatable or if it is an intermittent problem. If it is an intermittent

FIGURE 2.1   Sick PC

TABLE 2.1 Computer problem classifications

Reason for Failure	Description
Hardware failure	One or more components fails inside the computer.
Hardware incompatibility	One component is not compatible with another component. Note: This error may appear to be a hardware failure.
Improper hardware configuration	The hardware has not been installed or configured properly. This often happens when the user does not read the manual or does not have the knowledge to make use of the manual. Note: This error often appears to be a hardware failure.
Improper software configuration	The software (operating system or application software) is not installed or configured properly. This often happens when the user does not read the manual or does not have the knowledge to make use of the manual. Note: This error may appear to be a hardware failure.
Software failure	There is a glitch in the software. This can range from corrupted data to a flaw in the programming. Note: This error may appear to be a hardware failure.
Software incompatibility	The software is not compatible with the hardware or other software. Note: This error may appear to be a hardware failure.
Poor environment	The location of the computer and its environment (i.e., temperature, air flow, electromagnetic interference, magnetic fields) may affect the reliability of the PC and have a direct impact on the PC's life. Note: This problem may appear to be a hardware failure.
User error	This is a very common situation where the user hits the wrong keys or is not familiar with the computer or software. It could be something as simple as the user hitting the zero (0) key rather than the letter O key.

problem, does the problem follow a certain pattern (such as when the computer is on for a while) or does it occur randomly?

The more difficult problems are the intermittent problems. Since the intermittent errors do not happen on a regular basis, the computer may work fine when you test it, but as soon the customer takes it home, it will fail again. When dealing with intermittent problems, you make a change that might fix the system. You must then thoroughly test the system over a period of time to see if the problem actually goes away.

When gathering information, you must be observant by using four of your five senses. For example:

Seeing: Are all of the components present and are they connected properly? Are there any burn marks on any of the components, or is the cable physically damaged?

Hearing: Do you hear any excessive noise or electrical noises? In addition, do you not hear noises that you typically would hear, such as the fan or the hard drive spinning?

Smelling: Do you smell anything abnormal, such as something burning?

Feeling: Does the case feel excessively warm? Can you feel the hard drive spin?

After the problem has been repeated and verified, you need to test the system further to see the extent of the problem. For example, if your system doesn't boot properly, can you boot from the floppy drive and access the hard drive? If you can't print from a particular program, can you print using another program? If the mouse doesn't work in one environment, such as Windows, does it work using DOS?

You can gather additional information by trying to use software utilities to test your system and by using a **digital multimeter (DMM)** to measure certain electrical characteristics of the computer. Some of the utilities include software to test the computer components, check for viruses, look for formatting errors on a disk, or check software configuration.

In addition, find out if the computer was serviced or changed recently. Many times, servicing or changes can cause other problems.

2.1.4   ISOLATING THE PROBLEM

After you have gathered as much information as you can, you are now ready to make the repair or fix. Sometimes you will know exactly what to change or replace. Other times, you will have it narrowed down to several causes that will require you to isolate the problem. If you suspect a faulty component, you can replace the component with a known good component. If the system works with the new component, the problem was the item that you just removed. (Note: When a new item is taken off the shelf, it does not mean that the item is always good.) In addition, you can try "reverse swapping," which is trying a suspected faulty component with a second working system.

Other solutions include reconfiguring the software or hardware; reloading the operating system, application software, or drivers; or making changes to the CMOS setup program. Whatever course of action you choose, you should make only one change at a time. If the problem still exists, you will then make another change until the problem no longer exists. When determining which item to check or swap, you should first try to check items that are most likely to cause the problem and that are the easiest and quickest to check.

> **NOTE**   If the computer or device is under warranty, you should let the vendor fix the problem. If you open and try to repair a computer that is under warranty, you may void the warranty.

2.1.5   AFTER YOU FIX THE PROBLEM

After you fix the problem, you should always thoroughly test the computer before returning it to the customer or client. This will make sure that the problem did go away and that you did not cause another problem while fixing the first problem.

In addition, you should keep a log of changes made to a system and list any problems you encounter, as well as their solutions. The log can tell you if the system has gone through any recent changes, especially if you work for a department that has several PC support people. The log will also help you look for trends so that in the future you can make plans to minimize the problem and have the resources available when the problem occurs.

2.2   WHERE TO GET HELP WHEN NEEDED

When dealing with computer problems, there is no way that you are going to know everything about computers, nor are you expected to. What is expected is that you understand computers well enough to investigate and isolate problems, know when you need to find more information, and know how to get the information in a timely manner so that you can fix the problem. Some of the common places to find help include:

1. Documentation for the computer, device, or software package
2. HELP files, README files, and other text files
3. Fellow colleagues
4. Books
5. Popular computer magazines
6. The Internet
7. Computer and product technical support people

The documentation that comes with a computer, a device, or a software package usually contains valuable installation, configuration, and troubleshooting information. Software packages also often contain HELP files, README files, or other informational files describing installation procedures, troubleshooting problems, and last-minute changes to the

FIGURE 2.2 Internet web page showing the jumper settings for a hard drive (courtesy of Western Digital Corporation)

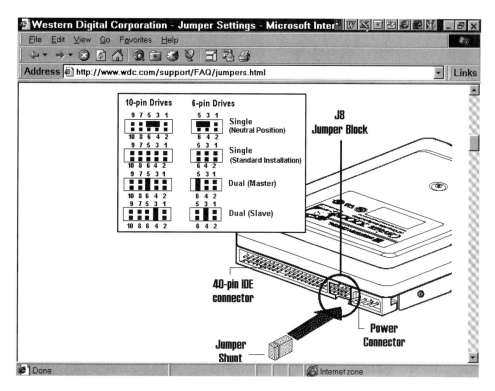

documentation. If you lose the documentation to a computer, device, or software package, the documentation can often be found on the manufacturer's website.

When working within a computer or information system (IS) department, you will be part of a team. An effective team uses teamwork. Since a colleague will have certain experiences and you will have certain experiences, it is common for colleagues to ask each other for help. Another source is to contact the company's technical support. Note: Not all technical support services are free. In addition, you may need to provide information such as the product license number, serial number or OEM number, the type of computer, and the type of software that is on the system.

Other sources of information are books, magazines, and the Internet. If you ever go into a large bookstore, you will usually find many PC books and magazines. Some of these include sections on installation, configuring, optimizing, troubleshooting, standards, and emerging technology. The Internet provides an easy way to find product documentation, software patches and fixes, tips, and troubleshooting utilities. (See Fig. 2.2.) The most common Internet services are shown in table 2.2 and some useful websites are listed in table 2.3.

TABLE 2.2   Internet services

Service	Description
Electronic Mail (E-mail)	Mail that can be sent to and from other Internet users.
Telnet	Remote logins to other machines on the Internet that allow you to work on the remote system or to try software.
File Transfer Protocol (FTP)	File transfer between machines that allows you to download software, graphics, and other files. Although hypertext transfer protocol (HTTP) can also download files, FTP specializes in downloading files.
World Wide Web (WWW)	A graphical information service. Usually uses HTTP to navigate web pages and to choose options.
Usenet Newsgroups	A set of bulletin boards for conversations on many different subjects, including computers.
Search Engines	An information search system.

TABLE 2.3   Useful computer troubleshooting web sites

Website	Name or Sponsor	Content
http://www.cnet.com	CNET: The Computer Network	Offers update news, tips, and software downloads
http://www.modems.com	Zoom Telephonics, Inc.	Valuable information on modems and related technology
http://www.pcwebopedia.com	PC Webopedia	An encyclopedia of computer and computer-related terms with many links to related sites
http://www.pcworld.com	*PC World Magazine*	Offers reviews, tips, and software downloads
http://www.tomshardware.com	Tom's Hardware Guide	Valuable technical information about major PC components
http://www.zdnet.com	Ziff-Davis, Inc., publisher of *PC Magazine, PC Computing,* and other magazines	Offers reviews, tips, and software downloads (note: to search their magazines, use http://xlink.zdnet.com/cgi-bin/texis/xlink/xlink/search.html)
http://www.ridgecrest.ca.us/~markee/home.htm	Mark's Computer Page	Valuable information about disks, microprocessors, networking, and operating systems
http://pcmech.pair.com	PC Mechanic	Online source for do-it-yourself computing
http://www.driverzone.com	The Driver's Zone	Provides easy access to find most drivers, as well as a search engine to identify a manufacturer by the product's FCC number
http://www.windrivers.com	WinDrivers.Com	Provides drivers, troubleshooting information, and identification information
http://www.winfiles.com	WinFiles.Com	Drivers, shareware patches, fixes, and other valuable information.
http://www.lemig.umontreal.ca/bios/bios_sg.htm	BIOS Survival Guide	Valuable information about configuring the CMOS setup program
http://www.ping.be/bios	WIM's BIOS Page	Valuable information about configuring the CMOS setup program and finding which BIOS to use with which motherboard
http://www.pcguide.com	The PC Guide	Offers detailed PC reference information

2.3   BACKUP

As a computer technician, you should always emphasize to your customers that they must back up all important files. A **backup** of a system is extra copies of data and programs. Unfortunately, it is often ignored by most people, and they do not think about doing it until it is too late.

Question: Why do a backup?

Answer: As you use the computer more and learn how the computer works, you will understand that the data generated by the computer and stored on disk is the user's most valuable item within the computer. The data usually represents hours of work and is sometimes irreplaceable.

As a computer technician or consultant, you may be the one that selects and installs the equipment, performs the actual backup, or trains other people in doing the backup. You need to make sure to select the equipment and method that will ensure that the backup is completed on a regular basis. Remember that even if you have the best equipment and software yet no one completes the backup, the equipment and software are wasted. Backup equipment and methods will be discussed in chapter 14.

2.4 SOFTWARE PIRACY

Software can be categorized into three categories—retail, freeware, and shareware. Retail software is software that is purchased from the software company or an authorized vendor. When purchasing retail software, a license is included in the user manual or on a separate piece of paper stating the legal use of the software. Freeware, or public domain software, is free software. Therefore, you can copy, install, and distribute it freely. Shareware is software that can be installed on your computer and tried for a time to see of you like it. If you decide to keep using the software, you are supposed to purchase it.

As a computer technician or consultant, you need to be aware of software piracy and its consequences. Software piracy (theft of intellectual property) is the illegal copying, distribution, or installation of software. It is copyright infringement. Some examples include:

1. Purchasing a software package that comes with a single-user license and loading it onto multiple computers or a network server.
2. Making, distributing, or selling copies that appear to be from an unauthorized source.
3. Distributing or selling software that has been unbundled from the products for which it was intended.
4. Downloading software from the Internet or bulletin boards without permission from the copyright holder.
5. Using a software package, purchasing an upgrade, and giving or selling the original software package to someone else.

If you are sued for civil copyright infringement, the penalty is up to $100,000 per title infringed. If charged with a criminal violation, the fine is up to $250,000 per title infringed and up to five years' imprisonment.

The Software Publishers Association (SPA) is an organization made up of software companies. One of its primary functions is to educate the public about software piracy and to catch companies and individuals pirating software. To accomplish this, they offer:

1. Easy ways to report software piracy by calling 1-800-388-7478 or sending an e-mail to piracy@spa.org.
2. Recommended software policy and employed usage guidelines, which can be utilized and adapted as needed. (http://www.spa.org/piracy/empguide.htm)
3. Several evaluation audit programs that can conduct hardware and software audits on network and stand-alone machines.

FIGURE 2.3   You should not pirate software

2.5 DEALING WITH THE CUSTOMER

When repairing computers, you may be repairing the computer for someone that works within the same company as you or for a customer who contacted you. One of your main responsibilities is to satisfy the customer or client. Since your job or business depends on the customers, you must be skilled at dealing with people.

You will find a wide range of computer users. Some of these people will be very knowledgeable about computers, while other people can barely turn them on. Some people will be easy to work with, and others will be more difficult. While you can show some people how to use the computer properly, you may find it is sometimes harder to fix people's attitudes than it is to fix a hardware or software problem.

When dealing with customers, you should follow certain guidelines. They are:

1. Always be courteous. Try to smile and say positive things to the customer whenever you can.
2. Focus on the customer and don't get distracted.
3. Be concerned about the customer's needs.
4. Don't belittle a customer, a customer's knowledge, or a customer's choice of hardware or software.
5. Don't complain to the customer and don't make excuses.
6. Stay calm. Don't get angry.
7. If you give a customer a component that appears to be defective or faulty, offer an immediate replacement.
8. Be professional. Dress appropriately for the environment. Don't take over a person's workspace without asking.
9. Be honest, especially if you caused a problem or you don't know the answer.
10. Be dependable and follow up on the service. If you will miss an appointment or will be late, call the customer to let him or her know.
11. Allow the customer to complain.
12. Allow the customer to explain the problem, and listen carefully.
13. If a customer is unhappy with you, your company, or a product, an apology can go a long way. If it is not your fault, you can still apologize for the situation. In addition, find out how you can make things better.

EXAMPLE 2.1   You are working for a help desk. At 8:45 A.M., you get a call from a customer saying that the printer they just bought from your company is not working.

When dealing with customers over the telephone, first gather certain information, such as the name of the company (if any), the name of the customer, a phone number to reach the customer, the type of hardware or software (in this case, the type of printer), and the nature of the problem. When the customer is done explaining the problem, you can then follow up with some of your own questions to gather more information. Next, you can ask the customer to check certain things, such as the printer connections and computer configuration. The customer's knowledge will determine the level at which you should communicate. For people who are not knowledgeable about computers, your explanations and directions need to be in easy-to-understand terms. If you can fix the problem over the phone, the customer will not have to bring the printer or system into your service department and you will not have to send someone to the customer.

If the customer cannot understand your directions, you can ask if there is anyone else to talk to, or you can get someone else from your department to talk to the customer. Don't be rude to the customer; stay calm. Whatever you do, don't yell at the customer and don't hang up on the customer.

EXAMPLE 2.2   After talking to the customer in example 1, the help desk personnel cannot fix the problem over the telephone. Therefore, they decide to send a service person to the customer's company. You are supposed to arrive at 11:30 A.M.

If the appointment is at 11:30 A.M., you need to show up at 11:30 A.M. If you can't make the appointment time because you are still finishing another service call, you need to call the customer to let him or her know what time you can make the appointment and apologize for the inconvenience. When you show up for the service call, you should be dressed appropriately for the environment. You should arrive with all the tools, test equipment, and software that is needed to effectively troubleshoot the problem. Don't take over the customer's work area and don't use the customer's telephone without permission. If you can't fix the problem because the printer is faulty, replace the printer immediately.

EXAMPLE 2.3   A customer brings in a computer saying that the computer will not turn on. What do you tell the customer when you cannot repeat or duplicate the problem?

If you cannot duplicate the problem, your people skills will be put to the test. First, you have to explain to the customer that you could not find anything wrong. This kind of news does not please most people. They feel that you do not know what you are doing, or they are angry with themselves for bringing in a system to be repaired that wasn't broken. In either case, they will usually be charged for the time and effort that you put into checking the machine.

To ease the customer's pain, show the customer what you did to try to duplicate the problem. Next, show the customer that the system is running properly. After assuring him or her that all is well, have the customer show you what he or she did when the computer failed. If the customer is able to duplicate the problem, you can then see the problem. If the user is causing the error by typing in the wrong key or doing something out of order, you can then show him or her the correct way to run the PC. In any case, you gave the customer excellent service.

ANECDOTES IN COMPUTER ILLITERACY

The next few stories will demonstrate some of the computer-illiterate people that you might deal with. Although these are extreme cases, they are all true stories. The first four anecdotes are based on stories that originally appeared in the *Wall Street Journal* and can be found throughout the Internet. The last story was told to me by a student of mine. Some of these stories might have happened to you when you were learning to use the computer!

Story #1. Many companies provide computer support over the telephone. One time, a customer was asked to send a copy of a defective disk. A few days later an envelope arrived from the customer with a photocopy of the disk.

Story #2. An exasperated caller to tech support could not get her new computer to turn on. After ensuring the computer was plugged in, the technician asked her what happened when she pushed the power button. Her response was, "I pushed and pushed on this foot pedal and nothing happens." The "foot pedal" turned out to be the computer's mouse.

Story #3. Technical support had a caller complaining that her mouse was hard to control with the dust cover on. The cover turned out to be the plastic bag the mouse was packaged in.

Story #4. A person called technical support on how to get his cup holder repaired since it broke off. The support person was puzzled and asked whether the cup holder was part of some special sales promotion or if it had any trademarks on it. The customer stated that he didn't know about any sales promotions and that it only had "4X" on it. Finally, the technician discovered that the customer broke off the load drawer of the CD-ROM drive.

Story #5. The last story is about a person who worked at a temporary service. The person's job was to fill out a form and fax the form to the central office. While sending the forms in a machine next to the computer, the temporary worker noticed that small strands came out the other side of the machine. When the owner discovered what the temporary worker did repeatedly, the owner asked, "Didn't you see the shredded paper?" The temporary worker's only response was, "Yes, but I thought that the paper was being shrunken down to fit through the wire."

2.6 PC TECHNICIAN TOOL KIT

To get a better understanding of what makes up a PC, you must first learn how to disassemble and reassemble a computer. To accomplish this, you will need a few basic tools. Many of these can be bought in a small tool kit made for PC technicians that sells for about $20.00. (See fig. 2.4.) The most common tools are described in table 2.4. Other useful tools include a flashlight, wire cutters, tamper-proof Torx drivers, file, electrical tape, can of compressed air, and lint-free cloth. A flashlight will help you identify PC components, especially in those hard-to-reach places. Wire cutters are useful for making or repairing cables or wiring. The Torx drivers are used to remove hex screws with a tamper-resistant pin in the center. A file is used to smooth rough or sharp edges. A roll of black electrical tape is used to wrap wire ends and insulate components.

You can use mild detergent and a damp cloth to clean the outside of the computer. To clean the monitor screen, use a damp cloth or special anti-static wipes. Use a can of compressed air to clean the inside of the computer. A can of compressed air is better than a vacuum cleaner because the compressed air can be directed more accurately and provides

FIGURE 2.4   Tool kit (courtesy
of Belkin Components)

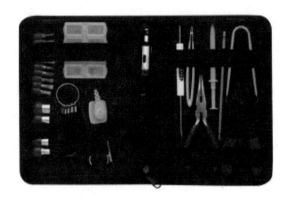

TABLE 2.4   PC technician's tool kit

Tool	Usage
Medium Phillips screwdriver (#2 head)	Probably the most commonly used tool. It is used to open most PCs and remove expansion cards, power supplies, motherboards, and drives.
Medium flat-edge screwdriver	
Small Phillips screwdriver	
Small flat-edge screwdriver	Can be used to pry chips from the motherboard. When using this tool to remove chips, take extreme care so that you do not bend or break any pins on the chips.
3/16-inch nut driver and 1/4-inch nut driver	Used to remove hexagonal-headed screws. These screws are used to secure the computer cover and expansion cards. Although you could use the screwdriver for most of these screws, a nut driver is easier and quicker to use.
Needlenose pliers	Useful for straightening pins on chips, changing jumper settings, crimping cables, or grabbing small parts.
Tweezers	Used to grab small parts.
Claw-type parts grabber	Used to grab small parts in tight places.
Chip puller (chip extractor)	Used to discharge NiCad (nickel-cadmium) batteries when needed or to remove keyboard key caps. Do not use the chip puller to remove chips since it will usually result in bent or broken pins.

more cleaning power. To clean the electrical contacts inside the computer, use metal contact cleaner or isopropyl alcohol with a cotton swab.

When using special cleaners or other chemicals, you should be aware of the proper usage, storage, and disposal of the chemicals and their impact on the environment. This information is usually found on the cleaner's container or on the Material Safety Directions Sheet (MSDS) that comes with the container or from the vendor.

2.7   TROUBLESHOOT-ING TOOLS

When a component fails to work, identifying what causes the failure is not always an easy task. However, several troubleshooting tools will help you isolate computer-related problems. They are:

1. POST error codes
2. POST cards
3. Software diagnostic packages
4. Measurements and inspection

2.7.1 POST ERROR CODES

During boot-up, the system ROM BIOS controls the power-on self-test (POST) during boot-up to perform a series of brief tests on major components. The purpose of the tests is to make sure the PC is functional before opening any files. If a test fails, an audio code consisting of a series of beeps will be heard or a video code consisting of a number or message will be displayed to identify the problem. This is known as a POST error code. Note: A single beep indicates a normal operation of the PC or speaker test.

> **Question:** You have turned on your computer, but you don't hear a beep upon a successful boot-up. What does this tell you?
>
> **Answer:** A single beep during boot-up usually indicates a successful boot, so there may be something wrong with the speakers or their connections. Check that the the speaker is connected properly and that the internal speaker is working properly. A good speaker should measure approximately 8 ohms.

When deciphering the meaning of a POST error code, you must first determine which system ROM BIOS manufacturer the computer has. Common manufacturers are IBM, AMI, Award, and Phoenix.

To identify which system ROM BIOS the machine has, you can:

1. Open the machine and look at the system ROM BIOS chip.
2. Look at the screen during boot-up. The manufacturer will be the second item listed on the screen. (The first item is the video ROM BIOS that activated the monitor.)
3. Use a software diagnostic package (assuming the computer can boot).

EXAMPLE 2.4 You have an IBM AT. The AT has a 286 microprocessor, 1 MB of RAM, 5¼-inch and 3½-inch floppy drives, and a 20 MB hard drive running DOS 5.0. You boot up the computer and you see *301* on the screen, and the computer seems to stop booting. What is the problem?

The problem is identified by the *301* error code. Since it is displayed on the screen, it is a video code. The first thing you need to know is which type of system BIOS your computer has. Since it is an IBM machine, it will, of course, have an IBM BIOS (this can also be verified by locating the ROM chips on the motherboard). Next, look in appendix C, table C.8 (IBM POST Error Codes), and look up the *301* code. The *301* error code means *stuck key or improper response*. By doing a quick inspection and checking the obvious, you may find that you left your keyboard unplugged.

EXAMPLE 2.5 You are using an ACME PC (PC clone) that contains a Pentium II microprocessor, 64 MB of RAM, 5¼-inch and a 3½-inch floppy drives, a CD-ROM drive, and a 4 GB hard drive running Windows 95. When the computer is booted up, you hear three short beeps and nothing appears on the screen. What is the problem?

Again, the first thing you need to know is which BIOS the Acme computer is using. After a quick inspection, you find that the BIOS is made by AMI. In this particular case, you have to locate the ROM chips on the motherboard because nothing showed up on the screen. Next, go to appendix C, table C.2 (AMI BIOS Beep Codes), and look up the three short beeps. The three short beeps mean it is *base 64 KB memory failure*. We will talk about what this means in following chapters.

Another tool to help diagnose problems with the PC during boot up is the **I/O POST Card.** (See fig. 2.5.) The POST card was originally designed to *burn in* systems (test new systems to find problems that would usually occur during the first few days of operation) on an assembly line. The POST card can also be used to diagnose a computer that does not boot and does not generate an audio or video error code.

During boot-up, the BIOS sends a test code to a special I/O (input/output) port address at the beginning of each test. These codes can be read and displayed (two or three numeric displays or a series of LEDs) with a special expansion card that is plugged into one of the expansion slots. If a test fails and the computer no longer boots, the code shown on the POST card will indicate what test failed.

EXAMPLE 2.6   We are using the same computer as in example 2.3. When you boot up the computer, it freezes. Nothing is displayed on the screen, and no beeps occurred. How can you isolate the problem?

The first thing to check is if there are any lights on and if the fan is running. If there are no lights on and the fan is not running, it is probably a power-related problem. For now, we will assume that power checks out and is not the source of the problem. Shut down the machine and insert an I/O POST card that will work with AMI BIOS into one of the expansion slots. Next, turn on the computer. When the computer boots, the POST card displays two characters, *52*. Look in appendix C, table C.3 (AMI POST Error Codes), and find that it says *Memory test above 1 M complete. Going to prepare to go back to real mode.* Since the computer froze at this point and this code is showing, the system could not switch back to real mode, for whatever reason. Therefore, it is probably a CPU or motherboard problem. If you don't understand what the microprocessor's real mode is, don't worry. It will be discussed in chapter 5.

> **NOTE**   POST error messages occur during boot-up, before the operating system is loaded into RAM. Error messages can also be generated by the operating system and software applications.

2.7.2   TROUBLESHOOTING DISKS

A valuable tool for the computer technician is a good set of troubleshooting disks. They can be used to gather information about a system or a computer problem, help to isolate a problem, and correct some of the problems. The troubleshooting disks can be divided into three categories:

1. Boot disk
2. Diagnostic package
3. Antivirus software

The **boot disk** is a disk that can load the operating system using the A drive. Therefore, if the hard drive is no longer bootable, you can boot using the A drive and then change over to the C drive to further investigate the problem and to perform repairs. You should have a boot disk for every operating system that you typically deal with, and it should contain common operating system files that will help you isolate or fix problems. (See exercises 1, 2, and 3 at the end of this chapter.)

TABLE 2.5 Common software diagnostic packages

Software Title	Company and Website	Comments
Checkit	TouchStone Software Corp. http://www.touchstonesoftware.com Evaluation copy is available at touchstonesoftware.com and zdnet.com	Good reporting and hardware diagnostic package. Hardware diagnostic software can also be executed at the command prompt.
First Aid 98	Cybermedia Inc. http://www.cybermedia.com	Good software troubleshooting and optimization package with hardware diagnostic.
Micro-Scope	Micro 2000, Inc. http://www.micro2000.com	Thorough reporting and hardware diagnostic package.
Norton Utilities	Symantec Corp. http://www.symantec.com Evaluation copy is available at zdnet.com	Good software troubleshooting and optimization package with hardware diagnostic and reporting. Well-known for Norton Disk Doctor (enhanced version of SCANDISK).
Nuts & Bolts	Network Associates http://www.nai.com Evaluation copy is available at nai.com and zdnet.com	Good software troubleshooting and optimization package with hardware diagnostic and reporting.
PC Care	American Megatrends http://www.ami.com	Good hardware diagnostic package.
QA Plus	Diagsoft http://www.diagsoft.com Evaluation copy can be ordered from diagsoft.com	Good hardware diagnostic and reporting package.

A software diagnostic package can report resources (I/O addresses, IRQs, DMAs, and memory addresses) used by devices, hardware diagnostics, software troubleshooting, and software optimization. (The hardware resources are explained in chapter 8.) The most common software diagnostic packages are shown in table 2.5. Note that DOS, Windows 95, Windows 98, and Windows NT provide some utilities (MSD, Device Manager, and Microsoft Diagnostic) to report and analyze the hardware. (See fig. 2.6.)

While some of the software packages can do a lot, they are really only tools that allow you to gather information. Software packages that test hardware components and try to troubleshoot software problems are far from foolproof. For example, when testing a hardware component, the software sends a predetermined code, signal, or pattern to the component being tested. If the component replies back with the correct response, it is considered a good component. However, if the problem is intermittent, you may run every test that the software has, but unless the problem occurs during the test, you will never know that the problem exists. In addition, even when a component test fails, it may not be bad—the problem could be caused indirectly by another bad component. Note that if the computer doesn't boot, you can't run any software, including software diagnostic packages.

Finally, you should have an up-to-date copy of **anti-virus software** on floppy disks. **Viruses** are small programs that can damage data on hard drives and floppy disks. Much like a virus attacking the human body and spreading from one person to another, these programs spread from computer to computer as they transfer themselves from disk to disk. When a virus is suspected, you need to boot with a clean (noninfected) disk and start the anti-virus program to check and clean the disk. The most popular anti-virus software packages are shown in table 2.6.

2.7.3 MEASUREMENTS AND INSPECTION

The last method in troubleshooting a computer involves measurements and inspection. Measurements are done with a **multimeter.** (For example, you can determine the voltage output of a power supply or electrical outlet or you can measure the continuity of a wire or speaker). To make proper measurements and to complete a thorough inspection, you will need to have a working knowledge of how the computer operates. You will also need to know what the measurements are supposed to read.

FIGURE 2.6   MSD utility

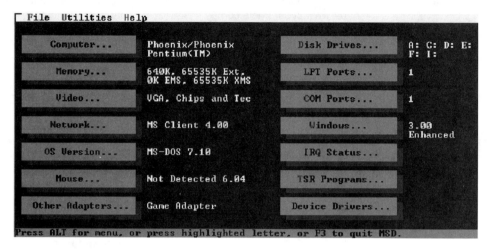

TABLE 2.6   Popular antivirus software packages

Software Title	Company and Website
Integrity Master	Stiller Research http://www.stiller.com Evaluation copy is available at stiller.com and zdnet.com
Norton AntiVirus (NAV)	Symantec Corporation http://www.symantec.com Evaluation copy is available at symatic.com and zdnet.com
Dr. Solomon Anti-Virus	Dr. Solomon's Software Inc. http://www.drsolomon.com Evaluation copy is available at drsolomon.com and zdnet.com
McAfee VirusScan	Network Associates http://www.networkassociate.com Evaluation copy is available at networkassociate.com and zdnet.com

SUMMARY

1. When troubleshooting computer problems, you must keep an open mind as to the cause of the problem. The problem could be hardware failure, a compatibility problem, an improper configuration, a software glitch, an environmental factor, or a user error.
2. Before trying to fix the problem, gather information.
3. After you have gathered as much information as you can, you are ready to make the repair or fix. Sometimes you will know exactly what to change or replace. At other times you will have to isolate the problem.
4. After you fix the problem, you should always thoroughly test the computer before returning it to the customer or client.
5. You are expected to understand computers well enough to investigate and isolate problems, know when you need to find more information, and know how to get the information in a timely manner so that you can fix the problem.
6. A backup of a system is an extra copy of data and programs.
7. Software piracy (theft of intellectual property) is the illegal copying, distribution, or installation of software.
8. The position of computer technician is a job that requires dealing with people.
9. The system ROM BIOS controls the power-on self-test (POST) during boot-up to perform a series of brief tests on major components.
10. You must first determine which system ROM BIOS manufacturer the computer has in order to decipher the meaning of a POST error code.
11. During boot-up, the BIOS sends a test code to a special I/O port address at the beginning of each test. These codes can be read with a special expansion card called a POST card.
12. A valuable tool for the computer technician is a good set of troubleshooting disks. They can be used to gather information about a system or a computer problem, help to isolate a problem, and correct some of the problems.

QUESTIONS

1. Before troubleshooting a problem, you must be able to (choose two answers):
   a. duplicate the problem
   b. replace the faulty component
   c. reformat the hard drive
   d. gather information
   e. run the CMOS setup program and change the number of wait states
2. Which of the following would be a logical first step in troubleshooting a PC?
   a. check the computer CMOS
   b. call the vendor
   c. define what applications are being used
   d. fire the user
   e. find the circumstances of the problem
3. The most important part of the computer to the user is the:
   a. microprocessor
   b. RAM
   c. keyboard
   d. data
   e. monitor
4. What is the most frequent cause of computer problems?
   a. hardware failure
   b. software glitches
   c. compatibility problems
   d. user errors
5. A customer complains because she has been on hold for a long time and has been transferred several times. What should you do?
   a. apologize for the inconvenience and offer to help her now
   b. give her your home phone number or cellular phone number
   c. tell her the best time to call back
   d. explain how busy you are
6. A customer calls and tells you that the hard drive you just sold him was defective. What should you do?
   a. tell the customer to call the manufacturer
   b. call the manufacturer for the customer

    c. tell him you will replace it if he can prove that it is defective

    d. replace the drive

7. A customer calls and complains that the computer you just repaired is still not working properly. What should you do?

    a. apologize and explain that it is a different problem than the one you repaired

    b. explain that the customer did something wrong

    c. refer the customer to another repair facility

    d. offer to replace any new components you installed or reservice the computer

8. A customer on the telephone can't understand your directions. What is the one thing that you should *not* do?

    a. ask if there is someone else you can speak to

    b. hang up on him because he can't follow directions

    c. refer him to a customer center

    d. tell him someone will call him back

9. What is the last thing you should do to complete a service call?

    a. hand the customer a bill

    b. thank the customer for his or her business

    c. explain why the repair took so long

    d. tell the customer how he or she could have repaired the problem

10. Why do we want a backup of the system?

    a. It is the best way to overcome data loss.

    b. Data may be erased during the fixing of computers.

    c. Data is the most important thing in the computer.

    d. all of the above

    e. none of the above

11. *True or false*—Before isolating a computer problem, you must be able to duplicate the problem.

12. You conclude that three components could be causing a particular problem. Which of the following is the best course of action?

    a. replace the one that you think is failing and return the system to the customer

    b. replace them one at a time to verify the failing part and then return the system to the customer

    c. replace the least expensive part and return the system to the customer

    d. replace all three and return the system to the customer

13. One of the first things to do when repairing a PC is:

    a. confirm that the 120 Vac power supply is filtered for noise

    b. confirm that the user is not part of the problem

    c. check the hard drive for correct format information in the CMOS setup program

    d. replace all components that can cause the problem

14. During boot-up, what does a single beep indicate?

    a. a hardware problem with the PC

    b. an operating system or application program problem

    c. an incompatible expansion card

    d. normal operation of the PC or speaker test

15. Which of the following could be a valuable source of information during troubleshooting?

    a. the customer

    b. hardware and software documentation

    c. the Internet

    d. all of the above

16. You have a computer that generates six beeps during boot-up. What is the first thing you must find out when determining the meaning of the beeps?

    a. the type of microprocessor

    b. the manufacturer of the system ROM BIOS

    c. the manufacturer of the video ROM BIOS

    d. the type of operating system on the hard drive

17. You have a computer that has a Pentium II microprocessor, an AMI system ROM BIOS, 64 MB of RAM, a 6 GB hard drive, and an All-Tech monitor. During boot-up, it generates six beeps. What is the problem?
    a. the read/write memory on the video card
    b. the A20 line
    c. the base 64 KB RAM
    d. a bad hard drive
    e. corrupt boot files
    f. a virus
18. You have a computer problem. What is the best method to determine if the problem is a hardware problem or a software problem?
    a. upgrade the operating system
    b. format the C drive and reload the operating system
    c. replace the motherboard
    d. move the hard drive to another computer
    e. boot the computer with a clean boot disk
19. What is the simplest and most efficient method of testing a component?
    a. run a software diagnostic test on the component
    b. make measurements with a multimeter or oscilloscope
    c. run the CMOS setup program
    d. boot the computer
    e. observe the component and see if it operates properly

HANDS-ON EXERCISES

Exercise 1: Making a DOS Troubleshooting Boot Disk

1. Label the outside of the disk as "DOS TROUBLESHOOTING DISK."
2. Format the practice disk in Drive A as a bootable disk.
3. Copy the FORMAT.COM, FDISK.EXE, MSD.EXE, EDIT.COM, EDIT.HLP, QBASIC.EXE, ATTRIB.EXE, SYS.COM, MEM.EXE, SCANDISK.EXE, and MSCDEX.EXE files from the C:\DOS directory to the disk in the A drive.
4. Copy the mouse driver executable file (.COM/.EXE extension) to the disk in the A drive. Example: MOUSE.COM or MOUSE.EXE file located in the MOUSE directory.
5. Write-protect the disk.
6. Boot from the floppy disk to make sure that it boots properly.

Exercise 2: Making a Windows 95/Windows 98 Troubleshooting Boot Disk

Note: You should create a troubleshooting boot disk for each version (Windows 95a, Windows 95b, Windows 95c, and Windows 98) that you work with.

1. Label the outside of the disk as "WINDOWS 95/WINDOWS 98 TROUBLESHOOT-ING DISK."
2. From the Control Panel, open the Add/Remove Programs applet/icon.
3. From the Startup Disk tab, click on the Create Disk button. Note: You may need a Windows 95 or Windows 98 CD-ROM disk or another source of the Windows installation files.
4. Write-protect the disk.
5. Boot from the floppy disk to make sure that it boots properly.

Exercise 3: Making a Windows NT Troubleshooting Boot Disk

1. Format a disk on a computer running Windows NT.
2. Copy the NTLDR, NTDETECT.COM, and BOOT.INI files from the root directory to the floppy disk in drive A.
3. If you are using SCSI cards with a BIOS-disabled SCSI adapter, copy the NTBOOTDD.SYS file. Ask your instructor if you don't know.

4. Write-protect the disk.
5. Boot from the floppy disk to make sure that it boots properly.

Exercise 4: Identifying PC Hardware Configuration I

1. Perform a cold boot (use the reset switch or on/off switch). If the computer displays information about the type of CPU, amount of RAM, the number and types of drives, and other useful information, press the pause key.
2. Identify the following:
     type of microprocessor
     type of math coprocessor
     size of all floppy drives and hard drives
     number of serial (COMX) ports
     number of parallel (LPTX) ports
     amount of conventional memory (base) and extended memory

Exercise 5: Identifying PC Hardware Configuration II

1. Start MSD.EXE. It should be in the C:\DOS directory, C:\WINDOWS\COMMAND directory, or C:\WIN95\COMMAND directory.
2. Identify the following:
     type of microprocessor
     type of math coprocessor
     size of all floppy drives and hard drives
     number of serial (COM) ports
     number of parallel (LPT) ports
     amount of conventional memory (base) and extended memory
3. Exit MSD.EXE.

Exercise 6: Identifying PC Hardware Configuration III

1. If you have Windows 95, go to the Control Panel and open the System applet.
2. From the General tab, identify the following:
     type of microprocessor
     amount of physical RAM
3. Click on the Device Manager tab.
4. Identify the following:
     number of serial (COM) ports
     number of parallel (LPT) ports
     type of mouse
     type of video card and monitor

Exercise 7: Using Software Diagnostic Packages

1. Run a software diagnostic package to identify the following:
     type of microprocessor
     manufacturer of the system ROM BIOS
     size of the hard drive
     number of serial ports (COMX)
     number of parallel ports (LPTX)
2. Run a software diagnostic package to test the following components:
     motherboard and CPU
     RAM
     floppy drives and hard drives
     video card and monitor
     serial and parallel ports

3. Run a software diagnostic package to check the speed of the following components:
   CPU
   floppy drives and hard drives
   system

Exercise 8: Create a Flowchart for Troubleshooting

Create a generic troubleshooting plan in the form of a flowchart.

Exercise 9: Software Piracy

Go to the website http://www.spa.org/piracy/pirnews.htm and read three articles on software piracy.

3 Basic Electronics

INTRODUCTION

To have a good understanding of the computer, you must have a basic knowledge of electricity and the basic electronic components that make up the PC. In addition, you need to take certain precautions when disassembling and reassembling the PC so that you do not damage the computer and are not injured.

OBJECTIVES

1. Explain how electrons relate to electricity.
2. Explain the differences between conductor, insulator, and semiconductor.
3. Define a circuit and list its primary parts.
4. Explain how an "open" and a "short" can affect a circuit.
5. Identify the basic electronic components and their schematic symbols and describe their basic characteristics.
6. Compare and contrast dc voltage and ac voltage.
7. Test an ac-power wall outlet.

8. Use a voltmeter to measure the voltage of an electronic device.
9. Use an ohmmeter to measure the resistance of an electronic device, including a wire.
10. Define electrostatic electricity.
11. Describe how to avoid electrostatic electricity.
12. Demonstrate proper ESD procedures when handling PC components.

3.1 ELECTRICITY

Atoms, very small particles that make up everything in the universe, themselves consist of three elementary particles. (See fig. 3.1.) In the center of the atom are the protons (positive-charged particles) and neutrons (neutral-charged particles), which make up the nucleus. Orbiting the nucleus are the electrons (negative-charged particles). Under certain conditions, the electrons can flow from one atom to another. This rate of flow of the electrons is known as **current** (electricity), which is measured in **amps (A).**

FIGURE 3.1   The atom

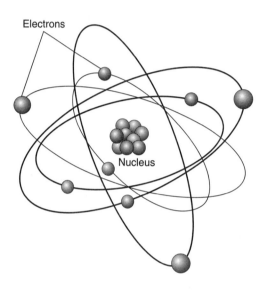

Electrons

Nucleus

3.2 ELECTRONIC COMPONENTS

Electronic devices are made using a combination of conductor, insulator, and semiconductor materials. A **conductor** is material in which current can flow easily. Most metals are good conductors, particularly silver and copper. Copper wire is often used as a conductor within electric circuits because it is inexpensive, yet very good. (See fig. 3.2.) An **insulator** is a poor conductor of electric current; therefore, insulators such as rubber are used to prevent current where it is not wanted. A **semiconductor** is a material that is neither a good conductor of electricity nor a good insulator. Computer chips, such as the microprocessor, RAM, and motherboard support chips, are composed of semiconductor materials.

3.2.1   VOLTAGE, RESISTANCE, AND CURRENT

Resistance is the characteristic of a material that opposes the flow of current. Components that are specifically designed to oppose current are known as *resistors*. Resistance is measured in **ohms (Ω).** The electrons flowing through a circuit are provided by an electronic power supply or a battery. The force that moves the electrons generated by the power supply or battery is called **voltage,** which is measured in **volts (V).**

FIGURE 3.2   A copper wire conductor surrounded by rubber insulator

Computers use many electrical circuits made up of integrated chips, transistors, resistors, capacitors, and inductors. Each of these electrical components reacts in a predictable way when a certain voltage is applied.

When a conductor, such as a wire, is moved through a magnetic field, a voltage is produced across the conductor and if the conductor is part of a circuit, current will flow through the circuit. This flow also produces an electromagnetic field. The amount of resistance in a circuit affects the amount of current. If the circuit has less resistance, the current will be more; if the circuit has more resistance, the current will be less. This can be shown by a common mathematical equation known as **Ohm's law:**

$$V = IR$$

where V is the voltage supplied by the battery,
              I is the current of the circuit, and
              R is the resistance of the circuit.

Power (P) is the rate of energy consumption or the amount of energy used in a certain length of time. In electronics, it is expressed in watts (W).

3.2.2 A CIRCUIT

The voltage source (power supply or battery) and electronic components are connected with a conductor such as a wire or metal trace to form a **circuit.** (See fig. 3.3.) Electrons leave the voltage source through the path of least resistance to a common return known as a ground. The **ground** is a reference point in electronic circuits.

The basic components of a circuit are a power source (such as a battery or power supply), the path (wire or metal traces on a circuit board), and a *load.* The load consists of resistors, capacitors, inductors, diodes, transistors, and other electronic components. (See table 3.1.) If there is a break in the conductor (known as an **open**) and there is no other pathway for the electrons to take, the current will not flow. When a circuit has zero or abnormally low resistance between two points, a **short** (excessive current) results.

3.2.3 INDUCTORS AND CAPACITORS

When a conducting wire is made into a coil **(inductor),** its magnetic field is intensified, which increases the voltage across the conductor. This capacity of an inductor, known as *inductance,* is measured in henrys (H). The electromagnetic field of an inductor is used to resist change in the current's polarity and flow rate.

A **capacitor** is a device that stores an electric charge. The amount of charge that can be stored per unit of voltage is known as *capacitance,* which is measured in farads (F). A capacitor can hold its charge for long periods. Therefore, before you work with any circuit containing capacitors, the capacitors should be discharged.

3.2.4 SWITCHES AND FUSES

A **switch** is an electrical or electronic device that opens and closes a current path. While the switch is open (off), the resistance across the switch is infinite and so the current cannot flow. While the switch is closed (on), the resistance across the switch is 0 ohms and so the current is able to flow.

FIGURE 3.3   A circuit

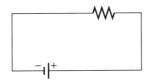

TABLE 3.1   Common electronic devices

Device	Description	How to Test the Electronic Device
Battery	A device that supplies dc power. Example: The CMOS battery that powers the CMOS RAM and real-time clock to function when the computer is off.	Set the voltmeter (or multimeter) to dc. Connect one lead to the positive end of the battery and the other lead to the negative end.
Power supply	A device that converts ac power into dc power. Example: The power supply converts ac power to +5 V dc, − 5 V dc, + 12 V dc, − 12 V dc.	Set the voltmeter (or multimeter) to dc. Connect one lead to a voltage output (such as +5 V or +12 V wire) and connect the other lead to ground.
Resistor	A device that resists current. Example: Resistors are used in most electronic devices.	To properly test a resistor, it must be removed from the circuit. Note: using an ohmmeter to test a resistor without removing it from the circuit could damage other electronic devices since the voltmeter uses voltage to determine resistance.
Wire (including metal traces)	A conductor that connects electronic devices and serves as an electrical pathway through which current can flow. Example: Wire is part of every circuit, including the power supply, motherboard, and expansion cards.	An ohmmeter (or multimeter) is used to test wires. Zero resistance in the wire indicates continuity (an unbroken circuit). If the wire has infinite resistance, it has an open and is considered defective.
Fuse	A protective device that melts when the circuit has too much current, causing an open in the circuit pathway. Example: Some fuses are contained within power supplies and motherboards.	An ohmmeter (or multimeter) will measure no resistance in a good fuse. A bad fuse with an open will measure infinity.
Capacitor	A device that stores electric charge (electrons). Example: Capacitors are used in RAM IC chips and power supplies.	To properly test a capacitor, it must be removed from the circuit. To remove a capacitor from a computer takes special skills and tools.

A **fuse** is a protective device in a circuit that melts when there is excessive current. (See fig. 3.4.) Therefore, under normal conditions, the fuse completes the circuit, but when the fuse melts open due to excessive current, the circuit is incomplete and current cannot flow.

3.2.5   TRANSISTORS AND INTEGRATED CIRCUITS

A **transistor** is a small electronic component that is found in virtually every electronic device. (See fig. 3.5.) It has two basic applications: amplifying an electric signal, and

FIGURE 3.4   A fuse

Device	Description	How to Test the Electronic Device
Inductor	A coil of wire that can transfer voltage or current using magnetic fields (without physical contact). It resists the change of current.\n\nExample: Inductors are used in power supplies and power protection devices.	To properly test an inductor, it must be removed from the circuit. To remove an inductor from a computer takes special skills and tools.
Transformer	A device that has two or more coil windings that are used to increase or decrease voltage.\n\nExample: Transformers are used in power supplies and power protection devices.	To properly test a transformer, it must be removed from the circuit. To remove a transformer from a computer takes special skills and tools.
Diode	A device that allows current to flow in one direction only.\n\nExample: Diodes are used in power supplies and power protection devices. Note: An LED light is a special diode.	To properly test a diode, it must be removed from the circuit. To remove a diode from a computer takes special skills tools.
Transistor	A device that can amplify signals or be used as an electronic on/off switch.\n\nExample: Transistors are used within power supplies and IC chips, such as the microprocessor and RAM chips.	To properly test a transistor, it must be removed from the circuit. To remove a transistor from a computer takes special skills and tools.
Integrated circuit (IC)	A device containing transistors, diodes, resistors, and capacitors in one miniaturized package.\n\nExample: Microprocessors, RAM chips, and motherboard support chips are all integrated circuits.	To properly test an integrated circuit, it must be removed from the circuit. To remove a integrated circuit from a computer takes special skills and tools.

fast switching. Switching is important to computers, which work by making millions of lightning-fast on-off changes.

An **integrated circuit (IC),** sometimes referred to as a *chip,* is a small electronic device made of semiconductor material (usually silicon) and consists of transistors, resistors, and capacitors. (See fig. 3.6.) The transistors on integrated chips are small, fast, and reliable and use relatively little power compared to other transistors. Integrated circuits are often classified by the number of electronic components they contain. (See table 3.2.)

There are two types of integrated circuits. The first type is the **transistor-transistor logic (TTL)** chip, which is based on two transistors. TTL chips run on +5 V dc power. The second type is the **complementary metal oxide semiconductor (CMOS)** chip. CMOS

FIGURE 3.5   A transistor

43

FIGURE 3.6   Integrated chip

TABLE 3.2   IC classification

IC Classification	Number of Components per Chip
Small-scale integration (SSI)	Up to 100
Medium-scale integration (MSI)	From 100 to 3,000
Large-scale integration (LSI)	From 3,000 to 100,000
Very large scale integration (VLSI)	From 100,000 to 1,000,000
Ultra–large scale integration (ULSI)	More than 1 million

chips are widely used in both NMOS (negative polarity) and PMOS (positive polarity) circuits. Since only one of the circuit types is on at any given time, and CMOS chips require less power than TTL chips, you will find CMOS chips running on +5.0 V dc or less.

> If you want more information on how computer chips are made, visit the following website:
> **http://www.chips.ibm.com/technology/makechip/**

3.3   POWER

Computers use **direct current** (dc) current that flows in only one direction and has a fixed polarity (positive or negative). If the voltage is steady, the graph of the voltage represents a straight, unchanging horizontal line in relation to time. (See fig. 3.7.)

FIGURE 3.7   Direct current (dc) voltage

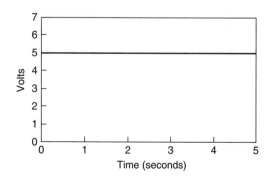

FIGURE 3.8 Alternating current (ac) voltage

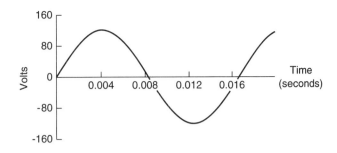

FIGURE 3.9 Outlet (ac)

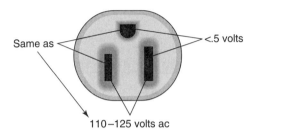

The opposite of a direct current voltage source is the **alternating current (ac)** voltage source, which uses ac power. Unlike dc voltage, ac current reverses directions in cycles, changing its polarity from positive to negative to positive again. (See fig. 3.8.) The frequency of an ac source is the number of complete cycles per second, measured in hertz (Hz).

Although most electronic devices use dc power, it is ac power that is sent to your house or place of work through the power lines to the ac power outlets. The reason ac power is used is that it can be sent over long distances much more efficiently than dc power. Its voltage is between 115 and 125 volts at a frequency of 60 Hz. (The 60 Hz means that there are 60 complete cycles per second in the current.)

The ac power outlet has three wires leading to three connectors. The power plug that connects to the ac power outlet has two blades and a ground. The smaller blade is for the hot wire, and the other blade is for the return. The wire leading to the slot used for the small blade is usually black; the wire leading to the slot used by the large blade is usually white. The ground wire is usually green.

The voltage between the two slots in a power outlet should test between 110 and 125 V ac. The voltage between the smaller slot and the ground should be the same as measured between the two slots. The voltage between the larger blade and the ground should be .5 V ac or less. (See fig. 3.9. Note: A $5–$10 outlet wire tester can be bought at any hardware store.)

It is important to have and use the ground connector. It makes electronic equipment (including computers) safer to work with, prevents electrical shock, and will minimize errors caused by electrical problems on the PC.

3.4 DECIMAL, BINARY, AND HEXADECIMAL NUMBER SYSTEMS

The most commonly used numbering system is the **decimal number system.** There are 10 different possible digits for each position in the decimal numbering system. Because there are 10 different possible digits—the digits are 0, 1, 2, 3, 4, 5, 6, 7, 8, and 9—the decimal number system is said to have numbers with *base 10*. In order to count values larger than 9, each position going away from the decimal point increases in value by a multiple of 10. (See table 3.3.)

TABLE 3.3 Decimal number system

7th Place	6th Place	5th Place	4th Place	3rd Place	2nd Place	1st Place
10^6	10^5	10^4	10^3	10^2	10^1	10^0
1,000,000	100,000	10,000	1,000	100	10	1

EXAMPLE 3.1 The value of decimal number 234 is shown by the following:

2	3	4
2×10^2	3×10^1	4×10^0
200	30	4

Therefore, the value is $200 + 30 + 4 = 234$.

3.4.1 BINARY NUMBER SYSTEM

The **binary number system** is another way of counting. The binary system is less complicated than the decimal system because it has only two digits, a zero (0) and a one (1). A computer represents a binary value with the electronic switch known as a transistor. If the switch is on, it allows current to flow through a wire or metal trace to represent a binary value of one (1). If the switch is off, it does not allow current to flow through a wire and represents a value of zero (0). (See table 3.4.) The on switch is also referred to as a *high* signal, while the off switch is referred to as a *low* signal.

If two switches are used to represent binary data, the first switch can be on or off and the second switch can be on or off, giving a total of four combinations or four binary values. (See table 3.5.) If four switches are used to represent data, 16 different binary values can be represented. (See table 3.6.)

Since each switch represents two values, each switch used doubles the number of binary values. Therefore, the number of binary values can be expressed with the following equation:

$$\text{Number of binary numbers} = 2^{\text{Number of binary digits}}$$

Therefore, one wire allows $2^1 = 2$ binary numbers, 0 and 1. Two wires allow $2^2 = 4$ binary numbers, 0, 1, 2, and 3. Four wires allow $2^4 = 16$ binary numbers.

Question: How many values can 1 byte represent?

Answer: Since a byte has eight binary digits, a byte can represent $2^8 = 256$ different characters.

TABLE 3.4 One-digit binary number

Switch 1	Binary Equivalent	Decimal Equivalent
Off	0	0
On	1	1

TABLE 3.5 Two-digit binary number

Switch 1	Switch 2	Binary Equivalent	Decimal Equivalent
Off	Off	00	0
Off	On	01	1
On	Off	10	2
On	On	11	3

TABLE 3.6 Four-digit binary
number

Switch 1	Switch 2	Switch 3	Switch 4	Binary Equivalent	Decimal Equivalent
Off	Off	Off	Off	0000	0
Off	Off	Off	On	0001	1
Off	Off	On	Off	0010	2
Off	Off	On	On	0011	3
Off	On	Off	Off	0100	4
Off	On	Off	On	0101	5
Off	On	On	Off	0110	6
Off	On	On	On	0111	7
On	Off	Off	Off	1000	8
On	Off	Off	On	1001	9
On	Off	On	Off	1010	10
On	Off	On	On	1011	11
On	On	Off	Off	1100	12
On	On	Off	On	1101	13
On	On	On	Off	1110	14
On	On	On	On	1111	15

Much like decimal numbers, the binary digits have placeholders that represent certain values, as shown in table 3.7.

EXAMPLE 3.2 Convert the binary number 11101010 to a decimal number.

1	1	1	0	1	0	1	0
1×2^7	1×2^6	1×2^5	0×2^4	1×2^3	0×2^2	1×2^1	0×2^0
128	64	32	0	8	0	2	0

Therefore, the binary number of 11101010 is equal to the decimal number of $128 + 64 + 32 + 8 + 2 = 234$.

EXAMPLE 3.3 Convert the decimal number 234 to a binary number.

Referring to table 3.7, you can see that the largest power of 2 that will fit into 234 is 2^7 (128). This leaves the value of $234 - 128 = 106$. The next largest power of 2 that will fit

TABLE 3.7 Binary number
system

8th Place	7th Place	6th Place	5th Place	4th Place	3rd Place	2nd Place	1st Place
2^7	2^6	2^5	2^4	2^3	2^2	2^1	2^0
128	64	32	16	8	4	2	1

into 106 is 2^6 (64). This leaves a value of $106 - 64 = 42$. The next largest power of 2 that will fit into 42 is 2^5 (32), which gives us $42 - 32 = 10$. The next largest power of 2 that will fit into 10 is 23 (8), which gives us $10 - 8 = 2$. The next largest power of 2 that will fit into 2 is 2^1 (2), which gives us $2 - 2 = 0$.

$$
\begin{array}{rl}
234 & \\
-128 & 2^7 \\
\hline
106 & \\
-64 & 2^6 \\
\hline
42 & \\
-32 & 2^5 \\
\hline
10 & \\
-8 & 2^3 \\
\hline
2 & \\
-2 & 2^1 \\
\hline
0 &
\end{array}
$$

Therefore, the binary equivalent of 234 is 11101010.

1	1	1	0	1	0	1	0
2^7	2^6	2^5	2^4	2^3	2^2	2^1	2^0

In computers, one of these digits is known as a **bit.** When several bits are combined, they can signify a letter, a number, a punctuation mark, a special graphical character, or a computer instruction. Eight bits make up a **byte.**

Since a byte is such a small unit, it is more convenient to use kilobytes (KB), megabytes (MB), and gigabytes (GB). The prefix *kilo-* indicates one thousand, *mega-* indicates one million, *giga-* indicates one billion, and *tera-* indicates one trillion. These measurements are not exact, however. A kilobyte is actually 1,024 bytes, not 1,000. This is because 2^{10} is equal to 1,024. A megabyte is 1,024 kilobytes, a gigabyte is 1,024 megabytes, and a terabyte is 1,024 gigabytes.

1 kilobyte = 1,024 bytes
1 megabyte = 1,024 kilobytes = 1,048,576 bytes
1 gigabyte = 1,024 megabytes = 1,048,576 kilobytes = 1,073,741,824 bytes

3.4.2 HEXADECIMAL NUMBER SYSTEM

The **hexadecimal number system** has 16 digits. One hexadecimal digit is equivalent to a four-digit binary number (4 bits, or a *nibble*), and two hexadecimal digits are used to represent a byte (8 bits). Therefore, it is very easy to translate between hexadecimal and binary, and the hexadecimal system is used primarily as a "shorthand" way of displaying binary numbers. (See table 3.8.) A number that represents a hexadecimal number will often end with the letter *H*. In order to count values larger than 15 in the hexadecimal system, each position going away from the decimal point in a decimal number increases in value by a multiple of 16. See table 3.9.

Question: What is the hexadecimal number that represents the binary number 1001 1010?

Answer: 1001 is equivalent to 9 and 1010 is equivalent to A, so the hexadecimal equivalent is 9AH.

To convert a hexadecimal number to a decimal number, you could first convert the hexadecimal number to binary and then convert the binary number to decimal. Another way to convert is to multiply the decimal value of each hexadecimal digit by its place and then take the sum of these products.

TABLE 3.8 Hexadecimal digit

Decimal	Binary	Hexadecimal
0	0000	0
1	0001	1
2	0010	2
3	0011	3
4	0100	4
5	0101	5
6	0110	6
7	0111	7
8	1000	8
9	1001	9
10	1010	A
11	1011	B
12	1100	C
13	1101	D
14	1110	E
15	1111	F

TABLE 3.9 Hexadecimal number system

7th Place	6th Place	5th Place	4th Place	3rd Place	2nd Place	1st Place
16^6	16^5	16^4	16^3	16^2	16^1	16^0
16777216	1048576	65536	4096	256	16	1

EXAMPLE 3.4 To convert EAH to a decimal number, you would multiply A by 16^0 and E by 16^1 and then add up the totals.

E	A
$E \times 16^1 = 14 \times 16^1 = 14 \times 16$	$A \times 16^0 = 10 \times 16^0 = 10 \times 1$
224	10

Therefore, the hexadecimal number EA is equal to the decimal number $224 + 10 = 234$.

EXAMPLE 3.5 To convert the decimal number of 234 to a hexadecimal number, refer to table 3.9 to see that the largest power of 16 that will fit into 234 is 16^1 (16). 16 goes into 234 a total of 14 (E) times, leaving a 10 (A).

$$234/16 = \mathbf{14}.625$$
$$234 - (\mathbf{14} \times 16) = 10$$
$$14 = EH$$

16^1	16^0
14×16^1	10×16^0
E	A

49

3.4.3 ASCII CHARACTER SET

In order to communicate, you need numbers, letters, punctuation, and other symbols. In the computer, an alphanumeric code represents these characters and various instructions necessary for conveying information. One commonly used alphanumeric code is the **ASCII (American Standard Code for Information Interchange) character set.** ASCII is based on eight bits, so there are 256 different possible combinations of 0s and 1s, allowing 256 ($2^8 = 256$) different characters. A partial listing of the ASCII characters is shown in table 3.10. The entire ASCII chart is shown in appendix B. For example, if a byte had the binary code 01000001, the byte would represent capital letter *A* (see fig. 3.10); 01100001 would represent lowercase *a*.

TABLE 3.10   A partial list of the ASCII character set

DEC	BIN	HEX	ASCII	DEC	BIN	HEX	ASCII	DEC	BIN	HEX	ASCII
32	00100000	20	space	64	01000000	40	@	96	01100000	60	`
33	00100001	21	!	65	01000001	41	A	97	01100001	61	a
34	00100010	22	"	66	01000010	42	B	98	01100010	62	b
35	00100011	23	#	67	01000011	43	C	99	01100011	63	c
36	00100100	24	$	68	01000100	44	D	100	01100100	64	d
37	00100101	25	%	69	01000101	45	E	101	01100101	65	e
38	00100110	26	&	70	01000110	46	F	102	01100110	66	f
39	00100111	27	'	71	01000111	47	G	103	01100111	67	g
40	00101000	28	(	72	01001000	48	H	104	01101000	68	h
41	00101001	29	)	73	01001001	49	I	105	01101001	69	i
42	00101010	2A	*	74	01001010	4A	J	106	01101010	6A	j
43	00101011	2B	+	75	01001011	4B	K	107	01101011	6B	k
44	00101100	2C	,	76	01001100	4C	L	108	01101100	6C	l
45	00101101	2D	-	77	01001101	4D	M	109	01101101	6D	m
46	00101110	2E	.	78	01001110	4E	N	110	01101110	6E	n
47	00101111	2F	/	79	01001111	4F	O	111	01101111	6F	o
48	00110000	30	0	80	01010000	50	P	112	01110000	70	p
49	00110001	31	1	81	01010001	51	Q	113	01110001	71	q
50	00110010	32	2	82	01010010	52	R	114	01110010	72	r
51	00110011	33	3	83	01010011	53	S	115	00111011	73	s
52	00110100	34	4	84	01010100	54	T	116	01110100	74	t
53	00110101	35	5	85	01010101	55	U	117	01110101	75	u
54	00110110	36	6	86	01010110	56	V	118	01110110	76	v
55	00110111	37	7	87	01010111	57	W	119	01110111	77	w
56	00111000	38	8	88	01011000	58	X	120	01111000	78	x
57	00111001	39	9	89	01011001	59	Y	121	01111001	79	y
58	00111010	3A	:	90	01011010	5A	Z	122	01111010	7A	z
59	00111011	3B	;	91	01011011	5B	[	123	01111011	7B	{
60	00111100	3C	<	92	01011100	5C	\	124	01111100	7C		
61	00111101	3D	=	93	01011101	5D	]	125	01111101	7D	}
62	00111110	3E	>	94	01011110	5E	^	126	01111110	7E	~
63	00111111	3F	?	95	01011111	5F	—	127	01111111	7F	Delete

FIGURE 3.10 A byte representing an ASCII character

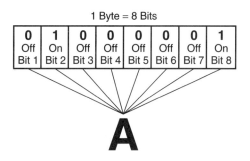

1 Byte = 8 Bits

0	1	0	0	0	0	0	1
Off	On	Off	Off	Off	Off	Off	On
Bit 1	Bit 2	Bit 3	Bit 4	Bit 5	Bit 6	Bit 7	Bit 8

A

3.5 USING A VOLTMETER AND OHMMETER

Voltmeters and ohmmeters are used to take certain electronic measurements of the computer. A **voltmeter** can be used to see if a device is generating the correct voltage output or signal. An **ohmmeter** can be used to check wires and connectors and measure the resistance of an electronic device. A **digital multimeter (DMM)** combines several measuring devices, including a voltmeter and an ohmmeter. Some DMMs also measure capacitance, check diodes and transistors, and act as frequency counters, but these features are usually not needed to repair individual computers.

When measuring voltage, three things must be set on the DMM before making the measurement. They are:

1. Voltage
2. Voltage type (dc or ac)
3. The expected range. If you don't know the expected range, set the DMM to the highest voltage range before taking the first measurement. This will prevent damage to the voltmeter. Note: Some voltmeters have an autorange feature.

After the DMM is configured, you then attach the red lead to the high-voltage, or positive, connector, and the black lead to the ground, or negative, connector. (See fig. 3.11.)

To measure the resistance of an electronic component, first switch the DMM to the ohms setting. Because the ohmmeter generates its own current to measure resistance, you must remove the electrical component from the circuit before taking a measurement—the comparatively large amount of current in the circuit could damage the ohmmeter or electronic component. Removing an electronic component requires special equipment and skills, and damage to the electronic device might result if done by an

FIGURE 3.11 Measuring voltage with a voltmeter or DMM

inexperienced electronics technician, so the resistance of an electronic device is not usually measured.

Question: How do you test the internal speaker?

Answer: First, disconnect the speaker from the motherboard and measure the resistance across the speaker. The measurement should be approximately 8 ohms.

The ohmmeter can be used to test a fuse or wire. Because a fuse or wire is a conductor, it should measure no resistance (0 ohms). This is known as a **continuity check,** a test to see whether the circuit is continuous—without breaks.

3.6 ELECTROSTATIC DISCHARGE

Electrostatic electricity is a potential electrical charge created by friction and separation. You experience **electrostatic discharge (ESD)** when you get a shock from touching a doorknob after walking across a carpet on a dry day or when your clothes cling to each other when you remove them from the dryer. If the proper steps are not taken to avoid ESD, it could damage the electronic components of a PC or cause the PC to lose data and programs.

ESD is caused by what is known as the *triboelectric effect.* Friction produces heat that excites molecular particles. When two materials are separated, electrons transfer from one material to the other, and the resulting imbalance of electrons generates a charge. The amount of static electricity generated depends upon the materials subjected to friction or separation, the amount of friction or separation, and the relative humidity of the environment. Common items that easily generate electrostatic discharge are waxed, painted, or varnished surfaces; plastics, including trays, bags, and wrap; common clothing items, including clean room smocks; paper, including documentation; and Styrofoam.

The electrostatic charge remains static until it comes into contact with a conductor. Most electronic components within a PC, for example, are integrated chips with metal pins and wires that carry electrical signals into and out of the chip. If material holding an electrical charge touches an electronic device, a small arc is formed, causing the circuit's semiconductor material to break down and its metal parts to short together.

PCs use two types of chips, transistor-transistor logic (TTL) and metal oxide semiconductor (MOS) chips. The TTL chips run at 5 V, and the CMOS chips run at 3.3 V or less. Although both are susceptible to ESD, MOS chips are more susceptible since they have a thin film of silicon dioxide that can easily break down.

When an ESD-damaged component is dissected and photographed with an electron microscope, the inside of the component looks much like metal that has been welded. Unfortunately, not all ESD damage is obvious from the outside. It may not show up for days, weeks, or even months, which may lead you to think that you did not cause the problem.

To give you an idea of how much charge can be generated from ESD, your body can generate up to 35,000 V on a dry day. The shock from touching a doorknob is at least 3,000 V. Lifting a foot or moving a chair can easily generate 1,000 V. Computer components can be destroyed or degraded by a charge as low as 10 to 20 V, depending on the type of chip. These voltages are not lethal because the discharge occurs within a fraction of a second. Table 3.11 shows charges generated from some everyday actions and that electrostatic discharge occurs more often at low humidity (less than 50%) than at high humidity.

It is imperative for a technician to avoid electrostatic discharge. This will allow you to keep fewer repair parts in stock, and the computer you work on will have less downtime. You will have fewer difficult-to-trace intermittent problems and fewer unnecessary service visits to make, which will lead to fewer disgruntled customers and therefore more job security and future business.

The best way to avoid electrostatic discharge is to wear a properly grounded wrist strap. The strap can be grounded by attaching it to the metal frame of a PC (preferably an area free of paint). The metal part within the strap must make good contact with the skin, since it is you who is being grounded, not your clothing. The strap should be kept clean and in good condition, and it should be tested daily to verify that there is continuity (a good connection) between you and the ground. In addition, you should roll up your sleeves and

TABLE 3.11 Electrostatic charges

Electrostatic Charges Generated by Technical Personnel		
Action	**High Humidity**	**Low Humidity**
Walking across carpet	1,500 V	35,000 V
Removing item from plastic bag	1,200 V	20,000 V
Sliding off of or onto plastic chair	1,500 V	18,000 V
Opening a vinyl envelope containing work instructions	600 V	7,000 V
Walking across vinyl floor	250 V	12,000 V
Sliding sleeve across laminated bench	100 V	6,000 V

secure your necktie so that they do not make contact with the electronic device. (See fig. 3.12.)

Some books recommend an alternative method if you do not have a wrist strap. You can touch the power supply or metal case before working within the computer. You should then touch the power supply or metal case often while you are handling computer components to reduce any charge buildup. This method is not as effective as using a wrist strap, however, and is therefore not recommended.

> **WARNING** When working on high-voltage devices such as monitors or power supplies, a wrist strap should *not* be used since the voltage stored in these devices can kill a person. Monitors and power supplies should only be serviced by trained, experienced electronic technicians.

Another device that you can use to avoid ESD is an **electrostatic mat.** The computer that you are repairing sits on top of the mat, which absorbs static electricity. Of course, the mat is grounded much like the electrostatic wrist strap.

When transporting and storing electronic devices, electrostatic bags should be used. (See fig. 3.13.) An electrostatic-shielded bag is usually either silver-colored or smoke-gray

FIGURE 3.12 An ESD wrist strap should be worn when handling any electrostaticlly sensitive components.

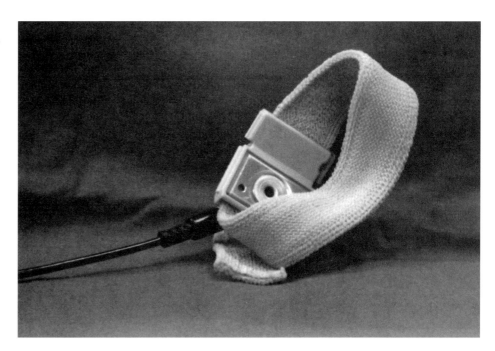

FIGURE 3.13 Electrostatic-shielded bag used to prevent electrostatic electricity from damaging the device inside the bag. Electrostatic-shielded bags should be used to transport and store electrostatic-sensitive devices.

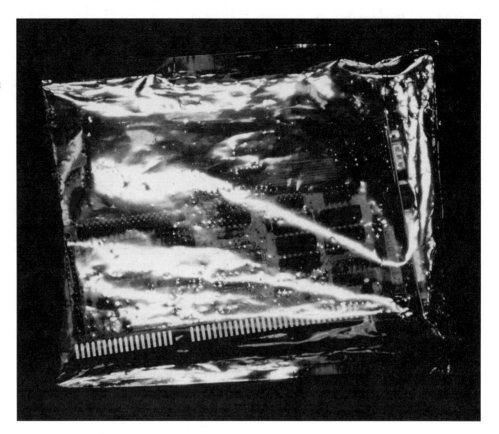

and is grid-lined. The static-shielded bag must be securely closed to be effective and should not have holes. Always keep spare static-shielded bags.

When handling integrated chips, you should avoid touching any of the metal parts. When handling circuit boards, you should avoid touching any of the chips, electronic components, metal traces, or edge connectors. When inserting or removing any integrated chips or expansion cards, you should make sure that the computer is turned off and unplugged.

3.7 ELECTRICAL SAFETY

There is always the chance of electric shock when working on computers. A device that uses high voltage will usually have a bright yellow-and-black sticker warning of the high voltage. (See fig. 3.14.) If you don't follow safety recommendations when working on a PC, the electricity from a device can cause shock, burns, blindness, or death as well as catastrophic equipment damage.

SAFETY GUIDELINES—ELECTRICITY
- Never use both hands to handle an electronic device.
- Wear rubber-soled shoes.
- Do not wear jewelry or any other articles that could accidentally contact circuitry and conduct current or get caught in moving parts.
- Connect or disconnect any test leads or connections with the equipment turned off and unplugged.
- Never assume anything without checking it out for yourself.
- Don't take shortcuts.

FIGURE 3.14   Warning of high voltage

FIGURE 3.15 A fire extinguisher

3.8 IN CASE OF FIRE

Although fires don't usually occur around computers, you should still know how to put out a fire correctly. The three major classes of fire extinguishers are: Class A, used for wood and paper; Class B, used for flammable liquids; and Class C, used for electrical fires. Since computers are electrical devices, you should use a Class C or an ABC-rated fire extinguisher. (See fig. 3.15.)

SUMMARY

1. The rate of flow of electrons is known as current (electricity), which is measured in amps (A).
2. A conductor is a material in which current can flow easily, and an insulator is a poor conductor of electric current.
3. A semiconductor, used in computer chips, is a material that is neither a good conductor of electricity nor a good insulator.
4. Components that are specifically designed to oppose current are known as resistors.
5. The force that moves the electrons generated by the power supply or battery is called voltage.
6. Power (P) is the rate of energy consumption or the amount of energy used in a certain length of time. In electronics, it is expressed in watts (W).
7. The voltage source (power supply or battery) and electronic components are connected with a conductor, such as a wire or metal trace, to form a circuit.
8. The ground is a reference point in electronic circuits.
9. A load is an element connected across the output terminals of a circuit that draws current from the circuit.
10. If there is a break in the conductor (known as an "open") and there is no other pathway for the electrons, the current will not flow.
11. A short occurs when a circuit has a zero or abnormally low resistance path between two points, resulting in excessive current flow.
12. A capacitor is a device that stores an electric charge. The amount of charge per unit of voltage that can be stored is known as capacitance.
13. A switch is an electrical or electronic device that opens and closes a current path.
14. A fuse is a protective device in a circuit that melts open when there is excessive current in the circuit.
15. A transistor is a small electronic component that can amplify an electric signal and perform fast switching.
16. An integrated circuit (IC), sometimes referred to as a chip, is a small electronic device made of semiconductor material (usually silicon) consisting of transistors, resistors, and capacitors.
17. In the decimal numbering system, each position can contain one of ten different possible digits—0, 1, 2, 3, 4, 5, 6, 7, 8, or 9.
18. The binary system is less complicated than the decimal system because it has only two digits, a zero (0) and a one (1).

19. One hexadecimal digit is equivalent to a four-digit binary number (4 bits, or a nibble). It is very easy to translate between the hexadecimal and binary systems, and so the hexadecimal system is used primarily as a "shorthand" way of displaying binary numbers.

20. An alphanumeric code represents binary and hexadecimal characters and the various instructions necessary for conveying information. One commonly used alphanumeric code is the ASCII (American Standard Code for Information Interchange) character set.

21. A digital multimeter (DMM) combines several measuring devices, including a voltmeter and an ohmmeter.

22. When measuring voltage and the expected range is unknown, the DMM is set to the highest voltage range before the first measurement is taken.

23. Since a wire or fuse essentially is a conductor, it should have no resistance (continuity check).

24. Electrostatic discharge, or ESD (electricity caused from friction), is easily generated by the technician and can damage electronic components.

25. The best way to minimize electrostatic discharge is to wear a grounded wrist strap and to use electrostatic-shielded bags when transporting electronic components.

26. When putting out a computer fire, you should use a Class C or an ABC-rated fire extinguisher.

QUESTIONS

1. Material through which current can flow easily is a(n):
   a. conductor
   b. insulator
   c. semiconductor
   d. resistor

2. A resistor is measured in:
   a. ohms
   b. hertz
   c. farads
   d. henrys
   e. volts
   f. resistance

3. Which of the following components will hold a charge even though power has been removed?
   a. diode
   b. transistor
   c. capacitor
   d. rectifier

4. The rate of energy consumption is measured in:
   a. ohms
   b. hertz
   c. watts
   d. henrys
   e. volts
   f. resistance

5. A (An) _____ consists of a power source, a path, and a load.
   a. power supply
   b. integrated circuit
   c. circuit
   d. multimeter

6. *True or false*—Multimeters should be set on the highest voltage range prior to the first measurement.

7. When measuring the value of a .5-amp fuse with a multimeter set at 1 k ohm, the value will be read as:
   a. 0
   b. 0.5
   c. 500
   d. 1000

8. Circuits used within the computer should not be tested with standard ohmmeters because:
   a. computer circuits use frequencies that cannot be measured by an ohmmeter
   b. ohmmeters provide their own current, which may damage ICs
   c. computer circuits require supply voltage when measuring resistance
   d. the internal resistance of the ohmmeter makes the reading of the ohmmeter completely unreliable when used on computers

9. To check the voltage in a wall outlet, you would set your meter to:
   a. dc voltage
   b. ac voltage
   c. resistance
   d. capacitance

10. When testing a 120 V ac wall outlet, which slot is considered hot?
    a. the larger of the two vertical slots
    b. the round opening
    c. both vertical slots
    d. the smaller of the two vertical slots

11. In the United States the wall power outlet is checked by placing one lead at the large slot and the other lead at the small slot. What voltage would indicate that the outlet is okay?
    a. 0 V
    b. 5 V
    c. 12 V
    d. 120 V
    e. 220 V

12. Which hole in a standard household wall outlet in the United States is for the safety ground connection?
    a. the small flat slot
    b. the round hole
    c. the large flat slot
    d. none of the above

13. The ASCII character (standard + extended) set contains _____ characters.
    a. 8
    b. 256
    c. 64
    d. 512
    e. 128
    f. 1,024

14. The most basic format in which data and programs are stored in a computer is the

    _____ format.
    a. ASCI
    b. octal
    c. binary
    d. hexadecimal

15. What is the binary code for the P character?
    a. 01010001
    b. 01010000
    c. 10100000
    d. 00100000
    e. 01110000

16. What is the decimal code for the dollar sign ($)?
    a. 100100
    b. 5A
    c. 36
    d. 44

17. Convert the decimal value 6 to binary:
    a. 00000101
    b. 01010101
    c. 00001111
    d. 00000110
    e. 00000111

18. Convert the decimal value 68 to binary:
    a. 10101010
    b. 11110000
    c. 00001111
    d. 01010101
    e. 01000010
    f. 01000100

19. Convert the binary value 10101010 to decimal:
    a. 170
    b. 224
    c. 165
    d. 128

20. Convert the hexadecimal number FH to binary:
    a. 1000
    b. 1010
    c. 1110
    d. 0001
    e. 1111

21. How many bits are represented by a single hexadecimal digit?
    a. 1
    b. 2
    c. 4
    d. 8
    e. 16
    f. 32

22. You have a file that is 2.2 megabytes in size. Exactly how many bytes is 2.2 megabytes?
    a. 22,000,000.0
    b. 2,252.8
    c. 2,252,800.0
    d. 2,306,867
    e. none of the above

23. Before opening a computer, removing a component, or installing a component, you should make sure that:
    a. the computer is turned off
    b. the keyboard is unplugged
    c. the monitor is unplugged
    d. the modem is unplugged

24. Static electricity is generated:
    a. by the triboelectric effect
    b. easily on dry days (low relative humidity)
    c. by rubbing certain materials together
    d. all of the above
25. Wrist straps will be useful only if:
    a. they are plugged into the wrist-strap jack
    b. they are clean and make good skin contact
    c. the cord has not been damaged
    d. all of the above
26. Before opening a static-shielding container, you should:
    a. look inside to see if it really is sensitive
    b. check for paperwork inside the container
    c. ground yourself in an ESD-protected area
    d. none of the above
27. If a ground strap fails the daily test, you should:
    a. get a new one from your supervisor
    b. use it for the rest of that day
    c. take the rest of the day off
    d. try to fix the test box
28. Before transporting an ESD-sensitive device, it must be:
    a. enclosed in a static-shielded container or bag
    b. put into a cardboard box
    c. thoroughly cleaned
    d. wrapped in newspaper
29. Which of the following could generate electrostatic voltages high enough to cause ESD damage?
    a. combing your hair
    b. walking across a carpeted floor
    c. taking off your coat
    d. all of the above
30. To avoid ESD when working on a PC, you should:
    a. make sure that you and the PC are at the same electrical charge level
    b. connect your grounding wire from the PC to a nonconductor
    c. connect your grounding wrist strap to the PC's motherboard
    d. connect your grounding wrist strap to your shoes
31. Carpeting can be one of the most static-prone surfaces in the office environment. Which type of mat will greatly reduce static problems?
    a. rubber   c. plastic
    b. nylon   d. vinyl
32. An ESD wrist strap contains which of the following to protect you from an electrical shock?
    a. a transistor   c. a capacitor
    b. a resistor   d. a fuse
33. Which of the following is most susceptible to ESD damage?
    a. CMOS chips   c. TTL chips
    b. the case   d. the power supply
34. To prevent ESD, humidity should be kept at least at:
    a. 10%   c. 50%
    b. 25%   d. 75%
35. *True or false*—When working with high voltages such as in monitors or the power supply, you should always use a wrist strap with at least a 1-megaohm resistor.
36. What is the best ground for a conductive work bench?
    a. an ac outlet   c. another device
    b. the floor   d. a chassis ground

37. What should a test of an internal speaker measure?
   a. 0 ohms
   b. 8 ohms
   c. infinite ohms
   d. 3.3 volts
   e. 5 volts
   f. 1 amp

HANDS-ON EXERCISES

Exercise 1: Checking the ac Power Outlet

Use a voltmeter to measure the following voltages:

a. hot slot and the neutral slot
b. hot slot and the ground
c. neutral slot and ground

Exercise 2: Measuring the Voltage of a Battery

Measure the voltage of a battery.

Exercise 3: Measuring for Continuity

1. If you have a wire, measure the resistance between the two ends.
2. If you have a small PC speaker, detach it and measure the resistance between the two leads.
3. If you have a resistor, measure its resistance.
4. If you have a push-button switch, measure the resistance between the two wires.
5. While measuring the switch connector, press the switch and measure the resistance again. Keep the switch pushed in long enough to get a steady reading.
6. If you have a fuse, measure the resistance between the two ends.

4 The Disassembly and Assembly of the PC

INTRODUCTION

To become a better technician and better understand how the computer works, you must learn how to identify its major components and how to disassemble and reassemble it in a timely manner while following ESD and safety guidelines. In addition, you must be able to determine which devices are field-replaceable units (FRUs) so that you can determine whether to fix the device or to replace it.

OBJECTIVES

1. Identify common ports and explain their primary function.
2. Identify standard PC components.
3. Demonstrate proper ESD procedures when handling PC components
4. Disassemble the PC to its basic FRU components and reassemble it.
5. Identify which are FRUs PC components.

4.1 THE PC CASE

The PC **case,** which contains most of the computer components, comes in many sizes and two orientations (desktop and tower). The **desktop case** lies flat; the **tower case** stands erect. (See fig. 4.1.) Today's PC cases usually have a turbo switch or turbo LED, a reset switch, and a lock. An LED is a small light that usually indicates if a component is on or active. The turbo switch slows the computer down for older programs that can't adjust to the faster speed of today's machines. The reset switch provides an easy way to reboot the computer. The lock is used to secure the system by disabling the keyboard or preventing entry into the case. (Caution: Many system locks can be opened with commonly used keys.)

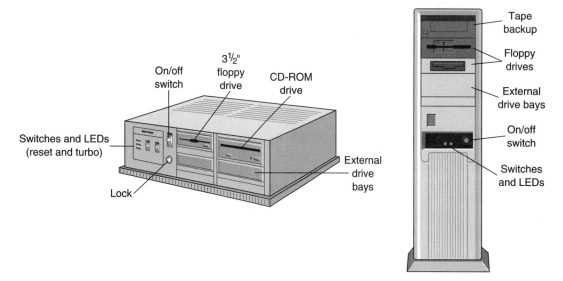

FIGURE 4.1   The desktop PC and tower PC

FIGURE 4.2   Ports found on the back of the computer

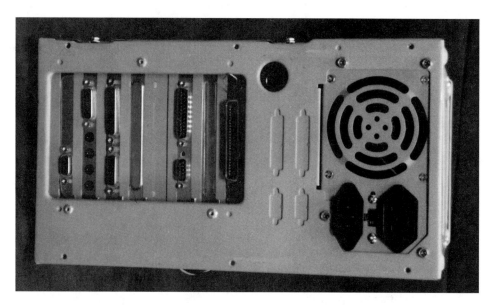

Before opening the PC, identify the **ports** that are located at the back of the case. (See fig. 4.2.) Ports are plug sockets that enable an external device, such as a printer, to be attached to the computer. These ports are usually identified by the shape of the plug socket, the number of pins, the number of rows in which the pins are aligned, and the orientation of the pins (male or female). The most common ports are shown in table 4.1.

4.2   DISASSEMBLING THE COMPUTER

To open the PC, you must remove the screws that hold the cover on. They are usually found on the back of the PC, near the edge of the case. Make sure not to remove the screws that hold the power supply in place. Some desktop cases have screws located at each corner, while other cases may include a fifth screw located at the top center. Other desktop cases have screws located near the bottom of the sides. Tower cases usually have their screws in the back, along the outer edge. Depending on how big the case is, it will have three to eight screws. (See fig. 4.3.) After the screws are removed, slide the cover off as you are lifting it up.

TABLE 4.1   Common PC ports

 **Parallel Port**	 **Serial Port**	 **Serial Port**
2-row, 25-pin female D connector The parallel port (also known as LPT1, LPT2, or LPT3) is used primarily to connect printers to the computer.	2-row, 25-pin male D connector The serial port (also known as COM1, COM2, COM3, or COM4) is used primarily to connect external modems, mice, and miscellaneous devices. Note that there are two types of serial ports.	2-row, 9-pin male D connector The serial port (also known as COM1, COM2, COM3, or COM4) is used primarily to connect external modems, mice, and miscellaneous devices. Note that there are two types of serial ports.
 Game Port	 **VGA or Super VGA Port**	 **Monochrome, CGA, or EGA Port**
2-row, 15-pin female D connector The game port is used to connect joysticks to the computer. If the 2-row, 15-pin female D connector is on a sound card, it is probably a MIDI port or game port.	3-row, 15-pin female D connector The VGA or Super VGA port is used to connect the VGA and Super VGA monitors to the computer.	2-row, 9-pin female D connector The DB-9F connector is used to connect the older monochrome, CGA, or EGA monitors.
 **SCSI Port**	 **SCSI Port**	 **Phone Jack Modem Port**
50-pin centronics port The SCSI port is used to connect SCSI printers, CD-ROMs, scanners, and hard drives. The SCSI-1 and SCSI-2 interfaces can connect up to 7 peripherals, while the SCSI-3 interface can connect up to 127 devices.	50-pin and 68-pin miniport The SCSI port is used to connect SCSI printers, CD-ROMs, scanners, and hard drives. The SCSI-1 and SCSI-2 interfaces can connect up to 7 peripherals, while the SCSI-3 interface can connect up to 127 devices.	RJ-11 Connector These two connectors are used to connect to the telephone wall jack and the telephone.
 **Keyboard**	 **PS/2 Mouse Port or PS/2 Keyboard Port**	 **Universal Serial Bus (USB)**
5-pin DIN This port is used to connect a keyboard to the PC. The keyboard port is always connected directly to the motherboard.	6-pin mini-DIN This port is used to connect a mouse without using a serial port or to connect a PS/2 keyboard.	This external port allows you to connect up to 127 external PC peripherals, including mice, keyboards, printers, modems, and external disk drives.
 10Base-T Network Port	 **BNC Connector**	
RJ-45 Connector These connectors are used to connect to a network using a 10Base-T cable.	Coaxial Connector These connectors are used to connect to a network using a coaxial cable.	

FIGURE 4.3 Screws used to open case

Screws

Screws

IMPORTANT NOTES

1. Before opening the computer and removing or installing components, make sure that the power is off and that the power cable is unplugged.
2. When removing the cover, do it with care. Sometimes parts of the case may snag some of the cables within the PC. As a computer technician, you should not introduce new problems.
3. Follow the ESD procedures discussed in chapter 3.

4.2.1 EXPANSION CARDS AND SLOTS

After opening the case, the major components are easily identified. They are the motherboard, the power supply, the drive bays (drives), and the expansion cards. (See fig. 4.4.)

The **motherboard,** the largest circuit board in the PC, contains the essential electronic components, including the microprocessor, the RAM, the system ROM BIOS, and support circuitry. To make the PC more configurable and expandable, the PC uses **expansion cards** (circuit boards), which are inserted into expansion slots on the motherboard. Expansion cards can be used to connect drives, I/O ports (parallel ports, serial ports, and game ports), mice, speakers, and monitors. Of course, they are usually identified by the type of ports and cable connectors they use.

Several types of **expansion slots** have been used over the years. The IBM PC used an 8-bit PC slot, and the IBM AT used a 16-bit ISA slot. Later, the Micro Channel Architecture (MCA) and the Extended Industry Standard Architecture (EISA), both having a 32-bit bus (a set of wires used to carry data and power), were introduced for use with the 386 machine. Today's desktop computers use a combination of ISA slots and local bus slots, mostly PCI (Peripheral Component Interconnect) with some VESA (Video Electronics Standards Association), while notebooks use a PC/CardBus slot.

To remove an expansion card, you must first disconnect any cables that may be attached to it. Next, remove the card's mounting screw. Grasp the board firmly along its top edge and rock it gently up and out. Avoid touching any of the chips, electronic components, or metal traces. Once the card is out of its slot, avoid touching the edge connector. Note: Make sure that the computer is off and unplugged before removing or inserting expansion cards.

To insert a card into an expansion slot, find an empty slot that matches the expansion card that you are inserting. If you have several matching slots to choose from, it should

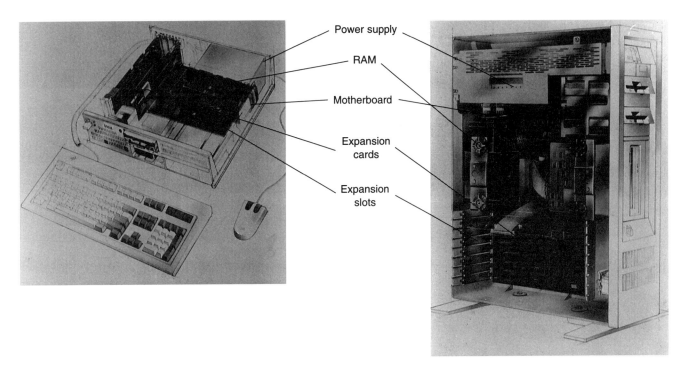

Power supply

RAM

Motherboard

Expansion cards

Expansion slots

FIGURE 4.4   Picture of desktop and tower computers (courtesy of International Business Machines Corporation; unauthorized use not permitted)

not matter which slot you use; they should all be the same. It is recommended that the cards be spaced out so that they can be accessed more easily in the future. (If there is a metal cover over the slot hole of the case, remove the screw that holds it in place to remove the slot hole cover.) Slide the card into the slot and insert the mounting screw. Note: Installing an expansion card is usually not this easy. Often, the cards need to be configured with jumpers or software. For more information on configuring expansion cards, see chapter 8.

4.2.2   RAM

RAM is packaged as DIPs, SIPPs, SIMMs, and DIMMs. A **DIP (dual in-line package)**, which resembles a bug with many legs, lies horizontally on the motherboard with metal leads extending down from its two long sides. The metal leads are inserted directly into the motherboard's DIP sockets. Note: Some RAM cache chips are DIPs.

To remove a DIP, you could use a special chip puller designed to grab and firmly hold the chip so that it can be pulled out of the IC socket. The chip puller that comes with most $10 to $50 tool kits does not work well, however, since it doesn't hold the chip firmly as it is pulled from the socket. Another way to remove a DIP is to use a small, flat-edge screwdriver blade. By gently sliding the screwdriver under one end of the chip and prying just a little, then going to the other end and prying that end up, you can prevent the legs from bending while you continue to alternate prying both ends until the chip can be easily removed.

To insert a DIP into an IC socket, you must first position the DIP so that pin 1 is in the proper orientation. Pin 1 of the chip and the socket is usually identified by a notch on one end of the DIP. (See fig. 4.5.) Next, align the pins with the socket and gently push the chip into its socket without bending any of its pins in the process. If a pin is bent by accident, the chip could be ruined.

A **SIPP (single in-line pin package)** is a small circuit board onto which several DIPs are soldered. The circuit board has a single row of pins for insertion into the motherboard. To remove a SIPP, you firmly grasp the small circuit board and pull straight up. To insert a SIPP, you must align the pins with the SIPP socket and gently press down on the SIPP so

FIGURE 4.5   IC chip. Notice the notch to indicate which end has pin 1.

that the pins go into the pin holes without bending. If the pins are bent by accident, the SIPP could be ruined.

SIMMs (single in-line memory modules) and **DIMMs (dual in-line memory modules)** are the most common forms of RAM. They consist of integrated chips soldered onto a small circuit board. A row of tin or gold metal plates (contacts) along the bottom of the module connects it to the motherboard. Metal pins on the motherboard make contact with the metal plates.

To install a SIMM chip, insert it into the slot at a 45° angle. Make sure the SIMM is seated properly in the slot. Push the SIMM until it clicks into place. (See fig. 4.6.) To remove a SIMM, pull apart the two clips located at the ends, tilt the SIMM back to a 45° angle, and pull it out. (See fig. 4.7.) Be careful not to bend, mangle, or break the clips. Turn the SIMM back to a 45° angle and lift it away from the slot.

To install a DIMM, line up the notches on the DIMM with the plastic tabs located in the DIMM socket. Once the notches are lined up, apply pressure to the module by pushing it into the socket until it is firmly seated. (See fig. 4.8.) To remove a DIMM, push the ejector tabs gently down and pull the DIMM out of the socket. (See fig. 4.9.) (For more information on RAM chips, see chapter 6.)

FIGURE 4.6   To install a SIMM chip, insert the SIMM into the socket at a 45° angle and snap it into place.

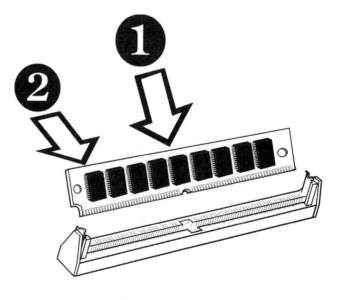

FIGURE 4.7   Remove a SIMM by pulling the two clips apart that keep the SIMM in place.

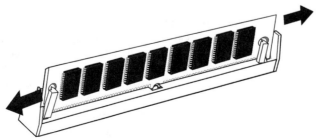

FIGURE 4.8 To insert a DIMM, put it into the socket and press down.

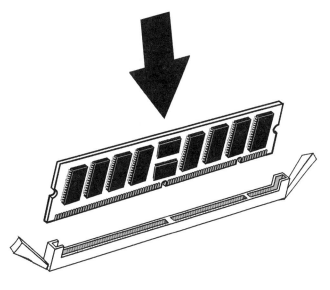

FIGURE 4.9 To remove a DIMM, pull the two ejector tabs apart.

4.2.3 DRIVES

The hard drives, CD-ROM drives, and floppy drives are connected to an expansion card or directly to the motherboard with a long, flat, gray cable known as a **ribbon cable.** The **floppy drive cable** has 34 pins, the **IDE cable** (used with IDE hard drives and IDE CD-ROM drives) has 40 pins, and the **SCSI cable** (used with SCSI hard drives, SCSI CD-ROM drives, and tape backup drives) has 50 or 68 pins. The ribbon cables use two-row connectors.

When connecting a ribbon cable, you must make sure the cable is correctly oriented. (See fig. 4.10.) Pin 1 of the cable (marked with a red or blue stripe along one edge) must be connected to pin 1 of the drive and pin 1 of the cable connector on the motherboard or expansion card. Pin 1 of the drive is designated by a small 1 or 2 printed on the drive's circuit

FIGURE 4.10 IDE hard drive. Notice the stripe on the cable that connects to pin 1. (Courtesy of Seagate Technology, Inc.)

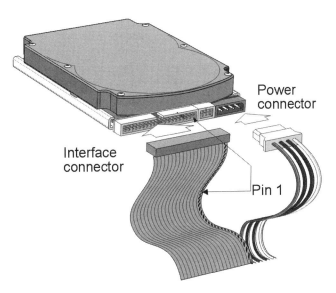

Power connector

Interface connector

Pin 1

FIGURE 4.11 34-pin floppy
drive ribbon cable

Drive B (3¹/₂″ and 5¹/₄″
floppy drive connectors)   Controller
card   Drive A (3¹/₂″ and 5¹/₄″
floppy drive connectors)

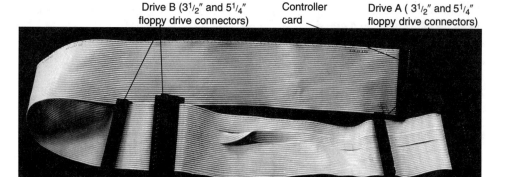

board. Pin 1 of the expansion card or motherboard connector can be identified by a small 1
or 2 printed on the circuit board or by a square solder (other pins have a round solder). Some
drives and cables are a notched to prevent the cable from being inserted incorrectly. If the
cable is connected incorrectly, the hard drive or compact disk may cause a short, preventing
the computer from booting. If the floppy drive is connected backwards, the floppy drive
light will remain on and any floppy disk inserted onto the drive will usually be unreadable.

When connecting **IDE (integrated drive electronics)** devices, it does not matter where
the IDE device is or where the IDE controller is connected to the ribbon cable. When connecting **SCSI (small computer system interface)** devices, including the SCSI expansion
card, the two devices with terminated resistors must be on the two ends of the chain. (For
more information on hard drives and terminating resistors, see chapter 10.) The floppy
drive controller goes on the long end of the ribbon cable, drive B goes in the middle, and
drive A goes on the other end. (See fig. 4.11. For more information on floppy disk drives,
see chapter 11.)

A drive is placed in a drive bay and is held in place by four screws. Openings in the
front of the computer case allow disks and tapes to be inserted and removed from the
floppy, compact disk, and tape drives. When the opening is not needed, it is usually covered with a removable plate.

4.2.4 MOTHERBOARDS

To remove the motherboard, you must first disconnect all external connectors (including
those for power, the keyboard, mouse, printer, and speakers). Next, disconnect the internal
connectors (including those for the battery, keylock, power light, and the reset button). If
you don't know which cable is connected to which plug, it is a good idea to record how
they are connected on a piece of paper or to label them with a piece of tape.

Most motherboards are attached with one to eight screws. In addition, most use white
plastic **standoffs,** as shown in fig. 4.12, to prevent the motherboard from shorting against
the computer case. After removing the screws, slide the motherboard away from the power
supply about one-half inch, until the standoffs have disengaged from their mounting slots.
Lift the motherboard up and out of the case. Some motherboards are mounted on a metal

FIGURE 4.12 White plastic
standoffs

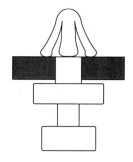

plate that swings open, while others have a removable bottom plate that allows the motherboard to slide out though the bottom of the case.

To install a motherboard, you perform the same actions but in reverse order. First, mount the motherboard onto the back plate of the case. To do this, lay the board down on top of the plate to see which of the holes in the board are above the mounting holes in the plate. Make sure the board is oriented correctly. Press the white plastic standoffs into the holes in the motherboard that correspond to the openings on the plate. Align the motherboard above the plate so that the spaces engage with the plate. You should be able to see the brass mounting sockets exposed through the holes in the motherboard. Place small insulating washers on top of these holes and screw finely threaded screws into the brass sockets. Lastly, install the expansion cards and connect all cables.

> **IMPORTANT NOTE** When connecting the two power connectors known as P8 and P9, make sure that the ground wires (black wires) are in the middle.

4.3 FIELD-REPLACEABLE UNITS (FRUS)

A **field-replaceable unit (FRU)** is any device that can be easily replaced in the field on a service call. No soldering or special equipment is needed to replace the component. FRUs include monitors, keyboards, most microprocessors, most RAM, motherboards, and expansion cards.

When a device is found to be faulty, the entire component (FRU) is replaced. Some computer technicians can do electronic repair, but there are several reasons why isolating and fixing a faulty electronic component (such as an integrated chip, capacitor, transistor, or resistor) on a circuit board is not cost effective. First, most electronic components require special skills or equipment to measure or replace. In addition, electronic documentation is not available for most circuit boards, and replacement components are not always obtainable. Finally, the labor to make such a repair costs more than a replacement device. Therefore, if you find a faulty power supply or video card, it is best to replace the failed item.

SUMMARY

1. A port is a plug-in socket that enables an external device, such as a printer, to be attached to the computer.
2. The parallel port (2-row, 25-pin female D connector) is used primarily to connect printers to the computer.
3. The serial port (2-row, 25-pin male D connector or 2-row, 9-pin male D connector) is used primarily to connect external modems, mice, and miscellaneous devices.
4. The game port (2-row, 15-pin female D connector) is used to connect joysticks to the computer.
5. The VGA or Super VGA port (3-row, 15-pin female D connector) is used to connect VGA and Super VGA monitors to the computer.
6. To make the PC more configurable and expandable, it has expansion cards (circuit boards) that are inserted into expansion slots on the motherboard.
7. Expansion cards, identified by type of port and cable connector, can be used to connect drives, I/O ports (parallel ports, serial ports, and game ports), mice, speakers, and monitors.
8. Pin 1 of a DIP chip and socket is usually identified with a notch on one end.
9. SIMMs and DIMMs, consisting of DIPs soldered onto a small circuit board, are the most common forms of RAM.
10. To remove a SIMM, pull apart the two clips located at the ends, tilt the SIMM backwards to a 45° angle, and pull it out.
11. To install a RAM chip, insert the SIMM into a slot at a 45° angle. Make sure the SIMM is seated properly in the slot. Push the SIMM until it clicks into place.
12. To remove a DIMM, push the ejector tabs down and pull the DIMM out of the socket.

13. To install a DIMM, line up the notches on the DIMM with the plastic tabs located in the DIMM socket. Once the notches are lined up, apply pressure to the module by pushing it into the socket until it is firmly seated.
14. When connecting ribbon cables, the cable must be correctly oriented.
15. Pin 1 of the cable (marked with a red or blue stripe along one edge) must be connected to pin 1 of the drive and pin 1 of the cable connector on the motherboard or expansion card.
16. Pin 1 of the drive is designated by a small 1 or 2 printed on the drive's circuit board, and pin 1 of the expansion card or motherboard connector can be identified by a small 1 or 2 printed on the circuit board or by a square solder (other pins have a round solder).
17. Motherboards are held in place by screws and white plastic standoffs.
18. When connecting the two power connectors known as P8 and P9, make sure that the ground wires (black wires) are in the middle.
19. A field-replaceable unit (FRU) is any device that can be easily replaced in the field on a service call.
20. When a device is found faulty, the entire component (FRU) is replaced.

QUESTIONS

1. A 25-pin female D connector on a computer is used to connect a:
   a. digitizer
   b. modem
   c. scanner
   d. printer
2. The parallel printer port on a PC is usually what type of connector?
   a. 9-pin male D
   b. 15-pin female D
   c. 25-pin male D
   d. 25-pin female D
3. Which port is usually used to connect printers?
   a. parallel
   b. serial
   c. game
   d. video
4. Which of the following ports would you use to connect a mouse?
   a. parallel
   b. serial
   c. game
   d. video
5. Before opening a computer, removing a component, or installing a component, you should make sure that:
   a. the computer is off
   b. the keyboard is unplugged
   c. the monitor is unplugged
   d. the modem is unplugged
6. Which of the following describes an IC chip that resembles a bug with many legs on the two long sides?
   a. SIPP
   b. SIMM
   c. DIMM
   d. DIP
   e. ESD
7. Pin 1 of the DIP is designated by:
   a. a notch on one end
   b. a red or blue stripe
   c. a square solder
   d. a small 1 printed on the DIP
8. When inserting SIMMs, which of the following statements is *false*?
   a. When inserting SIMMs, gently slide the SIMM into the SIMM socket at a 45° angle. Then tilt it up gently until it clicks into place.
   b. When inserting SIMMs, make sure *not* to bend or mangle the plastic or metal clips that hold the SIMM in place.
   c. When inserting SIMMs, make sure *not* to break the plastic or metal braces that hold the SIMM in place.
   d. When inserting a SIMM, you do not have to worry about ESD since SIMMs are on a circuit board.
9. When pulling a DIP or other chip from its socket, you should:
   a. pull the chip with a chip puller
   b. use a small screwdriver and gently pry on one side, then gently pry on the other side, and repeat this process until the chip is free
   c. press first, then pull gently
   d. have the computer on

10. An IDE hard-drive ribbon cable has _____ pins.
    a. 34
    b. 40
    c. 50
    d. 68
11. A ribbon cable has a red stripe along one edge. What does this mean?
    a. this is the positive lead
    b. this is the negative lead
    c. the cable carries hazardous voltage
    d. the conductor with the stripe connects to pin 1 of the connector
12. When connecting the power connectors to the motherboard, the connectors should:
    a. have the black cables together
    b. have the black cables on the outside
    c. have the black cables on the right
    d. have the red cables on the right
13. When inserting an expansion card into an expansion bus, you should:
    a. force it into the slot
    b. have the PC turned on
    c. wear an ESD wrist strap
    d. carry it down the hallway in your hand
14. Which of the following is *not* a FRU?
    a. math coprocessor
    b. video card
    c. hard drive
    d. resistor
15. Which of the following is a FRU? (Choose all that apply.)
    a. power supply
    b. keyboard
    c. a SIMM
    d. a DIP on a SIMM
16. Suppose that you have a failure caused by one of several possible field-replaceable units (FRUs). What should you do after turning the power off?
    a. replace the indicated parts one at a time until the problem is resolved and return the unused FRUs to stock
    b. replace all of the indicated FRUs at once and return the machine to the customer if the problem is resolved
    c. replace the indicated parts one at a time until the problem is resolved; if the motherboard is one of the FRUs, replace it first
    d. if multiple FRUs are indicated, then software is the most likely source of the problem

HANDS-ON EXERCISES   Exercise 1: Disassembling and Reassembling the PC

Be sure to follow ESD preventative measures.

1. Identify all the ports on the back of the computer. If any device is connected to the port, identify the device.
2. Open the PC.
3. Identify the type of hard drives used in your system (IDE or SCSI).
4. Identify pin 1 of the ribbon cables, the expansion card, and the drives. Disconnect and remove all the ribbon cables from the PC.
5. Disconnect the power connectors to the drive and remove the drives.
6. Remove all expansion cards from the expansion slots. As you take each one out, identify each card.
7. Remove the SIMMs and/or DIMMs from the motherboard.
8. Notice how the power connectors to the motherboard are connected. Disconnect the two power connectors from the motherboard.
9. Remove the motherboard from the system.
10. Find and identify the microprocessor and system ROM BIOS chip.
11. Reinstall the motherboard in the PC and reinsert the RAM chips into the motherboard. Be careful not to mangle the clips or the plastic backstops.
12. Reconnect the power connectors to the motherboard. Note: The power cables should be black to black.
13. Insert all of the expansion cards.

14. Reinstall the drives and reconnect the ribbon cables and power connectors.
15. Close and test the PC.

Exercise 2: Identifying Parts of the PC

Get various expansion cards from your instructor and identify them.

Exercise 3: Identifying Error Codes and Messages

1. Make sure the computer is off. Insert a POST card (if available) into one of the empty expansion slots.
2. Unplug the keyboard. Turn the system on and record what happens. If a series of beeps occurs or a message appears on the screen, look up the meaning of the beeps or message. If a POST code is shown on the POST card, look up the meaning of the code.
3. Turn the computer off and reconnect the keyboard.
4. Remove the video card. Turn the system on and record what happens. If a series of beeps occurs or a message appears on the screen, look up the meaning of the beeps or message. If a POST code is shown on the POST card, look up the meaning of the code.
5. Turn off the computer and reinsert the video card.
6. Remove one of the SIMMs. Turn the system on and record what happens. If a series of beeps occurs or a message appears on the screen, look up the meaning of the beeps or message. If a POST code is shown on the POST card, look up the meaning of the code.
7. Turn off the computer and reinsert the SIMM.
8. Disconnect the hard drive cable from the hard drive. Turn the system on and record what happens. If a series of beeps occurs or a message appears on the screen, look up the meaning of the beeps or message. If a POST code is shown on the POST card, look up the meaning of the code.
9. Turn off the computer and connect the hard drive cable to the hard drive backwards. Turn the system on and record what happens. If a series of beeps occurs or a message appears on the screen, look up the meaning of the beeps or message. If a POST code is shown on the POST card, look up the meaning of the code.
10. Turn off the computer and reconnect the hard drive cable to the hard drive correctly.
11. Disconnect the floppy drive cable from the 3½" floppy disk drive. Turn the system on and record what happens. If a series of beeps occurs or a message appears on the screen, look up the meaning of the beeps or message. If a POST code is shown on the POST card, look up the meaning of the code.
12. Turn off the computer and connect the floppy drive cable to the 3½" floppy drive backwards. Turn the system on and record what happens. If a series of beeps occurs or a message appears on the screen, look up the meaning of the beeps or message. If a POST code is shown on the POST card, look up the meaning of the code.
13. Turn off the computer and reconnect the floppy drive cable to the floppy drive correctly.

5   Microprocessors

INTRODUCTION

A microprocessor, also known as the CPU (central processing unit), is an integrated circuit that acts as the brain of the computer. Unlike most integrated chips, the microprocessor is programmable, so it can be made to perform many tasks. Through the years, the CPU has gone through many changes. Today's CPUs are far more complicated compared to the chips used in the 1981 IBM PC and are at least a thousand times faster.

OBJECTIVES

1. Explain what the microprocessor is and how it works.
2. Explain how the microprocessor interfaces with the rest of the computer.
3. List and explain the characteristics that determine the speed of the microprocessor.
4. Explain the difference between RISC and CISC chips.
5. List the characteristics of a microprocessor.
6. List and explain the microprocessor's operating modes.
7. Explain what a math coprocessor is and how it aids the microprocessor.
8. Describe MMX technology.
9. List the different ways to cool the microprocessor.
10. Install and remove a microprocessor.
11. List the problems caused by a faulty microprocessor.

5.1 MICRO-PROCESSORS

A **microprocessor,** also known as the **CPU (central processing unit),** is an integrated circuit that acts as the brain of the computer. It is made from a silicon wafer (see fig. 5.1) consisting of many transistors that act like tiny on/off switches (see figs. 5.2 and 5.3). Unlike most integrated chips, the microprocessor is programmable, so it can be made to perform

FIGURE 5.1   Silicon wafer

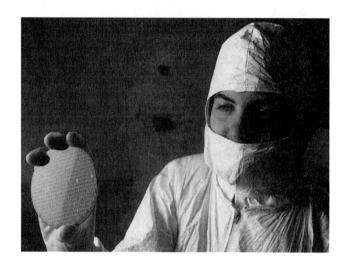

FIGURE 5.2   Pentium computer chip with MMX without the package (Intel and Pentium are registered trademarks and MMX is a trademark of Intel Corporation)

FIGURE 5.3 Intel Pentium with MMX Technology microprocessor with packaging (Intel and Pentium are registered trademarks and MMX is a trademark of Intel Corporation)

FIGURE 5.4 Inside the microprocessor

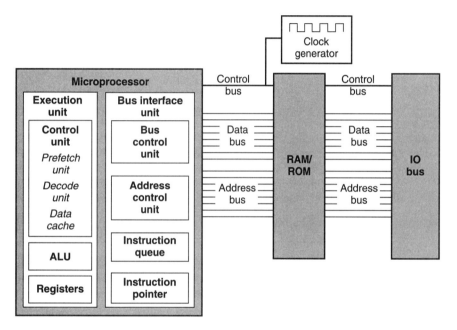

many tasks. The older 8088 and 8086 microprocessors had 29,000 transistors; the newer Pentium II microprocessor has 7.5 million transistors.

> To see how a microprocessor is made, you can visit the following website:
> **http://www.intel.com/intel/educate/chips/shock.htm**

The microprocessor has two major areas: the execution unit and the bus interface unit. The **execution unit** does the actual processing of data. It consists of the arithmetic/logic unit (ALU), the registers, and the control unit. The **bus interface unit (BIU)** links the microprocessor to the rest of the computer. It is divided into the bus control unit, the address control unit, the instruction queue, and the instruction pointer. Its purpose is to carry software instructions and data into and out of the CPU. Some of the more advanced microprocessors may contain a math coprocessor and a RAM cache. (See fig. 5.4.)

5.1.1 THE ALU AND REGISTERS

The **arithmetic/logic unit (ALU)** follows the instructions of the control unit and is the calculator part of the execution unit. It performs mathematical integer operations such as adding, subtracting, multiplying, and dividing and logical comparisons such as NOT, AND, OR, and exclusive-OR.

A **register** is a high-speed internal storage area that acts as the microprocessor's short-term memory and work area. Data must first be put in a register before it is processed by the ALU. For example, if two numbers are to be added, they are put into two different registers and then added together by the ALU. The result is stored in one of the two registers and can then be used for something else or stored in the RAM. In addition, registers can contain memory addresses—locations where data are stored.

The number of registers and their size (word size, or number of bits) help determine the power and speed of the microprocessor. For example, a 32-bit microprocessor, such as the 386DX and 486, has 32-bit registers, which can manipulate 32-bit data. Of course, if software is not written so as to make use of the entire register or the extra registers, the microprocessor will not perform at its peak.

The 8086 microprocessor has fourteen 16-bit registers. The general-purpose registers include the AX, BX, CD, DX, SI, DI, BP, and SP registers. Although these registers can serve any purpose, the have designated uses. For example, the AX (accumulator) register is used for most arithmetic and logical computations, and the CX (count) register is used to count things.

A 16-bit register can be addressed as two independent 8-bit registers. For example, the AX register can be accessed as the AL and the AH register. The H indicates the high byte (bits 8 through 15) and the L means the low byte (bits 0 through 7). Beginning with the 386, microprocessors contain 32-bit registers (EAX, EBX, ECX, and EDX), which can also be used as 16-bit registers (AX, BX, CX, and DX) and 8-bit registers (AL, AH, BL, BH, CL, CH, DL, and DH).

5.1.2 THE CONTROL UNIT

The **control unit** is a clocked logic circuit that controls the entire chip, including the ALU. It translates and follows the instructions contained in an external program (such as the ROM BIOS, the operating system, or application software) and keeps track of which step of the program is being executed. It consists of the following components:

- The *prefetch unit,* which decides when to get more data and instructions from the instruction cache or the computer's RAM based on its current tasks and the instructions that it is processing. In addition, it lines up the instructions to send off to the decode unit.
- The *decode unit,* which decodes and translates complex machine language instructions into simple commands (sometimes called microcode) understood by the ALU and the registers.
- The *data cache,* which is where data from the decode unit are stored for later use by the ALU and where the final results are prepared for distribution to different parts of the computer.

5.1.3 BUS INTERFACE UNIT (BIU)

The bus interface unit (BIU) manages three external connections: the data bus, the address bus, and the control bus. The **data bus,** which is managed by the bus control unit, is what actually carries the instructions and data into and out of the CPU. The size of the data bus is measured in bits. Each wire allows one bit of information to flow into or out of the microprocessor. A microprocessor with a data bus size of 32 bits has 32 wires connected to it for data transfer. If a microprocessor has more wires, it can transfer more data at the same time, making the microprocessor faster. The Intel 8088 microprocessor used in the IBM PC has an 8-bit data bus; the Intel Pentium and Pentium Pro have a 64-bit data bus.

The signals of the **address bus,** controlled by the address control unit, determine where the data bus signals are going to or coming from. Like the data bus, it is also measured in bits. For every wire or bit added to it, the amount of RAM that is addressable by the microprocessor is doubled. The amount of RAM the address bus can access is determined by the following equation:

$$\text{Amount of RAM} = 2^{\text{Size of address bus}}$$

Usually the motherboard (not the microprocessor) limits the amount of RAM that a system can recognize.

EXAMPLE 5.1 If you have a 20-bit address bus, the largest binary number that you can access is 1111111111 1111111111. If this is converted to the decimal number system, it is equivalent to 1,048,575 bytes (1 MB) of RAM. Note: The highest address that can be accessed in a 20-bit address bus is 1,048,575, not 1,048,576. This is because the numbering of bytes begins at 0, not 1.

The **control bus** coordinates the data transfer between the microprocessor and another device. It contains the address status lines, the data control lines, power lines, interrupt control lines, and operating control lines, including the clock signal input.

The *instruction pointer* contains the location or address of the next instruction to be executed. To help the microprocessor perform faster, instructions are placed in the instruction queue and held there until the execution unit needs them.

5.1.4 THE MICROPROCESSOR AT WORK

The instructions in a program are converted to machine code, which is what the CPU understands. Let's take as an example a sample program for adding two numbers together. Although this may seem like a simple operation to us, the computer must break it down to even simpler steps.

To add two numbers, such as 2 and 3, the computer would perform the following commands:

```
MOV AX,2
MOV BX,3
ADD AX,BX
MOV A2BFH,AX
```

The MOV and ADD commands are assembly language commands. Assembly language is low-level programming language that uses mnemonic abbreviations to represent machine operations and storage locations. It makes it possible to program the microprocessor directly without having to use machine language.

While performing these four commands, the microprocessor goes through the steps outlined in table 5.1.

> To see a more detailed description of how microprocessors work, visit the following website:
> **http://www.intel.com/education/mpuworks/index.htm**

5.2 MICROPROCESSOR PERFORMANCE

The microprocessor is the fastest component on the computer. The clock speed, the number of wait states, and the efficiency of the microprocessor determine the speed of the microprocessor.

5.2.1 CLOCK SPEED

The **clock speed** is the speed at which the microprocessor executes instructions; every computer contains an internal clock. More importantly, the clock synchronizes all of the various computer components. If the different components did not synchronize, they would get confused.

TABLE 5.1   How a micro-processor works

Step	
1	The CPU fetches the MOV AX,2 instruction (second software instruction) from the instruction queue. The instruction originally came from the RAM. If the instruction is not in the instruction queue, the prefetch unit will communicate with the bus interface unit to fetch the next instruction or instructions from RAM. The MOV command copies a value in one location to another location or will input a specified value into a location.	
2	The decode unit translates the instruction into a string of binary code.	
3	The MOV AX,2 instruction is executed and the value of 2 is stored in the AX register.	

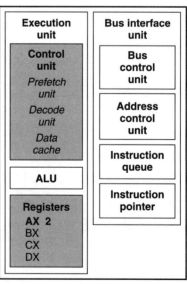

TABLE 5.1 *continued*

Step	
4	The CPU fetches the MOV BX,3 instruction (third software instruction) from the instruction queue. If the instruction is not in the instruction queue, the prefetch unit will communicate with the bus interface unit to fetch the next instruction or instructions from RAM. 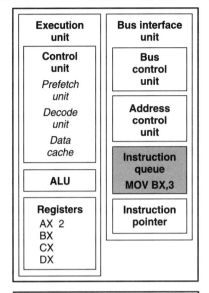
5	The decode unit translates the instruction into a string of binary code. 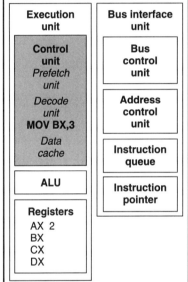
6	The MOV BX,3 instruction is executed and the value of 3 is stored in the BX register. 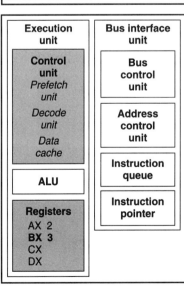

continued

TABLE 5.1 *continued*

Step		
7	The CPU fetches the fourth software instruction—the ADD AX,BX command. It indicates that the two numbers stored in the two registers should be added and the sum stored back into the first register.	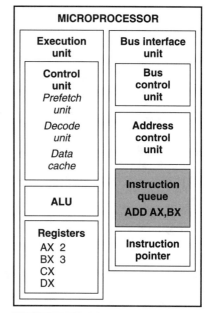
8	The decode unit decodes the ADD instruction and it is sent to the control unit.	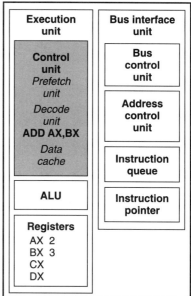
9	The control unit tells the ALU to add the two numbers together and store the sum in the first register or destination. This will replace the existing value.	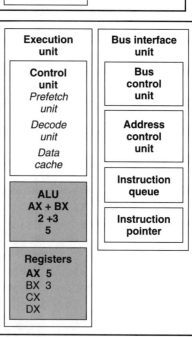

TABLE 5.1   *continued*

Step		
10	The CPU fetches the MOV instruction. The instruction specifies the RAM address that will hold the sum.	**Execution unit** **Control unit** *Prefetch unit* *Decode unit* *Data cache* **ALU** **Registers** AX 5 BX 3 CX DX **Bus interface unit** **Bus control unit** **Address control unit** **Instruction queue** **MOV A2BFH,AX** **Instruction pointer**
11	The CPU decodes the MOV instruction and reads the address of where to store the sum from the variable Z.	**Execution unit** **Control unit** *Prefetch unit* *Decode unit* **MOV A2BFH,AX** *Data cache* **ALU** **Registers** AX 5 BX 3 CX DX **Bus interface unit** **Bus control unit** **Address control unit** **Instruction queue** **Instruction pointer**
12	The bus interface unit activates the address bus and sets the control bus to indicate it is going to transfer the number from the CPU to the RAM. The address on the address bus is a memory address, which was assigned to the variable Z.	**Execution unit** **Control unit** *Prefetch unit* *Decode unit* *Data cache* **ALU** **Registers** AX 5 BX 3 CX DX **Bus interface unit** **Bus control unit** **Address control unit** **A2BFH** **Instruction queue** **Instruction pointer**

continued

TABLE 5.1   *continued*

Step	
13	The data bus transfers the sum back to the indicated RAM address. 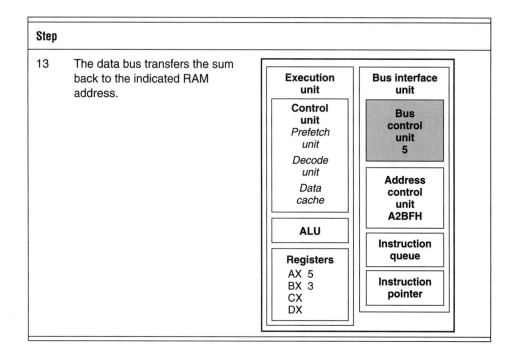

By now, you should have realized that the computer works by using many on/off switches made up of transistors. A bit is transferred by an on/off switch. When a switch switches from on to off or off to on, it takes a small amount of time for the change to occur. If a circuit tries to read a signal when the switch is in transition, the circuit gets confused since it is not on or off. The clock cycle (tick) indicates when a circuit is supposed to do its next task, such as reading a signal or performing a calculation. (See fig. 5.5.)

Clock speeds (frequency) are expressed in **megahertz (MHz),** 1 MHz being equal to 1 million cycles per second. The faster the clock speed, the more instructions the microprocessor can execute per second. The IBM PC had a clock speed of 4.77 MHz; today's machines exceed 600 MHz. The frequency of the clock and the time required for the transistors to switch from low to high or from high to low are related as shown in the following equation:

$$f = \frac{1}{t} \quad \text{or} \quad t = \frac{1}{f}$$

where t is time and f is frequency.

In a 4.77 MHz microprocessor, the transistor has to transition within $\frac{1}{4.77}$ MHz = 209.6 nanoseconds. In a 200 MHz microprocessor, the transistor has to transition within $\frac{1}{200}$ MHz = 5 nanoseconds, and in a 400 MHz microprocessor, the transistor has to transition within $\frac{1}{400}$ MHz = 2.5 nanoseconds. The maximum clock speed of the microprocessor is mostly determined by the speed of the switching transistor.

FIGURE 5.5   A clock signal is used by the microprocessor to indicate when it is to perform a task.

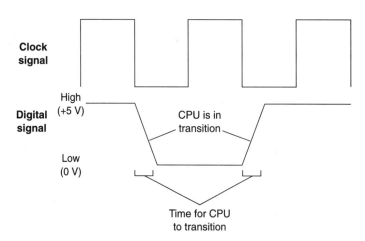

TABLE 5.2   Size of transistor in common microprocessors

CPU	Transistor Size (Microns)
8088	3
80286	1.5
80386	1
80486	.8
Pentium	.35
Pentium Pro	.35
Pentium II	.25 and .18

Overclocking is the process of running the microprocessor at a clock speed faster than specified. A clock signal that is too fast does not allow the transistors enough time to change states, so the microprocessor will experience errors.

> **IMPORTANT NOTE**   Some motherboards can accommodate several different CPU speeds, which can be changed by using jumpers or DIP switches on the motherboard or by using the CMOS setup program. If you choose a speed that is too fast, however, the microprocessor may be damaged or produce calculation errors and its life span will usually be shortened.

The size and spacing of the microprocessor's transistors partially determine the switching speed. The diameter of transistors is measured in microns; one micron is one-millionth of a meter. A human hair is, on average, 30 microns in diameter. Smaller transistors can be packed more tightly in a given area; if they are closer together, there is less distance for the electrical signals to travel, creating a faster microprocessor. Early microprocessors, such as the 8088, used transistors that were 3 microns in size. Today, the Pentium II uses transistors that are only .18 microns in size. (See table 5.2.)

5.2.2   MOORE'S LAW

Moore's law gives a better understanding of how the IC chip (including the microprocessor) has progressed over the years. In 1965, Gordon Moore, cofounder of Intel, stated that the number of transistors per square inch on integrated circuits had doubled and would double every year since the time the integrated chip was invented. Since his prediction, the number of transistors per square inch has doubled every 12 to 18 months. In the 26 years since the invention, the number of transistors on a microprocessor chip has increased more than 3,200 times—from 2,300 on the 4004 in 1971 to 29,000 for the 8086/8088 in 1978 to 7.5 million on the Pentium II in 1997. Between 1978 and 1997, the performance speed of the microprocessor has increased over a thousand times. Moore and other experts expect Moore's law to hold for approximately two more decades until technology restrictions prevent transistors from becoming any smaller. (See fig. 5.6.)

5.2.3   PIPELINING, WAIT STATES, AND SUPERSCALAR TECHNOLOGY

Every task that is done by the microprocessor is completed by the different parts of the microprocessor simultaneously. Some of the earlier microprocessors were not very efficient because they would bring in an instruction, decode it, process it, and output any results using the different parts of the microprocessor. Therefore, most of the microprocessor was idle while the different parts waited for the next instruction. For example, the 8088 or 8086 microprocessor used 12 clock cycles to execute a single instruction, such as adding two numbers together.

FIGURE 5.6   The number of
transistors and the performance
of the microprocessor throughout the years

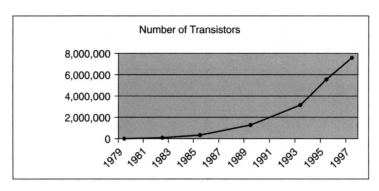

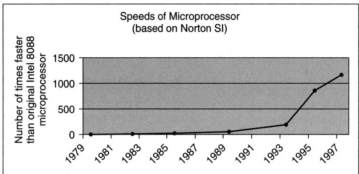

Later microprocessors used pipelines. **Pipelines** execute an instruction much like an assembly line. When one part of the microprocessor is done with the instruction, it hands it off to the next part of the microprocessor and starts on the next instruction. The 386 microprocessor can perform an instruction such as adding two numbers in about 4.5 clock cycles; the 486 can perform this instruction in 2 clock cycles. Pentium chips can add only two numbers together in one clock cycle, while the Pentium Pro can add three numbers. Consequently, a 486DX microprocessor running at 66 MHz can perform twice as fast as a 386DX running at 66 MHz. (See table 5.3.)

The microprocessor is the fastest component in the computer. Consequently, the microprocessor occasionally has to wait for other components to catch up. The catch-up period is called a **wait state,** in which the microprocessor lies idle. If a microprocessor is set to zero wait states, it is running at maximum speed without any timeouts to compensate for slow components such as memory.

A superscalar microprocessor can execute more than one instruction per clock cycle, typically by having more than one execution unit. Therefore, a superscalar microprocessor can literally perform two tasks at the same time.

5.2.4   CISC AND RISC

The commands recognized by the microprocessor are either the **complex instruction set computer (CISC)** commands or the **reduced instruction set computer (RISC)** commands. The CISC are used in many of the earlier Intel microprocessors; RISC are used in DEC Alpha, Power PC, and, to some extent, in recent Intel CPUs.

TABLE 5.3   Microcode
efficiency

CPU	Parameter	Clocks
8088/8086	Add two numbers	12
80286/80386	Add two numbers	4.5
80486	Add two numbers	2
Pentium	Add two numbers	1
Pentium Pro	Add three numbers	1

CISC commands are considered complex commands because they consist of several smaller commands (microcode) grouped together. As they are sent to the microprocessor, the microprocessor figures out how many bytes of processing room the commands require and then determines the correct way to load and store them. The final step is sending the commands to the decode unit, which translates them into the hard-wired microcode consisting of 1s and 0s. By grouping the commands together, CISC microprocessors do not have to access the slower RAM as much.

RISC commands consist of the smaller commands of the same size that are not grouped together. These can be performed in one clock cycle or less, and therefore the microprocessor does not have to determine the correct way to load and store the RISC commands and they do not have to go through a decode unit. Consequently, when RISC and CISC microprocessors perform the same tasks, the RISC microprocessor can execute the several smaller commands faster than the CISC microprocessor can perform the one complex command. Since the decode unit is not required by the RISC microprocessor, it also consumes less power and generates less heat.

5.3 INTEL MICROPROCESSORS

Due to the quick success in 1981 of the IBM PC, which used an Intel microprocessor, Intel became the manufacturer of choice for PC microprocessors. Since the introduction of the 8086 microprocessor in 1978, Intel has created many distinct versions of its microprocessor.

5.3.1 8088 AND 8086 MICROPROCESSORS

The 8088 microprocessor was used in the IBM PC (model 5150) and the IBM XT (model 5160). Any computers using the 8088 or 8086 microprocessor are known as XT computers. Both had 29,000 transistors, required 40 pins to connect to the motherboard, and were in the form of a DIP (dual in-line package). They were initially designed to run at 4.77 MHz. (See fig. 5.7.)

The 8088 and 8086 microprocessors are both 16-bit microprocessors since they use 16-bit registers and can process 16-bit numbers. In addition, they have a 20-bit address bus

FIGURE 5.7 Intel 8088 microprocessor (Intel is a registered trademark of Intel Corporation)

that allows the microprocessor to recognize up to 1 MB of RAM. The difference between these microprocessors is the size of the data bus. The 8088 microprocessor has an 8-bit bus, and the 8086 has a 16-bit bus. The larger bus gives the 8086 a 20% increase in performance over the 8088.

5.3.2 80286 MICROPROCESSOR

The 80286 (usually referred to as the 286) microprocessor was first used in the IBM AT. It had 134,000 transistors and required 68 pins to connect to the motherboard. Since the microprocessor was larger, the packaging of the chip had to be changed from dual in-line packaging (DIP) to the square pin grid array (PGA). The first 286 was designed to operate at 6 MHz. Although the clock speed was only 25.8% faster than the 8088's 4.77 MHz, its performance was five times greater.

The 286 had a 24-bit address bus that allowed the microprocessor to access up to 16 MB of RAM. Better yet, Intel also allowed the microprocessor to use up to 1,008 MB of virtual memory. **Virtual memory** is hard drive space pretending to be RAM. Even though the hard drive is much slower than RAM, allocating part of it to virtual memory does permit the running of programs that could not be run before because of memory constraints.

The 286 was designed to be backward compatible to the 8088 and 8086 microprocessors. Therefore, it could run all of the programs that were written for the XT computer. When running in **real mode,** the 286 microprocessor pretended to be an 8086 microprocessor. Unfortunately, it also inherited the limitations of the 8086 in that it recognized only 1 MB of RAM. When the 286 microprocessor switched from real mode to **protected mode,** it could recognize RAM above 1 MB. In protected mode, the microprocessor could run multiple programs in RAM and isolate them so that one program did not interfere with another. Unfortunately, the 286 could not switch back to real mode from protected mode without a resetting of the CPU. Therefore, software programmers mostly ignored protected mode.

5.3.3 80386 MICROPROCESSORS

The 80386 is considered the first modern microprocessor, although it is extremely outdated by today's standards. It has 32-bit registers, a 32-bit data bus, and a 32-bit address bus (allowing it to recognize up to 4 GB of RAM). Because of its increased power and improved capabilities, it made possible the GUI-based operating system in the PC. The instructions that the microprocessor recognizes, known as the x86 instruction set, has not changed much since it was introduced. There are three versions of the 80836 (usually referred to as a 386): the 386DX, 386SX, and 386SL. (See fig. 5.8.)

The 386 is backward-compatible with the 8086, 8088, and 286 microprocessors. Therefore, it includes real mode and protected mode. Unlike the 286, it can switch from real mode to protected mode and back to real mode without the microprocessor being reset. In addition, it introduced a third mode, called **virtual 8086 mode.** The virtual 8086 mode divides the RAM into several "pretend" 8086 machines, each consisting of 1 MB of RAM. The microprocessor then switches rapidly between the different virtual (pretend) machines so it appears that all of the machines are working at the same time (multitasking). The advantage of a virtual machine is that if one of the machines goes down, the microprocessor can terminate that machine without affecting the other virtual machines.

In addition to the protected and virtual 8086 modes, the 386 provided a new protection mechanism by its ability to assign data and instructions to a privilege ring, or level. The four privilege levels are 0, 1, 2, and 3, with the privilege level of 0 being the highest and level 3 the lowest. Programs in ring 0 can access programs in all of the rings, but the programs in ring 3 cannot access the programs in rings 0, 1, and 2. Some operating systems, such as Windows NT, assign the operating system to level 0 and other programs to level 3. Therefore, if a program becomes corrupted in RAM, that does not affect the operating system. The 386 also introduced instruction pipelining, which, as we have seen, allows the microprocessor to start working on a new instruction before it has completed the current

FIGURE 5.8   Intel 80386 micro-processor

one. To facilitate pipelining, the 386 included 16 bytes of pre-fetch cache memory to store the next few instructions.

The 386SX is a scaled-down 80386DX. Internally, the 386SX is nearly identical to the 386DX, including the 32-bit registers, but the 386SX has only a 16-bit data bus. Thus, the 386 SX is approximately 20% slower than the 386DX. In addition, the 386SX has only a 24-bit address bus, which can access up to 16 MB of RAM. Another variation on the 386 chip is the 386SL. This low-power microprocessor has the same capabilities as the 386SX but is designed for laptop systems, which require low power consumption. The SL chips offer special power-management features—for example, several sleep modes that conserve power—that are important to systems that run on batteries. The SL-type chip was used in every microprocessor after the 386.

5.3.4   80486 MICROPROCESSOR

The 486DX is a 386DX microprocessor with a math coprocessor and an 8 KB internal RAM cache (sometimes referred to as an L1 RAM cache), which is discussed below. (See fig. 5.9.) The 486SX, marketed as a low-end alternative to the 486DX, is identical to the 486DX, except it does not include a math coprocessor. Since the RAM cache and the math coprocessor are built into the microprocessor, signals do not have to be sent outside of the microprocessor (saving clock cycles), thus avoiding delays that might be encountered on the motherboard.

A **math coprocessor** is a chip that specializes in floating-point mathematical calculations. A floating-point number is a number with a decimal point or a number that includes exponents. **RAM cache** is ultrafast RAM that runs at the speed of the 486DX microprocessor and contains the data that it accesses most often. When the CPU needs some data, it will first search the RAM cache before searching the slower RAM. If the data are found in the RAM cache, a significant amount of time is saved. If it is not found in the RAM cache, the time it took to search there is small compared to the time required for searching the RAM.

The 486 microprocessor had a streamlined design. It used smaller silicon etchings to make up the internal circuits, which increased performance and used less power. In addition, it increased the execution pipeline and it supported burst mode. *Burst mode* is the state in which the microprocessor can lock in a single address and can access data that are sequential without resetting the address bus.

As the clock speed of the 486DX was increased, however, motherboard technology could not keep up. To allow for a faster computer without redesigning an expensive new motherboard, the 486DX2 and the 486DX4 were introduced. The DX2 microprocessor

runs at twice the clock speed of the motherboard. This means that while the motherboard is running at a speed of 33 MHz, the microprocessor runs at 66 MHz. This computer is faster even though the motherboard is the same. The "4" in the DX4 name does not mean what the "2" does in DX2. While the name DX2 meant that the microprocessor ran at twice the speed of the motherboard, the DX4 runs not at four times the speed of the motherboard, but only at three times the speed. Since the DX4 ran so much faster than the motherboard, its internal RAM cache was increased from 8 KB to 16 KB to make sure the information from the RAM was available to the microprocessor when needed.

5.3.5 THE PENTIUM MICROPROCESSOR

Intel introduced the Pentium microprocessor in 1993. (See fig. 5.10.) Although the industry expected it to be called the 80586 in keeping with the other names of Intel microprocessors, Intel chose the name *Pentium* so that the name could be trademarked.

The Pentium microprocessor uses two linked execution units. The first execution unit, similar to a 486DX, has a single 32-bit pathway known as the U pipeline. The second execution unit, similar to a 486SX, has a second 32-bit pathway known as the V pipeline. Since the microprocessor has more than one pipeline, it can perform two tasks at the same time. Of course, to utilize this superscalar technology, software had to be recompiled for the Pentium microprocessor.

The bus interface unit sends and receives data and code along two separate paths, each of which handles 64 bits at a time. One path leads to an 8 K storage unit, or cache, used for data. The other path leads to an identical cache used only for code that tells the processor what to do with the data. The data and code stay in the caches until other parts of the microprocessor need them. Other improvements included a math coprocessor that could process floating-point calculations three to five times faster than the 486DX and five levels of pipelining. Lastly, some of the internal links inside the microprocessor were as wide as 256 bits.

The second wave of Pentium chips used 3.3 V chips and .6-micron silicon traces. The third version of the Pentium chip ran at 2.9 V and eventually at 2.5 V. In addition, it had .25-micron silicon traces, which allowed the chip to be smaller.

The 75 MHz Pentium microprocessor allowed the microprocessor to become faster than the fastest motherboard—Pentium chips running at 75 MHz to 100 MHz run at 1.5 times the

FIGURE 5.10   Intel Pentium microprocessor (Intel and Pentium are registered trademarks of Intel Corporation)

speed of the motherboard, and Pentium microprocessors running at 120 MHz to 133 MHz run at 2.0 times the speed of the motherboard. Pentium chips running at 150 to 166 MHz are running at 2.5 times the speed of the motherboard, and faster microprocessors run 3 times faster. All of this demonstrates that the microprocessor has improved much more than any other PC component. In addition, there is a Pentium OverDrive microprocessor, which is a Pentium chip that can be installed in a 486-based computer that has an OverDrive socket. While the OverDrive chip is faster than a 486 microprocessor, it is not as fast as a Pentium chip in a Pentium computer.

5.3.6   THE PENTIUM PRO MICROPROCESSOR

The Pentium Pro microprocessor performs at a speed approximately 50% higher than a Pentium chip with the same clock speed. In addition, it is optimized for 32-bit operating systems, such as Windows NT. It is constructed with a Dual-Cavity PGA (pin grid array) package. (See fig. 5.11.) The Dual-Cavity PGA has a Pentium Pro microprocessor and a 256 or 512 KB L2 RAM cache. The L2 RAM cache, which is normally found on the motherboard, works very much like the L1 internal RAM cache, which buffers the RAM and the microprocessor. Of course, the 256 KB or 512 KB RAM cache is faster than the normal RAM cache chips found on the motherboard because the built-in RAM cache is running at the speed of the microprocessor, not the speed of the slower motherboard. The Pentium Pro microprocessor uses a Dual Independent Bus (DIB), one from the processor to RAM and the other from the processor to the L2 cache. The Pentium Pro chip can access both buses simultaneously.

Intel took a somewhat different approach in making the Pentium Pro chip compatible with the previous x86 microprocessors. Instead of hard-coding the computer's CISC instruction set, Intel built a RISC processor to implement each x86 instruction. Therefore, each CISC instruction is rebuilt out of the smaller and faster RISC instructions. Consequently, each x86 instruction is called a **RISC86 instruction.**

The Pentium Pro microprocessor incorporates three pipelines, rather than the two pipelines of the original Pentium chips. By breaking up instruction execution into 14 steps, Intel has made it possible to perform dynamic execution, which attempts to keep all three pipelines full. To keep the pipelines busy, the chip uses branch prediction and out-of-order execution.

Branch prediction is based on the fact that most programs have many instruction pathways. Depending on the results of calculations and the decisions made within the program, different pathways are chosen. To keep the pipelines full when it has nothing to do, the

FIGURE 5.11   Intel Pentium
Pro microprocessor (Intel and
Pentium are registered trade-
marks of Intel Corporation)

Pentium Pro tries to speculate which branch to use before it is actually needed. If it guesses correctly, there is a significant performance increase since it has already executed some of the needed instructions. If it is incorrect, it must discard the results executed from the speculated branch and execute the correct instructions.

Out-of-order execution means exactly what it sounds like—instructions are sometimes performed out of sequence. This also helps keep the pipelines full when an instruction can't be performed until another instruction is completed. Therefore, while the processor is waiting for the results, it will start on another instruction. Performing out-of-order execution takes a lot of coordination. Sometimes two different instructions may refer to the same register at the same time. When this happens, the CPU will produce confusing results and errors. To avoid this problem, the CPU can rename registers dynamically. If it needs two registers with the same name, it just renames the two registers with the same name.

5.3.7 MMX TECHNOLOGY

MMX technology, used in the Pentium microprocessor with MMX technology and the Pentium II, has the following improvements:

1. Fifty-seven new, powerful instructions specifically designed to manipulate and process video, audio, and graphical data previously handled by a separate sound or video card. These instructions are designed to handle the highly parallel, repetitive sequences often found in multimedia data.
2. Four 64-bit MMX registers.
3. Single instruction multiple data (SIMD), a technique that reduces the number of repetitive actions by loading several pieces of data into the microprocessor and performing the same command on them simultaneously. For example, if the microprocessor has several 16-bit numbers that need to have the same action performed on them, a Pentium chip can load four 16-bit numbers ($4 \times 16 = 64$ bits) and perform the same action on all four numbers at the same time.
4. A larger memory cache (32 KB), requiring fewer accesses to memory that is outside the microprocessor.

An MMX microprocessor can run a multimedia application that is written for MMX technology up to 60% faster than a microprocessor without MMX. In addition, an MMX microprocessor can run other applications 10% faster.

FIGURE 5.12   Intel Pentium II
microprocessor (Intel and Pentium are registered trademarks
of Intel Corporation)

The Pentium II processor (including the Pentium Xeon, Mobile Pentium II, and Pentium Celeron) is similar to a Pentium Pro processor with MMX technology. (See figs. 5.12 and 5.13.) The most obvious difference between the Pentium II and other Intel microprocessors is that it uses the single-edge contact (SEC) packaging, which connects to a motherboard via a single-edge connector. It includes a 512 KB L2 RAM cache, which connects to the microprocessor and runs at half the speed of the microprocessor. The SEC cartridge uses a retention bracket to hold the CPU and cache in place.

The flagship of the Pentium II processor family is the Pentium II Xeon processor, which connects to slot 2. It incorporates an L2 cache of 512 KB, 1 MB, or 2 MB that operates at the same speed as the processor core (400 MHz). The low-end Pentium II, the Celeron processor, is available in 266 MHz and 300 MHz but does not contain a Level 2 cache. The newer version of the Celeron processor contains a small amount of Level 2 cache.

One of the newer Pentium II microprocessors is the Mobile Pentium II. (See fig. 5.14.) Since the Pentium II microprocessor is designed for a notebook computer, a Mobile Pentium II 266 MHz processor consumes almost half the power of a Pentium II 333 MHz processor yet provides a 35% increase in performance over the Pentium MMX processor running at the same speed. In addition, it includes self-testing circuitry and thermal sensors that provide valuable data for managing software.

Intel's newest microprocessor is the Pentium III. It is available in speeds of 450 MHz and 500 MHz, and with improvements, it is expected to reach 600 MHz. The biggest performance increase comes from the new Katmai instructions, which are 70 multimedia instructions that improve 3-D graphics, video and audio performance, and speech recognition.

Table 5.4 summarizes the characteristics of Intel microprocessors. For more information on Intel microprocessors, you can visit the following website:
http://www.intel.com/intel/product/index.htm

FIGURE 5.13   Intel Celeron microprocessor (Intel and Pentium
are registered trademarks of Intel Corporation)

TABLE 5.4 Intel microprocessors

	Date	Intel (Register Size)	External (Data Bus)	Address Bus	Number of Transistors	FPU	Internal Cache	Speed Ratings*	Comments
8086 (4.77, 8, and 10 MHz)	6/78	16-bit	16-bit	20-bit (1 MB)	29,000	No	None	5 MHz—.33 MIPS 10 MHz—.75 MIPS	
8088 (4.77 and 8 MHz)	6/79	16-bit	8-bit	20-bit (1 MB)	29,000	No	None	5 MHz—.33 MIPS/1.0 Norton SI 8 MHz—.75 MIPS/1.7 Norton SI	Used in IBM PC and IBM XT
80286 (8, 10, and 12 MHz)	2/82	16-bit	16-bit	24-bit (16 MB)	134,000	No	None	6 MHz—.9 MIPS/3.1 Norton SI 12 MHz—2.66 MIPS/6.7 Norton SI	Used in IBM AT; 3 to 6 times faster than 8086; introduced virtual memory
80386DX (16, 20, 25, and 33 MHz)	10/85	32-bit	32-bit	32-bit (4 GB)	275,000	No	None	16 MHz—6 MIPS/15 Norton SI 33 MHz—11.4 MIPS/68 iCOMP/35 Norton SI	Introduced pipelining; 2 to 4 times faster than 286
80386SX (16, 20, 25, and 33 MHz)	6/88	32-bit	16-bit	24-bit (16 MB)	275,000	No	None	16 MHz—2.5 MIPS/22 iCOMP/11 Norton SI 33 MHz—2.9 MIPS/27 Norton SI	
80486DX (DX: 25, 33, and 50 MHz; DX2: 50 and 66 MHz; DX4: 75 and 100 MHz)	4/89	32-bit	32-bit	32-bit (4 GB)	1.2 million	Yes	8 KB; 16 KB for DX4	33 MHz—27 MIPS/166 iCOMP/72 Norton SI 50 MHz—41 MIPS/249 iCOMP/109 Norton SI DX2 66 MHz—41 MIPS/297 iCOMP DX4 100 MHz—70.7 MIPS/435 iCOMP	
80486SX (16, 20, 25, and 33 MHz)	4/91	32-bit	32-bit	32-bit (4 GB)	1.2 million	No	8 KB	16 MHz—13 MIPS/63 iCOMP/34 Norton SI 33 MHz—27 MIPS/136 iCOMP/72 Norton SI	

	Date				Transistors		Cache	Speeds	Notes
Pentium (60, 66, and 100 MHz)	3/93	32-bit	64-bit	32-bit (4 GB)	3.1 million	Yes	2 × 8 KB	60 MHz—100 MIPS/510 iCOMP/190 Norton SI 100 MHz—166.3 MIPS/815 iCOMP/317 Norton SI 133 MHz—218.9 MIPS/1110 iCOMP/421 Norton SI 166 MHz—278 MIPS/1308 iCOMP/529 Norton SI 200 MHz—142 iCOMP 2.0	5 times faster than than 486DX; introduced superscalar design
Pentium Pro (150, 166, 180, and 200 MHz)	9/95	32-bit	64-bit	36-bit (64 GB)	5.5 million	Yes	2 × 8 KB	200 MHz—450 MIPS/856 Norton SI	Introduced dynamic execution
Pentium with MMX (166 and 200 MHz)	1/97	32-bit	64-bit	32-bit (4 GB)	4.5 million	Yes	2 × 16 KB	166 MHz—278 MIPS/160 iCOMP 2.0/640 Norton SI 200 MHz—336 MIPS/182 iCOMP 2.0/770 Norton SI 233 MHz—203 iCOMP 2.0/890 Norton SI	Introduced multimedia commands
Pentium II with MMX (233, 266, 300, 333, 350, 400, and 450 MHz)	5/97	32-bit	64-bit	36-bit (64 GB)	7.5 million	Yes	2 × 16 KB	233 MHz—267 iCOMP 2.0/1170 Norton SI 266 MHz—303 iCOMP 2.0/1335 Norton SI 300 MHz—332 iCOMP 2.0/1506 Norton SI 400 MHz—440 iCOMP 2.0/2008 Norton SI 450 MHz—495 iCOMP 2.0/2259 Norton SI	

*iCOMP™—Intel Comparative Microprocessor Performance Index.

iCOMP 2.0™—Intel's revised iCOMP benchmark, used for Pentium 75 and later processors.

MIPS—Millions of instructions per second.

Norton SI—One of the earliest universal benchmarks relative to the first IBM PC.

FIGURE 5.14   Intel Mobile Pentium II microprocessor (Intel and Pentium are registered trademarks of Intel Corporation)

5.4   INTEL-COMPATIBLE PROCESSORS

Although Intel microprocessors are considered the de facto standard, Intel is not the only company that produces PC microprocessors. Two other manufacturers are Advanced Micro Devices (AMD) and Cyrix. Both AMD and Cyrix have 386, 486, and Pentium-like microprocessors, which offer CPUs with similar performance to Intel CPUs but cost less. Their microprocessors are also fully Intel-compatible, which means that all software that runs on an Intel microprocessor will also work on these microprocessors. Most of the chips are pin-compatible as well, although some require a customized motherboard.

5.4.1   AMD

AMD developed its own version of the 386DX and 486 microprocessors by using its own hardware design and Intel's microcode. One of the popular AMD microprocessors was the Am386DX-40. (See fig. 5.15.) It ran at 40 MHz—faster than Intel's fastest 386DX chip, which ran at only 33 MHz—yet the AMD chip consumed less power. The AMD 486DX40-

FIGURE 5.15   AMD Am386DX-40 microprocessor

120 used clock-tripling technology, which ran on a 40 MHz external clock, but the microprocessor itself ran at 120 MHz. The Intel counterpart, the 486DX4, ran only up to 100 MHz.

AMD's newest microprocessors include the AMD5K86 and AMD-K6. The AMD5K86, once called the K5, has a design similar to that of the Pentium Pro. It converts x86 code to RISC-like operations, which AMD calls RISC ops (ROPs). It also has other features, including superscalar design; out-of-order speculative execution; and dynamic cache, line-oriented branch prediction. In addition, it has a 16 KB instruction cache and an 8 KB data cache.

The newest AMD-K6 MMX processor is AMD's sixth-generation microprocessor. It is packaged in a ceramic pin grid array (CPGA) using C4 (Controlled Collapse Chip Connection) flip-chip interconnection technology that can be inserted in a standard Pentium socket. This technology permits a smaller chip, which helps performance since the signals have smaller distances to travel. Unlike the Pentium Pro microprocessor, the K6 is optimized for both 16- and 32-bit code. It contains two 32 KB RAM caches, one for data and one for code, and contains the MMX extensions.

The speed of both the AMD 5K86 and K6 is not rated in megahertz. Instead, the chips have a P rating system, which reflects performance relative to similar Intel Pentium microprocessors. A 5K86 runs at 133 MHz and has a P166 speed rating because it can perform similar to a Pentium chip running at 166 MHz.

The newest AMD microprocessor is the AMD-K6-2 processor with 3DNow! technology, which significantly enhances 3D graphics, multimedia, and other floating-point-intensive PC applications. 3DNow! technology is a set of 21 new instructions that use SIMD and other performance enhancements to open the performance bottleneck in the 3D graphics pipeline between the microprocessor and the 3D graphics accelerator card.

For more information on AMD microprocessors, visit the following website:
http://www.amd.com/products/cpg/cpg.html

5.4.2 CYRIX

The Cyrix MediaGX, introduced in February 1997, was created to be a low-cost multimedia chip that would run like a Pentium chip. (See Fig. 5.16.) To make it faster, Cyrix used six pipeline stages and included a 16 KB cache. Like Intel's Pentium chips, the MediaGX

FIGURE 5.16 Cyrix Media GX processor (the Media GX™ is a trademark and Cyrix® is a registered trademark of National Semiconductor Corporation)

has two 32-bit internal registers and a 64-bit external data bus. The chip's main boost comes from its built-in graphics system with its own pipeline and built-in support for SoundBlaster-compatible audio, a MIDI interface, and digital audio processing. In addition, the Cyrix CPU handles functions usually found on other support chips on the motherboard. These include a bridge logic to the ISA bus, four ATA ports to be used with the enhanced IDE drives, an AT-compatible timer, an interrupt controller, a DMA controller, and a PCI interface.

The newest version of the MediaGX family is the MMX-Enhanced Media GX processor (desktop version and mobile version). In addition to the many features of the Media GX processor, the MMX-Enhanced Media GX processor features support for MPEG1 and two USB ports, includes an integrated game port control, and supports MMX technology. The Cyrix 6x86, formerly code-named M1, does not convert the CISC instructions into RISC-like instructions. Instead, the 6x86 operates on a nonuniform-size x86 code more efficiently than other CPUs do. It has a superpipelined architecture with seven stages (instead of the Pentium chip's five stages). This allows the Cyrix CPU to start an instruction before the previous one is finished. Other features include multibranch prediction, speculative execution, out-of-order completion, and register renaming. Like the AMD chips, the recent Cyrix microprocessors also use the P rating system.

The newest CPU is the 6x86MX processor, formerly referred to as the M2. (See fig. 5.17.) It runs at a lesser voltage, can use the same slot as the corresponding Pentium chip, and is optimized for both 16-bit and 32-bit applications. Its pipeline has nine or ten stages, more than the seven stages used in the M1, and it includes a 64 KB cache. Unlike AMD, which licensed the MMX instruction set from Intel, Cyrix developed its own MMX-compatible instructions.

> For more information on Cyrix microprocessors, you can visit the following website:
>
> **http://www.cyrix.com/process/prodinfo/prodin-p.htm**

5.6 SYMMETRIC MULTIPROCESSING (SMP)

Symmetric multiprocessing (SMP) occurs in a computer consisting of two or more microprocessors that share the same memory. Using software written to use the multiple microprocessors, the computer can execute several programs at the same time or can execute multithreaded applications faster. A multithreaded application is an application that is broken into several smaller parts and executed simultaneously. For example, Microsoft Word uses one thread to respond to the keyboard input that places characters in a document; other threads are used to check spelling, paginate the document, and to spool a document to the printer. Newer versions of Windows NT, OS/2, NetWare, and some versions of UNIX can use SMP.

5.7 MATH COPROCESSORS

Math coprocessors, also known as floating-point units, floating-point numeric processors, or numeric processing units, are, as already stated, chips that specialize in floating-point mathematical calculations. A floating-point number is a number with a decimal point or a number that includes exponents.

Question: If a computer does not have a math coprocessor, can it still multiply two numbers with decimal points and exponents?

Answer: Yes. Remember that a microprocessor's ALU unit performs mathematical operations (including numbers with decimal points and exponents) and logical comparisons. Unfortunately, the microprocessor is designed to work exclusively with integers. Since microprocessors do not have commands that work on floating-point numbers, the floating-point numbers have to be broken down into integers before an operation can be performed. This, of course, takes much longer than operations involving just integer calculations.

The math coprocessor specializes in completing floating-point calculations. To be useful to the computer, it has to figure out which instructions are floating-point calculations, transfer the data to the math coprocessor, complete the calculation, and transfer the result back to the CPU faster than the CPU could do the whole calculation. The math coprocessor can perform floating-point calculations up to 200 times faster than the CPU. Of course, the software used must be able to employ the math coprocessor. CAD programs, spreadsheets, and graphic manipulation programs written to make use of the coprocessor significantly increase performance.

When the IBM PC was introduced in 1981, there was an empty socket next to the 8088 microprocessor on the motherboard. From 1981 to 1983, IBM wouldn't say officially what the empty socket was for, but eventually, it said the slot was designed for the 8087 math coprocessor. Since then, all succeeding Intel CPUs have offered some way of incorporating a floating-point coprocessor. Of course, by the time the 486DX was introduced, the math coprocessor was included in the CPU. When installing a math coprocessor, you must match the CPU speed and the math coprocessor speed. Table 5.5 shows the coprocessors that match up with various Intel CPUs.

Question: If a 486DX or Pentium chip motherboard has a large empty slot for a chip and the 486DX and Pentium have internal math coprocessors, what is the slot for?

Answer: The empty slot is for either an OverDrive chip or a faster, upgrade CPU. If the CPU is a 486DX, the slot may be used for a 486DX4 CPU or a Pentium chip.

Intel's 487 math coprocessor is different from the others because it is really a complete 486DX microprocessor with an extra pin added and some other pins rearranged. When the 487SX is installed in the extra socket provided in a 486SX system, the 487SX turns off the existing 486SX via a new signal on one of the pins. The extra pin actually carries no signal itself and exists only to prevent improper orientation when the chip is installed in a socket. The 487SX takes over all CPU functions from the 486SX and provides math coprocessor functionality to the system.

TABLE 5.5   Intel math coprocessors

CPU	Math Coprocessor
8088, 8086	8087
80286	80287
80386DX	80387DX
80387SX	80387SX
486DX	Internal
486SX	80487SX
Pentium, Pentium Pro	Internal

5.8 HEAT SINKS AND COOLING FANS

Most of today's faster microprocessors produce a lot of heat, and this heat has to be dissipated or the system will operate only intermittently or even fail completely. Heat is dissipated in several ways. The IBM PC and XT were cooled by adding holes in the side of the case, which allowed the heat to escape by convection.

When the 286 was introduced, it produced more heat, which could not be released fast enough. To alleviate this problem, fans were added to the power supply to suck the hot air out instead of letting it build up. If the fan of the power supply fails in a computer with a 386 microprocessor or better, the case of the computer will be warm to the touch.

By the time the 486 microprocessors were being introduced, the fan could not handle the load; it needed help. To overcome this problem, a heat sink was placed on top of the CPU. A **heat sink** is a finned piece of metal that is clipped or glued to the top of the processor. (See fig. 5.18.) Since the finned piece of metal has more surface area than a flat piece, it will pull the heat away from the CPU faster. (Note: For a heat sink to efficiently cool a microprocessor, a thermal transfer compound should be used between the heat sink and the fan.)

When the faster 486 microprocessors and the Pentium microprocessors were introduced, a small fan had to be added to the top of the heat sink to suck the heat away from the CPU. (See fig. 5.19.) Some newer motherboards, cases, and power supplies are designed to eliminate the need for a fan by blowing air into the computer. To improve the efficiency of the system, the fan is positioned to blow directly over the CPU.

FIGURE 5.18   Heat sink

FIGURE 5.19   CPU fan with heat sink (courtesy of PC Power & Cooling, Inc.)

5.9 INSTALLING A MICROPROCESSOR

First, when installing a CPU, avoid electrostatic discharge (ESD). This is even more important today than in the past because newer chips run at a lower voltage, which makes them more susceptible to ESD than the older CPUs. Second, keep in mind that not all CPUs use the same sockets. The older CPUs, of course, had fewer pins because of their smaller address and data buses and 5-volt operation. The newest CPUs have over 200 pins and use lower voltages. Therefore, make sure that the motherboard will accommodate the new CPU. Finally, avoid breaking or cracking the CPU and the motherboard, and avoid bending or mangling the chip pins.

Many motherboard manufacturers began using low-insertion-force (LIF) sockets, which typically require only 60 pounds of insertion force for a 169-pin chip. Today, nearly all motherboard manufacturers are using **zero-insertion-force (ZIF)** sockets. These sockets almost eliminate the risk involved in upgrading because no insertion force is necessary to install the chip. Most ZIF sockets are handle-actuated; you simply lift the handle, drop the chip into the socket, and then close the handle. This design makes replacing the original processor with the upgrade processor an easy task.

When installing a CPU or math coprocessor, the chip must be oriented properly on the motherboard. If a CPU is off by 90° or inserted backwards, it may damage the CPU or the motherboard. In either case, it will cause the computer not to boot. Pin A1 on the chip is designated by a slightly clipped corner or a small dot on one corner, and the socket for pin A1 will have a clipped corner, or the motherboard will be labeled. The sockets can also be described by the size, shape, and number of pin. Today, new motherboards will have either a socket 7 (for Pentium, 5x86, 6x86, K5, and K6 processors), socket 8 (for Pentium Pro processors), or a slot 1 (for Pentium II processors). (See fig. 5.20 and table 5.6.)

Inserting a microprocessor using a ZIF socket is quite easy. First, pull the handle up and place the CPU on top of the circuit, making sure that the pins are aligned with the holes of the socket. Gently press the CPU into the socket and push the handle down. Inserting a microprocessor using a LIF socket takes a bit more work and care since you must be sure to have the pins lined up properly with the holes of the socket. If they are not lined up and you press down with 60 to 100 pounds of force, the pins will bend. It will then take a pair of needle-nose pliers to straighten the pins, which may cause further ESD damage as you are working on the chip. Removing a CPU inserted into a LIF socket also takes a bit of care. The best technique is to use a small flat-edge screwdriver, inserted between the chip and the socket, to gently pry the CPU away from the socket. Each of the sides of the chip must be pried up until the chip can be easily pulled away from the socket.

FIGURE 5.20   Socket 7/ZIF socket. Pin 1 is located on the top left corner.

TABLE 5.6 Various microprocessor sockets and slots

Designation	Number of Pins	Voltage	Support Microprocessors
Socket 1	169	5 V	486DX, 486SX, 486DX2, 486DX4 OverDrive
Socket 2	238	5 V	486DX, 486SX, 486DX2, 486DX OverDrive, Pentium OverDrive 63 and 83
Socket 3	237	5 V/3.3 V	486DX, 486SX, 486DX2, 486DX4, AMD 5x85, Cyrix 5x86, Pentium OverDrive 63 and 83
Socket 4	273	5 V	Pentium 60-66, Pentium OverDrive 120/133
Socket 5	320	3.3 V	Pentium 75-133, Pentium OverDrive 125-166, Pentium with MMX OverDrive 125-166
Socket 7	321	2.5 V–3.3 V	Pentium 75-200, Pentium Over Drive, Pentium with MMX, Pentium with MMX OverDrive, 6x86, K5, K6, 6x86MX
Socket 8	387	3.1 V/3.3 V	Pentium Pro
Slot 1	242	2.8 V/3.3 V	Pentium II, Pentium Pro with socket 8 on daughtercard

After the CPU is inserted into the motherboard, the motherboard may need to be configured. Today's motherboards are designed to take various CPUs (for example, a 486DX or a Pentium microprocessor) or to run at different speeds. They must be configured using jumpers or DIP switches to set them to the proper CPU and speed. For some systems to work properly, the CMOS setup program may have to be run to configure the wait states if the motherboard cannot keep up with the CPU or set the clock speed.

5.10 TROUBLESHOOTING THE MICROPROCESSOR

Since the CPU is the brain of the computer and everything is centered around it, if it fails, either the entire computer will probably fail or failures will occur only when certain programs are being executed.

EXAMPLE 5.2 The LED lights come on, but the system does not boot.

Like most computer problems, this could be caused by several things. First, check the obvious. If you have just installed the CPU, make sure that pin 1 of the CPU is oriented properly (if not, the CPU can be damaged) and that the motherboard is configured properly for the microprocessor. If the CPU is correctly installed, the causes could be a bad microprocessor, bad motherboard, bad RAM chips, or a power-related problem. If the problem is a bad motherboard, RAM chip, or CPU, you will have to try them out one by one until the problem is found. If there is a power problem, you should measure the power supply to see if it is supplying the proper voltage and check to see if any of the components are causing a short or overload. The motherboard, RAM, and power-related problems will be discussed in later chapters.

EXAMPLE 5.3 You receive an audio or POST code indicating a CPU failure.

These codes can be caused by a faulty power supply, a bad motherboard, or a bad microprocessor. Again, check to see if the CPU is installed properly. Next, isolate the bad motherboard and CPU by swapping them for others one by one.

EXAMPLE 5.4 The PC crashes or freezes when certain applications are run.

Crashing can be caused by the CPU, motherboard, RAM chips, or corrupt files. Try reinstalling the software that is giving you the error message and reinstalling the operating system. If the problem still occurs, isolate the RAM chip, CPU, and motherboard.

EXAMPLE 5.5 The PC crashes after several minutes of operations.

The most likely cause is overheating. First, make sure that the PC has enough room around it so that it gets adequate ventilation. Next, feel the PC case to see if it is warmer than normal. If it is very warm to the touch, that probably means the power supply fan is faulty. If it is not, check to see if the CPU itself is overheating, including checking that the heat sink is in place and that the CPU fan is running.

SUMMARY

1. A microprocessor, also known as the CPU (central processing unit), is an integrated circuit that acts as the brain of the computer.
2. The microprocessor can be divided into two major areas: the execution unit and the bus interface unit.
3. The execution unit does the actual processing of data.
4. The bus interface unit (BIU) links the microprocessor to the rest of the computer.
5. The arithmetic/logic unit (ALU) is the calculator part of the execution unit that follows the instructions of the control unit.
6. A register is an internal storage area that acts as the microprocessor's short-term memory and work area.
7. The data bus, which is managed by the bus control unit, is what actually carries the instructions and data into and out of the CPU.
8. The signals of the address bus, controlled by the address control unit, define where the data bus signals are going to or coming from.
9. The clock speed, expressed in megahertz (MHz), is the speed at which the microprocessor executes instructions.
10. The commands known to the microprocessor are based on either the complex instruction set computer (CISC) commands or the reduced instruction set computer (RISC) commands.
11. CISC commands are considered complex because they consist of several smaller commands (microcode) grouped together.
12. RISC commands use the smaller, simpler commands that are the same size and that can be performed in one clock cycle or less.
13. The 8088 microprocessor was used in the IBM PC (model 5150) and the IBM XT. It had only a 20-bit address bus.
14. Virtual memory is hard drive space pretending to be RAM.
15. When running in real mode, the 80286 microprocessor pretends to be an 8086 microprocessor.
16. When the 286 microprocessor switched from real mode to protected mode, the microprocessor could have RAM above 1 MB, run multiple programs in RAM, and isolate the programs so that one program did not interfere with another program.
17. The virtual 8086 mode divides the RAM into several pretend 8086 machines, each having 1 MB of RAM.
18. The 486DX is a 386DX microprocessor with a math coprocessor and an 8 KB internal RAM cache (sometimes referred to as an L1 RAM cache).
19. A math coprocessor is a chip that specializes in floating-point mathematical calculations.
20. RAM cache is ultrafast RAM used to buffer the microprocessor and the slower RAM.
21. The Pentium microprocessor uses two execution units linked together.
22. The Pentium Pro microprocessor includes a 256 KB or 512 KB L2 RAM cache and performs branch prediction and out-of-order execution.
23. MMX technology includes 57 new instructions and SIMD (single instruction, multiple data) to run multimedia applications faster.

24. The Pentium II includes MMX technology and an L2 RAM cache that runs at half of the speed of the microprocessor. In addition, it comes in SEC (single-edge contact) packaging.

25. Advanced Micro Devices (AMD) and Cyrix produce Intel-compatible microprocessors.

26. Symmetric multiprocessing (SMP) refers to a computer consisting of two or more microprocessors that share the same memory.

27. A heat sink is a finned piece of metal that is clipped or glued to the top of the processor to diffuse heat more quickly.

28. Today, nearly all motherboard manufacturers are using zero-insertion-force (ZIF) sockets.

QUESTIONS

1. Another term for microprocessor is:
   a. motherboard
   b. system unit
   c. CPU
   d. RAM

2. The main integrated chip that the PC is built around is the:
   a. UART
   b. CPU
   c. RAM
   d. real-time clock
   e. system ROM BIOS

3. Which of the following describes a microprocessor? (Choose two.)
   a. executes software instructions
   b. performs arithmetic functions
   c. stores system configuration
   d. controls the hard drive

4. Data that are processed in the microprocessor are placed in small storage areas and manipulated. The small storage areas are called:
   a. RAM
   b. registers
   c. clipboard
   d. accumulator
   e. scratchpad

5. Computer clock speeds are expressed in:
   a. gigahertz
   b. megahertz
   c. hertz
   d. kilohertz

6. What determines the location of RAM that data are coming from or going to?
   a. data bus
   b. address bus
   c. registers
   d. control unit

7. What part of the CPU actually completes the mathematical calculations and logical comparisons?
   a. ALU
   b. instruction queue
   c. control init
   d. registers

8. Which of the following is *not* an advantage of the RISC commands over the CISC commands?
   a. RISC commands are smaller
   b. RISC commands can be executed in one cycle
   c. RISC commands have to be translated by the CPU before execution
   d. RISC commands can be executed out of order

9. Which of the following microprocessors was the first used for the PC?
   a. 8086
   b. 8088
   c. 286
   d. 386

10. What is the maximum amount of RAM that the 8086 microprocessor can access?
    a. 640 KB
    b. 1 MB
    c. 4 MB
    d. 16 MB

11. Which of the following CPUs is the first 32-bit microprocessor?
    a. 286
    b. 386DX
    c. 386SX
    d. 486DX

12. What are the word size and data path of the 80486DX CPU?
    a. 16-bit word size, 16-bit data path
    b. 16-bit word size, 32-bit data path
    c. 32-bit word size, 16-bit data path
    d. 32-bit word size, 32-bit data path
    e. 32-bit word size, 64-bit data path

13. What are the word size and data path of the 80386SX CPU?
    a. 16-bit word size, 16-bit data path
    b. 16-bit word size, 32-bit data path
    c. 32-bit word size, 16-bit data path
    d. 32-bit word size, 32-bit data path
    e. 32-bit word size, 64-bit data path
14. Which of the following does not have a math coprocessor?
    a. 486DX
    b. 486SX
    c. Pentium
    d. Pentium Pro
    e. Pentium II
15. Which of the following includes two execution units and two pipelines?
    a. 386DX
    b. 486SX
    c. 486DX
    d. Pentium
16. Which of the following microprocessors include MMX technology? (Choose all that apply.)
    a. 486DX
    b. Pentium
    c. Pentium with MMX
    d. Pentium Pro
    e. Pentium II
17. Which of the following have a built-in L2 RAM cache? (Choose all that apply.)
    a. 486SX
    b. 486DX
    c. Pentium
    d. Pentium Pro
    e. Pentium II
18. If a microprocessor has a 32-bit address bus, how much RAM can the computer work with?
    a. 1 MB
    b. 4 MB
    c. 16 MB
    d. 256 MB
    e. 4 GB
19. When the microprocessor starts in real mode, how much RAM can the CPU work with?
    a. 1 MB
    b. 4 MB
    c. 16 MB
    d. 256 MB
    e. 4 GB
20. Protected mode refers to the microprocessor's ability to:
    a. run two or more programs at the same time, with each program protected from the actions of the other
    b. protect the microprocessor from power surges and spikes
    c. pretend to be an 8086 microprocessor
    d. protect the data generated by the microprocessor
    e. protect the microprocessor from external damage
21. What are the word size and data path of the Pentium II microprocessor?
    a. 16-bit word size, 16-bit data path
    b. 16-bit word size, 32-bit data path
    c. 32-bit word size, 16-bit data path
    d. 32-bit word size, 32-bit data path
    e. 32-bit word size, 64-bit data path
22. What type of socket does the Pentium with MMX microprocessor use?
    a. socket 5
    b. socket 7
    c. socket 8
    d. slot 1
    e. slot 2
23. Which of the following uses a single-edge connector?
    a. Pentium
    b. Pentium with MMX
    c. Pentium Pro
    d. Pentium II
24. Which of the following enhances a computer's ability to process arithmetic operations quickly, particularly floating-point calculations?
    a. video controller
    b. SCSI controller
    c. math coprocessor
    d. DMA
25. Which of the following should be done when replacing a microprocessor?
    a. wearing an ESD wrist strap
    b. aligning the notch on the chip with the socket
    c. cleaning the pins before inserting
    d. all of the above

26. Which of the following affects the reliability of a microprocessor?
   a. ESD
   b. high temperatures
   c. too much current
   d. all of the above

27. Which component may be failing if the fan and hard drive run yet the system appears dead?
   a. the on/off switch
   b. the power supply
   c. the power cord
   d. the microprocessor
   e. the keyboard

28. Microprocessors since the 386 microprocessor use the Intel Protection model. Which ring allows the greatest access to the CPU?
   a. 0
   b. 1
   c. 2
   d. 3
   e. 7

29. *True or False*—A computer with an AMD K5 microprocessor can run MS-DOS and Windows 98.

HANDS-ON EXERCISES

Exercise 1: Identify the CPU

1. What kind of CPU do you have?
2. Look to see how pin A1 is designated on the motherboard and how pin A1 is designated on the CPU.
3. If the microprocessor has a heat sink, carefully remove the heat sink.
4. If the microprocessor is not soldered onto the motherboard, carefully remove the microprocessor from the motherboard. Do not bend or mangle the pins of the microprocessor.
5. Reinsert the microprocessor and reinstall the heat sink and test the system.

Exercise 2: Researching the Fastest CPU

1. Access the websites for Intel, Cyrix, and AMD to find out what their most advanced microprocessor is. Determine the maximum clock speed and identify at least two features that make the CPU faster than other microprocessors.
2. Ziff-Davis is the publisher of many of today's leading computer magazines, including *PC Magazine* and *PC Computing*. Access the ZDNet Search page (http://xlink.zdnet.com/cgi-bin/texis/xlink/xlink/search.html) to find the most recent article on the fastest CPU. Compare their choices of the fastest CPU to those you identified from the Intel, Cyrix, and AMD sites.

Exercise 3: How Microprocessors Work

For this exercise, you need Microsoft Internet Explorer or Netscape Navigator with Macromedia Shockwave plug-in or equivalent.

1. Access the following Intel website and run the tutorial "How Chips Are Made": http://www.intel.com/intel/educate/chips/shock.htm.
2. Access the following Intel website and run the tutorial "How Microprocessors Work": http://www.intel.com/education/mpuworks/index.htm.

Exercise 4: Using DEBUG to Create a File

1. At the command prompt, perform the following command:

```
DEBUG
```

2. At the DEBUG prompt or hyphen (-), perform the following command:

```
A
```

The A command means write a program in assembly language, compile it into machine code, and store it on a disk. A logical address will appear, such as 1B7B:0100.

3. Type in the following program. After each line, press the Enter key. Do not include the logical addresses in gray.

```
xxxx:100    nop
xxxx:101    mov AX,12AB
xxxx:104    mov BX,33CC
xxxx:107    mov CL,BB
xxxx:109    mov CH,F7
xxxx:10B    mov DX,BX
xxxx:10D    mov BP, CX
xxxx:10F    add CL,CH
xxxx:111    add AX,BX
xxxx:113    int 3
```

Note: The nop instruction is 1 byte and the mov instruction is 3 bytes in size. The last logical address after the int 3 will be xxxx:0114. This address is important because it tells you how many bytes are in the program. The start address was xxxx:0100 and the ending address was xxxx:0113. This means the program had 14 bytes (01130100) in hexadecimal.

4. Press the Enter key to get to the DEBUG prompt.
5. Put a disk into drive A.
6. To store the new program on the disk in drive A, you must name the file using the NAME (N) command. Perform the following command at the DEBUG prompt:

```
-n a:first.com
```

7. In order the write the program to disk, we need to tell the debugger how many bytes are in the program. This information is provided in two registers, the BX and CX. The BX holds the number that overflows the CX register.

   Since your program has only 14 bytes, we will put 0000 into the BX register and 014 into the CX register. You can do this by using the REGISTER (R) command. Therefore, perform the following command at the DEBUG prompt:

```
-r bx
```

   The response will be:

```
BX  XXXX
```
where XXXX is some value already in the BX register followed by a colon (:) on the next line

The first line tells you what is currently in the BX register and the second line with the colon is waiting for your input to the BX register.

   If the response is:

```
BX  0000
:  _
```

press the Enter key, since the BX register is already set to 0000.

   If the BX register is set to another value besides 0000, perform the following command at the colon (:) prompt:

```
:0000
```

8. To change the CX register to 0014, perform the following command at the DEBUG prompt:

```
-r cx
```

9. Perform the following command at the colon prompt:

```
:0014
```

10. After naming the file, telling it which drive to go to, and telling the debugger how many bytes to write, use the WRITE (W) command to write the program to the disk. Type the following command at the DEBUG prompt:

```
-w
```

The response will return:

```
Writing 00014 bytes
```

11. To quit DEBUG, perform the following command at the DEBUG prompt:

```
-q
```

12. Perform a directory listing of the A drive. Note that the file is 20 bytes in size, which is equivalent to 14H.

Exercise 5: Using DEBUG to Run a File

1. To load the FIRST.COM file (created in exercise 4) using the DEBUG command, perform the following command at the prompt:

```
debug a:first.com
```

2. Perform the following UNASSEMBLE (U) command at the DEBUG prompt to show the contents of the FIRST.COM file:

```
u 0100 0113
```

What you see on the screen should look like the following:

Logical Addresses	Machine Code (in Hexadecimal)	Assembly Language Command
2E80:0100	90	NOP
2E80:0101	B8AB12	MOV AX,12AB
2E80:0104	BBCC33	MOV BX,33CC
2E80:0107	B1BB	MOV CL,BB
2E80:0109	B5F7	MOV CH,F7
2E80:010B	89DA	MOV DX,BX
2E80:010D	89CD	MOV BP,CX
2E80:010F	00E9	ADD CL,CH
2E80:0111	01D8	ADD AX,BX
2E80:0113	CC	INT 3

3. Perform the following command at the DEBUG prompt:

```
-t
```

4. The program should show the following screen:

```
AX=0000  BX=0000  CX=0014  DX=0000  SP=FFFE  BP=0000  SI=0000  DI=0000
DS=2E7E  ES=2E7E  SS=2E7E  CS=2E7E  IP=0101  NV UP EI PL NZ NA PO NC
2E7E:0101 B8AB12    MOV    AX,12AB
```

The same registers should be used in every computer for this program:

```
AX=0000    SP=FFFE
BX=0000    BP=0000
CX=0014    SI=0000
DX=0000    DI=0000
           IP=0101
```

The BX and CX registers are indicating the total number of bytes in the program that was just loaded. The IP (instruction pointer) is pointing at the instruction MOV AX, 12AB. (Note: This instruction has not been executed—it is ready to be executed.)

5. Perform the TRACE (T) command at the DEBUG (-) prompt. The result should look like this:

```
AX=12AB  BX=0000  CX=0014  DX=0000  SP=FFFE  BP=0000  SI=0000  DI=0000
DS=2E7E  ES=2E7E  SS=2E7E  CS=2E7E  IP=0104   NV UP EI PL NZ NA PO NC
2E7E:0104 BBCC33     MOV     BX,33CC
```

Notice that the AX now has the 12AB and the IP has moved to the next instruction, MOV BX, 33CC.

6. Perform the TRACE (T) command again. The result should look like this:

```
AX=12AB  BX=33CC  CX=0014  DX=0000  SP=FFFE  BP=0000  SI=0000  DI=0000
DS=2E7E  ES=2E7E  SS=2E7E  CS=2E7E  IP=0107   NV UP EI PL NZ NA PO NC
2E7E:0107 B1BB      MOV     CL,BB
```

Notice that the BX now has 33CCH, the AX still has 12ABH, and the IP has moved to the next instruction at 0107 of MOV CL, BB.

7. Trace again. Note how the CX register changed. The CX register can be divided into two smaller registers, the CH register and the CL register.
8. Trace until the IP is 010F.
9. Trace once more to execute the ADD CL,CH instruction.
10. On your calculator or using the calculator in Windows 95, add the value in the CL register (BBH) to the value in the CH register (F7). Look at the result of this instruction:

```
AX=12AB  BX=33CC  CX=F7B2  DX=33CC  SP=FFFE  BP=F7BB  SI=0000  DI=0000
DS=2E7E  ES=2E7E  SS=2E7E  CS=2E7E  IP=0111   NV UP EI NG NZ AC PE CY
2E7E:0111 01DB      ADD     AX,BX
```

CL is B2, and the flag NC changed to CY to indicate a carry. The carry flag is set to show the 1 of the 1B2 answer.

11. Trace once more to execute the ADD AX, BX.
12. On your calculator or using the calculator in Windows 95, add 12ABH to 33CCH. Compare the result on your calculator to that in the AX register. (Note: The flag CY changed to NC to indicate that there was no carry out from this addition.) The IP is pointing at 0113 and you see INT 3.

Do not try to execute any more of this program.

13. Quit DEBUG by entering Q at the DEBUG prompt.

6

RAM

INTRODUCTION

Random Access Memory (RAM) is the computer's primary memory. This means that the programs are executed and data is created and manipulated in the RAM by the microprocessor. The amount of RAM determines how many programs you can run, how big each program can be, and how many documents you can have open at the same time. In addition, the amount of RAM is a big factor in your PC's performance.

OBJECTIVES

1. Define RAM and list the characteristics of RAM.
2. Compare and differentiate DRAM and SRAM.
3. Explain how RAM is addressed.
4. Explain why DRAM needs to be refreshed.
5. Compare and differentiate FPM RAM, EDO RAM, Burst EDO RAM, SDRAM, VRAM, and WRAM.
6. List and describe the memory areas.
7. Explain how RAM can increase PC performance.
8. Define virtual memory and explain how it interacts with RAM.
9. Compare and differentiate the different packages of RAM, including DIPP, SIPP, SIMM, and DIMM.
10. Install and remove RAM from a system.
11. List and explain the different forms of error control used in RAM.
12. Define what a bank of RAM is and explain how a bank relates to the data bus and size of the RAM chip.
13. Determine the speed and capacity of a RAM chip.
14. Define cache memory and explain how it increases PC performance.
15. List and describe the different symptoms caused by faulty RAM.
16. Explain how to isolate faulty RAM.

6.1 RANDOM ACCESS MEMORY (RAM)

Random access memory, more commonly referred to as **RAM,** consists of electronic memory chips that store information inside the computer. It is called *random access* memory because the information is accessed nonsequentially. Unlike a reel of data storage tape, which is accessed starting at one end until the location of the data is reached, information in the RAM can be accessed directly without going through preceding information.

RAM is known as *volatile* (changeable) memory. Much like a blackboard, information on RAM can be taken away from it and overwritten. In addition, RAM is known as *temporary* memory because when power is no longer supplied to RAM, its contents are lost. This is the reason that the user must save the contents of RAM to a disk.

RAM is considered the main memory or the *primary memory* because it is the memory that the microprocessor accesses directly. This means the program instruction that the CPU is executing must first be copied to the RAM from a device such as a disk. In addition, the data, such as letters, reports, and charts, generated by programs must be in the RAM to be manipulated. Therefore, it is the amount of RAM that determines how many programs can be executed at one time and how much data can be available to a program. In addition, the amount of memory is a major factor in determining how fast your computer will operate.

6.2 RAM ARCHITECTURE

RAM chips are based on two types of technology. The most common is dynamic RAM (**DRAM**), which is normally used for the primary memory; the other type is static RAM (**SRAM**), which is usually used for RAM cache.

6.2.1 DRAM

To store information, DRAM uses a storage cell consisting of a tiny solid-state capacitor and a MOS transistor. A **capacitor** is a simple electrical device, similar to a battery, that is capable of storing a charge of electrons. The charge or lack of charge represents a single bit of data. If the capacitor is charged, it has a logic state of 1. If it is discharged, it has a logic state of 0. A **transistor** is a tiny electronic switch that can be turned on or shut off by the flow of input voltage. When the input voltage is off, the switch is open and no current flows through the circuit. When the input voltage is turned on, the switch closes and current is permitted to flow.

The memory storage cells are organized into a large two-dimensional array or table made up of rows and columns. Similar to cells in a spreadsheet, each memory cell is identified by a row and column address, known as the **physical address.** Each row is activated with its own word line. After the row is activated, a pair of bit lines specifies which memory cell (column) to access within the activated row. Both the word lines and bit lines are controlled by the memory controller.

As the computer operates, the microprocessor follows a long series of software instructions. When the instructions call for information that needs to be written to RAM or read from RAM, a binary signal is sent along the address bus to the memory controller. The signal indicates the specific storage area that needs to be accessed. The memory controller enables the proper storage cell by first figuring out which row and column need to be accessed. It then sends a row address along the address bus to the RAM. A row address strobe (RAS) signal activates the specified row but deactivates all of the other rows. The column address is then placed on the address bus, which sends an input signal to the transistor, which in turn activates the individual storage cell. (See fig. 6.1.)

When a storage cell is accessed, a read/write signal defines the direction of data flow. To read the specified address, the read/write signal is turned on, while to write to a specified address, the read/write signal is turned off. A cell is read by precharging the two bit lines to an equal voltage with a precharge circuit. If the capacitor is charged, indicating a binary value of one (1), the capacitor drains off into one of the bit lines, causing its voltage to be higher than that of the other bit line. The output buffer circuit compares the two bit lines and sends the high signal, representing a binary value of one (1), through the data bus. If the capacitor is uncharged, representing a binary value of zero (0), the voltage of the bit line connected to the capacitor will decrease as it flows into the empty capacitor. Since the connected bit line has less voltage than the other bit line, it causes the output buffer circuit to produce a low signal, representing a binary value of zero (0), through the data bus. (See fig. 6.2.) Since the capacitor is drained during the read process, it no longer contains the actual data. Therefore, DRAM chips are designed so that after a one (1) is read from a capacitor, that capacitor is immediately recharged.

FIGURE 6.1 RAM interacting with the CPU

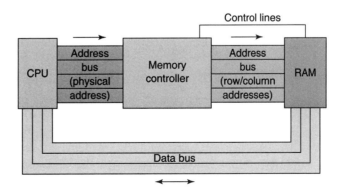

111

FIGURE 6.2 Memory controller accessing the RAM

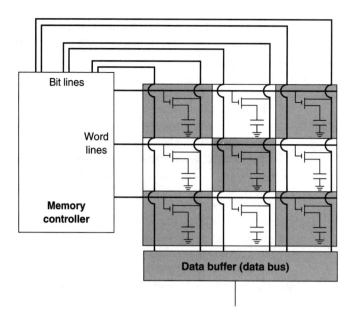

To write a value of a one (1) to a specified storage cell, the bit lines are charged. The address bus activates the transistor switch, and the charged bit lines charge the capacitor. To write a zero (0) to a specified storage cell, the bit lines are not charged. The address bus activates the transistor switch, and the transistor switch completes the circuit, causing the charged capacitor to drain out to ground.

After the read or write operations are completed, the column deactivates to get ready for the next read/write cycle. Unfortunately, during the time needed for deactivation, the microprocessor is waiting. The period during which the CPU is waiting is called a **wait state.**

A DRAM chip can contain millions of storage cells. That many capacitors in a small space requires that the capacitors be extremely small. Since they are extremely small, charges can be added or withdrawn from them in just a few nanoseconds, but unfortunately, their small size also means they can hold their charge only for a few milliseconds. Therefore, the DRAM must be refreshed (recharged) often to maintain its information. To recharge the DRAM storage cells, the computer uses a special circuit to run a **refresh routine.** The routine takes control of the data and address buses from the microprocessor and recharges all of the cells in each row by reading and rewriting each storage cell, row by row. While older computers use the DMA controller to run the refresh routine, newer computers use a special circuit within the chipset.

6.2.2 SRAM

Static RAM consists of storage cells, each having four transistors and two resistors that act as an electronic switch (flip-flop latch). If the switch is on, it allows electricity to flow, representing the binary value of one (1). If the switch is off, electricity stops flowing, and the circuit represents a binary value of zero (0). The advantage of SRAM over DRAM is that SRAM chips are faster and do not require refreshing. Unfortunately, SRAM storage cells (six components) are larger, more complicated, and cost more than DRAM storage cells (two components). SRAM also consumes more power because current is always flowing through the cells.

6.2.3 FAST PAGE MODE RAM (FPM RAM)

The typical access speed for a DRAM chip in the early PCs was 120 nanoseconds (ns) or slower. Newer machines, up through 1995, used **fast page mode RAM (FPM RAM),** which had typical speeds of 70 or 80 nanoseconds. A lower number indicates a faster speed. The fast page mode RAM works like the DRAM chip except that it tries to reduce the number of wait states. If data is accessed in the same row (sometimes referred to as a *page*) as the preceding data, the chip saves time by not deactivating and reactivating the row for the second piece of data. Ideally, a read from a 70-nanosecond FPM memory can achieve a burst cycle timing of 5-3-3-3, quicker than the 5-5-5-5 of DRAM. The 5-3-3-3 means that it takes the FPM RAM five clock cycles to access the first piece of data in a row and, after that row is activated, it takes three clock cycles each to access the next three pieces of data contained within the same row.

6.2.4 EXTENDED DATA OUTPUT RAM (EDO RAM)

Extended data output RAM, usually referred to as **EDO RAM,** takes the fast page mode RAM technology one step further. The two-stage pipeline of the EDO RAM chip lets the memory controller read data off the chip while it is being reset for the next operation. Instead of deactivating the column and turning off the output buffer, EDO RAM keeps the output data buffer on. If the data that needs to be transferred is sequential to the data just sent, it will be sent more efficiently. As a result of this design, the burst cycle timing of the EDO RAM chip is reduced to 5-2-2-2, giving it approximately 10%–15% better performance than FPM RAM. The speed of an EDO RAM chip is therefore either 50 or 60 ns.

A faster form of EDO RAM is burst extended data output RAM (**BEDO RAM).** It is faster because it allows the page-access cycle to be divided into two components. To achieve faster access time, data is read from the memory array at the same time data is transferred through the data bus. In addition, a counter on the chip is used to keep track of the next address so that sequential data can be accessed faster. As a result, burst EDO RAM offers an average of 15%–25% increase in efficiency over FPM RAM and reduces the transfer of sequential data to 1 clock cycle (5-1-1-1). Although EDO RAM and BEDO RAM are faster than FPM RAM, their popularity is already decreasing because they do not work well with the bus speeds higher than 66 MHz that some motherboards are already using.

6.2.5 SYNCHRONOUS DYNAMIC RAM (SDRAM)

A new form of RAM, called synchronous dynamic RAM (**SDRAM),** is synchronized to the external clock used on the motherboard, unlike previous forms of RAM. It works with bus speeds up to 100 MHz, and its fastest access speed in CPU cycles is 5-1-1-1. All of this is made possible by using an older technique of speeding RAM access called *interleaving.* Interleaving is two banks of memory chips working together to service a bus. (See section 6.6.2.). When one bank is getting ready for access, the other bank is being accessed. In addition, SDRAM uses internal pipelining (bringing additional data in while the previous data is being processed) to improve throughput. Both the interleaving and internal pipelining are designed to keep the SDRAM working at full capacity at all times.

6.2.6 VIDEO RAM (VRAM)

Another type of RAM chip is called video RAM (**VRAM).** Video RAM, usually used on video cards, is a special form of DRAM that has two separate data ports. One port is dedicated to updating the image on the screen while the other one is used for changing the image data stored in the RAM on the video card. This "dual-ported design" gives higher performance (up to 40%) than DRAM, which cannot read and write simultaneously.

A newer version of VRAM is windows RAM (**WRAM),** which was developed by Samsung. The chip uses a dual-color block write to perform very rapid pattern and text fills, and it can perform fast buffer-to-buffer transfers for video and double-buffered 3-D animation. As a result, WRAM offers a 40%–50% increase in performance over the VRAM chips.

TABLE 6.1   Types of RAM chips

Types of RAM Chip	Typical Access Time	Burst Cycle Timing	Time of First Access	Time of Sequential Access
DRAM	150 ns	5-5-5-5	750 ns	750 ns
FPDRAM	70 ns	5-3-3-3	350 ns	210 ns
EDO RAM	60 ns	5-2-2-2	300 ns	120 ns
BEDO RAM	50 ns	5-1-1-1	250 ns	50 ns
SDRAM	10 ns	5-1-1-1	50 ns	10 ns

6.3   MEMORY AREAS

When the IBM PC was first introduced, the RAM was divided into conventional and reserve memory. PC architecture changed through the years, and new techniques were developed to divide and address RAM. Today, the RAM in a PC is broken down into several memory areas: conventional memory, reserve memory, upper memory, expanded memory, and extended memory.

The early IBM PC was built around the Intel 8088 microprocessor. Because of the limitations of the microprocessor, the most RAM that the IBM PC could recognize was 1 MB. Therefore, when the PC was being developed, IBM, Intel, and Microsoft took that 1 MB of RAM and broke it into two memory areas: conventional memory and reserve memory. (See fig. 6.3.) Conventional memory was used to hold the operating system, application programs, and data, while the reserve memory was reserved for the hardware.

6.3.1   CONVENTIONAL MEMORY

Conventional memory is the first 640 KB of RAM. It is also known as *lower memory* and *base memory*. Although DOS could read and write to the entire first megabyte, it could only load application programs in conventional memory. Conventional memory, therefore, was used to store DOS itself, device drivers, TSRs (small programs that control hardware or perform a useful function), and application programs.

The first kilobyte of conventional memory stores the interrupt vector table, which is used to directly control hardware by accessing special low-level routines. When the routine needs to be accessed, its location is found in the interrupt vector table. The routine itself is part of either the BIOS or the operating system. The next 256 bytes are used for the BIOS data area, which is the work area for the ROM BIOS chips and includes the I/O address of the COM and LPT ports and a keyboard buffer area.

FIGURE 6.3   First one megabyte of RAM

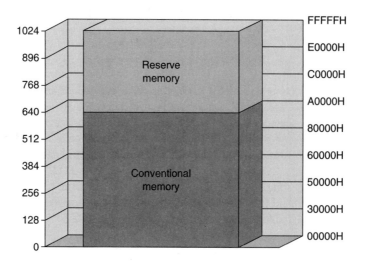

6.3.2 RESERVE MEMORY

Reserve memory, between 640 KB and 1 MB, is reserved for hardware. The reserve memory can be used as a working area for the expansion cards or can be used by the ROM BIOS chips, such as the system ROM BIOS, video ROM BIOS, and other ROM chips found on expansion cards.

The first 128 KB (A0000H to BFFFFH) of reserve memory is for the video RAM (this is not to be confused with the memory on the video card) and holds character and graphics information for display. The video ROM BIOS uses up to 32 KB of memory, starting at C0000H. Generally, if a video expansion card has a higher resolution and more colors, the card will use more reserve memory than is available. Since DOS could use only available contiguous (continuous) memory in the first megabyte as conventional memory, it is the memory location of the EGA, VGA, and super VGA cards that restrict the conventional memory to 640 KB.

The second 128 KB (C0000H to DFFFFH) is reserved for the BIOS chips found on expansion cards. During boot-up, the system ROM BIOS looks for additional ROM BIOS chips and uses them to expand its own instruction set. The more common cards that contain ROM BIOS chips include the hard drive controller (including SCSI controller cards), network cards, and sound cards. The memory areas used by ROM chips on the expansion cards are configured using jumpers, DIP switches, or a software configuration program, or the cards are plug and play. If ROM BIOS chips from two different expansion cards try to use the same memory area, the devices will usually fail.

The last 128 KB (E0000H to FFFFFH) is reserved for the system ROM BIOS, which controls the boot-up procedure and contains instructions for controlling basic hardware. (Note: Some system ROM BIOS chips use only 64 KB, located between F0000 and FFFFFH, even though 128 KB is reserved for the system ROM BIOS.) If the computer is accessing the memory between 640 KB and 1 MB, which is occupied by a ROM chip, it is accessing the ROM memory, not RAM memory. Since the ROM chips occupy the same memory address as RAM, the RAM is sometimes readdressed as extended memory. In other instances, since ROM chips are slower than RAM chips, the instructions within the ROM chips can be copied to the corresponding RAM address and accessed from the RAM. Since RAM is faster and usually has a bigger data path, performance can thus be greatly increased. This method of speeding up the computer is called **RAM shadowing.**

6.3.3 UPPER MEMORY (UMB)

After the conventional memory and reserve memory were divided up, engineers eventually discovered that not all of the 384 kilobytes of reserve memory were actually being used. Therefore, the memory between A0000H to FFFFFH not used by hardware is commonly referred to as the **upper memory.** It is divided into **upper memory blocks** or **UMB.** (See fig. 6.4.) In the later versions of DOS and Windows 95, **TSRs** (small programs that control hardware or perform a useful function) and **device drivers** (instructions that control hardware) were moved from conventional memory to the upper memory, freeing up conventional memory.

6.3.4 EXPANDED MEMORY (EMS)

Expanded memory was the first memory configuration that allowed computers to break the 1 MB boundary. In the early 1980s, many applications programs, such as spreadsheets, needed more RAM. Lotus and Intel, later joined by Microsoft, proposed EMS (expanded memory specifications), which became known as the LIM (Lotus/Intel/Microsoft) EMS. The LIM expanded memory specification (EMS version 3.0) used 64 KB of contiguous memory in the upper memory area as a window of up to 8 MB of expanded memory. The 64 KB window was further divided into four 16 KB page frames. Data is kept in expanded memory and is accessed using bank switching.

FIGURE 6.4   Memory areas

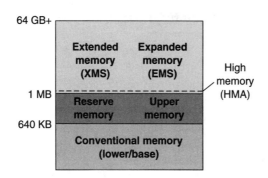

Since DOS could access only the first megabyte of RAM, the data had to be stored in the first 1 MB of RAM. So, instead of shuffling data back and forth between the page frame in upper memory and the expanded memory, bank switching was used to change the addresses of the storage cells so that a cell's address was between 640 KB and 1 MB. As far as the programs were concerned, the same memory areas were addressed—only the contents of each memory area were changed. Therefore, expanded memory involved mapping addresses of logical pages to physical pages.

Eventually, EMS version 4.0 was introduced. It increased the expanded memory from 8 MB to 32 MB, and it allowed any contiguous spaces located within upper memory that were 16 KB to be used as page frames. In addition, the expanded memory was enhanced so that it could contain both code (instructions) and data.

As with any new technology that is introduced, software had to be created or rewritten in order to use EMS 4.0. Software was written to request the expanded memory from a piece of internal software called an expanded memory manager (EMM). The 8088/8086 and 286-based machines contain an expanded memory board with an EMM manager. Today's computers (386 and above) use software like DOS's EMM386.EXE, which allows extended memory to emulate (pretend to be) expanded memory.

6.3.5   EXTENDED MEMORY (XMS)

The memory above 1 MB (FFFFFH) found on today's newer machines (386 and above) is known as **extended memory.** When the extended memory configuration was introduced, DOS could not normally use it except to provide a RAM disk (RAM pretending to be a disk) or to create a disk cache (buffer area between RAM and the slower hard drive). This was because DOS could run only in real mode, which can recognize only 1 MB of RAM. Some later programs, such as games, were able to switch the microprocessor from real mode to protected mode by means of the DOS protected mode interface (DPMI).

When Windows 3.XX was introduced, it would switch the microprocessor from real mode to protected mode by loading the HIMEM.SYS file during boot-up. Windows could then use the extended memory to hold data and code. (Note: Windows 3.1X will not run if HIMEM.SYS is not loaded.) Windows 95 and 98 operate mostly in protected mode but still make calls in real mode to access certain hardware components to keep the amount of RAM required to run Windows 95 smaller. Windows NT is a true protected-mode operating system and does not use real mode.

The extended memory specification (XMS) was developed in 1987 by Microsoft, Intel, AST, and Lotus to specify how programs would used extended memory. Although the XMS can function on a 286 chip or higher, it wasn't fully utilized until the 386. This was because the 286 could switch to protected mode but could not switch back to real mode (needed for the older programs not written for protected mode) without rebooting the computer. To ensure cooperation between programs using extended memory, HIMEM.SYS grabbed all of the extended memory for itself and distributed it to the programs that followed the XMS standard. It was the job of the HIMEM.SYS to make sure that no two programs overwrote each other's designated memory areas, and it allowed the microprocessor to switch back and forth between real mode and protected mode.

6.3.6 HIGH MEMORY (HMA)

The **high memory area (HMA)** is an area of 64 KB minus 16 bytes starting at the 1 MB boundary. The distinguishing feature of high memory is that it can be used to access a small part of extended memory while the microprocessor is in real mode, which can see only up to 1 MB of RAM.

The memory address of a computer running in real mode is 20 bits long (numbers 0 to 19). Unfortunately, early microprocessors had registers that were only 16 bits wide. Therefore, they had to use two registers and add them together to access the entire 20-bit line. When an 8088/8086 added the registers together and the value was larger than 1 MB, the carry (excess above 1 MB) was dropped. Newer microprocessors have 24-bit or larger address lines, which allow the carry to extend to the 21st address line (A20). This allows the CPU to access another 64 KB of RAM (HMA) while in real mode. To fully utilize the A20 line, special circuitry was built into the keyboard ROM BIOS chip, which controls the A20 line.

6.4 ADDRESSING RAM

When the microprocessor is in real mode (emulating an 8086 microprocessor), it can see only up to 1 MB of RAM. This is because the 8086/8088 microprocessor has only 20 address lines. When all lines are active (1111111111 1111111111 in binary form = 1 million in decimal form), the microprocessor is accessing the byte located at 1 MB. The address indicating the actual memory area designated by the address lines is called the **physical address.** As a computer technician, you will be seeing addresses other than the physical address.

6.4.1 ADDRESSING RAM IN REAL MODE

RAM addresses are sometimes given in a logical address form consisting of base address:offset address. The logical address was created by using two 16-bit registers because although the address line is 20 bits, the largest register (in the 8086/8088 microprocessor) was 16 bits. Therefore, the base address (which defines the beginning address of a 64 KB memory segment) had to be kept in one register, and the offset address (which defines the exact address within the 64 KB memory segment) was kept in another register. When combined, they created the physical address designated on the address lines.

EXAMPLE 6.1 What would be the physical address if the logical address is 5000H:2F3CH?

To calculate the logical address, take the base address and add a 0 to the end of it. Therefore, the base address in our example has a value of 50000. To calculate the logical address, add the base address and the offset address together. Note: When added, these numbers are hexadecimal numbers.

```
  50000    Base address of 5000 with 0 at end
+  2F3C    Offset address
  52F3C    Physical address
```

If you wanted to access RAM with the physical address 8BC3DH, you could use 8000H, which is the base address plus the offset address BC3DH, to get the desired address. The logical address could then be written as 8000H:BC3DH.

6.4.2 ADDRESSING RAM IN PROTECTED MODE

To access the extended memory, the microprocessor must be in protected mode. Addressing extended memory is very similar to addressing real memory, except that the locations of the blocks (segments of data and code) in extended memory are not kept in the CPU registers but are instead kept in a look-up table. The microprocessor register holds the location of the look-up table in which the instruction or code being sought is located.

The look-up table contains the location of the base address (segment), the limit (or size) of the segment, and its access rights. The base address indicates the starting location of the memory segment. The segment limit, which contains the last offset address found in the segment, indicates how big the segment is, which can be anywhere from 1 byte to 4 gigabytes in length. Access rights, used by the 386 microprocessor and above, are based on assigning privilege levels to code and data. The operating system is usually assigned the highest priority of 0, while the user and applications are assigned the lower priority of 3. With this scheme, if one of the program applications goes bad in RAM, the operating system is protected. Secure systems such as Windows NT and Novell NetWare are based on this design.

6.4.3   RAM LIMITATIONS

The amount of RAM in a system is limited by several things, first among them the size of the address bus, which determines the memory location. Since the 8088 microprocessor had only 20 address lines, the most that it could see was 1 MB of RAM. Today's 386DX, 486, and Pentium chips can see up to 4 GB of RAM, and the Pentium Pro, Pentium II, and Pentium III chips can see up to 64 GB of RAM.

However, even though the microprocessor can now address these large amounts of RAM, most motherboards are designed to recognize much less. For example, if a motherboard can recognize 64 MB DIMMs and it includes only eight DIMM slots, the most RAM that the motherboard can use is 512 MB. Of course, as time goes on, SIMMs and DIMMs with larger capacities will be created. Eventually, the PC will reach the maximum amount of RAM a CPU can recognize.

Question: How much RAM is enough?

Answer: DOS and Windows 3.XX require 2 MB of RAM, Windows 95 requires 4 MB of RAM, and Windows NT 4.0 requires 12 MB of RAM. Unfortunately, these minimum requirements are grossly understated. For usable performance, DOS and Windows 3.XX should have 8 MB or more, Windows 95 should have 12 MB or more, and Windows NT should have 16 MB of RAM. Of course, a system having more RAM will have better performance. Therefore, a system running DOS or Windows 3.XX should ideally have 16 MB or more, Windows 95 should have 24 MB or more, and Windows NT should have 32 MB or more. If you are running heavy graphical packages or other packages requiring a lot of RAM, you would need even more RAM.

RAM can be used for more than just programs. You can use it to enlarge a disk cache, which helps reduce the time it takes to access a disk. More RAM will also reduce the need for virtual memory. For example, graphical programs like Adobe Photo Paint need more memory, and working on several programs at the same time (such as Microsoft Word and Microsoft Excel) to create a single report requires more memory.

When Ziff-Davis Labs (ZD Labs, publishers of *PC Magazine* and *PC Computing*) tested the effect of RAM on the PC, it found that if a 75 MHz Pentium PC increased the RAM from 8 MB to 16 MB, performance was increased a minimum of 50%. When more RAM was added to a PC with a faster microprocessor, the performance increase was even more significant. Even a PC with a 75 MHz Pentium chip that had 16 MB of RAM delivered an approximately 50% higher performance than a 100 MHz Pentium machine with only 8 MB of RAM.

6.4.4   VIRTUAL MEMORY

Another major feature of the 386 chip was its ability to use up to 64 terabytes of virtual memory. **Virtual memory** is disk space that acts like RAM, which allows the operating system to load more programs and data. Parts of all the programs and data to be accessed are constantly swapped back and forth between RAM and disk so the virtual memory looks and acts like regular RAM. This is beneficial to the user because disk memory is far cheaper than RAM. Unfortunately, a disk is a thousand times slower than RAM, and since the disk consists of mechanical parts and pieces, it has a higher failure rate than RAM. Intel microprocessors use a technology called **demand paging,** which swaps data between the RAM and disk only on the demand of the microprocessor rather than trying to anticipate the needs of the microprocessor.

The RAM and virtual memory are broken down into chunks of information called **pages,** which are monitored by the operating system. When the RAM becomes full, the virtual memory system copies the least recently used programs and data to the virtual memory. Since this frees part of the RAM, it then has room to copy something else from virtual memory, load another program, or load more data. Windows 3.XX, Windows 95, and Windows 98 virtual memory takes the form of an ordinary file called a *swap file,* while Windows NT calls its virtual memory a *paging file.*

6.5   RAM PACKAGING

As RAM technology improved, so did its packaging. When the IBM PC was introduced, it used ICs (DIPs), which were inserted into the motherboard. Since then, SIPPs, SIMMs, and DIMMs have been developed. Table 6.2 describes the various types of chip packaging.

6.5.1   DUAL IN-LINE PACKAGE (DIP)

The form of RAM known as the **dual in-line package (DIP),** used on the original IBM PC and continued in the IBM XT and IBM AT, was inserted directly into the motherboard. Resembling a bug with many legs, these IC chips lie horizontally with metal leads extending down from the two long sides. (See fig. 6.5.)

DIPs can be inserted into IC sockets very easily. First, position the IC so that pin 1 is in the proper orientation. (Pin 1 of the chip and the motherboard will usually have a notch on one end.) Next, align the pins with the socket, and then gently push the chip into the socket. Avoid bending the pins in the process; a bent pin could easily ruin the IC. (Note: When handling RAM chips, remember to take precautions against ESD.) Removing a DIP is best done with a small, flat-edge screwdriver blade. Gently slide the screwdriver under the chip and pry just a little. Then alternately pry up the ends of the chip, which prevents the legs from bending, until the chip can be removed easily.

Some of the early PCs had problems with something called *chip creep.* This was caused by the constant expansion and contraction of the motherboard due to the temperature fluctuations associated with turning on and off the computer. Eventually, the chips would work themselves out of the sockets just enough so that they would not make a good

TABLE 6.2   Types of RAM packages

Type of RAM Package	Description
Dual in-line package (DIP)	DIP chips, resembling a bug with many legs, lie horizontally with metal leads extending down from the two long sides. The metal leads are inserted directly into the motherboard's DIP sockets. Note: Some RAM cache chips are packaged as DIP chips.
Single in-line pin package (SIPP)	SIPP is a small circuit board that has several DIPs soldered onto it. The circuit board has a single row of pins that are inserted into the motherboard.
Single in-line memory module (SIMM)	A SIMM is a small circuit board consisting of several DIP chips soldered together. The SIMM connects to the motherboard by means of a row of tin or gold metal plates (contacts) along the bottom of the module. As they are inserted into the motherboard, the metal pins make contact with its metal plates.
Dual in-line memory module (DIMM)	DIMMs closely resemble SIMMs.

FIGURE 6.5   DIPS

connection. When a memory problem occurred, a common solution was to gently press the DIP chips into the motherboard. Another solution to the chip creep problem was to solder the DIPs onto the motherboard. Although this did correct the initial problem, it often caused other problems later when a technician tried to desolder a bad RAM chip.

6.5.2   SINGLE IN-LINE PIN PACKAGE (SIPP)

To avoid the chip creep problem that occurred with the DIP chips, **the single in-line pin package,** sometimes called a SIPP, was created. A SIPP is a small circuit board that has several DIPs soldered onto it. (See fig. 6.6.) The name *single in-line pin package* came about because the small circuit board had a single row of pins for insertion into the motherboard. SIPPs soon gave way to SIMMs because they lacked a latching mechanism to retain the module, and the metal pins were easily bent and broken. SIPPs usually have 30 pins.

6.5.3   SINGLE IN-LINE MEMORY MODULE (SIMM)

Today, the majority of modern PCs use a **single in-line memory module,** usually referred to as a **SIMM.** Like the SIPP, the SIMM is a small circuit board consisting of several soldered DIP chips. Its connection to the motherboard is made by a row of tin or gold metal plates (contacts) along the bottom of the module. As the module is inserted into the motherboard, metal pins make contact with the metal plates. (See figs. 6.7 and 6.8.)

FIGURE 6.6   SIPPs

FIGURE 6.7   SIMM sockets

FIGURE 6.8   72-pin and 30-pin SIMMs

SIMMs are available in a wide range of capacities (from 256 K to 64 MB and higher) and in two pin configurations: 30-pin (8 or 9 bits) and 72-pin (32 or 36 bits). If a 30-pin uses parity for error control (see section 6.6), it will have nine bits; if it does not use parity, it will have eight bits. If a 72-pin uses parity, it will have 36 bits; if it does not, it will have 32 bits. The 72-pin SIMM is approximately 25% larger in size than the 30-pin SIMM and includes a notch in the center to identify it and so prevent the insertion of a 30-pin SIMM into a 72-pin socket. Both SIMMs also have notches that prevent them from being connected backwards. Four of the pins in the 72-pin SIMM are used to indicate the speed rating of the chip.

6.5.4   DUAL IN-LINE MEMORY MODULE (DIMM)

Dual in-line memory modules, or **DIMMs,** closely resemble SIMMs. (See fig. 6.9.) Like SIMMs, DIMMs are installed into a memory expansion sockets vertically. But the opposing pins on both sides of the SIMM circuit board are connected as one, while the pins of DIMMs are electrically isolated to form two separate contacts. Another difference between the two is that DIMMs support 64-bit pathways (72 bits with parity). The 168-pin DIMM, like the 72-pin SIMM, has electrical provisions for telling the PC the speed rating of the module. The module connector has eight pins for signaling this information. A smaller version of the DIMM, called the **small-outline DIMM (SODIMM),** which is narrower and thinner than the full-size DIMM, is usually found in notebook computers. A small-outline DIMM is like a 72-pin SIMM in a reduced-size package.

FIGURE 6.9   DIMM

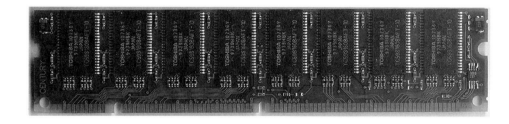

6.6   RAM ARCHITECTURE

RAM chips are arranged on the motherboard or within a SIPP, SIMM, or DIMM module in a special way. Some chips have parity while others don't; in addition, RAM is divided into banks, and RAM is arranged in many arrays of rows and columns. Depending on the microprocessor and the type of RAM, the system determines the size of the data and address bus.

6.6.1   PARITY VERSUS NONPARITY

RAM chips are arranged in sets of either 8 bits or 9 bits. In the 9-bit arrangement, eight of the nine bits are used for data and the ninth one is used to provide an error check on the other eight. The DIPs used in the IBM PC, IBM XT, and IBM AT were arranged in neat little rows of nine chips; some of the later SIMMs and DIMMs used a ninth bit for parity. **Parity** chips ensure accurate reading and writing of data, particularly on systems released prior to the introduction of Pentium motherboards. A PC using parity checking is using *odd* parity checking. As the eight individual bits in a byte are stored in memory, a parity generator/checker, which is either part of the microprocessor or is located in a special chip on the motherboard, evaluates the data bits by counting the number of 1s in a byte. If an even number of 1s is in the byte, the parity generator/checker creates a 1 and stores it in the ninth (parity) bit. This makes the total sum of all nine bits an odd number. If the sum of the eight data bits is an odd number, the parity bit created is 0, again keeping the 9-bit sum an odd number. The value of the ninth parity bit is always chosen so that the sum of all nine bits is an odd number.

When the system reads memory, it checks the parity information. If the stored 9 bits equal an even number, that byte must have an error. When a parity-check error is detected, the motherboard parity-checking circuits generate a **nonmaskable interrupt (NMI),** which halts processing and diverts the system's attention to the error. The NMI causes a routine in the system ROM BIOS chip to be executed. The routine clears the screen and then displays a message such as "PARITY ERROR" or "PARITY CHECK 1" in the upper-left corner of the screen.

There are two disadvantages of using parity for error control. First, RAM will only discover errors when one, three, five, or seven bits have changed. It will not discover a problem if two bits have been changed since the two bits cancel each other out. Second, it only detects the error but does not correct it.

Most systems do not halt the CPU when a parity error is detected; instead, they offer you a choice of either rebooting the system or continuing as though nothing happened. If you can, you should shut off the NMI (parity checking) and save your work. When saving your work, save it to a different name in case the file you are working on has become corrupted. This gives you the opportunity to first use the file you are currently working on. If it is too corrupted to use, you can then go back to the original file. (Note: You should save your work approximately every five to ten minutes to prevent loss of work from a technical difficulty.)

A computer system that checks for errors using parity must use RAM chips that contain the extra bit. An 8-bit chip may cause the computer not to boot and not to recognize all the RAM and can cause memory errors almost immediately during boot. The parity chip makes the computer more reliable, but it does cost a little bit more because of the extra chip. A computer system that does not check for parity can use a 9-bit chip, but it will not, of course, use the parity chip to hold information. One type of RAM offers fake parity. A computer system set up for parity checking can use RAM that sends a fake "parity good" signal. This saves money because you don't have to pay for the extra memory chip.

Other systems, such as many Pentium systems, use **error checking and correcting (ECC) memory** rather than parity checking. Every time data is stored in memory, this code is responsible for the generation of check bits, which are stored along with the data. When the content of a memory location is referenced, the ECC memory logic uses the check bit information and the data itself to generate a series of "syndrome bits." If these syndrome bits are all zeros, then the data is valid and operation continues. If any bits are 1s, then the data has an error and the ECC memory logic isolates the error and reports it to the operating system. In the case of a correctable error, the ECC memory scheme can detect single- and double-bit errors and correct single-bit errors. Of course, if you use ECC for parity, 1 bit of RAM is needed for every 8 bits, and 7 bits are needed to check 32 bits.

On many of today's machines, parity and ECC can be enabled or disabled in the CMOS setup program. Therefore, if parity is enabled in the CMOS setup program and a parity error occurs, make sure you are using RAM that uses parity.

6.6.2 BANKS OF RAM

When working with PCs and their RAM, it is common to hear the term *banks of memory* or *banks of RAM*. A **bank** is a collection of memory chips that make up a block of memory readable by the processor in a single bus cycle. The block must therefore be as large as the data bus of the particular microprocessor. In PC systems, the processor data bus is either 8, 16, 32, or 64 bits plus any parity bits that may be needed.

EXAMPLE 6.2 Let's say you have a 386DX chip. A 386DX has an external data bus of 32 bits. If it has 30-pin SIMMs, to fulfill the entire 32-bit data path, four SIMMs would be needed to fill a bank, since 30-pin SIMMS only have an 8-bit path. Of course, each SIMM would have to be the same size. If the SIMMs have different speeds, the entire bank would run at the slowest speed. Four 1 MB SIMMs and four 256 KB SIMMs would give a total RAM of 5 MB. If you wanted to upgrade the RAM, you would have to remove the four 256 KB SIMMs and insert bigger chips, such as four 4 MB chips, giving a total of 20 MB of RAM. Of course, the motherboard would have to accommodate the use of 4 MB SIMMs. You could not remove only one, two, or three chips; they must be in complete sets of four.

EXAMPLE 6.3 Let's say a 486DX uses the 72-pin SIMM instead of a 32-pin SIMM. Since the SIMMs have a 32-bit pathway, only 1 SIMM would be needed to make a bank.

With most computer models, mixing different-sized SIMMs will prevent the memory from booting or prevent the system from accurately detecting the total amount of RAM.

6.6.3 RAM ADDRESS AND DATA ORGANIZATION

It is important to note that RAM memory chips are defined by their address/data organization. For example, the label IC, indicating a chip that holds 1,024 KB, does not tell you how the chip is laid out. This 1,024 KB chip could be organized as 1,024K $\times$ 1 bit, 256K $\times$ 4 bits, 128K $\times$ 8 bits, and so on.

Today, a single DIP can contain millions of memory cells. As mentioned, these cells are organized into a large array of rows and columns. If it is a 1MB $\times$ 1 bit DIP, it contains 1,048,576 individual memory cells arranged in 1,024 rows and 1,024 columns. The engineers who designed it could, however, have used other arrangements, such as 512 rows and 2,048 columns or 2,048 rows and 512 columns. However, a square array (meaning the number of columns equals the number of rows) minimizes the number of address lines required and reduces the chip's size. The 1024K $\times$ 1 bit designation specifies that the chip holds 1,024 kilowords (1,048,576 words, or 1,024 $\times$ 1,024 words). Each word is 1 bit in length, as designated by the number after the multiplication sign. Therefore, this single chip can hold 128 kilobytes (eight bits in a byte) of data, with each bit accessed individually.

EXAMPLE 6.4 A motherboard or a SIMM has a single row of nine DIPs, each DIP labeled as a 1024K $\times$ 1. We know that each chip can hold 128 KB. We also know that the ninth DIP is used for parity. Therefore, the nine chips can hold 1 MB of information.

Some chips may actually contain several arrays of rows and columns. The 1024K $\times$ 4 chip is a common DRAM chip that holds 512 KB of data. In this case, the chip contains 1,024 $\times$ 1,024 (1,048,576) words, each word being 4 bits in size. Since each word is 4 bits in size, it contains four output lines. Although an individual storage cell cannot be accessed, four of them can be accessed in the time it would have taken to access one storage unit in another type of chip.

EXAMPLE 6.5 A SIMM has a single row of three DIPs. Two of the DIPs are designated 4096K $\times$ 4, and the third is designated 4096K $\times$ 1. The chips are arranged in a 9-bit pattern. The first two chips have four arrays of 4,096 KB, giving a total of eight arrays, while the third chip is the parity chip (array). The total capacity of the SIMM is 4,096 $\times$ 8 = 32,768 which is equal to 4,096 KB.

6.6.4 CHIP SPEED

One of the last things to look for when matching RAM chips is the access time (which indicates the speed) of the chips. The lower the number, the faster the chip. Therefore, if a PC requires a 100 ns DRAM, then 150 ns DRAM may be cheaper but most likely will not work. Generally, you can use DRAM chips with faster access times than those called for. A PC that requires 100 ns DRAM will work fine with 80 ns chips, but the faster chips will not deliver a speed boost. The PC will still operate as if you had installed 100 ns DRAM. (Note: Sometimes compatibility problems occur when using RAM chips with different speeds.)

6.6.5 READING THE CHIP LABEL

Determining how much RAM a system has is more of an art than a science. Some RAM chips can be identified with little difficulty, and others are impossible to decipher. The method is to determine the manufacturer of the RAM chip and use the Internet to access the manufacturer's home page to look up the part number.

If the part number is decipherable, it will look similar to the ones shown in fig. 6.10. In the top left corner is the logo of the company that made the RAM chip. In the first line of numbers and letters is the part number and the speed; the second line usually states the date (year and month or Julian date) when the RAM chip was created. As shown in table 6.3, the first digit of the part number acts as a placeholder. The second digit indicates if the chip is set up to contain a 1-bit (one data bus) word or a 4-bit word (four data buses). The rest of the part number indicates the number of words that the chip holds. To find out how much a RAM chip holds, you must look at the code of each DIP and add them together. The number after the dash indicates the speed of the RAM chip, either as the number stands or after adding a 0 to the end of it.

Let's look at two examples. A DIP labeled –70 means that the chip runs at 70 ns. But another DIP labeled –7 might run at 70 ns or 7 ns. Unless you contact the manufacturer (or use the Internet), you must use good judgment to determine which speed it is. If the chip is used for regular RAM, probably consisting of DRAM chips, the label must mean 70 ns because DRAM runs only between 50 and 70 ns. If the DIP is used for SRAM in RAM cache, the label could very well mean 7 ns. (Note: Some of the DIPs used in the XT and AT were labeled –3 and ran at 150 ns.)

> **NOTE** The capacity of a RAM chip can be as large as 64 megabits, but the part numbers are usually indecipherable.

FIGURE 6.10 Typical RAM chips found an SIMMs and DIMMS. The top left chip is a 4096K × 1 bit running at 60 ns. The top right chip is a 1024K × 1 bit running at 80 ns. The bottom left chip is an 8192 × 1 bit running at 60 ns. The bottom right chip is an SDRAM chip of 8192K × 8 bits running at 10 ns.

TABLE 6.3 **Common RAM chip labels**

Part Number	Capacity	Part Number	Capacity
4164	64K × 1 bit	4464	64K × 4 bit
41128	128K × 1 bit	44128	128K × 4 bit
41256	256K × 1 bit	44256	256K × 4 bit
411024	1024K × 1 bit	441024	1024K × 4 bit
41000	1024K × 1 bit	44000	1024K × 4 bit
414096	4096K × 1 bit	444096	4096K × 4 bit
418192	8192K × 1 bit	448192	8192K × 4 bit

> **NOTE** An excellent website to identify individual IC chips is:
> **http://icmaster.com/**

To determine the capacity of a SIPP, SIMM, or DIMM, you must determine the capacity (in bits) of each chip (see table 6.3) and add them together. To figure out the bytes, you must then divide by 8 bits (for nonparity RAM chips) or 9 bits (for parity RAM chips.)

6.7   RAM CACHE

Cache memory, usually made of SRAM, is a special ultrafast memory that acts as a buffer between the microprocessor and the slower RAM. On a typical 100 MHz Intel motherboard, it takes the CPU as much as 180 ns to retrieve information from the RAM, but as little as 45 ns to get information from cache memory. Since the RAM cache is faster and connects directly to the microprocessor, the data it holds can be accessed without any wait states. If more information is kept in the cache memory and is accessed from the RAM cache rather than from the slower RAM, the computer will perform better. It holds the most commonly used instructions and data so that the microprocessor doesn't always have to access the slower RAM. When information is found in the RAM cache, it is called a *cache hit.* When information is found not in the RAM cache but in the RAM, it is called a *cache miss.*

6.7.1   INTERNAL AND EXTERNAL CACHE

In general, there are two levels of cache memory: internal cache, which is usually located inside the CPU chip; and external cache, which is normally located on the motherboard.

Internal cache is sometimes referred to as *primary cache* or *level 1 (L1) cache.* Internal cache is faster than external RAM cache because it is a physical part of the microprocessor. Since it runs at the speed of the microprocessor, it runs at higher speeds than external RAM cache and has a larger data path. In 486 and Pentium microprocessors the data path between the internal cache and the rest of the microprocessor is 16 bytes (256 bits) wide. The internal RAM cache is quite small (8–32 KB). (Note: Some internal RAM caches are divided into separate instruction caches and data caches.)

External cache is sometimes referred to as *secondary cache* or *level 2 (L2) cache.* External cache is usually much larger than internal cache, ranging usually from 64 KB to 1 MB. If someone refers to upgrading the amount of cache, they are probably talking about the external cache. (Note: Since today's microprocessors are becoming much faster than today's RAM cache chips, the Pentium Pro and Pentium II microprocessors include both L1 and L2 RAM cache.) (See fig. 6.11.)

Internal or external cache can be characterized as a write-back cache or a write-through cache. The write-back cache, which is the faster of the two, allows the microprocessor to write changes to its cache memory. Eventually, the cache controller will write the changes back into the normal RAM. The write-through cache does not attempt to buffer the write

FIGURE 6.11   Different forms of RAM cache

operations. Instead, they write to the cache and also to the RAM. This is a safer approach because it guarantees that the RAM and cache are constantly in agreement. Most Intel microprocessors use write-through cache.

Question: How much cache should I have?

Answer: Most systems offer 256 KB or 512 KB of RAM cache. When using DOS or Windows 3.XX, 256 KB is plenty. When using Windows 95 or Windows NT, try 512 KB or more.

Tests done by Z-D Labs found that by adding 256 KB of pipelined-burst L2 cache to a Pentium system with 16 MB of EDO DRAM, performance increased 36%. Although increasing the RAM cache to 512 KB does increase PC performance, the increase is not as dramatic with the second 256 KB as for the first 256 KB.

6.7.2   CACHE MAPPING

Different RAM caches use different methods for copying instructions and data into the cache. The methods used depend on the amount of RAM cache, how it is arranged and addressed, and how information is found and accessed in the cache. The three most popular methods are fully associative, direct-mapped, and set-associative.

Fully associative cache is broken down into a table with two columns that hold the data. The first column, called the *tag,* stores the RAM address of the data; the second column holds the data associated with that tag. Each time the microprocessor attempts to read the RAM, the cache controller intercepts the request and checks to see if the requested address is in the tag column of the cache. It does this by searching the tag row by row. If the address is in the RAM cache, the information is accessed more quickly than if it were located in the RAM. If the controller doesn't find the address in the cache, it will retrieve the data from RAM and add it to the cache. If the cache is full, the new information will overwrite the oldest data. The reason the requested data is copied into the RAM cache is that since the data was accessed once, there is a good chance that it will have to be accessed again. The disadvantage of fully associative cache is that if there are a lot of rows to search, that will take up more time than going directly to the RAM.

Direct-mapped cache maps the RAM into small units that are the same size as the RAM cache. When a byte is accessed from RAM, the entire block is copied into the cache in the hope that the next information that it needs will be next to the byte just accessed. The tag lists a single memory address, which is the address of the entire memory block being cached. The disadvantage of the direct-mapped cache is that if programs are jumping between two different memory blocks, which is what occurs during multitasking, the cache is constantly being updated, which causes more cache misses.

The set-associative cache tries to take the best of both worlds. It maps the RAM into several smaller cache areas much as the direct-mapped cache does. Each cache area acts like a full-associative cache. Therefore, the set-associative cache can cache several areas at the same time yet keep the search through the tag smaller. This form of RAM cache is even faster because each cache area can be checked simultaneously by the cache controller.

6.7.3 TYPES OF CACHES

Today, RAM caches use some version of **burst mode.** Just as burst mode is used to read sequential RAM addresses, it can be used to read and write to RAM cache. Burst-mode cache can access information up to 54% faster. The RAM cache found within your computer will either be synchronous burst cache or pipelined burst cache.

Synchronous burst cache accesses a memory area from RAM but then uses its own internal clock, which is in sync with the RAM, to count up and access sequential addresses. In addition, synchronous burst cache will use pipelining, which allows the cache to access the next RAM address while transferring the current data. Cache speeds range from 15 ns to less than 6 ns. Unfortunately, when synchronous burst cache exceeds a bus speed of 66 MHz, the cache is overstrained. The other type of cache, **pipelined burst cache,** uses a register to hold the next piece of data to be read. While reading one piece of data, the RAM cache is already accessing the next piece of data. Therefore, the RAM cache can keep up with motherboards up to 133 MHz and offers access speeds of 4.5 to 8 ns.

6.8 TROUBLESHOOTING RAM

Memory problems can occur in many forms. Some error messages will be obvious (audio or video code), but others will not be so obvious. Some symptoms which may indicate a memory problem are as follows:

1. Random errors in programs
2. Unrecoverable application errors, general protection faults, or equivalent
3. Computer locking up every so often without any noticeable pattern or obvious explanation
4. Computer fails to activate even though the LED lights are on
5. Software problems

Memory problems are caused by one of three things, the most obvious being the RAM itself and the others being the motherboard (to which the RAM directly connects) and power-related problems (bad power supply or power fluctuations). You will need to isolate each of these components, one at a time, until you find the cause.

One way to test the RAM is to use a software diagnostic, such as QA Plus or Checkit Pro, and it is best to use it after booting the computer without loading a memory management program, such as HIMEM.SYS. If you load a memory manager, the memory goes into protected mode, and in that mode, memory above 1 MB cannot be tested. The other way to test the RAM is to run the comprehensive test (long test). By default, most of the software diagnostic packages perform the quick test. The comprehensive test takes longer, but it will do a much more thorough job. If a memory error is discovered during testing, it will usually be caused by a faulty RAM chip or a faulty motherboard.

EXAMPLE 6.6 When the IBM PC detects a memory error, it generates a 201 error code followed by a second four-number code identifying which DIP is causing the problem. The first two numbers indicate which bank (row) the problem occurred in, and the second two numbers indicate which chip within the bank is causing the problem. Therefore, if the following error message appears during boot:

```
0420 201
```

the 201 identifies it as a RAM error while the 0420 identifies which chip is causing the problem. (See fig. 6.12.)

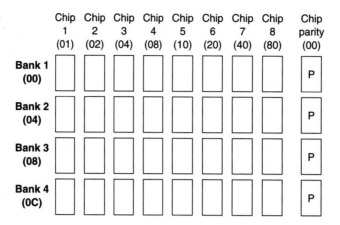

FIGURE 6.12 A diagnostic diagram used to identify PC RAM errors in XT computers

From the diagram in fig. 6.12, the 04 indicates that the problem is happening within the 2nd bank. The 20 indicates that it is located in the 6th chip over. The first thing you should do in this situation is push down on the chip to make sure that it is seated properly in the motherboard. If the error goes away, the problem was caused by chip creep. If the error does not go away, replace the RAM chip. If the problem still occurs after replacing the chip, you have to replace the motherboard.

EXAMPLE 6.7 A computer produces three beeps (AMI BIOS) during boot-up and nothing appears on the screen.

If you look up the error code, you will find that it means "Base 64 KB Error," which is a very common error message. It indicates that the first bank of chips (DIP, SIPP, SIMM, or DIMM) is faulty. To isolate the actual cause of the problem, you should first check to see if all the RAM chips are seated properly. If one of the chips is not connected or seated properly, the entire bank may not be recognized. After you check this, you should swap the suspected RAM chip with one that you know is good. If the problem still exists, it is most likely a motherboard problem.

EXAMPLE 6.8 The computer won't boot, nothing appears on the screen, and no audio codes are generated.

Check the obvious first, which in this case is making sure that the computer is plugged in and turned on. Next, make sure that you actually have power from the outlet. The third thing to do is open the machine and make sure the speaker is still connected to the motherboard. This is important so that you will be able to hear an audio code if it is generated.

If all of these things check out, you have to isolate. When a computer doesn't boot, it can be a power problem, a memory problem, or a motherboard problem. You should first suspect a power-related problem, such as a component causing a short or overload. To check for short or overload, you need to remove every expansion card except the video card and disk controller. If the problem still exists, it must be caused by one of the components still in the system. Therefore, the next logical step would be to remove the disk controller. If the problem still exists, it has to be caused by the video card or something on the motherboard, so the next step would be to replace the video card. Again, if the problem continues, it is has to be caused by something on the motherboard. This could be the CPU, the RAM, or the motherboard itself. Isolate these components until you find the problem.

EXAMPLE 6.9 All the RAM doesn't show up during the POST.

This is usually caused by either a faulty RAM chip or module or a faulty motherboard. Check the obvious first by making sure that the RAM is seated properly in the RAM slots. If the RAM is seated properly, replace each of the banks of RAM one at time until the problem goes away. After you find out which bank is causing the problem, you can then swap one RAM chip back into the system until you find out which individual chip is causing the problem.

EXAMPLE 6.10 You get an "Incorrect Memory Size" message during boot after you either increased or decreased the amount of RAM in the system.

This is usually not a major problem. During boot, the system instructs the ROM BIOS, which controls the boot procedure, to look in the CMOS RAM to see how much RAM the computer is supposed to have. It then tests the specified amount of RAM. When you change the amount of RAM, therefore, the information within the CMOS RAM does not match the actual amount of RAM. To fix this problem, go into the CMOS setup program and enter the standard CMOS settings. The new amount of RAM will automatically be written to the CMOS RAM when you save the changes and exit the program. The computer should then boot properly. (Note: Newer systems will automatically update the CMOS values when the amount of RAM is changed.)

If the *incorrect memory* message appears but you did not change the amount of RAM, then the CMOS value changed (because of bad CMOS battery or bad CMOS chip), the RAM became bad, or the motherboard became faulty.

EXAMPLE 6.11   You turn on the computer and the system indicates a "Gate A20 Failure."

This error message indicates in a 286 or higher machine that the computer must change to protected mode to utilize more than 1 MB of RAM. The first 1 MB of RAM is indicated with 20 address lines, identified A0 to A19; therefore, A20 is the 21st address line, which is the beginning of the extended memory. The gate A20 failure error indicates that the system, for whatever reason, could not activate the A20 line and change to protected mode. Since the A20 line is controlled by the keyboard controller, the gate A20 failure may be caused by either a faulty keyboard or a faulty motherboard.

To isolate the problem, check to see if the keyboard is configured correctly (XT versus AT). Next, replace the keyboard with a known good one. If the problem still exists, replace the motherboard.

EXAMPLE 6.12   You get a "Cache Memory Failure" during boot-up.

This error message could be generated if the system does not have RAM cache but it is enabled in the CMOS setup program. If the PC does have RAM cache, then the RAM cache, the cache controller, or the motherboard has gone bad. The first thing you should do is replace the RAM cache. If that does not correct the problem, replace the motherboard. (Note: You could also disable the RAM cache in the CMOS setup program. This will stop the error message from appearing but, unfortunately, it will also slow the computer down.)

SUMMARY

1. Random access memory, more commonly referred to as RAM, consists of electronic memory chips that store information inside the computer.
2. RAM is known as volatile (changeable) memory.
3. The RAM is considered the main memory or the primary memory because it is the memory that the microprocessor accesses directly.
4. Primary RAM usually consists of dynamic RAM (DRAM) chips, which use tiny capacitors to store information.
5. Dynamic RAM needs to be constantly recharged (refreshed).
6. RAM cache consists of static RAM (SRAM) chips, which are faster than DRAM.
7. VRAM, usually used in video cards, is a special form of DRAM that can read and write at the same time.
8. Conventional memory is the first 640 KB of RAM.
9. Reserve memory, between 640 KB and 1 MB, is reserved for hardware.
10. Upper memory is memory between 640 KB and 1MB not being used by hardware. It can be used to load small programs (TSRs and device drivers).
11. Expanded memory was the first form of memory that allowed users to break the 1 MB boundary.
12. The memory above 1 MB found on today's newer machines (386 and above) is known as extended memory.
13. The amount of RAM determines how many programs can be run at the same time, how big each program can be, and how many documents can be open at the same time. In addition, the amount of RAM is a big factor in the speed of the PC.
14. Virtual memory is space reserved on the hard drive to act like RAM.

15. Dual in-line package (DIP) chips, found on the original IBM PC, are inserted directly into a motherboard designed for them.
16. SIPPs, SIMMs, and DIMMs are small circuit boards with several DIP chips soldered onto them.
17. RAM is divided into 8- or 9-bit patterns. The 8 bits represent a byte of data; the 9th bit is a parity bit used for error control.
18. A bank is a collection of memory chips (data bus size) that make up a block of memory readable by the processor in a single bus cycle.
19. RAM chips contain millions of memory cells that are organized into a large array of rows and columns.
20. Cache memory, usually made of SRAM, is a special ultrafast memory that acts as a buffer between the microprocessor and the slower RAM.
21. Internal cache—primary cache or level 1 (L1) cache—is part of the microprocessor.
22. External cache—secondary cache or level 2 (L2) cache—is located on the motherboard and is much larger than internal cache.
23. Memory problems are caused by faulty RAM chips, a faulty motherboard, or power-related problems (bad power supply or power fluctuations).

QUESTIONS

1. RAM is considered volatile memory. Which of the following best describes volatile memory?
   a. UV light is used to erase the contents of the chip
   b. data in RAM is permanent and can't be erased
   c. data in RAM can be changed and is not permanent
   d. the data is maintained by a small battery when the power is shut off
2. Which type of memory involves mapping addresses of logical pages to physical pages?
   a. extended
   b. expanded
   c. conventional
   d. reserve
   e. high
3. Which of the following is the fastest form of RAM?
   a. FPM RAM
   b. EDO RAM
   c. Burst EDO RAM
   d. SDRAM
4. Which of the following does not require the RAM to be refreshed?
   a. FPM RAM
   b. EDO RAM
   c. Burst EDO RAM
   d. SDRAM
   e. SRAM
5. Which of the following best describe DRAM? (Choose two.)
   a. chips that use tiny capacitors to represent bits of information
   b. chips that use tiny electronic switches to represent bits of information
   c. chips that need to be constantly recharged
   d. chips that do not need recharging
   e. DRAM is faster than SRAM
6. Which type of RAM is used for RAM cache?
   a. DRAM
   b. VRAM
   c. SRAM
   d. EDO RAM
7. Which of the following best describes burst mode?
   a. one memory address is sent followed by several sequential pieces of data
   b. the memory and data addresses are sent simultaneously
   c. data is sent at a faster speed
   d. memory reads and writes at the same time
8. VRAM is faster than DRAM because:
   a. VRAM supports burst mode
   b. VRAM can read and write at the same time
   c. VRAM does not need recharging
   d. VRAM runs at a higher speed than DRAM

9. The first 640 KB of memory is known as:
   a. conventional memory
   b. CMOS memory
   c. extended memory
   d. reserve memory
10. Memory between 640 KB and 1 MB used by hardware is known as:
    a. conventional memory
    b. upper memory
    c. reserve memory
    d. expanded memory
    e. extended memory
11. Which of the following was developed to work around some of the limitations of DOS and early microcomputers?
    a. upper memory area (UMA)
    b. expanded memory (EMS)
    c. high memory area (HMA)
    d. extended memory (XMS)
12. Which memory area is above 1 MB and is found on any new IBM PC or compatible?
    a. upper memory
    b. reserve memory
    c. extended memory
    d. expanded memory
13. What is the hexadecimal range for conventional memory?
    a. A0000 to 7FFFF
    b. 00000 to A0000
    c. 00000 to 9FFFF
    d. 00000 to A0000
14. The video ROM BIOS memory address is commonly located between:
    a. A0000 and AFFFFH
    b. B0000 and BFFFFH
    c. C0000 and CFFFFH
    d. D0000 and DFFFFH
    e. F0000 and FFFFFH
15. Virtual memory is:
    a. extended memory pretending to be expanded memory
    b. ROM chips pretending to be memory
    c. extended memory being used for video RAM
    d. hard disk space pretending to be RAM
16. A small circuit board consisting of several DRAM chips and small metal plates that is inserted into the motherboard is known as a:
    a. DIPP
    b. SIPP
    c. SIMM
    d. SRAM
    e. none of the above
17. Which of the following has a 64-bit data path?
    a. DIPP
    b. SIPP
    c. SIMM
    d. DIMM
18. Which of the following has a 32-bit data path? (Choose two.)
    a. 30-pin SIMM
    b. 72-pin SIMM
    c. DIMM
    d. SODIMM
19. After adding two 8 MB SIMM (72-pin) chips to the banks of memory in a 486 DX machine, the memory will perform like:
    a. two individual banks of 8 MB RAM
    b. a single bank of 8 MB RAM
    c. a single double-bank (8 MB × 32) of 64 MB RAM
    d. a single bank of 16 MB RAM
20. After adding four 1 MB SIMMs (30-pin) to the banks of memory in a 386DX machine, the memory will perform like:
    a. four individual banks of 1 MB RAM
    b. a single bank of 4 MB RAM
    c. a single bank of 1 MB RAM
    d. a single double-bank (1 MB × 8) of 8 MB RAM
21. A memory chip on a SIMM has the marking 45096-6. The 6 after the dash means an access time of:
    a. 6 μs
    b. 6 ns
    c. 60 ns
    d. 6 ms
    e. 60 ms

22. Generally, how many 72-pin SIMMs are needed to make a bank in a Pentium micro-processor?
    - a. 1
    - b. 2
    - c. 4
    - d. 8
23. RAM is often divided into a 9-bit pattern. Eight of the bits represent one byte of data. What is the ninth bit used for?
    - a. a spare bit
    - b. error control
    - c. data storage
    - d. the address of the data
24. Cache memory is:
    - a. spare storage
    - b. virtual memory
    - c. ultrafast memory that acts as a buffer between the microprocessor and the slower RAM
    - d. shadow RAM
25. RAM cache that is inside the microprocessor is known as:
    - a. L1 cache
    - b. fast cache
    - c. local cache
    - d. extended cache
26. Some IC chips mounted in sockets can work loose over time because of:
    - a. thermal cycling of the chip and the socket
    - b. metal stresses from the leads of the chip
    - c. vertical mounting of chips on circuit boards
    - d. vibration caused by disk drive and cooling fan motors
27. Which of the following will not cause a memory error?
    - a. faulty hard drive
    - b. faulty RAM chip
    - c. power fluctuations
    - d. faulty power supply
    - e. faulty motherboard
28. Which component may be failing if the fan and hard drive run, yet the system appears dead?
    - a. the on/off switch
    - b. the power supply
    - c. the power cord
    - d. the RAM
    - e. the floppy drive

HANDS-ON EXERCISES

Exercise 1: Identifying the Memory Areas Using MEM and MSD

1. At the command prompt, use the MEM command to identify the total amount and the free amount of the following memory areas:
   conventional memory
   reserve memory
   upper memory
   extended memory
   expanded memory
2. Boot to the command prompt. Use MSD to analyze the memory. Determine:
   the total amount of memory
   the total amount of conventional memory and free amount of conventional memory
   the amount of extended and expanded memory
   the memory addresses used by the ROM chips

Exercise 2: Analyzing Memory in Windows 3.1X

1. Start Windows 3.1X.
2. Look under the About Program Manager option under the Help menu. Determine the total amount of memory.
3. In the Control Panel, double click on the Enhanced 386 icon.
4. Determine the amount of virtual memory used by Windows. Determine why the amount of actual memory found using the MEM command and MSD is different from the amount reported in Windows 3.1X.

Exercise 3: Analyzing Memory in Windows 95 or 98

1. Start Windows 95 or 98 (if available).
2. Within the Control Panel, start the System applet. Determine the actual amount of memory.
3. Click on the Virtual Memory button under the Performance tab. Determine what drive the virtual memory file is stored on and how big the virtual memory can be.

Exercise 4: Testing the RAM Using a Software Diagnostic Package

1. Using a software diagnostic package, determine the amount of RAM your system has.
2. Using a software diagnostic package, test the RAM. Note: If the software has a short/quick test and a long/comprehensive test, run both.

Exercise 5: Identifying the RAM Chips and RAM Cache Chips

1. Open your computer and remove the RAM chips.
2. Identify the size and speed of each RAM chip.
3. Reinsert the RAM chips.
4. Identify the RAM cache on the motherboard.
5. Identify the microprocessor on the motherboard. Does the microprocessor have an internal L1 or L2 RAM cache? If it does, how much cache memory does the microprocessor have?

Exercise 6: Enabling/Disabling the RAM Cache

1. Using the CMOS setup program, make sure the RAM cache is enabled.
2. Reboot the computer and start Windows, Windows 95, or Windows 98. Time it to see how long it takes Windows to load.
3. Using the CMOS setup program, disable the RAM cache.
4. Reboot the computer and start Windows, Windows 95, or Windows 98. Time it to see how long it takes Windows to load.
5. Using the CMOS setup program, enable the RAM cache.

Exercise 7: Troubleshooting

1. Shut off the computer and remove all the RAM chips.
2. Turn on the computer. What kind of error, if any, occurred?
3. Shut off the computer and reinsert all the RAM chips.
4. Remove the first RAM chip.
5. Turn on the computer. What kind of error, if any, occurred?
6. Shut off the computer and reinsert the first RAM chip.
7. Turn on the computer. What kind of error, if any, occurred?
8. Shut off the computer and, if possible, remove the second RAM chip.
9. Turn on the computer. What kind of error, if any, occurred?
10. Shut off the computer and, if possible, remove a chip from the second bank.
11. Turn on the computer. What kind of error, if any, occurred?
12. Determine how many RAM chips make up a bank.
13. If possible, install different-capacity RAM chips within a bank.
14. Reinstall the RAM the way it was before you started.

7

The Motherboard Support Chips

INTRODUCTION

The motherboard acts as the central nervous system of the computer and allows the microprocessor to connect to other components. The motherboard holds the microprocessor, the RAM, expansion slots, and a wide array of chips known as the motherboard chipset. These support chips allow all the different components to work together.

Two important motherboard support chips are the system ROM BIOS chip and the CMOS RAM chip. The system ROM BIOS chip might be said to represent the "instincts" of the computer; it works very closely with the CMOS RAM chip, which holds valuable hardware configuration information.

OBJECTIVES

1. Identify and describe the motherboard.
2. Explain the advantages of a printed circuit board.
3. Describe what the form factor of a motherboard is.
4. List the different forms of memory and their advantages and disadvantages.
5. List the different BIOS chips used in a PC and describe their function.
6. Describe the boot-up procedure of the PC.
7. List and describe how the system ROM BIOS is supplemented.
8. Using the motherboard documentation, configure the DIP switches and jumpers of a motherboard.
9. Describe the function of the CMOS RAM and how it relates to the system BIOS.
10. Describe the function of the real-time clock (RTC) and the CMOS battery.
11. Describe the chipset/PC support chips.
12. Describe and differentiate the system clock, crystal oscillator, and timer chip.
13. Enter and configure the CMOS setup program.
14. Describe common problems caused by a faulty motherboard.
15. Describe how to determine if the motherboard is faulty.

7.1 MOTHERBOARDS

The **motherboard,** also referred to as the *main board* or the *system board,* is the primary printed circuit board located within the PC. It includes connectors for attaching additional boards (expansion slots) and additional devices (ports). In addition, it contains the microprocessor, the RAM chips, the RAM cache, several ROM BIOS chips, CMOS RAM, the real-time clock, and several support chips.

Printed circuit boards have thin metal traces embedded within their glass-epoxy construction that connect the different electronic components. Since the microprocessor talks to the other components by sending signals through the metal traces, the motherboard can be thought of as the PC's nervous system. Since so many electronic devices require many connections, modern motherboards will usually contain several layers of metal traces.

> **Question:** Why don't PC designers use wires instead of metal traces?
>
> **Answer:** The motherboard as well as other printed circuit boards actually simplifies the insides of a computer. Without the printed circuit board, the PC would have hundreds of wires, which must be connected and soldered, making the computer cost more. Wires are also more fragile, and it would be difficult to troubleshoot hundreds of wires. (See fig. 7.1.)

Motherboards are often described by their **form factor** (physical dimensions and sizes). The main form factors are shown in table 7.1. The two most common form factors used today are the Baby AT motherboard and the ATX motherboard. The **Baby AT** motherboard is approximately the same size and has the same dimensions as the IBM XT motherboard.

The **ATX motherboard** is similar to the Baby AT motherboard, except the components are placed differently. The expansion slots are parallel to the short side of the board, which allows more space for other components. The microprocessor and RAM are next to the power supply so that the airflow generated by the power supply runs over the microprocessor. Lastly, the ATX motherboard contains integrated I/O port connectors and an integrated PS/2 mouse connector and supports 3.3 volts coming from an ATX power supply.

Expansion cards for **LPX motherboards** are inserted into a *riser card* that protrudes from the motherboard. Consequently, the expansion boards are parallel to the motherboard rather than at right angles to it, allowing for smaller cases. Some motherboards that have a planar design also use a riser card to hold the expansion slots. The **NLX motherboard,** though similar to the LPX, contains several improvements. It supports larger memory modules and newer microprocessors and provides better access to motherboard components. (See fig. 7.2.)

Some computers, including most name-brand computers, use proprietary motherboards. The motherboards will therefore not normally fit into another case, and cases will not accommodate most nonbrand motherboards.

FIGURE 7.1 The original IBM PC prototype motherboard before it was made into a printed circuit board

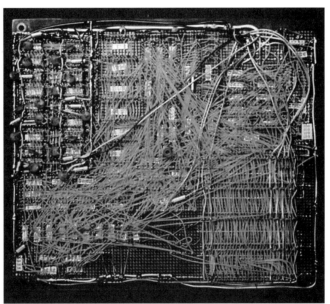

TABLE 7.1 Motherboard form factors

Style	Dimensions	Comments
Full AT	12″ × 11–13″	Used in older PCs
Baby AT	8.5″ × 11–13″	Most common form factor
ATX	12″ × 9.6″	Common in today's newer Pentium systems; allows better cooling of CPU
Mini ATX	11.2″ × 8.2″	Smaller version of the ATX
LPX	9″ × 11–13″	Uses riser card
Mini LPX	8.9″ × 10–11″	Uses riser card
NLX	9″ × 13.6″	Provides better access to motherboard components

FIGURE 7.2   NLX motherboard (courtesy of Intel Corporation)

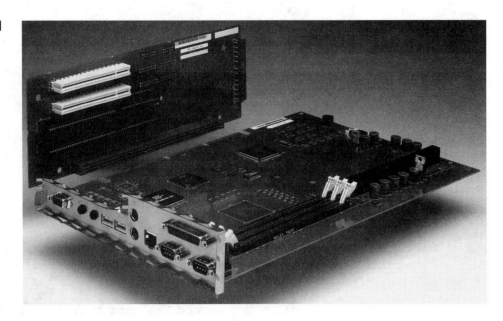

7.2   FORMS OF MEMORY

7.2.1   RAM AND DISKS

RAM, which stands for **random access memory,** is the computer's short-term or temporary memory. It stores instructions and data that the microprocessor accesses directly. If power is discontinued to the RAM, such as when you shut off your PC, the contents of the RAM disappear. This is the reason we use disks (floppy disks and hard disks) for long-term storage.

Disks (hard drives and floppy drives) are the PC's long-term memory. They consist of mechanical parts that use magnetic patterns to store information on specially coated platters. Although they can hold large amounts of information, they are slow and have a high failure rate as compared to other nonmechanical components.

7.2.2   ROM CHIPS

Read-only memory (ROM) chips contain instructions and data that the microprocessor accesses directly. Unlike the contents of the RAM, the contents of the ROM are permanent. They can't be changed or erased by normal means and are not lost when there is no power. Although they are much faster than any disk, ROM chips are slower than RAM chips. There are several types of ROM chips, including:

1. Mask ROM
2. Programmable read-only memory (PROM)
3. Erasable programmable read-only memory (EPROM)
4. Electrically erasable programmable read-only memory (EEPROM)
5. Flash ROM

Mask ROM chips are programmed during manufacturing; PROM chips are manufactured as a blank chip and are programmed later by using a PROM burner. Both chips are permanent and nonchangeable after programming and are therefore unsuited to today's fast-changing PC.

Erasable programmable read-only memory (EPROM) is a special type of PROM that can be erased by shining ultraviolet light through a clear window on top of the chip. Once the chip is erased, it can be reprogrammed. Since the EPROM chip holds instructions that allow a device to run properly, erasing the chip will cause the device to not function properly, so the chip has to be reprogrammed with an EPROM burner or replaced. **Electrically erasable programmable read-only memory (EEPROM)** chips (pronounced "double-E PROM") can also be reprogrammed. The chips are erased using higher-than-normal voltage instead of ultraviolet light. Unfortunately, EPROM chips can be erased only a set number of times.

Flash RAM chips are similar to EEPROM chips except they can be reprogrammed by running a BIOS update program using the normal voltage found in the PC. The first generation of flash RAM chips was limited to a finite number of changes but was eventually improved to act more like normal RAM. There are many different uses for flash RAM. Today, flash RAM can be used in plug-and-play systems to store the expansion card configuration information and as upgradable ROM BIOS chips.

7.3 ROM BIOS CHIPS

ROM chips in the computer provide instructions and data to the microprocessor. The instructions and data in the ROM chip that control the boot process and hardware are known as the **basic input/output system (BIOS),** sometimes called *firmware.*

FIGURE 7.3 Keyboard ROM BIOS

Every PC has several BIOS chips, including the system ROM BIOS, the keyboard ROM BIOS, and the video ROM BIOS. The **system ROM BIOS,** which is located on the motherboard, directs the boot-up and allows basic control of the majority of the hardware. The **keyboard ROM BIOS** (see fig. 7.3), which is also found on the motherboard, controls the keyboard. The **video ROM BIOS,** which is located on the video card, or on the motherboard if the video card is built into the motherboard, controls the video systems.

Other ROM chips, which are often found on expansion cards, supplement the instructions of the system ROM BIOS. They provide instructions used to control new or nonstandard hardware not included in the original system ROM BIOS and include SCSI controller cards, enhanced IDE controller cards, sound cards, proprietary CD-ROM drive controller cards, and network cards.

The ROM chips, which are mapped with the RAM, occupy the reserve memory between 640 KB and 1 MB. The reserve memory got its name because it was reserved for the BIOS. The system ROM BIOS uses up to 128 KB of reserved RAM; it may use as little as 64 KB (F0000–FFFFF). The video BIOS has 128 KB of reserved memory (C0000–C7FFF), and other expansion cards use the last 128 KB. Therefore, when these memory locations within reserve memory are accessed, it may be the ROM chip that is accessed instead of the RAM chip.

7.4 SYSTEM ROM BIOS

The primary ROM BIOS chip is the system ROM BIOS. (See fig. 7.4.) On today's PCs, there is only one system ROM BIOS chip; older systems may have up to four ROM BIOS chips. The system ROM BIOS has the following functions:

1. Controlling the boot-up procedure
2. Performing a series of diagnostic tests known as the power-on self-test (POST) during boot-up
3. Generating hardware error codes (audio and video) if a problem is found during boot-up
4. Finding other ROM BIOS chips on the expansion cards
5. Finding a boot sector or boot files to boot an operating system
6. Providing the most basic commands to control hardware
7. Providing compatibility between the operating system and the hardware
8. Containing the CMOS setup program

FIGURE 7.4   AMI system ROM BIOS (courtesy of American Megatrends Inc.)

7.4.1   BOOT-UP PROCEDURE

The computer performs a quick power check when it is first turned on. When the microprocessor receives a power-good signal, it starts reading and executing the instructions in the system ROM BIOS on how to boot the computer. The microprocessor will then initialize and test the essential PC components (RAM and motherboards) and perform an inventory of the hardware devices installed in the computer. When a component does not respond correctly to the test, the failure will be identified as a series of beeps (audio codes) or a number code or message (video code), as described in chapter 2.

BOOT PROCEDURE

HARDWARE INITIALIZATION

Step 1. After the PC is turned on, the microprocessor timer chip generates a reset signal.

Step 2. The power supply performs a self-test to make sure that all voltages and current levels are acceptable. The power supply indicates that the power is stable by sending the power-good signal to the microprocessor timer chip.

Step 3. The microprocessor timer chip stops generating a reset signal to the microprocessor and starts executing the instructions at address FFFF:0000H.

Step 4. The microprocessor begins executing instructions located within the system ROM BIOS. These instructions perform tests of the central hardware to verify basic system functionality. Any errors that occur are indicated by audio codes because the video system has not yet been initialized.

Step 5. The system ROM BIOS performs a search for the video ROM BIOS, which is located on the video card. If it does not find the video ROM BIOS, it uses the system ROM BIOS to initialize the monitor. A cursor will appear on the screen.

Step 6. The system ROM BIOS searches for other ROM chips (C0000H to EFFFFH) located on other adapter cards. A checksum test is done on the ROM modules. If the test fails, it will give a message (XXXX ROM Error), the XXXX being the segment address of the failed ROM module.

Step 7. The system ROM BIOS reads the information stored in the CMOS RAM. The CMOS RAM stores hardware information, such as the number and size of the drives and the amount of RAM in the system. If the information in the CMOS does not match the actual hardware found during testing, an error message will be generated stating what hardware could not be found.

Step 8. The ROM BIOS checks to see if the start is cold or warm. If a cold start, it will do the memory (RAM) test. If it is a warm start, it will skip the memory test. The test can be seen on the screen as the memory counts up from zero.

Step 9. If it is a cold start, the POST (power-on self-test) executes. The POST performs additional tests on the system. If an error occurs, it will be identified by a combination of audio and video codes. A successful POST is indicated by a single beep.

BOOTING FROM DISK

Step 10. The ROM BIOS searches for a volume boot sector at cylinder 0, head 0, sector 1 (the very first sector) on the A drive. This sector is loaded into the RAM and tested. If a disk is in the drive but the sector cannot be read or no disk is present, the BIOS continues to the next step. If the PC cannot boot from the floppy disk, a disk boot failure occurs or a "Nonsystem Disk or Disk Error" message is generated. Note: The boot order can be changed in some systems (the A drive followed by the C drive, the C drive followed by the A drive, or another combination of boot devices); the A drive followed by the C drive is the default order.

Step 11. If no volume boot sector can be read from the A drive, the BIOS looks for a master boot record (MBR), located at cylinder 0, head 0, sector 1, to find out which partition to boot from. If an active partition cannot be found, it will generate a "Missing Operating System" error message.

Step 12. If there is a problem at this point, a message will appear. Depending on the BIOS manufacturer, the message will say that there is no boot device available, no ROM BASIC, or an invalid partition. If the system does boot from this drive, it will go to step 14.

Step 13. The system then goes to the active partition and tries to boot from it. If it can't boot from the partition, a loading operating system or a missing operating system error message will be generated.

LOADING DOS

Step 14. After finding the drive or partition to boot from, the system then goes to the root directory and finds the boot files for the operating system. For DOS, it is IO.SYS (or IBMBIO.COM for PC DOS) and MSDOS.SYS (or IBMDOS for PC DOS). If a problem occurs, a "Nonsystem Disk or Disk Error" message is generated.

Step 15. The IO.SYS file will then read the CONFIG.SYS and then load the COMMAND.COM followed by the AUTOEXEC.BAT file. If the CONFIG.SYS file or AUTOEXEC.BAT file is missing, it will continue to boot. If the COMMAND.COM file is missing, a "Bad or Missing Command Interpreter" message appears.

Step 16. When the computer is finished booting, a prompt will appear on the screen (usually C:\> if DOS) or a GUI environment will appear (if Windows 3.XX is loading from within the AUTOEXEC.BAT file).

LOADING WINDOWS 95 AND 98

Step 14. After finding the drive or partition to boot from, the system then goes to the root directory and finds the boot files for the operating system. For Windows 95 and 98, it is IO.SYS. If a problem occurs, a "Nonsystem Disk or Disk Error" message is generated.

Step 15. IO.SYS then reads the MSDOS.SYS, CONFIG.SYS (if it exists), COMMAND.COM, and AUTOEXEC.BAT (if it exists) files. (Note: Windows 95 and 98 load certain CONFIG.SYS entries automatically.) Lastly, control is given to the VMM32, which will load the other Windows 95 and 98 files.

Step 16. When the computer is finished booting, a GUI environment (default) or a prompt will appear on the screen.

LOADING WINDOWS NT

Step 14. After finding the drive or partition to boot from, the system then goes to the root directory and finds the boot file called NTLDR.

Step 15. The NTLDR reads the BOOT.INI file and displays the boot menu. When Windows NT is selected from the boot menu, NTDETECT.COM and NTOSKRNL.EXE are loaded.

Step 16. When the computer is finished booting, a GUI environment or a prompt appears on the screen.

During this time, the system ROM BIOS has instructions to search for additional ROM BIOS chips. Since the system ROM BIOS cannot possibly hold instructions for every piece of hardware or include instructions for all the new pieces of hardware that are introduced every day, a way to store additional instructions to control hardware was needed. These additional hardware instructions are located in the other ROM BIOS chips found on the expansion cards.

The last thing that the system ROM BIOS chip does during boot-up is to find a boot device to load the operating system. If all goes well, the system will finish with a prompt waiting for a command input (DOS or UNIX) or will display a GUI interface (Windows 3.XX, Windows 95, or Windows NT).

7.4.2 HARDWARE CONTROL

The system ROM BIOS and the other ROM chips found during boot-up contain many small individual programs called **system routines** or BIOS services. They are low-level programs that directly manipulate the PC hardware. (See table 7.2.)

The system routines located within the system ROM BIOS provide a level of compatibility between hardware and the system software. With so many different PCs of many different designs, you would expect that there would have to be several different versions of the operating system and software applications, one for each PC design. Yet when you buy a copy of DOS 6.22 or Windows 95, it operates on any PC as long as the PC has the minimum CPU, RAM capacity, and hard disk space. The reason only one version is needed is that the system ROM BIOS provides a translation between the operating system and the many different types of hardware. Even today's latest and most powerful PCs still duplicate everything the old AT did, so older software that ran on the AT also runs on the newer PCs.

Several companies specialize in developing compatible IBM system ROM BIOS chips. The most popular are American Megatrends Incorporated (AMI), Phoenix, and Award. (See table 7.3.) After a system ROM BIOS is developed, these companies license their ROM BIOS chips to a motherboard manufacturer. The motherboard manufacturer matches the hardware to a chosen system ROM BIOS or has one developed specifically for its motherboard.

The routines of the ROM BIOS are executed using interrupts. An **interrupt** is something that causes the CPU to stop its current task so that it can do another task. When the second task is completed, it will go back to the original task to continue where it left off. There are three types of interrupts: processor interrupts, software interrupts, and hardware interrupts. Processor interrupts occur when something unexpected happens or a program gives an erroneous result. See table 7.4 for a list of processor interrupts. Some of the main processor interrupts are:

- **Divide Error (Int 00)**—If a program tries to divide a number by zero, the CPU will generate INT 00H that causes a "Divide by Zero" error message.
- **NMI Interrupt (Int 02)**—NMI stands for *nonmaskable interrupt.* A nonmaskable interrupt is an interrupt that cannot be masked or switched off in the normal operation of the system through software. It is usually used to indicate a parity error.
- **General Protection Fault (Int 0D)**—A **general protection fault** indicates that the program has been corrupted, often terminating the application
- **Page Fault (Int 0E)**—A page fault occurs when the PC needs to access information that is stored in virtual memory or a program requests data that is not currently in RAM or virtual memory.

The PC supports 256 types of software interrupts and 15 hardware interrupts. Software interrupts are generated when a hardware device must be checked or manipulated by the PC. Each type of software interrupt is associated with a routine that takes control when the interrupt occurs. The complete list of interrupts and the location of the routine are stored in the interrupt vector table, which is located in the first 1 KB of RAM.

TABLE 7.2 System routines (BIOS services)

Interrupt	Type of Interrupt	Event
00H	Processor	Divide by zero
01H	Processor	Single-step interrupt handler
02H	Processor	Nonmaskable interrupt (NMI)
03H	Processor	Breakpoint
04H	Processor	Arithmetic overflow handler
05H	Software	Print screen
06H	Processor	Invalid op-code
07H	Processor	Coprocessor not available
08H	Hardware	System timer service routine
09H	Hardware	Keyboard device service routine
0AH	Hardware	Cascade from 2nd programmable interrupt controller (IRQ2)
0BH	Hardware	Serial port service (COM2–IRQ3)
0CH	Hardware	Serial port service (COM1–IRQ4)
0DH	Hardware	Parallel printer service (LPT2–IRQ5)
0EH	Hardware	Floppy disk drive service (IRQ6)
0FH	Hardware	Parallel printer service (LPT1–IRQ7)
10H	Software	Video service routine
11H	Software	Equipment list service routine
12H	Software	Memory size service routine
13H	Software	Hard disk drive service
14H	Software	Serial communication service routines
15H	Software	System services support routines
16H	Software	Keyboard support service routines
17H	Software	Parallel printer support services
18H	Software	Load and run ROM BASIC
19H	Software	DOS loading routine
1AH	Software	Real-time clock service routines
1BH	Software	<Ctrl><Break> service routine
1CH	Software	User timer service routines
1DH	Software	Video control parameter table
1EH	Software	Floppy disk parameter table
1FH	Software	Video graphics character table
20H–3FH	Software	DOS interrupt points
40H	Software	Floppy disk revector routine
41H	Software	Hard disk drive C parameter table
42H	Software	EGA default video driver
43H	Software	Video graphic characters
44H	Software	Novell NetWare API
46H	Software	Hard disk drive D parameter table
4AH	Software	User alarm
64H	Software	Novell NetWare IPX
67H	Software	EMS support routines
70H	Hardware	Real-time clock (IRQ8)
71H	Hardware	Redirect interrupt cascade (IRQ9)
72H–73H	Hardware	Reserved (IRQ10–11)
74H	Hardware	Bus mouse (IRQ12)
75H	Hardware	Math coprocessor exception (IRQ13)
76H	Hardware	Hard disk support (IRQ14)
77H	Hardware	Suspend request (IRQ15)
7AH	Software	Novell NetWare API

TABLE 7.3   Popular BIOS manufacturers

BIOS Manufacturer	Description
IBM	IBM represents today's personal computer standard. All other ROM BIOS chips need to be compatible with the IBM BIOS if they wish to be truly IBM compatible.
AMI	AMI is the most popular BIOS. Its success is due to its many features and enhancements.
Award	Award is unique among BIOS developers because it sells its BIOS code to other vendors and allows those vendors to customize the BIOS for their particular systems.
Phoenix	Phoenix was one of the first BIOS developers to design its own IBM-compatible BIOS and has become the standard for IBM-compatible BIOS. Phoenix ROM BIOS is efficient and very reliable.

IBM, AMI, Award, and Phoenix are by far the most popular. You should note that there are many other companies that sell their own BIOS. These BIOSes are proprietary or compatible with common ROM BIOS. Some of the more popular are DTK, Epson, Hewlett-Packard, NCR, Compaq, Wang, and Zenith.

7.4.3   ROM BIOS SHORTCOMINGS

All PCs are compatible to the ROM BIOS level, but ROM BIOS chips have two shortcomings. First, the BIOS cannot hold every instruction for every hardware device, nor can it handle devices based on newer technology. To overcome this problem, PC designers use several techniques to supplement the standard ROM BIOS:

1. Additional ROM BIOS chips located on expansion cards to supplement the instructions of the system ROM BIOS
2. Software written to access and control the hardware directly
3. Device drivers that enhance the BIOS instructions and TSRs that modify the interrupt vector table

To see examples of these techniques, let's examine IDE hard drives and enhanced IDE (EIDE) hard drives. Older computer systems, specifically the system ROM BIOS, were designed to see IDE hard drives only up to 504 MB of capacity. This is considered an extremely small size today but was considered large when it was introduced. Enhanced IDE drives were developed to extend the size of IDE hard drives and to make them faster. If you had a computer with an IDE controller card (expansion card) and tried to connect a 1 GB EIDE hard drive, the hard drive would not work properly. To overcome this problem, you would have to do one of the following:

1. Obtain a system with a newer system ROM chip or purchase a replacement system ROM BIOS chip, which includes instructions for handling EIDE hard drives
2. Update the ROM chip using special software if the system ROM BIOS is flash RAM
3. Purchase an EIDE controller card, which includes a ROM BIOS chip, to supplement the system ROM BIOS chip
4. Set the computer to recognize a 10 MB hard drive and to use a device driver that includes instructions for handling EIDE hard drives

As you can see, the ROM BIOS chips are vitally important to the operation of the computers and are in continuous use. Unfortunately, ROM BIOS chips are slow for performing these essential tasks, which causes the performance of the PC to be slow. ROM BIOS chips run as slowly as 200 ns and are accessed 8 bits at a time. To increase the speed of the ROM BIOS chips, the contents of the chips can be copied to the faster RAM during boot-up and accessed directly from RAM. RAM runs much faster than ROM (50 ns versus 80 ns) and can be accessed up to 32 bits at a time. This process of copying the ROM instructions to the RAM is called **ROM shadowing,** which can be activated or deactivated within the CMOS setup program.

TABLE 7.4   Processor interrupts

Interrupt	Microprocessor				
	8086/8088	286	386	486	Pentium
00	Divide error	Divide error	Divide error	Divide error	Divide error
01	Single step	Single step	Single-step debugging exceptions	Single-step debugging exceptions	Single-step debugging exceptions
02	Nonmaskable interrupt	Nonmaskable interrupt	Nonmaskable interrupt	Nonmaskable interrupt	Nonmaskable interrupt
03	Breakpoint	Breakpoint	Breakpoint	Breakpoint	Breakpoint
04	Info detected overflow	Info detected overflow	Info detected overflow	Info detected overflow	Info detected overflow
05	Bound range exceeded	Bound range exceeded	Bound range exceeded	Bound range exceeded	Bound range exceeded
06	Invalid instruction	Invalid instruction	Invalid instruction	Invalid instruction	Invalid instruction
07	Coprocessor not available	Coprocessor not available	Coprocessor not available	Coprocessor not available	Coprocessor not available
08	Double exception detected	Double exception detected	Double exception detected	Double exception detected	Double exception detected
09	Coprocessor	Coprocessor	Coprocessor	Coprocessor	Coprocessor
0A	Invalid task state segment	Invalid task state segment	Invalid task state segment	Invalid task state segment	Invalid task state segment
0B	Segment not present	Segment not present	Segment not present	Segment not present	Segment not present
0C	Stack fault	Stack fault	Stack fault	Stack fault	Stack fault
0D	Protection fault	Protection fault	Protection fault	Protection fault	Protection fault
0E			Page fault	Page fault	Page fault
10	Coprocessor error	Coprocessor error	Coprocessor error	Coprocessor error	Coprocessor error
11				Alignment check	Alignment check
12					Machine check

A second way to increase PC performance is to have the applications (usually the operating system) work directly with the PC hardware rather than go through the ROM BIOS chips. Of course, this causes more work for software programmers, especially considering the number of hardware components available.

Question: Are all system ROM BIOSes the same?

Answer: No, they are not. First, when a company makes an IBM-compatible ROM BIOS chip, it must do so from scratch since the IBM ROM BIOS program code is copyrighted. Second, the ROM BIOS codes have been designed for specific hardware. Next, some BIOS chips are better optimized for hardware than other BIOS chips, and therefore allow the PC to operate faster. Lastly, some ROM BIOS chips may include instructions for handling newer hardware, while others do not.

Occasionally, you may need to upgrade or replace the system ROM BIOS. Reasons to upgrade the system BIOS are:

1. New hardware is introduced and the system ROM BIOS does not know how to work with the new hardware
2. There are programming glitches
3. The newer system ROM BIOS runs more efficiently than the older system BIOS

When replacing system ROM BIOS, you must use one that is compatible with the motherboard. The system ROM BIOS can be identified by the manufacturer, serial numbers, and dates, which are printed on the label.

7.4.4 ROM BASIC CHIPS

When the IBM PC was introduced in 1981, the BASIC language could be used to create simple programs for the PC. The BASIC language interpreter was stored on a ROM chip located on the motherboard. Instead of saving the programs to a disk, the user would save them to a cassette tape. The use of the cassette tape is why ROM BASIC was also called Cassette BASIC. If an IBM PC did not have a system disk in any of the bootable drives, the machine would start executing the BASIC language from the ROM BASIC chip. Compatible computers (PCs using AMI, Award, or Phoenix BIOS) and newer IBM computers do not include the ROM BASIC chip. AMI BIOS strives to be as compatible as possible to the IBM ROM BIOS, including looking for a BASIC ROM chip if a bootable device (drive A or drive C) can't be found. If a computer with AMI BIOS boots and can't find a bootable device, it will display the following error message:

```
NO ROM BASIC - SYSTEM HALTED
```

To fix this problem, check the CMOS settings. In addition, check to see if the partition that contains the operating system is set to "active." See section 7.9 (CMOS Setup Program) and chapter 10 (The Hard Drive) for more information.

7.5 CHIPSETS

One essential yet inexpensive part of the PC is the motherboard chipset. (See fig. 7.5.) A **chipset** consists of the chips and other components on the motherboard that allow different PC components, including the microprocessor, to communicate with each other. It consists of the bus controllers, peripheral controllers, memory controllers, cache controllers, clocks, and timers. Although the chipset consists of several components, they may all be contained on several integrated chips or combined into one or two VLSI integrated chips (chips with over 20,000 circuits). The chipset used in a motherboard design greatly influences the performance and limitations of the PC. It defines how much RAM a motherboard can use and what type of RAM chips it will accommodate, cache size and speed, processor types and speed, and types of expansion slots.

Chipsets are constantly being introduced and improved and enhanced over time to allow for new technology. Since the chipsets are constantly changing, the older chipsets become harder to find. Therefore, if a component of a chipset is faulty, the difficulty of finding a replacement, not to mention the work and skill of replacing the component, will most likely lead to the replacement of the entire motherboard.

The most common chipsets produced today are by Intel. Intel has the most advanced CPU, PCI expansion bus, and universal serial bus (USB) and produces the fastest chipsets. Other major manufacturers include VIA, OPTi, and SIS. Table 7.5 lists a number of chipset manufacturers and how to locate their products.

TABLE 7.5   Common chipset manufacturers

Manufacturer	Website
Acer Labs	**Home:** http://www.ali.com.tw **Product:** http://www.ali.com.tw/ep.htm **Driver Downloads:** http://www.ali.com.tw/es.htm
Advanced Micro Devices, Inc.	**Home:** http://www.amd.com/
Intel	**Home:** http://www.intel.com **Chipset products:** http://www.intel.com/design/pcisets/
OPTI	**Home:** http://www.opti.com/
Silicon Integrated Systems Corp. (SiS)	**Home:** http://www.sisworld.com/
VIA Technologies	**Home:** http://www.viatech.com/ **Product:** http://www.viatech.com/products/index.htm

7.5.1   OSCILLATORS AND TIMERS

The **system clock** acts as the heartbeat of the computer. The system clock allows the many circuits of the PC to work in harmony with each other. Every time it beats, they react.

PCs mostly consist of digital electronics made up of switching circuits. Each switch in the circuit usually represents bits that are either being processed, stored, or transported. When a switch turns on or off, it takes a miniscule amount of time for it to change from one state to the other. If a circuit tries to read the voltage of the switch during this transition, a mistake could occur because the voltage of the switch is not high or low but somewhere in between. The *clock signal* prevents this problem by telling the circuits when to react. The clock signal is generated by a **quartz crystal (oscillator)** and a *timer* chip. The quartz crystal is made of piezoelectric material, which vibrates in the presence of electricity. The frequency of this vibration is controlled by varying the size and shape of the piezoelectric material. The signal from the quartz crystal is fed into the timer chip, which is connected to the various PC components. (See fig. 7.6.)

The original IBM PC used a 14.31818 MHz crystal oscillator. This odd number was chosen because back then the idea was that color televisions would eventually be used as color monitors and so the IBM oscillator was four times the frequency used in color televisions. The timer chip, 8284A, sent a 4.77 MHz signal (CLKIN) to the microprocessor, a 4.77 MHz signal to the expansion bus, and a 1.19 MHz signal to the PC's timer/counter

FIGURE 7.6   Three common crystal oscillators and one common timer chip

circuit (used by other PC components). The IBM AT and later machines use two or more oscillators. The main oscillator (CLK2IN), which runs at twice the speed of the CPU, synchronizes the CPU. Therefore, a CPU running at 33 MHz has an oscillator running at 66 MHz. A second signal, known as the ATCLK, is a separate clock for the ISA bus. This second signal is derived from either a second clock crystal or from the CL2IN signal. It is used to control the real-time clock and the RAM refresh circuitry and to adjust the frequency of the internal PC speaker.

Today, most clock signals are provided by a frequency synthesizer that combines a voltage controller oscillator (VCO) and a programmable divider to derive a high-speed clock from a much lower-speed crystal oscillator. Instead of the clock generator chip running at twice the speed of the microprocessor, it runs at the same speed because the timers use both edges of the timing signal rather than the rising edge.

Beginning with the 486 microprocessors, the motherboard or external bus runs at a fraction of the speed of the microprocessor. This means that the data moving between the microprocessor and the other parts of the computer, such as the RAM and peripherals, are running at a slower speed than the microprocessor. For example, the 486DX2-66 microprocessor runs at 66 MHz, but the motherboard runs at 33 MHz; the 486DX4-75 microprocessor runs at 75 MHz, but the motherboard runs at 25 MHz. The Pentium microprocessor runs between 2 and 4.5 times faster than the motherboard. Common motherboard speeds used today (known as the *bus speed*) are 66 MHz, 100 MHz, and 133 MHz.

7.5.2   BUS CONTROLLERS AND PERIPHERAL CONTROLLERS

Expansion cards are inserted into expansion slots (also known as the *expansion bus*) on the motherboard to extend the reach of the CPU. There are several types of expansion slots: ISA, MCA, EISA VLB, PCI, and PC Bus. The speed and frequency of the signals on the motherboard and the signals on the expansion bus usually do not match. Therefore, when a signal on the expansion card needs to be read by the CPU, it is translated by the **bus controller.** For example, the ISA expansion bus runs at 8.33 MHz. It therefore uses a fraction of the signal from the clock generator chip. If the clock generator chip is running at 33 MHz, the ISA bus would be running at CLKIN/4, which is equivalent to 33 MHz/4 = 8.33 MHz.

The expansion card uses hardware interrupts and DMAs to communicate with the rest of the system. **Hardware interrupts,** known as **IRQ,** consist of wires that connect the CPU, RAM, and expansion slots. When the expansion cards need the CPU to do something, a signal is sent through one of the hardware interrupt wires to get the CPU's attention. The purpose of the hardware interrupt controller is to manage the interrupts and keep track of which one has the highest priority.

Another way the expansion card moves data from one location to another is by using a **direct memory address (DMA),** which consists of wires leading from the expansion slot to the RAM. The DMA controller moves the data from an expansion card to the RAM without any direction from the CPU. The performance of the PC improves because the CPU can use the time saved to do something else.

Newer motherboards may also include a peripheral controller to control built-in serial ports, parallel ports, bus mouse ports, floppy drive connectors, and IDE hard drive connectors. In older systems, these components were installed into the PC by using expansion cards.

7.5.3 MEMORY CONTROLLER AND CACHE CONTROLLERS

Compared to the other devices, the microprocessor is the fastest component of the PC. When signals are sent between the microprocessor and the slower RAM, it is the job of the **memory controller** to translate the signals between the two. The RAM is connected to the CPU and expansion slots or ports via a data bus and address bus. The data bus carries the data while the address bus carries a signal defining the location of the data on the RAM. The memory controller translates the needed memory address and controls the address lines. In addition, the memory controller defines what capacity and type of RAM chips (standard, EDO, burst EDO, SDRAM, or other) the motherboard can use.

A second purpose of the memory controller is to provide a refresh signal every few milliseconds to the DRAM chips (RAM). DRAM chips use small capacitors within the chips to store information. A charged capacitor represents an *on* bit (switch) and a discharged capacitor represents an *off* bit (switch). Capacitors cannot hold their charge permanently. Therefore, they need to be constantly recharged so that they do not forget their content.

The **RAM cache** is ultrafast RAM that buffers the CPU and the RAM by keeping copies of instructions and data. When the CPU needs some information, it will first look in the RAM cache before searching the slower RAM. Finding the needed information in the RAM cache is much faster than searching the RAM for it, and little time is wasted if the information is not in the RAM cache. The purpose of the cache controller is to anticipate what information is needed by the CPU and to place it into the RAM cache.

7.6 MOTHERBOARD JUMPERS AND DIP SWITCHES

IBM wanted to design the IBM PC (model 5150) and IBM XT (model 5160) to be flexible and allow for growth. Consequently, IBM used expansion slots and cards to expand the system as needed. In addition, these computers could have different amounts of RAM and up to two floppy disk drives. DIP switches were used to specify the amount of RAM or the number of floppy disk drives within a system. (See fig. 7.7.)

DIP switches are small devices consisting of 4 to 12 on/off switches. The IBM PC used two banks of DIP switches (designated as switch block 1 and switch block 2); the IBM XT used one bank. Each bank consisted of 8 on/off switches. DIP switches come in two forms: sliding switches and rocker switches. To indicate which direction is on and which direction is off, the bank will be labeled on, off, open, or closed. When a switch is on, the circuit is closed, allowing current to flow. When a switch is off, the circuit is open, allowing no current to flow.

EXAMPLE 7.1 You want to install two 5¼″ floppy disk drives and you want to increase the RAM to 640 KB. In addition to physically installing the floppy drives and RAM chips, you have to change the DIP switches.

To set the floppy disk drives, you must first look at table 7.6. The settings on the floppy disk drives are located on bank 1, switches 7 and 8. The next task would be to find switch block 1 on the motherboard. After finding switch block 1, you must then set switch 7 to off and switch 8 to on. No other jumper settings are changed at this time because they are used to configure other things.

The next task is to configure the RAM. On the IBM PC, RAM consists of integrated chips (ICs) that are inserted directly into the motherboard. The IBM PC and IBM XT could accommodate four rows of nine chips, each row being a bank of RAM. To get 640 KB of RAM, you would have to have two rows consisting of 256 KB each and two rows consisting of 64 KB each. Therefore, you would have to go to switch block 1 to set switches 3 and 4 to off. This will enable all four memory banks.

FIGURE 7.7 DIP switches

TABLE 7.6 Partial listing of switch settings for the IBM PC (Model 5150)

Switch Block 1		
IBM PC Function	**Switch 1**	
Boot from floppy drive	Off	
Do not boot from floppy drive	On	
Math Coprocessor	**Switch 2**	
Installed	Off	
Not installed	On	
Installed Motherboard Memory	**Switch 3**	**Switch 4**
Bank 0	On	On
Bank 0 and 1	Off	On
Bank 0, 1, and 2	On	Off
All 4 banks	Off	Off
Video Adapter Type	**Switch 5**	**Switch 6**
Monochrome (MDA)	Off	Off
Color (CGA)—40×25 mode	Off	On
Color (CGA)—80×25 mode	On	Off
Any video card w/onboard BIOS (EGA/VGA)	On	On
Number of Floppy Drives	**Switch 7**	**Switch 8**
1 floppy drive	On	On
2 floppy drives	Off	On

Switch Block 2								
	Switch Number							
Memory	**1**	**2**	**3**	**4**	**5**	**6**	**7**	**8**
16 KB	On	On	On	On	On	Off	Off	Off
32 KB	On	On	On	On	On	Off	Off	Off
64 KB	On	On	On	On	On	Off	Off	Off
128 KB	On	Off	On	On	On	Off	Off	Off
192 KB	On	On	Off	On	On	Off	Off	Off
224 KB	Off	On	Off	On	On	Off	Off	Off
256 KB	On	Off	Off	On	On	Off	Off	Off
320 KB	On	On	On	Off	On	Off	Off	Off
384 KB	On	Off	On	Off	On	Off	Off	Off
448 KB	On	On	Off	Off	On	Off	Off	Off
480 KB	Off	On	Off	Off	On	Off	Off	Off
512 KB	On	Off	Off	Off	On	Off	Off	Off
576 KB	On	On	On	On	Off	Off	Off	Off
608 KB	Off	On	On	On	Off	Off	Off	Off
640 KB	On	Off	On	On	Off	Off	Off	Off

FIGURE 7.8 Motherboard jumpers

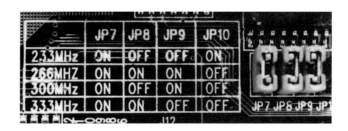

	JP7	JP8	JP9	JP10
233MHz	ON	OFF	OFF	ON
266MHZ	ON	ON	ON	OFF
300MHz	ON	OFF	ON	OFF
333MHz	ON	ON	OFF	OFF

Lastly, you need to tell the system how much RAM it actually has. As you can see by looking at the configuring tables, to get 640 KB of RAM, you must find switch block 2 on the motherboard. On switch block 2, you would then set switch 1 to on, switch 2 to off, switches 3 and 4 to on, and switches 5, 6, 7, and 8 to off. Again, the other switches should be left alone.

The designers of the 386 and 486 computers tried to make their motherboards even more flexible. Some of these motherboards could accommodate several different types of micro-processors running at different speeds and having different amounts of RAM cache.

DIP switches are no longer used on today's motherboards to specify the number of floppy drives or the amount of RAM a PC has. Instead, this is done electronically by running a CMOS setup program from a floppy disk (AT and early 386 computers) or from the system ROM BIOS. To configure these motherboards, **jumpers** (sometimes called *shunts*) are used. A jumper is a small, plastic-covered metal clip that is used to connect two pins protruding from the motherboard. The jumper (which is the same as an on switch) closes the circuit, allowing current to flow. (See fig. 7.8.) Some motherboards now use the CMOS setup program in place of the jumpers to specify the CPU speed, the amount of RAM cache, port settings (COMX and LPTX), and drive controller settings.

7.7   CMOS RAM

The PC tests the major components of the PC during boot-up. In order to properly test a computer, the PC needs to know what there is to test (the amount of RAM, the number of floppy drives, the presence of a math coprocessor, the type of monitor, and so forth). Therefore, the PC must have this information available during boot-up.

As mentioned, when the IBM PC was released in 1981, the computer had two sets of eight DIP switches that defined the system configuration information. When the IBM XT was introduced, only one set of eight DIP switches was needed. As new technology became available, newer systems had more options available. A system with more options required more DIP switches, which meant the motherboards had more complicated designs and configurations. To make things worse, DIP switches would occasionally fail simply because they are small mechanical devices.

Starting with the IBM AT, IBM replaced the DIP switches with a special chip that combined 64 bytes of **CMOS RAM** with a **real-time clock.** CMOS chips (such as MC146818) operate at 3.3 volts, which consumes less power than the older TTL chips. The real-time clock keeps track of the time and date. (See fig. 7.9.)

> **Question:** Why does the computer care what time it is?
>
> **Answer:** The computer does not actually care; it has no understanding of date or time. However, date and time can be used by the operating systems and application programs. Operating systems use the date and time to time-stamp each file to indicate when it was created and last edited. In addition, some programs can use the date and time within a document, keep track of appointments, or automatically time-stamp activities involving a database.

The RAM portion of the chip holds the basic system configuration. As motherboards have become more complicated by the addition of more configuration options, the size of the CMOS RAM chip has had to be increased. (See fig. 7.10.)

To change the configuration options contained in the CMOS RAM, you must run a **CMOS setup program.** At the time the IBM AT was introduced, the CMOS setup

FIGURE 7.9 Dallas CMOS with real-time clock next to the Award system ROM BIOS

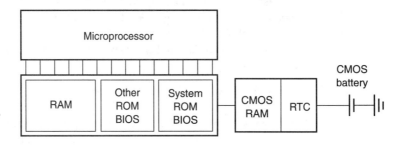

FIGURE 7.10 The micro-processor communicates with different forms of memory, including the system ROM BIOS. The CMOS RAM (powered by a CMOS battery) stores the hardware configuration information.

program was kept on a floppy disk. Unfortunately, if the floppy disk configuration was incorrect, accessing the disk to run the setup program might not be possible. The CMOS setup program could not be kept in the RAM (including the CMOS RAM) because if power is discontinued to RAM, the contents will disappear, losing the setup program. Therefore, the CMOS setup program was placed in the system ROM BIOS.

Question: If the CMOS setup program is stored in the system ROM BIOS, why can't the configuration information be stored in the system ROM BIOS?

Answer: The configuration information can't be stored in the system ROM BIOS because the system ROM BIOS is a permanent form of memory. Therefore, if a second floppy drive is added or a hard drive replaced, the configuration information could not be changed.

7.8   CMOS BATTERY

The configuration information is stored in CMOS, a special form of RAM. When you disconnect the power from the RAM, it will forget its content. Yet, when you turn the system on later, the PC still remembers the configuration information and the clock still has the correct date and time. This is because the CMOS chip is connected to a battery, which keeps the CMOS circuit powered while the PC is off. This battery is often referred to as the **CMOS battery.**

The most common batteries used in the PC are lithium and nickel-cadmium (NiCd). (See fig. 7.11.) Lithium batteries are small and light and offer a high energy density. When used as a CMOS battery, they last up to five years. NiCd batteries don't last as long as

FIGURE 7.11   Common CMOS batteries

152

FIGURE 7.12 External battery pack

FIGURE 7.12 External battery pack

lithium batteries but can be recharged every time you turn on your computer. Both types of batteries usually do not leak, which could damage other PC components.

Three types of CMOS batteries are available: the coin cell, the battery pack, and the soldered battery. Coin cells are disc-like batteries that resemble a coin. The external battery pack is connected to the motherboard via a four-prong connector. (See fig. 7.12.) The soldered battery is permanently soldered onto the motherboard. When replacing a battery, you must match not only the battery type but also the voltage. The batteries used in PCs are normally either 3.6 V, 4.5 V, or 6 V. Another important issue when replacing the batteries is to make sure that the polarity is correct. If the battery is connected backwards, it will damage the CMOS RAM chip. Since the CMOS RAM chip is soldered onto the motherboard, this could be an expensive mistake.

When the CMOS battery is replaced or when the motherboard is removed, the information in the CMOS RAM will usually be lost. Therefore, *it is recommended that all the CMOS configuration information stored in the CMOS RAM be recorded by using the CMOS setup program.*

A few newer systems don't require a CMOS battery. Some of these systems have a special capacitor that automatically recharges any time the system is plugged in. If the system is unplugged, the capacitor will power the CMOS RAM chip for up to a week or more. If the system remains unplugged for a long time, the CMOS RAM information will be lost. Fortunately, the contents of the CMOS RAM can be restored from a backup copy kept in a flash ROM chip. Other systems contain a CMOS chip (such as those produced by Dallas Semiconductor Corporation) that includes nonvolatile SRAM technology (low-power SRAM and a tiny lithium battery) that does not require an external battery.

7.9 CMOS SETUP PROGRAM

The CMOS setup program, which is stored in the system ROM BIOS, varies greatly from computer to computer. Even PCs from the same manufacturer containing a CPU and system ROM BIOS made by the same supplier may also have major differences.

To access the CMOS setup program, you need to know which keys to press and when to press them. Most systems will display on the screen during boot-up how to enter the CMOS setup program. AMI BIOS and other systems will display a "Hit <DEL> if you want to run SETUP" message. (See fig. 7.13.) Therefore, when this message is displayed, you will press the DEL key. Often, these systems include the option of enabling or disabling the message. If the message is not displayed, the best time to press the DEL key is when the memory is counting.

FIGURE 7.13 Boot-up screen of PC using AMI BIOS. Note the instructions to press the DEL key to enter the CMOS setup program.

```
PhoenixView(tm) VGA-Compatible BIOS Version B 1.00 07
Copyright © 1984-1990 Phoenix Technologies Ltd.
All Rights Reserved

ROM BIOS © 1995 American Megatrends Inc.

003712


Hit <DEL>, if you want to run SETUP
```

Other ways to start the CMOS setup program might include:

- Award and Phoenix BIOS: F2, Ctrl+Alt+Esc or Ctrl+Alt+S during the POST
- Zenith machines: Ctrl+Alt+Ins
- Dell machines: Ctrl+Alt+Enter
- Some computers, such as Compaqs, IBMs, and NECs: either F1 or F10 (depending on the system ROM BIOS) while a rectangular cursor flashes during boot-up
- PS/2 uses a reference diskette to access the CMOS setup program

The best way to find out how to enter the CMOS setup program is to look either at the screen or in the documentation.

> **WARNING** Since incorrect CMOS settings can cause the computer not to run properly, record the CMOS settings before making any changes. In addition, if you don't know what a CMOS setting does, it is usually best to leave it at its default settings.

Today's setup programs include many options. To organize them, they are often grouped together. Most CMOS setup programs are menu-based, although AMI has introduced a newer GUI interface similar to Windows. (See figs. 7.14 and 7.15.) Modern PCs will include a standard CMOS setup and an advanced CMOS setup. Other commonly used options include chipset setup, power management, PCI setup, and peripherals.

Although ISA and PCI local bus are the most popular designs, there are a large number of Micro Channel (MCA) and Extended ISA (EISA) computers still being used. These systems have a sophisticated setup program that store motherboard and expansion card configurations. With these motherboards, the setup program can save the CMOS settings to a file on floppy disk so they can be restored later.

7.9.1 STANDARD CMOS SETUP

The standard CMOS setup has not changed too much through the years. It includes the information for the date, time, floppy drives, hard drives, keyboard, and video card. (See fig. 7.16.)

FIGURE 7.14 Text-based CMOS setup program main menu

```
BIOS SETUP PROGRAM - AMI BIOS SETUP UTILITIES

© 1990 American Megatrends Inc., All Rights Reserved
─────────────────────────────────────────────────────
              STANDARD CMOS SETUP
              ADVANCED CMOS SETUP
              ADVANCED CHIPSET SETUP
      AUTO CONFIGURATION WITH BIOS DEFAULTS
    AUTO CONFIGURATION WITH POWER-ON DEFAULTS
              CHANGE PASSWORD
              HARD DISK UTILITY
             AUTOSELECT HARD DRIVE
             WRITE TO CMOS AND EXIT
          DO NOT WRITE TO CMOS AND EXIT
─────────────────────────────────────────────────────
 Standard CMOS Setup for Changing Time, Date, Hard Disk Type, etc.

      Esc: Exit  Sel:      F2/F3: Color  F10: Save & Exit
```

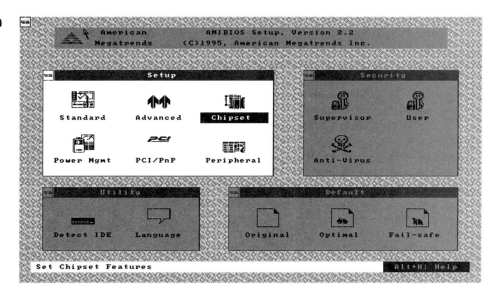

Date and Time

The time and date appear at the top of the standard CMOS setup screen. The date and time
displayed in the setup program is the date and time in the real-clock chip. It can be changed
with the setup program, with commands (DOS's DATE and TIME commands), or with a
GUI interface (Windows' Control Panel). (Note: Most modern system ROM BIOSes account for daylight savings time.)

Hard Drive

The next set of options is the hard disk settings, which must define the parameters of the
hard drive. The options are hard drive type, number of cylinders, number of read/write
heads, number of sectors per track, write precompensation, and landing zone. Note: the

FIGURE 7.16 AMI standard
CMOS setup screen

BIOS SETUP PROGRAM - STANDARD CMOS SETUP

© 1990 American Megatrends Inc., All Rights Reserved

Date (mm/date/year): Tue, Jan 15, 1991   Base memory size: 640 KB

Time: (hour/min/sec): 12:24:38   Ext. memory size: 3072 KB

Daylight saving   : Disable   Cyln Head WPcom LZone Sec Size

Hard disk C: type   : 47   1024   8   0   0   57   228

Hard disk D: type   : Not Installed

Floppy drive A: : 1.44 MB 3$\frac{1}{2}$"

Floppy drive B: : 1.2 MB 5$\frac{1}{4}$"

Primary Display   : VGA/EGA

Keyboard   : Not Installed

Sun	Mon	Tue	Wed	Thu	Fri	Sat
30	31	1	2	3	4	5
6	7	8	9	10	11	12
13	14	15	16	17	18	19
20	21	22	23	24	25	26
27	28	29	30	31	1	2
3	4	5	6	7	8	9

Month	: Jan, Feb,...Dec
Date	: 01, 01, 03,...31
Year	: 1901, 1902,...2099

ESC: Exit   :Select F2/F3: Color PU/PD: Modify

standard CMOS setup screen shows only two hard drives. Newer system ROM BIOSes may show four types because enhanced IDE can have up to four hard drives.

The hard drive types are disk parameters predefined in the system ROM BIOS. The type, number of cylinders, number of read/write heads, number of sectors per track, and other parameters are automatically set. For example, if you select a type 1, you will get the following information:

```
Type    Cylinders    Heads    Write Precomp    LZ    Capacity (MB)
 1         306          4          128         305        10
```

There is a limited number of drive types, but there is literally an unlimited number of drives with different CMOS parameters. Instead of making more drives, companies created a user-definable type. By selecting type 47 or type 48, you could then input the rest of the hard drive parameters. The number of cylinders, number of read/write heads, and number of sectors per track, multiplied together, define the number of sectors. The computer than takes the number of sectors times the 512 bytes per sector to determine the capacity. Write precompensation and landing zone are not usually defined on today's hard drives. SCSI hard drives are a little different. When installing a SCSI hard drive, the CMOS is set to No Hard Drive Defined. The BIOS on the SCSI controller card and the firmware on the hard drive run the hard drive.

If you do not enter the correct hard disk information in the CMOS setup program, the hard drive may not boot and the information may not be accessible. Common error messages include "Missing Operating System" and "Drive C Error." In addition, you could permanently damage the hard drive. When working inside a system, it a very good idea to record the CMOS parameters before opening the system.

Some setup programs feature a hard drive autodetect feature. This feature will automatically look in the firmware of the hard drive and set the CMOS accordingly.

Floppy Disk Drives

The floppy drives define the type of floppy disks to be used. The choices include 1.44 MB, 720 KB, 1.2 MB, and 360 KB; newer systems include 2.88 MB. If the wrong type of drive is selected, the drive may not function and you may get an "FDD Controller Failure" or similar message.

Video and Keyboard

The monitor type is always set to EGA/VGA. Other choices include monochrome and CGA, which are extremely outdated. Keyboard options are "installed" and "not installed," which determine whether a keyboard is looked for during boot-up.

7.9.2   ADVANCED CMOS SETUP AND ADVANCED CHIPSET SETUP

The advanced CMOS setup and advanced chipset setup are used to fine-tune the hardware setup of the system. Hardware differs from computer to computer, so these options also are differ. Most of these settings are used to enable or fine-tune the cache system, memory system, or I/O system. (See tables 7.7, 7.8, 7.9, and 7.10.)

TABLE 7.7　General settings

Setting	Description
System boot-up Num Lock	When this option is set to off, the Num Lock key will be off automatically after boot. Therefore, you can use the arrow keys on both the numeric keypad and the keyboard. When the option is off, the keypad can be used for quick number input.
Numeric processor test	Although this is not needed for newer PCs, when enabled it will test the math coprocessor during boot-up.
CPU speed	Since many motherboards can accommodate different CPU speeds, some use the CMOS setup program to specify the speed rather than jumpers on the motherboard. Unfortunately, if you set the CPU speed too fast, it may burn out the microprocessor. Some people may also tell you that you can increase the microprocessor a little. Although this may work with some microprocessors, it will shorten the lifespan of others and may introduce errors.
Boot-Up sequence	This option sets the sequence of boot drives. The standard boot sequence is the A drive followed by the C drive. With this option, you can change the sequence to the C drive followed by the A drive. Note: Newer setup programs allow booting from CD-ROM drives, LS-120 drives, and Zip drives.
Password checking option	These options are Disable, Always, and Setup. When set to the Always option, the system will prompt for a password during the POST. The setup password option means the system will prompt for a password when the user accesses the CMOS setup program.
Antivirus	When enabled, this option will issue a warning when anything attempts to write to the boot sector of the hard disk drive. When the warning is issued, you must then determine if you are writing to the boot sector or whether it is a virus.

TABLE 7.8　Cache memory settings

Setting	Description
Cache memory	One option is to disable the cache, enable the internal L1 (CPU) cache, enable the external L2 (motherboard) cache, or enable both caches. Another option is to have separate controls for the internal and external cache. Both of these include options for WriteBack and WriteThru options.
Cache timing	This option determines the speed that the chipset will use for reading data from the external (level 2) cache. It usually appears in the form x-y-y-y (for example: 3-1-1-1). The x is the number of clock cycles to read the first 64-bit value from the RAM cache, and the y is the number of clock cycles to read the next three sequential values in the RAM cache. In general, the lower these numbers, the faster your system will be. If the values are too fast, you may experience system problems.
Level 2 cache size	Some older motherboards have a specific setting to indicate how much level 2 cache you have on your motherboard. Most newer motherboards automatically detect the amount of RAM cache.
Level 2 cacheable DRAM size/Cache over 64 MB of DRAM	This setting determines how much of the RAM is cache by the size of the level 2 cache. For best performance, the value should be set to the total amount of RAM in the system. Note: This setting will not be present on Pentium Pro motherboards because the Pentium Pro processor uses an integrated level 2 cache.

TABLE 7.9   Memory Settings

Setting	Description
System ROM shadow/System BIOS cacheable	When this option is enabled, it copies the system ROM BIOS chip into the RAM so that it will be accessed from the faster RAM. Normally, this option should be enabled unless a problem is fixed by turning it off.
Video ROM shadow/Video BIOS cacheable	When this option is enabled, it copies the video ROM BIOS chip into the RAM so that it will be accessed from the faster RAM. Normally, this option should be enabled unless a problem is fixed by turning it off.
ROM BIOS shadow	When these options are enabled, they will copy the ROM BIOS chips found on expansion cards into the RAM so that they will accessed from the faster RAM. Normally, this option should be enabled for cards using ROM BIOS chips. Therefore, you must know the memory addresses used by the expansion cards.
Wait states	Each wait state slows the CPU one clock cycle so that slower RAM can function properly. The fastest setting would be no wait states.
Turn-around insertion	This option inserts a wait state between consecutive DRAM read cycles. For best performance, this option should be disabled, unless wait states are needed to prevent system problems. Note: This setting is normally controlled by the dynamic automatic timing setting.
RAM access time or DRAM read timing/DRAM burst read timing/DRAM read wait states or DRAM write timing/DRAM burst write timing/DRAM write wait states	These settings determine how many clock cycles it takes to access RAM. Examples would be 5-5-5-5, 5-2-2-2, 4-1-1-1, etc. The first number is the number of clock ticks it takes to access a storage cell within the RAM. The next three numbers indicate the number of clock ticks it takes to access data if storage cells are sequential to the first storage cell. Again, if the speed is set too fast, the PC may not boot, memory errors may occur, or the PC may lock up often.
Parity checking	Some systems have RAM with 9 bits per byte, while others have 8 bits per byte. Eight bits represent a byte of data. If a ninth (parity) bit is used, it is for error control. Note: If the RAM does not have parity capability and the parity option is turned on, the system will experience parity error.
DRAM parity/ECC mode	To check the integrity of memory, some systems will use parity checking or ECC error detection/correction mode. If the system supports both, you can select Parity, ECC, or None. Note: The parity setting is ignored if parity checking is disabled.
Dynamic automatic timing	If the system is set to Auto, the chipset will detect the type of memory and cache during POST and dynamically set all the timings automatically. Other chipsets let you choose a common memory speed (such as 60 or 70 ns) or a memory type (such as FPDRAM or EDO). Note: If the memory chips are of different speeds, the slower memory should be in the first bank. Otherwise, the system may set the RAM speed too fast for the slower RAM chips.
DRAM speculative leadoff	When enabled, this option reduces first access of system memory because the memory controller will start the initial read request before the address for the read has been completely resolved. Normally, this option should be enabled unless it causes system problems. Note: This setting is normally controlled by the dynamic automatic timing setting.
DRAM R/W leadoff timing	This setting controls how many clock cycles are required for the first access to memory during a four-read burst. On some systems, this setting will refer to the actual number of clock cycles used for the first acess, while others will be the additional cycle required for the first access. The lower this setting, the faster the system will work. If this setting is too low, the system may experience some problems.
Memory hole	Some expansion cards require access to particular memory addresses in order to function properly. This option lets you reserve the appropriate memory area for these cards. The typical memory areas that can be set aside are 512–640 KB and 15–16 MB. The default setting is Disabled.

TABLE 7.10 Bus settings

Setting	Description
Bus clock	Some ISA systems allow you to adjust the clock speed of their expansion buses although the default clock speed is 8.33 MHz. In a CPU that runs at 33 MHz, you would set the clock speed to CLOCKIN/4, which implies one-quarter the microprocessor clock speed. Higher speeds, which have a lower divisor (such as CLOCKIN/3, giving a clock speed of 11 MHz), will usually deliver better performance, but some expansion cards may not adjust to the faster speed.
ISA (or AT bus) clock speed/ Divisor	This setting controls the speed of the ISA bus. Options will include the speed in MHz (such as 6 MHz or 8 MHz) or the fraction of the PCI clock speed (such as PCICLK/3, PCICLK/4 or PCICLK/6). The accepted standard maximum speed for the ISA bus is 8.33 MHz.
8-Bit I/O recovery time and 16-bit I/O recovery time	This setting allows additional clock cycles to be inserted after an ISA I/O request, which is sometimes needed to slow the processor after completing activity on the ISA bus. The default setting for this is usually 1 cycle.
Peer concurrency	When enabled, this setting allows multiple PCI devices to be active at the same time. The default for this setting is Enabled.

7.9.3 MISCELLANEOUS CMOS SETUP PROGRAM OPTIONS

TABLE 7.11 Miscellaneous settings

Setting	Description
Power management	Power management includes several options designed to extend the battery life of notebook computers. Some options control how many minutes of nonuse before the monitor shuts off and the hard drive winds down. When these features are enabled, they may slow the PC.
Peripheral setup	Onboard floppy disk drives, parallel ports, and serial ports can be disabled or configured using the CMOS setup program. This includes defining the IRQ and I/O addresses. In addition, parallel ports can be configured to be normal, bidirectional, EPP, or ECP.
PCI control/Plug and play	These options will enable the plug-and-play features and will enable or disable PCI expansion slots. In addition, they will define the IRQ and DMA, which the PCI slots use. Other options may enable or disable built-in IDE controller cards.

Note: For more information on particular CMOS setup settings, refer to the following websites:
BIOS Survival Guide   http://www.lemig.umontreal.ca/bios/bios_sg.htm
WIM's BIOS Page   http://www.ping.be/bios/

7.9.4 BIOS DEFAULTS AND POWER-ON DEFAULTS

The BIOS defaults and power-on defaults are used to automatically set the CMOS settings. When the BIOS defaults are chosen, the CMOS settings will be optimized for the quickest speed possible. When the power-on defaults are selected, the CMOS will be set to the most conservative settings. Although the conservative settings are slower, this may allow some hardware to function that did not function under the BIOS defaults. Systems with the CMOS setup program that have the GUI interface call these optimal and fail-safe BIOS setup settings. They are designated by a rabbit and a turtle icon.

Question: A user sets the password option to Always so that whenever the computer is turned on, it will ask for the password. Unfortunately, the user forgot the password. What can you do?

Answer: To remove the password, you need to remove or short out the battery while the computer is off. Unfortunately, this will remove all the contents of the CMOS RAM, so they will have to be reentered. To erase the contents of the CMOS RAM, you would do one of the following:

1. If there is a coin package battery, remove it and let the computer sit without the battery for 15 to 30 minutes.
2. If you have access to the motherboard documentation, look for a password or CMOS jumper. Remove the jumper, then put the jumper back in place.
3. If there is a soldered-in battery, there should be a four-prong jumper connecting to an external battery pack. Remove the jumper for 15 to 30 minutes.
4. If you cannot find a jumper next to the soldered-in battery, use a wire to short both ends of the battery for 30 seconds.

7.10 YEAR 2000 PROBLEM

The Year 2000 problem is a programming problem involving programs that are not written to handle dates for the year 2000 and beyond. The most common and most potentially damaging problem arises from software that has been written to store or manipulate dates using only two digits for the year. Therefore, the software will store the date for the year 2001 as 01, which will be later interpreted as 1901. In addition to programs using only two digits to keep track of the year, some programs are not written to recognize the year 2000 as a leap year.* These programs cause all dates following February 29, 2000, to be offset incorrectly by one day. Table 7.12 lists some websites where you can find more information on the Year 2000 problem.

TABLE 7.12 Information on the Year 2000 problem

Source	Website
Microsoft	**Home:** http://www.microsoft.com **Year 2000 Product Guide:** http://www.microsoft.com/technet/topics/year2k/product/ product.htm **Microsoft Year 2000 Resource Center:** http://www.microsoft.com/technet/topics/year2k/default.htm
The Year 2000 Information Center	http://www.year2000.com/

7.11 TROUBLESHOOTING THE MOTHERBOARD AND MOTHERBOARD SUPPORT CHIPS

Since the motherboard contains the majority of the system components and acts as the central point of connection, it is a suspect in every problem that you encounter. To help eliminate the motherboard as a suspect, the system ROM BIOS is written to test each major component on the motherboard during boot-up. The testing doesn't eliminate the motherboard as the source of a problem, but it does help to identify obvious problems with the motherboard. When an error code or message indicates that the motherboard is faulty or that one of the support chips on the motherboard is faulty, it means only that a specific response to a code sent out to test the component was expected back. The problem may be in the device actually tested or in some other, related device.

Troubleshooting individual components on the motherboard is usually quite difficult and can be done only by an experienced electronics technician. Motherboards contain several layers of metal traces (metal trails acting as electrical wires to connect to the different components), and it is impossible to peel apart the layers to get to the metal traces. In ad-

*Years evenly divisible by four are normally leap years, *unless* they are also evenly divisible by 100. However, if the year is evenly divisible by 400, that "overrides" the 100 rule, and it is a leap year.

TABLE 7.13 Common mother-board manufacturers

Manufacturer	Website
American Megatrends	**Home:** http://www.megatrends.com **Technical support:** http://www.megatrends.com/
ASUS	**Home:** http://www.asus.com **Product information:** http://www.asus.com/products.asp
First International Computer	**Home:** http://www.fica.com/
Giga-Byte Technology	**Home:** http://www.giga-byte.com **Technical Support:** http://www.giga-byte.com/support.html
Intel Corporation	**Home:** http://www.intel.com **Motherboards:** http://developer.intel.com/design/motherbd/index.htm **Motherboard manuals:** http://www.x86.org/intel.doc/IntelMotherBoards.html
Micronics Computers	**Home:** http://www.micronics.com **Product:** http://www.micronics.com/micronics/products/index.asp **Support:** http://www.micronics.com/micronics/support/index.html
Supermicro Computer, Inc.	**Home:** http://www.supermicro.com **Technical support:** http://www.supermicro.com/TechSupport.htm
Tyan Computer	**Home:** http://www.tyan.com

Note: For other motherboard manufacturers, Intel and ASUS manuals, and identifying motherboards using the Award and AMI BIOS ID number, consult the following website: http://www.sysopt.com/mboard.html.

dition, most of the time you do not have electronic diagrams of the motherboard, nor do you usually have replacement parts. Also, the majority of the components on the motherboard are soldered to it using surface mount technology. Special equipment and skill are required to desolder and solder surface mount chips. For all these reasons, it is not worth the time and effort to find the problem and fix it; the motherboard should just be replaced. Table 7.13 lists useful web addresses for several motherboard manufacturers.

Of course, before throwing the motherboard away, you should still check for the obvious things. First, make sure that everything is connected properly, particularly the ribbon cables and the power connectors (P8 and P9 should have the grounds next to each other—black to black). In addition, check the voltage levels of the power supply and make sure that none of the expansion cards is causing a short or overload. Next, make sure the microprocessor is inserted properly and that the proper speed and voltage have been selected for it by checking the settings for the DIP switches and the positions of the jumpers on the motherboard or by using the CMOS setup program.

Problems may also have been caused by inserting the motherboard without properly using the white spacers. The spacers prevent the motherboard from shorting out against the metal case. A foreign object, such as a screw or paper clip, may have fallen into the case. Loosen the motherboard mounting screw that holds the motherboard in place. If after loosening it the problem goes away, the overtight screw was causing some part of the motherboard to short against something.

EXAMPLE 7.2 You turn on the computer and nothing happens. The fan does not spin and no lights come on in the front.

First, make sure that the power cord is connected, the power cord is good, and the outlet is supplying power. Shut off the computer and open the case to check for the obvious: all the connectors are attached correctly (especially the ribbon cables and the power cables) and no foreign objects are in the case. After checking this make sure the power supply is good and that there is a load on the power supply. (For more information on power supplies, see chapter 9.)

Next, you need to figure out which component is preventing the computer from starting. Remove all of the nonessential expansion cards and leave the video card and disk drive controller card in the case. If the system starts, then one of the removed expansion cards was causing a short or overload. Identify the faulty card by inserting them in the system one at a time. If none of the cards is faulty, the problem has to be the motherboard, the video card, or the disk controller card.

Remove the disk controller card; if the computer starts to boot, then one of the drives or the controller card itself was causing the short. If the machine still doesn't work, the problem has to do with either the video card or the motherboard. If the video card is not part of the motherboard, the next step would be to replace the video card with a known good video card. If the system boots, the video card that you removed was faulty; if it still doesn't work, it is the motherboard.

To narrow down the source of the problem even further, first make sure the motherboard is placed in the case properly and then remove its mounting screw. If the problem goes away, the mounting screw was causing a short on the motherboard. If the problem still occurs, it has to do with the motherboard itself, the microprocessor, or the RAM. The easiest thing to check is the RAM. Replace the first bank of RAM and see if the machine will boot. If the microprocessor is not soldered to the motherboard, try replacing the microprocessor. If the problem still occurs, you are left only with the motherboard, which will have to be replaced.

EXAMPLE 7.3   You get an error code or message indicating a BIOS ROM checksum error.

During boot-up and when using a software diagnostic package, a checksum (a mathematical computation) is performed on the ROM contents and compared with a number stored within the ROM chip. If the two numbers are equal, then the ROM is considered good. If the two numbers are not equal, the error message appears. To fix the problem, the ROM chip will have to be replaced with one that matches the motherboard, or the entire motherboard will have to be replaced.

EXAMPLE 7.4   You get an error message that says your CMOS battery is low, the date and time are off, or you have invalid settings in the CMOS setup program.

This indicates that the CMOS battery, for some reason, lost its charge. If you were working within the computer, it is very possible that you shorted out the CMOS battery. This usually happens when you remove and replace motherboards. All that you have to do is reset the settings in the CMOS setup program.

If the computer uses a NiCd battery, which requires recharging, and it has not been turned on for several weeks, the battery ran out of power. Again, reset the settings in the CMOS setup program and leave the computer on for several hours so that the battery can be fully recharged.

If the problem still exists or occurs often, either the battery or the motherboard is the source. A lithium battery (coin or battery pack) is easily replaced. If the battery is a NiCd battery soldered unto the motherboard, it is best to purchase an external battery pack. If the problem still exists after replacing the battery, replace the motherboard.

EXAMPLE 7.5   The CMOS information has been erased and you do not know the correct settings for the hard drive. Trying settings that are not the same as the original ones gives a "Drive C Failure" error message and the hard drive will not boot.

The hard drive was originally prepared (partitioned and formatted) with certain parameters in the CMOS. Therefore, if the CMOS parameters are later changed for some reason, the drive may not boot and may not be accessible. The only way to fix this and access the information is to enter the same parameters as before. If you don't know what those parameters were, you will probably need to reprep the drive. This means you will have to repartition and reformat the drive. Unfortunately, this will erase all of the existing data.

EXAMPLE 7.6   After having some jumpers and DIP switches on the motherboard adjusted or some of the CMOS settings changed, the computer does not boot.

This problem is usually caused by trying to improve performance by adjusting the wait states, bus speed, clock speed, or RAM settings. If you were working on the motherboard, put the jumpers back to where they were originally. If you don't know what the original positions were, consult the motherboard manual to figure out the correct settings. If you were making changes in the CMOS setup program, restore the original settings. If you don't know what the original settings were, the best approach would be to set the BIOS defaults or the power-on defaults. Try the BIOS defaults first since they will give the quickest speed. If this doesn't work, then try the power-on defaults. If this works, then you can proceed to change the settings one at a time to achieve the most speed possible for the system.

SUMMARY

1. Motherboards are large printed circuit boards made of glass-epoxy layers. They contain metal traces instead of wires to connect a large array of electronic circuits and devices.
2. Motherboards come in several different physical dimensions and sizes known as *form factors*. The common form factors include full-size AT, Baby AT, ATX, mini-ATX, LPX, and mini-LPX.
3. Read-only memory (ROM), also known as *firmware*, is considered a permanent form of memory that contains software (instructions).
4. Erasable programmable ROM (EPROM) can be erased with ultraviolet light so that it can be reused.
5. Flash ROM, rewritable ROM that retains its contents even without power, is used within plug-and-play systems and as ROM BIOS chips.
6. Basic input/output system (BIOS) chips include special instructions that control the hardware.
7. The primary ROM BIOS chip is the system ROM BIOS, which controls the boot-up procedure and hardware, provides compatibility between the operating system and the hardware, finds the sector/boot files to boot an operating system, and stores the CMOS setup program.
8. Every system has a minimum of two other ROM chips, the video ROM BIOS, which controls the video system, and the keyboard ROM BIOS, which controls the keyboard.
9. The system ROM BIOS uses other ROM BIOS chips found on expansion cards to supplement itself.
10. CMOS RAM is used to store hardware configuration information. The contents are changed using a CMOS setup program.
11. Since CMOS RAM is RAM, it uses a battery to keep the chip powered while the PC is off.
12. Motherboard chipsets consist of the additional chips on the motherboard that allow the CPU to communicate with the rest of the system.
13. The system clock acts as the heartbeat of the computer, keeping the chips in sync with each other.
14. The CMOS setup program is used to configure the hardware.

QUESTIONS

1. XT-type motherboards configure the amount of RAM by:
   a. setting jumpers
   b. running the CMOS setup program
   c. setting DIP switches
   d. reading a text file on the floppy drive
2. Most AT-type motherboards configure the size of the hard drives by:
   a. setting jumpers
   b. running the CMOS setup program
   c. setting DIP switches
   d. reading a text file on the floppy drive

3. After replacing a faulty motherboard to repair a computer, what is the first thing you do before returning the computer to the customer?
   a. edit the CONFIG.SYS and AUTOEXEC.BAT files
   b. repartition and reformat the hard drive
   c. run the CMOS setup program
   d. record the serial number of the motherboard
4. What type of memory is usually maintained by a battery?
   a. dynamic RAM (DRAM)   c. CMOS
   b. ROM   d. cache RAM (SRAM)
5. Flash ROM chips can be:
   a. erased when power is discontinued
   b. used as normal RAM
   c. programmed once using quick jolts of electricity
   d. upgraded as needed
6. What does BIOS stand for?
   a. beginning instruction operating system
   b. basic input/output system
   c. basic interpreter output system
   d. beginning interpreter operating system
7. Which of the following functions is performed by the system ROM BIOS? (Choose all that apply.)
   a. containing application programs
   b. controlling the POST
   c. containing the CMOS setup program
   d. containing the operating system
   e. containing the microprocessor
8. The system ROM BIOS contains which of the following?
   a. the PC's real-time clock
   b. the file allocation table for the boot device
   c. device drivers and TSRs
   d. instructions for communicating with I/O devices
9. Which of the following is not a manufacturer of system ROM BIOS?
   a. Microsoft   d. IBM
   b. Phoenix   e. HP
   c. AMI
10. Where is the system ROM BIOS chip located?
    a. on the motherboard   c. on the video card
    b. within the microprocessor   d. on an expansion card
11. What type of memory stores the BIOS?
    a. dynamic RAM (DRAM)   c. CMOS
    b. ROM   d. cache RAM (SRAM)
12. How can you disable the CMOS password in a computer that has a coin-cell CMOS battery?
    a. call the company that makes the system ROM BIOS and ask for the secret password
    b. shut off the computer
    c. disconnect the battery
    d. remove the battery
13. When shadowing is enabled in the computer's CMOS setup program:
    a. the conventional memory is moved to the top of extended memory
    b. everything in RAM is stored twice
    c. the contents of the system ROM BIOS or other ROM chips are copied into the extended memory
    d. the contents of the system ROM BIOS or other ROM chips are copied into reserve memory

14. Which component may be failing if the fan and hard drive run, yet the system appears dead? (Choose two.)
   a. the on/off switch
   b. the power supply
   c. the power cord
   d. the motherboard
   e. the RAM
15. When the computer is powered up, POST (power-on self-test) does what first?
   a. resets the CMOS RAM
   b. finds and reads the boot device
   c. resets the microprocessor and sets the program counter to F000
   d. finds and initializes the video controller
   e. resets the RTC
16. The CMOS holds only:
   a. BIOS
   b. drivers
   c. hardware commands
   d. configuration data
17. The following process determines the amount of memory present, the date/time, and which communications ports and display adapters are installed in a PC:
   a. start-up utility test
   b. power-on self-test
   c. power-up boot process
   d. power-on start-up process
18. If the date and time clock have stopped even though the battery has been replaced, which of the following may be causing the problem?
   a. hard drive
   b. motherboard
   c. video controller
   d. keyboard controller
   e. RAM
   f. corrupted CMOS data
19. You activated the CMOS password but don't know or remember it. How can you disable the password?
   a. boot from a floppy disk and format the hard drive
   b. press Ctrl+Alt+Del to reboot the computer and enter the CMOS setup program to disable the password
   c. discharge the CMOS battery by removing the battery or by shorting the CMOS jumper
   d. enter the default password used by the manufacturer of the system ROM BIOS
20. After you upgrade the hard disk drive from 540 MB to 4 GB, you get a "Drive Mismatch Error" message during boot-up. What happened?
   a. the information stored with the CMOS setup program does not match the new hard drive
   b. the new hard drive is incompatible with the hard disk controller
   c. the system ROM BIOS does not accommodate drives over 540 MB
   d. the controller cable on the hard drive is damaged, missing, or not connected
21. What keeps the chips on the motherboard in sync with each other?
   a. the CMOS battery
   b. the clock crystal/oscillator
   c. the microprocessor
   d. the system ROM BIOS
   e. the RTC
22. The bulk of the chips on the motherboard that allow the microprocessor to communicate with the rest of the computer and determine what technology can be used are known as:
   a. the CMOS RAM
   b. the system chipset
   c. the clock crystal
   d. the RTC
23. What is most likely the problem if the system date and time seem to be always off every time you turn on your computer?
   a. faulty CMOS RAM
   b. faulty CMOS battery
   c. faulty clock crystal
   d. faulty power cable
24. The motherboard contains which of the following? (Choose all that apply.)
   a. the microprocessor
   b. expansion slots
   c. the hard drive
   d. the clock oscillator
25. Hardware error codes are generated by:
   a. the crystal oscillator
   b. RAM
   c. the system ROM BIOS
   d. video ROM BIOS
   e. CMOS

HANDS-ON EXERCISE

Exercise 1: Identifing the System ROM BIOS and CMOS Battery

1. Open the computer case and identify the system ROM BIOS.
2. Identify any VLSI chips or chipsets in the computer.
3. Determine if the motherboard has any jumpers or DIP switches. By using the motherboard manual, find out what their settings are.
4. Boot the computer and identify the system ROM BIOS during boot-up.

Exercise 2: Testing the Motherboard Components with Software Diagnostics

Test the system components.

Exercise 3: Using the CMOS Setup Program

1. Start the computer and enter the CMOS setup program.
2. If the option is available, enter the standard CMOS setup.
3. Record the hard drive and floppy drive settings. For hard drives, include the hard drive type, the number of cylinders, the number of read/write heads, and the number of sectors per track.
4. Change the A drive to a 1.44 MB disk drive and the B drive to a 1.2 MB disk drive.
5. Change the A drive and B drive back to their original settings.
6. Change drive C or the primary master to type 1.
7. Exit the CMOS setup program and save the changes. Reboot the computer. Notice the error message, if any, and check whether the hard drive boots.
8. Reboot the computer and enter the CMOS setup program. Set the hard drive parameters to a user-definable type/type 47 and set the following parameters:
   Number of cylinders: 2,700
   Number of read/write heads: 32
   Number of sectors per track: 63
9. Exit the CMOS setup program and save the changes. Reboot the computer. Notice the error message, if any, and check whether the hard drive boots.
10. Reboot the computer and enter the CMOS setup program. Reset the hard drive to its original settings. Notice the size of the drive.
11. Divide the number of cylinders by 2 and enter this number for the C drive.
12. Multiply the number of read/write heads by 2 and enter this number for the C drive. Notice the size of the drive.
13. Exit the CMOS setup program and save the changes. Reboot the computer. Notice the error message, if any, and check whether the hard drive boots.
14. Determine whether your hard drive has different addressing modes, such as normal, large, and LBA mode.
15. Find and run the HD autodetect within the CMOS setup program.
16. Exit the CMOS setup program and save the changes. Reboot the computer. Notice the error message, if any, and check whether the hard drive boots.
17. Reboot the computer and enter the CMOS setup program. Reset the hard drive to its original settings.
18. Set drive D or primary slave to a type 10.
19. Exit the CMOS setup program and save the changes. Reboot the computer. Notice the error messages, if any, and check whether the hard drive boots.
20. Reboot the computer and enter the CMOS setup program. Reset the hard drive to its original settings. Save the changes and reboot the computer.
21. Boot the computer from a floppy disk.
22. Enter the CMOS setup program. Set the boot sequence to C followed by A, which is probably under the advanced CMOS setup screen (or equivalent). Save the changes and reboot the computer with the bootable floppy disk in drive A.
23. Enter the CMOS setup program and change the boot sequence back to A followed by C.
24. Determine if your system has shadow ROM/RAM options. If the option is available and either system or video ROM chips are not shadowed, enable them.

25. If the options are available, record the settings for wait states and memory speeds.
26. If the motherboard has built-in serial ports, find and reconfigure the first serial port to COM3 with IRQ 3.
27. Change the first serial port back to COM3 and IRQ 4.
28. If the motherboard has built-in parallel ports, change the parallel port to LPT2 and reboot the computer.
29. Change the parallel port from bidirectional or normal mode to ECP mode.
30. Change the parallel port back to its original configuration.
31. If the motherboard has a built-in diskette controller, disable the diskette controller.
32. Exit the CMOS setup program and save the changes. Try to reboot from the floppy disk.
33. Reboot the computer and enter the CMOS setup program. Enable the floppy drive controller.
34. Using the CMOS setup program, make sure the RAM cache is enabled.
35. Reboot the computer and start Windows, Windows 95, or Windows 98. Time how long it takes Windows to load.
36. Using the CMOS setup program, disable the RAM cache.
37. Reboot the computer and start Windows, Windows 95, or Windows 98. Time how long it takes Windows to load.
38. Using the CMOS setup program, enable the RAM cache.
39. Activate the LOAD BIOS DEFAULT or equivalent. View the advanced CMOS setup and the CMOS chipset setup. Save the changes in the CMOS setup program and reboot the computer and see how long it takes to boot.
40. Enter the CMOS setup program and activate the LOAD SETUP DEFAULTS or equivalent option. Try to find at least four different options that were changed between the two defaults.
41. Save the changes in the CMOS setup program, reboot the computer, and time how long it takes to boot. Reboot the computer and see how long it takes to boot.
42. Activate the LOAD BIOS DEFAULT or equivalent.
43. Make sure the computer boots. If it doesn't boot, use the LOAD SETUP DEFAULTS and see if the problem goes away. If it does, make adjustments until you find out which parameter or parameters stopped the system from booting.

Exercise 4: Discharging the CMOS Battery

1. Enter the CMOS setup program and record the hard drive and floppy drive settings. For hard drives, include the hard drive type, the number of cylinders, the number of read/write heads, and the number of sectors per track.
2. Enter the CMOS setup program and change the CMOS setup program to PC.
3. Reboot the computer and notice what happens during boot-up.
4. Shut off the computer. Using a voltmeter, measure the voltage of the CMOS battery.
5. If it is a removable battery, remove the battery. After a couple of minutes, reinstall the battery. If the battery is soldered onto the motherboard, discharge the battery.
6. Start the computer and record any messages that may appear.
7. Enter the CMOS setup program and reenter the CMOS information.

8 The Expansion Slots and Cards

INTRODUCTION

The expansion slot, also known as the I/O bus, extends the reach of the microprocessor so that it can communicate with peripheral devices. They are called expansion slots *because they allow the system to be expanded by the insertion of circuit boards, called* expansion cards, *into the motherboard. When an I/O device (including expansion cards) is installed into a system, it must not use the same resources allocated to another device. If it does, the two cards will most likely not work properly or at all. Therefore, when installing an expansion card, you must be familiar with the different types of expansion slots and be able to configure the expansion card using jumpers, DIP switches, and software. Consequently, you must be able to interpret the documentation that comes with the PC and expansion card.*

OBJECTIVES

1. Explain the purpose of the expansion slot and card.
2. List and describe the resources used by an expansion card.
3. List the different methods of configuring an expansion card.
4. Configure an expansion card for use within a PC using its documentation.
5. Determine which resources are free by using software diagnostic packages.
6. Identify a particular expansion slot.
7. List the different types of expansion slots and describe their characteristics.
8. Describe how plug-and-play systems work.
9. List the different methods of locating documentation if documentation is not available for an expansion card.
10. Locate and correct the problem of a failed expansion card within a system.

8.1 MOTHERBOARD DESIGN

When the IBM PC was being designed in 1981, two major motherboard designs were being used: the single-board design and the bus-oriented design.

The single-board motherboard included all of the electronic devices on a single circuit board. The advantage of a single-board design was that it required less labor and fewer materials and so was cheaper to produce. In addition, since connections and slots are more prone to failure and the single-board design had fewer of them, it was considered more reliable. But that usually meant that upgrades to the system or partial failures in the board required that the entire board be replaced.

The bus-oriented design had a different approach. Instead of having one circuit board containing everything, it used one primary circuit board to connect several smaller circuit boards. The main advantage to this design was expandability, since an individual circuit board could be added or a faulty board could be replaced with a new one without affecting the rest of the boards. The disadvantage of the bus-oriented design was that it had a higher failure rate than the single-board design because it relied on connections and slots, which are more prone to failure. The bus-oriented design also cost more because it required more material and more labor to produce.

The design that IBM chose had the best features from both designs. The central part of the computer was the motherboard, which contained the essential circuitry. Expansion slots were added to it to expand the system (video cards, disk drive connectors, and other devices).

8.2 EXPANSION SLOT OPERATION

The **expansion slot,** also known as the **I/O bus,** extends the reach of the microprocessor so it can communicate with peripheral devices. Expansion slots are so named because they allow the system to be expanded by the insertion of circuits boards, called **expansion cards.** These are essential to the computer because a basic system cannot satisfy everyone's needs, and they allow the system to use new technology as it becomes available. Expansion slots consist of connectors and metal traces that carry signals from the expansion card to the rest of the computer, specifically the RAM and CPU. These connections are used for power, data, addressing, and control lines.

8.2.1 DATA BUS AND ADDRESS BUS

The primary purpose of the data and address bus slots is to carry data between the expansion cards and the CPU and RAM. The **data bus** carries the actual data between the expansion card, the RAM, and the CPU, and the **address bus** determines the memory location of the data—where the data is going to or coming from. Ideally, the size of the expansion slot's data bus should match the size of the CPU's data bus.

Much like the other digital electronic components of the PC, the expansion buses coordinate their actions with an oscillator. It requires at least two clock cycles to transfer a piece of data. The first clock cycle is used for the address bus to signify the memory address where the data is going to or coming from. After the address is sent, the data is sent along the data bus into the RAM. The data and address buses can carry only one set of signals at a time. If two signals were sent at the same time, they would collide and both would be corrupted. To prevent two devices from using the address and data buses at the same time, certain steps must be taken.

8.2.2 HARDWARE INTERRUPTS

The first method of preventing two devices from communicating at the same time is the **hardware interrupt (IRQ).** When a device needs the attention of the microprocessor, it sends a special signal to the CPU. The microprocessor recognizes only two types of interrupt. The first is microprocessor interrupts, such as divide error (when it tries to divide by zero) or a nonmaskable interrupt (used to identify RAM parity errors). The second type of interrupt understood by the CPU is connected to the interrupt controller, which branches to several other devices.

When a device (such as a modem, mouse, keyboard, hard drive controller, floppy drive controller, or sound card) needs the attention of the microprocessor, the device sends a signal through an interrupt line to the **interrupt controller.** When this happens, the CPU saves all the data located in the CPU register (small storage areas within the CPU) to a stack (area in RAM used to store the contents of the CPU). It then goes to the interrupt vector table to determine the location of the routine (stored in either a device driver or a ROM BIOS chip) that controls the device and then interacts with the device. When the CPU has completed interacting with the device, it will restore to the register the information that had been moved to the stack. The CPU can then continue with its previous task. In short, the interrupt is used to interrupt the CPU in order to complete another task.

The first two device interrupts are reserved for the system timer and the keyboard controller. IRQ 0 is controlled by the system timer, which generates a periodic interrupt at a rate of 18.2 times per second. The microprocessor uses it to keep track of the date and time and to check the status of a device, such as an alarm. IRQ 1 is used every time a key is pressed on the keyboard. The other device IRQs are wired by metal traces to the expansion bus, specifically each of the expansion slots. A single expansion card is set to use a single interrupt. When the device needs to interrupt the CPU, it sends a signal through the selected interrupt. If two devices are set to use the same interrupt, the cards will function improperly since the microprocessor will not know which device needs its attention.

The first IBM PC had eight interrupts (IRQ 0–7), which were managed by the Intel 8259 interrupt controller. Since two devices may need the CPU at the same time, interrupts are prioritized. Generally, the interrupt with a lower number has a higher priority than one with a higher number (See table 8.1.).

TABLE 8.1 XT default interrupt assignments

IRQ	Default Use	Bus Slot
0	System timer	No
1	Keyboard controller	No
2	Available	Yes
3	Serial port 2 (COM2)	Yes
4	Serial port (COM1)	Yes
5	Hard disk controller	Yes
6	Floppy disk controller	Yes
7	Parallel port 1 (LPT1)	Yes

Question: The CPU is performing a task. A device using IRQ 5 sends an interrupt signal to the CPU. As result, the CPU saves its registers to the stacks and begins interacting with the device using IRQ 5. What happens if a device using IRQ 3 sends an interrupt signal?

Answer: When an interrupt of higher priority interrupts another interrupt, the CPU must stop what it is doing to divert its attention to the second device. This is called a *nested interrupt*. The CPU then saves its registers again onto the stack. The reason they are called *stacks* is that sets of information are stacked on top of each other much like a stack of plates. If a second set of information is stacked on top of a first set of information, the second set of information must first be removed before the first set of information can be accessed.

In this example, the CPU has already put information into the stack and is working on a second task. It will stop doing the second task (device using IRQ 5) and store its information to the stack. The CPU will then interact with the device using IRQ 3. When it is done interacting with the device using IRQ 3, it will restore the information for the device using IRQ 5 and finish interacting with that device. Lastly, it will restore the last of the information kept in the stack to the CPU registers to continue working on its original task.

If too many devices are generating interrupts, the stacks can't hold all of the CPU information. As a result, operating systems such as DOS will generate an "Internal Stack Overflow" error message.

When the IBM AT with its 16-bit ISA slots was introduced, the computer had to have more interrupts. These machines (and machines since the IBM AT) had 16 interrupts (IRQ 0–15). To increase the number of interrupts without redesigning the entire motherboard, a second Intel 8259 interrupt controller (IRQ 8–15) was added by wiring IRQ 2 and IRQ 9 together. Unfortunately, this reduced the number of interrupts available by one. Since the last eight interrupts are accessed through IRQ 2, the order of priority is modified. IRQ 0 and 1 have the highest priority, followed by IRQ 8 through 15, since these all go though IRQ 2. IRQ 3–7 have the lowest priority. See table 8.2 for a description of which devices are assigned to the interrupts.

With the wide assortment of devices available, it is possible to run out of interrupts. Therefore, some bus designs allowed for interrupt sharing. Interrupt sharing allows two different devices to use the same interrupt. The interrupt-handling software or firmware

TABLE 8.2   AT default interrupt assignments

IRQ	Default Use	Bus Slot
0	System timer	No
1	Keyboard controller	No
2	2nd IRQ controller (cascade)	No
3	Serial port 2 (COM2)	Yes (8-bit)
4	Serial port 1 (COM1)	Yes (8-bit)
5	Parallel port 2 (LPT2)	Yes (8-bit)
6	Floppy disk controller	Yes (8-bit)
7	Parallel port 1 (LPT1)	Yes (8-bit)
8	Real-time clock	No
9	Available	Yes (8–16-bit)
10	Available	Yes (8–16-bit)
11	Available	Yes (8–16-bit)
12	Bus mouse (or available)	Yes (8–16-bit)
13	Math coprocessor	No
14	Primary IDE	Yes (8–16-bit)
15	Secondary IDE (or available)	Yes (8–16-bit)

distinguishes for the microprocessor which device is making the request. (Note: Unless sharing interrupts is unavoidable and only if two devices are made to be shared with each other, it is best not to have two devices use the same interrupt.)

> **NOTE**   Instead of using interrupts, data may be transferred by the microprocessor by polling. Polling is the microprocessor going to each device in turn and asking if it has anything for the microprocessor to do. Of course, this is very wasteful of clock cycles since the microprocessor is occupied with asking each device instead of doing something useful. Joysticks use polling.

8.2.3   DIRECT MEMORY ADDRESS

Direct memory address (DMA) channels are used by high-speed communication devices that must send and receive large amounts of information at high speed (sound cards, some network cards, and some SCSI cards). The DMA controller takes over the data bus and address lines to bring data from an I/O device to the RAM without any assistance or direction from the CPU. Since the CPU can perform other tasks while the data transfer is taking place, the PC performs better.

A device using a DMA address channel is very similar to a device using an IRQ. DMA lines link the DMA controller to each of the expansion slots. When a device uses DMA to transfer data using a DMA channel, it will first send a signal along a single DMA channel to the DMA controller. The DMA controller will then send a request to the CPU. When the CPU acknowledges the request, the DMA controller takes control of the data bus and the address bus. The DMA controller then sends another signal to the device, telling the device to start sending information (up to 64 KB of data). After the transfer is done, the DMA controller will release the data bus and address bus back to the CPU.

As with IRQs, devices that want to make a DMA transfer are assigned a priority level. If its DMA has a low number, it has a higher priority than a device that has a higher number. The IBM PC and IBM XT had four DMA channels when they used an 8237A DMA controller. When the AT needed more DMA channels, IBM cascaded (connected) two DMA controllers together through the DMA 4 channel, giving the IBM AT eight DMA channels, of which seven were available for use. See tables 8.3 and 8.4 for a comparison of DMA channel assignments in the XT and AT. Note that the DMA channel reserved for the

TABLE 8.3   XT default DMA assignments

DMA	Default Use	Bus Slot
0	DRAM refresh	No
1	Available	Yes
2	Floppy disk controller	Yes
3	Hard disk controller	Yes

TABLE 8.4   AT default interrupt assignments

DMA	Default Use	Bus Slot
0	Unused	Yes (8-bit)
1	Unused	Yes (8-bit)
2	Floppy disk controller	Yes (8-bit)
3	Unused	Yes (8-bit)
4	First DMA controller	No
5	Unused	Yes (16-bit)
6	Unused	Yes (16-bit)
7	Unused	Yes (16-bit)

hard drive controller in the XT was taken away in the AT. This happened because the microprocessors became faster but the speed of the DMA channels stayed at 4.77 MHz. Therefore, the hard drive (and other devices) needed a faster method of moving data.

Another difference between the XT and AT designs was the removal of the refresh function from DMA 0. The XT used DMA 0 to perform the dynamic RAM (DRAM) refresh. This was essential to the computer because the tiny capacitors in the DRAM chips used to store data would lose their charge after a short period. To prevent the loss of the DRAM contents, DMA 0 was used to recharge each capacitor cell by cell. Systems newer than the XT use other circuits to refresh the contents of DRAM.

8.2.4 BUS MASTERING

Bus mastering is the taking of temporary control of the data and address bus by an expansion card with its own processor to move information from one point to another. This makes the PC faster. This is not the same as the DMA controller taking control of the buses. If several devices try to use the data and address bus at the same time, the data being transferred would, of course, become corrupted, so the bus is managed by the integrated system peripheral (ISP) chips. As with IRQs and DMAs, the devices using the bus are assigned priorities. These are as follows:

1. RAM refresh
2. DMA transfers
3. CPU
4. Bus master expansion cards

EISA, MCA, and PCI support bus mastering.

8.2.5 I/O ADDRESSES

As the microprocessor communicates with a device, it will use either an OUT command or an IN command. The OUT command is an assembly language command used to send data or a command to an I/O device. The IN command is used to read data from the device or to check the status of a device. In either case, the IN and OUT commands must include the **I/O address,** which identifies the device. To make sure that the PC doesn't confuse an I/O address with a RAM address, a special signal is sent with the I/O address.

Each device is configured to respond to a range of addresses known as **ports.** Generally, a device will respond to a range of addresses. For example, the COM1 port responds to addresses 03F8 to 03FF, with 03F8 handling all of the data. Four of the remaining addresses are used to configure the line (speed and parity), to control the telephone (hang up and begin), to check modem status, and to perform other housekeeping tasks. (Note that the addresses are expressed in hexadecimal form.) The I/O address, therefore, is a memory address used to identify the input/output (I/O) device much like a street address identifies a house or building. Of course, no two devices can be set to use the same I/O address or range of addresses. See table 8.5 for examples of I/O addresses for various devices. Intel designed 65,536 I/O ports, each address being 16 bits long, into its microprocessors. The engineers didn't think all those ports would be needed, so they limited the usable addresses to 1,024.

8.2.6 MEMORY ADDRESSES

Many expansion cards need to use a range of **memory addresses** in the reserve memory between 640 KB and 1MB of RAM. The reserve memory will either be used as a working area for the expansion card or it will used by the ROM BIOS chips. Again, no two devices can be set to use the same memory areas.

TABLE 8.5 Common IBM PC AT I/O addresses

Hex 000-0FF for System I/O Board		Common Expansion Cards and Ports	
000-01F	DMA cntroller #1	1F0-1F8	Fixed disk
020-03F	Interrupt controller #1	200-207	Game port
040-05F	Timer	278-27F	Parallel port #2 (LPT2)
060-06F	Keyboard	2F8-2FF	Serial port #2 (COM2)
070-07F	Real-time clock, NMI mask	378-37F	Parallel printer port #1 (LPT1)
0A0-0BF	Interrupt controller #2	3B0-3BF	Monochrome display and printer adapter
0C0-0DF	DMA controller #2		
0F8-0FF	Math coprocessor	3C0-3CF	Enhanced graphics adapter
		3D0-3DF	CGA monitor adapter
		3F0-3F7	Diskette controller
		3F8-3FF	Serial port #1 (COM1)

8.2.7 POWER CONNECTIONS AND CONTROL SIGNALS

Connections essential to the expansion slots are the power connections that provide the cards with the power to operate. The power supply provides $+5$, $+12$, -5, and -12 dc voltage. Most expansion cards have either TTL chips, which use 5 volts, or CMOS chips, which use 3.3 volts. The TTL chips can use the $+5$ volts directly, but the 3.3-volt chips must use an on-board voltage regulator. A handful of devices, such as the hard drive card (expansion card with a hard drive mounted on it), use the $+12$ volts to power the drive's motor. Very few devices actually use the -5- and -12-volt power. (Note: There are several more $+5$ voltage lines than there are for the other voltage levels.)

For electricity to flow, a circuit must be a complete loop. Therefore, two wires are needed, one to send the power to the card and one to send it back (ground). Although all circuits inside the PC share a common system ground, which appears in several places, the additional ground wires are needed to allow more current to flow and reduce signal interference like crosstalk. Less interference means that engineers can design faster bus speeds.

Expansion slots also carry control signals. These can range from the system clock signal to the read/write signals that indicate if data is going from the device or to the device.

8.3 TYPES OF EXPANSION SLOTS

Through the years, several types of expansion slots have been developed. The original IBM PC used the 8-bit PC slot, and the IBM AT used the 16-bit ISA slot. Later, the micro channel architecture (MCA) and the EISA were introduced for 386 machines. Today's desktop computers use a combination of ISA slots and local bus slots (VESA and PCI); notebooks use a PC slot/CardBus slot. See table 8.6 for some common types of expansion slots.

8.3.1 PC BUS

Most technology used for personal computers in the early 1980s was based on 8-bit technology. Therefore, IBM chose the 8088 microprocessor, which had an external 8-bit data bus. This became known as the **PC slot** or the 8-bit ISA bus. (See figs 8.1 and 8.2.) Since the bus was controlled directly by the microprocessor, both ran at 4.77 MHz. To move information back and forth between the bus and the RAM or the bus and the CPU, the bus used 62 contacts, which included connections for the various data lines, address lines, power lines, IRQs, DMAs, and the various control lines. Instead of making its PC a

TABLE 8.6   Common expansion slots

Name	Date	Bus Width	Operating Speed	Maximum Bandwidth	Comments
PC Bus	1981	8	4.77 MHz	2.385 MB/s	Used in IBM PC and XT
ISA	1984	16	8.33 MHz	8.33 MB/s	Used in IBM AT
MCA	1987	32	10 MHz	20 MB/s	Used in PS/2
EISA	1988	32	8.33 MHz	16.6 MB/s	Created to compete against MCA
VL Bus	1992	32	33 MHz	105.6 MB/s	Used mostly in 486 computers
PCI*	1992	32	33 MHz	66.6 MB/s or higher (non-burst mode) 133 MB/s (burst mode)	Used in 486 and some pentium machines
PCI*	1992	64	66 MHz (or higher)	264 MB/s or higher (non-burst mode) 528 MB/s (burst mode)	Used in Pentium machines
AGP	1998	32	66 MHz (or higher)	1X - 266 MB/s 2X - 533 MB/s 4X - 1.07 GB/s	Used in newer Pentium systems
PC Card	1990	16	8 MHz	16 MB/s	Used in notebook computers
CardBus	1994	32	33 MHz	133 MB/s	Used in notebook computers

*As the PCI bus matured, the bus speed increased and is still being increased today.

FIGURE 8.1   PC slot (top), sometimes known as the 8-bit ISA slot, and the 16-bit ISA slot (bottom)

FIGURE 8.2   Expansion card used in the 8-bit PC slot

proprietary machine, IBM opened up the PC's architecture, which means it licensed the technology for a small fee. This strengthened the architecture because other companies could then produce IBM-compatible computers and develop add-on devices.

8.3.2 INDUSTRY STANDARD ARCHITECTURE (ISA) BUS

In 1984, Intel released the 286 microprocessor. The 286 used an external 16-bit data bus and a 24-bit address bus, which allowed the microprocessor to see up to 16 MB of RAM. This gave IBM two choices. First, it could choose to develop a new motherboard from scratch to take advantage of the new technology. Unfortunately, this would have meant that the large base of 8-bit cards could not be used. The second choice was to somehow modify the older design to use both the 8-bit cards and the new 16-bit cards.

IBM's solution was the IBM AT. The AT motherboard still used the older 8-bit connector to accommodate the 8-bit cards. To accommodate 16-bit cards, the 8-bit slots were extended by adding a second 36-pin connector. The second connector contained the additional data and address lines. In addition, there were five more interrupt lines and four additional DMA channels. At this time, microprocessors were getting faster. Therefore, IBM tried to increase the speed of the expansion bus to match the speed of the microprocessor but quickly discovered that some expansion boards failed at 10 MHz and most of them failed at 12 MHz. Since the expansion cards did not use chips that could transition from high to low or low to high, the new 16-bit slot stayed at the 8.33 MHz speed. Even today, computers that run at 300 MHz or faster have ISA slots that still can run only at 8.33 MHz. Because of the difference in speed between the microprocessor and the expansion bus, IBM had to use several oscillators in the AT. One oscillator was used to control the CPU speed and the other oscillator controlled the bus speed. By 1987, a committee of the Institute of Electrical and Electronic Engineers (IEEE) approved the AT bus as the **industry standard architecture (ISA).** Even though the ISA slot is considered old technology, even the most advanced motherboards contain some of them. Other names for it include the *classic bus,* the *AT bus,* or the *legacy bus.* (See fig. 8.3.)

As has been discussed, the data bus carries data back and forth between the microprocessor, RAM, and the input/output devices. The ISA slot has a total of 16 bits to match the data bus of the microprocessor. Eight data bus lines are in the first connector and eight are in the second connector. Each 16-bit line is numbered from 0 to 15. The zero indicates the least significant bit in each data transfer. To specify the location where data is going to or coming from, the connector uses the address bus. The original connector has 20 address lines and the extension connector has an additional 4 address lines. The address lines in the extension are different from the original 20 address lines because they do not latch. When an address latches, the value is held by the motherboard throughout the memory cycle. By not latching, the address is given only after the memory read or write command is given,

FIGURE 8.3   ISA card and bus

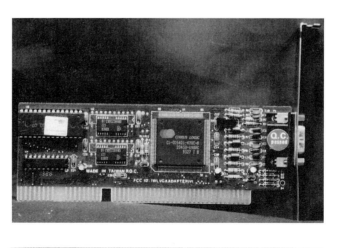

which allows faster operation on the bus. The 24 total lines are identified with the numbers 0 through 23, again with line zero being the least significant.

To read or write to memory, the microprocessor first sends the memory address through the address lines. If the microprocessor is communicating with an 8-bit card, it will send a signal down the Address Latch Enable line telling the motherboard to remember this address. Next, the microprocessor will send either a Memory Read signal or a Memory Write signal. If the Memory Read signal is sent, the memory controller enables the path to the storage cell within the RAM and sends the data to the microprocessor using the data bus. If a Memory Write signal is sent, the microprocessor sends the address followed by the data to the memory controller. It is the job of the memory controller then to store the data in the proper storage cell.

To read or write to an input/output port, the microprocessor sends an I/O Read command or an I/O Write command. When the I/O Read signal is sent, the data lines will feed directly into the microprocessor, which stores the data in a register. The I/O Write signal indicates that data is coming to an input/output device to be sent out of the output port. When a device using a DMA channel wants to send data, it will send a signal to the DMA controller. Each line is assigned a priority based on its number, with 0 having the highest priority and 7 the lowest. To indicate that the request has been received by the DMA controller, a DMA acknowledgment is sent back using a different wire. The DMA controller then tells the microprocessor to disconnect itself from the device so that it does not interfere with the transfer. When the microprocessor has been disconnected, a signal is sent along the Address Enable line. At this point, the DMA controller is controlling the data and address buses and the related control lines. Before the data is transferred, the number of bytes must be declared. The transfer then takes place, with the number of bytes transferred being counted during the transfer. When the transfer is complete, as indicated by reaching to the specified number of bytes, a Terminal Count signal is sent. Finally, the DMA controller sends a signal back to the microprocessor telling it that the DMA transfer is complete and that it is again in control of the data and address lines.

Another signal, the Refresh signal, is used to indicate the RAM is being refreshed using the data and address buses. This will prevent interruptions so that the RAM doesn't lose its contents.

Finally, the ISA bus has 11 Interrupt Request lines out of a total of 16 interrupts. Numbers 0, 1, 2, 8, and 13 are reserved for the motherboard. These lines are used by devices to signal the microprocessor to stop what it is doing and to perform a different process with the device. In addition, the ISA design allows **interrupt sharing** so that one interrupt can be used by several devices. Level-sensitive interrupt signals used in the ISA design signal the interrupt condition by shifting the voltage on the interrupt request line from high to low or low to high. It is not whether the signal is on or off, but whether it has changed that triggers the interrupt-handling software or firmware to direct the microprocessor to take action to service the device making the interrupt and to run the proper interrupt routine. The high or low level of the signal is maintained throughout the processing of the interrupt.

Several signals are used in the ISA bus to distinguish between 8-bit and 16-bit expansion cards. The first signal is the System Bus High Enable signal, which must be active for 16-bit data transfers to take place. The expansion card will use either a Memory 16-Bit Chip Select or an I/O 16-Bit Chip Select signal to indicate RAM or an I/O device. In addition, Memory Read and Memory Write signals are used for PCs running in real mode memory (which sees only up to 1 MB of RAM) and Memory Read and Memory Write signals for 16-bit transfers. Memory transfers within the 1 MB real addressing range require that both the new and old Memory Read or Write lines be activated. When a Read or Write request is made to the area above the 1 MB limit of real memory, however, only the supplementary connector Memory Read or Write lines are activated. Therefore, an 8-bit card never receives a command, nor is it able to issue one that it cannot act upon. If the data in the RAM or the input/output device is intact, a signal is sent along the I/O Channel Check line. If a parity check error occurs, than the signal is stopped. If this signal becomes grounded, the entire system will crash. When the PC is shut off or power is interrupted, a Reset signal is sent which instructs the entire system to reset or reinitialize itself. Table 8.7 lists the pin and signal connections in the ISA bus.

TABLE 8.7   ISA bus pin-out

Signal	Pin	Pin	Signal
Ground	B1	A1	−I/O Channel Check
Reset	B2	A2	Data Bit 7
+5 V dc	B3	A3	Data Bit 6
IRQ 9	B4	A4	Data Bit 5
−5 V dc	B5	A5	Data Bit 4
DMA Request 2 (DRQ 2)	B6	A6	Data Bit 3
−12 V dc	B7	A7	Data Bit 2
−0 Wait	B8	A8	Data Bit 1
+12 V dc	B9	A9	Data Bit 0
Ground	B10	A10	−I/O Channel Ready
Real Memory Write (−SMEMW)	B11	A11	Address Enable (AEN)
Real Memory Read (−SMEMR)	B12	A12	Address Bit 19
−I/O Write	B13	A13	Address Bit 18
−I/O Read	B14	A14	Address Bit 17
DMA Acknowledge 3 (−DACK 3)	B15	A15	Address Bit 16
DMA Request 3 (DRQ 3)	B16	A16	Address Bit 15
DMA Acknowledge 1 (−DACK 1)	B17	A17	Address Bit 14
DMA Request 1 (DRQ 1)	B18	A18	Address Bit 13
−REFRESH	B19	A19	Address Bit 12
Clock (8.33 MHz)	B20	A20	Address Bit 11
IRQ 7	B21	A21	Address Bit 10
IRQ 6	B22	A22	Address Bit 9
IRQ 5	B23	A23	Address Bit 8
IRQ 4	B24	A24	Address Bit 7
IRQ 3	B25	A25	Address Bit 6
DMA Acknowledge 2 (−DACK 2)	B26	A26	Address Bit 5
Terminal Count (T/C)	B27	A27	Address Bit 4
Address Latch Enable (BALE)	B28	A28	Address Bit 3
+5 V dc	B29	A29	Address Bit 2
Memory 16-Bit Chip Select (−MEM CS16)	D1	C1	−System Bus High Enable (SBHE)
I/O 16-Bit Chip Select (−I/O CS16)	D2	C2	Unlatched Address Bit 23
IRQ 10	D3	C3	Unlatched Address Bit 22
IRQ 11	D4	C4	Unlatched Address Bit 21
IRQ 12	D5	C5	Unlatched Address Bit 20
IRQ 15	D6	C6	Unlatched Address Bit 19
IRQ 14	D7	C7	Unlatched Address Bit 18
DMA Acknowledge 0 (−DACK 0)	D8	C8	Unlatched Address Bit 17
DMA Request 0 (DRQ 0)	D9	C9	Memory Read (−Mem R)
DMA Acknowledge 5 (−DACK 5)	D10	C10	Memory Write (−MEM W)
DMA Request 5 (DRQ 5)	D11	C11	Data Bit 8
DMA Acknowledge 6 (−DACK 6)	D12	C12	Data Bit 9
DMA Request 6 (DRQ 6)	D13	C13	Data Bit 10
DMA Acknowledge 7 (−DACK 7)	D14	C14	Data Bit 11
DMA Request 7 (DRQ 7)	D15	C15	Data Bit 12
+5 V dc	D16	C16	Data Bit 13
−MASTER	D17	C17	Data Bit 14
Ground	D18	C18	Data Bit 15

Since the microprocessor is faster than the bus, it can easily generate or demand more data than the bus and devices can handle. Therefore, when the I/O Channel Ready line is shut off, that tells the microprocessor to pause for one or more clock cycles. It will wait as long as the ready signal is not present. IBM specifications do not allow these delays to extend for longer than 10 clock cycles. In addition to this slow-down signal, there is a speed-up signal. The Zero Wait State signal indicates that the current bus cycle can be completed without wait states.

The ISA bus did not change significantly until 1993 when Intel and Microsoft introduced the **plug-and-play (PnP) ISA.** The PnP ISA bus allows a PnP ISA card to be inserted and its resources automatically assigned without any need to use jumpers or DIP switches to configure the card. (Note: ISA cards that are not plug-and-play are referred to as **legacy cards.**) A plug-and-play manager (software) identifies the card and assigns the resources it needs. This is possible because the PnP cards have a ROM chip that contains a number. The number identifies the type of card, not the model number, so several cards can be used within the same system, such as two network cards or two hard drive controllers. After the card is identified, the plug-and-play manager assigns the required I/O and memory addresses, IRQs, and DMAs to the card. The ISA slot, therefore, does not need to be changed physically.

8.3.3 MICRO CHANNEL ARCHITECTURE (MCA)

The 386DX was introduced in 1985. It ran at 16 MHz and used a 32-bit data bus and a 32-bit address bus. Again, IBM was faced with designing a computer that would use all of the features of the new microprocessor. In addition, the development of graphics programs made evident that video performance was becoming a major concern in PC performance. And IBM at this time was trying to regain its dominance in the PC market from companies such as Compaq. As a result, IBM introduced the PS/2. (See fig. 8.4.) On the outside, it was a sleek, modern-looking PC. On the inside, it was redesigned to accommodate the new features of the 386DX and overcome some of the limitations of the original IBM PC. It integrated the display adapter, disk controller, serial port, parallel port, and mouse port on the motherboard. In addition, it used the 3½″ disk drive and introduced the new VGA graphics adapter standard. Lastly, it introduced the **micro channel architecture (MCA).**

The MCA was a 32-bit expansion bus. Its standard operating speed was 10 MHz, but it had the capability of increasing its speed to match the speed of the card to the speed of the microprocessor. To improve performance, MCA increased the speed of the DMA channel up to 2.5 times, and it used a form of bus mastering called *central arbitration point,* which

FIGURE 8.4 IBM PS/2

allowed the microprocessor to complete other things while other devices used the data and address lines. IBM also added a burst mode to the bus that allowed a device to send a steady flow of data for up to 12 milliseconds.

Because the PS/2 ran at greater speeds than previous PCs, there was a need for better signal shielding. A ground or power supply conductor was placed within three pins of every signal to reduce frequency interference. The use of jumpers and DIP switches to configure the MCA expansion cards was avoided by including a unique identifying number written on a ROM chip. A PS/2 reference disk configured the card by keeping its configuration information in a CMOS RAM. To increase video performance, the MCA motherboard included MCA Video Extensions built into a special video-extension connector. A video card made to use the special slot could take advantage of special VGA circuitry built into the motherboard.

Unfortunately, the PS/2 and the Micro Channel Architecture had some disadvantages, which led to its discontinuance. The MCA did not accommodate the older 8-bit and 16-bit ISA cards, and IBM tried to charge heavy licensing fees to companies who wanted to use the new technology, which drove them away. And, even though the MCA expansion slots were faster, the system performance was not significantly increased. Customers did not want to pay extra money for such a small increase in performance.

8.3.4 EISA

IBM's hefty licensing fees drove several companies to form the "gang of nine" to design a bus to compete against the Micro Channel Architecture. The "gang" was led by Compaq and consisted of AST Research, Epson, Hewlett-Packard, NEC, Olivetti, Tandy, Wyse, and Zenith Data Systems. The new bus they developed was the **extended industry standard architecture (EISA).**

The EISA consisted of two slots in one: the 16-bit slot, used by ISA cards, on top and the 32-bit slot on the bottom. Since the ISA card connectors were shorter and thicker, they could go only part way into the new slot. The EISA cards were longer and thinner, so they could make contact with the new 32-bit bus. (See fig. 8.5.) Although the EISA slot ran at 8 MHz, newer technology was used to increase performance. Instead of reacting only when the clock signal rose, EISA cards would lock their address when the clock signal rose and would transfer data when the clock signal fell. Also, much like the MCA, the EISA offered bus mastering. EISA systems were also one of the early attempts to produce a plug-and-play system. To avoid IRQ and I/O address conflicts, the EISA setup software would automatically configure the expansion cards.

FIGURE 8.5   EISA expansion cards

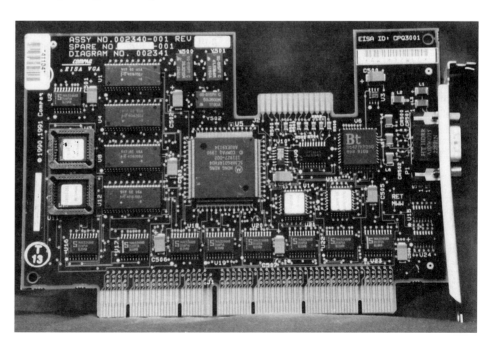

Unfortunately, not very many EISA cards were developed. Many companies felt they did not have to develop new EISA cards for a machine that already supported their ISA cards. In addition, instead of designing a complete line of EISA cards, companies waited to see if the EISA standard was to become successful. As a result, only a handful of EISA cards was created, mostly for network servers (disk array controllers and network cards), and the EISA slot is no longer manufactured.

8.3.5 LOCAL BUS (VESA AND PCI)

By the time Windows 3.XX with its GUI interface emerged, it was evident that video performance had to be improved. Since both the MCA and EISA did not achieve great success, another bus needed to be developed that would be accepted by everyone and give the video performance that was needed.

The **local bus** is a modern bus but is similar to the one used in the original PC. To maximize performance, it has the same data path size as the microprocessor, connects directly to the microprocessor, and runs at the same speed. After some early attempts, two standards emerged: the VESA local bus and the PCI local bus.

The first widely accepted local bus was the **VESA local bus (VL bus)** created by the Video Electronics Standards Association (VESA), which had formed originally to standardize Super VGA monitors. The association's interest in developing a local bus was to improve video performance. The VESA local bus was built around the 486 microprocessor and was intended to supplement the existing ISA, EISA, and MCA slots. (See figs. 8.6 and 8.7.) When coupled with the ISA slot, the VESA slot aligned directly with it. Because the VESA architecture was built around the faster 486, it used a 32-bit data bus to match the microprocessor and ran at the same speed.

Much like the MCA architecture, the VESA bus can run in a faster burst mode. While in burst mode, sequential data is transferred by specifying one memory address followed by up to four bits of data. This means that when it is in burst mode running at 33 MHz, it can transfer up to 105.6 MB/second; in nonburst mode it transfers only up to 66 MB/second. In either case, both speeds are far greater than the ISA's 8.33 MB/second. In addition, the VESA supports bus mastering.

The VESA local bus can run at speeds up to 66 MHz, but since it is connected directly to the 486 microprocessor, connecting another device caused loss of data integrity and timing problems. Therefore, the maximum speed was usually limited to 33 MHz for up to three devices, not including the microprocessor (video, disk controller, and network card).

FIGURE 8.6   VESA local bus slot

FIGURE 8.7   VESA local bus expansion card

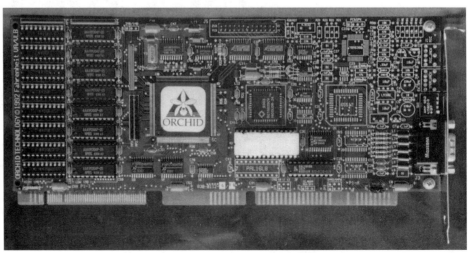

FIGURE 8.8 PCI slot

FIGURE 8.9 PCI video card

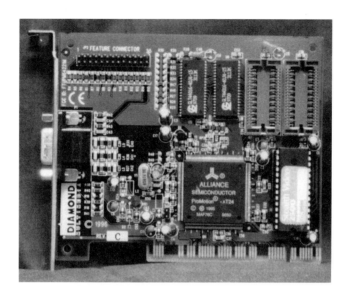

When you hear the term *local bus* today, it probably refers to the **peripheral component interconnect (PCI) local bus.** The PCI slot was developed by Intel to eventually replace the older bus designs. Unlike the VESA, the PCI local bus is not an extension of any other slot; it is offset from the normal ISA, MCA, or EISA connector. In addition, the PCI design provides between three and five slots. (See figs. 8.8 and 8.9.) Unlike the VESA bus, the PCI is not a true local bus. Instead, it occupies an intermediate level between the CPU local bus (processor/memory/cache subsystem) and the standard expansion bus (ISA), which is why it is sometimes called the *mezzanine* bus.

The PCI bus is controlled by a PCI bridge/controller. To increase performance, the microprocessor writes data to a PCI device by immediately storing the data in the bus controller's buffer. While the microprocessor goes on to its next operation, the stored data is then fed to the PCI device. Since the bus was made to run at incredible speeds, Intel chose reflected signaling rather than direct signaling for the PCI. Therefore, a card that would run at 5 V dc under the ISA design would send a 2.5 V signal instead of a 5 V signal in the PCI design. These signals bounce back when they get to the end of a wire, and the reflected signal combines with the original signal to bring the value up to 5 V.

To reduce the number of pins needed for the PCI slot, the address bus and the data bus use the same pins. When the Cycle Frame (FRAME#) signal is inactive, the address/data pins carry the address. When the address is valid, the Cycle Frame becomes active, indicating that the address/data pins will be carrying data. The PCI bus's built-in burst mode will keep sending data as long as the Cycle Frame is active and until the address/data bus is needed by another device, such as RAM refresh. Consequently, while in burst mode, the transfer rate is 132 MB/second for the 32-bit PCI design and 264 MB/second for the 64-bit PCI design. Table 8.8 lists the pin and signal connections in the 64 bit PCI bus.

Like the other newer slot designs, PCI supports bus mastering. The DMA controller and each device gets its own dedicated Request and Grant lines. When a device needs to use the data/address bus, it sends a signal to the central resource (the PCI bus-mastering arbitrator), which grants the device permission. Several flow control signals ensure that the PCI bus speed does not exceed the speed of the expansion card. A Target Ready (TRDY#) signal indicates that the device is ready to read or write data. An Initiator Ready (IRDY#) signal indicates information will be sent over the address/data bus. When the device has completed its data transfer, a Stop (STOP#) signal is sent.

Unlike most of the other bus designs, the PCI specification uses parity-checking to ensure the integrity of the data being sent. For 32-bit transfers, it uses a single parity bit (PAR) signal; for 64-bit transfers it uses two parity bits. If a parity error is detected, it will

TABLE 8.8 64-bit PCI bus pin-out

Pin	Signal Function	Signal Function	Pin
	Rear of the Computer		
B1	−12 V dc	Test Reset (−TRST)	A1
B2	Test Clock (TCK)	+12 V dc	A2
B3	Ground	Test Mode Select (TMS)	A3
B4	Test Data Output (TDO)	Test Data Input (TDI)	A4
B5	+5 V dc	+5 V dc	A5
B6	+5 V dc	Interrupt A (−INTA)	A6
B7	Interrupt B (−INTB)	Interrupt C (−INTC)	A7
B8	Interrupt D (−INTD)	+5 V dc	A8
B9	−PRSNT1#	Reserved	A9
B10	Reserved	+3.3 V dc I/O	A10
B11	−PRSNT2#	Reserved	A11
B12	Access key	Access key	A12
B13	Access key	Access key	A13
B14	Reserved	Reserved	A14
B15	Ground	Reset	A15
B16	Clock	+3.3 V dc I/O	A16
B17	Ground	Grant	A17
B18	Request (−REQ)	Ground	A18
B19	+V I/O	Reserved	A19
B20	Address/Data 31	Address/Data 30	A20
B21	Address/Data 29	+3.3 V dc	A21
B22	Ground	Address/Data 28	A22
B23	Address/Data 27	Address/Data 26	A23
B24	Address/Data 25	Ground	A24
B25	+3.3 V dc	Address/Data 24	A25
B26	C/BE 3	Init Device Select (IDSEL)	A26
B27	Address/Data 23	+3.3 V dc	A27
B28	Ground	Address/Data 22	A28
B29	Address/Data 21	Address/Data 20	A29
B30	Address/Data 19	Ground	A30
B31	+3.3 V dc	Address/Data 18	A31
B32	Address/Data 17	Address/Data 16	A32
B33	C/BE 2	+3.3 V dc	A33
B34	Ground	Cycle Frame (−FRAME)	A34
B35	Initiator Ready (−IRDY)	Ground	A35
B36	+3.3 V dc	Target Ready (−TRDY)	A36
B37	Device Select (−DEVSEL)	Ground	A37
B38	Ground	−STOP	A38
B39	−LOCK	+3.3 V dc	A39
B40	Parity Error (−PERR)	Snoop Done	A40
B41	+3.3 V dc	Snoop Backoff	A41
B42	System Error (−SERR)	Ground	A42
B43	+3.3 V dc	PAR	A43
B44	C/BE 1	Address/Data 15	A44
B45	Address/Data 14	+3.3 V dc	A45
B46	Ground	Address/Data 14	A46
B47	Address/Data 12	Address/Data 11	A47

TABLE 8.8 *continued*

	Rear of the Computer		
Pin	**Signal Function**	**Signal Function**	**Pin**
B48	Address/Data 10	Ground	A48
B49	Ground	Address/Data 9	A49
B50	Access key	Access key	A50
B51	Access key	Access key	A51
B52	Address/Data 8	C/BE 0	A52
B53	Address/Data 7	+3.3 V dc	A53
B54	+3.3 V dc	Address/Data 6	A54
B55	Address/Data 5	Address/Data 4	A55
B56	Address/Data 3	Ground	A56
B57	Ground	Address/Data 2	A57
B58	Address/Data 1	Address/Data 0	A58
B59	+5 V I/O	+3.3 V dc I/O	A59
B60	Acknowledge 64-bit (−ACK64)	Request 64-bit (−REQ64)	A60
B61	+5 V dc	+5 V dc	A61
B62	+5 V dc Access key	+5 V dc Access key	A62
B63	Reserved	Ground	A63
B64	Ground	C/BE 7	A64
B65	C/BE 6	C/BE 5	A65
B66	C/BE 4	+3.3 V dc I/O	A66
B67	Ground	Parity 64-bit	A67
B68	Address/Data 63	Address/Data 62	A68
B69	Address/Data 61	Ground	A69
B70	+V I/O	Address/Data 60	A70
B71	Addres/Data 59	Address/Data 58	A71
B72	Address/Data 57	Ground	A72
B73	Ground	Address/Data 56	A73
B74	Address/Data 55	Address/Data 54	A74
B75	Address/Data 53	+3.3 V dc I/O	A75
B76	Ground	Address/Data 52	A76
B77	Address/Data 51	Address/Data 50	A77
B78	Address/Data 49	Ground	A78
B79	+V I/O	Address/Data 48	A79
B80	Addres/Data 47	Address/Data 46	A80
B81	Address/Data 45	Ground	A81
B82	Ground	Address/Data 44	A82
B83	Address/Data 43	Address/Data 42	A83
B84	Address/Data 41	+3.3 V dc I/O	A84
B85	Ground	Address/Data 40	A85
B86	Address/Data 39	Address/Data 38	A86
B87	Address/Data 37	Ground	A87
B88	+V I/O	Address/Data 36	A88
B89	Address/Data 35	Address/Data 34	A89
B90	Address/Data 33	Ground	A90
B91	Ground	Address/Data 32	A91
B92	Reserved	Reserved	A92
B93	Reserved	Ground	A93
B94	Ground	Reserved	A94

then send a Parity Error signal (PERR#), which prompts other actions, depending on the system. Much like the other expansion slots, PCI supports hardware interrupts and interrupt sharing. PCI includes four level-sensitive interrupts (INTA# through INTD#), which are assigned to the slots by the CMOS setup program. PCI also supports plug-and-play technology. Unlike other expansion bus designs, PCI expansion cards store their own configuration information. Most are therefore not configured using jumpers or DIP switches but by software or a true plug-and-play system.

A newly developed high-performance PCI standard is the compact PCI, which uses the rugged Eurocard packaging and a high-quality 2 mm metric pin and socket connector. The new compact PCI supports hot-swap—inserting and extracting the card while the system is on.

8.3.6 ACCELERATED GRAPHICS PORT (AGP)

The **accelerated graphics port (AGP)** is a spinoff of the PCI slot (based on the PCI 2.1 specification). It is called a *port,* not a bus, because a bus can support multiple devices and the AGP cannot—it is made exclusively for video cards. It is similar to the PCI slot in shape and size but is offset further from the edge of the motherboard than PCI slots are. (See fig. 8.10.)

Current PCI cards are still able to run at only 33 MHz; the AGP uses a 32-bit path running at 66 MHz (with the capability of increasing to 100 MHz). It can handle 266 megabits per second, and this flow can be doubled by sending information on both the rising and falling edges of the clock signal. A 4X mode is planned, which will perform four transfers per clock cycle, allowing a bandwidth of 1.07 gigabits per second. By comparison, the Pentium microprocessor, which uses a 64-bit bus running at 66 MHz, supports only 533 megabits per second, and a 64-bit bus running at 100 MHz supports only 807 megabits per second. Since the video card is removed from the PCI bus, in addition to the faster speed for the video system, other PCI devices also benefit from the improved bandwidth. To increase performance still further, the AGP uses video pipelining. Video pipelining means that while the video card works on one task, it will start on a second task. Therefore, pipelining allows sequential parts of tasks to overlap.

AGP has the ability to allow the video chipset to share the system RAM, allowing the video system access to larger amounts of RAM for 3-D and other processing without requiring large amounts of special video memory. For example, textures, which can be as large as 128 KB, previously had to be loaded into the video card's RAM and processed by the graphic processor. With AGP, textures can be loaded into the main memory without impacting performance. Since the main memory is faster than the memory being accessed on a video card through the PCI slot, the processing of graphical data is faster. (Note: The main memory provided by the AGP doesn't replace the screen buffer of the graphic accelerator; it is additional memory specifically used for processing.)

8.3.7 PC CARD

Users buy laptop and notebook computers because they are small and portable. Unfortunately, their size does not permit use of any of the traditional expansion cards (ISA, MCA,

FIGURE 8.10 AGP port next to a PCI slot

FIGURE 8.11   PCMCIA/PC card

EISA, and local bus). Therefore, a new type of expansion slot had to be created specifically for portable systems.

The Personal Computer Memory Card International Association (PCMCIA) established several standards for a laptop expansion system that was later developed and implemented by over 300 manufacturers, including IBM, Toshiba, and Apple. Consequently, there are four types of **PC cards** (formerly known as **PCMCIA cards**): Type I, II, III, and IV. (See fig. 8.11.) All PC cards are about the size of a credit card (3.4 × 2.1 inches) and use a 68-pin (two rows) connector and a 16-bit data bus. The Type I cards, which are 3.3 mm thick, are memory expansion cards. Unlike a SIMM or DIMM, which expand a system's RAM, the Type I card acts more like a RAM drive. Type II cards, which are 5 mm thick, are the most common and are the standard expansion card. They are the cards used for modems, fax/modems, SCSI, networks, and sound. (See fig. 8.12.) Some cards include two functions in one package (fax/modem and network or sound and SCSI). Since the Type I and Type II cards have the same type of connector, the Type II slot can accommodate Type I cards. The Type III and Type IV cards are small hard drives. Type III cards are up to 10.5 mm thick; Type IV cards are thicker than 10.5 mm. Most machines will accommodate two

FIGURE 8.12   Inside a fax/modem PC (PCMCIA) card

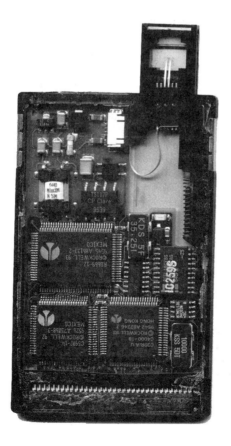

Type II cards or one Type III card. Since the Type III cards are much larger than the Type II cards, one Type III card takes up the space of two Type II cards. Type III slots can accommodate Type I and Type II cards, and Type IV slots can accommodate Type I, II, and III cards. (Note: The Type IV cards are not described in the PC card specification.)

PC cards have power-saving capabilities to increase battery life. The cards operate at 3.3 V and support APM (advanced power management). The PC cards are **hot-swappable,** which means they can be inserted and removed while the power is on. Hot-swappable technology is possible because the pins used to connect the PC card vary in length. The power and ground connectors are longer and the two activation pins are shorter, ensuring that the power is connected before anything else is.

The original PC cards were 16-bit, and there soon was a need to create a 32-bit version, which would operate at a faster speed. By 1995, the **CardBus** had been introduced with speeds up to 33 MHz (133 MB/second). To make it backward compatible with the 16-bit PC cards, the address pins and data pins were multiplexed. To increase MPEG (Motion Picture Experts Group) and video performance, the CardBus uses **zoomed video (ZV),** which is a direct connection to the system's VGA controller. The zoomed video is used for videoconferencing applications and MPEG decoders.

To enable the PC card and to allow it to be recognized by the operating system, two programs need to be loaded. The first one is a socket services program that activates the PC socket itself. The program can be implemented within a ROM BIOS chip, a device driver, a TSR, or a service running on an operating system (such as Windows 95 or 98). The second program is card services. Card services are responsible for assigning the appropriate hardware resources to the PC cards by means of a configuration file/software driver, by typing a command at the prompt, or by using plug-and-play.

8.3.8 UNIVERSAL SERIAL BUS (USB)

A new, emerging technology is the **universal serial bus (USB),** an external port allowing connection of up to 127 external PC peripherals in series and offering a data transfer rate of up to 12 megabits/second. The USB connector will accept any USB peripheral, including mice, keyboards, printers, modems, and external disk drives. Seven devices can be connected directly using the standard four-pin connector. These seven devices can then be connected to others, to a total of 127 devices, by connecting external hubs (each hub accommodates another seven devices) in a chain (hence, the term *daisy chain* for this type of serial connection). (See figs 8.13 and 8.14.)

USB is already supported by specific chipsets on Pentium and Pentium Pro processor-equipped host PCs, and there are software device drivers for it available in Windows 95 and 98. With the proper chipset and drivers, a USB device will work without rebooting or reconfiguring every time a peripheral is added or removed. USB devices can also be hot-swapped.

FIGURE 8.13   A USB connector

FIGURE 8.14   USB port

8.3.9 IEEE 1394 (FIREWIRE)

Another external bus standard is **IEEE 1394,** sometimes called **FireWire.** IEEE 1394 supports data transfer rates of up to 400 megabits per second. A single 1394 port can connect up to 63 external devices. It can deliver data at a guaranteed rate, which makes it ideal for devices that need to transfer large amounts of data in real-time, such as video cameras and other video devices. Like USB, 1394 supports plug-and-play and hot-swapping and provides power to IEEE 1394 devices. The 1394 port uses a tree topology (physical layout) whereby any device can be connected to any other device as long as there are no loops. Unfortunately, IEEE 1394 costs a lot more than USB.

8.4 EXPANSION CARDS

When an expansion card is inserted into a system, it must be configured to use the proper resources. The resources include I/O addresses (including COMX/LTPX), IRQs, DMAs, and memory addresses. One general rule applies when configuring a card: No two devices can use the same resource. Therefore, two expansion cards should not be set to use the same DMA channel or the same I/O address. If two devices are using the same setting, they will not work properly or will not work at all. The available resources can be determined by using diagnostic software, such as QA Plus or Checkit Pro, or utilities that come with the operating system, such as Microsoft Software Diagnostic (MSD) or the Windows 95 and 98 System icon located within the control panel. The card itself can be configured in one of several ways:

1. With DIP switches and/or jumpers
2. With a software setup program
3. Using plug-and-play (PnP)

Determining which resources the card can use and how to select them most likely will require the expansion board documentation. Most documentation is included in a manual; some will be silk-screened on the card itself or placed within a file on a disk. Without the documentation, a lot of trial and error is usually required to figure out the correct settings. (Note: Many expansion cards require software drivers to function. DOS drivers are typically loaded by running the install program from disks that come with the expansion card or by copying the appropriate files to the hard drive and modifying the CONFIG.SYS and AUTOEXEC.BAT files. Windows 3.XX drivers are typically loaded by running the install program from disks that come with the expansion card. Windows 95 and 98 drivers are typically loaded by running the Add New Hardware Driver icon or by using the installation disks that come with the expansion card.)

If you, your customers, or your clients lose the documentation or drivers, you can look for information on the Internet, contact the manufacturer of the device, or consult the Microhouse Technical Library/On-line Service. Many companies post their documentation on the Internet for quick-and-easy access. Microhouse Incorporated publishes a technical library (book/CD-ROM) and has an on-line service for motherboard, expansion card, and hard drive documentation.

8.4.1 DIP SWITCHES

DIP switches, found on the motherboard or on the expansion card of many older computers, consist of a bank of tiny on/off switches.

EXAMPLE 8.1 When installing a fax/modem card, you must specify which COM port and IRQ the modem will use.

Figure 8.15 shows a Zoltrix fax/modem card. As you can see, in this case the DIP switches are with the ports at the end of the card (although they could have been on the circuit board surface). The IRQ and the COM port the modem uses must be configured. As you can see the documentation that comes with the modem, when the COM port is

FIGURE 8.15 A fax/modem with documentation

COM PORT ADDRESSES

Each COM port in your computer uses a specific computer address. The addresses for each COM port are:

COM1   3F8–3FF
COM2   2F8–2FF
COM3   3E8–3EF
COM4   2E8–2EF

IRQ	SW1	SW2	SW3	SW4	SW7	COMPORT	SW5	SW6
2	Off	Off	Off	Off	On	COM1	On	On
3*	Off	Off	Off	On	Off	COM2*	Off	On
4	Off	Off	On	Off	Off	COM3	On	Off
5	Off	On	Off	Off	Off	COM4	Off	Off
7	On	Off	Off	Off	Off			

*Indicates the factor (default) setting

selected, the I/O address is also chosen. Therefore, if the card is set to COM2, the modem will use the I/O address of 2F8 to 2FF. Modems can use COM1, COM2, COM3, or COM4. Whichever port you choose, including the 9-pin and 25-pin ports, make sure it is not being used by another device and that the software that will be running the modem will support it. (Note: If the serial port is not being used but is still active, it is still assigned a COM port and an IRQ.)

To select the COM port, you must look at the accompanying documentation. In our example, to set the modem to COM2, you must find switches 5 and 6. Switch 5 must be off (up) and switch 6 must be on (down). The on position of a DIP switch is indicated by the word *on* stamped on the DIP switch bank. When changing these two switches, remember not to change any of the others since they are used to configure other parameters. The standard IRQ for COM2 is IRQ 3. Unless there is a good reason for not using the standard assignments (such as to get all of the expansion devices to work), you should always use the standard. To configure the modem as IRQ 3, again look at the documentation. The IRQ requires setting switches 1, 2, 3, 4, and 7. The settings for COM2 are:

Switch 1	Switch 2	Switch 3	Switch 4	Switch 7
Off (Up)	Off (Up)	Off (Up)	On (Down)	Off (Up)

Most documentation will indicate what the default settings for the DIP switches are. These should be the settings when you first open the box, but even though the switches are supposed to be preset correctly, check the settings before inserting the card.

8.4.2 JUMPERS

A **jumper** is a small, plastic-covered metal clip used to connect two pins protruding from an expansion card. (See fig. 8.16.) The jumper (which operates the same as an on switch) connects the pins closing the circuit and allowing current to flow. Two pin configurations that need to be jumped are the two-pin configuration and the three-pin configuration.

The two-pin configuration will either be connected with a jumper or will not be connected. If the jumper is to be used, the documentation will either indicate on or closed or include a small diagram showing where the jumper should be placed. If a jumper is not to be placed over the two pins, the documentation will indicate off or open or include a small diagram showing that a jumper should not be used. (Note: To avoid losing jumpers that are not being used, they can be placed over one pin.) The three-pin connection has a high/low configuration. If the documentation indicates high, you will jumper the two pins on the side indicated with an H. If the documentation indicates low, you will jumper the two pins on the side indicated with a L. In either case the center pin is used.

EXAMPLE 8.2 The expansion card shown in figs. 8.17, 8.18, 8.19, and 8.20 is an example of a standard I/O card found in many systems. It holds an IDE hard disk controller, a floppy disk controller, two serial ports, one parallel port, and a game port. Since the card houses so many devices on one circuit board, it also includes many jumpers.

Let's take a look at the serial ports and the parallel ports that also require an IRQ. As already mentioned, the card has two serial ports, designated as Serial Port I/RS-232 I and Serial Port II/RS-232 II. Note that these names do not designate the COM ports. The COM ports are set with jumpers. The ports (9-pin male and 25-pin male) connect to a 10-pin connector on the card. The 9-pin port is usually connected to the Serial Port I connector and is usually configured as COM1. The 25-pin port is usually connected to the Serial Port II and is usually configured as COM2. If you wish the 25-pin connector to be connected to Serial Port I and the 9-pin connector to Serial Port II, you just have to change the connection.

To configure Serial Port I as COM1 using IRQ4, the documentation indicates the jumpers used to do this are the set of jumpers designated JP2, specifically, jumpers 1 and 2. As you can see, to set Serial Port I to COM1, jumper 1 must be set to low and jumper 2 must be set to high. If you wanted to truly disable Serial Port I, you would set both jumpers to high. Again, the other jumpers should be left alone since they are used to control other items. To set the IRQ, the documentation indicates you must use jumper set J5, jumpers 1,

FIGURE 8.16 Jumpers on an expansion card

FIGURE 8.17   Common multi-function I/O card

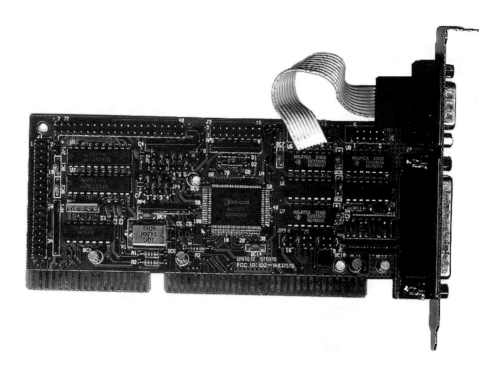

2, and 3. To set the port to use IRQ 4, you must have a jumper on 1 and no jumpers on 2 and 3. (Note: The jumpers are numbered from the left, not the right. Jumper 1 is designated by a small number 1.)

8.4.3   SOFTWARE CONFIGURATION AND PLUG-AND-PLAY

To simplify the configuration of expansion cards, new technology was developed that allowed the cards to be configured electronically. This is done by running a software setup program from a disk that comes with the expansion card. These cards are not to be confused with preset plug-and-play cards since the settings for the resources they use must be physically activated. Today, many motherboards contain built-in serial ports, parallel ports, and video cards. Some motherboards even have a sound card. Since the serial ports, parallel ports, and sound cards use hardware resources, they are usually configured using the CMOS setup program.

Another way to configure an expansion card is to let the computer to do it by using plug-and-play (PnP). However, the system has to support plug-and-play, which means that the computer must have a system ROM BIOS/plug-and-play BIOS, the expansion card must have a plug-and-play ISA and PCI and PC Cards/PCMCIA, and the operating system (or the appropriate drivers) must support plug-and-play. If all this is in place, then during boot-up, the plug-and-play BIOS will track the insertion and removal of plug-and-play devices. If the device can identify itself and its system requirements to the system, the plug-and-play BIOS will assign the needed resources and avoid conflicts with the known legacy cards. Operating systems such as Windows 95 and 98 that support plug-and-play will allow you to overcome the resources assigned to the plug-and-play device if there is a conflict.

To make sure that the resource assignments and device placements are the same each time the computer is powered on, the system uses the extended system configuration data (ESCD) method, which stores the legacy information and the last working configuration (LWC) of configurable devices. This is important when using device drivers that get their resource allocation information from a static source, such as the command line parameters in the CONFIG.SYS file.

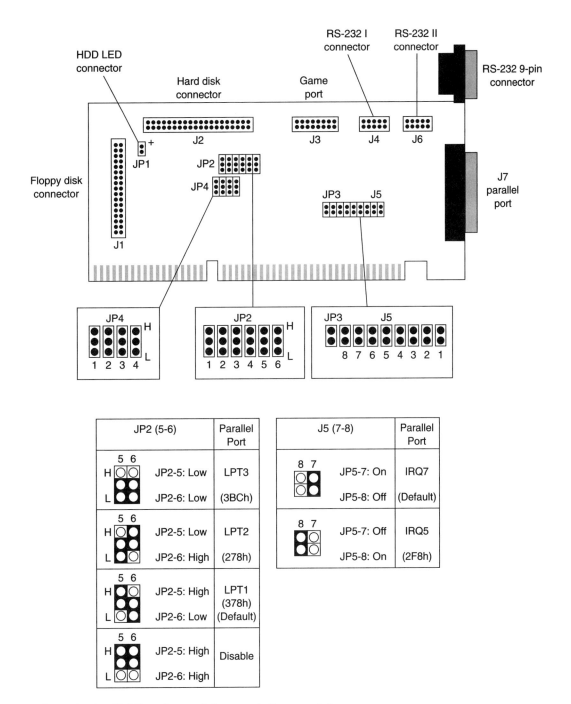

FIGURE 8.18   Multifunction card documentation—part A

FIGURE 8.19   Multifunction card documentation—part B

JP3	Parallel Port Function
On	Output (Default)
Off	Input

JP2 (1-2)	Serial Port I	JP2 (3-4)	Serial Port II
JP2-1: Low, JP2-2: Low	COM4 (2E8h)	JP2-3: Low, JP2-4: Low	COM3 (3E8h)
JP2-1: Low, JP2-2: High	COM1 (3F8h) (Default)	JP2-3: Low, JP2-4: High	COM2 (2F8h) (Default)
JP2-1: High, JP2-2: Low	COM3 (3E8h)	JP2-3: High, JP2-4: Low	COM4 (2E8h)
JP2-1: High, JP2-2: High	Disable	JP2-3: High, JP2-4: High	Disable

FIGURE 8.20   Multifunction card documentation—part C

J5 (1-3)	Serial Port I	J5 (4-6)	Serial Port II
J5-1: On, J5-2: Off, J5-3: Off	IRQ4 (Default)	J5-4: On, J5-5: Off, J5-6: Off	IRQ3 (Default)
J5-1: Off, J5-2: On, J5-3: Off	IRQ3	J5-4: Off, J5-5: On, J5-6: Off	IRQ4
J5-1: Off, J5-2: Off, J5-3: On	IRQ5	J5-4: Off, J5-5: Off, J5-6: On	IRQ5

JP4-1	Hard Disk Address Selection	JP4-2	IDE Hard Disk
High	3F6-3F7 / 1F0-1F7	Low	Enabled (Default)
Low	376-377 / 170-177	High	Disabled

JP4-3	Hard Disk Address Selection	JP4-4	IDE Hard Disk
High	3F0-3F7 (Default)	Low	Enabled (Default)
Low	370-377	High	Disabled

8.5 TROUBLESHOOTING EXPANSION CARDS AND SLOTS

When an expansion card fails to work, it is because of the card itself or the motherboard. The card could be physically damaged, or it could be in conflict (I/O address, IRQ, DMA, memory usage) with another card. Or it may not function because the proper software drivers (built into the operating system or as drivers or TSRs) are not installed to activate the card.

EXAMPLE 8.3 You just inserted an expansion card and the system does not work.

The first thing to do is to check the obvious: Is the card inserted properly? Are the cables connected properly? Does the card require any drivers or TSRs, which must be loaded for the card to function? Wipe off any oxides or dust that may have accumulated on the metal connectors of the expansion card. Then try the card again.

Try inserting the card into another expansion slot. If the card starts working, then the first expansion slot is most likely bad. The metal fingers within the slot, which provide the contact with the expansion card, eventually wear out if expansion cards are frequently inserted and removed or if an expansion card is inserted with excessive force, which would break the connector or even the motherboard. If the expansion slot is bad, you should label it and be sure to tell your customer. If you choose to repair it, the best course of action would be to replace the motherboard. Replacing the expansion slot would require some special knowledge, skill, and equipment as well as time. It is quicker and more cost-effective to replace the motherboard.

After trying the obvious, look elsewhere. Since you just inserted the card, check the resources used by the expansion card. If the card uses jumpers or DIP switches, remove the card and verify that they are configured properly. If the card is software-configurable, rerun the configuration software and verify the card's resources. If the card is plug-and-play, use the plug-and-play manager (DOS) or use the Windows 95 or 98 System icon to verify the settings of the card. Make sure that the plug-and-play software chooses nonconflicting resources. In either case, remove the card and run diagnostic software (such as QA Plus or Checkit Pro), run the System icon within the Control Panel (Windows 95 and 98), or use Microsoft Diagnostic (Windows NT) to verify that the resources chosen are not being used by another device. If there is no conflict, then the card must be physically bad. Try to install another card.

EXAMPLE 8.4 After you inserted a card, the computer does not boot.

First, remove the card to see if the computer boots properly. If it does, try reinserting the card. If the same problem occurs, the card is most likely causing the problem or the card is causing the motherboard to short against some part of the case. Look at the card carefully for bad solder and burn marks. If you find bad solder, the card is probably being shorted out by the solder as it bridges two circuits that shouldn't be connected (referred to as a *bridge*). If you find burn marks, the card probably heated up, which usually indicates the card is bad.

If the visual inspection of the card is fine, the next thing to do is to verify the resource configuration (IRQ, DMA, I/O address, and Memory address) used by the card. If the card appears to be good, try it in another system. If the same problem occurs, the card is probably bad. If the system has been booting properly, this would indicate that when the card is inserted into the slot, it is somehow causing the motherboard to short against the case. Check the motherboard to see whether there are any loose screws or paper clips within the computer; then check to see whether the motherboard is positioned correctly against the spacers.

SUMMARY

1. The single-board motherboard, which required less labor and materials to produce, includes all electronic devices on a single circuit board.
2. The bus-oriented design, which allowed for expandability, uses one primary circuit board to connect several smaller circuit boards.
3. The expansion slot, also known as the I/O bus, extends the reach of the microprocessor so that it can communicate with peripheral devices.
4. The data bus carries the actual data between the expansion card, the RAM, and the CPU; the address bus determines the memory location for the data.

5. No two devices can generally share the same resources (IRQ, DMA, IO address, and memory addresses).

6. A hardware interrupt (IRQ) is a signal sent to the microprocessor to redirect its attention to another task.

7. The XT system had 8 interrupts and the AT and above had 16 interrupts.

8. Direct memory address (DMA) channels are used to take over the data bus and address lines to bring data from an I/O device to the RAM without any assistance or direction from the CPU.

9. The XT had four DMA channels, and the AT has eight DMA channels.

10. Bus mastering is a process by which an expansion card with its own processor takes temporary control of the data and address bus to move information from one point to another.

11. The I/O address is a memory address used to identify the input/output (I/O) device.

12. Many expansion cards need to use a range of memory addresses in the reserve memory between 640 KB and 1 MB of RAM.

13. The IBM PC and IBM XT used an 8-bit expansion bus called the PC slot or the 8-bit ISA bus.

14. The IBM AT introduced a 16-bit expansion bus called the industry standard architecture (ISA) bus.

15. Micro channel architecture (MCA) and extended industry standard architecture (EISA) were developed to increase the speed of the PC, specifically video speed, but both failed.

16. The local bus, such as VESA local bus and PCI local bus, was originally designed to run at or near the speed of the microprocessor.

17. The VESA bus, found mostly on 486 machines, has a 32-bit data bus. The PCI bus, found on Pentium and later machines, has either a 32- or 64-bit data bus.

18. Notebook and laptop computers use PC (formerly PCMCIA) cards and CardBus cards.

19. Expansion cards can be configured with DIP switches, jumpers, or special setup software. Today, some are automatically configured with plug-and-play (PnP) technology.

QUESTIONS

1. COM 1 is usually assigned which interrupt?
   a. IRQ 1
   b. IRQ 2
   c. IRQ 3
   d. IRQ 4
   e. IRQ 9

2. The DMA channel used for the floppy controller is:
   a. DMA 1
   b. DMA 2
   c. DMA 3
   d. DMA 5

3. The Type II PC bus card:
   a. fits in a Type 1 slot.
   b. is 3 mm thick.
   c. is 5 mm thick.
   d. is 10.5 mm thick.

4. After installing a new sound card, the system fails to boot. Which of the following could be causing the problem?
   a. the operating system does not support the sound card
   b. the cables to the sound card are connected wrong
   c. there is an IRQ conflict
   d. none of the above

5. The ISA bus was made for which microprocessor?
   a. 8088
   b. 8086
   c. 80286
   d. 80386
   e. 80486
   f. none of the above

6. How many hardware interrupts does a Pentium PC have?
   a. 4
   b. 8
   c. 12
   d. 16

7. Bus mastering is similar to a(n):
   a. I/O address
   b. IRQ
   c. DMA
   d. memory address
   e. none of the above

8. How many hardware interrupts does an XT PC have?
   a. 4
   b. 8
   c. 12
   d. 16

9. The MCA bus is predominately used in the:
   a. IBM AT
   b. IBM PS/2
   c. Compaq Presario
   d. HP DESKPRO

10. Another term for VESA local bus is:
   a. PCI
   b. VLB
   c. VM bus
   d. VLSI

11. PC (PCMCIA) cards were designed for use in:
   a. notebook and subnotebook computers
   b. desktop computers
   c. tower computers
   d. palmtop computers
   e. none of the above

12. The most common expansion slot found on new and old machines is:
   a. MCA
   b. EISA
   c. ISA
   d. PC
   e. PCI
   f. VESA

13. Which type of slot is the fastest?
   a. ISA
   b. EISA
   c. MCA
   d. PCI local bus
   e. PCMCIA

14. Which of the following are *not* possible conflicts when installing an expansion card?
   a. port conflict
   b. I/O address conflict
   c. IRQ conflict
   d. power conflict
   e. memory conflict

15. You suspect an IRQ conflict when installing a sound card. How would you check to see which IRQs are free?
   a. reboot the computer
   b. install the operating system
   c. run a software diagnostic program, such as QA Plus or MSD
   d. enter the CMOS setup program

16. Which of the following describes an IRQ?
   a. an address that points to an input or output device
   b. a line that allows access to memory without using the CPU
   c. a line that temporarily stops the CPU from doing something so that it can give its attention to something else
   d. a line that supplies power to an interface card

17. Which of the following describes a DMA?
   a. an address that points to an input or output device
   b. a line that allows access to memory without using the CPU
   c. a line that temporarily stops the CPU from doing something so that it can give its attention to something else
   d. a line that supplies power to an interface card

18. The device I/O address:
   a. must be unique and correspond to a port or device
   b. must be the same for each device
   c. is not needed for some devices
   d. is only needed for devices that do not require or use a DMA

19. Expansion boards are configured in which of the following ways? (Choose all that apply.)
   a. with jumpers that need to be set
   b. with DIP switches that need to be set
   c. with a special preprogrammed ROM chip
   d. with software

20. When installing an expansion board, what is the best method of determining the current settings?
    a. run MSD to view the IRQs after the board is installed
    b. consult the documentation for the board
    c. systematically change the DIP switch settings on the board
    d. remove all the jumpers on the expansion card and reinstall them one by one until the board functions
21. Which of the following statements is true about IRQs? (Choose two answers.)
    a. under the correct conditions, several devices on a PC can share the same interrupt
    b. IRQ settings are stored in the system ROM BIOS
    c. after processing an IRQ, the CPU must find where it left off with processing other tasks
    d. each device on a PC must have a unique IRQ number
22. How many DMA channels does a 486 computer have?
    a. 2
    b. 4
    c. 8
    d. 16
23. What is the standard I/O address for LPT1?
    a. 3F8-3FF
    b. 2F8-2FF
    c. 3F0-3F7
    d. 278-27F
    e. 378-37F
24. What is the standard I/O address for COM1?
    a. 3F8-3FF
    b. 2F8-2FF
    c. 3F0-3F7
    d. 278-27F
    e. 378-37F
25. What is meant by the term *memory address* in relation to expansion boards?
    a. an area above 640 KB that a device can use exclusively for its operations
    b. an address in RAM that alerts the CPU to an expansion board's presence
    c. a unique number assigned to a device to identify the expansion card to the computer
    d. ROM that specifies what drivers are needed
26. Which of the following does *not* support data paths of 32 bits?
    a. ISA
    b. MCA
    c. EISA
    d. VLB
    e. PCI
27. After installing and configuring an expansion card, such as the sound card or fax/modem, to activate the card you will need to:
    a. run the CMOS setup program
    b. turn on the expansion card's power switch
    c. load the appropriate drivers
    d. insert a ROM chip into the expansion card
    e. insert a ROM chip into the motherboard
28. Which of the following statements about PC cards are true? (Choose all that apply.)
    a. Type 1 cards are memory cards and are accepted by Type 1, Type 2, and Type 3 slots
    b. Type 2 cards are normally expansion cards, such as fax/modems and sound cards, and are accepted by Type 2 and Type 3 slots
    c. Type 3 cards often support small hard drives and are not accepted by Type 1 and 2 slots
    d. all three types of cards have the same physical dimensions and plug into a 68-pin connector
29. PCMCIA/PC cards are characterized by their:
    a. small size, low power, and hot-swap capability
    b. portability and bus-mastering capabilities
    c. ability to fit both ISA and EISA buses
    d. small size and 32-bit data bus

30. Which of the following is made for and is only used by video cards?
    a. AGP
    b. PCI
    c. ISA
    d. VLB
    e. none of the above
31. Which of the following support data paths of 64 bits?
    a. MCA
    b. EISA
    c. VLB
    d. PCI
    e. CardBus
32. Which of the following will automatically choose card resources such as IRQ and DMA?
    a. plug-and-play systems
    b. IRQ and DMA controllers
    c. I/O manager
    d. device driver
33. How do you configure a PC card?
    a. set jumpers or DIP switches
    b. run the CMOS setup program
    c. install software drivers
    d. write a program and transfer it to the PC card using the parallel or serial port
34. You just installed a sound card that causes the computer to lock up when a parallel port Zip drive is used. What is most likely the problem?
    a. an I/O addresses conflict
    b. an IRQ conflict
    c. a DMA conflict
    d. a defective sound card
    e. a defective parallel port
    f. a defective Zip drive
35. Which of the following is used to connect up to 127 external devices such as mice, keyboards, printers, hard drives, tape drives, and removable drives?
    a. AGP
    b. PCI
    c. PC
    d. USB
    e. none of the above
36. Which of the following is used to connect devices that transfer large amounts of data in real-time?
    a. AGP
    b. PCI
    c. PC
    d. USB
    e. FireWire
    f. none of the above

HANDS-ON PROJECTS

Exercise 1: Using Diagnostic Software

Using diagnostic software, such as QA Plus or Checkit Pro, answer the following questions:

1. What device is actually using IRQ 4?
2. What device is actually using IRQ 5?
3. What device is actually using IRQ 7?
4. What device is actually using IRQ 11?
5. What device is actually using DMA 2?
6. What device is actually using DMA 3?

Exercise 2: Using the Operating System Internal Software

Using DOS's Microsoft Diagnostic (MSD), Windows 95 or 98's System icon within the control panel, or Windows NT's Microsoft Diagnostic software, answer the following questions:

1. What device is actually using IRQ 4?
2. What device is actually using IRQ 5?
3. What device is actually using IRQ 7?
4. What device is actually using IRQ 11?
5. What device is actually using DMA 2?
6. What device is actually using DMA 3?

Exercise 3: Configuring a Modem or I/O Card

1. Make sure the computer is off. If your system has a modem, remove it.
2. By looking at the back of the computer, determine how many serial ports your system has.
3. Turn the computer on. If you have a COM1 and a COM2, run some form of diagnostic software that shows hardware resources. What are the IRQs for COM1 and COM2?
4. Install the mouse to COM1, and load the mouse driver in the appropriate configuration file.
5. Test the mouse to make sure that it is working properly.
6. Shut off the computer. By looking at the modem's documentation, set the modem to COM1 and insert the modem card into an available expansion slot.
7. Turn the computer on. Test the mouse. Does the mouse work? If it doesn't, what is the problem?
8. Shut the computer off. Using the I/O controller card documentation, or the motherboard documentation if the serial ports are part of the motherboard, disable COM2. (Note: If the serial ports are part of the motherboard, this is probably done with the CMOS setup program.)
9. If possible, use the modem documentation to change the modem to COM2 and to use the same IRQ as the mouse. Remember that the mouse is plugged into COM1.
10. Turn the computer on. Test the mouse. Does the mouse work? If it doesn't, what is the problem?
11. Shut the computer off. Using the modem documentation, change the modem's IRQ to an available one. (Hint: You should use the IRQ that is standard for COM2.)
12. Turn the computer on. Test the mouse again. Does the mouse work?
13. Shut off the computer and remove the modem.
14. Enable COM2 on the I/O controller card and reinsert the card into the expansion slot.
15. Turn on the computer and test the mouse to make sure it is working properly.

Exercise 4: Installing a Network Card

1. By using some form of diagnostic software, determine which I/O addresses, IRQs, DMAs, and memory addresses are available to install the network card.
2. By reading the network card's documentation, configure the card to an available I/O address, IRQ, DMA (if needed), and memory address (if needed).
3. Insert the card in the expansion slot.
4. Turn the computer on. Did it boot?
5. If the card is plug-and-play, determine what resources the card is using.

Exercise 5: Installing a Sound Card

1. By using some form of diagnostic software, determine which I/O addresses, IRQs, DMAs, and memory addresses are available to install the network card.
2. By reading the sound card's documentation, configure the card to an available I/O address, IRQ, DMA, and memory address (if needed).
3. Insert the card in the expansion slot.
4. Turn the computer on. Did it boot?
5. If the card is plug-and-play, determine what resources the card is using.

9

The Case and Power Supply

INTRODUCTION

The computer consists of three obvious parts: the case, the keyboard, and the monitor. The case (sometimes known as the CPU) is the box that most of the computer components rest in. It will usually contain the power supply, the motherboard, the floppy drives, the hard drive, and the RAM.

The power supply is the "blood" of the computer. It takes ac power from an outlet and converts it into clean (without fluctuation) dc power to run the computer chips. In addition, the power supply helps keep the computer cool so that heat will not prematurely destroy any of the electronic circuitry.

OBJECTIVES

1. List and describe the two main functions of the case.
2. List and describe the major characteristics to look for when choosing a case.
3. Identify the basic electronic components and their schematic symbols and describe their basic characteristics.
4. Describe the function of the power supply.
5. Compare and contrast dc voltage and ac voltage.
6. Describe the function of the power supply.
7. List the common voltages supplied by a PC power supply and describe their use.
8. Describe the major characteristics of the switching power supply.
9. Properly connect and disconnect the power connectors.
10. Install and remove a power supply from a PC.
11. Determine and correct a power-related problem in a PC.
12. List and describe the different types of power fluctuations.
13. List and describe the power protection devices.

9.1   THE CASE

The **case** of the PC is a large metal or plastic box designed to hold and protect the motherboard, the drives, and the power supply. Like motherboards and microprocessors, cases come in many different configurations, which are characterized by the orientation of the box, the number of drives and expansion slots it can hold, and the size of the expansion cards it can take (See fig. 9.1).

9.1.1   CHOOSING THE RIGHT CASE

Cases come in two orientations. A PC that lies flat is known as a **desktop case** (much like the IBM PC); a case that stands erect is known as a **tower case.** The desktop case comes in two sizes, the slim-line and regular, while the tower comes in three sizes, the minitower, the medium tower, and the full-size tower. It stands to reason the larger the case, the more room for expansion. Before choosing a case, you must be sure that the case will fulfill all of your needs.

FIGURE 9.1   Case (Courtesy of PC Power & Cooling, Inc.)

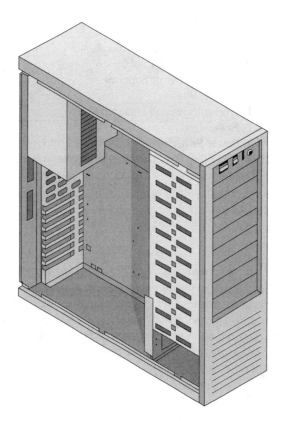

Cases come in different form factors. The **form factor** describes the general layout of the case, the positioning of the slots in the back of the case, and what type of motherboard it will accommodate. The baby AT form factor, which accommodates the baby AT motherboard, is the most popular built within the last few years. A slim-line case, which has a lower profile, uses an LPX motherboard. The newest form factor is ATX. It accommodates an ATX motherboard, which has integrated I/O ports. In addition, it is designed for easier access to common components and better placement of air flow.

When looking for a case, you should ask the following questions:

1. Does the case have enough drive bays (including open drive bays)?
2. Does your motherboard fit into the new case?
3. How many expansion slots does the case have and how are the expansion slots oriented?
4. What type of power supply does the case have and what is the wattage rating of the power supply?
5. If the case doesn't come with a power supply, what kind of power supply and on/off switch will it accommodate?

The case must have enough closed and open drive bays to accommodate all of the hard drives, floppy drives, and miscellaneous peripherals. A drive bay is an empty space where a drive or other peripherals sit. An open drive bay has an opening in the front of the case. The opening is used to insert a floppy disk or CD into the drive. The closed drive bay is completely enclosed by the case. Drive bays come in two sizes, $5\frac{1}{4}''$ and $3\frac{1}{2}''$. The $5\frac{1}{4}''$ drive bay will hold $5\frac{1}{4}''$ floppy disk drives, internal stereo speakers, CD-ROM drives, and some hard drives. The $3\frac{1}{2}''$ drive bays hold $3\frac{1}{2}''$ floppy disk drives and some hard drives.

You should choose a case that has at least three drive bays, including an open $5\frac{1}{4}''$ drive bay (for a CD-ROM drive), an open $3\frac{1}{2}''$ drive bay (for a $3\frac{1}{2}''$ disk drive), and a closed drive bay (for the hard drive). Be sure to pick a case that has extra drive bays. This will allow you to add other peripherals to your system, such as additional drives (hard drives, tape backups, or removable drives such as Zip drives) or some internal speakers.

A second criterion in choosing the case is how well it accommodates the motherboard. The motherboard is mounted to the bottom of the case by standoffs and screws. **Standoffs** are small plastic or metal pieces that keep the motherboard from touching the case. If the motherboard touches the case, it will short itself out and could damage the electronic chips. Make sure that the screws and standoffs line up with the holes drilled in the motherboard. (Note: Some proprietary cases will accommodate only proprietary motherboards.) Another factor in matching a case with a motherboard is how many expansion slots the case will accommodate. More importantly, if the motherboard is inserted properly into the case, do the expansion slots line up with the expansion gaps located at the back of the computer, which allows you to access your expansion cards from the outside?

The last criterion for choosing the case concerns the power supply. Most cases today come with power supplies. If you are installing a power supply into a case, make sure it has the same type of on/off switch and is located in the same place. Some systems may use a toggle switch or a push-button switch. The switches may be located on the side, front, or back of the system.

Cases will usually have other options. One option is a reset switch, which allows you to reset the computer without actually using the on/off switch. Using the reset switch is a little easier on the system's power supply. Another option cases can have is a locking device that can lock the case so that no one can open it. It can also prevent anyone from typing on the keyboard. The locking devices can be locked and unlocked with a key. Unfortunately, most keys are generic keys, which are mass-produced.

9.1.2 RFI RADIATION

Protecting the PC components is not the only function of the case. It also limits the flow of **RFI radiation** (radio frequency interference) from the computer. Since some of the radiation is broadcast as radio and television signals, an electronic component can interrupt a radio, a television set, or the navigation equipment used in aircraft.

The amount of RFI generated by an electronic device is monitored by the Federal Communications Commission (FCC). The FCC divides electronic devices into two classifications. Class A digital devices are those suited only for business, commercial, and industrial applications. They include mainframes and minicomputers. For a device to be accepted as a class A device, it must not cause interference to radio or television reception when separated from the television set or radio by one wall and 300 feet or more. These standards are considered to describe the average business or industrial site. Class B devices are those likely to be used in the home. Personal computers are class B devices. Class B equipment cannot produce interference with a radio or television reception when separated from the television set or radio by one wall and 30 feet. The 30 feet and the one wall are considered to describe the average household. Naturally, for a device to achieve a class B certification, it must be better designed and have better quality control than a class A device. (Note: The FCC does not classify motherboards, cases, and power supplies by themselves but all three of them together.)

Computer manufacturers use several techniques to minimize the RFI radiation. A steel case does a fair job of limiting RFI. A plastic case is treated with conductive paint made with silver to minimize radiation. The chassis is grounded to the case, and the cables are shielded. As the frequencies of the PC increase, so does the radiation. Radio signals can leak out through any cracks in the case or if parts of the chassis are not electrically connected to the case. Cables attached to the computer can act as an antenna, sending out radio signals. To reduce the emissions, special metal fingers on the edge of the case and its lid ensure that the two pieces have good electrical contact and that the cables are shielded.

9.2 THE POWER SUPPLY

Since the power outlet supplies ac power and the computer needs dc power, something is needed to convert the ac power to dc. The primary function of the PC power supply is to convert ac power to clean dc power (± 5 V and ± 12 V). Clean power has very little voltage variation, or *noise*. The $+5$ V is used by most of the integrated chips that make up the PC. Therefore, power supplies are designed to produce large amounts of 5 V current (20 or more amperes).

As stated back in chapter 1, computers transfer information by means of binary code–based on/off switches. An *on* switch represents a 1, which is a high logic state; an *off* switch represents a 0, which is a low logic state. The most common type of digital integrated chip (IC) used in the computer is the transistor-transistor logic (TTL) chip, which is characterized by its fast switching speed. All TTL ICs use a $+5$ V power supply. The high logic state is indicated by a signal measuring between 2 and 5 V, while the low logic state signal uses 0 to .8 V. The voltage between .8 and 2 V is the undefined region. This voltage range is used as the signal changes from high to low or low to high.

The $+12$ V are used by the hard drives and floppy drives. The higher voltage is needed to operate the motors, which spin the drives, and is used to generate the output voltages of older serial ports. The -12 V is also used to generate the output voltages for older serial ports, while -5 V was used in older floppy disk-drive controller cards. Most modern PCs do not usually use -5 V and -12 V signals, even though you will find -5 V within the ISA expansion slot because it is part of the ISA standard. The Micro Channel Architecture and the local bus slots do not include a connection for -5 V.

Some chips that include the newest microprocessors use 3.3 V to operate. The motherboard has to convert the 5 V of older power supplies to 3.3 V. Newer power supplies, such as the ATX power supply, include a 3.3 V power line.

Much like cases, power supplies come in many different sizes and shapes. The traditional ones are the XT, AT, baby AT, tower, baby tower, and mini-style power supplies; the most common is the baby AT power supply. (See fig. 9.2.) The newest type of power supply is the **ATX power supply.** Instead of blowing air out of the system, it blows air into the system directly over the microprocessor. This helps cool the microprocessor, eliminating the need for a microprocessor fan, and pressurizes the inside of the case, keeping it clean. In addition, it provides software control of the power on/off signal so that it can shut down the system with software and a 5 V standby signal so that the system can be turned on with the keyboard.

FIGURE 9.2 XT (left) and AT (right) power supplies (Courtesy of PC Power & Cooling, Inc.)

There are two kinds of power supplies, linear power supplies and switching power supplies, and they have several common characterisitics. Power supplies need to rectify, filter, regulate, and isolate electronic signals. **Rectification** is the process by which ac current is turned into dc current. It is usually coupled with **filtering,** the smoothing of the ripple of the rectified voltage. Without filtering, the computer would not provide clean dc power. **Regulated power supplies** are those whose output voltages are independent of line and load variations. This means that no matter how many items are connected to the power supply, it will provide the voltage needed by each item up to the capacity of the power supply. *Isolation* means that the output devices are separated from the ac lines.

9.2.1 LINEAR POWER SUPPLIES

Linear power supplies consist of ac electricity being sent through a step-down transformer. The transformer reduces the voltage to a value slightly higher than what is required by the computer's circuits. Next, several rectifiers and filters consisting of diodes, capacitors, and transistors convert the low-voltage ac to dc.

The linear power supply uses an output pass transistor to regulate the dc power. The transistor acts like a variable resistor to control the output voltage. If the power supply is generating too much power, the resistance of the transistor will increase, which decreases the voltage. The excess voltage is dissipated as heat. Finally, the dc is sent through a linear voltage regulator, which adjusts the voltage created by the power supply to the level required by the computer's circuits.

One advantage of a linear power supply is that it is easier to service than other types of power supplies and it has no hazardous voltages stored in large capacitors like other types of power supplies. A disadvantage of the linear power supply is that it dissipates excess voltage through heat, making the efficiency low (usually under 50%).

9.2.2 SWITCHING POWER SUPPLIES

Most personal computers use a **switching power supply,** also known as a *self-resetting, foldback power supply.* These power supplies are smaller yet more efficient than the linear power supply.

In a switching power supply, the ac voltage is sent through a rectifier and a filter, which convert the ac voltage into high-voltage dc power. The rectifier usually consists of a diode bridge or a voltage doubler. The voltage leaving the rectifier is between 150 and 300 V. The power is sent through an oscillator, which switches on and off at high rates of speed (20 to 40 kHz). The oscillation will vary depending on the dc output required. If the output voltage needs to increase, the oscillator will remain on longer, supplying more power. If the output voltage needs to decrease, the oscillator will not stay on as long. The resulting voltage is then bridged to form dc power by means of capacitors and a second set of filters, which are both are used to even out current flow. (See fig. 9.3.) In PCs, this output is then

FIGURE 9.3   Block diagram of a switching power supply

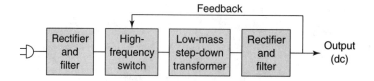

sent across a second transformer, which breaks down the output voltage into the needed voltages ($+/-5$ V and $+/-12$ V).

The switching power supply gets its name from the switching action of the oscillator. The oscillator is not an ideal switch for this system, but it does produce little heat, so efficiency can be as high as 85%. The switching power supply is ideal for personal computers because of another, unique characteristic—overload protection. If a power supply is either shorted or overloaded, it kicks into idle mode and does not supply power to the computer. The idle mode helps protect the computer circuitry from damaging power fluctuations. (See fig. 9.4.)

9.2.3   THE POWER-GOOD SIGNAL AND THE RESET SWITCH

In addition to supplying power to the PC components, the power supply also provides the **power-good signal.** You may recall from chapter 7 that the microprocessor timer chip tells the computer to reset constantly. As soon as the power supply performs a self-test, testing whether all voltage and current levels are acceptable, it will send a power-good signal ($+5$ V) to the microprocessor timer chip. When the power-good signal is sent, the computer will finish the boot process.

If the power supply experiences a short or overload, the switching power supply will go into idle mode by stopping the power-good signal. The purpose of the power-good signal is to prevent the computer from running on intolerable voltages. If the power-good signal is grounded with a wire and the power supply goes into idle mode, the PC will shut down. If the same ground wire has a switch (for example, a push button) added to it, the switch will re-boot the computer. This push button, called a **reset button,** is found on most cases. This is useful when the computer "freezes up" and a soft boot (Ctrl-Alt-Del) does not work.

9.2.4   POWER SUPPLIES OVERSEAS

As already stated, most power supplies designed to be used in the United States operate at 120 V with a frequency of 60 Hz. In other nations, the supply voltage and frequency may be different. In Europe, 230 V with a 50 Hz frequency is the standard. Most modern switching power supplies are willing to operate at either voltage. Some can automatically switch over to the proper voltage, while most are adjusted by a small switch on the rear of the power supply. Make sure when plugging in your PC and before turning it on that the

FIGURE 9.4   Picture of inside power supply

correct voltage is selected. If the power supply is switch to 230 V and the voltage is 120 V, there will be no problem, except the PC will not boot. If, however, the power supply is set to 120 V and it is connected to a 230 V outlet, the power supply and other important components will be seriously damaged.

Inexpensive voltage converters should not be used to convert a PC's power supply. Even though the voltage levels will be correct, the frequency usually will not be adjusted, which may damage the PC.

9.2.5 POWER SUPPLY CONNECTIONS

The IBM PC had four connectors coming from the power supply; newer power supplies usually have more. Two of these connectors attach to the motherboard and the others connect to the floppy drives, hard drives, CD drives, and other devices.

Many motherboards have two motherboard connectors, identified as P8 and P9, that use **Burndy connectors.** (See fig. 9.5 and table 9.1) These connectors are supposed to be keyed—that is, they have small tabs sticking out—so that you cannot put one in the wrong

FIGURE 9.5   Power supply connectors (P8 and P9) that connect to the motherboard. Note that the black cables are together.

TABLE 9.1   Motherboard power connectors

	Connector	AT, XT-286 Voltages*	PC, XT Voltage	Typical Colors
P8 (motherboard connector #1)	P8-1	+5 V (power-good signal)	+5 V (power-good signal)	Orange
	P8-2	+5 V	Not connected	Red
	P8-3	+12 V	+12 V	Yellow
	P8-4	−12 V	−12 V	Blue
	P8-5	0 V (ground)	0 V (ground)	Black
	P8-6	0 V (ground)	0 V (ground)	Black
P9 (motherboard connector #2)	P9-1	0 V (ground)	0 V (ground)	Black
	P9-2	0 V (ground)	0 V (ground)	Black
	P9-3	−5 V	−5 V	White
	P9-4	+5 V	+5 V	Red
	P9-5	+5 V	+5 V	Red
	P9-6	+5 V	+5 V	Red

*Acceptable voltage ranges are 4.5 to 5.4 for 5 V, and 10.8 to 12.9 for 12 V.

FIGURE 9.6 ATX power supply connector

place. Unfortunately, some replacement power supplies are shipped without the proper keying. Therefore, a good rule to follow is to place the black wires of each connector together. If you fail to do this, you will destroy the motherboard or the microprocessor, or both. ATX motherboards have a single 20-pin connector. (See fig. 9.6 and table 9.2.) It supplies all the standard voltages that older previous power supplies do, but it also supplies 3.3 V, so the motherboard does not have to convert 5 V to 3.3 V.

Not all motherboards use the two Burndy connectors or the ATX connector. Some use a Molex connector, which is slightly different from a Burndy, while others use a connector that combines the two Burndy connectors into one large connection. The Molex connectors use smaller, square pins; the combined Burndy connection has rectangular pins. The only way that you can plug in the wrong connector is by forcing it.

The remaining connectors are used for floppy drives, hard drives, tape drives, and other peripherals and come in two sizes. The 5¼″ connector was part of the IBM PC. It has a rectangular shape with two corners clipped off. When the connector is plugged into the drive, the two clipped corners prevent it from being connected upside down. The other connector is smaller and is used to connect 3½″ drives. This connector has a ridge that allows the plug to be inserted in only one way. (See fig. 9.7 and table 9.3.)

TABLE 9.2 ATX power supply motherboard power connector

Pin	ATX Voltage	Color	Pin	ATX Voltage	Color
1	+3.3 V	Orange	11	+3.3 V	Orange
2	+3.3 V	Orange	12	−12 V	Blue
3	0 V (ground)	Black	13	0 V (ground)	Black
4	+5 V	Red	14	+5 V (power supply on)	Green
5	0 V (ground)	Black	15	0 V (ground)	Black
6	+5 V	Red	16	0 V (ground)	Black
7	0 V (ground)	Black	17	0 V (ground)	Black
8	+5 V (power-good signal)	Gray	18	−5 V	White
9	+5 V (stand-by signal)	Purple	19	+5 V	Red
10	+12 V	Yellow	20	+5 V	Red

FIGURE 9.7 5¼″ and 3½″ power connectors

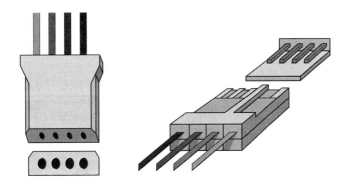

TABLE 9.3 Disk drive power connectors

Connector	Voltage	Color
P10-1	+12 V	Yellow
P10-2	0 V (ground)	Black
P10-3	0 V (ground)	Black
P10-4	+5 V	Red

Acceptable voltage ranges are 4.5 to 5.4 for 5 V, and 10.8 to 12.9 for 12 V.

> **WARNING** Be careful to plug these in the correct way and not force them in the wrong way. If they are improperly connected, 12 V will enter components that are made for 5 V. This will result in damaged or blown chips, and the cable may catch on fire.

9.2.6 POWER SUPPLY CAPACITY

The power supply capacity is measured in watts (W). The wattage rating of a power supply is the maximum amount of electric power a device can safely handle continuously. If the amount of power exceeds the wattage rating of the power supply, the power supply detects an overload and shuts down into idle mode.

When the IBM PC was introduced, it had a small (63.5 W) power supply. This power supply could handle two floppy drives, a video card, and the XT motherboard. If a hard drive and a memory expansion card were added, the power supply would sometimes kick into idle mode because the power supply was overloaded.

The IBM XT and IBM AT had larger power supplies (130 W), which allowed expandability. Most power supplies today have ratings between 200 W and 300 W. The more devices connected to the computer, the more wattage the PC will need. (See table 9.4.)

9.2.7 ON/OFF SWITCH

If you buy a case with a power supply, the power supply is already connected to the on/off switch. The on/off switch is either a push button or a paddle switch. If you have to add a power supply to the case or replace a power supply, you must connect four cables to the on/off switch. The colors of the connectors in the switch are brown, blue, white, and black. (See fig. 9.8.) If the cables are connected 90° off (such as the brown cable connected where blue is supposed to be, black connected where brown is supposed to be, white connected where black is supposed to be, and blue connected where white is supposed to be), you will blow a fuse in the fuse box and knock out all power to the ac outlet as well as any other power outlets on the same circuit. (Note: Since some on/off switches use nonstandard

TABLE 9.4   Maximum output for various power supplies

Specified Output Wattage	Voltage of Devices Powered				Calculated Output Wattage
	+5 V	**−5 V**	**+12 V**	**−12 V**	
100 W	10.0 A	0.3 A	3.5 A	0.3 A	97.1 W
150 W	15.0 A	0.3 A	5.5 A	0.3 A	146.1 W
200 W	20.0 A	0.3 A	8.0 A	0.3 A	201.1 W
250 W	25.0 A	0.5 A	10.0 A	0.5 A	253.5 W
300 W	32.0 A	1.0 A	10.0 A	1.0 A	297.0 W
450 W	45.0 A	0.5 A	15.0 A	1.0 A	419.5 W

Example: A power supply rated at 100 W could simultaneously power +5 V devices requiring a maximum of 10 A, −5 V devices requiring a maximum of 0.3 A, +12 V devices requiring a maximum of 3.5 A, and −12 V devices requiring a maximum of 0.3 A.

FIGURE 9.8   On/off switches

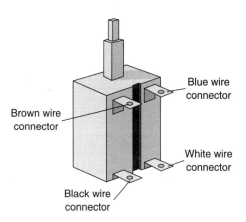

Blue wire connector

Brown wire connector

White wire connector

Black wire connector

color schemes, it is important to record how the wires are connected before disconnecting them.)

9.2.8   POWER EQUIPMENT CERTIFICATION

To make sure that power supplies are safe to use, several testing and certification organizations have set up standards for their design and manufature. One of the most well known of these organizations is **Underwriters Laboratories Inc. (UL),** an independent, nonprofit organization. The purpose of UL is to act as a safety engineering consultant and provide certification. Owing to UL's strict standards and solid reputation, companies pay UL to detect flaws and defects in their products before the products hit the market.

Underwriters Laboratories deals with all electronic devices. Computers and other related equipment, including desktop PCs, disk drives, printers, main frame computers, desktop calculators, and electric typewriters, come under the UL 1950 standard. UL gives a product a UL Listing or UL Recognition. A UL Listing applies to a complete product, such as a desktop PC, a monitor, or a power supply. UL Recognition applies to a component used to make up products such as the power supply.

9.2.9   KEEPING THE PC COOL

One of the biggest enemies of the PC, and particularly of its semiconductor circuits, is heat buildup. Heat is generated when a current flows against electrical resistance and whenever an element of a computer circuit changes logical states. Inside the case, heat cannot escape, so it builds up, driving up the temperature. Heat shortens the life span of the circuits, which will lead to computer failure. Therefore, keeping a system cool means prolonging its life.

Ventilation holes were added to the case of the IBM PC to keep the PC cooler by letting the heat out. When setting up a PC, remember to allow good ventilation and to not block or restrict the ventilation holes. The ventilation slots in the case should have at least three feet of free space. Additionally, if the power supply is run close to its full capacity or exceeds it, it tends to overheat.

Most PCs produce heat faster than heat can escape through the ventilation holes. Therefore, they need some active cooling to force the heat away from the circuits. A fan has been added to the power supply to circulate the air around the case. To ensure adequate cooling in a computer system, the case should always be kept closed and the card blockoff plates (the plates that cover an expansion card hole in the back of the computer when an expansion slot is not being used) should be in place so that the airflow within the case will be maintained. (See fig. 9.9.) One fan is not enough, however, for the newer microprocessors. Some power supplies use two fans; others use a heat sink and/or fan on the microprocessor. The **heat sink** is a piece of metal with a large surface area. It takes heat away from the microprocessor and dissipates it faster than a fan system.

Question: Should you shut off your computer when you leave your desk or should you keep it on all day?

Answer: If you are coming and going from your desk, leave the computer on all the time. Studies show that computers will last longer if you leave them on. It is not the sudden electrical surge that does the damage when the system is turned on, but the sudden heating and cooling. Of course, at the end of the day, you can shut off your computer.

9.3 TROUBLESHOOTING POWER SUPPLIES

Since the power supply is a half-electronic and half-mechanical component, it is considered a high-failure item compared to other items within the PC that do not have any mechanical parts. The mechanical part of the power supply is the fan. If the fan fails, the PC will heat to a level that can damage other components. In addition, if the power supply is supplying the proper power and the fan has failed, the PC may have boot-up failures, boot-up errors, memory errors, and device failures and may give off electrical shock when the case or connections are touched.

As a general rule, when a power supply fails, it is easier, quicker, and usually cheaper to replace it than to repair it. Replacement is usually cheaper because it takes more time to diagnose and repair a power supply. It is the time spent that drives the cost up. In addition, you need to have some skills as an electronic technician to be able to successfully repair a power supply.

When checking a system that has no power, the first thing to do is to see if the power supply is plugged into the ac outlet and the PC is on. Remember that the power should be 120 V ac at 60 Hz. Next, check the ac power cord to see if it is good.

Before opening the power supply, check that the fan is running and that the power supply is generating the proper dc voltages. The best way to check for proper voltages is to use a voltmeter or a digital multimeter (DMM). To check the voltage level, the power supply must have a load. This can be done by connecting a nonexpensive peripheral or using a dummy load. Floppy drives should not be used because they are devices that come on only when they are being accessed. A dummy load may be a 2- or 3-ohm 15 W resistor on the +5 output (red wire). If there is no load on the power supply, the power supply will falsely detect a short, which causes it to go into idle mode. (Note: Power supplies that do not go into idle mode without a load are not well designed and do not offer as much protection against power problems.) Next, set the voltmeter to the proper dc scale and measure the voltage. Be sure to check multiple connections. If the power is bad on one connection but is good on the others, that indicates a power cable and/or connector is bad.

The large filter capacitors are second only to the fan as a common source of failure within the power supply. To test the capacitors, you would set a voltmeter to the ac scale to measure ripple (ac fluctuations). The ac scale will show how clean the output voltage is. The ac voltage should be 200 mV or less (zero or almost zero). If the capacitors are dried up or have an open in them, this will cause a pulsing at 60 or 120 Hz and all kinds of regulation problems.

If you choose to repair the power supply rather than replace it, there are certain things that you must consider.

> **WARNING** The filter capacitors used in switching power supplies can store an amount of energy that can kill. What makes things more dangerous is that these capacitors can store the energy for months after nonuse of the power supply. In addition, if the capacitors are discharged into other components of the power supply, there is a good chance that those components will be damaged. Always discharge the capacitors before working within the power supply.

Many books recommend using a screwdriver to short out the two connecting wires to discharge the capacitor. A better method is to use a high-wattage resistor. This resistor will prevent an electrical arc yet allow the capacitor to be discharged within a few seconds. After discharging the capacitor, check to see if there is a fuse within the power supply that may have been blown. The fuse protects against an overload resulting from a short circuit. If there is excessive current, the heat generated by the excessive current will melt the fuse, which will, of course, shut down the power supply and, in turn, protect the computer. A blown fuse is easy to diagnose and repair. What you need to be concerned with is why there was an overload that caused the fuse to blow in the first place. After checking the fuse, inspect the other components (resistors, capacitors, and diodes) and visually check the solder joints and traces for damage. Lastly, remember that damage that cannot be seen can occur inside the chip or component.

9.4 POWER FLUCTUATIONS

When you turn on a PC, you expect the power to be there. Unfortunately, the power that you get from the power company is not always 120 V ac. The voltage level may drop or increase. While the power supply can handle many of these power fluctuations, other power fluctuations may shut down or damage the computer, corrupt the data, and lose unsaved work. (See fig. 9.10.)

Studies done by IBM show that a typical computer is subject to more than 120 power problems per month. The most common of these are voltage sags. Obvious power problems such as blackouts and lightning make up only 12% of power problems. American Power Conversion states that power problems cause 45.3% of data losses.

Symptoms of bad power are frozen computers or keyboards, errors in data transmissions, corrupted or lost data, frequently aborted modem transfers, and total failure of a computer or computer component.

9.4.1 OVERVOLTAGES AND UNDERVOLTAGES

Power line irregularities can be classified into two categories: overvoltages and undervoltages. The more dangerous is overvoltage, which is defined as voltage in excess of 10% of

FIGURE 9.10　Power irregularities

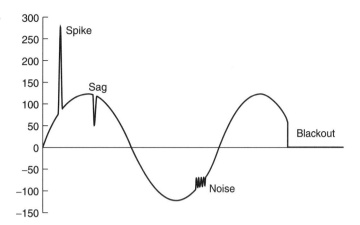

the power supply rating. The worst of these is a spike, which lasts only a nanosecond but can measure as high as 25,000 V (normally caused by lightning). A **spike** is sometimes defined as transient overvoltage. A **surge,** which can stretch into milliseconds, is overvoltage of longer duration. Spikes and surges can visibly damage the electronic components or can cause microdamage, which cannot be seen. Other causes of overvoltage besides lightning include when overburdened power grids switch from one source to another and when a high-powered electrical motor tries to grab power.

Undervoltages (including total power failure) make up 87% of all power problems and occur when the computer gets less voltage than is needed to run properly. Most PCs are designed to withstand prolonged voltage dips of about 20% without shutting down. Power outages and short drops in power typically do not physically damage the computer. Unfortunately, they do result in lost and corrupted data.

Undervoltage takes the form of sags, brownouts, and blackouts. **Sags,** which usually are not a problem, are very short drops lasting only a few milliseconds. **Brownouts** last longer than sags and can force the computer to shut down, introduce memory errors, and cause unsaved work to be lost. (Note: Brownouts or power failures of 200 milliseconds are sufficient to cause power problems with the PC. These problems can be caused by damaged power lines and by equipment that draws massive amounts of power, such as air conditioners, copy machines, laser printers, space heaters, and coffee makers.) **Blackouts** are total power failures.

9.4.2　NOISE

In addition to power line overvoltages and undervoltages, the computer may experience electrical **noise,** radio frequency interference (RFI), caused by telephones, motors, fluorescent lights, and radio transmitters. Noise can introduce errors into executable programs and files. (Note: To limit the chance of ac line noise, a computer should be installed on its own power circuit.)

9.4.3　POWER PROTECTION

Most voltage fluctuations can be prevented from doing any damage. There are several devices that can protect the computer from overvoltages and undervoltages: surge protectors, line conditioners, standby power supplies, and uninterruptible power supplies.

The most common of the power protection devices is the **surge protector.** A surge protector is designed to prevent most short-duration, high-intensity spikes and surges from reaching the PC by absorbing excess voltages. (See fig. 9.11.) The most common surge protector uses a metal oxide varistor (MOV). A MOV looks like a brightly colored plastic-coated disk capacitor and works by siphoning electricity to ground when the voltage exceeds 200 V. Consequently, the voltage spike is "clipped" and the excess electricity is then converted into heat. Other devices used to suppress overvoltages are gas discharge tubes,

FIGURE 9.11   Surge protector

pellet arrestors, and coaxial arrestors. The better surge protectors use a combination of these.

When purchasing a surge protector, you should consider its clamping voltage and clamping speed. The **clamping voltage** is the voltage at which the surge protector will clip the overvoltage, and the **clamping speed** is the amount of time it takes to respond to an overvoltage. Some surge protectors also use a circuit breaker. A circuit breaker is a mechanical fuse that opens the circuit when there is too much current. Unlike a fuse, the breaker can be manually reset without replacing it. Phone line surge protectors are also available. If a modem, fax/modem, or fax is connected to the PC, consider getting one. It will prevent surges and spikes that travel through the telephone lines.

Surge protectors have several drawbacks. First, they protect only against overvoltages, not undervoltages. In addition, the life expectancy of a MOV is limited. With every spike, the MOV gets weaker and weaker until it can't protect the PC anymore. When buying a surge protector, make sure it has some kind of indicator (LED light or a beep) to indicate when it can no longer protect. In addition, be extremely careful that the device is not one that just provides extra power connections, like an extension cord.

The next level of protection is the **line conditioner.** It uses the inductance of transformers to filter out noise, and capacitors (and other circuits) to "fill in" brownouts. In addition, most line conditioners include surge protection.

The last two forms of protection are the standby power supply (SPS) and the uninterruptible power supply (UPS). Both of these are based on a large battery. The **standby power supply (SPS)** consists of a battery connected in parallel to the PC. When the SPS detects a power fluctuation, the system switches over to the battery. Of course, the SPS requires a small but measurable amount of time to switch over (usually one-half of one cycle of the ac current, or less than 10 milliseconds). Most built-in surge protection devices are SPSs. The **uninterruptible power supply (UPS)** differs from the SPS in that the battery is connected in series with the PC. The ac power is connected directly to the battery. Since the battery always provides clean dc power, the PC is protected against overvoltages and undervoltages. (See fig. 9.12.) When the SPS and UPS send dc power from the battery, it has to be converted back to ac power before reaching the PC's power supply. Most SPSs and UPSs will generate a sine wave. (Note: Poorer quality SPSs and UPSs generate a square wave instead of a sine wave and should be avoided.) Uninterruptible power supplies are usually not designed to keep the PC running for hours without power. Instead,

FIGURE 9.12   UPS

they are usually intended to give the user or users enough time to save all files and to properly shut down the PC. Laser printers should not be connected to a UPS since they have large current demands and can generate line noise.

> **NOTE** If a UPS or SPS has not been used for a long period of time, do not discharge the battery. If you do, the battery may lose some of its capacity to store power or may be unable to accept a charge at all. Of course, always check the manufacturer's documentation.

One ideal situation for a UPS is local area networks (LANs) and wide area networks (WANs), which consist of many computers connected together, usually with cable. The computers on the network are divided into servers and workstations. Since the main function of the server is to provide file services (multiple users accessing data files, large databases, and application programs), the server accesses disks constantly. If a power disturbance occurs when a file is open or a file is reading or writing, the file can easily become lost or corrupted. If the file allocation table is corrupted, it could lead to losing the entire disk. It is probably not cost-effective to have UPSs for every PC, but it is important that each server have a UPS to help protect against power-related problems.

9.5 TROUBLESHOOTING POWER-RELATED PROBLEMS

When troubleshooting the PC, you should always be concerned with power-related problems. As you have seen, the power problems may be caused by a power supply, bad power provided by the ac power outlet, or a PC component that causes a short or overload. Power problems can cause errors and may cause failure in RAM chips, microprocessors, and hard drives. Power-related problems may be harder to diagnose because they are sometimes not obvious and are often intermittent.

EXAMPLE 1 You turn on the PC and it does not boot, nor do the lights on the front panel light up. After a quick inspection, you notice that the fan is not spinning.

The first thing to check is the obvious. Is the power cord plugged into the ac power outlet and into the back of the computer? You will be amazed how many times this is the problem. Next, make sure that the ac outlet power is on and not shut off with an on/off light switch somewhere within the room.

If the machine is properly connected, make a list of what can cause total failure:

1. A bad power supply
2. The ac outlet
3. The power cable connecting the PC to the ac outlet
4. The power plugs that connect the power supply to the motherboard and drives
5. A short or open in the computer
6. Overloading the power supply

Remember that this is only a list and may not represent the order in which you want to check everything.

Make sure you have ac power from the power outlet. Use a voltmeter or connect another device to the outlet. If the other device works properly, the power is probably good. It may be a good idea to check the voltage at the other end of the power cable or use the same power cable when connecting the other device. This will verify the presence of ac power and verify that the power cord is good.

After checking everything outside of the computer, it is time to open the computer up and take a look inside. After opening the case, check the power connectors leading to the motherboard (P8 and P9) to see if they are connected properly (black to black) and that the drives are connected properly. Remember, to run most switching power supplies, you must have a load. In addition, inspect the floppy drive and hard drive ribbon cables for proper connection.

If the computer is connected properly, you should test the power supply. Disconnect everything connected to the power supply and put a load (inexpensive device or a dummy load) on the power supply. If the power supply does not operate, it is bad. If the power comes on, then there is a short or overload, which is causing the power supply to go into idle mode.

To check for shorts and overloads, you need to use isolation. First take out all of the expansion cards except the video card and the floppy drive/hard drive controller card and disconnect all drives except the floppy disk drive and primary hard drive. If the machine powers on with the minimum devices, one of the components that were removed or disconnected is causing a short or overload, or all of the components together are too much for the power supply. To find out the cause of the problem, insert one expansion card or connect one drive at a time and turn on the machine to find out if that device is the one causing the power supply to go into idle mode.

If the computer still does not work after removing all of the extra devices, the motherboard/RAM, video card, floppy drive/hard drive controller card, floppy drive, or hard drive must be causing the problem. In this case, you must use isolation and replace one device at a time until you find out which one is causing the problem.

9.6 PORTABLE BATTERIES

The power requirements of portable computers (laptops and notebooks) differ from those of a desktop computer because portable computers are designed to decrease power consumption to provide a longer battery life. Therefore, portable computers use a +5 V motor for their hard disk, which eliminates the need for a plug for +12 V. Most newer microprocessors are designed to operate at 3.3 V or less. Finally, portable computers need little power protection because the battery within the portable computer always provides clean low-voltage dc power. (See fig. 9.13.)

To stretch the power of the battery, most notebook and laptop computers have their own power management functions to conserve power. Some may dim the screen down, much like a screen saver, or stop the hard drive from spinning if a certain time of nonuse has passed. If the computer does not have built-in power management features, many of the operating systems have software that helps prolong the life of the battery. For example, you can enable DOS's power management feature by loading POWER.EXE in the

FIGURE 9.13 Notebook battery

TABLE 9.5 Common types of portable batteries

Nickel-cadmium (NiCad)	NiCad batteries provide considerable power but last only two to four hours. Older NiCad batteries can take as much as twelve hours to recharge; newer batteries take only a few hours. NiCads also suffer from memory effects, where if they are partially drained and then recharged, they lose about 40% of their charge. Lastly, NiCad batteries can only be recharged about 1,000 times.
Nickle-metal hydride (NiMH)	NiMH batteries store up to 50% more power than NiCad batteries, and they do not suffer from memory effects. In addition, they do not use the dangerous substances found in NiCads. They can be recharged as many as 500 times; they take nearly twice as long to recharge as NiCads.
Lithium-ion (Li-ion)	Lithium is the lightest metal and has the highest electrochemical potential. Since lithium itself is unstable, lithium-ion batteries are made from lithium ions produced from chemicals. These batteries do not use poisonous metals. *Note:* Do not insert a Li-ion battery into a system designed for a NiCad or NiMH battery; it can result in fire.

CONFIG.SYS file or you can enable Windows 95 and 98's power management feature by using the Power Management applet in the Control Panel.

The most common types of portable batteries are described in table 9.5. Since many of these batteries contain harmful or poisonous chemicals and improper handling and disposal can result in fire or explosion, you should always check the battery label for information on special disposal procedures.

SUMMARY

1. The case of the PC is a large metal or plastic box that protects most of the major PC components and limits the flow of RFI radiation.
2. When choosing a case, you must consider the size, orientation, form factor, the number of drive bays, the number of slots, and the type of power supply.
3. The PC power supply converts ac power into clean dc power. Clean power has very little voltage variation, or noise. The power supply produces ± 5 V and ± 12 V power.
4. Most PCs have switching power supplies. Switching power supplies are small, efficient, and go into idle mode when a short or overload is detected.
5. Two Burndy connectors connect many motherboards to the power supply. When you connect a Burndy connector, the ground wires (black) need to be together.
6. Heat shortens the life span of a circuit, which leads to computer failure.
7. The secondary function of the power supply is to cool the system.
8. Power irregularities cause frozen computers and keyboards, errors in data transmission, corrupted or lost data, frequently aborted modem transfers, and total failure of a computer or computer component.
9. Surge protectors protect against overvoltages; line conditioners protect against undervoltages.
10. Standby power supplies (SPSs) and uninterruptible power supplies (UPSs) use a battery to power the PC during power irregularities.

QUESTIONS

1. Which of the following is *not* true about cases?
   a. they protect the components inside the PC
   b. they reduce RFI emanating from the PC
   c. they are not important for computer operations
   d. they include the power supply, motherboard, RAM, and expansion cards
2. What should you do to ensure adequate cooling in a computer system?
   a. turn off the system when not in use
   b. keep the system fan well lubricated
   c. always keep the case closed
   d. remove an empty slot cover
3. The primary function of the power supply is to:
   a. produce clean dc power
   b. convert ac power into clean dc power
   c. act as a large battery
   d. cool the PC
4. The type of power supply most computers use is:
   a. standby power supply
   b. turn-down power supply
   c. linear power supply
   d. switching power supply
5. When the switching power supply detects a short or overload, the power supply:
   a. will display a message on the monitor
   b. will go into idle mode
   c. compensates by providing more power
   d. keeps on working without change
6. To check the output of the power supply, you would set the meter to:
   a. dc voltage
   b. ac voltage
   c. resistance
   d. capacitance

7. A switching power supply steps down voltage by means of:
   a. a transformer
   b. a network of resistor conduits
   c. turning off and back on in rapid cycles
   d. a network of capacitors

8. When you purchase a replacement power supply for a PC, you should pay particular attention to:
   a. how P8 and P9 are connected
   b. the form factor, including shape, size, mounting holes, and power switch location and its capacity
   c. its voltage rating
   d. the type of regulation used

9. Which of the following voltages is *not* normally present at the output of a personal computer power supply?
   a. +5 V
   b. −5 V
   c. +12 V
   d. −12 V
   e. 120 V

10. The wires coming from the power supply in a personal computer are color coded. What color is used for the ground (or common) wires?
    a. red
    b. black
    c. yellow
    d. blue

11. The wires coming from the power supply in a personal computer are color coded. What color is used for the +5 V wires?
    a. red
    b. black
    c. yellow
    d. blue

12. You have a Windows NT workstation. When you insert a CD-ROM disk and boot up the computer, the computer starts to spin the CD but then reboots. What is the most likely cause of the problem?
    a. a bad CD
    b. a bad power supply
    c. an improperly loaded driver
    d. a bad drive
    e. a bad motherboard

13. Which of the following is the smallest power interruption that can cause memory errors or cause the computer to lock up?
    a. 1 second
    b. ⅕ second
    c. 10 seconds
    d. 1 minute

14. What is the best way to protect a PC during an electrical storm?
    a. back up the hard drive
    b. use a surge protector
    c. power off the system
    d. unplug the power cord

15. To test for ripple on a PC power supply, you should set the multimeter for:
    a. dc voltage
    b. ac voltage
    c. ohms
    d. farads

16. Which of the following can be caused by power fluctuations? (Choose all that apply.)
    a. random memory errors
    b. damaged components inside the computer
    c. hard disk read/write errors
    d. computer lock-up

17. After turning on the computer, it does not boot. You notice that no LEDs are lit on the computer and the fan is not spinning. What is the most likely cause of the problem?
    a. the hard drive has been reformatted
    b. the CMOS battery failed
    c. the LED lights are not connected
    d. the hard drive partition has been deleted
    e. the power supply is bad or the power supply is not receiving any power

18. What is the difference between a sag and a brownout?
    a. a sag typically lasts a few seconds, while a brownout lasts a few hours
    b. a sag typically lasts less than a few milliseconds, while a brownout lasts for a prolonged period
    c. sags are measured in nanoseconds, while brownouts are measured in milliseconds
    d. *sag* and *brownout* are terms that describe the same condition
19. What is the difference between a spike and a surge?
    a. a spike is a very short overvoltage condition measured in nanoseconds, while a surge is measured in microseconds or minutes
    b. a spike is a very short overvoltage condition measured in nanoseconds, while a surge is measured in milliseconds
    c. a surge occurs when the power first drops and then overcorrects within 5 milliseconds, while a spike drops and overcorrects in less than 10 milliseconds
    d. *spike* and *surge* are terms that describe the same condition
20. When purchasing a surge protector, what main factors should be considered?
    a. clamping speed and switching time
    b. switching time and clamping voltage
    c. switching voltage and clamping time
    d. clamping speed and clamping voltage
21. Which of the following contains a battery that is connected between the ac line and the computer and provides constant surge protection?
    a. a power conditioner
    b. a surge suppressor
    c. an uninterruptible power supply (UPS)
    d. a standby power supply (SPS)
22. The output of a UPS should be:
    a. dc voltage
    b. sine wave
    c. square wave
    d. saw wave
23. To limit ac line noise, you should:
    a. use extension cords and surge protectors
    b. install the computer system on its own power circuit
    c. install the computer system on a circuit with other high-wattage units
    d. avoid using a ground connection
24. Which of the following items would require you to comply with EPA disposal guidelines?
    a. keyboard
    b. system board
    c. power supply
    d. battery
25. PCs are:
    a. FCC class A devices
    b. FCC class B devices
    c. FCC class C devices
    d. FCC class D devices
    e. not rated by the FCC

HANDS-ON EXERCISES

Exercise 1: Checking the ac Power Outlet

Use a voltmeter to measure the following voltages:

    hot slot and neutral slot
    hot slot and ground
    neutral slot and ground

Exercise 2: Checking the Power Supply

1. Make sure the computer is off.
2. Disconnect the connectors that lead to the motherboard.
3. Turn on the computer and measure the following voltages from the motherboard power connector: red wire and black wire; yellow wire and black wire.

4. Turn off the computer and reconnect the motherboard connectors.
5. Turn on the computer and measure the following voltages from one of the drive power connectors: red wire and black wire; yellow wire and black wire.
6. Using the drive power connectors, measure the ac voltage between the yellow wire and black wire.
7. Turn off the computer.
8. If your power supply has a voltage selector switch, change the switch to 220 V. (Note: If your computer is designed to use 220 V, do not switch it to 110 V.)
9. Turn on the computer.
10. Shut off the computer and change the voltage selection switch back to 110 V.

Exercise 3: Removing and Installing a Power Supply

1. First see if there is any documentation on the power supply indicating how the on/off switch is connected.
2. Find the power cables connected to the on/off switch and study how they are connected. Compare this connection to the documentation for the power supply. (Note: You may choose to draw a sketch of how the connectors are connected.)
3. Remove the power supply from the computer, including all cables.
4. Reinstall the power supply from the computer. Make sure that the on/off switch is connected properly and that the connectors leading to the motherboard are connected properly.

Exercise 4: Measuring the Voltage of the CMOS Battery

1. Access the CMOS setup program and record the hard drive settings.
2. If the PC has a CMOS battery, measure its voltage while the computer is off.

10 The Hard Drive

INTRODUCTION

Hard drives are half-electronic, half-mechanical devices that store information on rotating platters. They are considered long-term storage and are the primary mass storage system. Of course, since the hard drive contains the bulk of the data files used within the PC, its failure could be disastrous unless the data files have been backed up.

OBJECTIVES

1. Describe the function of the hard drive.
2. List and describe the characteristics of a hard drive platter.
3. Describe the read/write head and how it reads and writes to the platter.
4. Describe the head actuators.
5. Compare and contrast the two types of head actuators.
6. Define tracks, sectors, and cylinders.
7. Calculate the capacity of a hard drive given the number of read/write heads, the number of sectors and tracks, and the number of cylinders.
8. Explain zone recordings and sector translation.
9. Compare and contrast CHS addressing, translation addressing, and LBA.
10. Define encoding.
11. List the factors that contribute to hard drive performance.
12. List and describe the basic steps in installing a hard drive.
13. Configure and install an IDE or SCSI hard drive in a system.
14. Perform a low-level format, partitioning, and high-level format on a hard drive.
15. Describe RAID and list and describe its levels.
16. Explain the need for terminating resistors and explain where they are needed in a daisy chain.
17. Determine and correct hard drive problems.

10.1   WHAT IS A HARD DRIVE?

Hard drives are half-electronic and half-mechanical devices that use magnetic patterns to store information on rotating platters. They are considered long-term storage devices because they do not "forget" their information when power is disconnected. They are also considered the primary mass storage system because they hold all the programs and data files that are fed into RAM. The first hard drive used in a PC had a capacity of only 5 MB. Today, hard drives can be 10 GB or larger. Hard drives are sometimes referred to as *fixed disks* because they usually cannot be removed from the PC easily like a floppy disk. This term does not describe all hard drives because there are external hard drives (disks that rest outside the case) and removable hard drives.

Hard drives communicate with the rest of the computer by means of a cable connected to a controller card, which is either an expansion card or built into the motherboard. All hard drives consist of the following components: rotating platters, read/write heads, and head actuators. (See fig. 10.1.) Another type of hard drive is the hard card. A **hard card,** made for systems that do not have available drive bays, is a hard disk drive and controller on a single expansion card. The capacity of a hard card is usually limited.

10.1.1   PLATTERS

The name *hard drive* is derived from the fact that the platters are solid. The **platters** rotate around a spindle with speeds as low as 3,600 rotations per minute (rpm) and as fast as 7,200 rpm or more. A typical speed is 5,400 rpm. A faster speed usually means that the access time (the time it takes to find the data) and throughput time (the time needed for data transfer) are greater.

The platters do not store the actual data. Instead, they store patterns of 0s and 1s. The platters are coated with a magnetic material (iron oxide or a thin-film material) that can hold many tiny magnetic fields. When these fields are placed in certain patterns, they represent 0s and 1s. The bits of information are written and read using a read/write head.

The size of the drive is partially determined by the size of each platter and the number of platters stacked on top of each other. When drives were first used in the IBM PC, the platters were 5¼″ in diameter. Later drives were reduced to 3½″. Today, there are 2½″ and 1.8″ drives that hold more information than the older models.

The platters are made of aluminum, glass, or ceramic material, chosen because they are light, inexpensive, inherently flat, nonmagnetic, and rugged and have a low thermal coefficient. The platters must be light to minimize the power required to spin them. Their low thermal coefficient means that temperature changes do not have much effect on the size

FIGURE 10.1 Inside a hard drive

Platter   Spindle

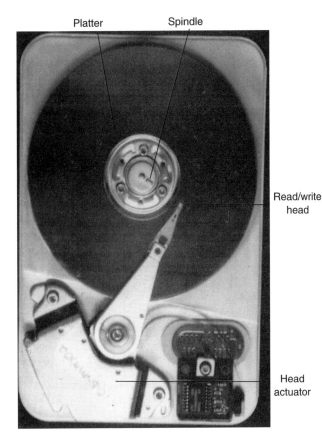

Read/write
head

Head
actuator

and shape of the platters. If they are inherently flat, the read/write heads can get closer to the surface without touching it. If a read/write head is closer to the platter, it can generate a denser magnetic field, which allows more information to be stored in a smaller area. The platters need to be nonmagnetic because it is the coating that needs to be magnetized, not the platter. Lastly, the platters must be rugged enough to withstand the high rotational speeds without changing size or shape. Some drives use aluminum platters and others use a newer glass-ceramic composite. These glass platters resist cracking better than normal glass and are more rigid than aluminum platters, permitting the platters to be half as thick as aluminum platters or less. In addition, they resist expanding and contracting with temperature changes better than aluminum.

Older hard drives had platters coated with syrup containing iron oxide particles (fine rust). After the syrup was applied to the entire surface, it was cured and polished to make it as smooth as possible and coated with carbon to make it harder. The smoother the surface, the closer the read/write head can be positioned to the platter, allowing denser magnetic fields and so increasing storage capacity. By the time the coating process is completed, it is about 30 millionths of an inch thick and has a brownish or amber color. (See fig. 10.2.) The softness of the iron oxide coating is a disadvantage. If the read/write head touches the platter while it is spinning at high speeds, the surface of the platter could easily be scratched. If the disk drive runs constantly, the magnetic oxide may move outward because of centrifugal force, resulting in track shifting. If the drive overheats, the iron oxide coating will soften even more, and when the computer is shut off, the read/write head could get stuck in the coating as it hardens. If that happens, you would have to hold the hard drive firmly in your hand and "flick your wrist" very hard in hope of freeing the read/write head.

Newer hard drives use a thin-film medium that appears as a smooth, shiny silver surface. The thin-film medium is thinner and smoother than the older iron oxide coating and is much harder. This allows for read/write heads to be closer to the platters, and the platter is more resistant to surface damage if the read/write head makes contact with the surface.

Two techniques are used to apply the thin-film coating to the platter. *Plated* thin-film coatings are electroplated to the platter, much as chrome is applied to automobiles. The platters are immersed in a series of chemical baths. When an electric current is applied, the platters

FIGURE 10.2   Older hard drive with iron oxide coating and stepper motor

attract the cobalt (magnetic material) in the bath, which plates the surface of the platters. The coating is approximately 3 millionths of an inch thick. *Sputtered* thin-film coating is applied in two layers, nickel phosphorus followed by cobalt alloy. Sputtering, which must be done in a near vacuum, is a form of vapor plating in which metal is ejected from a hot electrode and electrically attracted to the platter. To protect the surface, a third coat of carbon is applied. The surface of sputtered platters contains magnetic layers as thin as 1 millionth of an inch.

Do not take a hard drive or any other type of medium that uses magnetism to store data through a metal detector. Since metal detectors use strong magnetic fields to find metal objects, the magnetic media could easily be destroyed.

10.1.2   READ/WRITE HEADS

A read/write head reads the data from a platter and writes the data to a platter. (See fig. 10.3.) A hard disk drive usually has one read/write head for each side of a platter. If, therefore, a drive has three platters, it could have up to six read/write heads. The read/write heads are connected by a head rack, which resembles a "multifingered" arm. The arm is moved back and forth by the head actuator.

FIGURE 10.3   Read/write head

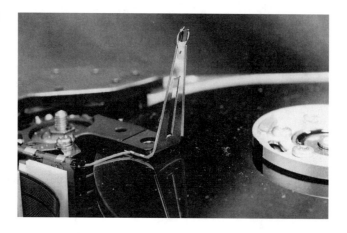

FIGURE 10.4   Objects that can cause head-to-disk interference (HDI)

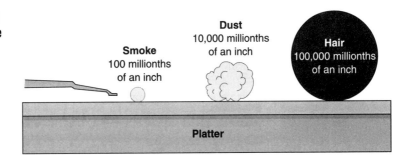

The basic read/write head is a wire shaped like a coil winding (inductor). When electricity is applied to the coil, it acts as an electromagnet. To write to a disk, current is sent through the wire and an electromagnetic field forms around the wire. As it passes through the coil, the electromagnetic field is intensified. When this electromagnetic field crosses the magnetic material on the platters, the magnetic material also becomes magnetized. To read from the platter, the process is reversed. The read/write head approaches the magnetized material, and when the coil detects a magnetic charge, it causes a small amount of current to flow in the coil. After this signal is amplified and filtered, the current is translated into 0s and 1s.

When the computer is shut off, the heads, which are spring-loaded, touch the platter. When the computer is turned on, air pressure caused by the spinning of the platters within the sealed drive causes the read/write head to rise off the platter. Therefore, the read/write head does not actually touch the platter while it spins. The distance between the read/write head and the platter is between 3 to 20 millionths of an inch. Since the gap is so small, the smallest particle of dust or cigarette smoke would act like a boulder placed between the read/write head and platter. These tiny boulders could cause the heads to read improperly and could cause physical damage to the read/write head and the platter. A grinding noise might be heard. This damage is called **head-to-disk interference (HDI).** (See fig. 10.4.) A hard drive should therefore not be opened except in a clean-room environment (a specially designed room or area from which most of the particles in the air have been filtered out). For hard drives, the clean room cannot contain more than 100 particles larger than 19.7 millionths of an inch per cubic foot. A typical person just breathing puts out approximately 500 of these particles in a single minute. Therefore, when working in a clean room, a technichian must wear special clothing and a mask to reduce the number of particles in the air.

The basic read/write head used in the early PC drives could be categorized as an inductive read/write head because it was based on the concept of an electromagnet and the law of induction. One type was the composite ferrite head, which had a small ferrite core bonded with glass in a ceramic housing. Another type was the metal-in-gap (MIG) head. MIG heads were formed much like the composite heads, but since newer techniques (sputtering) were used in making them, they were smaller and lighter. This allowed them to get even closer to the surface, which increased the magnetic field and allowed more data to be written to a smaller area.

Today, most drives have thin-film (TF) heads. These read/write heads are made with a photolithographic process much like the one used in chip manufacturing. This process starts with a mask (picture outline) of the read/write head. A special lens reduces the illuminated mask image to a smaller image on the surface of a silicon wafer coated with light-sensitive material. Acid is then used to eat away the surface covered by the light shining through the read/write head pattern. A single circular wafer can create thousands of tiny, high-quality read/write heads.

Unlike previous read/write heads, TF heads do not actually have a coil. Instead, the heads are completely enclosed by a hard aluminum material, which makes them much more resistant to damage if they touch the surface of the platter while it is spinning. The core of the head is a combination of iron and nickel, making the magnetic field two to four times more powerful than that of a ferrite head core. Because of its small size and powerful magnetic field, the TF head can get as close as two millionths of an inch to the surface of the platter, and the platters can be closer together, which allows more platters to be stacked in a drive.

Magnetoresistive (MR) heads are really two read/write heads in one. The MR part of the head is optimized to read, while the TF part of the head is optimized to write. Instead of measuring the current, MR heads are made of a material that changes its electrical resistance in the presence of a magnetic field. When the small current sent through the head encounters a magnetic field, the resistance changes, resulting in a voltage change. The voltage changes are then interpreted as 0s and 1s. These heads are extremely sensitive to magnetic fields, but electromagnetic shields allow it to focus on the area to be read. Most drives today are MR drives.

The proximity or semicontact head is a new type of read/write head. Proximity heads are inductive read/write heads and come as close as .8 millionths of an inch to the platter. Since the proximity head rides so low, it makes contact with the platter often, but these heads and newer platters are more rugged than previous heads and platters, which helps them avoid physical damage when they make contact.

Areal density is the term for the physical amount of data that can be held on an area of a platter; it is expressed in bits per square inch. It is calculated by multiplying the bit density (bits per inch, or BPI) by the track density (tracks per inch, or TPI). Hard drives are capable of areal densities of 500 to 1,000 megabits per square inch. **Coercitivity** measures the strength of the magnetic field used to store data on the platters. The coercitivity of hard drive media usually exceeds 1,400 oersteds compared with 600 oersteds for floppy media. If the coercitivity of a magnetic platter is high, it will take a stronger magnetic field to change it. The coercitivity is influenced by the type of platter, the magnetic material on the platter, the type of read/write head, the amount of current through the head, and the distance between the head and the platter.

10.1.3   HEAD ACTUATOR

The **head actuator** is the component that moves the read/write heads back and forth. There are two types: the stepper motor actuator and the voice coil actuator.

Stepper motors are electrical motors that move from one position to another in steps. Unfortunately, the stepper motor cannot take half steps. If the stepper motor is to move the read/write heads to a particular location, it counts the appropriate number of steps, but it has no way of determining whether it has arrived at the correct location. If, for instance, the platters had been left overnight in a cold building, they would contract (shrink). Consequently, when the stepper motor moves the read/write heads the appropriate number of steps, the data would have shifted inward. When the read/write heads try to read the data, they are actually reading between tracks, resulting in read/write errors.

Stepper motor drives are also slow compared to today's voice coil actuators and are sensitive to their physical orientation. This means that after a drive has been prepped while lying flat and it is moved to its side, the read/write head moves a little downward, causing read/write errors. In addition, the magnetic material on these older drives shifts outward over time, so a low-level format must be performed periodically to prevent read/write errors from occurring.

Lastly, most stepper motors are not autoparking; that is, the read/write heads do not move to a safe area (area containing no data) when the system is shut down. They instead rest on the platter. Consequently, if the computer is moved or bumped hard enough, the read/write heads could be damaged or the platters could be scratched. A landing zone (safe zone) has to be specified to avoid this damage during the low-level formatting of the drive; the landing zone can also be specified with the CMOS setup program by stating where the read/write head should go when the power is shut off. A PARK.COM or equivalent program would then have to be run to move the read/write head to the landing zone just before the computer is shut off. (Note: A few higher-end stepper motor hard drives do include an extra device to autopark the read/write heads.)

Most newer hard drives, including the IDE and SCSI hard drives, use voice coil actuators. Instead of using a physical motor to move the read/write heads, voice coil actuators use electromagnetic force. An electromagnetic coil is attached to the end of the head rack and placed near a stationary magnet. As current is sent through the coil, a magnetic field is created that attracts or repels the stationary magnet and moves the head rack.

Voice coil actuators are quicker, more efficient, and quieter than stepper motors. Instead of moving in steps, the voice coil actuator moves directly to the needed location because it gets constant feedback of its location from a closed loop, allowing the read/write heads to adjust their position. The feedback comes from servo information—magnetic markings written on the platters—placed there during manufacturing. These markings are unaffected by temperature changes.

10.1.4 LOGIC BOARDS AND CONNECTORS

The drive contains several connectors to the rest of the computer. Older hard drives (ST-506 and ESDI drives) require two gray ribbon cables for direct connections with the computer; newer hard drives (IDE and SCSI) require one. The hard drive also uses a 5½″ power connector for power. The power connector has a +12 V line to power the motor and a +5 V line to power the chips on the drive.

Commands and instructions are issued by the operating system and sent through an expansion card (sometimes referred to as the *controller card* or *I/O card*) through the gray ribbon cable to the hard drive—specifically, to the hard drive's logic board. The logic board is the printed circuit board located under the drive. It makes sure that the platters are rotating at a constant speed, and it translates the commands received from the controller card into voltage fluctuations that control the head actuator and read/write heads.

As mentioned at the beginning of the chapter, the hard drive is a half-mechanical, half-electronic device. Since it is half-mechanical, the device has a high failure rate compared to nonmechanical devices. This is because mechanical parts and pieces eventually wear out. Although most failures are mechanical in nature, some hard drive problems occur in the logic board. If this is the case, the drive can easily be repaired by removing and replacing the logic board, not the entire drive. Although this is not the most cost-effective solution (since drives are so inexpensive), it may be the only choice if the data stored on the disk is irreplaceable and the drive was not backed up as it should have been. Of course, the new logic board must match the drive.

A few older drives include a grounding tab that connects to a grounding wire. Grounding is important because it provides a positive ground connection between the drive and the system's chassis. Improper grounding of the drive may result in improper operation, intermittent failure, or general read/write errors. Most drives do not need a grounding tab because they are grounded when screwed into a metal case. If a drive has plastic or fiberglass rails, which do not provide proper grounding, the grounding wire must be attached to the grounding tab.

10.1.5 TRACKS, CYLINDERS, AND SECTORS

Information is stored on the platters according to a system of tracks and sectors forming a circular grid. (See fig. 10.5.) The platters are first divided into concentric circles called **tracks.** (*Concentric* means circles that share the same center—much like rings in a tree.) A platter can have anywhere between 312 and 3,000 or more tracks. Tracks are numbered starting at 0 for the outside track. The tracks are then divided into **sectors;** each sector contains 512 bytes of usable data. A hard drive track can have as few as 17 sectors per track or may have more than 100 sectors per track. Sectors on a track are numbered starting with 1.

So far, tracks and sectors have been described as the division of one side of a platter into a circular grid. But actually, each side of a platter has a track 0, a track 1, a track 2, and so on. As the platters are stacked on top of each other, the track 0s are also stacked on top of each other, and these start to form a cylinder (much like a can). Therefore, the number of tracks equals the number of cylinders. Of course, tracks are two-dimensional and cylinders are three-dimensional—a cylinder would be able to hold more data because it has the third dimension, height.

FIGURE 10.5 Track and sector

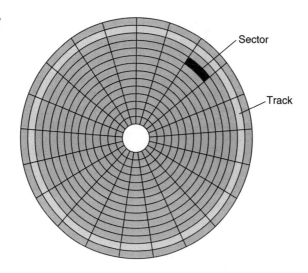

Since the AT computer, computers have included a CMOS setup program to specify the number and size of hard drives and floppy drives, the amount of RAM, and other important hardware configuration information. The hard drive option in the program includes the type of hard drive, the number of cylinders, the number of read/write heads, and the number of sectors and tracks. By selecting the type of hard drive, the other parameters are automatically chosen. Today, most computers have the Type 47/48 or User-Definable Type option, which allows (and requires) the other parameters to be selected.

EXAMPLE 10.1   How much data can a hard drive that has 4,092 tracks, 16 read/write heads, and 63 sectors per track hold?

Multipling the three numbers together gives the total number of sectors used by the hard drive. (Note: The number of read/write heads indicates that there are 8 platters since each side of the platter has a read/write head.)

4,092 tracks × 16 read/write heads × 63 sectors per track = 4,124,736 sectors

Since each sector contains 512 bytes of data, multiply the number of sectors by 512 to find the number of bytes:

4,124,736 sectors × 512 bytes per sector = 2,111,864,832 bytes

Most people think mega- means 1 million and giga- means 1 billion, so the companies selling hard drives will state that this hard drive is a 2.1 GB drive. But the computer is based on the binary numbering system, in which $2^{10} = 1,024$, and so

1,024 bytes = 1 kilobyte
1,024 kilobytes = 1 megabyte
1,024 megabytes = 1 gigabyte

Therefore,

2,111864,832 bytes ÷ 1,024 bytes per kilobyte = 2,062,368 kilobytes
2,062,368 kilobytes ÷ 1,024 kilobytes per megabyte = 2,014.03 megabytes
2,014.03 megabytes ÷ 1,024 megabytes per gigabyte = 1.97 gigabytes

The companies are not lying, they are just using numbers based on 1,000 (the decimal system), but computers use numbers based on 1,024.

On older hard drives, all the tracks have the same number of sectors even though the tracks are much larger toward the outside of the platter than the inside. This is known as a *fixed-sector-per-track system*. Although this simplifies the organization of the sectors on the drive, it does waste a lot of usable disk space. If the sectors were the same distance apart on all the tracks, the outer tracks would hold more sectors. Today's hard drives divide the tracks into zones. The tracks within the outer zones have more sectors per track than the tracks within the inner zones. Consequently, the capacity of the hard drive is

FIGURE 10.6   Zoned recordings

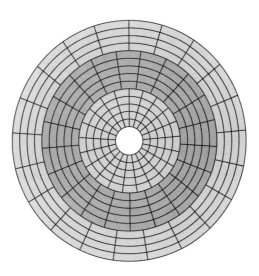

increased by 20% to 50%. Today, most IDE and SCSI drives use **zoned recordings.** (See fig. 10.6.)

Older hard drives, such as the ST-506 and ESDI, place the electronics that control them on the expansion card connected to the hard drive. As result, the controller cards had to be generic to accommodate all of the different hard drives. Newer drives, such as IDE and SCSI hard drives, have their controlling electronics on the logic board located on the drive. Since the electrical connections are significantly shorter, they are more resistant to noise. This makes the drive faster and more reliable. In addition, the performance of the drive can be further increased if the controlling electronics are designed for the specific drive rather than for many different types of drives.

Several sector-addressing schemes are used in hard drives. The simplest addressing scheme identifies each sector by its exact physical address. It is known as *cylinder–head–sector* addressing or **CHS addressing.** When using the CHS addressing mode, the CHS parameters must be specified at some point during the installation of the hard drive. On modern systems, this will be done with the CMOS setup program; in older systems the parameters will be entered during low-level formatting (see section 10.3.2). The CHS addressing mode can't be used in many situations. First, it can't be used in systems with ROM BIOS because these do not recognize more than 1,024 cylinders. Second, it can't be used with drives using zoned recording because in that system the number of sectors varies with different tracks. To accommodate these two situations, hard drive manufacturers developed sector translation, which makes CHS addresses usable by these other two systems.

EXAMPLE 10.2   A drive has 1,600 cylinders, 4 read/write heads, and 49 sectors per track. How much data can it hold?

Multipling the three numbers together gives the number of sectors per track:

$$1,600 \text{ cylinders} \times 4 \text{ heads} \times 49 \text{ sectors per track} = 313,600 \text{ sectors}$$

Since each sector is 512 bytes, the total disk capacity is

$$313,600 \text{ sectors} \times 512 \text{ bytes per sector} = 160,563,200 \text{ bytes}$$

Unfortunately, when you format the disk with some systems, it will format only to 102,760,448 bytes because older system ROM BIOSes can recognize only up to 1,024 cylinders. To fix this problem, you "lie" to the system and say that you have 800 cylinders and 8 read/write heads. These values still give you the same number of sectors and the same number of bytes:

$$800 \text{ cylinders} \times 8 \text{ heads} \times 49 \text{ sectors per track} = 313,600 \text{ sectors}$$

$$313,600 \text{ sectors} \times 512 \text{ bytes per sector} = 160,563,200 \text{ bytes}$$

Of course, since the drive has translating electronics, the entire capacity can be seen when it is partitioned and formatted.

The newest addressing scheme is **logical block addressing (LBA).** LBA uses a 28-bit number to indicate the total number of sectors on a hard drive. The 28-bit number used to indicate the number of sectors is equivalent to the number of bits used to list the number of cylinders, the number of read/write heads, and the number of sectors per track in CHS. It allows up to 268,435,456 sectors, or 128 GB. Instead of using the cylinder number, read/write number, and sector number to identify the sector, LBA numbers each sector sequentially starting at 1. Unfortunately, some software can access the hard drive only by using the CHS addressing scheme. In these systems, the system ROM BIOS has to translate the CHS address to the LBA address and the ROM BIOS recognizes only up to 7.9 GB.

10.1.6   DISK STRUCTURE

Information written to the platters of the disk is represented by tiny magnetic fields (flux) that flow from the north to the south or the south to the north magnetic poles of the electrical field. The read/write heads are designed to measure not the polarity of the magnetic fields but the flux reversals. Encoding is the method or pattern used to represent the bits of data on the platter. An efficient encoding method allows more bits to be encoded per flux reversal. The magnetic fields cannot be too close together because the bits will start to run together, and they can't be too far away from each other because the read/write heads may lose track of which bit they are reading or writing. The heads may also lose track if there are several values that have no flux reversals grouped together.

Several different encoding methods have been used. The first, used before the IBM PC, was frequency modulation (FM). During FM encoding, the value of 1 was represented by two flux reversals, the first for the clock and the second for the 1. A 0 was represented by a flux reversal (clock) followed by a no reversal. FM encoding is therefore wasteful since each bit requires two flux reversal positions. Early hard drives and floppy disks used **modified frequency modulation (MFM),** which, instead of inserting a clock reversal before each bit, inserted one only between consecutive zeroes. This meant far fewer reversals were needed on average per bit, allowing approximately double the storage capacity of FM. Hard drives that use MFM encoding (ST-506) have 17 sectors per track. An improvement to MFM encoding is **run length limited (RLL).** Instead of working with individual bits, RLL works with groups of bits. The two parameters that define RLL are the run length and the run limit (hence the name). The run length is the minimum spacing between flux reversals, and the run limit is the maximum spacing between them. As mentioned, the amount of time between reversals cannot be too large or the read/write head can become out of sync and lose track of which bit is where. The most common type of RLL is 1,7 RLL. Early RLL hard drives (ST-506 and ESDI) usually had 25 or 26 sectors per track. IDE and SCSI hard drives use RLL encoding.

Disk capacity may be expressed in unformatted and formatted terms. Unformatted capacity is the total number of bytes an unformatted hard drive is designed to handle before the tracks and sectors are defined on the disk. The formatted capacity is the amount of data that can be stored on the disk after the tracks and sectors have been defined.

Each track is identified with a track identifier. Each sector of the track contains a sector header, 512 bytes of data, and some form of error control. The sector header, which identifies the sector, contains the cylinder, head, and sector number of the sector. The **cyclical redundancy check (CRC)** is used to verify the address, while **error correction code (ECC)** is used to verify the actual data.

There is a small gap within each track that allows the read/write heads time to move from the end of one track to the next. If the gap didn't exist and the read/write head just missed the first sector in the next track, it would have to wait until the first sector came around again. If the read/write heads cannot move fast enough, some hard drives can be formatted to use head skewing. Head skewing offsets the first logical sector on each track from the first sector on the next track. (See fig. 10.7.)

FIGURE 10.7   Sector skewing

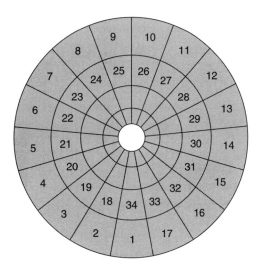

10.2   HARD DRIVE CHARACTERISTICS

The worth of a hard drive can be determined by several criteria. Most of these are concerned with the speed of the hard drive.

10.2.1   HARD DRIVE PERFORMANCE

Since programs and data files are larger than ever, more and more information has to be stored on hard drives. Therefore, the overall performance of the PC is partially dependent on how long it takes to get the information from the hard drive into the RAM so that it can be processed by the microprocessor. Hard drive performance can be measured by the access time (consisting of seek time and latency period), the data transfer rate, the drive rpms, and PC data handling, as shown in fig. 10.8.

The **access time** is the average amount of time it takes for the read/write head to move to the requested sector. It is the sum of the seek time and latency period. The **seek time** is the average time it takes the read/write head to move to the requested track—usually the time it takes the read/write head to move one-third of the way across the platter. The **latency period** is the time it takes for the requested sector to spin underneath the read/write head after the read/write head moves to the requested track. The latency period is usually one-half the time it takes for a single revolution of the disk platter. All of these intervals are measured in milliseconds (ms).

The disk transfer rate is the speed at which data is transferred to and from the platters. This is usually measured in bits per second (bps) or bytes per second and is dependent on the speed of the disk (rpm) and the density of the data on the disk (bpi, bits per inch). Since most modern drives use zoned recording, the outer zones have a faster disk transfer rate because they have more bytes per track. The maximum disk transfer rate can be calculated by the following equation:

FIGURE 10.8   Hard drive performance factors

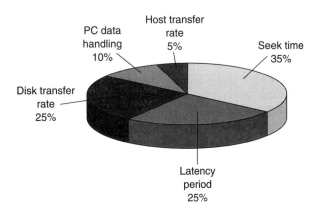

$$\text{Disk transfer rate in Mbps} = \frac{(\text{Sectors per track})(512 \text{ bytes})(\text{rpm})}{(60 \text{ seconds})(1,000,000 \text{ bits})}$$

The host transfer rate is determined according to the method by which data is transferred through the hard drive interface (IDE, EIDE, SCSI, etc). IDE hard drives use either a processor input/output mode or a direct memory access (DMA) mode; SCSI drives use either SCSI I, SCSI II, or SCSI III. These topics will be discussed later in the chapter.

Data handling occurs after the data has been transferred to the controller card. The time it takes for the data to be transferred to the RAM is not necessarily a factor of the hard drive but of the PC itself. It depends on the type and speed of the microprocessor, the speed and amount of the RAM, the speed and amount of RAM cache, and the speed of the hard drive controller card (expansion card).

The speed of the hard drive can be enhanced by using a software cache or buffer area, or both. A buffer area, a software disk cache, and a 32-bit disk access operating system must be set up.

The buffer area, usually set up with the BUFFERS command, is a block of memory (RAM) used to store data temporarily. It collects large amounts of data as it is being moved between the microprocessor and the controller card. The data transfer rate is increased since the data is accessed in larger chunks from the RAM, and since the data is being accessed in larger chunks, which helps to fill up the data transfer pathways, the buffer area moves data more efficiently.

Like the buffer area, the software disk cache (set up with SMARTDRV.EXE, VCACHE, or equivalent program) sets aside a cache area to store both data and instructions. But the software controlling the disk cache tries to anticipate what the microprocessor needs next. One method it uses is to keep a copy of information that has been recently accessed on the assumption that if it has already been accessed, there is a good chance that it will be accessed again. Another method is to read ahead to the next sector after one has been accessed. Whatever the method used, when data need to be accessed, the cache area will be searched first before the slower hard drive. The time it takes to search the cache area (RAM) is almost negligible compared to the time required to access the hard drive. Therefore, finding the needed information in the RAM greatly increases PC performance. Another form of cache is the hardware cache located on the hard drive controller card or the hard drive logic board. This cache is not to be confused with the hardware cache located on the motherboard or within the microprocessor. The hardware cache on the controller card or logic board fulfills the same functions as the software disk cache—that is, it speeds up the processing of data. Instead of sending a hard drive software interrupt to the microprocessor, the controller card physically completes the task.

Another way to increase performance is to use 32-bit access. (This is not to be confused with Windows 3.XX 32-bit disk access and 32-bit file access.) Some drives typically transfer only 16 bits at a time, a legacy from the original IBM AT design, which used the 16-bit ISA bus. If a system is designed to enable 32-bit disk access (through the CMOS setup program or some other method), it allows a PCI hard disk controller card to transfer two 16-bit chunks at the same time.

10.2.2 HARD DRIVE RELIABILITY

So far, most of the characteristics discussed have dealt with speed issues. The final hard drive characteristic concerns reliability. Mean time between failure (MTBF) is the statistically derived prediction of the amount of time the drive will operate before a hardware failure occurs. If, for example, a drive has a 300,000-hour MTBF period, then it would, on average, run for approximately 34 years before it failed. These numbers are more of a guess than anything else because they are not based on real statistics. In the case just mentioned, drives have not been around for 34 years so data is not available with which to calculate the real MTBF period.

10.3 INSTALLATION OF HARD DRIVES

When installing a hard drive, there are some basic steps to take when configuring it:

1. Physically install and configure the hard drive system
2. Low-level format the drive
3. Partition the drive
4. High-level format the drive (and make bootable if needed)
5. Install and configure the operating system and application programs

10.3.1 INSTALLING AND CONFIGURING THE HARD DRIVE SYSTEM

After physically installing the hard drive and its related components, they must be configured to work with the rest of the computer. The hard drive is connected to one or two gray ribbon cables that are connected to a hard drive controller, which is either an expansion card or is built into the motherboard. The hard drive is held in the drive bay with screws. Try to use the shortest screws possible since some hard drive logic boards or circuit boards are placed directly behind the screw holes. Therefore, if the screw is too long, it will short the hard drive.

To configure the hard drive controller (expansion card), you must select its resources, such as IRQs, DMAs, I/O addresses, and memory usage, which you will do with the appropriate arrangement of jumpers and DIP switches or with a software configuration program or a plug-and-play card. Many controller cards also include a floppy disk drive controller and an I/O controller (serial, parallel, and game ports), which also need to be configured. Extra steps may be required by some controller cards to prepare the hard drive for use. Many controller cards have ROM BIOS chips, and some of the ROM BIOS chips include low-level format programs and drive activation programs that must be run. If the hard drive controller is part of the motherboard, it will be configured with either jumpers and DIP switches or the CMOS setup program. The hard drive also needs to be configured to work with the other devices connected to the controller card. The drive and devices must have proper designation numbers and terminating resistors.

The gray ribbon cable must be connected properly. To indicate the correct way to connect the cable, pin 1 of the cable is designated with a red or blue stripe. The expansion card/motherboard connectors will either have a small number 1 or 2 to designate which end has pin 1 or will use a square solder (other pins use a round solder). Pin 1 of the drive is also designated by a small 1 or 2. If one of the cable ends is connected backward, the hard drive will not function and the computer may not boot. In addition to the gray ribbon cable, a hard drive also uses a power connector. Most hard drives use the 5¼″ connector, which supplies +5 V and +12 V. The +5 V are used to power the chips, while the +12 V power the motors.

The final step in installation is to enter the proper CMOS parameters for the hard drive or drives. For AT ST-506 and IDE drives, the number of cylinders, the number of read/write heads, and the number of sectors per track must be defined. For SCSI hard drives, Hard Drive Not Installed or SCSI would be selected. (See table 10.1.) Most newer CMOS setup programs have an autodetect option that will automatically detect the CMOS parameters for any IDE drive connected. If the drive is using this option, it is installed properly. If the drive is not, it is installed incorrectly or there is a faulty component, such as the driver, controller card, or cable.

10.3.2 LOW-LEVEL FORMATTING

Low-level formatting (LLF) is the process that defines the tracks and sectors on the platters of the hard drive. Any information already on the platters will be completely replaced with new tracks and sectors. (See fig. 10.9.)

When a disk drive is manufactured, it is thoroughly tested by special equipment for any areas that might have errors. The sectors with errors are called *bad sectors* or *bad blocks*. The bad sectors are considered unreliable and are listed in a special table called the defect

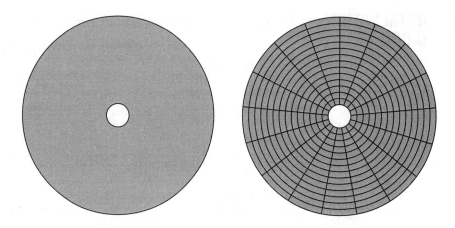

FIGURE 10.9 Low-level formatting (before and after)

mapping. On older hard disks, these bad sectors were actually listed on a label located on the top of the drive. When a low-level format is performed, the program will ask the user to enter the location of the bad sectors. If any other bad sectors are discovered at a later time, they should be written on the label. On newer hard drives, the bad sectors are listed within the hard drive. When formatting these hard drives, the proper low-level format program must be used, one that is made for that specific drive. If the right program is not used, it may erase the table listing the bad sectors and may damage the drive.

TABLE 10.1 CMOS parameters

CMOS

Older computers will recognize two hard drives (drive C and drive D). Newer computers will recognize four hard drives (drive C/Primary Master, drive D/Primary Slave, drive E/Secondary Master, drive F/Secondary Slave).

HARD DRIVE PARAMETER

Type number—Most CMOS programs have type numbers 1 through 46. By selecting a type number, common CMOS parameters are selected (number of tracks for each platter, number of read/write heads, and the number of sectors per track). Today, most computers will use Type 47/User Definable, which allows the common CMOS parameters to be entered by the user.

Cylinders—Number of tracks for each platter

Heads—Number of read/write heads

Sectors—Number of sectors per track

LZ (landing zone)—The cylinder used as a safe area for read/write heads when the computer is shut off. It is needed for nonautoparking hard drives.

Wpcom (write precompensation)—The write precompensation is used only in older hard drives. Since the bits are stored much closer together, the magnetic fields start to run together. Therefore, when writing, the current in the read/write heads is increased to strengthen the magnetic fields. The Wpcom specifies which cylinder starts the increased current. Note: In modern hard drives (IDE and SCSI) this entry is useless. Set it to either −1 or 65535. The IDE HDD will ignore it because it has its own built-in parameters.

TYPE OF HARD DRIVE

ST-506/ESDI using an XT controller—Set CMOS to No Hard Drive Installed.

ST-506/ESDI using an AT controller—Select the correct hard drive type. If the drive is set to Type 47/User Definable, enter the appropriate cylinders, heads, sectors, LZ, and Wpcom.

IDE—Select the correct hard drive type. If the drive is set to Type 47/User Definable, enter the appropriate number of cylinders, heads, and sectors. LZ should be set to 0 and Wpcom should be set to either −1 or 65535. Some drives will use CHS (normal), translated (large), or LBA mode.

SCSI—Select SCSI (if available) or No Hard Drive Installed.

TABLE 10.2 Useful websites for hard drives and hard drive controllers

Company		Websites
Adaptec	Home:	http://www.adaptec.com
	Support:	http://www.adaptec.com/support/index.html
IBM	Home:	http://www.ibm.com
	Storage:	http://www.storage.ibm.com/
	Hard drive support:	http://www.storage.ibm.com/techsup/hddtech/hddtech.htm
Maxtor	Home:	http://www.maxtor.com
	Product information:	http://www.maxtor.com/products/products.html
	Download library:	http://www.maxtor.com/library/index.html
Quantum	Home:	http://www.quantum.com/
	Support:	http://support.quantum.com/
Seagate	Home:	http://www.seagate.com/
	Support:	http://www.seagate.com/support/disc/discsupt.shtml
Western Digital	Home:	http://www.westerndigital.com/
	Support web page:	http://www.westerndigital.com/support/

Most people don't like the idea of having a hard drive with bad sectors. Therefore, modern drives use spare sectoring. **Spare sectoring** is the setting aside of extra sectors on a drive. When the drive finds an unreliable sector, it will mark the sector as bad and then move the data to one of the spare sectors. Therefore, when the drive is analyzed by the user, it still has the same capacity with no visible errors. If a drive is using spare sectoring, bad sectors should not show up during normal operations. If they do, this means that all of the spare sectors have been used, which indicates a far greater problem. It is highly recommended to perform an immediate backup of the hard drive and to start looking for a replacement drive.

A critical area of the hard drive is track 00, which stores the hard drive's master boot record and other vital disk information. If a bad sector occurs on Track 00, the hard drive will usually become unusable. If this happens, try a low-level format to correct the problem. If it doesn't, the entire hard drive will have to be replaced. (Note: Track 00 can always be checked with diagnostic software.)

The low-level format process also sets the interleaving of the hard drive. Interleaving establishes the interleave ratio, or the number of sectors that pass beneath the read/write heads before the next numbered sector arrives. Today's hard drives have a 1:1 ratio, meaning that each sector is read in sequence. Many older drives, such as the ST-506, used 3:1 interleaving. This means that a sector was read, then two sectors were skipped, and then the 3rd sector was read as the next numbered sector. The fastest interface is 1:1, assuming that the read/write heads are fast enough to read each sector in sequence. If they cannot, the read/write heads will read the first sector but have to wait an entire revolution before they can read the next sector. (See fig. 10.10.) (Note: IDE and SCSI hard drive interleaves cannot be changed since they are established electronically.)

Low-level formats are completed with special software. Since there is no one software package that will low-level format every hard drive, you must be sure that the software package used will correctly handle the drive to be formatted. The software can be executed from disk (manufacturer's own software, On-Track's Disk Manager, MicroScope's Micro 2000, or Microhouse's Drive Pro), with the CMOS setup program, or by means of the ROM BIOS chip on the controller card (accessed through DOS's DEBUG program or by pressing specific keys during boot-up). But unless you are formatting an older ST-506 or ESDI drive as part of maintenance, there is not much reason to low-level format a hard drive. One reason for doing it would be to completely erase all information from a drive so that it could not be used or seen by someone else. Another reason would be to remove a corrupted or non-DOS partition or operating system or to remove a virus that could not be removed by normal means.

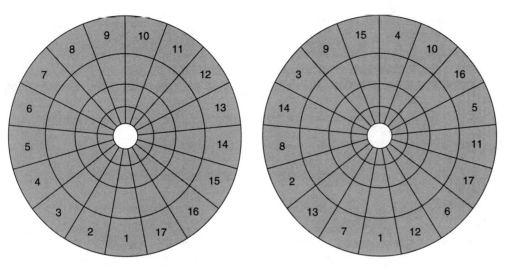

FIGURE 10.10   Disk interleaving: the left image shows 1:1 interleaving; the right image shows 3:1 interleaving

10.3.3   PARTITIONING THE HARD DRIVE

Partitioning is defining and dividing the physical drive into logical volumes called *partitions*. Each partition functions as if it were a separate hard disk. (See fig. 10.11.) It is the physical drive that is installed and configured, but the logical drive (the partitions) is what the system "thinks" it has. Every drive must include at least one partition. The reason for partitioning hard drives is to overcome operating system size limits, to use a drive more efficiently, to have multiple operating systems, and to isolate data areas.

EXAMPLE 10.3   The first step in installing and configuring a 4 GB hard drive would be to install the controller card, connect the cable, configure the hard drive, and run the CMOS setup program. If the drive requires a low-level format, it must be done with the proper software. The drive is then partitioned into two hard drives, drive C and drive D. Although only one hard drive was installed, the operating system, including File Manager/Explorer, recognizes drives C and D.

The information about how a hard drive is partitioned is stored in the master boot record (MBR), which is located in the first sector of the disk. The MBR contains a small program that reads the partition table, checks which partition is active (marked as bootable), and reads the first sector of the bootable partition. The most common utility used to partition a hard drive is the FDISK utility, which is found in DOS, Windows 95 and 98, and Windows NT. FDISK can create a primary partition and an extended

FIGURE 10.11   Partitioning (before and after)

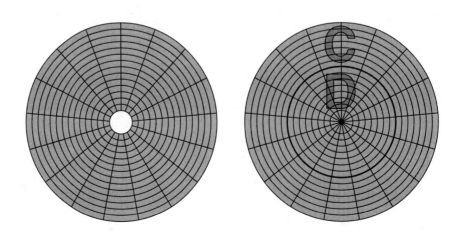

partition. The primary partitions are the drives that can be made active. The extended partitions can be used to designate logical drives, which are actually assigned a drive letter. (Note: If you want to change the partition size, you have to delete the partitions and recreate them. Unfortunately, all data is lost during this process.) The primary partition on the first hard drive is assigned to be drive C. Any other primary partitions are assigned drive letters before any logical partitions. The drive letters assigned are not permanent. If you install another hard drive and define a primary partition on that drive, it will grab the next drive letter after the first primary partition. The logical drives are reassigned new drive letters as well. Unfortunately, programs configured to look under a certain drive letter to find a particular directory or file will not find them, causing all kinds of software execution errors.

10.3.4 FINAL STEPS FOR PREPARING THE HARD DRIVE

High-level formatting is the process of writing the file system structure on the disk so that it can be used to store programs and data. This includes creating a file allocation table (an index listing all directories and files and where they are located on the disk) and a root directory to start with. In addition, high-level formatting creates a volume boot sector, which is used to store the boot files of an operating system. (Note: If you high-level format a disk that already has files and a directory, you will usually recreate the file allocation tables. Of course, without the index used to find the files, the previous information becomes inaccessible.) During high-level formatting, the partition can be made bootable by copying the operating system's boot files, such as DOS's IO.SYS, MSDOS.SYS, and COMMAND.COM. High-level formatting is usually performed with the FORMAT.COM command. If the disk was not made bootable during formatting, it will have to be reformatted, which of course will erase all data on the partition, or it will have to be done with a special operating system utility or command, such as the SYS command.

Much of the installation can be simplified by using the operating system's installation disks (or CD-ROM). If there are no partitions, the installation program will usually partition the drive. If there are partitions but they have not been formatted, the installation disks will format the individual partitions. They will also transfer the boot files to the disk, making it bootable, and copy the operating system files to the hard drive.

If you try to access a drive and you receive an Invalid Media Type error message, the drive has not been high-level formatted. If the drive was high-level formatted and is no longer, you need to check the hard drive for viruses and other problems.

10.4 DATA PROTECTION OF HARD DRIVES

The best method of protecting the data on the hard drive is to do a complete backup on a regular basis. Therefore, if the hard drive physically fails or the data become corrupt, the drive can be repaired or replaced and the data can be restored to the hard drive.

To help with data protection, there is **RAID (redundant arrays of inexpensive disks)**—two or more drives used in combination to create a fault tolerance system to protect against physical hard drive failure and to increase hard drive performance. A RAID can be accomplished with either hardware or software and is usually used in network servers. (Note: RAID does not replace a good backup since it does not protect against data corruption or viruses.)

There are several levels of RAID. (See table 10.3.) A common one used in networked PCs is RAID level 1, known as disk mirroring. **Disk mirroring** copies a partition onto a second hard drive. As information is written, it is written to both hard drives simultaneously. If one of the hard drives fails, the PC will still function because it can access the other hard drive. Another kind of disk mirroring is disk duplexing. **Disk duplexing** not only duplicates the hard drive but also the controller card and cable. Therefore, if the hard drive, controller card, or cable fails, the computer will still function.

TABLE 10.3   Levels of RAID

Level 0—Disk striping	Data striping is the spreading out of blocks of each file across multiple disks. It offers no fault tolerance, but it increases performance. Level 0 is the fastest and most efficient form of RAID.
Level 1—Disk mirroring/disk duplexing	Disk mirroring duplicates a partition onto two hard drives. When information is written, it is written to both hard drives simultaneously. It increases performance and provides fault tolerance. Disk duplexing is a form of disk mirroring. Disk mirroring uses two hard drives connected to the same card; disk duplexing uses two controller cards, two cables, and two hard drives.
Level 2—Disk striping with ECC	Level 2 uses data striping plus ECC to detect errors. It is rarely used today since ECC is embedded in almost all modern disk drives.
Level 3—ECC stored as parity	Level 3 dedicates one disk to error correction data. It provides good performance and some level of fault tolerance.
Level 4—Disk striping with large blocks	Level 4 offers no advantages over RAID-5 and does not support multiple simultaneous write operations.
Level 5—Striping with parity	RAID-5 uses disk striping and includes byte error correction on one of the disks. If one disk goes bad, the system will continue to function. After the faulty disk is replaced, the information on the replaced disk can be rebuilt. This system requires at least three drives. It offers excellent performance and good fault tolerance.

10.5   ST-506/412 AND ESDI HARD DRIVES

Hard drives are characterized by their interface. The ST-506/412 and ESDI drives are old-style hard drives; IDE and SCSI are modern drives.

The ST-506 interface was developed by Shugart Associates. It works at 5 megabits per second and uses MFM encoding, allowing 17 sectors per track. (See fig. 10.12.) By 1981, Seagate, improving on the original ST-506 interface, had developed the 10 MB ST-412

FIGURE 10.12   ST-506 hard drive

hard drive. Since IBM chose to use Seagate hard drives in the IBM XT computer, the ST-506/412 became the standard interface. Later on, the ST-506/412 came with RLL encoding, which offered 25 or 26 sectors per track and a buffered seek feature. As a result, the data transfer rate increased to 7.5 megabits per second. Most of these drives had a 3:1 interleave factor.

The original 8-bit MFM controller card used in the IBM XT was the Xebec 1210. The controller's ROM chip contained an 8 KB hard disk BIOS with an internal table that had entries for four different hard drives. For the AT, IBM used the Western Digital WD1002 and WD1003 16-bit controller cards, which had MFM encoding and no ROM BIOS chip to control the hard drive. BIOS support was built instead into the motherboard system ROM BIOS.

In 1983, the **ESDI (Enhanced Small Drive Interface)** drives were introduced by Maxtor Corporation to replace the ST-506/412. This interface had RLL encoding, allowing 34 sectors per track, and a 1:1 interleave factor. Unlike the ST-506/412 drives, the ESDI drives have the separator/encoder circuitry on the drive, not the expansion card. Since this simplifies the information sent through the cable and controls the motion of the read/write heads directly, the data transfer rate could go as high as 24 megabits per second, although most are designed for 10 megabits per second. ESDI drives are often found on servers.

Both the ST-506/412 and ESDI drives connect to a controller card with two gray ribbon cables, a 34-pin control cable and a 20-pin data cable, which can handle one or two drives. The control cable carries the operating signals, such as the drive select, step, head select, etc., while the data cable carries the data to and from the drive. Unlike newer drives, the controlling electronics are on the expansion card, which is generic to handle several different types of hard drives. The ST-506/412 controller cards will support MFM or RLL encoding. Since the RLL interface is newer, the RLL controller card will usually support an MFM hard drive. The MFM interface will not support an RLL hard drive.

There are two kinds of control cables for these drives: one control cable has a twist in it, and the other does not. The twist is located closer to pin 34. (Make sure that you don't get this cable confused with the floppy drive cable, which also has 34 pins. Its twist is located closer to pin 1.) The end drive of the cable without the twist should be configured as drive 0, and the drive connected to its middle connector should be set as drive 1. The cable with the twist is configured so that both drives are set to drive 1. The twist in the cable determines that the end drive is drive 0 and the other drive is drive 1. As with SCSI drives, terminating resistors are needed on both ends of these cables to prevent signals from bouncing back when they reach the end of the cable. One end, attached to the controller card, is already terminated. The other end, located at the far end away from the expansion card, is attached to drive 0 and is also already terminated. The terminating resistor on drive 1 (the drive using the middle connector), however, needs to be removed. If it is not, the signals will not be able to flow to drive 0.

The controller card for the ST-506/412 is either XT or AT. ESDI drives have AT cards. The XT cards have a ROM BIOS chip, which contains a table of drive parameters. When the drive is selected during the low-level formatting, this in turn selects the number of cylinders, the number of read/write heads, and the number of sectors per track. If the drive were not listed within the ROM BIOS chip, it could not be used. (Note: If an XT card is used in an AT, set the CMOS parameter to No Hard Drive Installed because the ROM BIOS chip on the XT controller card controls the drive, not the system ROM BIOS.) For AT cards, the number of cylinders, the number of read/write heads, and the number of sectors per track are selected using the CMOS setup program.

After the drives, controller cards, and CMOS are configured and connected, they must then be low-level formatted. All ST-506/412 and ESDI drives require a low-level format when first installed. In addition, a low-level format should be completed as part of a maintenance routine (approximately every six months) because the older hard drives use the platters coated with magnetic oxide, and as the platters spin, the bits stored on the magnetic oxide move outward, resulting in track shifting. The low-level formatting realigns the bits. If this isn't done, read/write errors will eventually occur.

A low-level format for these drives is done using the BIOS routine, which is usually accessed through an old DOS utility, DEBUG. When the DEBUG.EXE file is executed at the prompt, DEBUG displays a hyphen (-) prompt. To start the low-level format program from the ROM BIOS chip, a specific command based on the type of controller card used is executed. Western Digital, DTC, and Seagate controller cards use g=c800:5; Adaptec controllers use g=c800:CCC; and SMS-OMTI controllers use g=c800:6. Some CMOS setup programs and specialized programs can also format the ST-506/412 drives.

10.6   IDE HARD DRIVES

IDE (integrated drive electronics) was developed in 1988 as a fast, low-cost hard drive interface. Three modifications were developed to connect the new IDE hard drives to the existing architecture: the AT attachment (ATA), made for the 16-bit ISA slot; the XT IDE interface, made for the 8-bit PC slot; and the MCA IDE for the IBM Micro Channel architecture.

10.6.1   ATA IDE HARD DRIVES

All of the controlling electronics of the IDE drive are located on the drive itself, not the controller card as in older drives. The BIOS instructions that control the IDE drives are contained in the system ROM BIOS. Therefore, the controller card is only a paddleboard used to connect the cable to the rest of the computer. The hard drive is connected to the controller card with a 40-pin cable, which should not exceed 61 centimeters (24 inches). (Note: Some older IBM computers use a 44-pin and a 76-pin cable.) IDE drives have data transfer rates of up to 2–3 MB per second. (See fig. 10.13.)

The IDE drive is considered an intelligent drive because it can support drive translation. While in translation mode, any combination of cylinders, heads, and sectors can be used in the CMOS setup program as long as the total number of sectors is equal to or less than the actual number of sectors on the drive. The controller electronics on the drive translate the CHS sector to the actual sector on the drive and support zoned recordings since each track uses a different number of sectors. If a drive with translating electronics is installed, configured, partitioned, and formatted with one set of CMOS parameters and then changed to another, the drive may not boot (a "Drive C: Error" message may appear) or be accessible. Therefore, it is important to record the CMOS information and store it in a safe place. To find the correct CMOS parameter to use for a hard drive, it is best to use the documentation (some documentation is listed on the drive) that comes with the drive or to check the manufacturer's website or bulletin board. Newer CMOS setup programs can do an excellent job of automatically detecting the correct CMOS parameters.

The ATA IDE interface was modeled after the WD1003 controller used in the IBM AT. In addition to supporting the WD1003 commands, the ATA specification added other commands to increase performance and enhance capabilities. One important command is the Identify Drive command, which displays important identification information stored

FIGURE 10.13   Connector ribbon cable and power connector (courtesy of Seagate Corporation, Inc.)

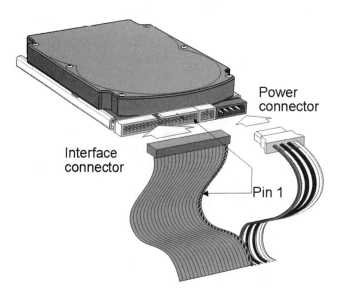

TABLE 10.4 Limitations of IDE
hard drives

	BIOS Limitation	IDE Limitation	Combined Limitation
Number of cylinders	1,024	65,536	1,024
Number of read/write heads	255	16	16
Maximum sectors per track	63	225	63
Maximum capacity	7.9 GB	112.5 GB	504 MB

within the firmware of the drive. This information includes the drive manufacturer, the model number, and the operating parameters (number of cylinders, number of read/write heads, and number of tracks) of the drive. This is the reason that most modern CMOS setup programs and other hard drive–configuring software can automatically detect the drive and set the CMOS parameters.

When working with ATA IDE hard drives, you will often encounter two limitations. First, because of the limitation of their older ROM BIOS chips (some dating back to 1996), the system cannot see more than 1,024 cylinders. This can be overcome with translating electronics (extended CHS), however. Second, due to the ROM BIOS and the limitations of the IDE hard drive itself, IDE hard drives cannot be bigger than 504 MB. (See Table 10.4.)

Up to two hard drives can be connected with the IDE cable. If one drive is installed, it is known as a *stand-alone drive.* If two hard drives are installed, the physical drive C is known as the *master drive* while the physical drive D is known as the *slave drive.* The master drive got its name because its controlling electronics on the logic board control both the master drive and the slave drive. The stand-alone, master, and slave drives are determined by jumper connections on the hard drive. It makes no difference where the drive and controller card are connected to the cable. (See fig. 10.14.) The jumpers most commonly used to determine a drive as a stand-alone, master, or slave are the master (M/S) jumper and the slave present (SP). (See fig. 10.15 and table 10.5.)

After the hard drive, controller card, and system are configured, the IDE drive must then be partitioned and high-level formatted. Since the drive is already low-level formatted by the manufacturer, that does not have to be done during installation.

Many people say never low-level format any hard drive. In reality, an IDE hard drive can be low-level formatted if it is done properly and with the correct software. The correct software will not erase the servo information or the defect-map information, and it will set the optimal head and sector-skew factor. To prevent improper formatting, some IDE hard drives require special codes to unlock the format routines. In addition, while the drive is in translation mode, which always occurs in zone recordings, the skew factors cannot be changed and the defect map cannot be overwritten. (Note: If a low-level format is done while the drive is under warranty, it may void the warranty.)

FIGURE 10.14 IDE hard drive connected to controller card (courtesy of Seagate Corporation, Inc.)

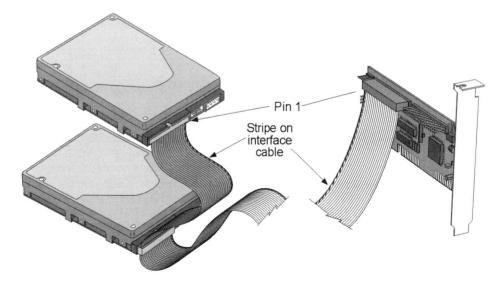

Pin 1

Stripe on interface cable

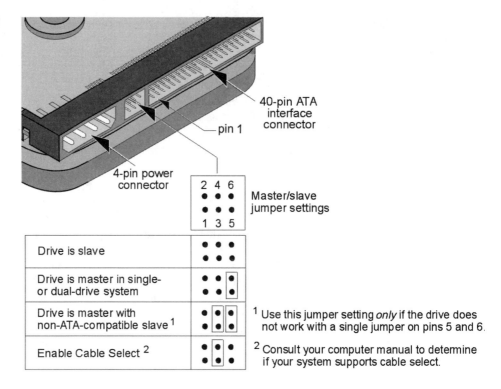

FIGURE 10.15 Typical jumper setting of an IDE hard drive (courtesy of Seagate Corporation, Inc.)

The best place to get the proper low-level format software is the manufacturer's website (such as Seagate, Western Digital, or Maxtor) or bulletin board. Conner hard drives (owned by Seagate) are different from the others in that a special device must be connected to the serial port to unlock the low-level format capabilities. If the proper low-level format program cannot be found on the Internet or manufacturer's bulletin board, a commercial package like Ontrack's Disk Manager, Microscope's Micro 2000, or Microhouse's Drive Pro can be used.

Some compatibility issues may prevent IDE drives from working properly. Some IDE hard drives are incompatible with IDE hard drives made by other manufacturers. This is usually true of older IDE drives, which did not adhere to the ATA IDE specification. Also, only PCs made since 1990 are fully compatible with ATA IDE drives. Therefore, if working on a machine made before 1990, you should consider upgrading the system ROM BIOS.

10.6.2 ENHANCED IDE (EIDE) HARD DRIVES

To compete against SCSI drives and to overcome some of the limitations of the IDE, **enhanced IDE (EIDE)/AT attachment interface with extensions (ATA-2)** was developed. The EIDE interface supports up to four IDE devices using two IDE cables. Each cable is its own channel, consisting of its own master and slave device. Instead of supporting only hard drives, EIDE supports nondisk peripherals that follow the ATAPI (ATA packet interface) protocol. ATAPI is the protocol used on the enhanced IDE devices (IDE CD-ROM drives, IDE tape backup drives, and other IDE storage devices).

TABLE 10.5 Typical jumper settings for an ATA IDE hard drive

	Master (M/S)	Slave Present (SP)
Stand-alone (master with no slave drive)	On	Off
Master	On	On
Slave	Off	Off

The 504 MB capacity limitation of the IDE was broken by the introduction of **logical block addressing (LBA).** LBA uses the 28 bits of the CHS address as a binary number. LBA numbers each sector starting at 0 and continuing to the last physical sector. Its binary number base allows up to 268,435,456 sectors, or 128 GB. To maintain compatibility with older operating systems like DOS, the system ROM BIOS must translate the CHS addresses generated by software into the LBA address. However, since the older operating systems communicate with the BIOS and the BIOS recognizes only up to 7.9 GB, a drive must be ATA-2 compatible and the BIOS must understand LBA to access the increased capacity. If the system ROM BIOS does not support EIDE/ATA-2 drives, the system ROM BIOS needs to be either updated or modified, which can be done by:

1. Adding a newer system ROM chip that includes instructions for handling EIDE/ATA-2 hard drives
2. Updating the ROM chip (if the system ROM BIOS is flash ROM) by using special software
3. Inserting an EIDE controller card that includes a ROM BIOS chip to supplement the system ROM BIOS chip
4. Configuring the computer to recognize the drive and using software or a device driver (sometimes called a *dynamic drive overlay*) that includes instructions for handling EIDE hard drives

Modern CMOS setup programs include several hard drive options or modes: normal, large, or LBA mode. The normal mode, for older IDE drives, uses CHS translation mode for drives that do not exceed 1024 cylinders. The large mode uses CHS mode under translation mode, making it possible for drives to exceed 1,024 cylinders. The LBA mode allows the sectors to be numbered in sequence.

The limited data transfer rate of the IDE also had to be overcome. Enhanced IDE, depending on the transfer mode, allows a transfer rate up to 33.3 MB per second. The two methods of transferring data are **processor input/output (PIO)** and **direct memory access (DMA).**

PIO is the transfer method used on most IDE drives, with the microprocessor using in and out instructions to handle data transfers. There are currently five PIO modes in use: PIO modes 0, 1, and 2 use the old ATA specification; PIO modes 3 and 4 use the ATA-2 specification. (See table 10.6.) Modes 3 and 4 run at such high speeds that the EIDE interface can experience some errors. Therefore, the higher modes have an IORDY hardware flow control signal to slow the interface when necessary. (Note: PIO modes 3 and 4 require local bus access because the ISA bus cannot handle transfer rates of over 10 MB per second.) ATA-2 also allows block mode PIO, sometimes referred to as *multisector data transfer.* Rather than generating one interrupt for each sector being transferred, block mode PIO will process up to 32 multiple sectors using one interrupt. This greatly reduces the number of interrupts sent to the microprocessor, which reduces the traffic. (Note: Block mode PIO requires a local bus connection, a compatible drive and controller, and software that supports multisector data transfers.)

The other mode of data transfer is DMA, specifically bus mastering. Bus mastering transfers the information through the address and data bus without any direction from the microprocessor. In older DMA transfers were performed by the DMA controller on the motherboard; the bus mastering transfer is controlled by the controller card. Since the

TABLE 10.6   PIO modes used with EIDE devices

PIO Mode	Average Transfer Rate	Cycle Time	Flow Controlled	Specification
0	3.3 MB/s	600 ns	No	ATA
1	5.2 MB/s	383 ns	No	ATA
2	8.3 MB/s	240 ns	No	ATA
3	11.1 MB/s	180 ns	Yes	ATA-2
4	16.6 MB/s	120 ns	Yes	ATA-2

TABLE 10.7   DMA mode used with EIDE devices

DMA Mode	Average Transfer Rate	Cycle Time	Requirements	Standard
0—Single word	2.08 MB/s	960 ns		ATA
1—Single word	4.16 MB/s	480 ns		ATA
2—Single word	8.33 MB/s	240 ns		ATA
0—Multiword	4.16 MB/s	480 ns	Local bus controller	ATA
1—Multiword	13.33 MB/s	150 ns	Local bus controller	ATA-2
2—Multiword	16.6 MB/s	120 ns	Local bus controller	ATA-3
3—Multiword	33.3 MB/s	60 ns	Local bus controller	Ultra ATA/Ultra DMA/ATA-4

microprocessor can perform other tasks during the data transfer, DMA transfers are ideal for multitasking operating systems. Single-word DMA transfer uses DMA "handshaking," consisting of requests and acknowledgements for each transfer. Multiword DMA transfer reduces the traffic by handling several DMA transfers at the same time without using the DMA requests and acknowledgements. (See table 10.7.)

The latest advancement to the ATA specification (ATA-4) and the fastest mode is the Ultra DMA/33 mode. It supports a burst mode data transfer rate of 33.3 megabits per second, which is twice is fast as previous modes. In addition to increasing throughput, Ultra DMA/33 improves data integrity by using a **cyclic redundancy check (CRC)** to flag any data transfer errors that may have been made over the ATA bus. Systems on which the master and slave devices are running at different speeds may be limited to the speed of the slower device. Therefore, it is best to isolate the slower device by putting it on a different channel.

The ATA interface is designed for the AT's 16-bit ISA bus, which, of course, transfers data 16 bits at a time, but the local bus can transfer at a 32-bit rate. Therefore, if the system includes a 32-bit Access option in the CMOS setup program and it is enabled, it will allow two 16-bit chunks of data to be transferred at the same time. (Note: this is not to be confused with Windows 3.XX 32-bit disk and file access.)

10.7   SCSI HARD DRIVES

Another very popular hard drive and system interface is the **small computer systems interface (SCSI,** pronounced "skuzzy"), which evolved from Shugart Associates standard interface (SASI). Much like the IDE devices, SCSI devices also have the controlling electronics on each of the drives. SCSI is a much more advanced interface than the ATA/ATA-2 IDE drives and is ideal for high-end computers, including network servers. (See fig. 10.16.)

FIGURE 10.16   Typical SCSI adapter

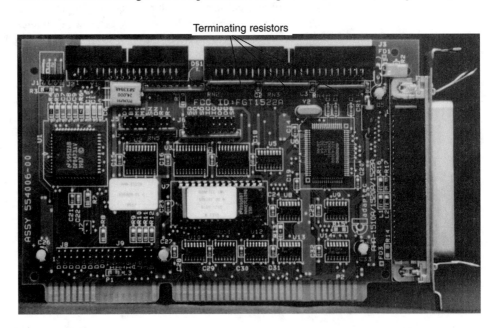

FIGURE 10.17 Typical SCSI connectors (Centronics and Mini-SCSI port)

The standard SCSI interface allows up to seven devices (hard drives, tape drives, CD-ROM drives, removable drives and disks, and scanners) to be connected to one SCSI adapter/controller. This would be eight devices if the controller card is counted. The SCSI controller cards usually contain a ROM BIOS chip to supplement the system ROM BIOS. When enabled, the SCSI adapter intercepts all hardware interrupt 13 calls and passes the non-SCSI interrupt to the system ROM BIOS. SCSI devices are connected in series, forming a chain (daisy chain). The cables are characterized by the number of pins (50-, 68-, or 80-pin) and by whether they are made to be used inside (internal) or outside (external) the computer. The 50-pin connector (type A) has an 8-bit data path; the 68-pin (type P) and 80-pin cables have a 16-bit (wide) data path. (See fig. 10.17 and table 10.8.)

Each device, including the adapter/controller card, is numbered with a SCSI ID number from 0 to 7. The numbers are selected with jumpers, DIP switches, or a thumb wheel. The SCSI adapter is usually set to ID #7. The primary SCSI hard drive (or any other boot device) is set to ID #0. The SCSI ID numbers do not have to be in order, nor do they have to be sequential. Of course, no two devices within the same chain can use the same SCSI ID number.

The two SCSI devices at either end of the chain must be terminated; the other devices should not be terminated. If only an internal cable is used, the adapter card and the device at the end of the cable need to be terminated, but the other devices in between should not be terminated. If using an internal cable and an external cable, the two devices located at the end of each cable should be terminated, but the other devices, including the adapter/controller card, should not be terminated. To terminate or not terminate a device, the terminators are inserted/removed or enabled/disabled with jumpers or DIP switches. Some SCSI devices can be automatically terminated. (See figs. 10.18, 10.19, 10.20, and 10.21.)

The SCSI standard (SCSI-1) was approved in 1986 by the American National Standards Institute (ANSI). It specified an 8-bit bus with a 5 MB/s transfer rate. Unfortunately, the standard included only the hardware connection and did not specify the driver specification or Common Command Set required to communicate with the SCSI hard drive. Therefore, manufacturers used their own communication standard, which led to many compatibility problems among different devices, drivers, and adapters. Most of the earlier Apple Macintosh computers used the SCSI interface instead of expansion slots for expanding the system. But this line of computers did not suffer from compatibility problems because Apple made a SCSI adapter for its computers.

TABLE 10.8   Types of SCSI devices and interfaces

SCSI Type	SCSI Specification	Connector	Maximum Number of Devices	Bits	Maximum Throughput
Standard	SCSI-1/SCSI-2	A cable	8	8	5 MB/s
SCSI Fast	SCSI-2	A cable	8	8	10 MB/s
SCSI Wide	SCSI-2	P cable	16	16	10 MB/s
SCSI Fast-20 (Ultra SCSI)	SCSI-3	P cable	8	8	20 MB/s
SCSI Fast-40	SCSI-3	P cable	16	8	40 MB/s
SCSI Fast-Wide	SCSI-3	P cable	16	16	80 MB/s
Fiber Channel	N/A	Fiber channel	127	Serial	100 MB/s

FIGURE 10.18   Terminating resistors and jumpers in a typical SCSI hard drive

FIGURE 10.19   Internal daisy chain

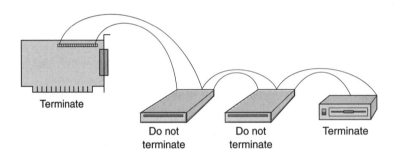

FIGURE 10.20   External daisy chain

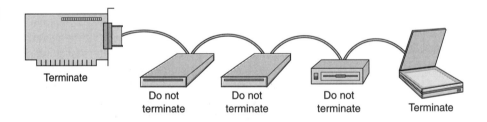

FIGURE 10.21   Internal and external daisy chain

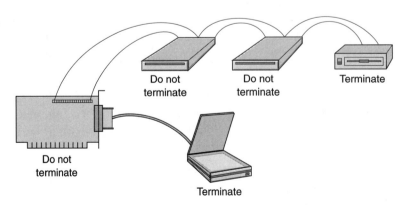

FIGURE 10.22 SCSI terminating resistor. Pin 1 is indicated by the square block on the left.

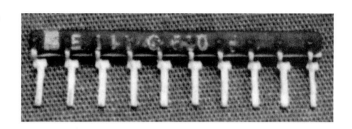

Question: What are terminating resistors?

Answer: Terminating resistors are used to control the signal in the SCSI pathway. There are two kinds of terminating resistors, passive and active.

The classic, or standard, terminator is the passive terminator. The passive terminator uses special electrical resistors that act as voltage dividers. Since they help ensure that the chain has the correct impedance load, the terminators prevent signals from reflecting, or echoing, when they reach the end of the chain. Passive terminating resistors work well for chains of short distances (2 to 3 feet) and slower speeds (SCSI-1 specification). The chain should never exceed 20 feet.

A newer type of termination is active termination. Active termination functions like a voltage regulator to maintain a stable voltage through the chain by utilizing the termination power lines to compensate for voltage drops. Since active termination helps reduce noise, it allows for longer cable lengths and faster speeds. The chain should never exceed 25 meters. The newest form of terminating resistor is the **forced perfect terminator (FPT).** The FPT attempts to remove reflections by automatically matching the line impedance, thus allowing "perfect" termination.

When installing a terminating resistor, make sure pin 1 is oriented properly. Pin 1 will be marked with a small square or rectangle, and the device will be marked with a small number 1 or a small arrow. (See fig. 10.22.)

To correct some of the shortcomings of the SCSI-1 interface, ANSI approved the SCSI-2 in 1992. It included a set of 18 basic SCSI commands, called the *Common Command Set* (CCS), to support different peripherals, including CD-ROM drives, tape drives, removable drives and disks, and scanners. In addition, SCSI-2 used command queuing. Command queuing allows a device to accept multiple commands and execute them in the most efficient order rather than in the order received, which increases the performance of computers running multitasking operating systems. In addition, SCSI-2 established faster SCSI variations, such as Fast SCSI and Wide SCSI, which increased the data path and improved data transfer to 10 MB/s.

SCSI-3 is a set of standards still under development. It specifies a high-speed synchronous transfer called Fast SCSI (10 MB/s) and Fast-20 SCSI or Ultra (20 MB/s) using a type A cable (8-bit data bus). In addition, the wide formats of Fast SCSI and Fast-20 SCSI allow twice the data transfer rate and up to 16 devices if the P cable (16-bit data bus) is used. A new kind of SCSI, the Fiber Channel SCSI, which is a serial connection made of fiber or coaxial cable, allows greater cable lengths, has a 100 MB/s data transfer rate, and supports up to 126 devices.

Like the IDE hard drives, SCSI drives do not have to be low-level formatted. If low-level formatting is needed, it can be done with software from the controller card's manufacturer or it can be executed from the SCSI setup program located within the SCSI ROM BIOS chip.

10.7.1 HOT-SWAPPABLE HARD DRIVES

A new type of drive is the hot-swappable drive that can be removed or installed while the computer is running. The ability to hot-swap a disk drive is beneficial in those situations where computers cannot be shut off for even a few minutes, such as network servers. Currently, SCSI drives are the only ones available that are hot-swappable.

10.8 TROUBLE-SHOOTING HARD DRIVES

Because hard drives are half-mechanical, half-electronic devices, they have a high failure rate compared to nonmechanical devices. They include most of the data created by the computer, so it is essential to keep them operating properly and to keep a timely backup of all data on the hard drive. The hard drive can fail because of its own internal problems or because of problems in the cable, the card, the motherboard, or the power connector. Failures can also be caused by power fluctuations or improper configuration of the drive, controller card, CMOS setup program, or motherboard. Data can also be lost by other means, such as viruses or badly written software.

EXAMPLE 10.3 The computer is turned on. During bootup, an "HDD Controller Failure" error message or equivalent appears on the screen or a "No Fixed Disk Present" error message appears while running FDISK. The "HDD Controller Failure" error message (or 1701 error message) indicates that the controller card tried to control the hard drive during boot-up but could not. The reason that it could not still needs to be determined.

First check the obvious: Before opening the system, check the CMOS values to see if they are correct. Remember that SCSI drives should have the CMOS set to SCSI (if available) or No Hard Drive Available. Check this first because it does not require the system to be opened. If the CMOS values keep disappearing, check the CMOS battery. The next step would be to see if the cables (ribbon cables and power connectors) are connected properly.

If nothing has been recently changed or added, replace the cable to see if the problem goes away. If not, replace the controller card. If the problem persists, the next step would be to measure the voltage level of the power connector to make sure that the cable is supplying +5 and +12 V. If it is, the next thing to do would be to replace the hard drive.

If it is a new installation or changes have been made to the hard drive system, verify the configuration, including the controller card resources (I/O address, IRQ, DMA, and memory usage) and the hard drive configuration (master/slave settings, the SCSI ID number, and terminating resistors). If there is no resource conflict, replace the cable to see if the problem goes away. If not, replace the controller card. If the problem persists, the next step would be to measure the voltage level of the power connector to make sure that the cable is supplying +5 and +12 V. If it is, the next thing to do would be to replace the hard drive.

EXAMPLE 10.4 The master boot record is corrupted, FDISK causes the computer to lock up, or changes to the partition cannot be saved.

The first thing to check is the CMOS settings. If the master boot record is corrupted, it can be recreated with the following command:

```
FDISK  /MBR
```

If this corrects the problem, you should be concerned with what caused the corruption of the master boot record. It could have been caused by a virus, power fluctuations when the drive was being accessed, or a failing hard drive. If the problem still exists, try a low-level format.

EXAMPLE 10.5 During boot-up, a "Disk Boot Failure," "Non-System Disk," "No ROM Basic—System Halted," or "Missing Operating System" error message appears.

If you are trying to boot from the floppy disk drive, you need to make sure that the floppy disk drive has the proper boot files. If you are trying to boot from the hard drive, make sure there is no floppy disk in drive A. Next, check the CMOS settings to make sure the proper hard drive parameters are being used and that the correct boot order is set. Next, boot using the A drive and make sure the hard drive boot files are in place and intact. If the boot files are missing or corrupted, use the SYS command from a floppy disk or equivalent to restore the files. Lastly, make sure that the hard drive has an active primary partition.

EXAMPLE 10.6 You turn on the computer and nothing happens. The fan does not spin and no lights come on in the front.

First, shut off the computer and open the case to check for the obvious: whether all the connectors are on correctly and whether any foreign objects are in the case. (Note: Incorrectly connected hard drive cables could cause the computer not to boot.)

Next, figure out which component is keeping the computer from starting. Remove all the unnecessary expansion cards and leave the video card and disk drive controller card in the case. If the system starts, then one of the expansion cards that you just took out is causing a short or overload. Isolate each card by inserting them into the system one at a time. If the problem still exists, you know it has to be caused by the motherboard, the video card, or the disk controller card. Next, remove the disk controller card. If the system starts to boot but does not finish, one of the drives or the controller card itself is causing the short.

If after replacing the drives and the controller card the machine still doesn't work, either the video card or the motherboard is at fault. If the video card is not part of the motherboard, the next step would be to replace the video card with a known good video card. If the system boots, the video card that you removed was faulty. If the system still doesn't work, it is the motherboard that is the cause of the problem.

Make sure the motherboard is placed in the case properly and remove the mounting screw. If the problem goes away, the mounting screw is causing a short on the motherboard. If the problem still occurs, it is the motherboard itself, the microprocessor, or the RAM. The easiest thing to check is the RAM. Replace the first bank of RAM. If the system still does not boot, try replacing the microprocessor if the microprocessor is not soldered onto the motherboard. If the problem still occurs, you are left with the motherboard, which will have to be replaced.

EXAMPLE 10.7 The computer does not boot and the hard drive light stays on.

First, make sure that the drive and controller card are connected properly and that the card and drives are configured properly. If the problem still exists, it is most likely a hard drive or controller card problem. Replace the card, cable, and hard drive one at time to see if the problem goes away. If the problem still exists, suspect the motherboard or one of the other expansion cards.

EXAMPLE 10.8 During boot-up, a "No SCSI Controller Present" error message appears.

This indicates that the SCSI controller card is bad or the card is not configured properly (I/O addresses, IRQs, DMAs, and memory addresses) and that another card is causing a conflict. If the card is configured correctly, replace the card.

EXAMPLE 10.9 During boot-up, a SCSI device is not recognized.

Make sure the device is connected and configured properly. This means checking the SCSI ID number and the terminating resistors for all SCSI devices connected to the chain. If the problem still exists, make sure that the proper drivers (if any) are loaded correctly. Next, replace the device to see if that fixes the problem. If the problem still exists, there is probably a compatibility problem between the SCSI adapter and the SCSI device.

SUMMARY

1. Hard drives are half-electronic, half-mechanical devices that use magnetic patterns to store information onto rotating platters.
2. Hard drives are considered long-term storage devices because they do not "forget" their information when power is disconnected. They are considered the primary mass storage system because they hold all the programs and data files that are fed into RAM.
3. Hard drives communicate with the rest of the computer by means of a cable connected to a controller card (either an expansion card or card built into the motherboard).
4. The rotating platters are covered with a magnetic material (iron oxide or a thin-film material) that can hold many tiny magnetic fields.
5. A read/write head, one for each side of a platter, reads the data from a platter and writes data to a platter.
6. A head-to-disk interference (HDI) occurs when particles cause the read/write head or platters to read improperly.
7. The head actuator is the component that moves the read/write heads back and forth.
8. Stepper-motor actuators are electrical motors that move from one position to another in steps. They are slow, sensitive to drive orientation and temperature fluctuations, do not have autoparking capability, and need to be low-level formatted as part of a maintenance routine.

9. Voice coil actuators use electromagnetic force to move the read/write heads back and forth. They are quicker, more efficient, able to constantly adjust position, and are autoparking.

10. A platter is divided into a circular grid consisting of tracks (concentric circles) and sectors (512 bytes).

11. The encoding of the data on the platter is the method or pattern used to represent the bits.

12. The capacity of the hard drive is the product of the number of cylinders, number of read/write heads, number of sectors per track, and 512 bytes per sector.

13. Hard drive sectors are addressed in CHS (cylinder–head–sector), translation mode, or LBA mode.

14. Hard drive performance is often measured in access time (average seek time + latency period) and data transfer rate.

15. The basic steps for installing and configuring a hard drive are physical installation of the hard drive system, low-level formatting, partitioning, high-level formatting (and making bootable if necessary), and installing and configuring the operating system and application programs.

16. Low-level formatting (LLF) is the process that defines the tracks and sectors of the hard drive. It must be done with special software.

17. Partitioning is defining and dividing the physical drive into logical volumes called partitions. Each partition functions as if it were a separate hard disk.

18. High-level formatting is the process of writing the file system structure on the disk so that it can be used to store programs and data.

19. Data protection is improved by RAID (redundant arrays of inexpensive disks), that is, by using two or more drives in combination as a fault tolerance system to protect against physical hard drive failure and to increase hard drive performance.

20. Hard drives are characterized by their interface. The ST-506/412 and ESDI drives are old-style hard drives; IDE and SCSI are modern drives.

21. The hard drive is connected to the controller card using a 40-pin cable.

22. The IDE drive is considered an intelligent drive because it can support drive translation. IDE hard drives can connect one drive (stand-alone) or two hard drives (master and slave).

23. The EIDE interface supports up to four IDE devices (IDE CD-ROM drives, IDE tape backup drives, and other IDE storage devices) using two IDE cables. It is faster than the IDE interface and can use LBA mode.

24. If the system ROM BIOS does not support EIDE/ATA-2 drives, it needs to be either updated or modified.

25. The standard SCSI interface allows up to seven devices (hard drives, tape drives, CD-ROM drives, removable drives or disks, and scanners) to be connected to one SCSI adapter/controller.

26. Each SCSI device, including the adapter/controller card, is identified with a SCSI ID number from 0 to 7.

27. When using SCSI devices, the two devices at both ends of the chain must be terminated; the other devices are not.

28. Since hard drives are half-mechanical, half-electronic devices, they have a high failure rate compared to nonmechanical devices.

29. Hard drive failure can be caused by failure of the hard drive itself, the cable, the card, the motherboard, or the power connector. It can also be caused by power fluctuations or improper configuration (drive, controller card, CMOS setup program, or motherboard). In addition, data can be lost through other means, such as viruses or badly written software.

QUESTIONS

1. Which type of head actuator is autoparking and found on all modern hard drives?
   a. stepper motor
   b. metal-in-gap
   c. magneto-resistive
   d. voice coil

2. Magnetic fields can:
   a. distort the circuitry within the microprocessor
   b. shut down the PC
   c. cause a RAM error message
   d. cause problems with data integrity on magnetic media
3. A hard drive HDI means:
   a. hard drive interference
   b. hard drive interface
   c. head-to-disk interference
   d. head distortion inside
   e. none of the above
4. The hard drive makes a grinding noise. The cause is probably:
   a. HDI
   b. resource conflict
   c. a corrupted file
   d. a SCSI ID number conflict
   e. incorrect CMOS configuration
5. A ribbon cable has a red stripe along one edge. What does this mean?
   a. it is the positive lead
   b. it is the negative lead
   c. the cable carries hazardous voltage
   d. the conductor with the stripe connects to pin 1 of the connector
6. How many bytes are in a sector?
   a. 256 bytes
   b. 512 bytes
   c. 1,024 bytes
   d. 4 KB
7. If a hard drive has three platters, 5,600 cylinders, and 63 sectors per track, what is the capacity of the hard drive?
   a. 1,058,400 bytes
   b. 1,033.6 MB
   c. 516.8 MB
   d. 2,116,800 bytes
8. Which of the following pertain to the speed with which data can be transferred to the PC from a hard drive?
   a. disk seek time
   b. rotational latency period
   c. interleaving
   d. data transfer rate
9. The time it takes for the hard drive to find data is called:
   a. rotational latency period
   b. access time
   c. data transfer rate
   d. seek time
10. What is the latency period?
    a. the time it takes the head to be positioned over the proper track
    b. the time it takes the desired sector to move under the head
    c. the time it takes the data to be sent to the PC
    d. the time required for the disk to make one rotation
11. The time required for positioning the head over the proper track is:
    a. seek time
    b. access time
    c. latency period
    d. data transfer rate
12. Which of the following should be done before replacing a hard drive?
    a. back up the hard drive
    b. run the CMOS setup program
    c. run CHKDSK
    d. erase the hard drive
13. What does RAID stand for?
    a. random access interrupt driver
    b. redundant array of interchangeable disks
    c. redundant array of inexpensive disks
    d. redundant access information data
14. Which program partitions a hard drive?
    a. SCANDISK
    b. DISKCOPY
    c. FORMAT
    d. FDISK
    e. SETUP
15. When configuring a system with preloaded software, formatting the primary hard disk will:
    a. improve system performance
    b. erase the partitions
    c. compress preloaded programs
    d. provide additional partition and format options

16. CHS mode is:
    a. physical CMOS parameters for cylinders, heads, and sectors
    b. physical CMOS parameters using translating electronics
    c. a fast method of data transfer
    d. a 28-bit binary number indicating the physical number of sectors on a drive
17. What is the first step in configuring the hard disk drive?
    a. partition the drive
    b. format DOS
    c. format the drive physically
    d. set the jumpers on the drive
18. What is it called when a hard drive writes a sector, skips one or more sectors, and then writes another sector?
    a. sectoring
    b. interweaving
    c. interleaving
    d. sector skipping
19. When older disk drives are run constantly, which of the following is likely to occur?
    a. the platter will warp from vibrations caused by the drive motor
    b. the magnetic oxide may move outward, resulting in tracks shifting
    c. the read/write heads can overheat from surface friction
    d. the drive belt is damaged from excessive heat
20. Which of the following must be checked when replacing an ESDI hard drive? (Choose all that apply.)
    a. the cable
    b. the controller address
    c. the drive select jumper
    d. voltage
21. When you replace an IDE hard drive, you must:
    a. set the ID jumper on the drive
    b. set the master/slave jumper on the drive
    c. set the speed jumper on the drive
    d. set the speed jumper on the mother board
22. The boot IDE hard drive is known as the:
    a. stand-alone
    b. master
    c. slave
    d. active
23. Which of the following would be the correct configuration for a dual IDE drive system?
    a. the primary drive would have the M/S jumper and the SP jumper on, while the secondary drive would have the M/S jumper and the SP jumper on
    b. the primary drive would have the M/S jumper and the SP jumper on, while the secondary drive would have the M/S jumper and the SP jumper off
    c. the primary drive would have the M/S jumper on and the SP jumper off, while the secondary drive would have the M/S jumper off and the SP jumper on
    d. the primary drive would have the M/S jumper off and the SP jumper on, while the secondary drive would have the M/S jumper on and the SP jumper off
    e. the primary drive would have the M/S jumper and the SP jumper off, while the secondary drive would have the M/S jumper and the SP jumper off
24. How many devices do EIDE controllers support?
    a. 2
    b. 4
    c. 7
    d. 8
25. Which of the following was created to overcome the 504 MB IDE drive limitation?
    a. PIO
    b. CHS
    c. translation mode
    d. LBA
26. What is the maximum number of devices that can be connected to a standard SCSI-2 adapter?
    a. 2
    b. 4
    c. 7
    d. 8
27. When installing a system with four SCSI drives on one cable, where should the terminator be installed? (Assume the controller card is already terminated.)
    a. on the last drive on the cable
    b. on the first drive on the cable
    c. on the first and last drive
    d. none of the above
28. When you replace a SCSI hard drive, you must (choose all that apply):
    a. set the ID jumper on the drive
    b. set the master/slave jumper on the drive

c. set the speed jumper on the drive

d. set the terminating resistors on the SCSI devices

29. What is the ID number commonly assigned to the boot device in a PC?

    a. 0   c. 7

    b. 15   d. 8

30. What is the jumper setting on a SCSI device to configure it to use the fifth SCSI ID? Remember, SCSI IDs start with 0.

    a. 010   d. 101

    b. 110   e. 001

    c. 011

31. The total length of your standard SCSI cables should not exceed:

    a. 3 feet   c. 20 feet

    b. 6 feet   d. 100 feet

32. You are installing a SCSI hard drive as your boot drive. How should you configure the hard drive?

    a. set the SCSI ID number to 0

    b. set the SCSI ID number to 1

    c. set the SCSI ID number to 7

    d. set the SCSI ID number to any number that is free

    e. enable the boot jumper

33. Which of the following IRQ's would probably be free so that it could be used by a SCSI card if the system has a standard IDE controller card? (Choose two answers.)

    a. IRQ 7   d. IRQ 14

    b. IRQ 6   e. IRQ 15

    c. IRQ 10

34. What is the highest binary number that can be referred to on a three-position jumper block?

    a. 4   c. 5

    b. 6   d. 7

35. An internal SCSI device uses which type of cabling?

    a. 34-pin ribbon cable   d. 50-pin Centronics cabling

    b. 40-pin ribbon cable   e. 25-pin shielded cable

    c. 50-pin ribbon cable

36. Which implementation of SCSI has a transfer rate of 20 MB/s?

    a. Fast SCSI-2

    b. Fast-Wide SCSI-2

    c. SCSI-3

    d. Ultra SCSI

37. Which of the following will not cause an HDD controller failure?

    a. ribbon cable not on properly   d. bad controller card

    b. bad ribbon cable   e. power cable not connected

    c. bad hard drive   f. bad RAM chip

38. Which of the following are the most likely failing components if the hard drive activity light is on solid and the system fails to boot? (Choose two answers.)

    a. hard drive   c. hard drive controller

    b. motherboard   d. power supply

39. After upgrading a hard disk drive from 540 MB to 2.1 GB, a "Drive Mismatch Error" message appears when you power up the system. What has happened?

    a. the information stored in the CMOS setup program does not match the new hard drive

    b. the new hard drive is incompatible with the hard disk controller

    c. the new hard drive requires a local bus

    d. the controller cable on the hard drive is damaged or missing from the new installation

    e. the driver needs to be loaded

40. Suppose you had an incurable computer virus and decided to wipe out all the data and partitions on your hard drive and reformat. What is the order in which you must delete the partitions?
    a. extended, logical, primary
    c. logical, extended, primary
    b. primary, extended, logical
    d. logical, primary, extended
41. A single hard drive has a primary hard drive (drive C) and two logical drives (drives D and E). You add a second hard drive and create a primary partition. Which of the following is correct?
    a. the second drive becomes drive D and the logical drives become E and F
    b. the second drive becomes F and the logical drives are unchanged
    c. the second drive becomes D and the logical drive D is deleted
    d. the second drive becomes E and the logical drive E is deleted
    e. the second drive becomes C and the first primary partition is deleted
42. During boot-up, you get an "HDD Controller Failure" error message. Upon further investigation, you cannot hear the hard drive. Therefore, you should:
    a. check to make sure that the power cable is connected
    b. replace the hard drive
    c. replace the hard drive controller
    d. replace the hard drive cable
    e. use the CMOS setup program

HANDS-ON PROJECTS

Exercise 1: Installing an IDE Hard Drive

1. Make sure that the computer can boot to drive C.
2. With the CMOS setup program, record the drive type, number of tracks, number of read/write heads, number of sectors per track, and hard drive mode (if any).
3. Using the FDISK utility, view the partitions (option 4; see figure below and figure at top of next page). Look for the number and type of partitions.
4. Using the FDISK utility, delete all partitions (option 3; see second figure on next page). (Note: This is done by deleting any logical partitions, then deleting the extended partition and the primary partition.)
5. After the partitions are deleted, press the ESC key several times until a request is made to insert a system disk.
6. If the drive is set to a type 47, type 48, or a user-definable type, set the number of tracks, number of read/write heads, and number of sectors per track to 0.
7. Go into the CMOS setup program and set drive C to type 1.
8. Save the changes to the CMOS setup program and shut down the computer.

```
                    Microsoft Windows 98
                   Fixed Disk Setup Program
               (C)Copyright Microsoft Corp. 1983 - 1998


                        FDISK Options

Current fixed disk drive: 1

Choose one of the following:

1. Create DOS partition or Logical DOS Drive
2. Set active partition
3. Delete partition or Logical DOS Drive
4. Display partition information

Enter choice: [4]


Press Esc to exit FDISK
```

```
                    Display Partition Information

Current fixed disk drive: 1

Partition  Status  Type       Volume Label   Mbytes   System   Usage
C: 1       A       PRI DOS                    1039     FAT16    50%
   2               EXT DOS                    1024     FAT32    50%

Total disk space is 2067 Mbytes (1 Mbyte = 1048576 bytes)

The Extended DOS Partition contains Logical DOS Drives.
Do you want to display the logical drive information (Y/N)......?[Y]

Press Esc to return to FDISK Options
```

```
              Delete DOS Partition or Logical DOS Drive

Current fixed disk drive: 1

Choose one of the following:

1. Delete Primary DOS Partition
2. Delete Extended DOS Partition
3. Delete Logical DOS Drive(s) in the Extended DOS Partition
4. Delete Non-DOS Partition

Enter choice: [ ]

Press Esc to return to FDISK Options
```

9. Shut off the computer. Disconnect the power cable and remove the hard drive, cable, and controller card from the system. Observe how the cable, particularly pin 1, is connected to the card and the drive.
10. Reinstall the hard drive, cable, and controller into the system and connect the power to the hard drive.
11. Set the proper CMOS settings for the hard drive.
12. Try to boot the computer with the C drive. Record the error message.
13. Boot the computer with the A drive.
14. Run FDISK to create (option 1; see figure below) a primary DOS partition. Do not maximize the partition and do not make it active. Specify the size of the primary DOS partition to be 75%. (Note: You must include the % sign. If you don't, it will create a partition of 75 MB instead of 75%.)
15. Go back to the main menu. Notice the warning at the bottom of the screen.
16. Use the rest of the free disk space to create an extended DOS partition. Assign one logical drive (drive D).

```
              Create DOS Partition or Logical DOS Drive

Current fixed disk drive: 1

Choose one of the following:

1. Create Primary DOS Partition
2. Create Extended DOS Partition
3. Create Logical DOS Drive(s) in the Extended DOS Partition

Enter choice: [1]

Press Esc to return to FDISK Options
```

17. Press the ESC key until a request is made to insert a system disk.
18. Boot the computer using drive C. Record the error message.
19. Using FDISK, make the primary DOS partition active (option 2).
20. Boot the computer using drive C. Record the error message.
21. Boot the computer using drive A. Switch over to the C drive. Perform a DIR command. Record the error message.
22. Use the Abort/Fail options to move back to the A drive.
23. Boot the computer using drive A. Format the hard drive, but do not make it bootable.
24. Boot the computer using drive C and record the error message.
25. Boot the computer using drive A. Make the hard drive bootable with either a FORMAT command or a SYS command.
26. Format the D drive.
27. Boot the computer using drive C.
28. Using the CMOS setup program, reduce the number of cylinders by 50% and double the number of read/write heads. (Note: You may need to use a user-definable type if you are not already using one.) Save the changes.
29. Boot the computer using drive C. Record any error messages or if it doesn't boot.
30. Using the CMOS setup program, put the original settings back.
31. Boot the computer to drive C.
32. Shut off the computer. Remove the cable connector from the hard drive and place it on backwards.
33. Boot the computer using drive C. Record any error messages or if it doesn't boot.
34. Shut off the computer. Reconnect the cable properly.
35. Disconnect the gray ribbon cable.
36. Boot the computer to drive C. Record any error messages or if it doesn't boot.
37. Shut off the computer. Reconnect the gray ribbon cable and disconnect the power connector.
38. Boot the computer to drive C. Record any error messages or if it doesn't boot.
39. Shut off the computer. Reconnect the power cable.
40. Go into the CMOS setup program and set drive D to be a type 1 drive.
41. Boot the computer to drive C. Record any error messages or if it doesn't boot.
42. Go into the CMOS setup program and disable drive D.
43. Make sure that the computer boots properly.

Exercise 2: Installing a Second IDE Hard Drive

1. Make sure that the computer can boot to drive C.
2. With the CMOS setup program, record the drive type, number of tracks, number of read/write heads, and number of sectors per track.
3. Shut off the computer. Remove the hard drive that is already in the computer. Examine the jumpers on the hard drive. They should be set to be a stand-alone hard drive.
4. Set the jumpers on the original hard drive to master and set the jumpers on the second hard drive to slave.
5. Connect both hard drives to the cable and connect the power cables.
6. Set the CMOS parameters for drives C and D.
7. Boot the computer using drive C.
8. Using FDISK, switch to the second hard drive (option 5). Create a primary DOS partition (option 1).
9. Press the ESC key until a request is made to insert a system disk.
10. Boot the computer using drive C. Change over to the D drive. Remember that all primary partitions are given drive letters first.
11. Use the Abort/Fail options to move back to the A drive. Format the D drive.
12. Change to the E drive, which should be the extended DOS partition on the first hard drive.
13. Remove the second hard drive.
14. Change the first drive back to a stand-alone drive.
15. Disable drive D in the CMOS setup program.
16. Make sure that the computer boots properly.

Exercise 3: Recreating a Master Boot Record

1. Using FDISK, recreate the master boot record.
2. Create a primary DOS partition. Use the entire drive for the partition and make it active.
3. Format the C drive and make it bootable.
4. Make sure that the computer boots properly.

Exercise 4: Low-Level Formatting the IDE Hard Drive

1. Access the Internet and download the proper low-level format program for your hard drive.
2. Low-level format the hard drive.
3. Boot the computer using the A drive.
4. Run FDISK to create a primary DOS partition (80 MB) and an extended DOS partition (remaining amount). In addition, make the primary DOS partition active.
5. Boot the computer to the A drive.
6. Format the C drive.
7. Make sure that the computer boots properly.

Exercise 5: Installing a SCSI Hard Drive

1. Remove any IDE drives from your system.
2. Disable drive C in the CMOS setup program.
3. Set the resources of the SCSI expansion card. Use the card's documentation and a software diagnostic to determine the I/O addresses, IRQs, and DMA.
4. Locate the terminating resistors on the SCSI expansion card. Make sure that they are installed and enabled.
5. If the SCSI controller card has a floppy disk drive controller and one already exists in the computer, disable the one on the SCSI controller card.
6. Install the SCSI controller card.
7. Using the drive's documentation, set the boot drive to SCSI ID 0. Make sure that the terminating resistor is installed and enabled.
8. Install the boot drive to the end of the chain (cable) and connect the power.
9. Using the drive's documentation, set a second SCSI hard drive or a SCSI CD-ROM to SCSI ID 5.
10. Disable or remove the terminating resistor on the second drive.
11. Connect the second drive to the middle of the chain and connect the power.
12. Boot the computer using drive A.
13. Create a primary DOS partition. Use the entire drive for the partition and make it active.
14. Format the hard drive and make it bootable.
15. Using the correct software, low-level format the first SCSI hard drive.
16. Remove all SCSI drives, including the controller card.
17. Reinstall the IDE hard drive.
18. Enter the correct parameters in the CMOS setup program.
19. Make sure that the computer boots properly.

Exercise 6: Common Drive Problems

1. Delete all partitions on the hard drive.
2. Create a primary partition (80%) and make it active.
3. Create a logical drive (drive D—20%).
4. Format drive C and drive D.
5. Create a DOS directory on the D drive.
6. Copy the FORMAT.COM, CHKDSK.EXE, and SCANDISK.EXE files to the D:\DOS directory.
7. Create an AUTOEXEC.BAT file on the C drive and include the D:\DOS directory in the PATH statement.
8. From the C:\ directory, start the SCANDISK program and check the D drive.

9. Install a second hard drive. On the second hard drive, create a Primary DOS partition.
10. From the C:\ directory, start the SCANDISK program and note the error.
11. Determine the drive letter for the primary DOS partition on the first hard drive, the logical drive on the first hard drive, and the primary DOS partition on the second hard drive.
12. Restart the computer and enter the CMOS setup program.
13. Double the number of sectors per track for drive C and halve the number of read/write heads.
14. Boot the computer using the C drive.
15. If the hard drive does not boot using the C drive, reboot the computer using the A drive.
16. Try to access the C drive and perform a DIR command.

Exercise 7: Internet Research

1. Find the CMOS parameters for the Western Digital Caviar AC33200 (3.2 GB EIDE) hard drive.
2. Find the jumper settings to make the Western Digital Caviar AC33200 (3.2 GB EIDE) a master drive.
3. Find the jumper settings to make the Western Digital Caviar AC33200 (3.2 GB EIDE) a slave drive.
4. Find and download the low-level format program for the Western Digital Caviar AC33200 (3.2 GB EIDE).
5. Find the jumper settings to make a Seagate ST-11900N (1.7 MB SCSI hard drive) SCSI ID 0.
6. Find the jumper settings to make a Seagate ST-11900 N (1.7 MB SCSI hard drive) SCSI ID 5.
7. Find how to terminate the resistance on a Seagate ST-11900N (1.7 MB SCSI hard drive).
8. Find and download the software to make a Seagate Medallist Pro hard drive overcome certain system BIOS and operating system limitations.
9. Find and download the Windows NT driver for the AHA-2940 SCSI card.
10. Find and download the installation guide for the Adaptec 2940 Ultra SCSI card.

11 The Floppy Disk Drive and Other Removable Media

INTRODUCTION

Floppy drives are half-electronic, half-mechanical devices that use magnetic patterns to store information on a removable disk consisting of a single rotating platter.

Floppy drives are essential to a computer technician because they are needed to prepare the hard drive for first-time use (partitioning and formatting), to load essential device drivers, and to analyze a system that has failed.

OBJECTIVES

1. Describe the function of the floppy drive.
2. List and describe the characteristics of a floppy drive platter.
3. Describe the read/write head and how it reads and writes to the platter.
4. Describe the head actuators.
5. List and describe the different kinds of floppy disks and their capacity.
6. Define track and sectors.
7. List and describe the basic steps in installing a floppy disk drive.
8. Determine and correct a floppy drive problem.
9. List at least three different removable media drives.
10. Determine and correct a removable media drive problem.

11.1 WHAT IS A FLOPPY DRIVE?

A **floppy disk drive** is a half-electronic, half-mechanical device that uses magnetic patterns to store information on a removable disk consisting of a single rotating platter. It is considered a long-term storage device because it does not lose information when power is disconnected. Today, floppy drives are considered secondary storage systems because of their size limitations and slow speeds.

Although floppy drives do not play as important a role as they did when the IBM PC was introduced, they are still an essential component of the PC. They are used to prepare the hard drive for first-time use (partitioning and formatting) and to load essential device drivers such as the one needed for the CD-ROM drive since it is the CD-ROM drive that is used to load Windows 95 and 98 and Windows NT. The floppy disk is a valuable tool for the PC technician in analyzing a hard drive that isn't booting or is not accessible. Lastly, the floppy drive can be used for storing and backing up small files and is still a common way to transfer files from one computer to another.

Floppy disk drives communicate with the rest of the computer by means of a 34-pin ribbon cable connected to a controller card. The controller card could be an expansion card or could be built onto the motherboard. All floppy drives consist of the following components: floppy disks, read/write heads, and head actuators.

11.1.1 FLOPPY DISKS

Unlike hard drives, floppy disk drives use **floppy disks,** which are removable from the system, to store data. The reason they are called *floppy disks* is because they are flexible platters made of mylar. Some people wrongly call the 3½″ floppy disk a *hard disk* because of its sturdy protective casing. Of course, the terms *floppy* and *hard* are based on the platter, not the casing for the platter. The mylar platters don't actually store data. Instead, it is their coating of magnetic material, such as iron oxide, that stores data. The magnetic coating is made up of tiny particles that can hold magnetic fields. When these fields are placed in certain patterns, they represent 0s and 1s. The bits of information are written (stored) and read (retrieved) using a **read/write head.**

All floppy disk platters rotate around a **spindle** at 300 rotations per minute (rpm) except the DS/HD 5¼″ floppy disk drive, which rotates at 360 rpm. The faster the drive spins, the less time it takes to access data. The spindle motor, which spins the platter, uses very little power and generates very little heat.

Disks have come in two sizes and two densities since the introduction of the PC. These are shown in table 11.1. The 5¼″ disk consists of two parts, the platter and the protective jacket. (See fig. 11.1.) As the lever of the disk drive is closed, the drive clamps down around a large hole in the middle of the platter, sometimes referred to as the *spindle access hole.* When the disk is accessed, the platter is spun around the spindle. A slot cut in the jacket allows the read/write heads to read the surface of the platter. Below the center of the spindle hole, there is a small round hole called the *index hole.* When a hole on the platter is lined up with the index hole, that indicates that the read/write heads are at the beginning of the track. To write-protect the disk, the write-protect notch located on the side of disk is covered with a piece of tape. To make the disk read/write, the tape would be removed from

TABLE 11.1 Different floppy disk drives

Disks	Capacity	Sectors per Track	Tracks per Inch	Bits per Inch	Coercivity
DS/DD 5¼″	360 KB	9	48	5,876	290 oersteds
DS/HD 5¼″	1.2 MB	15	96	9,869	660 oersteds
DS/DD 3½″	720 KB	9	135	8,717	650 oersteds
DS/HD 3½″	1.44 MB	18	135	17,434	720 oersteds

Note: There are also double-sided, *extra-density* (DS/ED) 3½″ disks and drives, which have a 2.88 MB capacity. Although these disks can hold twice as much as other floppy disks, they aren't widely used.

FIGURE 11.1 5¼″ floppy disk

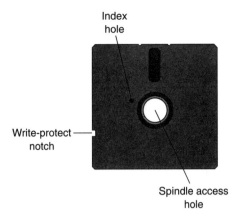

Index
hole

Write-protect
notch

Spindle access
hole

the notch. There is a liner, made of soft woven cloth, between the platter and the jacket. The cloth reduces the friction between the platter and the jacket and collects dust and particles from the surface of the platter, reducing the potential for errors caused by surface dirt. Unfortunately, the jacket doesn't do a very good job of protecting the platter. The disk can be bent easily, and writing on the label of the jacket with a ballpoint pen could cause impressions on the platter that would produce read/write errors.

The standard floppy disk today is the 3½″ disk. (See fig. 11.2.) It is smaller yet holds more information than the 5¼″ disk. The platter is enclosed in a sturdy protective casing. Rather than part of the platter being exposed so that the read/write head can access it, the 3½″ platter includes a metal shutter that opens as it slides into the drive. When the disk is removed from the computer, a small metal spring automatically closes the shutter. The disk is made so that it can't be inserted upside down or backwards. The 3½″ disk is write-protected by a small hole with a sliding plastic cover. When the cover is open, the disk is write-protected; when the cover is closed, it is not write-protected.

The *density* of a disk refers to the amount of data that can be stored in a given amount of space, which depends on how many tracks can fit on the disk and how many bits can fit on each track. A density hole on 3½″ disks identifies the disk as a DD disk or a HD disk. If a density key or hole is present, the disk is a 1.44 MB disk; if the density key is not present, the disk is a 720 KB disk.

To store information on a platter, it is divided into a circular grid consisting of tracks and sectors. The platter is first divided into concentric circles called **tracks.** (*Concentric* means circles that share the same center, much like rings of a tree.) A floppy disk platter will have either 40 or 80 tracks. Tracks are numbered starting with the outside track as track 0. The tracks are then further divided into **sectors;** each sector contains 512 bytes of usable data. A floppy disk has 9 to 18 sectors per track. Sectors are numbered on a track starting with 1. Information written to the platter is represented by tiny magnetic fields

FIGURE 11.2   3½″ floppy disk

(flux) whose polarity flows from north to south or south to north. The read/write heads do not measure the polarity of the magnetic fields, but instead the flux reversals.

Encoding the data on the platter is the method or pattern used to represent the bits. The first encoding method, used before the IBM PC, was frequency modulation (FM). In FM encoding, the value of 1 is represented with two flux reversals, the first for the clock and the second for the 1. A 0 is represented by a flux reversal (clock) followed by a no reversal. Unfortunately, FM encoding is wasteful since each bit requires two flux-reversal positions. Modern floppy disks use MFM encoding. Instead of inserting a clock reversal before each bit, one is inserted only between consecutive zeroes. This means far fewer reversals are needed on average per bit and allows approximately double the storage capacity of FM encoding. This is why the early floppy disks were called *double-density* disks.

Although floppy drives are quite reliable, the same can't be said about floppy disks. Since the magnetic fields used to represent data are not very strong and the platter, the magnetic coating, and the protective case are not as sturdy as a hard drive, the floppy disk will often develop unreadable areas. These errors may appear as read/write errors during disk reading and writing or can appear as bad blocks when using software to analyze the disk. These types of problems are usually caused by stray magnetic fields or certain areas of the platter losing their magnetic properties. In addition, the surface of the platter is exposed to the open air, which can contaminate the surface and damage the magnetic material on the platter. (Note: Since floppy disks are so inexpensive and not very reliable, a disk should be thrown away if it develops any read/write errors.)

11.1.2 READ/WRITE HEADS

The read/write head is an iron core with wire (a coil) wrapped around it. When electricity is applied to the coil, it acts as an electromagnet. To write to a disk, current is sent through the wire, which causes an electromagnetic field to form around the wire. The coil intensifies the electromagnetic field. As the electromagnetic field crosses the platter, the magnetic material on the platter becomes magnetized. To read from the disk, the process is reversed. The read/write head passes over the magnetized material, and as the coil detects the changes (flux) in the magnetic charge, a small amount of current is caused to flow in the head. After this signal is amplified and filtered, it is translated into 0s and 1s.

Compared to the read/write head of a hard drive, the read/write head of a floppy drive is larger and much less precise. This is because they are generic so that they can work on disks made by different manufacturers. As a result, the density of the floppy disk is much lower. Since the floppy read/write heads are not as precise, floppy disk drives must use tunnel erasing to keep the tracks well defined. (See fig. 11.3.) The floppy read/write assembly consists of a single read/write head and two erase heads (placed on each side of the read/write head). The erase heads erase any stray magnetic information that the read/write head might have recorded outside the designated track. If tunnel erasing were not done, interference might result between the tracks.

Since data can be stored on both sides of a platter, a read/write head is used for each side. The bottom head is the first read/write head while the top head is the second. Because the operations of the read/write heads may affect one another, the top read/write head is offset by four or eight tracks (depending on the type of drive) inward from the bottom head. Unlike those in most hard drives, the floppy drive heads make contact with the platter. The platters do not spin at high speeds and are flexible, so the read/write heads and the

FIGURE 11.3 Tunnel erasing used in floppy disk drive

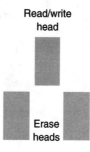

Read/write head

Erase heads

platter are not damaged when the two make contact. Unfortunately, since the read/write heads are exposed to the air and make contact with the platters, magnetic oxide and dirt build up on the heads. This is the reason that the floppy drive read/write heads have to be cleaned with a special cleaning disk made of a soft cloth platter that uses a special cleaning solution.

11.1.3 HEAD ACTUATOR

The **head actuator** is the component that moves the read/write heads back and forth. Floppy drives use the **stepper motor** head actuator. Stepper motors are electrical motors that move from one position to another in steps. Unfortunately, the stepper motor cannot take half steps. If the stepper motor is to move the read/write heads to a particular location, it counts the appropriate number of steps, but unfortunately, it has no way of determining whether it has arrived at the correct location. If, for instance, the platters have been left overnight in a cold building, they would contract (shrink). Consequently, when the stepper motor moves the read/write heads the appropriate number of steps, the data would have shifted inward. When the read/write heads try to read the data, they are actually reading between tracks, resulting in read/write errors. But since floppy disks have a lower track density, this is usually not a problem.

The head actuators on a floppy disk drive are very slow compared to those on hard disk drives. It takes the read/write heads about 200 milliseconds to move from the outer track to the inner track, a distance of approximately 1 inch. This is one reason why floppy disks are much slower than hard disks.

11.1.4 FLOPPY DRIVE CHARACTERISTICS

The 5¼″ floppy drive first used in the IBM PC was a full-height drive bay, which is 3½″ high. Later, the 5¼″ drive was reduced to a half-height device, which is 1¾″ high. The 3½″ drive is much smaller and is considered a one-third-height device measuring 1″.

As disks are inserted into the disk drive, a spindle clamp clamps around the spindle hub. This is done manually with a latch or lever in the 5¼″ drive; it is done automatically in the 3½″ disk drive. The button on the 3½″ disk drive is used to release the disk. Since floppy drives use a clamping mechanism to hold the disk in place, the drive can be placed horizontally or vertically.

On the underside of each floppy drive, there is an integrated logic board. It controls the read/write heads, the spindle motor, and head actuator and communicates with the floppy disk controller.

11.1.5 FLOPPY DISK CONTROLLER

The floppy disk controller electronically interfaces the floppy disk drives to the rest of the PC. It manages the flow and transfer of information from the floppy disk drives to the microprocessor and RAM. The controller card will be either an expansion card (usually part of a multifunction expansion card) or built into the motherboard.

Today a floppy disk controller will run every type of standard floppy disk drive. Older controllers will not always work on newer drives since some cannot run at the faster speeds required by the newer drives. The speed required of the controller is directly related to the density of the floppy disk media being used, in particular the bit density per track. The closer the information is, the faster the controller must work to read and write information within the same time frame. There are currently three different controller speeds. The older controllers perform at 250 kilobits per second and support the 360 KB 5¼″ and 720 KB 3½″ drives. The newer controllers perform at 500 kilobits per second and support the 360 KB, 1.2 MB, 720 KB, and 1.44 MB drives. The most modern floppy disk controller performs at 1 megabit per second. It supports all standard floppy drives, including the 2.88 MB floppy and proprietary floppy drive devices such as tape backups.

As with any other disk, the files on a floppy disk are located by reading the FAT (file allocation table) and directory information. Every time a disk is inserted in the drive, a change-disk signal is sent to the controller through pin 34 of the floppy drive cable. The controller then copies the FAT and directory information to the RAM. Every time the disk is accessed, the location of the file is read from the RAM. Consequently, the performance of the disk is increased.

11.2 INSTALLING A FLOPPY DISK DRIVE

The first step to installing any floppy drive is to physically install the controller card and floppy drive. The floppy drive is usually held in an external drive bay with screws. The disk controller could be an expansion card (possibly the same card as the hard drive controller) or it could be already incorporated on the motherboard. The resources used by the floppy disk drive controller are quite standard and universal. The floppy disk drive controller uses IRQ 6, DMA channel 2, and I/O address 3F0-3F7H. Most of the time, these resources can't be changed, and most computer component manufacturers avoid using these resources since they know that these are used for the floppy disk drive controller.

The drive and controller are connected with a gray 34-pin ribbon cable, which must be connected properly. (See fig. 11.4.) The first floppy controller card and the 5¼″ floppy disk drives used a 34-pin edge connector. (See fig. 11.5.) To make sure that the cable was not inserted into the edge connector, the edge connector had a key consisting of a slit cut into the connector. If you tried to connect the cable backwards, a thin piece of plastic meant for the slit would prevent the connector from going on. The thin piece of plastic was known to fall out, however. Forcing the 5¼″ connector onto the drive when the cable was on backwards caused the thin piece of plastic to shear the edge connector.

Newer controller cards and 3½″ floppy disk drives use a 34-pin connector. (See fig. 11.6.) Pin 1 of the cable is designated with a red or blue stripe. The controller card and drive are marked with either a small number 1 or 2 to designate which end has pin 1, or they use a square solder (other pins use a round solder). If one of the cable ends is connected backward, the floppy drive light or lights remain on. If a 5¼″ disk is inserted, the drive will make a hideous grinding noise while it destroys the disk. If a 3½″ disk is inserted, the drive will not make any unnecessary noise yet will still destroy the disk. (Note: The drive itself is rarely damaged if the ribbon cable is connected backwards.)

In addition to the gray ribbon cable, the floppy drive also uses a power connector. A 5¼″ floppy drive will use a 5¼″ power connector, and a 3½″ floppy drive will use a 3½″ power connector. In both cases, the drive requires +5 V to power the chips and +12 V to power the motors. Floppy disk drives in notebook computers use +5 V for the motor. The power cable must be connected properly. To ensure proper orientation, the 5¼″ power cable connector has a rectangular shape with two corners clipped off; the 3½″ power connector has a ridge on the bottom. If the cable is improperly connected, 12 V will enter components that are designed for 5 V, which will result in damaged or blown chips and a possible fire in the cable.

The gray ribbon cable will have three, four, or five connectors grouped into three sets. A set could be one connector or two connectors. The connector or connector set located on the long end will connect to the controller card, the set of connectors on the other end is for drive A, and the set in the middle is for drive B. If a set has two connectors, one connector is the 3½″ connector and the other the 5¼″ connector, only one of which would be used at a time.

The last step in installing the floppy disk drive is to set the floppy drive parameters using the CMOS setup program. The possible options are Not Installed, 360 KB, 720 KB, 1.2 MB, 1.44 MB, and 2.88 MB. On newer systems, the advanced CMOS setup screen has other parameters that will affect the floppy disk drives. The Boot Sequence controls which drive it will boot from first. By default, the boot order is the A drive followed by the C drive, although this can be changed to the C drive followed by the A drive. Newer systems will include other boot drives such as SCSI drives and CD-ROMs. (Note: You cannot boot with the B drive.)

Although most floppy drives are easy to connect, there are a few older, nonstandard floppy drives that require additional configuring. Since these drives use a 34-pin ribbon

FIGURE 11.4   34-pin floppy drive ribbon cable

Drive B (3½" and 5¼" floppy drive connectors)   Controller card   Drive A (3½" and 5¼" floppy drive connectors)

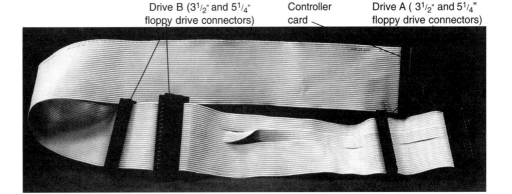

FIGURE 11.5   5¼" floppy drive connector

Key

FIGURE 11.6   3½" floppy drive connector

cable that does not include a twist, a drive select (DS) jumper is used to select whether the drive is drive A or drive B.

11.3   PREPARING THE FLOPPY DISK

Before a floppy disk can store files, it must be properly prepared. This includes low-level and high-level formatting. Low-level formatting defines the tracks and sectors on the disk. High-level formatting is the process of writing the file system structure on the disk so that it can be used to store programs and data, including a root directory to start with and a file allocation table (an index listing all directories and files and where they are located on the disk).

Both types of formats can be done with the FORMAT command or equivalent. If the drive has never been formatted, the FORMAT command will low-level format the disk and follow it by a high-level format. Normally, if a floppy disk has already been formatted, only a high-level format will be completed. If you wish to redraw the tracks and sectors, you must specify the unconditional format. Of course, whichever type of formatting is done, all information on the disk will be lost. Today, most disks are preformatted.

11.4 TROUBLE-SHOOTING FLOPPY DISK DRIVES

A floppy disk drive problem is most likely caused by a faulty disk, drive, cable, or controller card. Incorrect power and incorrect CMOS values can also cause problems. Since the drive and controller card are inexpensive, it is best to replace the faulty components rather than repair them.

EXAMPLE 11.1 The computer is turned on. During boot-up, an "FDD Controller Failure" error message or equivalent appears on the screen.

The "FDD Controller Failure" error message (or 601 error message) indicates that the controller card tried to control the floppy drive during boot-up and could not. The reason that it could not needs to be determined.

Check the obvious first: Before opening the system, check the CMOS values to see if they are correct. This should be checked first because it does not require opening the system. If the CMOS values keep disappearing, check the CMOS battery. The next step would be to see if the cables (ribbon cables and power connectors) are connected properly. Make sure that the A drive is located at the end of the cable and that the B drive is located in the middle.

If nothing has been recently changed or added, replace the cable. If the problem does not go away, replace the controller card. The next step would be to measure the voltage level of the power connector to make sure that the cable is supplying +5 and +12 V. If the voltage level is correct, replace the floppy drive.

If the installation is new or changes have been made to the hard drive system, verify the configuration, including the controller card resources (I/O address, IRQ, DMA, and memory usage), and that no other devices are using the same resources. If there are no conflicts, replace the cable. If the problem does not go away, replace the controller card. The next step would be to measure the voltage level of the power connector to make sure that the cable is supplying +5 and +12 V. If the voltage is correct, replace the drive.

EXAMPLE 11.2 The system can't read the floppy disk and the drive lights will not shut off.

The most common cause for this problem is the cable not being connected properly (a connector is backwards or the cable is not connected to all of the pins). If the cable is connected properly, then the problem is a bad cable, controller card, or floppy disk drive. To isolate these, you would swap them one by one until the problem is fixed.

EXAMPLE 11.3 *First Scenario:* You place a disk in drive A and perform a DIR command. You then remove the first disk and place a second disk in drive A. When you perform the DIR command again, the same directory listing as the one for the first disk appears. *Second Scenario:* When installing a program, you insert disk 1 and start the installation program. When it asks for disk 2, you put the second disk in drive A and press the Enter key, but the installation program still asks you to place disk 2 in the A drive.

This problem is called a *phantom directory,* and it occurs when the change-disk signal through pin 34 is not being received when a new disk is inserted, which should indicate to read the second disk's FAT and directory areas into RAM for faster access. The cause will be a bad cable, controller card, or floppy drive. A temporary solution when using DOS would be to press Ctrl+Break or Ctrl+C to force the system to reread the FAT and directory areas. It is important not to save to the disk when the second disk is in the drive. (Note: When running Windows 3.XX, you must not change a disk while working in an application.)

EXAMPLE 11.4 You get a read/write error when accessing a floppy disk.

Since floppy disks are not very sturdy, floppy read/write errors are common. To determine whether the disk is bad or the computer itself is bad, take the floppy to another machine and try to access the disk in the same way. If the same error occurs, then the disk is bad. If the disk works with no problems, then the floppy drive system must be at fault. The first thing to do would be to clean the read/write heads with a special cleaning disk that uses denatured alcohol pads. If the problem still occurs, it is caused by the floppy disk drive, the controller card, or the cable. (Note: If the disk starts showing bad sectors, it is recommended that it be thrown away.)

EXAMPLE 11.5   A disk works fine on one system. When the disk is taken to another computer, read/write errors occur. Yet, when it is taken back to the first system, the disk again works fine.

The problem is that the disk drive system of the second computer is bad or that the floppy disk read/write heads in the first computer are misaligned. To determine which problem it is, try the disk in a third machine. If the problem does not occur, the second computer has a floppy drive problem. If the same problem occurs, the read/write heads in the first computer are misaligned.

A head alignment problem occurs when the floppy disk head actuator drifts. To fix the alignment problem, you could realign the read/write heads by adjusting the drive with the aid of a special disk and software, but it is easier and cheaper to replace the floppy disk drive. Of course, this does not fix the floppy disks themselves, which were prepared with the faulty disk drive. To fix this problem, copy the contents of all floppy drives prepared with the faulty drive to another drive. Then replace the drive.

EXAMPLE 11.6   You try to boot the computer using the A drive. Instead, the computer boots from the C drive.

The first thing to check is the CMOS setup program, specifically the boot order. Although the default boot order is the A drive followed by the C drive, it could have been changed to the C drive followed by the A drive. If the CMOS setup program is fine, check the disk on another machine to make sure that it is readable. (If the disk can't be read, the system goes to the C drive.) If the problem still exists, it has to be due to the floppy disk drive, the cable, or the controller card.

EXAMPLE 11.7   A disk is stuck in the drive and will not eject.

This is usually caused by the label, which has peeled and stuck to the inside of the drive, or the metal slider on the disk which has come loose and has snagged on something inside the drive. Using a small flat-edge screwdriver or knife, carefully pry the disk out of the drive. After the disk is removed, test the drive with another disk to make sure that the drive itself was not damaged. (Note: If the metal slider is loose, you can remove it from the disk and can then make a copy of the disk.)

Occasionally, the metal slider will come completely off and become stuck in the drive. Again, use a small flat-edge screwdriver or knife to carefully pry the disk out of the drive. You can also use a small hook made out of a large paperclip to grab the metal slider. After the disk is removed, test the drive with another disk to make sure that the drive itself was not damaged.

11.5   REMOVABLE MEDIA DRIVES

Today, it is very easy to create a large document or picture that is several megabytes in size. Floppy disks are obviously too small to store these large files. Currently, several companies make high-capacity removable magneto-optical disk drives. (See table 11.2.) Some of these are designed to replace the floppy disk drive.

Magneto-optical media drives have read/write heads that are similar to the read/write heads of a floppy disk drive. Since the magneto-optical disk contains many more tracks than a floppy disk, its capacity is considerably greater. To guide the read/write heads to the correct track, the platters include servo information, which is read by a laser beam. The servo information, placed there during manufacturing, consists of magnetic markings used to identify the track.

The first magneto-optical drive was the floptical, developed by Insite. The floptical disk held 20 MB, rotated at 720 rpm, and offered a 10-Megabit-per-minute transfer rate. The drive used a SCSI interface. Therefore, when connecting this drive, a SCSI ID number that

TABLE 11.2 Websites for manufacturers of removable media

Company	Website
Iomega	**Home:** http://www.iomega.com/ **Support:** http://www.iomega.com/support/index.html **Software:** http://www.iomega.com/support/software/index.html
SyQuest Technology	**Home:** http://www.syquest.com/index.html **Support:** http://www.syquest.com/support/index.html
Imitation (LS-120/ Super disk)	**Information:** http://www.imation.com/dsp/ls120/index.html

FIGURE 11.7 Iomega Zip drive

was not being used had to be selected and the terminating resistors had to be checked. (For more information on SCSI devices, see chapter 10.) Unfortunately, this drive was not supported by any major companies, including Microsoft and IBM, and therefore, the drive was not widely used.

One of the newest magneto-optical drives is the LS-120, a drive developed by 3M and Matsushita-Kotobuki Electronics Industries, Ltd. and currently controlled by Imitation (LS stands for *laser servo*). The LS-120 disk is the same size and shape as a 1.44 MB 3½″ floppy disk yet has a track density of 2,490 tracks per inch and a 120 MB capacity. The LS-120 drive is an IDE device that can also read and write 720 KB and 1.44 MB floppy disks at three times the speed and access the 120 MB disk at five times the speed of a standard floppy drive. Since the LS-120 floppy drive can act as the PC's bootable drive and is fully compatible with Windows NT and Windows 95, it may eventually replace the floppy disk drive.

Another popular type of drive is the Bernoulli removable media drive, which was developed by Iomega. The Bernoulli drive is connected to the computer as an IDE device or as an external SCSI card. The original Bernoulli drive is approximately the same size as a 5¼″ floppy disk drive, although it includes a large shutter, similar to the shutter on a 3½″ floppy disk. The disks come in several capacities, up to 230 MB. Unlike floppy disk drives, air pressure is used to pull the disk toward the drive heads. The airflow is controlled by a Bernoulli plate. The disk spins at approximately 3,600 rpm and has an average seek time of 18 ms.

One of the more popular removable drive systems is the Iomega **Zip drive.** (See fig. 11.7.) The Zip disk is about twice as thick as a standard 3½″ floppy disk, can hold 100 MB of data, has an access time of 29 ms, rotates at 2,968 rpm, and has a transfer rate of 1 MB/s. The Zip drive comes with a SCSI, IDE, or parallel port interface. Iomega also produces the 1 GB and 2 GB Jaz drive.

When installing LS-120, Zip, and Jaz drives, you usually have to install drivers to activate the devices. Today, some system ROM BIOS chips support and activate the Zip drives during boot-up, while others support and activate the LS-120 MB drive (either as a 1.44 MB floppy drive or as a 120 MB drive). Therefore, it is possible to boot from these drives.

SUMMARY

1. Floppy drives are half-electronic, half-mechanical devices that use magnetic patterns to store information on a removable disk consisting of a single rotating platter.

2. Although they are considered long-term storage devices, floppy disks are considered to be secondary storage systems because of their size limitations and slow speeds.

3. Floppy disk drives are used to load essential device drivers, to analyze a hard drive that isn't booting or is not accessible, to back up small files, and to transfer files from one computer to another.

4. Floppy disk drives communicate with the rest of the computer by means of a 34-pin cable connected to a controller card.

5. A floppy disk is a flexible platter made of mylar and coated with a magnetic material such as iron oxide.

6. All floppy disk platters rotate around a spindle at 300 rotations per minute (rpm) except the DS/HD 5¼″ floppy disk drive, which rotates at 360 rpm.

7. To write-protect a 5¼″ disk, you must cover the write-protect notch; to write-protect a 3½″ disk you must uncover the write-protect hole.

8. The floppy disk platter is divided into a circular grid consisting of tracks (40 or 80 tracks) and sectors (9 to 18 sectors per track).

9. Since their read/write heads are not as precise, floppy disk drives must use tunnel erasing to keep tracks well defined.

10. The floppy disk drive read/write heads make contact with the platter.

11. Since floppy drive read/write heads are exposed to the air and make contact with the platter, magnetic oxide and dirt build up on the heads, making it necessary to clean the heads occasionally.

12. The head actuator is the component that moves the read/write heads back and forth. Floppy drives use the stepper motor head actuator.

13. The resources used by the floppy disk drive controller (IRQ 6, DMA channel 2, and I/O Address 3F0-3F7H) are quite standard and universal.

14. If one of the cable ends is connected backward, the floppy drive light or lights remain on.

15. The connector or connector set located on the long end of the connector cable will connect to the controller card; the set of connectors on the other end is for drive A, and the set in the middle is for drive B.

16. An FDD Controller Failure error can be caused by a faulty floppy drive, cable, controller card, power cable, or motherboard or incorrect CMOS settings.

17. A phantom directory (the second disk showing the same FAT listing as the first disk) is caused by a faulty ribbon cable, controller card, or floppy drive.

18. Floppy drives may be replaced by either the Zip drive or LS-120 drive.

QUESTIONS

1. The DMA channel used for the floppy controller is:
   a. 1
   b. 2
   c. 3
   d. 5
   e. 6

2. The IRQ used for the floppy controller is:
   a. IRQ 2
   b. IRQ 3
   c. IRQ 4
   d. IRQ 6
   e. IRQ 11
   f. IRQ 14

3. The storage capacity of a 3½″ high-density diskette is:
   a. 360 KB
   b. 720 KB
   c. 1.2 MB
   d. 1.44 MB
   e. 2.88 MB

4. A red stripe on one of the edges of the ribbon cable indicates:
   a. the positive/hot lead
   b. the ground lead
   c. pin 1
   d. the cable is made for the hard drive

5. When not being used, the 5¼″ disk should:
   a. be kept in the box that it came in
   b. be kept in its protective sleeve
   c. be kept near or on the computer
   d. be kept in a standing position

6. What moves the read/write heads in and out on a floppy disk drive?
   a. stepper motor
   b. voice coil
   c. spindle
   d. hub
   e. head springs
7. How do you write-protect a 3½″ disk?
   a. by covering the write-protect notch.
   b. by uncovering the write-protect notch.
   c. by closing the write-protect hole
   d. by opening the write-protect hole
   e. with special software
8. How does the PC identify a high-density 3½″ floppy disk?
   a. by a label with a magnetic strip
   b. by a metallic label
   c. by an extra hole in the case
   d. by a small arrow along one side
9. How does a computer know where to start reading data on a 5¼″ floppy disk?
   a. by using the write-enable notch
   b. by using the head-access slot
   c. by using the index hole
   d. by using a line embedded on the platter
10. A customer says that she cannot slide her hard disk into the drive. Which component is she probably talking about?
    a. hard drive
    b. 5¼″ floppy disk
    c. 3½″ floppy disk
    d. Zip disk
    e. CD-ROM disk
11. During boot-up, you get a "Non-System Disk or Disk Error. Replace and Strike any Key When Ready" error message. What is the first thing you should check or do?
    a. check the operation of the hard drive
    b. reinstall DOS
    c. check if a disk is in drive A
    d. check to see if the proper drivers are loaded
12. What is the most likely problem when you connect two floppy drives in the computer and both drive lights are on at the same time?
    a. bad cable
    b. cable is on backwards
    c. bad power connection
    d. CMOS parameters are reversed
    e. none of the above
13. You insert a disk in drive A, perform a DIR, and find out that it is not the disk you wanted. Therefore, you insert a second disk and perform another DIR command, yet you get the same listing as for the first disk. Which of the following could *not* cause this problem?
    a. the RAM
    b. the floppy disk drive
    c. the floppy ribbon cable
    d. the floppy drive controller
14. Which of the following should be used to clean floppy drive heads?
    a. sandpaper
    b. water and mild soap
    c. a general purpose cleaner such as Windex or 409
    d. denatured alcohol
    e. a paper clip

HANDS-ON PROJECTS

Exercise 1: Reinstalling a Floppy Disk Drive

1. Enter the CMOS setup program and set the floppy disk drives to Disabled/Not installed.
2. Shut off the computer.
3. Disconnect the floppy disk drive ribbon cable.
4. Disconnect the floppy disk drive power connectors.
5. Remove the floppy disk drives from the PC.
6. Remove the floppy disk drive controller card.
7. Reinstall the floppy disk drive controller card.

8. Reinstall the floppy disk drives.

9. Reinstall the floppy disk drive ribbon cable and the drive power connectors.

10. Turn on the PC. Enter the CMOS setup program and set the floppy disk drives to the correct CMOS settings.

Exercise 2: Troubleshooting the Floppy Disk Drive

1. Shut off the computer and disconnect the power connector from the A drive.
2. Turn on the PC and record the error message.
3. Shut off the computer and reconnect the power connector.
4. Disconnect the floppy ribbon cable from the A drive.
5. Turn on the PC and record the error message.
6. Turn off the PC and reconnect the ribbon cable, but connect it backwards.
7. Turn on the PC and notice the drive lights.
8. Turn off the PC and reconnect the ribbon cable properly.

Exercise 3: Troubleshooting the Phantom Directory

1. Format one floppy disk and give it disk1 as its volume label; format a second floppy disk and give it disk2 as its volume label.
2. Shut off the computer and remove the ribbon cable.
3. Get a special floppy drive ribbon cable (pin 34 is clipped) and install it in the computer.
4. Turn on the computer and boot from the C drive.
5. Insert the first disk in drive A. Switch over to drive A and perform a DIR command. Notice the volume label of the disk.
6. Remove the first disk and insert the second disk. Perform a DIR command. Notice the volume label of the disk.
7. Press Ctrl+Break on the keyboard. Perform a DIR command. Notice the volume label of the disk.

12　The Compact Disk Drive

INTRODUCTION

The compact disk (CD) is a 4.72" encoded platter that is read by laser. Since the CD can hold a combination of data tracks, audio tracks, and video tracks, it can store large amounts of information. CDs are commonly used to distribute programs (operating systems, application software, device drivers, and multimedia libraries), so knowing how to install and troubleshoot a CD drive is essential.

OBJECTIVES

1. Define a compact disk and explain how it stores information on the platter.
2. List and describe the different types of compact disks.
3. Differentiate between CLV and CAV.
4. Install an IDE and SCSI CD-ROM drives.
5. Identify and correct CD-ROM problems.

12.1 WHAT IS A COMPACT DISK?

A **compact disk (CD)** is a 4.72″ encoded platter that is read by laser. A CD drive is needed to read a CD. Since they can hold large amounts of information and are very inexpensive, CDs are used to distribute programs, including:

1. Operating systems (such as Windows 95 and 98 and Windows NT)
2. Application software (Microsoft Office 97, Adobe Photoshop, various encyclopedias, and most games)
3. Device drivers
4. Multimedia libraries (pictures, sound clips, and video clips)

Several different kinds of compact disks have been developed. The more common ones include the audio CD, CD-ROM, CD-R and CD-W, and DVD.

12.1.1 CD-DIGITAL AUDIO (CD-DA)

The **CD-Digital Audio (CD-DA)** was jointly developed by Philips and Sony Corporation and was introduced in the United States in 1983. The CD-DA, also known as the audio CD and the Red Book (its specifications were originally put into a red binder), is the standard for the compact disk used in a stereo system. Even though the compact disk measures only 4.72″ across, it can hold up to 74 minutes of high-fidelity audio. (Note: most CD-ROM drives can play an audio CD.)

The compact disks, or platters, are made of a polycarbonate wafer coated with an aluminum alloy. The data is stored as lands (similar to ridges) and pits, which are etched into the aluminum coating. Each pit is about 0.12 microns deep and about 0.6 microns wide. A pit and land together are 1.6 microns long, allowing 16,000 tracks per inch. To protect the data, the aluminum alloy is coated with a plastic polycarbonate coating. Currently, audio CDs are single sided, storing data only on the bottom side. Once an audio compact disk is recorded, the data cannot be changed.

Similar to hard disks, the pits and lands do not translate directly into 0s and 1s. Instead, the CD-ROM disk uses eight-to-fourteen modulation (EFM) encoding. An EFM binary 1 is represented by a transition (pit-to-land or land-to-pit). When fourteen lands and pits are put together, the EFM pattern will represent 8 bits (1 byte) of information. (See table 12.1.)

CD-ROM drives use laser light (class 1 laser) to read the disks, so the disks are not affected by magnetic fields. In addition, they are subject to less wear and tear since the read assembly does not actually make contact with the disk. However, dirt on the surface of the platter or dirt on the read assembly can cause errors. And even though CDs are sturdier than floppy disks, the platters must be handled with care. Scratching the surface, specifically the bottom half, should be avoided, and the disks should not be left in direct sunlight on a hot day or bent or otherwise handled carelessly.

TABLE 12.1 Partial listing of EFM encoding

Number	Binary Pattern	EFM Pattern
0	00000000	01001000100000
1	00000001	10000100000000
2	00000010	10010000100000
3	00000011	10001000100000
4	00000100	01000100000000
5	00000101	00000100010000
6	00000110	00010000100000
7	00000111	00100100000000
8	00001000	01001001000000
9	00001001	10000001000000
10	00001010	10010001000000

Much like the old vinyl records, CDs store data in a single, long spiral track. There are a maximum of 99 tracks on a CD. Part of each track has a pause area, which separates each of the audio selections. Each track is divided into large frames consisting of 2,352 bytes of information. It takes 75 large frames to make one second of recorded sound. Each frame includes a synchronization field (12 bytes), sector address tag field (12 bytes), and auxiliary field (288 bytes) and has at least 2,048 bytes of data. The auxiliary field is used for additional data and error detection and correction. The large frames are further divided into 98 small frames containing 24 bytes of information. This is enough data to store about 136 microseconds of music containing six samples (layers of sounds) for each stereophonic channel. Each sample is 16 bits of data, so there is a total of 65,536 different levels, giving the audio CD the quality of FM radio.

Since audio compact disks are time-sensitive, they use **constant linear velocity (CLV)** to access data. The outer tracks hold more information than the inner tracks, so the platter spins faster on the inner tracks than the outer tracks to keep a constant data rate. If it didn't, parts of the compact disk would play too slow or too fast. No matter which track is being read, the drive reads 75 blocks of data per second, giving the drive a transfer rate of 150 KB per second. Some compact disk drives use **constant angular velocity (CAV);** that is, they rotate at a constant speed and have different data transfer rates depending on which location on the CD is being read.

Since errors on a CD can cause significant problems for the PC and the compact disk is considered permanent, several techniques are used to find and correct errors. The primary error detection and correction method is error correcting code (ECC). ECC is a special data encoding protocol that uses extra bits to provide a redundancy of information. If a bit is missing or is bad within a byte, special algorithms can correct it while the data is being accessed. (Note: Since the CD-ROM is read-only, an ECC correction is only a soft fix.) For audio CDs, another technique used in error correction is called *linear interpolation*. When data is missing, the drive estimates the missing value. Since thousands of values are being read each second and the interpolated value is probably close to the missing value, it is impossible to tell when the drive is making the substitution.

12.1.2 THE CD-ROM

The **CD-ROM (compact disk–read-only memory)** is the standard compact disk used in the PC. It follows the CD-DA (digital audio) standard, also known as the Yellow Book. CD-ROMs are used to install operating systems, application software, device drivers, and large amounts of data. Each disk can store up to 682 MB of data, or up to 333,000 pages of text, and can hold sound, video, and digital data (in separate tracks). CD-ROMs must follow a standard so that they can be read by all CD-ROM drives. Two standards are used today. The standard known as the "High Sierra" standard became, after some modifications, the official adopted standard, known as the ISO-9660 standard. When someone refers to the "High Sierra" standard, he or she usually means ISO-9660.

Since video and digital data used by the PC is not based on time like audio data is, the compact disk drive can spin the disk at a higher linear velocity. Drives that spin twice as fast as the single-speed drive are known as *double speed* (2X); drives that spin at four times the speed of the single-speed are known as *quad speed* (4X). (See table 12.2.)

As mentioned the data is stored on the CD as lands and pits. To read the data, a low-powered laser is emitted from an infrared laser diode and aimed at a reflecting mirror that is part of the head assembly moving linearly along the surface of the disk. The read assembly is moved back and forth by a microcontroller, which uses a servo system to determine its location. Written on the platter is servo data, consisting of markings used to guide the read assembly to the right location. (See fig. 12.1.) The laser beam reflects off the mirror and is sent through a lens that focuses it onto a specific point on the disk. The light is reflected back from this area of the disk into a series of collectors, mirrors, and lenses, which focus it on a photodetector, an electronic device that is sensitive to light. When light hits a land and is reflected back to the detector, its signal is strong and the photodetector produces a strong output signal. When a light strikes a pit, it is diffused and scattered in all directions, causing the photodetector to produce a very weak output signal.

TABLE 12.2   Drive speeds

Drive Speed	Transfer Rate (KB/s)	Access Time (ms)
Single-speed (1X)	150	400
Double-speed (2X)	300	300
Triple-speed (3X)	450	200
Quad-speed (4X)	600	150
Six-speed (6X)	900	150
Eight-speed (8X)	1,200	100
Ten-speed (10X)	1,500	100
Twelve-speed (12X)	1,800	100
Sixteen-speed (16X)	2,400	90
Twenty-four speed (24X)	3,600	90
Thirty-two speed (32X)	4,800	80

FIGURE 12.1   Inside the CD-ROM drive

(See fig. 12.2.) The electrical signals are finally decoded by the microprocessor into a binary code.

The loading mechanism is the mechanical component that loads the CDs into the CD-ROM drive. The most popular type is the tray. When the user presses the eject button, the tray slides out, and after the CD is placed in the tray, the tray is retracted into the drive when the user presses the eject button a second time or gently presses against the tray. (Note: While the tray is out, it can be easily broken if it is bumped with enough force or if enough weight is placed on it.) Older systems and some high-end drives use a caddy, a small plastic cartridge. A CD is placed inside the caddy, which is inserted into the CD-ROM drive. The advantage of a caddy is that it protects the disk. (See fig. 12.3.)

CD-ROM drives will also play audio CDs and most drives come with a headphone jack so that you can listen to audio disks. Unfortunately, the sound quality through the headphone jack is poor, so it is best to connect to the sound card.

FIGURE 12.2   Lands and pits

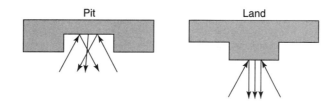

FIGURE 12.3   CD tray and caddy

12.1.3   RECORDABLE CD (CD-R)

In 1990, Philips introduced the **recordable CD,** also known as CD-WORM (write once, read many) and CD-WO (write once). As the *write once* name implies, the disks can be recorded only once and cannot be changed after that. The standard for the recordable CD is also known as the Orange Book.

CD-R disks have a polycarbonate substrate, much like a regular CD, but the spiral is already stamped on the surface. The disk is then coated with a special photosensitive dye followed by a metal reflective layer, usually made of gold or silver alloy. Finally, a plastic protective layer to help protect the disk is applied.

The process that writes data to the CD-R is called *burning the disk.* The data is written to disk by an intense laser beam (contained within a CD-R drive), which heats the surface rapidly. The burned areas reflect less light (pit) than the unburned areas (land). (Note: Some older CD-ROM drives cannot read the CD-R.) Some drives record in a single session; others allow multisession recording. Multisession recording allows additional information to be recorded on the unused portions of the disk at a later time.

Since most drives are faster than single speed, CD-R disks can be read faster than they can be written to. A 4X drive, for example, might be 4X when reading but only 2X when writing to a disk. A CD-R moves at a constant speed as the laser writes the data, and the data flow can't be interrupted. This means that the disk can't be stopped and it can't wait for data. Therefore, the faster the disk spins, the more data flow it will require. To generate the required amount of data flow, most CD-R drives use the SCSI interface, and a few use the faster ATAPI (IDE) interface.

12.1.4   ERASABLE CD (CD-E)

The **CD-E** is a CD that can be written to more than once. It is sometimes referred to as the *rewriteable* CD or CD-RW. Much like the CD-R, the CD-E is a polycarbonate disk with a molded pregrooved spiral. The disk is then covered with special phase-change recording layer. When the surface is heated to a certain temperature and is then cooled, the special layer crystallizes. In its crystalline form, it reflects more light, much as a land does. If it is heated to a higher temperature and then cooled, it forms a noncrystalline structure. The noncrystalline form does not reflect light very well and therefore acts as a pit. However, the media doesn't emulate the pits and lands as well as the CD-R disk does, so CD-Es do not work on all CD-ROM drives. The CD-E is not a perfect storage medium. Although the disk is being improved, it can be written to only a set number of times before the special layer does not change states any more. The speed at which the CD-E is read is slow compared to the speed of a hard drive, and the writing of a CD-E disk is usually limited to 2X speed.

12.1.5 DIGITAL VERSATILE OR VIDEO DISK (DVD)

The **digital video disk,** also called the digital versatile disc, is the newest type of compact disk, and it has the capability to store massive computer applications, such as a full multimedia encyclopedia, or a feature-length movie on one disk. The standard DVD-5 can hold up to 4.7 GB on a single-sided disk, and the DVD-10 can hold up to 9.4 GB on a double-sided disk. The increased capacity is the result of reduced track pitch and pit size and reduced error correction overhead. To increase the storage capacity even further, DVD technology allows a single side to be double layered. Distinguishing the individual layers requires focusing the laser on the desired layer, which increases the capacity of the disk to 8.5 GB on a side, or 17.0 GB total for a two-sided disk.

There are two basic types of DVD devices currently available: DVD-ROM drives and DVD-Video players. DVD-ROM drives attach to a computer and function like CD-ROM drives; DVD-Video players attach to a TV and function like a VCR. Depending on whether a disk is single or double sided and single or dual layered, the DVD disk can store up to 17.0 GB (enough for a 480-minute movie at 60 frames per second and $1,280 \times 720$ resolution) using MPEG-2 compression. (See table 12.3.) DVD standards are under development for DVD-Recordable drives (write once) and DVD-RAM drives (rewritable). To get the full benefit of a DVD system, a DVD-Video board and an MPEG-2 decoder board are required, and in order to get Dolby AC-3 Digital Surround Sound, Dolby Pro Logic speakers or an AC-3-capable stereo receiver have to be added to the system. A single-speed (1X) DVD has a transfer rate of 1,250 KB per second, which is almost nine times faster than the 1X CD-ROM. Therefore, a 2X DVD drive could have a transfer rate of 2,500 KB per second, but when playing back video, the 2X DVD drive still performs at the 1,250 KB rate because, like the audio CD, the video CD is time-sensitive.

12.2 PERFORMANCE

Since hard drives can attain transfer rates of 16 MB per second and have access times as low as 9 milliseconds, the fastest CD drives are significantly slower than even the slowest hard drives. Most CD drives use constant linear velocity (CLV), but some newer drives are using constant angular velocity (CAV). While CLV varies the rotational speed of the disk depending on the track being read, CAV does not. Therefore, when reading the outside of the disk, where there is more data, the CLV drive will have a higher transfer rate than when it is reading the inside of the disk. A CLV drive is faster than a CAV drive—a 12X CLV

TABLE 12.3 DVD drive standards

Standard	Sides	Layers	Capacity	Playing Time
DVD-5	1	1	4.7 GB	133 minutes
DVD-9	1	2	8.5 GB	240 minutes
DVD-10	2	1	9.4 GB	266 minutes
DVD-18	2	2	17.0 GB	480 minutes

drive, for example, is faster than a 16X CAV drive because the 16X CAV is equivalent to a 6X to 16X CLV drive, depending on which track is being read.

Another factor in defining the performance of the CD drive is its access time. Access time is the average amount of time it takes to find a piece of data, and it is based on the speed change time, access time, and latency period. The speed change time is the time it takes for the spindle motor to change to the correct speed, depending on which track it is reading. The seek time is the time it takes for the drive to move the heads to the right location on the disk. The latency period is the amount of time it takes for the correct block of data to spin under the read assembly. The access time tends to be faster on the higher-speed drives.

Although the CD drive is slower than a hard drive, its performance can be significantly increased if parts of the RAM are used to cache the CD. As with the hard drive, the microprocessor's controller software controls the RAM cache area, which tries to anticipate what the microprocessor needs next. One method it uses is storing a copy of information that has been recently accessed. Information that has already been accessed may well be accessed again. Another method it uses is to read ahead an additional sector after the one being accessed. Whatever the method or methods used, when the disk needs to be accessed, the microprocessor will look in the cache area first. If it can't find the information, it will access the slower CD drive. The time it takes to search the cache area (RAM) is almost negligible compared to the time it takes to access the CD drive. If the needed information is found in the RAM, therefore, PC performance is greatly increased. Another form of cache is the hardware cache located on the CD controller card or the CD drive logic board. (This cache is not to be confused with the hardware cache located on the motherboard or within the microprocessor.) Much like its software counterparts, it fulfills the same functions as the RAM cache.

12.3 INSTALLATION

Internal CD drives are half-height devices designed to fit into a standard 5.25″ open drive bay. Like other drives, it is typically held in place with four screws. External drive bays, of course, sit outside the computer. Much like hard drives, every CD drive contains a logic board. The logic board controls the drive and allows it to connect to the rest of the PC. Most drives today are either IDE/ATAPI or SCSI devices; some older systems connected through the parallel port or had a proprietary interface. Because compact disk drives are much slower than hard drives, connecting a compact disk drive and a hard drive on the same cable is not recommended.

12.3.1 IDE/ATAPI CD DRIVES

The most common interface used in the CD drive is the AT attachment packet interface (ATAPI) protocol associated with the enhanced IDE standard. The enhanced IDE is an improvement over the standard IDE interface and allows for CD drives, tape drives, and other storage devices.

When connecting IDE devices using a 40-pin IDE cable, the drives must be configured as stand-alone, master, or slave. (Note: An older sound card may have a 40-pin connector that is usually not an IDE connector but a proprietary CD-ROM connector.) If one drive is installed on a cable, that drive is a stand-alone drive. If two drives (hard drive, CD-ROM, or any other IDE device) are installed on the same cable, the primary drive is the master drive and the secondary drive is the slave drive. The master drive is so called because the controlling electronics on the logic board of the master drive control both the master drive and the slave drive. The stand-alone, master, and slave drives are determined by setting the jumpers on the hard drive. (Note: It does not matter where the drive and controller card are connected to the cable.) The enhanced IDE standard supports up to four IDE devices and two IDE cables. Each cable is its own channel with its own master and slave device. (Note: Performance may be improved if the IDE hard drive and the CD drive are installed on separate channels.)

In order to use an enhanced IDE device such as a CD-ROM drive, the BIOS must use the ATAPI protocol. If the system ROM BIOS does not support ATAPI, it needs to be either updated or modified, which can be done the following ways:

1. Install a newer system ROM chip that includes instructions in handling EIDE/ATA-2 hard drives
2. If the system ROM BIOS is flash ROM, update the ROM chip using special software
3. Supplement the system ROM BIOS chip with an EIDE controller card, which includes a ROM BIOS chip
4. Set the computer to recognize the drive and use software or a device driver (sometimes called a dynamic drive overlay) that includes instructions for handling EIDE hard drives

12.3.2 SMALL COMPUTER SYSTEMS INTERFACE (SCSI)

The standard SCSI interface allows up to seven devices (hard drives, tape drives, CD drives, removable drives and disks, and scanners) to be connected to one SCSI adapter/ controller. It is most commonly used in higher-end systems and tends to provide better performance, though at a higher cost, than ATAPI drives. (Note: The SCSI-3 standard still under development has a single controller that can connect 16 or 128 devices, depending on its specification.) The SCSI devices are connected in series, forming a chain (daisy chain). The cables are characterized by the number of pins (50, 68, or 80 pins) and whether they are intended for internal or external use. The 50-pin connector (type A) has an 8-bit data path; the 68-pin (type P) and 80-pin cables have a 16-bit (wide) data path.

The SCSI devices, including the SCSI controller card and CD drive, are identified with a SCSI ID number ranging from 0 to 7, which are selected with jumpers, DIP switches, or a thumb wheel. The SCSI adapter is usually set to ID 7, and the primary SCSI hard drive (or any other boot device) is set to ID 0. The SCSI ID numbers do not have to be in order, nor do they have to be sequential. Of course, no two devices within the same chain can use the same SCSI ID number.

The SCSI devices at each end of the chain must be terminated; the other devices are not. On an internal cable, the adapter card and the device at the end of the cable need to be terminated but all the other devices in between are not. On an internal cable and an external cable, the two devices located at the end of each cable will be terminated, while other devices, including the adapter/controller card, will not be terminated. Terminating and not terminating a device is accomplished by either inserting or removing the terminators or enabling or disabling them with jumpers or DIP switches. Some SCSI devices have automatic termination.

12.3.3 PROPRIETARY INTERFACES

Some of the early CD-ROM drives were sold as part of a multimedia kit. These kits included a sound card that had a 40-pin proprietary interface for the CD-ROM drive, a cable, and a set of speakers. The three main proprietary interfaces are those developed by Panasonic, Sony, and Mitsumi. The biggest disadvantage of the proprietary interface is that it works only with a specific drive. Therefore, if the original drive is replaced, the interface probably will not work with the new drive. Its also difficult to tell the different proprietary interfaces apart, causing a lot of confusion for the service technician.

Another type of CD drive is the CD-ROM connected to the parallel port, specifically bidirectional parallel ports. Although these drives are portable and easily moved from computer to computer, they are much slower than the IDE and SCSI drives.

12.3.4 SOFTWARE DRIVERS

After the CD drive is physically installed and configured, the final step to activating it is to load the device drivers and configure the operating system so that it recognizes the CD drive. This is usually done with an installation disk that comes with the CD drive or the controller card. Some operating systems will install the proper drivers automatically during installation. Some newer systems do not require drivers and will even boot from the CD-ROM drive.

In DOS and Windows 95 and 98 machines, EIDE CD drives require a device driver, which allows the operating system to control the CD-ROM drive, to be loaded in the CONFIG.SYS; SCSI drives usually require a device driver for the controller card and a device driver for the CD-ROM drive. Since there are many drives on the market, make sure that the driver matches the CD-ROM drive. Another driver needed to activate the CD drive is a file system extension, which enables the operating system to identify and use data from CDs attached to the system. For DOS, the file system extension is the Microsoft compact disk extension (MSCDEX.EXE), which is loaded in the AUTOEXEC.BAT. The file system extension is built into Windows 95 and 98. (Note: If you boot a Windows 95 machine to Windows 95 DOS mode, the CONFIG.SYS will have the necessary device drivers but will not have the file system extension, MSCDEX.EXE, loaded. Therefore, it needs to be executed at the command prompt.)

12.3.5 BOOTABLE CD DRIVES

Some system ROM BIOS chips support a bootable CD drive (El Torito standard) without any CD drivers being loaded. A bootable compact disk can be inserted in the drive and, if the CMOS setup program is set to search the CD drive for a bootable disk, it will boot just like the A drive or the C drive.

12.4   TROUBLE-SHOOTING CD DRIVES

Problems with a CD drive or compact disk can be caused by the drive, compact disk, cable, power supply, drive configuration, or software configuration.

EXAMPLE 12.1   The computer cannot read the CD.

Most problems with the CD drive are caused by compact disks, such as dirty or scratched disks. Determine if the problem is with the drive or the disk by trying the disk in another computer. If the disk works, then the problem is with the drive. If the disk does not work, the problem is with the disk.

Many disk problems can be corrected by cleaning the disk with a special compact disk cleaning kit or by using a soft cloth. Compact disk cleaning solutions are also available. When cleaning the disk with a cloth, it is best to wipe the disk in a radial pattern beginning with the center and working toward the edge. Remember that the data on a standard compact disk is on the bottom of the disk, not the top. Deep scratches can sometimes be buffed out with a commercial plastic polish or cleaner that has a very mild abrasive.

A read problem caused by the drive could be corrected by cleaning the read lens. This is best done with a CD drive cleaner or with a can of compressed air. If the problem still exists, the drive, cable, or controller board should be replaced.

> **NOTE:**   CD drives use a laser beam, and you should never make eye contact with the beam. Always turn the power off before working inside a CD drive.

EXAMPLE 12.2   The computer does not recognize the CD-ROM drive.

This problem is caused by incorrect drive configuration, controller configuration, software configuration, a cable problem, or a power problem.

The easiest thing to check is the software configuration since that doesn't require opening the computer. For DOS and Windows 95 and 98, a device driver (a SYS file loaded in the CONFIG.SYS file) is needed for the IDE CD drive; a SCSI or proprietary drive needs a device driver for the SCSI controller card (if any). In addition, DOS needs the MSCDEX.EXE file loaded in the AUTOEXEC.BAT file, which should have the same drive signature as the device driver for the CD drive.

If the software configuration does not show a problem, the problem must be with the hardware. After opening the PC, the first thing to do is make sure the data and control cables are connected properly and that the drive has power. If everything is fine, the next item to check is the drive and controller card configuration. If the problem still exists, the drive, the controller card, or the cable must be bad. Therefore, each needs to be replaced, one at a time, until the bad component is discovered.

EXAMPLE 12.3   The CD drive will not accept or reject the compact disk.

When the drive will not accept or reject a disk, it usually has a mechanical problem. Of course, before replacing the drive, make sure that the power cable is connected to the drive and that nothing is jammed in the drive. If it appears the problem is with the drive, the drive would have to be replaced or repaired. Although you could try to repair the drive, it is easier to replace it. (Note: Some CD-ROM trays and caddies can be manually opened by inserting the end of a paper clip in a tiny hole located in the front of the drive.)

SUMMARY

1. The compact disk (CD) is a 4.72″ encoded platter that is read by laser.
2. The CD-DA, also known as the audio CD, is the standard for the compact disk used in a stereo system. It can hold up to 74 minutes of high-fidelity audio.
3. Data is stored on a CD as lands and pits, which are etched into the aluminum coating.
4. Since the CD drive uses light to read the surface of the platter, dirt on the surface of the platter or on the read assembly can cause errors.
5. Most CD drives use constant linear velocity (CLV) to access data, which allows for a constant data flow rate.
6. The CD-ROM (compact disk–read-only memory) is the standard compact disk used in the PC. It can hold up to 682 MB of data.
7. The standard for the CD is the ISO-9660 standard.
8. The CD-R, also known as CD-WORM (write once read many) and CD-WO (write once), can be written to only once and cannot be changed after that.
9. The CD-E is a CD that can be written to more than once.
10. Digital video disk (DVD), the newest type of compact disk, has the capability of storing up to 17 GB of information.
11. CD disk drives will use an EIDE (most common), SCSI, or proprietary interface.
12. An IDE CD drive must be configured as a master, slave, or stand-alone drive upon installation.
13. The SCSI ID number of the SCSI CD drive and the terminating resistors must be configured on the drive upon installation.
14. Most CD drives require software drivers in order to function.

QUESTIONS

1. Which type of compact disk is most commonly used to install applications and device drivers or to access multimedia libraries?
   - a. CD-DA
   - b. CD-ROM
   - c. CD-R
   - d. CD-E
   - e. DVD
2. Which of the following is sometimes referred to as a WORM (write once, read many)?
   - a. CD-DA
   - b. CD-ROM
   - c. CD-R
   - d. CD-E
   - e. DVD
3. Which of the following has the greatest capacity?
   - a. CD-DA
   - b. CD-ROM
   - c. CD-R
   - d. CD-E
   - e. DVD
4. Which of the following will you *not* find as a CD drive interface?
   - a. EIDE
   - b. SCSI
   - c. floppy drive
   - d. proprietary
5. To make sure that all drives can read a CD, the CD must follow the:
   - a. Amiga standard
   - b. High Sierra standard
   - c. ISO-9660
   - d. DOS standard

6. Which speed should the CD be playing at when playing an audio track?
   a. single speed
   b. double speed
   c. 12X speed
   d. 24X speed
7. A single-speed CD-ROM drive transfers data at:
   a. 1 KB per second
   b. 100 KB per second
   c. 150 KB per second
   d. 1 MB per second
   e. 1.5 MB per second
8. When installing an EIDE CD-ROM drive, you must configure the drive's (choose all that apply):
   a. terminating resistors
   b. SCSI ID number
   c. type (stand-alone, master, or slave)
   d. frequency modulation
9. When installing a SCSI CD-ROM drive, you must configure the drive's (choose all that apply):
   a. terminating resistors
   b. SCSI ID number
   c. type (stand-alone, master, or slave)
   d. frequency modulation
10. If the CD has a read/write error, you should:
    a. throw the disk away
    b. clean the disk
    c. throw the CD drive away
    d. replace the RAM
11. When the CD drive is not being recognized by the system, the first thing you should check is:
    a. the power connector
    b. the ribbon cable
    c. the drive
    d. the drivers
12. You insert a Microsoft Office installation CD in your computer running DOS. The computer does not recognize the CD drive, although you can play audio compact disks by using the headphone jack in the front of the drive. During boot-up, you notice that the driver is loaded. What is the problem?
    a. the installation CD is not compatible with the drive
    b. the installation CD is bad
    c. the CD drive is bad
    d. although the device driver is loaded, MSCDEX.EXE is not loaded

HANDS-ON PROJECTS

Exercise 1: Installing an IDE CD-ROM Drive

1. Configure the IDE CD-ROM drive as either a master, slave, or stand-alone, as appropriate.
2. If the system already has an IDE device, configure the device as either a master, slave or stand-alone, as appropriate.
3. Connect the CD to the appropriate IDE channel.
4. Boot the system and install the appropriate drivers for the CD drive.
5. Insert a CD into the drive and test it.
6. Remove the CD-ROM drive and reconfigure the system.

Exercise 2: Installing a SCSI CD-ROM Drive

1. Configure the SCSI drive's SCSI ID number and terminating resistors.
2. Connect the CD to the appropriate SCSI connector.
3. Boot the system and install the appropriate drivers for the CD drive.
4. Insert a CD into the drive and test it.
5. Remove the CD-ROM drive and reconfigure the system.

Exercise 3: Loading the Drivers from a Floppy Disk Drive on a DOS Machine

1. On a DOS system, install and configure the CD drive.
2. Boot the system and install the appropriate drivers for the CD drive onto the hard drive.

3. After studying the CONFIG.SYS and AUTOEXEC.BAT files, copy the appropriate files needed to activate the CD disk drive to a bootable floppy disk in drive A.
4. Create new CONFIG.SYS and AUTOEXEC.BAT files that will load the drivers from the A drive.
5. Boot with the floppy disk in drive A and make sure the CD drive is working properly.
6. Remove the CD drive and reconfigure the system back to the way it was.

13

The Disk Structure

INTRODUCTION

Since the data on the disk is the most important part of the computer, it is necessary to protect the integrity of the disk. Disk problems and errors can occur without warning and may easily result in data loss. To recognize and correct problems with the disk structure, you must have a good understanding of the general layout of the disk.

OBJECTIVES

1. Describe the disk boot sequence.
2. Describe the master boot record and describe how it relates to the partition table.
3. Partition a hard drive to one or more partitions as needed.
4. Describe the file allocation table.
5. Describe how the file allocation table relates to a cluster.
6. Describe how a file is retrieved using a file allocation table and directory.
7. List the contents of a directory.
8. List and describe the common file systems.
9. Explain how disk compression works.
10. Compress a hard drive.
11. Identify and correct disk problems.
12. Run the SCANDISK and DEFRAG programs on a volume.

13.1 WHAT IS DISK STRUCTURE?

The disk structure does not describe how a hard drive or floppy disk physically works but how it stores files on the disk. In other words, it describes the formatting of the disk (file system, partitions, the root directory, and the directories). Since the data on the disk is the most important part of the computer, it is necessary to protect the integrity of the disk. Disk problems and errors can occur without warning and may easily result in data loss.

13.2 BOOT SEQUENCE

To boot the computer is to make it operational and to load the operating system into RAM. The process begins with turning on the on/off switch, and, if everything goes well, it usually ends with a command prompt or a GUI interface. During this time, the system ROM BIOS is looking for an operating system to boot.

By default, the system ROM BIOS will begin searching the volume boot sector of drive A, which is the first sector on the A drive (cylinder 0, head 0, sector 1), for the operating system boot files. If a disk is in the drive but the sector cannot be read or there is no disk in the drive, the system ROM BIOS continues to the hard drive. The system ROM BIOS looks for the master partition boot sector at cylinder 0, head 0, sector 1 of the first physical drive (drive C) and then reads the partition table to see which partition is active (marked as bootable).

It then searches the volume boot sector of the active partition and looks at the first sector for the operating system boot files. Depending on the operating system, some of the boot files are:

DOS	IO.SYS and MSDOS.SYS
Windows 95 and 98	IO.SYS
Windows NT	NTLDR

13.3 BOOT SECTORS AND PARTITIONS

The **master boot record (MBR)** is always found on the first sector of a hard drive (master boot sector). It tells the system ROM BIOS how the hard drive is divided and which part to boot from. The first 466 bytes consist of a special program code called the **bootstrap loader,** which locates the first active or bootable partition on the disk. The next 2 bytes of this 512-byte sector are an identification header, and the last 44 bytes contain the **master partition table,** which lists all partitions on the hard drive.

Partitioning is the defining and dividing of the physical drive into logical volumes called *partitions*. Each partition functions as if it were a separate hard disk. Therefore, although it is the physical drive that is installed and configured, the logical drive is the drive the system "thinks" it has. All hard drives must have at least one partition. (Note: Because floppy disks are small, they do not have partitions; the entire disk is considered a volume.)

The partition table is defined with the FDISK utility or an equivalent program. (See section 13.9.) Each entry in the partition table is 16 bytes of data and contains the following:

1. Start of the partition in CHS coordinates
2. End of the partition in CHS coordinates
3. Start of the partition in LBA coordinates
4. Number of sectors for the partition
5. Partition type
6. Active flag

CHS coordinates express a location in cylinder-head-sector terms; the LBA (logical block addressing) coordinate defines the actual number of the sector. The boot sector is in the first sector. Where the partition expressed in LBA mode ends can be calculated by adding the start of the partition in LBA coordinates and the number of sectors in the partition. The partition type defines the type of file system being used; for example, 12-bit FAT, 16-bit FAT, HPFS, NTFS, and extended partitions. (See section 13.6.) The partition table can hold up to four primary partitions and two extended partitions. Of the primary partitions, only one can be marked active since the computer can boot from only one partition. If the MBR cannot locate a bootable partition, it will issue the "Missing Operating System" error message.

In most versions of FDISK, the first sector of a partition, the volume boot sector, will be aligned so that it is at head 0, sector 1 of a cylinder. This means that there may be unused sectors on the track prior to the first sector of a partition and unused sectors following a partition table sector. Some software packages and drivers will use these spaces to "lock down," or secure, the system or to overcome limitations of the hard drive or system ROM BIOS. Unfortunately, these unused spaces are also good places for boot sector virus programs to hide. The **volume boot sector (VBS),** the first sector of any partition or the first sector of a floppy disk, is created by a high-level format program (DOS's FORMAT program or equivalent). Within the VBS, the media parameter block or disk parameter block contains information used by the operating system to verify the capacity of the disk volume as well as to determine the location of the file allocation table. The VBS also contains the partition's boot program, which checks and executes the necessary boot files (IO.SYS or MSDOS.SYS, WINBOOT.SYS, or NTLDR).

13.4 FILE ALLOCATION TABLES

When you save a file, the file can be stored at the beginning, the middle, or the end of the disk. When you retrieve a file, you do not worry about its physical location. Instead, you specify a name (and sometimes the path) and the operating system finds the file. The directory structure, methods for organizing a volume (a partition or floppy disk), and how the system stores and retrieves a file is called the *file system.*

Disks are divided into a circular grid consisting of tracks and sectors. **Tracks** are concentric circles; that is, the circles share the same center, much like rings in a tree. Tracks are numbered sequentially, starting with the outside track as track 0, and are further divided into **sectors,** 512-byte chunks of usable data. Sectors on a track are numbered starting with 1. For operating systems, the most basic storage unit is not a sector but a **cluster** (also called an *allocation unit*). It consists of one or more sectors (usually more than one), the size of the cluster depending on the operating system, the version of the operating system, the file system the operating system is using, and the size of the volume (partition or floppy disk).

The **file allocation table (FAT)** is an index used to "remember" which file is located in which cluster. It lists each cluster in a partition (or floppy disk), whether the cluster is being used by a file, the name of the file in the cluster, and all the clusters the file takes up.

Question: Why doesn't the file allocation table list each sector?

Answer: Grouping sectors into clusters reduces the number of entries in the file allocation table, making the table smaller and thus enabling it to be searched faster. This allows the operating system to retrieve a file more quickly.

Unfortunately, since an entry in the file allocation table can be only one file, the space remaining is unused and wasted if a file doesn't use the entire cluster.

EXAMPLE 13.1 A partition is using clusters consisting of eight sectors (4,096 bytes). A file that is 2,048 bytes will have an entry for the cluster and the file belonging to the cluster in the file allocation table. Although the file is only half the size of the cluster, the file allocation table can list only one file for that allocation unit. Therefore, the entire 4,096-byte sector will be used for the 2,048-byte file.

EXAMPLE 13.2 A partition is using clusters consisting of eight sectors (4,096 bytes). A file of 8,193 bytes would therefore be listed as three entries in the file allocation table. The first part of the file is stored in one cluster. After the first cluster is filled, there are still 4,097 bytes left over. Therefore, the entry for the first cluster will list the location of the second cluster occupied by the file. (Note: The cluster may or may not be the next one.) The second cluster would then be filled up, but 1 byte would be left over. Again, the second cluster would list the third cluster, where this last byte of the file resides. Since the file allocation table can list only one file per cluster, the single byte would take up the entire 4,096 bytes of disk space in the third cluster.

The larger the cluster, the more disk space the system tends to waste. Therefore, some people divide their hard drives into smaller partitions to use space more efficiently.

The file allocation table is created during the high-level format process—when using the FORMAT.COM command or equivalent program, for example. The table is stored in the space immediately following the volume boot sector. Each volume actually has two file allocation tables, the second being a duplicate of the first one. When an entry is changed in one file allocation table, both allocation tables are changed. The second table is read only when the first one can't be read. Unfortunately, most operating systems place the two file allocation tables next to each other, and so if one becomes physically damaged, there is a good chance the other table would also be damaged. Of course, if the file allocation table is lost, there is no index of where the files are located, resulting in a loss of data.

13.5 DIRECTORIES, FILES, AND ATTRIBUTES

The model for storage in the PC is based on an inverted directory tree structure. Every volume has a starting point called the **root directory,** located at the top of the tree structure. The root directory holds files and directories. The **directories** under the root directory are also referred to as **subdirectories.** (Note: Newer operating systems may refer to a directory as a *folder.*) Each directory can also hold files and more subdirectories.

13.5.1 THE ROOT DIRECTORY

The root directory is typically located directly after the two copies of the file allocation tables. It is not like the other directories within a volume. First, there can be only one root directory for any disk volume. In addition, the root directory is usually limited to a certain size and therefore can have only a certain number of entries. (See table 13.1.) When the maximum number of files and subdirectories in the root directory is reached, no more can be added even though plenty of disk space may be left. Subdirectories and root directories in newer operating systems such as FAT32 do not have to follow the file allocation table and so have no limits on the number of entries in the root directory. (Note: Long file names in the older file systems use multiple directory entries.)

13.5.2 DIRECTORIES AND FILES

Every file on the system is stored in a directory. The directory, a specially marked file, is a table that contains information about the files and subdirectories stored within it.

For DOS systems, every directory, including the root directory, consists of a small database. Each entry in the database contains 32 bytes of information. (See table 13.2.) Although in most operating systems the number of entries in the root directory is fixed, the number of entries in directories is not fixed. If a directory needs more space for more

TABLE 13.1   The maximum
number of root directory entries
under FAT

Volume Type	Maximum Number of Root Directory Entries
360 KB 5¼" floppy disk	112
720 KB 3½" floppy disk	112
1.2 MB 5¼" floppy disk	224
1.44 MB 3½" floppy disk	224
2.88 MB 3½" floppy disk	448
Hard disk	512

entries, it will expand to another cluster. A directory entry in DOS will use 11 bytes for the entire file name, 8 bytes for the file name and 3 bytes for the extension. The file name is meant to identify the file, so the name should represent the contents of the file. The extension is used to identify the type of file. For example, files that have a DOC extension are usually Microsoft Word documents, and files that have an EXE extension are executable files. (Note: To indicate that a file is deleted, the operating system changes the first character of the file name to a lowercase sigma (σ). This way, assuming that all of the clusters are intact and have not been used by other files, a file can be undeleted by substituting another character for the sigma). If all eight characters (bytes) available for the file name are not used and the three characters for the file extension are not used, the leftover bytes become spaces. (Note: The dot separating the file name and the extension is not stored as part of the file allocation table or the directory. It is shown by the operating system to indicate a separation between the two.)

After the bytes reserved for the file name and extension, one byte is used for file attributes. The **file attribute** field stores a number of characteristics about each file, the most common attributes being read-only, hidden, system, and archive. (See table 13.3.) Attributes can be either on or off. If the file has the particular characteristic, the file attribute is on; if it doesn't, the file attribute is off. (Note: One of these attributes indicates whether the file is a real file or a directory.) Since DOS reserves one byte for attributes, it can keep track of up to eight attributes (remember, one byte equals 8 bits.) The ATTRIB command, File Manager, or Explorer is used to change file attributes.

Next, DOS and other operating systems also record the date and time that the file or directory was created or modified and the size of the file in bytes. The files are stamped with the date and time from the real-time clock (RTC) on the motherboard. If, of course, the RTC clock is not set to the correct date and time, the file will also have the incorrect date and time.

The last part of the entry is the number of the cluster that starts the file or subdirectory. When a file is retrieved from a subdirectory, the system reads the directory first to find the starting point of the file and, since files are often bigger than one cluster, it then goes to the file allocation table to find the location of the second cluster, the third cluster, and so on until the file has been retrieved into RAM.

TABLE 13.2   DOS directory
format

Content	Size
File name	8 bytes
File extension	3 bytes
File attributes	1 byte
Reserved	10 bytes
Time of creation	2 bytes
Date of creation	2 bytes
Starting cluster	2 bytes
Size in bytes	4 bytes

TABLE 13.3 DOS file attributes

Attributes	Abbreviations	Description
Read-only	R or RO	When a file is marked as read-only, it cannot be deleted or modified. (Note: The opposite of read-only is read-write.)
Hidden	H	When a file is marked as hidden, it cannot be seen during normal directory listings.
System	S or Sy	When a file is marked as system, it should not be moved. In addition, it usually can't be seen during normal directory listings.
Volume label		The name of the volume.
Subdirectory		A table that contains information about files and subdirectories.
Archive	A	When a file is marked as archive, it has not been backed up. Any time a file is new or has been changed, the operating system automatically turns the archive attribute on, indicating that the file needs to be backed up. When the archive attribute is off, the file is not new or changed and does not have to be backed up.

Every directory, excluding the root directory, has two additional entries. The first one is the "." (single dot), which indicates the current directory and its location. The second one is the ".." (double dot), which indicates the parent directory and its location. When performing the CD.. command at the prompt or by clicking on the .. within Windows dialog boxes, the double-dot entry tells the operating system to jump to the location of the parent directory.

Each file, a collection of related information that is referenced by name, or directory on a volume can be uniquely identified by using the file name (including the file extension, if any) and the path (or location on the tree). Files are stored in clusters. Since files are often larger than a cluster, a file will be spread among many clusters. On the last cluster, to indicate the end of a file, a special end-of-file (EOF) character is used so the operating system knows to ignore the rest of the cluster since it does not have any valid data. The file allocation table and the directory work very closely together. The file name is entered to open a file. The system looks in the specified directory. If no directory is specified, it looks in the current directory. After the system finds the file name, it looks at the starting cluster and reads the data. The operating system then jumps to the file allocation table, specifically the starting cluster, to read the next cluster where the file is located. It then jumps to the next cluster and retrieves that data. It will continue jumping between the file allocation table to find the next cluster and the clusters to retrieve the data until it gets to the EOF.

13.6 FILE SYSTEMS

Different file systems have been used for the PC. The most common systems today include:

FAT	Used by DOS and most other operating systems
HPFS	Used by OS/2 and earlier versions of Windows NT
VFAT	Used by Windows 95 and Windows NT 3.5X
FAT32	Used by Windows 95B and Windows 98
NTFS	Used by Windows NT

13.6.1 FAT

The most common file system is the **file allocation table (FAT).** It is the standard file system used by DOS, Windows 95, OS/2, and Windows NT. FAT is a simple and reliable file

TABLE 13.4   Cluster size for floppy disks

Disk Type	Number of Sectors	Number of Bytes
5¼" DS/DD disk (360 KB)	2	1,024
5¼" DS/HD disk (1.2 MB)	1	512
3½" DS/DD disk (720 KB)	2	1,024
3½" DS/HD disk (1.44 MB)	1	512

TABLE 13.5   Cluster size for hard drives

Volume Size	Number of Sectors	Number of Bytes	FAT Type
0 MB to 16 MB	8	4,096	12-bit
More than 16 MB to 128 MB	4	2,048	16-bit
More than 128 MB to 256 MB	8	4,096	16-bit
More than 256 MB to 512 MB	16	8,192	16-bit
More than 512 MB to 1,024 MB	32	16,384	16-bit
More than 1,024 MB to 2,048 MB	64	32,768	16-bit

system and uses minimal memory. Because of its cluster sizes, it is not as efficient for partitions larger than 32 MB. It supports file names of 11 characters, which include 8 characters for the file name and 3 characters for the file extension.

Older DOS systems used FAT12. In FAT12, a 12-bit binary number is used to number each cluster. The biggest cluster number that FAT12 could see, therefore, was 4,086, which would have been 4,096 except that some clusters are reserved. FAT12 is still used on floppy disks and hard disk partitions smaller than 16 MB. (See table 13.4.) Most current DOS systems use FAT16, which, instead of a 12-bit number uses a 16-bit number to number the clusters, giving 65,526 clusters. References to FAT probably mean FAT16. It is used for volumes up to 2 GB. (See table 13.5.)

13.6.2   VFAT

VFAT is an enhanced version of the FAT structure that allows Windows 95 and Windows NT to support long file names (LFN) of up to 255 characters. Because it is built on ordinary FAT, each file has to have an 8-character name and 3-character extension to be backward compatible to DOS and Windows 3.XX applications. Programs running in DOS and Windows 3.XX will not see the longer file names. WIN32 programs (programs made for Windows 95 and 98 or Windows NT) can see and make use of the longer names. To accommodate both the DOS file names and the long file names, VFAT uses additional directory entries to store the long file names. When a long file name is saved, the first entry will be a truncated name (known as the *alias*) for the file. Additional directory entries will hold the rest of the long file name. Each entry is 32 bytes in length. A single long file name can use many directory entries (since each entry is only 32 bytes in length), and for this reason it is recommended that long file names not be placed in the root directory, where the total number of directory entries is limited.

EXAMPLE 13.3   The first entry for a file called *The Budget for 1999 and 2000.DOC* saved in Windows 95 or 98 will use the first 6 characters, ignoring the spaces and adding a tilde (~) followed by a number, and appear in the directory as *THEBUD~1.DOC*. A DOS or Windows 3.XX program would see *THEBUD~1.DOC;* Windows 95 and 98 and Windows NT programs would see *The Budget for 1999 and 2000.DOC*. Of course, it would take several directory entries to store the alias and a couple more to save the long file name. A second file saved with the name *The Budget for 2000 and 2001.DOC* would have the alias *THEBUD~2.DOC*.

To make sure that DOS and Windows 3.XX do not use the directory entries that hold the long file names, the entries have the read-only, hidden, system, and volume attributes enabled. With all of these labels active, older software basically ignores the extra directory entries being used by VFAT. Disk problems can be caused by older utilities in an operating system that does not know how to handle VFAT because they will usually truncate the long file names or cause other problems. Make sure that Windows 95 or 98 SCANDISK, DEFRAG, or similar utilities made specifically for Windows 95 and 98 or VFAT are installed.

13.6.3 FAT32

FAT32, with 32-bit FAT entries, was introduced with the second major release of Windows 95 (OSR2/Windows 95B) and is an enhancement of the FAT file system. It supports hard drives up to two terabytes and uses space more efficiently. It has, for example, 4 KB clusters for drives up to 8 GB, which results in a 15% more efficient use of disk space in large FAT drives. Unlike VFAT, all of Microsoft's disk utilities (DEFRAG and SCANDISK) have been revised to work with FAT32.

FAT32's root directory is an ordinary cluster chain and can, therefore, be located anywhere in the drive. In addition, the system allows dynamic resizing of FAT32 partitions (without losing data) and the disabling of FAT mirroring, which allows a copy of the FAT other than the first to be active. Consequently, FAT32 drives are less prone to the failure of critical data areas such as the FAT.

The FDISK utility from Windows 95 OSR2/Windows 95B must be used to install FAT32 on a volume on a hard drive over 512 MB. The utility will ask whether to enable large disk support. If the answer is yes, any partition that is greater than 512MB will be marked as a FAT32 partition. At this time, Windows 95 (OSR2/Windows 95B), Windows 98, and Windows NT 2000 are the only operating systems capable of accessing FAT32 volumes. Windows 3.l, MS-DOS, the original version of Windows 95, and Windows NT do not recognize FAT32 partitions and are not able to boot from a FAT32 volume. (Note: There is a good chance that FAT32 might be added to Windows NT.)

13.6.4 HPFS

HPFS (high performance file system) is a file system that was developed for OS/2. It allows long file names of up to 256 characters and volume sizes up to 8 GB. In addition, it allows additional extended attributes. Because there is no room for these additional attributes in the FAT directory, OS/2 creates a separate hidden file on the disk volume named EA DATA. SF and stores the additional information there. HPFS provides better performance than FAT on larger disk volumes. However, it requires more memory than FAT. OS/2 and Windows NT 3.51 or earlier can recognize HPFS, but DOS cannot. DOS and Windows applications, however, do recognize HPFS.

13.6.5 NTFS

NTFS (NT file system) is a new file system for Windows NT. Since it was designed for both the server and workstation, it has many enhancements and features built into it. It supports long file names, yet maintains an 8.3 name for DOS and Windows 3.XX programs. The NTFS is a 64-bit architecture and is designed to support drive sizes up to 2^{64} bytes (18,446,744,073,709,551,616 bytes = 16 exabytes).

Windows NT includes enhanced security and supports a variety of multiuser security models. It allows computers running other operating systems, including DOS, Windows 3.XX, Windows 95, Windows NT Workstation, UNIX, POSIX, and even Macintosh computers, to save files to the NTFS volume on an NT server. It does not allow DOS to access an NTFS volume directory directly but only through the network (assuming the operator has the proper permissions or rights to access the volume). It can compress individual files or directories, including infrequently used files or directories. To make an NTFS volume more resistant to failure, NTFS writes updates to a log area. If a system crash occurs, the log area can be used to quickly clean up problems.

Although FAT is simpler and smaller than NTFS, NTFS is generally faster because it minimizes the number of disk accesses required to find a file, which makes access to the file faster, especially if it is a large folder. In addition, it tries to keep the hard drive unfragmented. Unlike the other file systems, NTFS supports a "volume set," the combination of several hard drives (or parts of hard drives) into a single volume. If the volume needs to be expanded, another hard drive is added.

(Note: You can set up a computer to dual-boot between Windows 95 and Windows NT 4.0 and have both operating systems access the same files if they are both running VFAT. Remember that Windows 95 cannot read or access NTFS and Windows NT 3.51 or 4.0 cannot read or access FAT32. In addition, drive compression for Windows 95 and Windows NT are not compatible.)

13.7 DISK COMPRESSION

Disk compression expands the amount of space on a disk and is accomplished in two ways: first, by reducing the amount of wasted and unused space created by large clusters; second, by squeezing the files on the disk so that they will take up less space.

When a volume is compressed, a compression interface (DBLSPACE, DRVSPACE, or Stacker, among others) simulates a file allocation table for the compressed drive. The normal file allocation table allocates a fixed number of clusters to a file. The simulated file allocation table allocates a variable number of sectors to a cluster. Therefore, if a small file fits within one sector, it will use only one sector, not an entire cluster.

When a drive is compressed, the compression software changes the drive letter. The compression software might change the drive letter of the existing C drive to H, for example. The drive with the new drive letter is known as the *host drive* for the compressed volume. A large hidden file created on the host drive, which usually uses most of the volume space, is called the **compressed volume file (CVF).** It is at the beginning of the hidden file that the simulated file allocation table is created and stored. The rest of the hidden file is used to store files in compressed format. The reason that the CVF does not include the entire volume is because some files, such as certain boot files and Windows 3.XX swap files, need to be uncompressed.

File compression works by substitution. It starts by locating repetitive patterns and replacing the repetitive data with another, shorter pattern. Most operating systems and disk compression software packages will compress files as they are written to disk. When a compressed file is accessed, it has to be uncompressed in RAM before it can be used. If a file stored on a compressed drive is copied to another drive that is not compressed, the file is uncompressed in RAM and stored on the target drive uncompressed. As far as the user is concerned, the compressed drive is drive that works just like any other drive. But although the amount of space for a volume is expanded through file compression, the performance of the PC will be slower since it has to process the compression and decompression of files. In addition, the disk compression software must remain in RAM to handle the compression and decompression, which uses up resources that could have been used for something else.

13.8 DISK PROBLEMS

Since the data on the disk is the most important part of the computer, it is necessary to protect the integrity of the disk. Disk problems and errors can occur without warning and may easily result in a data loss. Some causes include power fluctuations, viruses, parts of the hard drive wearing out, badly written software, user wear and tear, and user errors. Some of the errors these problems can cause include:

Invalid entries in the file allocation table
Invalid directory entries
Bad sectors (unreadable areas on the disk)
Corrupt MBR or corrupt volume boot sector

Corrupt compressed header, compressed file structure, compression structure, and signatures

Lost clusters

Cross-linked files

The file allocation table and directory entries are databases. Therefore, if part of these databases becomes corrupted, part or all of the databases may be unusable. Without these two databases, the operating system would not be able to find the clusters belonging to a file. Consequently, the data would be lost.

Bad sectors are areas on the disk that cannot reliably store the magnetic patterns that make up data. If an area of the disk becomes unreliable, the operating system marks as bad those sectors on the file allocation table and will not use these areas in the future to avoid data loss.

If the master boot record, which consists of the startup program to boot from the disk, becomes unreadable, the volume boot sector will not be found during boot-up. Of course, if the volume boot sector becomes corrupt, the computer cannot load the operating system's boot files. In either case, the computer does not boot.

If the compressed header, compressed file structure, compression structure, or signatures become corrupt, the files within a compressed volume may not be accessed and could be permanently damaged.

Lost clusters are clusters that get "lost" or detached from a file when a program unexpectedly stops running or isn't shut down properly, when there are power fluctuations, or when disk system problems occur. Unfortunately, the lost clusters may be a very important part of the file (an executable file or a data file). When the cluster is no longer part of the file, it may cause the computer to "lock up" or act erratic when the system tries to execute the missing instructions or it may make a data file inaccessible. If the disk system is going bad or the system is experiencing power problems, the system may generate lost clusters. When lost clusters are found on a system, the most likely cause is that the user may be shutting off the computer without closing all programs and performing the proper shutdown procedure (File, Exit in the Windows 3.XX Program Manager or Start, Shutdown in Windows 95 and 98). Some utilities that search for and retrieve lost clusters will make them available as a file on the disk. Unfortunately, since most files are in machine code, you cannot reattach them to the file they came from, you would have to figure out not only which files they came from but exactly which part of the files they are. Therefore, it is best to delete the file. If the lost cluster was vital to the proper running of a program, the program would have to be reinstalled or the data file would have to be restored from a backup.

A **cross-link file** is the opposite of a lost cluster. Instead of the cluster being separated from a file, cross-linked errors occur when two or more files use the same cluster. Usually, the cluster belongs to only one of the files, so repairing cross-linked files usually results in only one file remaining usable.

13.9   DISK UTILITIES

There are several utilities that can help fix disk errors. Some of these utilities are FDISK, CHKDSK, SCANDISK, and DEFRAG.

13.9.1   FDISK UTILITY

The FDISK is the standard utility used to partition a hard drive. When the hard drive does not boot, FDISK causes the computer to lock up, or the changes to the partition table cannot be saved; this may indicate that the master boot record (MBR) may be bad. What most people who use FDISK don't know is that it can also be used to recreate the master boot record without changing the partition table. To recreate the MBR, boot with a bootable floppy containing the FDISK.EXE program, change to the drive with the corrupt MBR, and perform the command FDISK /MBR. If this corrects the problem, you should be concerned with what caused the corruption of the master boot record. Perhaps the cause is a virus, power fluctuations when the drive is being accessed, or a failing hard drive. If the problem still exists, try a low-level format.

13.9.2 CHKDSK UTILITY

CHKDSK has been around since DOS 1.0. It is probably the first utility that was developed to analyze a disk. It shows the disk statistics, including the amount of space being used, the amount of free space, the number of files and directories, and the size of the clusters. It also inspects directories and FATs to see if there are any discrepancies and will check if a file is contiguous or fragmented. CHKDSK can identify and recover (if the /F is used) lost clusters, cross-linked files, FAT allocation errors, and invalid directories. Since CHKDSK is an old utility, it is recommended for DOS 6.00 and above to run SCANDISK to fix disk problems.

13.9.3 SCANDISK UTILITY

SCANDISK, Norton Disk Doctor, and similar utilities are intended to fix disk errors, including invalid entries in the file allocation table, invalid directory entries, lost clusters, cross-linked files, problems with the compressed volume, files left in an open status, and bad sectors. Unlike FDISK and CHKDSK, SCANDISK is a menu-based utility. (See fig. 13.1.) As SCANDISK checks a hard drive, it first checks disk structure and then completes a surface scan.

With SCANDISK, you can choose to save the lost clusters to files or to delete them to free up disk space. If you choose to save them, they will be saved with a CHK extension (for example, FILE0000.CHK, FILE0001.CHK, FILE0002.CHK) in the root directory. If you find that you do not need the converted files, they can be deleted at any time. The surface scan test identifies any sector that may be failing. It accomplishes this by reading the data of a sector, writing a predetermined pattern to the sector, and rereading the sector to make sure that the pattern is the same. If the data is the same, the original information is placed back in the sector. If the sector is unreliable, SCANDISK marks the sector as bad and moves the data to another sector.

Whichever disk utility is used, it must be made for the operating system and file system. If not, the long file names may be truncated or corrupted, the file allocation table and

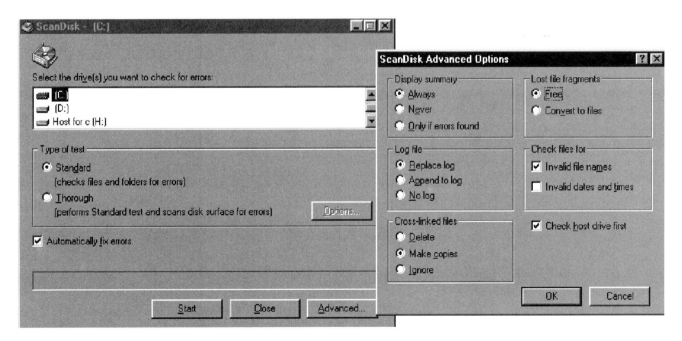

FIGURE 13.1 Windows 95's SCANDISK utility

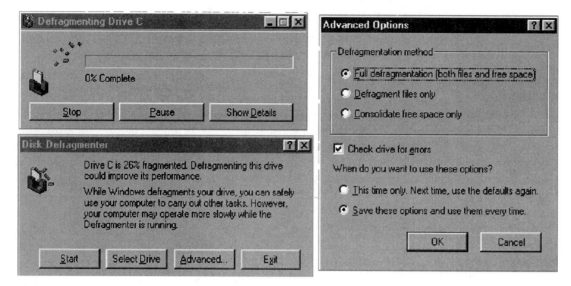

FIGURE 13.2   Windows 95's disk defragmenter utility

directories may be corrupted, or files may become inaccessible. (Note: You should not run SCANDISK while running Windows 3.XX.)

13.9.4   DEFRAG UTILITY

When a file is created, it is assigned the number of clusters needed to hold the amount of data. After the file is saved to the disk, other information is usually saved to the clusters following those assigned to the saved file. Therefore, if the original file is changed or more information is added to it, the bigger file doesn't fit within the allocated clusters when it is saved back to the disk. Part of the file will be saved in the original clusters and the remaining amount will be placed elsewhere on the disk. Over time, files become fragmented as they are spread across the disk. The fragmented files are still complete when they are opened, but it takes longer for the computer to read them, and opening them causes more wear and tear on the hard disk. DEFRAG fixes this fragmentation problem by bringing these scattered segments of a file back into a more efficient order on the storage medium. (See fig. 13.2.)

DEFRAG and other similar utilities reorganize the files on the hard drive to optimize disk performance. It does this by gathering all parts of a file and placing them in continuous sectors. If the drive is badly fragmented, the program may take several hours to finish. DEFRAG cannot move files that are marked as system (system file attribute) or hidden (hidden file attribute) because some of these files are placed in a particular position on the disk.

13.9.5   OTHER UTILITIES

The remaining utilities worth mentioning are the UNDELETE and UNFORMAT utilities. The UNDELETE utilities can be used to recover files (not subdirectories) that were deleted with the DEL command because a file is not actually deleted but rather marked as deleted by changing the first character of the file name to a sigma (σ). The file can be undeleted as long the entire file is intact and has not been replaced with another file.

Windows environments like to create a lot of temporary files so the chances of undeleting a file are reduced significantly. But Windows 95 and 98 and Windows NT have a recycle bin, which is actually a subdirectory where deleted files are stored. Therefore, if you need to undelete the file, look in the recycle bin and restore it back to the drive. (See fig. 13.3.) If the hard drive starts to become full, it will start to delete the oldest files first.

FIGURE 13.3   Windows 95's
recycle bin

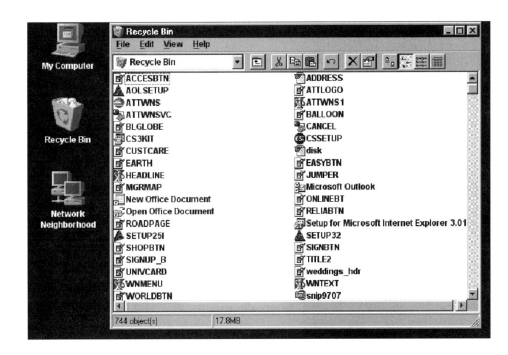

Most of the time when the FORMAT command is used to format a disk, it performs a safe format. A safe format copies the file allocation table to an unused portion of the disk and then erases the original file allocation table. The UNFORMAT utility can recover a disk that has been accidentally formatted with a safe format by copying the copy of the file allocation table back to the file allocation table position on the disk.

13.10   TROUBLE-SHOOTING DISK PROBLEMS

When troubleshooting any kind of disk problem, keep in mind that it could be either a hardware problem or a formatting problem, such as a corrupt file allocation table, corrupt partition table, or corrupt file. If the problem is a formatting problem, then you need to investigate to determine how the disk acquired its problems. This may lead back to a hardware problem or to a virus or user error.

EXAMPLE 13.4   A client is using Windows 95 or 98 on the computer. While Microsoft Word for Windows is running, it locks up often, and occasionally an exception error occurs.

This is most likely a software problem, probably with Word. Check for viruses and run SCANDISK on the hard drive. If there are lost clusters, most likely they are clusters from important Word files. Therefore, the best thing to do would be to reinstall Word. If the problem still exists, try to reinstall Windows. If this clears up the problem, make sure that the user knows how to properly shut down Windows. If SCANDISK detects a lot of bad sectors on the hard drive, that indicates the hard drive is going bad. Therefore, it is best to back up the hard drive immediately and start looking for a replacement drive. If the problem still exists after replacing the drive, it is probably caused by the the RAM, microprocessor, or motherboard.

EXAMPLE 13.5   A file name consists of strange ASCII characters. It cannot be deleted with DEL, DELTREE, File Manager, or Explorer.

To correct this problem, run SCANDISK on the drive. In addition, it is probably not a bad idea to check for viruses.

SUMMARY

1. By default, the system ROM BIOS will begin searching the volume boot sector of drive A followed by the volume boot sector of drive C for the operating system boot files.

2. The master boot record (MBR), always found on the first sector of a hard drive, tells the system ROM BIOS how the hard drive is divided (master partition table) and which partition to boot from.

3. Partitioning is the process of defining and dividing the physical drive into logical volumes called *partitions*. Each partition functions as if it were a separate hard disk.

4. FDISK (or an equivalent program) can create the master boot record and define the partition table.

5. The file system consists of the directory structure, methods for organizing a volume (partition or floppy disk), and methods of storing and retrieving files.

6. Disks are divided into a circular grid consisting of tracks (concentric circles) and sectors (512-byte chunks of usable data).

7. The most basic storage unit for an operating system is a cluster or allocation unit. A cluster is one or more sectors that make up one entry in the file allocation table.

8. The file allocation table is an index used to "remember" which file is located in which cluster.

9. The file allocation table is created during a high-level format, such as when using the FORMAT.COM command or an equivalent program.

10. Every volume has a starting point called the *root directory,* which is located at the top of the tree structure.

11. The directories under the root directory are also referred to as *subdirectories.*

12. Every directory, including the root directory, consists of a small database. The database stores the file name, file attributes, starting cluster, size of the file, and the date and time that the file was created or last modified.

13. The file attribute field stores a number of characteristics about each file, such as read-only, hidden, system, and archive.

14. The file allocation table (FAT) is the most common file system (used by DOS, Windows 95, OS/2, and Windows NT).

15. VFAT is an enhanced version of the FAT structure that allows Windows 95 and Windows NT to support long file names (up to 255 characters).

16. FAT32 is an enhancement of the FAT file system. It supports hard drives up to two terabytes and uses space more efficiently on large hard drives.

17. HPFS (high performance file system) is a file system that was made for OS/2.

18. NTFS (NT file system) is a new file system for Windows NT. Since it was made for a server and workstation, it offers many enhancements and features.

19. Disk compression is expanding the amount of space on a disk.

20. Disk compression works by reducing the amount of wasted and unused space created by large clusters and by squeezing the files on the disk so that they will take up less space.

21. Since the data on the disk is the most important part of the computer, it is necessary to protect the integrity of the disk.

22. Disk problems and errors can occur without warning and may easily result in a data loss.

23. Lost clusters are clusters that get "lost," or detached, from a file.

24. A cross-link is two or more files using the same cluster.

25. SCANDISK and similar utilities are made to fix disk errors.

26. DEFRAG and other similar utilities reorganize the files on the hard drive to optimize disk performance.

QUESTIONS

1. By default, the BIOS will boot from:
   a. the A drive followed by the C drive
   b. the A drive followed by the B drive followed by the C drive
   c. the C drive followed by the A drive
   d. the C drive followed by the B drive followed by the A drive
   e. the CD-ROM drive

2. A cluster is a collection of:
   a. heads
   b. tracks
   c. sectors
   d. cylinders

3. The small unit of storage for an operating system is a:
   a. sector
   b. cluster
   c. cylinder
   d. track
4. The master boot record holds the:
   a. partition table
   b. volume boot sector
   c. file allocation table
   d. root directory
5. What utility is used to partition the drive?
   a. FORMAT
   b. FDISK
   c. SCANDISK
   d. CHKDSK
   e. DEFRAG
6. The index of the disk is the:
   a. partition table
   b. file allocation table
   c. directory
   d. root directory
7. The file allocation table is created during the:
   a. low-level formatting
   b. partitioning
   c. high-level formatting
   d. CMOS setup
8. The top of a file structure tree is the:
   a. partition table
   b. root directory
   c. subdirectory
   d. MBR
9. Which of the following is not listed in the directory?
   a. starting cluster
   b. file name and extension
   c. attributes
   d. date and time that the file was created or edited
   e. ending cluster
10. What kind of file cannot be deleted or changed?
    a. read-only
    b. system
    c. hidden
    d. archive
11. Which DOS attribute is used by backup programs?
    a. R
    b. S
    c. H
    e. A
12. The most common file system used in DOS, Windows 95 and 98, and Windows NT is:
    a. FAT
    b. HPFS
    c. VFAT
    d. NTFS
13. Which of the following does *not* support long file names?
    a. FAT
    b. VFAT
    c. FAT32
    d. NTFS
    e. HPFS
14. What is the maximum number of files and directories in the root directory supported by Windows 95 using the FAT file system?
    a. 128
    b. 256
    c. 512
    d. 1,024
15. What is the maximum partition size used in DOS or Windows 95 running FAT?
    a. 512 MB
    b. 1 GB
    c. 2 GB
    d. 4 GB
    e. 8 GB
16. The compressed volume file is located on:
    a. drive C
    b. CD-ROM
    c. the host drive
    d. a floppy disk
    e. the first partition of the first hard drive
17. When a cluster becomes detached from its file, it is called a:
    a. lost cluster
    b. cross-linked file
    c. bad sector
    d. corrupt volume boot sector
18. Which utility identifies and corrects files that are not contiguous?
    a. SCANDISK
    b. DEFRAG
    c. MEMMAKER
    d. BACKUP

19. Which best describes a fragmented hard drive?
    a. the platters are bad or cracked
    b. the platters are slipping on the spindle
    c. data files are corrupted
    d. files are not stored in consecutive clusters
20. SCANDISK can be used to:
    a. locate lost clusters and provide the option to save or delete them
    b. look for viruses
    c. reconfigure and optimize the programs in RAM
    d. locate a specific program on a disk or drive
21. A hard drive has slowed down considerably over time. What should be done to improve the performance of the hard drive?
    a. use DriveSpace or DoubleSpace
    b. use Fast Disk
    c. use Disk Defragmenter
    d. use CHKDSK
    e. increase the maximum amount of virtual memory
22. What are some advantages of using SCANDISK rather than CHKDSK? (Choose two answers.)
    a. SCANDISK can perform a surface scan
    b. SCANDISK can repair CD-ROM disks
    c. SCANDISK can repair physical damage to a disk
    d. SCANDISK can repair lost clusters on a compressed drive
    e. SCANDISK can repair a corrupt partition table

HANDS-ON EXERCISES

Exercise 1: Running SCANDISK and DEFRAG

1. Using DOS or Windows 95 or 98, run SCANDISK on the hard drive.
2. Using DOS or Windows 95 or 98, run DEFRAG on the hard drive.
3. If they are available, run Norton's Disk Doctor and Norton's SpeedDisk utilities.

Exercise 2: Finding and Correcting Disk Problems with SCANDISK

1. Using a test disk and the DIR command, view the contents of the disk.
2. Using SCANDISK, find and correct any problems on the disk.

Exercise 3: Using the CHKDSK Command

Use the CHKDSK utility with the Fix option.

Exercise 4: Using the FDISK Command

Use the FDISK utility to create a new master boot record.

Exercise 5: Looking at Clusters

1. Insert a formatted DS/HD 3½″ disk in drive A. Use the CHKDSK command to find the size of the clusters on the A drive.
2. Delete all partitions on the hard drive. Create and format a 10 MB primary partition on the hard drive.
3. Using the FDISK command, find the type of file system being used on the C drive.
4. Using the CHKDSK command, find the size of the clusters on the C drive.
5. Delete the primary partition on the hard drive.
6. Create and format a 300 MB primary partition on the hard drive.
7. Using the FDISK command, find the type of file system being used on the C drive.
8. Using the CHKDSK command, find the size of the clusters on the C drive.
9. Record the number of bytes free on the C drive.
10. Using the COPY command or EDIT utility, create a file consisting of the word "SCHOOL."

11. Record the size of the file.
12. Using the CHKDSK command, record the number of bytes free on the C drive.
13. Determine the difference between the bytes of free space before the file was added and the bytes of free space after the file was added. Compare the result with the size of the cluster.
14. Delete the primary partition on the hard drive.
15. Create a primary partition on the hard drive. Maximize the size.
16. Format the primary partition.
17. Using the FDISK command, find the type of file system being used on the C drive.
18. Using the CHKDSK command, find the size of the clusters on the C drive.
19. Record the number of bytes free on the C drive.
20. Using the COPY command or EDIT utility, create a file consisting of the word "SCHOOL."
21. Record the size of the file.
22. Using the CHKDSK command, record the number of bytes free on the C drive.
23. Determine the difference between the bytes of free space before the file was added and the bytes of free space after the file was added. Compare the result with the size of the cluster.

Exercise 6: Using a FAT32 Partition

1. Create a primary partition on the hard drive using DOS's FDISK. Maximize the size.
2. Format the primary partition.
3. Using the FDISK command, find the type of file system being used on the C drive.
4. Using the CHKDSK command, find the size of the clusters on the C drive.
5. Record the number of bytes free on the C drive.
6. Using the COPY command or EDIT utility, create a file consisting of the word "SCHOOL."
7. Record the size of the file.
8. Using the CHKDSK command, record the number of bytes free on the C drive.
9. Take the difference between the bytes of free space before the file was added and the bytes of free space after the file was added. Compare the result with the size of the cluster.
10. Delete the primary partition.
11. Create a primary partition using FDISK from the Windows 95 (OSR2) startup disk. Maximize the size.
12. Format the primary partition with the Windows 95 startup disk.
13. Using the FDISK command, find the type of file system being used on the C drive.
14. Using the CHKDSK command, find the size of the clusters on the C drive.
15. Record the number of bytes free on the C drive.
16. Using the COPY command or EDIT utility, create a file consisting of the word "SCHOOL."
17. Record the size of the file.
18. Using the CHKDSK command, record the number of bytes free on the C drive.
19. Determine the difference between the bytes of free space before the file was added and the bytes of free space after the file was added. Compare the result with the size of the cluster.
20. Perform the following command at the C:\> prompt:

```
MD "FAT32 USES THE LONG FILE NAME SCHEME"
```

21. Perform a DIR command at the C:\> prompt.
22. Boot with a DOS boot disk.
23. Perform a DIR command at the C:\> prompt.

14

Tape Drives and Data Protection

INTRODUCTION

Data is the most important thing on the computer. It represents hours of work, and the information is sometimes irreplaceable. The best way to protect data is to back up, back up, back up. Because the data can be lost due to hardware failure, software glitches, viruses, and user error, as a technician, consultant, or support person, you need to emphasize to the customer or client the importance of a good backup. Backups can be performed with floppy disks, hard disks, compact disks, removable disks, and tapes. One of the best, easiest, and most inexpensive ways to back up a system is with a tape drive.

OBJECTIVES

1. Depending on the situation, recommend the best device for backup.
2. Install an antivirus software package.
3. Look for, detect, and remove a virus.
4. List and describe the various tape recording methods.
5. Describe the two types of quarter-inch cartridges.
6. Install a tape drive and back up the hard drive.
7. Identify and correct a tape drive problem.

14.1 DATA

Data are the raw facts, numbers, letters, or symbols that the computer processes into meaningful information. Examples of data include a letter to a company or a client, a report for your boss, a budget proposal for a large project, and an address book of your friends and business associates. Whatever the data, it can be saved (or written to disk) so that it can be retrieved at any time, printed on paper, or sent to someone else over the telephone line.

As mentioned throughout this book, data is the most important part of the computer. Your data usually represents hours of work and is sometimes irreplaceable. Since data is the most important part of the computer, it is essential that you protect it. Data loss can be caused by many things. Previous chapters have discussed how hardware failure, especially drive failure, disk failure, or power fluctuations can cause data loss. Data loss can also be caused by software problems, viruses, and user error.

14.2 VIRUSES

A virus is a program designed to replicate and spread, generally without the knowledge or permission of the user. Computer viruses spread by attaching themselves to other programs or to the boot sector of a disk. When an infected file is executed or accessed or the computer is started with an infected disk, the virus spreads into the computer. Some viruses are cute, some are annoying, and others are disastrous. (See fig. 14.1.) Some of the disastrous symptoms of a virus include the following:

> The computer fails to boot
> Disks have been formatted
> The partitions are deleted or the partition table is corrupt
> A disk can't be read
> Data or entire files are corrupt or are disappearing
> Programs don't run anymore
> Files become larger
> The system is slower than normal
> The system has less memory available than it should
> Information being sent to and from a device is intercepted

Question: How does a virus spread?

Answer: Since viruses are small programs that are made to replicate themselves, they spread very easily. For example, you are handed an infected disk or you download a file from the Internet or a bulletin board. When the disk or file is accessed, the virus replicates itself to RAM. When you access any files on your hard drive, the virus again replicates itself to your hard drive. If you shut off your computer, the virus in the RAM will disappear, but unfortunately, because your hard drive is infected, the RAM becomes infected every time you boot from the hard drive. When

**FIGURE 14.1 Viruses can
cause a wide range of problems**

TABLE 14.1   Virus facts

Viruses can't infect write-protected disks.	Viruses can infect read-only, hidden, and system files.
Viruses don't typically infect a document (except macro viruses).	Viruses typically infect boot sectors and executable files.
Viruses do not infect compressed files.	A file within a compressed file could have been infected before being compressed.
Viruses don't infect computer hardware, such as monitors or chips.	Viruses can change your CMOS values, causing your computer not to boot.
You cannot get a virus just by being on the Internet or a bulletin board.	You can download an infected file.
Viruses cannot be activated by reading an e-mail message.	Viruses can be part of a file attached to e-mail.

you insert and access another disk, that disk also becomes infected. You then hand the disk or send an infected file to someone else and the cycle repeats itself.

Symantec, developer of Norton Antivirus, says that most current infections are caused by viruses that are at least three years old. Stiller Research, developer of Integrity Master, states that viruses are very widespread but only a relatively small number (about 100) account for 90% of all infections. Table 14.1 lists a number of facts about viruses.

14.2.1   TYPES OF VIRUSES

Computer viruses can be categorized into five types:

1. Boot sector
2. File
3. Multipartite
4. Macro
5. Trojan horse

Every logical drive (hard drive partition and floppy disk) has a boot sector with both bootable and nonbootable components. The boot sector contains specific information relating to the formatting of the disk and a small program called the *boot program,* which loads the operating system files. On hard drives, the first physical sector (side 0, track 0, sector 1) contains the master boot record (MBR) and partition table. The master boot program uses the partition table to find the starting location of the bootable partition (active partition). It then tells the computer to go to the boot sector of the partition and load the boot program. A **boot sector virus** is transmitted by rebooting the machine from an infected diskette. When the boot sector program on the diskette is read and executed, the virus goes into memory and infects the hard drive, specifically the boot sector or the master boot program.

File infector viruses attach themselves to or replace executable files (usually files with the COM or EXE filename extension), but they can also infect SYS, DRV, BIN, OVL, and OVY files. Uninfected programs become infected when files are executed with the virus in memory; in other cases, programs are infected when they are opened, including from the DOS DIR command. Or the virus simply infects all of the files in the directory from which it was run.

A **multipartite virus** has the characteristics of both boot sector viruses and file viruses. It may start as a boot sector virus and spread to executable files, or start from an infected file and spread to the boot sector.

A macro, or formula language, used in word processing, spreadsheets, and other application programs, is a set of instructions that a program executes on command. Macros group several keystrokes into one command or perform complex menu selections. They therefore simplify redundant or complex tasks. The **macro viruses** are the newest strain and are currently the most common type of virus. Unlike previous viruses, macro viruses

TABLE 14.2   General information about viruses

Title	Website
Dr. Solomon's Virus Central	http://www.drsolomon.com/vircen/index.cfm
All About Viruses	http://www.drsolomon.com/vircen/vanalyse/va002.html
Technical Papers from Dr. Solomon	http://www.drsolomon.com/vircen/vanalyse/index.cfm
Introduction to Macro Viruses	http://www.drsolomon.com/vircen/vanalyse/macvir.html
Computer Virus Information and Virus Description Database	http://www.datafellows.com/vir-info/
Hoax Warnings on the Run	http://www.datafellows.com/news/hoax/

are stored in a data document and spread when the infected documents are accessed or transferred. Currently, the most vulnerable applications are Microsoft Word and Microsoft Excel. Some macro viruses modify the contents of the document and can even cause documents to be sent out via e-mail.

The fifth type of virus is the **Trojan horse virus,** which, by definition, is not really a virus since it does not replicate itself. Nonetheless, the Trojan horse virus is a program that appears to be legitimate software, such as a game or useful utility. Unfortunately, when you run the Trojan horse and the trigger event occurs, the program will do its damage, such as formatting your hard drive.

Some viruses can be characterized as polymorphic viruses or stealth viruses. A **polymorphic virus** mutates, or changes its code, so that it cannot be as easily detected. **Stealth viruses** try to hide themselves by monitoring and intercepting a system's call. For example, when the system seeks to open an infected file, the stealth virus uninfects the file and allows the operating system to open it. When the operating system closes the file, the virus reinfects the file.

For more information on viruses, how they work, and how they affect your computer and for descriptions of particular viruses, check out the websites in table 14.2.

14.2.2   VIRUS HOAXES

A virus hoax is a letter or e-mail message warning you about a virus that does not exist. For example, the letter or warning may tell you that certain e-mail messages may harm your computer if you open them. In addition, the letter or message usually tells you to forward the letter or e-mail message to your friends, which creates more network traffic.

14.2.3   ANTIVIRUS SOFTWARE

Antivirus software will detect and remove viruses and help protect the computer against viruses. Whichever software package is chosen, it should include a scanner-disinfector and an interceptor-resident monitor. The scanner-disinfector software will look for known virus patterns in the RAM, the boot sector, and the disk files. If a virus is detected, the software will typically attempt to remove the virus. The interceptor-resident monitor is piece of software that is loaded and remains in the RAM. Every time a disk is accessed or file is read, the interceptor-resident monitor software will check the disk or file for the same virus patterns that the scanner-disinfector software does. In addition, some interceptor-resident monitor software will detect files as you download them from the Internet or bulletin board.

Unfortunately, scanner-disinfector software has three disadvantages. First, it can detect only viruses that it knows about. Therefore, the antivirus software package must be continually updated. The easiest way to do this is through the Internet. Second, it cannot always remove the virus. Therefore, the file may need to be deleted or a low-level format may need to be performed on the hard drive. Lastly, if it succeeds in removing the virus, the file or boot sector may still have been damaged. Therefore, the infected file still needs to be deleted or replaced, the boot sector needs to be recreated, or a low-level format needs to be performed on the disk.

If you think a virus is present even though interceptor software is installed, boot from a clean write-protected disk. This will ensure that the RAM does not contain a virus. Without changing to or accessing the hard drive, run an updated virus scanner-disinfector from the floppy disk. If a virus is detected and removed, it is then best to reboot the computer when the scanner-disinfector has finished checking the hard drive. (Note: Also boot from a bootable floppy and check the hard drive before installing any antivirus software.)

14.2.4 PROTECTING AGAINST VIRUSES

To avoid viruses, do the following:

1. Do not use pirated software because there is more of a chance that such software will have a virus.
2. Treat files downloaded from the Internet and bulletin boards with suspicion.
3. Do not boot from or access a floppy disk of unknown origin.
4. Educate fellow users.
5. Use an updated antivirus software package that constantly detects viruses.
6. Back up your files on a regular basis.

14.2.5 REMOVING A VIRUS

If you suspect a virus, immediately check the hard drive and disk with a current antivirus software package. If you think that the hard drive is infected, use a noninfected, write-protected bootable floppy disk that contains the antivirus software to boot the computer without accessing the hard drive. Next, run the software to check the hard drive and remove the virus. If you think that there is a virus on a floppy disk, boot the computer using the hard drive. If you have been using the possibly infected disk, first check the hard drive for viruses. Then execute the antivirus program to check the floppy disk.

14.3 WHAT IS A TAPE DRIVE?

The main storage device within a PC is the hard drive. It contains the operating system, applications, and data generated by the applications. Since the data represent hours of work and the information is sometimes irreplaceable, data is the most important part of the computer. The best way to protect data is to perform a **backup,** which is an extra copy of data. Unfortunately, most people fail to do this and do not think about it until it is too late. As a technician, consultant, or support person, you need to emphasize to the customer or client the importance of "backup, backup, backup." You may have to select and install the backup equipment, perform the backup, or train other people to perform the backup. Whichever method and equipment are chosen and whichever person is selected to perform the backup, make sure that backup is completed on a regular basis. Remember that even with the best equipment and software, if no one completes the backup, the equipment and software are wasted.

Backups can be performed with floppy disks, hard disks, compact disks, removable disks, and tapes. Although floppy disks can be easily moved from computer to computer, it would take hundreds, maybe thousands, of them to back up today's computer. This method would also be slow and require a lot of work, as each disk would have to be inserted one at a time. Hard drives have large capacities but are usually permanently installed within the system. Compact disks also have large capacities for storage but are slow and are limited in terms of the number of times they can be written to. In either case, both devices are relatively expensive compared to others that can be used for backup. In some situations, hard drives configured in a RAID system can enhance data protection. **RAID,** which stands for **redundant arrays of inexpensive disks,** uses two or more drives in combination to create a fault tolerance system. But because this system simply duplicates information with the extra hard drives, it protects only against physical hard drive failure. If a file gets infected with a virus or becomes corrupt, the duplicated information becomes infected and corrupt on all hard drives within the RAID system.

A newer way to back up a system is with removable disks like Zip disks, Jaz disks, and LS-120 disks. These disks have a large capacity, great speed, and are relatively inexpensive, so they are an excellent choice for some systems. Unfortunately, they are not yet widely accepted and their capacity, though large, is still limited.

Tape drives are ideal for backing up hard drives on a regular basis. (See fig. 14.2.) They read and write to a long magnetic tape and so offer large storage capacities. They are also relatively inexpensive. To back up a hard drive with tape, insert a tape into the tape drive, start a backup software package, and select the drive or files you want to back up and it will be done. If a drive or file is lost, the backup software can be used to restore the data from the tape to the hard drive. Some tape drives and backup software automatically back up the hard drive at night, when it is being used least. The only thing to remember is to replace the tape each day. (Note: Tapes have been known to fail, and there have been times when people think they have selected a drive or file to be backed up only to find that they have a blank tape when disaster occurs. Therefore, it is important to occasionally test the tapes by choosing a nonimportant file and restoring it to the hard drive.)

14.3.1 THE TAPE MEDIUM

Magnetic tapes were used on older mainframes as a primary storage device and as a backup storage device. Eventually, magnetic tape evolved into the floppy disk and then the hard drive. When the IBM PC was introduced, it included a drive port for a cassette tape storage device.

Floppy disks as a medium are the most similar to a tape. They are made of a mylar platter coated with a magnetic substance to hold magnetic fields. Floppy disks are random-access devices, which means that no matter where the data is located on the disk, the read/write heads can move directly to the proper sector and start to read or write. Instead of being a mylar platter, **tapes** are a long polyester substrate coated with a layer of

FIGURE 14.2   Tape drive

FIGURE 14.3   A quarter-inch cartridge (QIC) and digital audio tape (DAT)

magnetic material. Unlike a floppy disk, a tape stores and retrieves data sequentially. Therefore, when a file needs to be retrieved, the read/write head has to start at the beginning of the tape and read each area to get to the correct file. Because it takes so much time to find the appropriate file, tapes are completely inappropriate as a PC's primary storage device.

Tapes come in different sizes and shapes and offer different speeds and capacities. As a result, several standards have been developed, including the quarter-inch cartridge (QIC) and the digital audio tape (DAT). (See fig. 14.3.)

14.3.2 RECORDING METHODS

A tape is divided into parallel tracks across its width. The number of tracks varies with the drive and the standard it follows. The data is recorded either in a parallel, serpentine, or helical scan fashion.

Parallel recording spreads the data throughout the different tracks. For example, if a tape is divided into 9 tracks, a byte of information with parity could be spread throughout all 9 tracks (one bit per track). Newer tape systems may lay 18 or 36 tracks across the tape, totalling two or four bytes of information over the tracks. Although such a tape offers high transfer rates, data retrieval time is slow because the drive might have to fast-forward across the entire tape before retrieving all of the data required. The read/write assembly for these tapes is also quite complicated because it has to consist of several poles and gaps, one for each track. This complexity increases the cost of the drive.

Most PC tape systems use **serpentine recording.** The tape is still divided into several tracks, but the data is first written onto one track, and when the end of the track is reached, the drive moves to the next track and writes to it. It repeats this process until it runs out of tracks. A serpentine tape drive can access data quickly by moving its head among the different tracks. The read/write assembly requires only one pole and gap, so the drives are cheaper.

The newest method of recording is **helical scan.** Much like a VCR read/write head, tape backup drives with helical scan use heads mounted at an angle on a cylindrical drum. The tape is partially wrapped around the drum, and as the tape slides across the drum, the read/write heads rotate. As each head approaches the tape, it takes swipes at the tape to read or write the data. The tape is moved only slightly between swipes, allowing data to be packed very tightly. In addition, since each head is skewed slightly from the others, they respond well to signals written in the same orientation but not to other signals. Blank spaces are therefore are not needed. And if two more heads are added to the drum, data can be read immediately after it is written. Therefore, if any errors are detected, the data can be rewritten immediately on the next piece of tape.

14.3.3 QUARTER-INCH CARTRIDGE (QIC)

The first tape drives, used before the PC, were reel-to-reel systems. A tape mounted on one spool was threaded through an open disk drive and fed onto another spool. Later, the tape was enclosed in a cassette and inserted into a capstan drive system. The cassette consisted of two spools (a supply and a takeup spool) and a rubber drive wheel, all connected with a small belt. When the drive wheel turned, the belt caused the spools to move, moving the tape across a linear read/write head.

In 1972, 3M company introduced the first quarter-inch tape cartridge (QIC) designed for data storage. The cartridge measured $6'' \times 4'' \times \frac{5}{8}''$. Although the cartridge became the standard, each tape drive manufacturer used different encoding methods, varied the number of tracks, and varied the data density on the tape, causing all kinds of compatibility problems. As a result, in 1982 a group of manufacturers formed the QIC Committee to standardize tape drive construction and application. The full-size quarter-inch cartridge standardized by the QIC Committee is the DC 6000 cartridge (the DC stands for data cartridge.) The first tape that the QIC committee approved was the QIC-24, which used serpentine recording. It had nine tracks and a density of 8,000 bits per inch, giving it the total

TABLE 14.3 QIC data cartridges

QIC Standard Number	Capacity without Compression	Tracks	Interface	Original Adoption Date
QIC-24-DC	45 MB or 60 MB[1]	9	SCSI or QIC-02	4/83
QIC-120-DC	125 MB	15	SCSI or QIC-02	10/85
QIC-150-DC	150 MB or 250 MB[1]	18	SCSI or QIC-02	2/87
QIC-525-DC	320 MB or 525 MB[1]	26	SCSI or SCSI-2	5/89
QIC-1350-DC	1.35 GB	30	SCSI-2	5/89
QIC-1000-DC	1.0 GB	30	SCSI or SCSI-2	10/90
QIC-6000C	6 GB	96	SCSI-2	2/91
QIC-2100-DC	2.1 GB	30	SCSI-2	6/91
QIC-5010-DC	13 GB	144	SCSI-2	2/92
QIC-2GB-DC	2.0 GB	42	SCSI-2	6/92
QIC-5GB-DC	5 GB	44	SCSI-2	12/92
QIC-4GB-DC	4 GB	45	SCSI-2	3/93
QIC-5210-DC	25 GB	144	SCSI-2	8/95

[1]Depending on length of tape.

storage capacity of 60 MB. It achieved a read/write speed of 90 inches per second and, with the QIC-02 interface, offered a data transfer rate of 720 kilobits per second.

The data density and number of tracks have increased over the years. The QIC-1000-DC packed 30 tracks across the tape at 36,000 bits per inch, allowing up to 1.2 GB per tape cartridge. Its speed was also increased to 2.8 megabits per second. Yet the QIC-1000-DC drives could read earlier QIC tapes. By 1989, the QIC committee had revamped the original QIC standard by approving 1,7 RRL encoding and higher coercivity, which allowed higher bit density, a higher number of tracks, and faster transfer rates. By 1995, the QIC standard became the QIC-5210-DC, which had 144 tracks and 76,200 bits per inch, producing 25 GB storage space. (See table 14.3 for a description of QIC data tapes and cartridges.)

The full-size QIC is too large to fit into a drive bay, so the QIC committee created the minicartridge, which measured 3.25″ × 2.5″ × 1.59″. Minicartridges are also referred to as DC 2000 cartridges. The QIC-40-MC was the first cartridge standard adopted. It fit into the 5.25″ drive bay and connected to the computer by using the floppy drive controller. Since floppy disk drives use MFM encoding, so did the QIC-40-MC. Unlike earlier tapes, QIC-40 specified the format for the data recorded on the tape, including how sectors were assigned to files and FAT for listing bad sectors. Thus the tapes had to be formatted, but they could be bought formatted or unformatted. These tapes could also be accessed randomly. The tape had to be moved to the proper sector, but each file did not have to be read sequentially. To increase storage capacity even further, the Sony Corporation introduced the 8 mm (.315-inch) tape. It used the same size cartridge, but the extra width allowed for more tracks. It became known as the QIC-Wide minicartridge. (See table 14.4 for a description of QIC minicartridges.)

In 1995, a number of tape and drive manufacturers, including Conner, Iomega, HP, 3M, and Sony, introduced Travan technology, which, unlike the standard QIC cartridge, measured 0.5″ × 3.6″ × 2.8″. The smaller front was inserted into the drive; the larger back contained the tape spools. The larger size allowed longer tapes and more data capacity. In addition, the Travan drive accepts standard DC 2000 cartridges and QIC-Wide cartridges.

TABLE 14.4 QIC minicartridges

Type of Cartridge	Capacity without Compression	Tracks	Interface	Original Adoption Date
QIC-40-MC	40 MB or 60 MB[1]	20	Floppy or optional card	6/86
QIC-80-MC	80 MB or 120 MB[1]	28	Floppy or optional card	2/88
QIC-128- MC	86 MB or 128 MB	32	SCSI or QIC	5/89
QIC-3030-MC	555 MB	40	SCSI-2 or QIC	4/91
QIC-3020-MC	500 MB	40	Floppy or IDE	6/91
QIC-3070-MC	4 GB	144	SCSI-2 or QIC	2/92
QIC-3010-MC	255 MB	40	Floppy or IDE	6/93
QIC-3040-MC	840 MB	42/52	SCSI-2 or QIC	12/93
QIC-3080-MC	1.6 GB	60	SCSI-2 or QIC	1/94
QIC-3110-MC	2 GB	48	SCSI-2 or QIC	1/94
QIC-3230-MC	15.5 GB	180	SCSI-2 or QIC	6/95
QIC-3095-MC	4 GB	72	SCSI-2 or QIC	12/95

[1]Depending on length of tape.

14.3.4 DIGITAL AUDIO TAPES (DAT)

The newest type of audio tape is the 8 mm **digital audio tape (DAT),** which uses the same helical scan technology as VCR tapes and has a storage capacity of up to 35 GB. The DAT standard has been developed and marketed primarily by Hewlett-Packard, which chairs the DDS (Digital Data Storage) Manufacturers Group that developed the DDS standards. Data is not recorded on the DAT tape in the MFM or RLL format; instead, bits of data received by the tape drive are assigned numerical values, or digits. These digits are then translated into a stream of electronic pulses that are placed on the tape. Later, when information is being restored to a computer system from the tape, the DAT tape drive translates these digits back into binary bits that can be stored on the computer.

Digital Data Storage (DDS) tapes are the newest standard for the digital audio tape. DDS-3 can hold 24 GB (the equivalent of over 40 CD-ROMs) and supports data transfer rates of 2 megabits per second, and it is only slightly larger than a credit card. In a DDS drive, the tape barely creeps along—it requires about three seconds to move one inch. The head drum spins at 2,000 revolutions per minute, putting down 1,869 tracks across a linear inch of tape, which can store 61 kilobits per inch. The main advantage of the DAT is its access speed and capacity.

One of the newest tapes is the *DLT (digital linear tape).* Designed for high-capacity, high-speed and highly reliable backup, DLTs are ½″ wide, have capacities of 35–70 GB compressed, and support data transfer rates of 5–10 megabits per second or more. Unfortunately, the drives are quite expensive and so are used primarily for network server backup.

14.3.5 INSTALLING TAPE DRIVES

Installing tape drives is not much different from installing other drives. They fit into an open drive bay or will be connected externally though the back of an expansion card. The power connected to the drive will be either a 3½″ or 5¼″ power connector for internal devices and an ac adapter for external devices. (Note: A few proprietary external tape drives are powered through the interface cable.)

Tape drives will usually use one of four interfaces: (1) QIC-standard (external), (2) floppy (internal), (3) SCSI adapter (internal and external), or (4) EIDE (internal). The floppy disk interface either connects to the unused connector on the floppy drive ribbon cable or will be attached with a special cable link-splitter. SCSI tape drives will have to have their termination and SCSI ID numbers configured; EIDE tape drives will have to be configured for either stand-alone, master, or slave. (See chapter 10.) Some drives will also require a SCSI-to-parallel port converter.

The next step in installing and configuring a tape drive is to install any drivers. This may involve running a setup program, adding lines to the AUTOEXEC.BAT/CONFIG. SYS file, and using the control panel (Add New Hardware or SCSI Devices). Lastly, backup software that will recognize the tape drive must be installed. Most drives include a backup software package, but you may choose to purchase a commercial package, which may offer more "bells and whistles."

14.3.6 TROUBLESHOOTING TAPE DRIVES

All tape drives are half-mechanic, half-electronic devices. Therefore, like any other drive, they can be a high-failure item. Also, the tapes and tape cartridges do not last forever. If a problem does occur, check the drive and drive interface documentation and the backup software documentation for help in diagnosing problem and interpreting error symptoms and messages.

Since tape drives and tape cartridges go bad, sometimes without warning, it is important to test the drive system from time to time. First, make sure that the files are actually on the tape. Many times, people have thought they were backing up the files only to find out when the computer fails that the tape is blank. Test the system by choosing a file that is not important and try to restore it to the hard drive. Lastly, since tapes do go bad, keep several backups.

EXAMPLE 14.1 The system does not recognize the drive.

First check the obvious. Make sure that the correct drivers are installed and the correct drive is selected. Next, make sure the power cable is connected properly and is supplying power. Lastly, check to see if the data or control cable is attached properly.

If the problem still exists and the drive had been working before and no hardware changes have been made to the computer, it is probably a hardware failure (the interface card or port, the power cable, the data or control cable, or the drive itself). To determine which one is causing the problem, swap one component at a time until the problem is discovered.

If the tape drive is being installed for the first time, it could be hardware failure or it could be a resource or drive conflict. The resource conflicts include I/O addresses, IRQs, DMAs, or memory addresses. The drive conflicts include terminating resistors (SCSI), SCSI ID numbers, and stand-alone/master/slave (EIDE) configurations.

EXAMPLE 14.2 The tape does not load or eject.

When the drive will not accept or reject a tape, there is usually a mechanical problem with the drive. Of course, before replacing the drive make sure that the power cable is connected to the drive and that nothing is jammed in the drive. If the problem appears to be the drive, it is easier to replace the drive than to repair it.

EXAMPLE 14.3 The drive writes to a write-protected tape.

To check the obvious, make sure that the tape *is* write-protected. If it is, the problem must be with the drive, specifically the sensor that detects the write-protect lever or the drive's logic board. In either case, it would be best to replace the drive.

EXAMPLE 14.4 You get read/write errors on the tape.

A read/write error is caused by the drive or the tape. As with floppy disk drives, the read/write heads become covered with magnetic oxide (caused by the contact of the read/write heads with the tape), dust particles, or smoke contamination. To remove these contaminations, you need to use a prepackaged cleaning cartridge. If the problem still exists, the tape must be bad or the drive must be bad. If the tape works in another tape drive, then you know the tape drive is bad. If not, the tape is bad.

14.4 BACK UP, BACK UP, BACK UP

The best method of recovering lost or corrupted data is to back up, back up, back up. When the system does not have a backup of its important files, it is often too late to recover them when disaster occurs. A backup of a system is an extra copy of data and programs. As a technician, consultant, or support person, you need to emphasize at every moment the importance of backing up a system. There are three important parts of a backup system:

1. Developing a backup plan
2. Sticking to the backup plan
3. Testing the backup system

When developing a backup plan, consider the following:

1. What equipment will be used?
2. How much data needs to be backed up?
3. How long will it take to do the backup?
4. How often must the data be backed up?
5. When will the backup take place?
6. Who will do that backup?

Whatever equipment, person, or method is chosen, make sure that the backup will be done. If the backup is not done for whatever reason, the best equipment, the best software, and the brightest person are wasted resources and the data is put at risk.

Backups can be done with floppy disks, extra hard drives (including network drives), compact disk drives, tape drives, and other forms of removable media. Due to the size of floppy disks, they are used to copy only a few files. Extra hard drives, compact disks, tape drives, and other forms of removable media are ideal for the storage of large or many files. If the entire hard drive is backed up on a regular basis, a backup software package can be used. A basic software package comes with Windows 95 and 98 and Windows NT, and one usually comes with the tape drives. There are also other commercial packages with more bells and whistles.

Question: How often should the backup be done?

Answer: How often the backup is done depends on the importance of the data. If many customers are loaded into a database that is constantly changed or the files represent the livelihood of a business, they should be backed up every day. If only a few letters are sent out during the week and none are vitally important, backing up once a week is enough.

Table 14.5 describes the four types of backup.

TABLE 14.5 Types of backup

Type	Description
Full	The full backup will back up all files selected and shut off the archive file attribute, indicating the file has been backed up.
Incremental	An incremental backup will back up the files selected if the archive file attribute is on (files changed since the last full or incremental backup). After the file has been backed up, it will shut off the file attribute, indicating that the file has been backed up.
Differential	A differential backup will back up the files selected if the archive file attribute is on (files changed since the last full backup). Unlike the incremental backup, it does not shut off the archive attribute.
Copy	A copy backup will back up the files selected regardless of the archive attribute and it will not shut off the archive attribute after the file has been copied. The copy backup is not typically used as part of a backup procedure. Instead, it would be used as an interim backup in case something goes wrong during major changes or upgrades.

EXAMPLE 14.5 You decide to back up the entire hard drive once a week on Friday, and you decide to use the full backup method. If the hard drive goes bad, you use the most recent backup to restore the hard drive.

EXAMPLE 14.6 You decide to back up the entire hard drive once a week on Friday, and you decide to use the incremental method. Therefore, you perform a full backup on week 1. This will shut off all of the archive attributes, indicating that all of the files have been backed up. On week 2, week 3, and week 4, you perform incremental backups using a different tape or disk. Since the incremental backup turns the archive attribute off, only new files and changed files are backed up. Therefore, all four backups make up the entire backup. It is much quicker to back up a drive using an incremental backup than a full one. Of course, if the hard drive fails, you must use backups 1, 2, 3, and 4 to restore the entire hard drive.

EXAMPLE 14.7 You decide to back up the entire hard drive once a week on Friday, and you decide to use the differential method. Therefore, you perform a full backup on week 1. This will shut off all the archive attributes, indicating that all the files have been backed up. On week 2, week 3, and week 4, you perform differential backups using a different tape or disk. Since the differential backup does not turn off the archive attribute, it backs up the new files and the files changed since the last full backup. Therefore, the full backup and the last differential backup make up the entire backup. It is much quicker to back up a drive using a differential backup than a full backup but slower than using an incremental backup. If the hard drive fails, you must restore backup 1 and the last differential backup to restore the entire hard drive.

After the backups are complete, check to see that they actually worked by selecting a nonessential file and restoring it to the hard drive. This will reveal empty backups or a faulty backup/restore device. Keep more than one backup. Tapes and disks do fail. One technique is to rotate through three sets of backups. If you perform a full backup once a week, you would then use three sets of backup tapes or disks. During week 1, you would use tape or disk 1. During week 2, you would use tape or disk 2, and during week 3, you would use tape or disk 3. On week four, you start over and use tape or disk 1. If you have to restore a hard drive and the tape or disk fails, you can always go to the tape or disk from the week before. If the data are important enough, consider keeping a backup set in a fireproof safe off-site.

SUMMARY

1. Because data represent hours of work and the information is sometimes irreplaceable, data is the most important part of the computer.
2. A virus is a program designed to replicate and spread, generally without the knowledge or permission of the user.
3. Some viruses are cute, some are annoying, and others are disastrous.
4. A boot sector virus infects the computer by rebooting from an infected diskette.
5. File infector viruses attach themselves to or replace executable files.
6. A multipartite virus has the characteristics of both boot sector viruses and file viruses.
7. The macro viruses are the newest strain of viruses and currently are the most common type of virus. Unlike previous viruses, macro viruses are stored in a data document and spread when the infected documents are transferred.
8. The Trojan horse virus is a program that appears to be legitimate software, such as a game or useful utility. Unfortunately, when you run the Trojan horse and the trigger event occurs, the program will do its damage.
9. A virus hoax is a letter or e-mail message warning you about a virus that does not exist.
10. Antivirus software will detect and remove viruses and help protect the computer against viruses.
11. Antivirus software must be continually updated.

12. Backing up a system is making an extra copy of data and programs.
13. The best way to protect data is to perform a backup.
14. Backups can be performed with floppy disks, hard disks, compact disks, removable disks, and tapes.
15. Tapes are ideal for backing up hard drives on a regular basis because they are relatively inexpensive, easy to use, and offer large storage capacities.
16. Tape drives read and write to a long magnetic tape.
17. Several standards have been developed for tapes and tape drives, including the quarter-inch cartridge (QIC) and the digital audio tape (DAT).
18. Tapes are divided into parallel tracks across the width of the tape. The number of tracks varies with the drive and the standard (parallel, serpentine, or helical scan) it follows.
19. The full-size quarter-inch cartridge standardized by the QIC Committee is also referred to as the DC 6000 cartridge. The DC stands for data cartridge.
20. Because the full-size QIC is too large to fit into a drive bay, the QIC committee created the minicartridge, also referred to as the DC 2000 cartridge.
21. Digital audio tape (DAT) uses the same technology as a VCR tape (helical scan).
22. A tape backup will use a QIC, floppy, SCSI, or EIDE interface.
23. After backups are completed, you should check that the backups actually worked.

QUESTIONS

1. What is the most important part of the computer?
   a. the microprocessor
   b. the hard drive
   c. the RAM
   d. the data
2. The best method for protecting the data is:
   a. RAID
   b. back up, back up, back up
   c. a surge protector
   d. antivirus software
3. A small program that replicates itself and sometimes has destructive tendencies is:
   a. a macro
   b. a TSR
   c. a device driver
   d. a virus
4. Which of the following is *not* a symptom of a virus?
   a. the computer fails to boot
   b. files are corrupted
   c. the system is slower than normal
   d. a disk cannot be read
   e. the monitor bursts into flames
5. Which of the following statements is *not* true?
   a. a virus cannot infect a write-protected disk
   b. a virus can hide in the CMOS RAM
   c. opening an e-mail message cannot infect a system with a virus
   d. a virus cannot infect a compressed file
6. Which statement best describes a boot sector virus?
   a. boot sector viruses are spawned from a bad sector in the boot sector
   b. a boot sector virus replaces the volume's boot sector program with its own and is loaded into RAM upon boot-up
   c. unlike file infector viruses, the boot sector virus does not replicate
   d. boot sector viruses only cause the volume not to boot but are not harmful to data
   e. boot sector viruses only cause the volume not to be a volume but are not harmful to data
7. A virus that infects both the boot sector and a file is known as a:
   a. multipartite virus
   b. macro virus
   c. stealth virus
   d. polymorphic virus
   e. Trojan horse virus
8. A Trojan horse virus is:
   a. a virus that uses the term *Trojan* or shows a wooden Trojan horse before doing damage
   b. the first recorded virus

    c. a virus that appears as a legitimate program but harms the computer when it is executed

    d. a virus that replicates when it is executed

9. To protect yourself from a virus, you should do the following *except:*
    a. use pirated software
    b. not boot from or access a floppy disk of unknown origin
    c. use an antivirus software package
    d. educate your fellow users

10. You suspect a virus has entered your computer. Where can the virus *not* reside?
    a. ROM BIOS   c. floppy disks
    b. boot sector   d. program files

11. Which is ideal for backing up an entire hard drive?
    a. Zip drive   c. RAID
    b. second hard drive   d. tape drive

12. Which of the following records using one track then gets to the end of the tape and proceeds to the next track?
    a. parallel   c. helical scan
    b. serpentine   d. none of the above

13. Which of the following records data much like a VCR does?
    a. parallel   c. helical scan
    b. serpentine   d. none of the above

14. The full-size quarter-inch cartridge is known as:
    a. DC 2000   c. Travan
    b. DC 6000   d. DAT

15. The newest type of tape, which offers large capacities within a small cartridge, is:
    a. DAT   c. CD
    b. quarter-inch   d. open-face

16. When installing an EIDE tape drive, you must configure the drive as a:
    a. master   c. stand-alone
    b. slave   d. depends on the system

17. *True or False*—When troubleshooting a tape drive, never suspect the tape because they rarely go bad.

18. You have tried several tapes and the tape drive does not read any of them. What is the first thing you should do?
    a. buy a new pack of tapes and try them   c. replace the tape drive
    b. format the tape   d. clean the tape drive

19. After backing up a drive, you should occasionally:
    a. restore a nonessential file to the hard drive
    b. reformat the hard drive
    c. shut down the system
    d. reformat the tape

20. The archive attribute is the attribute that indicates whether a file is backed up. Which of the following backups does *not* shut off the archive attribute?
    a. full   c. differential
    b. incremental   d. none of the above

HANDS-ON EXERCISES

Exercise 1: Installing an Antivirus Software Package

1. Install an antivirus software package.
2. Find and download the update for the package.
3. Install the update.

Exercise 2: Finding and Removing Viruses

1. Use the antivirus software package to check your hard drives for viruses.
2. Insert a formatted floppy disk in drive A and use the antivirus software package to check the disk for viruses.
3. Get an infected disk from your instructor and remove the virus from the disk.

Exercise 3: Researching Viruses

1. Read the following Internet document on viruses:

    http://www.drsolomon.com/vircen/vanalyse/va002.html

2. Read the following Internet document on macro viruses:

    http://www.drsolomon.com/vircen/vanalyse/macvir.html

3. Load the following Internet document:

    http://www.datafellows.com/news/hoax/

    and read the introduction section on virus hoaxes and the section on the Good Times Virus hoax.

4. Load the following Internet document:

    http://www.drsolomon.com/vircen/enc/

5. Research the following viruses:

Michelangelo	Stoned
Junkie	Monkey
Wazzu	CAPS
Melissa	

6. Load the following Internet document:

    http://www.microsoft.com/msoffice/antivirus.asp

7. Download the available Microsoft Antivirus Tools for Microsoft Word.

Exercise 4: Installing a Backup Tape Drive

1. Configure and physically install the tape backup drive using a floppy, EIDE, SCSI, or proprietary interface.
2. Install any drivers needed to activate the tape backup drive.
3. Install a backup software package that supports the tape drive.
4. Back up the entire hard drive using the backup software package (full backup).
5. Choose several nonessential files from the hard drive and delete them.
6. Using the tape drive, restore the deleted files.
7. Create or add three files and change at least two others.
8. Select all files on the hard drives, but choose an incremental backup to back up only the new or changed files.
9. Remove the tape drive from the system.

Exercise 5: Backing Up the Hard Drive

This exercise requires Windows 3.XX or Windows 95 and 98 loaded on drive C.

1. Create a DATA directory on the C drive.
2. In the DATA directory, create a PICTURE directory and a TEXT directory.
3. Copy all files that have a BMP filename extension from the C:\WINDOWS directory to the PICTURE directory.
4. Copy all of the files that have a TXT filename extension from the C:\WINDOWS directory to the TEXT directory.
5. Create a CHANGE.TXT file in the TEXT directory. Include your name in the text file.
6. Start the backup software that comes with tape drive or the Windows 95 and 98 Backup program.
7. Select the entire hard drive so that it can be backed up. Determine the total number of bytes. (Do not back up the drive.)
8. Deselect the hard drive.

9. Select the PICTURE and DATA directories, including the files within the PICTURE and DATA directories. Determine the total number of bytes.
10. Back up the selected files to a tape or to floppy disks.
11. Determine the status of the Archive attribute of the CHANGE.TXT file.
12. Edit the CHANGE.TXT file, add today's date into the file, and save the file.
13. Determine the status of the archive attribute of the CHANGE.TXT file.
14. Create a file called NEW.TXT in the TEXT directory.
15. Determine the status of the archive attribute of the NEW.TXT file.
16. Back up the first name directory using an incremental backup.
17. Delete the TEXT directory.
18. Restore the TEXT directory from the tape or disks.

15   The Video System

INTRODUCTION

The video system, consisting of the monitor and video card, displays the results of computing. The monitor, a device similar to a television, is the computer's primary output device and the user's direct link to the computer. The video card is the component that connects the monitor to the rest of the computer. The quality of the monitor greatly affects the productivity of the user.

OBJECTIVES

1. Compare and contrast the two types of video display.
2. Using the monitor controls, adjust the contrast, brightness, horizontal and vertical positioning, horizontal and vertical size, and pincushioning.
3. Compare and contrast passive LCD screens and active LCD screens.
4. Define pixels, aspect ratio, resolution, dot pitch, and convergence.
5. List the advantages and disadvantages of text mode and graphics mode.

6. Define refresh rate and explain how it relates to flicker.
7. Enable and adjust the power management features within the CMOS setup program.
8. Given a bit depth, calculate the total number of colors that can be used by the system.
9. Given the resolution and bit depth of a video system, calculate the amount of video RAM needed.
10. List the resolution and number of colors used by the different video systems.
11. Explain the difference between a standard VGA card and a video accelerator.
12. List and compare the different forms of RAM used on video cards.
13. List the different buses used with video cards and explain which is the best one to use.
14. Install a video card and monitor.
15. Open a monitor and discharge it.
16. Test a video system.
17. Determine and correct video system problems.

15.1   THE MONITOR

The video system, which displays the results of computing, consists of the monitor and video card. The **monitor,** which connects to the video card, is the computer's primary output device. It is sometimes referred to as a *display* or *video*. Since the user must use the monitor to see results, the monitor is the user's direct link to the computer.

Like televisions, the size of the monitor is measured diagonally across the screen. (See fig. 15.1.) The most popular sizes for monitors are 14″, 15″, 17″, and 21″. Since some monitors become significantly distorted near the edges of the screen, they have a black border around the edges, reducing the size of the actual picture.

Monitors are of two types, cathode ray tube (CRT) and liquid crystal display (LCD). CRTs are the displays that resemble a television. They are usually found on desktop and tower computers. LCD displays are usually found on laptop and notebook computers and are the most expensive component of a portable computer.

15.1.1   THE CRT MONITOR

The **cathode-ray tube (CRT)** inside the monitor consists of an electronic screen that is lined with a phosphorescent material. (See fig. 15.2.) An electron gun shoots electrons at the phosphorescent material and the material glows as it is struck. The intensity of the electron beam determines the intensity of the color produced. Since the phosphorescent material will glow for only a fraction of a second, it has to be constantly recharged.

To aim and focus the beams of electrons, the CRT uses a magnetic deflection yoke to bend the path of the electrons with electromagnetic fields. (See fig. 15.3.) To keep the electron beams from affecting nearby pixels on the screen, the CRT uses a shadow mask or an aperture grill to focus the beams. The most commonly used is the **shadow mask,** a fine metal mesh with openings that line up with the pixels. The **aperture grill** is made up of hundreds of fine metal strips that run vertically from the top of the screen to the bottom. The aperture grill allows for a brighter monitor and less glare from a flat vertical screen,

FIGURE 15.1   Monitor size is determined by measuring diagonally across the screen

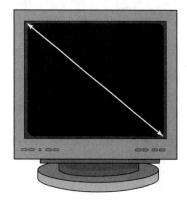

FIGURE 15.2   Inside the CRT
monitor

but it requires one or more stabilizing wires, which run horizontally across the screen, to prevent the grill from vibrating. The stabilizing wires may show as extremely faint lines on the screen, although they usually are noticeable only on a full white screen.

Some monitors have a curved screen; some newer monitors are flat. The curved screens are less expensive, but they tend to have more glare from overhead lights than flat screens do. The glare makes it harder to see the image on the screen and eventually leads to eyestrain and fatigue. To reduce the surface glare, most monitor screens have a special film or coating. (Note: The screen should be cleaned only with a water-dampened cloth or a cloth with a special cleaning solution made for monitors that will not remove the coating. Do not use Windex glass cleaner or 409 multipurpose cleaner.)

The CRT monitor can generate a lot of heat, so every monitor case has special ventilation holes to allow for the cooling of the system components. If the holes are covered or blocked, the monitor will overheat, causing damage to the monitor. CRT monitors also produce large amounts of electromagnetic radiation. To someone who spends a lot of time around a monitor that is on, the electromagnetic radiation can be harmful over a period of time. Today, monitors are being designed to reduce the amount of electromagnetic radiation.

As on a television, the sharpness, brightness, contrast, vertical and horizontal position (sometimes known as vertical and horizontal center), vertical and horizontal size, and pin cushioning (straightness of the vertical and horizontal lines) of a monitor can be adjusted with analog or digital controls. Most of these controls are located at the front of the monitor, but they may also be found at the back or the side of the monitor or inside the monitor.

FIGURE 15.3   A CRT uses an electron gun to shoot electrons at a phosphorescent screen

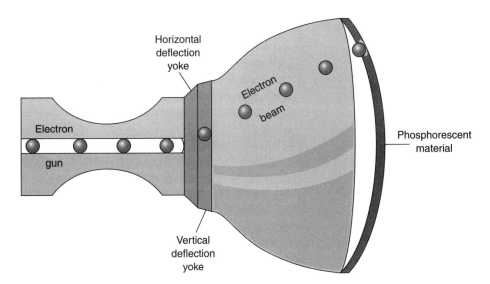

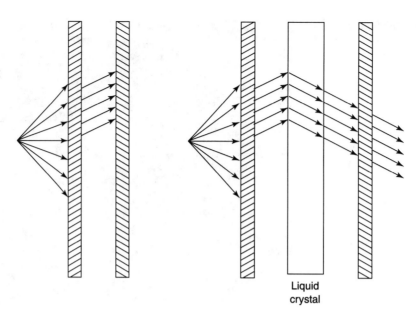

FIGURE 15.4 In the left-hand picture, light is not allowed through because the polarizing filters let light in at two different angles. In the picture on the right, liquid crystal bends the light to the angle of the second filter.

Liquid crystal

Analog controls are usually knobs; a digital control is a single menu button that selects the feature to change with up and down arrows for adjusting the feature. The digital controls are not always intuitive, but they do reduce the number of analog controls on the monitor.

15.1.2 THE LCD PANEL

LCD stands for **liquid crystal display,** which uses **liquid crystal (LC),** an organic material that has the characteristics of both a liquid and a solid. Liquid crystal consists of a large array of rod-shaped molecules. It appears to be a liquid but has a crystalline molecular structure usually found in solid objects. In an LCD display, the liquid crystal material is pressed between two pieces of clear plastic, which are polarized. The polarized plastic allows light to vibrate in only one way. Tiny grooves in the plastic sheets align the molecules. When electricity is sent through the LC material, the molecules twist, which will bend any light shown through them. When the electricity is stopped, the molecules go back to their normal orientation.

As a light **(backlit light)** is shone through the first layer of polarized plastic, it passes through a filter (allowing the light to shine in only one direction) and into the LC material. The second polarized sheet bends the light to a different angle from that of the first sheet. Normally, when electricity is not being applied to the LC material, the light passes through the first sheet and LC material but cannot pass through the second polarized sheet. When electricity is applied, the LC molecules twist, bending the light to the proper angle so that it can pass through the second sheet. The amount of electricity controls the amount of the twist and the intensity of the light. (See fig. 15.4.)

Passive matrix displays use row and column electrodes to send electricity through the LC material. An electrode is a conductor used to establish electrical contact with a non-metallic part of a circuit. Much like CRT monitors, each cell in the matrix has to be constantly refreshed and in sequence. Unfortunately, the electrical charges fade quickly, causing colors to look faded. To increase the brightness, some passive matrix displays use double-scan, a technique that splits the screen into a top half and a bottom half and allows both halves to be refreshed at the same time. Since the cells can be refreshed quicker, the screen is brighter and has a quicker response time.

Active matrix displays, known as *thin-film transistor (TFT) displays,* have a rear glass screen to hold the electrodes for each cell and a front glass screen that contains a single, large common electrode for every screen element. To control the flow of electricity, each cell uses a transistor, which acts as an on/off switch. Since the transistor can provide a constant charge that does not need refreshing, colors are brighter. As a result, the screen can be viewed at an angle of up to 45° and has a contrast of 40:1. This means that the brightness of an "on" pixel is 40 times greater than that of an "off" pixel. The disadvantage of active matrix displays is cost and, because the TFTs block a fraction of the light, the need for a more intense backlighting system.

When handling an LCD display, be careful not to scratch the surface and make sure that you do not expose the screen to high amounts of force or pressure, since this may crack the LCD panel. Lastly, to clean the LCD screen, you should use a water-dampened lint-free cloth or a lint-free cloth with isopropyl alcohol or ethyl alcohol.

15.1.3   PIXELS AND THE MONITOR RESOLUTION

The image (text, lines, boxes, and pictures) on the monitor is made up of many dots called **picture elements** or **pixels.** (See fig. 15.5.) The number of pixels that can be displayed on the screen at one time is called the **resolution** of the screen. The resolution consists of two numbers, the number of pixels going from left to right and the number of pixels going from top to bottom. The **aspect ratio** of most monitors is 4:3. This means that for every four pixels going across the screen, there are three pixels going down. The horizontal number of pixels divided by the vertical number of pixels is 1.33; therefore, if there are 480 pixels vertically, the number of pixels going across would be $480 \times 1.33 = 640$ pixels. (See table 15.1)

Another term relating to the resolution of the monitor is the monitor's **dot pitch.** Dot pitch is the distance between the pixels. (See fig. 15.5.) Typical values range from .25 mm to .41 mm. If the dot pitch is too large, the picture may be "grainy." If the dot pitch is too small, the monitor tends to have decreased brightness and contrast. A good dot pitch is between .28 and .31 mm. **Convergence** describes the clarity and sharpness of each pixel. It is the capability of the color monitor to focus the three colored electron beams into a single point. If a monitor has poor convergence, the picture will be fuzzy and blurry.

Question: If a VGA monitor has a resolution of 640×480, how many pixels does it have?

Answer: A screen with a resolution of 640×480 has 640 pixels going across and 480 pixels going down. Multiplying these two numbers gives a total of 307,200 pixels on the screen.

FIGURE 15.5   Picture elements (pixels) make up images on the screen

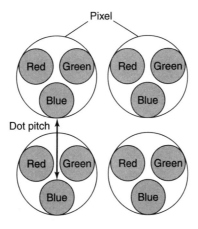

TABLE 15.1   Typical resolution and aspect ratios

Resolution	Number of Pixels	Aspect Ratio
320 × 200	64,000	8:5
640 × 480	307,200	4:3
800 × 600	480,000	4:3
1024 × 768	786,432	4:3
1280 × 1024	1,310,720	5:4
1600 × 1200	1,920,000	4:3

Question: Is a monitor with a higher resolution better than a monitor with a lower resolution?

Answer: Typically, a monitor with a higher resolution is a better monitor, although the higher resolution may not always be the best resolution to use. Most programs are made to work with a certain resolution and will not adjust for a different one. For example, a Windows application that takes up the entire 640 pixels going across and 480 pixels going down would fill the entire screen. At a higher resolution, such as 1024 × 768, the program still displays the box using 640 pixels going across and 480 pixels going down. The problem is that the box would be 38% smaller. If software is made for a monitor with a higher resolution and can adjust to the higher resolution proportionately, the picture tends to be sharper and more detailed than it is on a monitor with a lower resolution.

As the computer is operating, the video system runs in either text mode or graphics mode. When the computer is first turned on or when it is running a command-driven operating system (such as DOS), the video system uses text mode, typically displaying 25 rows of 80 characters (80 × 25). Most monitors can also support other modes, such as 43 rows of 80 characters (80 × 43). The instructions (ROM BIOS, operating system, or software programs) specify what characters are to be shown on the screen by sending the ASCII character and its location (row and column) to the video card. The pixel information, defined in the video ROM BIOS, is then sent from the video card to the monitor. Text mode is simple and fast, but its simplicity limits it to the set of predefined ASCII characters.

Question: How much information is used by a video system that runs in 80 × 25 text mode?

Answer: In this mode, there can be a total of 80 × 25 = 2,000 characters at any one time. Since each character (ASCII character) uses one byte to define it, the entire screen can display 2,000 bytes of data.

The GUI operating system or environments (Windows 3.XX, Windows 95 and 98, and Windows NT) and most programs run in graphics mode. In graphics mode, the information that is to be displayed is broken down into pixels and the pixel information is sent to the video card. The video card will then send the proper signals to the monitor. Graphics mode is more complicated than text mode and can use the pixels to make any form of text or picture.

All video systems support the text and graphics modes at different resolutions. This allows one program to use one resolution while another program uses another resolution. The maximum resolution that a monitor can display is determined by its technology, its size (larger monitors can contain more pixels), the capabilities of the video card (including the amount of video memory), and the software being used. (Note: The resolution supported by the monitor must match the resolution supported by the video card.)

15.1.4 REFRESH RATE

In order to draw the entire screen before the phosphorescent material fades, the electron guns must be fast. The number of times that the screen is redrawn in a second is referred to as the **refresh rate,** which is measured in hertz (Hz). If the refresh rate is too low, the electron guns do not recharge the phosphorescent material before it fades, which causes the monitor to flicker. Although the flicker is hardly noticeable, it can lead to eyestrain. To avoid flickering, a refresh rate with at least 70 Hz is required. The Video Electronics Standards Association (VESA) has established an 85 Hz refresh rate as the standard for flicker-free monitors. Unfortunately, few video systems support 85 Hz at high resolutions.

High-quality monitors that support high resolutions refresh the screen one line at a time, from top to bottom. This is called **noninterlacing** or conventional mode. Some monitors use **interlacing** to refresh the screen, which redraws the screen in two sweeps, refreshing every other line. During the first sweep, the monitor refreshes the odd-numbered lines; during the second sweep, it refreshes the even-numbered lines. The refresh rate is lower as a result, allowing for a cheaper monitor. Unfortunately, the monitor's reaction speed is reduced, which may introduce flicker.

15.1.5 MONITOR BURN-IN AND SCREEN SAVERS

Older monitors, particularly monochrome monitors, were susceptible to burn-in when a particular image was displayed on a screen for a long time, which burned out the phosphorescent material and left behind a ghost image. To prevent this problem, **screen savers** were used to blank the screen or to provide a constant moving pattern. Although screens savers are not needed today, hundreds are available and with every conceivable theme. The screen saver has therefore progressed to a form of entertainment.

15.1.6 DPMS

The monitor, like the computer case, uses a power supply. To help reduce power consumption, the Environmental Protection Agency (EPA) began a program called Energy Star to certify PCs and monitors that reduce power consumption. These PCs are sometimes called **green PCs,** and the Energy Star logo appears on the screen when the monitor is initialized by the computer.

In an effort to conserve power, Intel and Microsoft created the **advanced power management (APM)** standard that allows the system ROM BIOS (enabled in the CMOS setup program) or software to manage the power consumption of the system. Part of the APM standard is the **display power management system (DPMS)** standard, which was introduced by the Video Electronics Standard Association (VESA). DPMS allows the monitor to go into stand-by mode (which uses less power than the normal operational state) and suspend or shut-down mode (which turns the monitor off) during periods of inactivity.

15.2 THE VIDEO CARD

The **video card** is the component that takes the visual output of the computer and sends it to the monitor. It tells the monitor which pixels to light up, what color the pixels should be, and what intensity they should have. The video card is an expansion card or is built into the motherboard. It is identified with its 3-row, 15-pin female port (VGA or SVGA) and 2-row, 9-pin female port (monochrome, CGA, or EGA). (See fig. 15.6.)

15.2.1 NUMBER OF COLORS

All monitors can be classified as either monochrome or color. **Monochrome** monitors display two colors, one for the background and one for the foreground. The background color is black, and the foreground color is white, green, or amber. A gray-scale monitor, a special

FIGURE 15.6 PCI video card

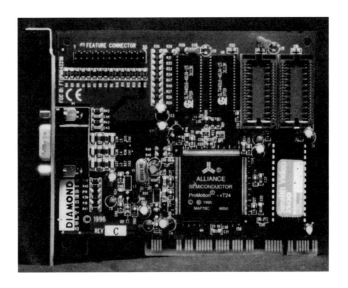

TABLE 15.2　Color depth

Common Name	Color Depth	Number of Displayed Colors	Bytes of Storage per Pixel
Monochrome	1 bit	2	⅛ byte
16 colors (VGA mode)	4 bits	16	½ byte
256 colors	8 bits	256	1 byte
High color	16 bits	65,536	2 bytes
True color	24 bits	16,777,216	3 bytes

kind of monochrome monitor, can display different shades of white. Depending on the type of video system, it can support either up to 64 or up to 256 different shades.

The most common type of monitor is the color monitor. Depending on the monitor and video card, the monitor can display from 4 to 16 million colors. The pixel of a color monitor is actually made of a red, a green, and a blue dot. As the three colors are mixed at various intensities, they can produce virtually any color. When all three colors are at the highest intensity, the color displayed is white. If all colors are at the lowest intensity, the color displayed is black.

Color depth, or bit depth, is the amount of information that determines the color of a pixel. The more colors each pixel can show, the more colors the screen can show and the more shades of the same color, which can produce a more realistic, detailed picture. However, the higher number of bits required to give each pixel a higher color depth requires more video memory for the video system to store the pixel's information and more processing by the computer. (See table 15.2.)

Question: How much memory is required for a monochrome monitor with a resolution of 640 × 480?

Answer: A monochrome monitor displays a single color, which represents either *on* or *off*. The data to describe the status of the pixel is stored as one bit of information (the 0 indicates the pixel is off and the 1 indicates the pixel is on). A 640 × 480 screen resolution with 307,200 dots will require 307,200 dots, or 38,400 bytes (8 bits per byte).

Early color monitors were digital devices that could show only a set number of predetermined colors. The color of the pixel was specified by a binary code. VGA monitors and Super VGA monitors are analog devices capable of showing an unlimited number of colors. The VGA system can display 16 colors at a resolution of 640 × 480 or 256 colors at a resolution of 320 × 200. As an image is drawn on the screen, a binary code is sent to the video card. The video card then looks up the color in a palette (preselected colors) to define the intensities of the red, green, and blue colors of the pixel and sends that information to the monitor. If a picture has more than 256 unique colors, it can still be displayed on a 256-color video system. The other colors are created by choosing the 256 closest colors and using dithering. Dithering is the process of creating more colors and shades by intermixing colors. Unfortunately, these pictures often look grainy or patchy.

Question: How much information is required for a monitor with a resolution of 640 × 480 that displays up to 256 colors?

Answer: A binary number of eight 0s and 1s has 256 different combinations (each combination representing a particular color), so each pixel uses 1 byte of information. The monitor has 307,200 pixels, so it requires 307,200 pixels × 1 byte per pixel, or 307,200 bytes.

For high-quality pictures, the computer would use high color or true color. **High color** uses 16 bits to define the color of the pixel, and the 16 bits allow 65,536 different combinations of 0s and 1s, or 65,536 different colors. Blue and red use 5 bits each to specify 32 different intensities or shades, while green uses 6 bits to define 64 intensities. (Note: Some systems may use a 15-bit model, which allows only 32,768 different colors.) **True color** uses three bytes to define each pixel, which allows up to 16,777,216 colors. Since each pixel uses three bytes of data, each color (blue, red, and green) is defined with a 1-byte binary code that specifies 256 different intensities.

15.2.2 VIDEO MEMORY

The amount of information sent to the monitor in the early PCs was extremely small. A monitor in text mode (25 rows of 80 characters) had only 2,000 characters, which required only 2,000 bytes of data. On these older systems, the video data was generated by the microprocessor and stored in the reserve memory. The data was then constantly read by the video card and sent to the monitor to be displayed.

As computers shifted from text mode to graphics, and systems with higher resolutions and more colors were developed, the reserve memory was not big enough to hold the increased video data. Therefore, the modern video card contains **video memory** (also called **frame buffer**). For example, a VGA video system with a maximum resolution of 640 × 480 (307,200 pixels) can show 16 colors (4 bits), requiring a minimum of 153,600 bytes of video memory. Because video cards do not come with exactly 153,600 bytes, a card with 256 KB (or higher) would be used. If the monitor is set at 1024 × 768 (786,432 pixels) and displays 16 million colors (24 bit), the video card requires a minimum of 2,359,296 bytes. Therefore, a 3 or 4 MB (or more) video card would have to be used. (Note: Modern video cards perform some of the video processing, so some higher-end video cards also use the video memory for processing.)

The **RAMDAC** (RAM digital–analog converter), located on the video card, translates the digital information into the analog information used by the monitor. It uses a lookup table located within the video ROM BIOS to determine the voltage intensities for each of the primary colors (red, green, and blue). The speed of the video card, or video card bandwidth, is the amount of data that can be generated by the video card and sent to the monitor. It depends mainly on the speed of the RAMDAC, the speed of the RAM, and the speed of the PC interface.

> **Question:** A monitor has a resolution of 640 × 480 and a bit depth of 4 bits (16 colors). How much bandwidth is required if the picture is being redrawn at a rate of 10 updates per second?
>
> **Answer:** There are 307,200 pixels on the screen using 307,200 pixels × .5 bytes = 153,600 bytes of data at one time. Since the screen must be redrawn 10 times per second, there is required bus bandwidth of 153,600 bytes × 10 = 1.54 MB per second.

> **Question:** A monitor is using a resolution of 1,024 × 768 with a bit depth of 24 bits (16 million colors). How much bandwidth is required if a real-time video is being shown at 30 frames per second?
>
> **Answer:** There are 786,432 pixels on the screen using 786,432 pixels × 3 bytes = 2,359,296 bytes of data at one time. The screen must be redrawn 30 times per second, so there is a required bandwidth of 2,359,296 bytes × 30 = 70.8 MB per second.

15.2.3 VIDEO RAM

Video RAM, much like regular RAM, can be described by the memory technology used and its access time. The older and slower video cards use the standard **dynamic RAM (DRAM)** chip, specifically **fast page mode DRAM (FPM DRAM)** and **extended data out (EDO) RAM.** It is single ported (it can do only one access at a time) and has a low speed and small access width. Another type of RAM chip is **video RAM (VRAM).** Video RAM, usually used on video cards, is a special form of DRAM that has two separate data ports. One port is dedicated to updating the image on the screen while the other one is used for changing the image data stored in the RAM on the video card. This dual-ported design gives higher performance (up to 40%) than DRAM. (Note: Don't confuse VRAM, a type of memory used in video cards, and the generic term *video memory,* which refers to memory in the video system.)

A newer type of video RAM is **synchronous graphics RAM (SGRAM).** Memory transfers take place faster with SGRAM, and it incorporates performance-enhancing features like the acceleration features built into the video card. Although it is single ported, it offers performance close to VRAM because it can open two memory pages at the same time, simulating a dual-port design.

A newer version of VRAM is **Windows RAM (WRAM)** developed by Samsung and used on high-end video cards. It has a dual-color block write to perform very fast pattern and text fills and can perform fast buffer-to-buffer transfers for video and double-buffered 3D animation. As a result, WRAM offers 25% more bandwidth than VRAM and up to a 40% to 50% increase in performance when doing text drawing and block fills. In addition, WRAM is cheaper than VRAM.

Lastly, there is **multibank DRAM (MDRAM).** Rather than using a single block of video memory, MDRAM breaks its memory into multiple 32 KB banks that can be accessed independently. This allows interleaving of the RAM. (Interleaving is two banks working together.) When one bank is getting ready for access, the other bank is being accessed. MDRAM also allows video cards to have customized memory sizes, so there is no wasted RAM, which reduces the cost of the video card.

Much like normal RAM used on the motherboard, the video RAM chips are available in different access speeds. The lower the access speed, the faster the RAM. Although the access speed is a factor in video card performance, it is not as important as the type of technology used in the RAM chip.

15.2.4 VIDEO CARD INTERFACE

The video card interface is *the* interface to the rest of the computer. Initially, the PC used the PC bus or 8-bit ISA and 16-bit ISA bus to transfer data between the system and the video card. The 16-bit ISA bus had a 16-bit data path, ran at 8 MHz, and had a maximum bandwidth of 8.33 MB per second. As higher resolutions were introduced and the number of colors was increased, the ISA bus quickly became a bottleneck in the transferring of data between the microprocessor and the video card. To overcome the video bottleneck, the Micro Channel Architecture (MCA) and the EISA buses were introduced. Although these cards had 32-bit access and could transfer data more quickly than the ISA bus, the performance increase was not great enough to justify the increased cost.

Newer machines use a local bus video card. Since the local bus was initially designed to run at or near the speed of the microprocessor and had at least a 32-bit data bus, it was far faster than anything previously used in the PC. The first widely accepted local bus was the **VESA local bus (VL bus)** created by the **Video Electronics Standards Association (VESA),** which was originally formed to standardize Super VGA monitors. Its interest in developing a local bus was to improve video performance. The VESA local bus was built around the 486 microprocessor and was intended to supplement the existing slots (ISA, EISA, or MCA). When coupled with the ISA slot, the VESA slot was directly in line with it. Because it was built to accommodate the 486, the VESA used a 32-bit data bus to match the microprocessor and ran at the same speed. In addition to its faster speed and larger data bus, the VESA also offered burst mode and bus mastering. While in burst mode, sequential data was transferred faster by accessing one memory address to transfer up to four pieces of data. In burst mode at 33 MHz, the VESA bus could transfer up to 105.6 MB per second. In nonburst mode it could transfer only up to 66 MB per second. Both speeds were far greater than the ISA's 8.33 MB per second. Bus mastering is an advanced form of DMA that allows a data transfer to occur without aid from the microprocessor. As a result, the microprocessor can do something as the data transfer takes place, increasing the overall performance of the system.

Today, the term *local bus,* usually refers to the **peripheral component interconnect (PCI)** local bus, which is usually found on Pentium machines. The PCI slot was developed by Intel and designed to eventually replace the older bus designs. Unlike the VESA, the PCI local bus is not an extension of any other slot; it is offset from the normal ISA, MCA, or EISA connector. The PCI bus is available in 32 bits (486 machines and some early Pentium machines) and 64 bits. The PCI bus is controlled by a PCI bridge or controller. To increase performance, the microprocessor writes data to a PCI device by immediately storing the data in the controller buffer of the bus. While the microprocessor goes on to its next operation, the stored data is then fed to the PCI device. Much like the VLB, the PCI bus also supports burst mode and bus mastering.

The newest type of bus or interface is the **accelerated graphics port (AGP).** AGP is based on the PCI 2.1 64-bit extension, which has a 64-bit interface that will run at 66 MHz and 100 MHz. It quadruples the theoretical bandwidth of current PCI buses and has the potential to go even higher. (See chapter 8 for more information.)

15.2.5 VIDEO ACCELERATORS AND COPROCESSORS

As previous sections have pointed out, modern video systems with their high resolution and number of colors require massive amounts of information that must be processed by the microprocessor and transferred to the video card and monitor. Video cards now include coprocessors to help process the video data. Instead of the microprocessor processing each individual pixel and then sending the information to the video card, these cards, usually referred to as *accelerators,* perform the same processing with instructions consisting of only a few bytes. For example, let's say you need to draw a line 100 pixels long on the computer screen. Instead of the microprocessor calculating all 100 pixels one by one, the microprocessor would send an instruction to the coprocessor on the video card. The instruction would include the starting point and ending point of the line. The coprocessor would then process each pixel. Because the microprocessor has much less to do, it can do something else and the bus traffic is greatly reduced.

The video chipset, which includes the video coprocessor, is the logic circuit that controls the video card. More advanced chipsets are more efficient, include more acceleration features, and may also include 3D acceleration or MPEG decoding. The chipset is a major factor in determining overall video performance. For example, 3D accelerator cards perform many complicated calculations. The picture on the monitor is a two-dimensional (2D) image that has a height and width. To make the 2D image appear to be three-dimensional (3D)—that is, having height, width, and depth—requires a complex interaction of visual effects (relative position, size, light levels, shadowing, relative motion, and sharpness). Very complex mathematical equations are used to determine when an object is visible in a scene, at what angle, in what color, etc. For smooth animation in a 3D game or presentation, these calculations must be redone 20 or more times per second since a typical movie will have a minimum of 20 frames per second. Each time the screen is recalculated (due to movement on the screen) it is necessary to recalculate the color and intensity of each pixel on the screen. This is done by applying different 3D computations to a scene in a process that is called *rendering.*

15.3 INSTALLING A VIDEO CARD

A video card is probably one of the easiest devices to install into a computer. The video card is physically installed into an empty expansion slot, the holding screw for the expansion card is secured, and the monitor is connected. Because every computer must have a monitor and most monitors are VGA or SVGA, the VGA/SVGA card resources (I/O addresses: 3B0–3BBH and 3C0–3DFH) are well established.

As with many other hardware devices, after the card is installed the correct driver usually needs to be loaded to take full advantage of the card's capabilities. If the correct driver is not loaded, the higher resolutions, higher number of colors, higher refresh rates, and coprocessing capabilities of the video card may not be available.

15.4 TYPES OF VIDEO SYSTEMS

Most computers today use VGA or Super VGA video systems. Like other computer components, the video system has gone through significant changes since the IBM PC was introduced in 1981. Table 15.3 describes a number of common video systems and their characteristics.

TABLE 15.3   Common video systems

Name	Year Introduced	Resolution	Colors
Monochrome display adapter (MDA)	1981	720 × 350 (25 × 80 characters)	Mono
Hercules graphics card	1982	720 × 350	Mono
Color graphics adapter (CGA)	1982	320 × 200 640 × 200	4 2
Enhanced graphics adapter (EGA)	1984	640 × 350	16
Variable graphics array (VGA)	1989	640 × 480 320 × 200	16 256
Super VGA (SVGA)	1990	800 × 600 1024 × 768	256 16
Extended VGA (XVGA)	1992	800 × 600 1024 × 768	65,536 256

The first video system, used with the original IBM PC, was the **monochrome display adapter (MDA).** It was a text system and could display 25 rows of 80 characters (80 × 25 characters). Although the monitor could not display graphics, it had a resolution of 720 × 350. (Note: The IBM MDA video card also included a parallel port.) The next monitor introduced by IBM was the **color graphics adapter (CGA).** It supported several modes, including a 16-color 80 × 25 character text mode, and could display up to 16 colors in several resolutions (320 × 200, 640 × 200, 160× 200). The monitors had a refresh rate of 60 Hz. Although this system introduced color to the PC for the first time, the low resolution, blurry screen, and lack of software support significantly limited its utility. Upgrading a system to CGA also required the replacement of the video card and monitor.

The next improvement to the PC video system was the **Hercules graphics card,** developed by Hercules Computer Technology Inc. Upgrading to this system required replacing only the video card; it worked with the same monochrome monitor used with the MDA video system. The video system could display in graphics mode with a resolution of 720 × 350. The CGA video system had been developed independently, but the Hercules card was developed in partnership with Lotus for the next version of their 1-2-3 spreadsheet to display graphs and charts on the computer screen.

Eventually, IBM answered the Hercules with the enhanced graphics adapter (EGA) video system, the first successful color video system. It included a 16-color 80 × 25 text mode and 16-color 640 × 350 graphics mode. (Note: EGA cards are the minimum requirement for Windows 3.XX.) IBM then developed **video graphics array (VGA)** as part of the PS/2 line. It was the first modern monitor, and all of today's monitors are derived from it. It supports a resolution of 640 × 480 at 16 colors or a resolution of 320 × 200 at 256 colors (chosen from a palette of 262,144 colors) and was also the first analog monitor used for the PC (all previous monitors had been digital). Standard VGA did not, however, include any kind of coprocessor or acceleration feature on the card. Table 15.4 lists the VGA pins and their function. The VGA standard became widely accepted but it was the last standard developed by IBM. Computer users wanted still higher resolutions and more colors. IBM did try to create several new video standards, but, unfortunately for IBM, these were not widely accepted because they were based on the failing Micro Channel Architecture. These standards included the 8514/A, which supported a resolution of 1024 × 768 at 256 colors but had a refresh rate of only 43.5 Hz (interlaced), or a resolution of 640 × 480 at 256 colors with a refresh rate of 60 Hz (noninterlaced). In addition, the 8514/A had some acceleration features. Another card introduced by IBM was the XGA and the XGA-2. The XGA supported a resolution of 1,024 × 768 at 256 colors or 640 × 480 at high color, and the XGA-2 had a resolution of 1,024 × 768 at high color. Both of these cards supported bus mastering.

IBM was no longer the computer leader as it had once been, and no company replaced it as the leader, so many companies made VGA video cards with higher resolution and more colors. But a video card made by one company and a monitor made by another

TABLE 15.4   VGA pinout

	Pin	Function	Direction
	1	Red	Out
	2	Green	Out
	3	Blue	Out
	4	Monitor ID2	In
	5	Digital ground (monitor self-test)	N/A
	6	Red analog ground	N/A
	7	Green analog ground	N/A
	8	Blue analog ground	N/A
	9	Key (plugged hole)	N/A
	10	Sync ground	N/A
	11	Monitor ID 0	In
	12	Monitor ID1	In
	13	Horizontal sync	Out
	14	Vertical sync	Out
	15	Monitor ID 3	In

company had all sorts of compatibility problems. To overcome these compatibility problems, the Video Electronics Standard Association (VESA) was formed by major computer, monitor, and video card manufacturers. VESA developed a Super VGA (SVGA) standard, called the *VESA BIOS extension (VBE)*. If a system has a resolution higher than 640×480 or can display more than 16 colors at the 640×480 resolution, the video system is probably Super VGA (SVGA), not VGA.

15.5 TROUBLESHOOTING A VIDEO SYSTEM

Most video system problems are caused by incorrect monitor control settings (the brightness and the contrast controls), incorrect video drivers, a failed video card, or a failed monitor. The obvious solutions to a failed video system should be checked first:

1. Are the computer and monitor on?
2. Is the monitor plugged into the power outlet and the computer?
3. Is the power outlet supplying sufficient power?
4. Are the brightness and contrast controls set properly?
5. Is the screen saver on or is the monitor in a power-saving mode, such as DPMS?

If the monitor is on but the display is acting very erratically, the wrong video driver may have been selected. This is probably the case if the monitor comes on during boot-up (text mode) but starts to act erratic when a GUI operating system or environment (Windows 3.XX, Windows 95 and 98, and Windows NT) is being loaded. The correct driver must be loaded to take full advantage of the card's capabilities, and a well-written driver will allow the video card to be faster and more reliable. If the wrong video driver has been selected, or an "Unable to initialize display adapter" message is displayed, Windows 3.XX, Windows 95 and 98, and Windows NT will allow you to go into standard VGA mode (640×480 with 16 colors), which will then allow you to choose the correct video driver.

Windows 3.XX   If the display is readable, you can run the Windows Setup icon located in the main group to change video drivers. If not, you must exit Windows (possible rebooting) to get back to the DOS prompt. Next, change to the Windows directory (or the directory that is holding the Windows files). Run the SETUP.EXE program. This will allow you to change the video driver while in text mode.

Windows 95 and 98   To start Safe Mode, press the F5 key (or F8 and choose Safe Mode) when the "Starting Windows 95/98" message appears on the screen during boot-up. The display settings can then be changed by using the Display icon/applet within the control panel.

Windows NT   If you have made a change in the Windows NT system and the machine does not boot properly, you can choose Last Known Good Configuration during boot-up. This will restore the previous driver setup and configuration. If you have not made a change, you must choose the Windows NT Server or Windows NT Workstation VGA mode. The display settings can then be changed from within the Display icon/applet within the Control Panel.

If the card is bad and is still under warranty, you can get a replacement card. If it is not under warranty, it is probably best to throw the card away and get a new one because you will most likely not have its schematic diagram, replacement parts, or surface mount soldering and desoldering equipment. Having the video card repaired usually costs more than purchasing a new one.

Monitors, on the other hand, cost more than a video card, and so it may be best to try to have a bad monitor repaired. You won't usually have the schematic or replacement parts, so it is best to have the manufacturer or its representatives fix the monitor or to send it to a monitor repair depot. A monitor should be opened and repaired only by an experienced technician—the monitor can hold a lethal charge (enough to kill a person) for long periods, even after it has been unplugged. If you do choose to open a CRT monitor, certain guidelines must be followed. First, make sure that the monitor is unplugged, and allow at least 15 minutes for it to discharge before disassembling it. Second, do not wear an ESD wrist strap—the monitor can contain high charges that can flow through the ESD strap into you. You should also not wear any jewelry. Do not operate the monitor without its X-ray and RF shields in place. Lastly, have a second person nearby in case the unexpected happens.

The case of the monitor is usually held together by several screws located in the back. To disassemble the monitor, remove the screws and carefully remove the rear enclosure. Make sure that you have removed all the screws; if you don't you may break the neck of the CRT when you pull on the rear enclosure. Since the CRT can store up to a 50,000 V dc charge, it is important to discharge the monitor before touching any wiring (especially the red wire that connects to the top of the CRT) or boards. Use a regular flat-blade screwdriver or a high-voltage logic probe with a heavy-duty alligator clip that is connected to a 1-megaohm resistor connected to ground. The resistor will prevent damage to some of the monitor components from a sudden surge of electricity. While grasping the insulated handle of the screw driver only, gently insert the screwdriver blade or a high-voltage logic probe under the anode cap until it touches the metal contacts. The **anode cap** is a flat, circular object resembling a suction cup located on the top of the CRT. Do not rotate the screwdriver or force it into the CRT. You will usually hear a mild crackle as the CRT is being discharged. Once the crackle stops (a couple of seconds), remove the screwdriver. After the monitor is discharged, it is a good idea to connect a grounded alligator clip to the anode cap to avoid any charge that may rebuild inside the monitor. (See fig. 15.7.) If the anode lead needs to be removed, such as when replacing the CRT, squeeze the lead while rocking it back and forth. Note: If you are adjusting some of the monitor controls, you shouldn't have to discharge the monitor, although you should make sure not to touch anything else.

> **NOTE**   CRT monitors are considered hazardous waste and are not allowed in landfills in most states. The frit, which joins the front and back panels of the monitor, is made of almost pure lead. Therefore, when disposing of a CRT monitor, ship it to a computer or electronics recycler or donate it to a needy organization.

Magnetic fields, such as those generated by stereo speakers, can distort images and cause discoloration of isolated areas on the screen. Strong magnetic fields can also cause the internal components of the monitor to become magnetized. The process of eliminating

FIGURE 15.7 Discharging a CRT monitor

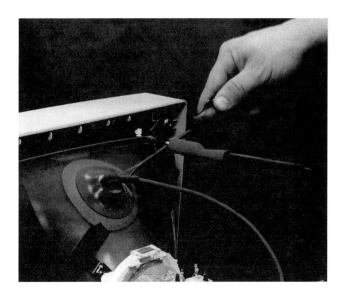

magnetization on a CRT is called *degaussing.* Some monitors have a built-in degaussing circuit, which can be activated automatically or by pressing a button or switch. If the degaussing circuit does not work, a **degausser,** which is a special demagnetizing device that is moved over the outside surface of the CRT to eliminate magnetic fields, should be used.

If an LCD display is cracked or broken and liquid crystal material leaks out, use rubber gloves to wipe up the spill with soap and water. Immediately wash off any LC material that makes contact with your skin.

One way to test a video system is to use a software diagnostic package such as QAPlus or Checkit Pro. These packages contain several tests that will display a grid to test pincushioning and several color blocks to test the purity of the colors. Unlike most tests, many of the video tests are interactive in that you have to determine if the system passed or failed.

EXAMPLE 15.1 You turn on the computer and during boot-up, you get an audio beep code (such as AMI's 8 beeps) indicating "Display Memory Read/Write Test Failure."

The first thing to check is whether the system has a video card. If there is a video card, then the error message indicates that the RAM on the video card failed. The video card will have to be replaced. If the problem persists, check the motherboard.

EXAMPLE 15.2 The sides of the images on the screen bulge inward or outward.

Check the monitor controls first, specifically the pincushioning controls. If the problem still exists, plug the monitor into another computer to see if the problem is with the monitor. If the problem does not appear on the other system, replace the video card in the original system.

EXAMPLE 15.3 The image is shifted over, or the image is shifted over and part of it looks distorted.

Check the monitor controls first, specifically the horizontal and vertical size and horizontal and vertical positioning. If the problem still exists, plug the monitor into another computer to see if the problem goes away. If the problem still exists, it must be the monitor. If the problem does not appear on the other system, replace the video card in the original system.

EXAMPLE 15.4 The image is wavy.

This is most likely a monitor power supply problem. To isolate this problem, plug the monitor into another computer to see if the monitor is causing it. Also, try another monitor with the computer to see if the computer is causing the problem. If the monitor appears to be the problem, then the power supply will have to be replaced. Again, this should be attempted only by experienced technicians who have the proper training on monitors.

EXAMPLE 15.5 The image is red, cyan (greenish-blue), blue, yellow, green, or magenta (bluish-red).

First, check the cable, especially if the monitor uses a coaxial cable that has connections for the red, green, and blue. After the cable has been checked, plug the monitor into another computer to see if the monitor is the problem. Also try another monitor with the computer to see if the computer is causing the problem. If the monitor appears to be the problem, it will have to be opened and the specific problem diagnosed. Most likely, one of the color video circuits is faulty. Again, to fix the problem requires an experienced technician who has access to schematics and parts.

EXAMPLE 15.6   A high-pitched noise comes from the computer when it is turned on.

The noise is most likely caused by the video system (monitor or video card), although it can also be caused by the hard drive or power supply. Before taking the machine apart, try to determine if the sound is coming from the monitor or the computer case. This will help you isolate it. To determine which component is causing the problem, swap each component one at a time.

15.6 VIDEO SYSTEM ERGONOMICS

If you use the computer for long stretches of time, you need to develop some good habits to reduce eyestrain, muscle stiffness, back problems, and headaches. When viewing the monitor, you should sit high enough so that your eyes are slightly higher than the screen. To reduce eyestrain, your eyes should be between 24 and 30 inches away from the screen (compared to the 16-inch distance recommended for reading books). In addition, if you are typing from hard copy, such as a report or a book, try to keep them the same distance from you as the computer screen.

Another key to being comfortable is controlling glare. Although glare itself won't lead to permanent eye damage, it can cause eyestrain and headaches. To control sources of glare on your screen, adjust the colors on your monitor to differentiate foreground from background. Position your monitor so that the bright light from a lamp or the sun is neither directly in front of you nor behind you (causing glare to be reflected in the screen). If your monitor doesn't have a built-in antiglare feature, consider buying an antiglare device.

Lastly, control the refresh rate of the monitor. It should be 70 Hz or higher.

15.7 VIDEO AND TELEVISION

Television signals are analog because analog signals can carry a lot of information using a low bandwidth. In the United States and Japan, the color TV signal is the **NTSC (National Television System Committee).** In many parts of Europe, the color TV signal is **PAL (phase alternate line).** As computers become more powerful, more and more software applications are using animation and video, and people want to display computer images on a large television screen and incorporate television images or television clips in the computer. These interactions require some form of signal conversion.

To display a computer image on a television, a VGA-to-NTSC adapter is needed. In addition, if you are recording to a VCR tape, the VGA-to-NTSC adapter must include genlocking. Genlocking enables the board to synchronize signals from multiple video sources or video with PC graphics and provides signal stability. Some VGA-to-NTSC converters are expansion cards; others are external boxes that are connected to the VGA or SVGA port. Many of these adapters have an S-Video and composite video interface, and some may include an antiflicker circuit to help stabilize the picture.

To capture a still image from a television, camcorder, or VCR, a still-image **video capture card** (NTSC-to-VGA converter) is used. Although image quality is limited by the input signal, the results are good enough for presentations and desktop publishing applications. These devices usually accept video input from VHS, Super VHS, and Hi-8 devices.

A video digitizer or video grabber is used to capture an entire video clip from the NTSC television signal. The video images within an NTSC television signal allows for approximately 32,000 colors and requires 30 frames per second. As a result, to display full-motion video requires a fast microprocessor, large amounts of RAM, huge amounts of disk space, and a local bus connection. Without these resources, images are often jerky or less than full screen.

Because full-motion video consumes huge amounts of disk space, most full-motion video systems use **compression and decompression (codec).** By using compression and decompression, files take up less space and perform better because there is less data to process. There are two forms of codecs: hardware codecs and software codecs. Hardware codecs require additional hardware but offer high-quality images and a high-compression ratio. Software codecs don't require special hardware but usually do not offer the same high-quality images, compression ratio, and performance as the hardware codec. Two common forms of compression are the **Joint Photographic Experts Group (JPEG)** and the **Motion Pictures Expert Group (MPEG).** JPEG, originally developed for pictures, compresses each frame by eliminating redundant data for each individual image. JPEG offers rates acceptable for nearly full-motion video (30 fps), a compression ratio of 30:1, and easy editing. MPEG can compress up to 200:1 at high quality levels yet is faster than JPEG. It compresses movies by storing only incremental changes. Unfortunately, because it does not include full information for every frame, it does not allow for easy editing.

There are several other video file formats. A common format on the PC is Video for Windows (developed by Microsoft), which uses **audio video interleave (AVI)** files. Just as the name implies, it interleaves video and audio data. This means that it has a segment of video data followed by a segment of audio data. AVI files are limited to 320 × 240 resolution and 30 frames per second, neither of which is adequate for full-screen, full-motion video. However, Video for Windows does not require any special hardware, making it a popular format. Another popular format is **QuickTime,** developed by Apple Computers, which uses a MOV filename extension. It can be played with the software on most common platforms and supports a variety of encoding types, including JPEG, Indeo, Cinepak, Animation, etc. In February 1998, the ISO standards body gave QuickTime a boost by deciding to use it as the basis for the new MPEG-4 standard being defined. Two of the newer popular formats are the **Real video** and **Real audio** formats developed by Real Networks. Unlike the other formats, the Real video and audio format supports streaming, so the files can be played over the Internet. The Real video and Real audio files have a RA filename extension and are played with RealPlayer.

SUMMARY

1. The monitor, a device similar to a television, is the computer's primary output device.
2. Like televisions, the size of the monitor is usually measured diagonally across the screen.
3. Monitors are of two types, cathode-ray tube (CRT) and liquid crystal display (LCD), which is mostly used on notebook and laptop computers.
4. The cathode-ray tube (CRT) consists of an electronic screen that is lined with a phosphorescent material that glows when struck by electrons.
5. To clean the screen, you should use a water-dampened cloth or a cloth with a special cleaning solution made for monitors.
6. Liquid crystal (LC) is an organic material made up of rod-shaped molecules that can bend light under the proper conditions.
7. The image (text, lines, boxes, and pictures) on the monitor is made up of many dots called *picture elements* or *pixels.*
8. The number of pixels that can be displayed on the screen at one time is called the *resolution* of the screen. It is expressed by two numbers.
9. While in text mode (the simplest operating mode), the system will usually display 25 rows of 80 characters (80 × 25).
10. Dot pitch is the distance between the pixels.
11. The number of times that the screen is redrawn in a second is referred to as *refresh rate.* It is measured in hertz (Hz).
12. Interlacing monitors will redraw the screen in two sweeps, refreshing every other line in each sweep.
13. To prevent screen burn-in, screen savers are used to blank the screen or to provide a constant moving pattern.
14. The video card can be identified by its 3-row, 15-pin female port (VGA or SVGA) and 2-row, 9-pin female port (monochrome, CGA, or EGA).

15. The amount of information that determines the color of a pixel is known as *color depth* or *bit depth*. The more bits used to define the number of colors for each pixel, the greater the number of colors the screen can show.
16. The amount of video memory determines the resolution and number of colors available.
17. Video cards can use DRAM, EDO RAM, VRAM, SGRAM, SDRAM, WRAM, and MDRAM.
18. Modern video cards include coprocessors to help process video data. These are known as *video accelerators*.
19. 3D accelerator cards calculate an object's relative position, size, light levels, shadowing, relative motion, and sharpness.
20. The video graphics array (VGA) system supports a resolution of 640 × 480 at 16 colors or a resolution of 320 × 200 at 256 colors (chosen from a palette of 262,144 colors).
21. Most video system problems are caused by incorrect monitor control settings (the brightness and the contrast controls), incorrect video drivers, a failed video card, or a failed monitor.
22. Before touching any wiring (especially the red wire that connects to the top of the CRT) or boards in the monitor, it is important to make sure that the CRT is fully discharged.
23. To discharge a monitor, use a regular flat-blade screwdriver with a heavy-duty alligator clip grounded in series with a 1-megaohm resistor. Gently insert the screwdriver blade under the high-voltage anode cap and keep it there for a few seconds.
24. Do not wear an ESD wrist strap when working within a monitor.
25. When viewing the monitor, your eyes should be slightly higher than your computer screen and be between 24 and 30 inches away from the screen.
26. In the United States and Japan, the color TV signal is the NTSC (National Television System Committee) signal.

REVIEW QUESTIONS

1. Which of the following is the primary output device of the computer?
   a. keyboard
   b. monitor
   c. printer
   d. mouse
2. The size of the monitor is measured in:
   a. inches diagonally across the screen
   b. square inches of the screen
   c. dots going across and dots going down
   d. pounds
3. Which of the following uses electrons to energize a phosphorescent material to display images on the screen?
   a. VGA
   b. LCD
   c. MDA
   d. CRT
4. Dots on the screen are known as (choose two):
   a. pixels
   b. dot pitch
   c. resolution
   d. picture elements
   e. lights
5. Which of the following statements are correct if a monitor has a .28 dot pitch?
   a. each dot is .28 cm wide
   b. each dot is .28 mm wide
   c. each dot is .28 cm apart
   d. each dot is .28 mm apart
6. A monitor has a refresh rate of 72 Hz. Which of the following statements are true? (Choose all that apply.)
   a. the refresh rate is 72 times per second
   b. the number of vertical lines is 72 per inch
   c. the monitor probably produces more flicker than a 60 Hz monitor
   d. the monitor probably produces less flicker than a 60 Hz monitor
7. Which of the following describes a noninterlaced monitor?
   a. the pixels on the screen are illuminated from left to right and from top to bottom
   b. three electron guns shoot electrons beams that are not in sync with one another
   c. three electron guns shoot electron beams that are not interlaced with one another

d. the lines on the screen are scanned in two or more passes

e. all the lines on the screen are scanned in one pass

8. If characters on a monitor are squashed to one side, which adjustment will correct this problem?

    a. vertical size

    b. horizontal centering

    c. horizontal hold

    d. vertical linearity

    e. pincushioning

9. Which of the following will prevent screen burn-in?

    a. increasing the refresh rate

    b. decreasing the refresh rate

    c. reducing the screen resolution

    d. using a screen saver

    e. increasing the number of colors used

10. Which of the following best describes the VGA connector on the PC?

    a. 25-pin male connector

    b. female connector with 3 rows of 5 pins each

    c. 9-pin female connector

    d. 25-pin female connector

11. Which of the following best describes the EGA connector on the PC?

    a. 25-pin male connector

    b. female connector with 3 rows of 5 pins each

    c. 9-pin female connector

    d. 25-pin female connector

12. How many different colors can a video system show with a 16-bit color depth?

    a. 256

    b. 65,536

    c. 16,777,216

    d. 4,294,967,296

13. You want to display high color with a resolution of 800×600 on a 15″ monitor. (The monitor has a refresh rate of 72 Hz.) How much video RAM would you need?

    a. 937.5 kilobytes

    b. 7.4 megabytes

    c. 13.8 megabytes

    d. 66.0 megabytes

14. Which of the following types of RAM used in video cards is dual-ported?

    a. VRAM

    b. SGRAM

    c. EDO

    d. MDRAM

15. Which is the best bus to use when choosing a video card?

    a. ISA

    b. MCA

    c. EISA

    d. PCI

16. Which of the following best describes a video accelerator?

    a. the video accelerator uses a faster bus speed

    b. the video accelerator does all of the video processing

    c. the video accelerator has a microprocessor that does a lot of the video processing

    d. the video accelerator bypasses the microprocessor

17. Which of the following best describes 3D accelerator cards?

    a. the 3D video accelerator is three cards in one

    b. the 3D video accelerator compresses the data sent to the monitor by a ratio of $1:3$

    c. the 3D video accelerator performs many of the complicated video calculations that relate to size, relative position, and relative motion

    d. the 3D video accelerator uses a clock crystal that is three times faster than the motherboard clock crystal

18. What are the number of characters per line and the number of lines that may be displayed in text mode?

    a. 64 characters by 28 lines

    b. 120 characters by 40 lines

    c. 75 characters by 30 lines

    d. 80 characters by 25 lines

19. A monitor has a fixed resolution of 640×350. This means that it is:

    a. a CGA monitor

    b. an EGA monitor

    c. a VGA monitor

    d. a monochrome monitor

20. Which mode is a video resolution of 800×600?

    a. CGA

    b. EGA

    c. VGA

    d. SVGA

21. Which of the following produces an image that has a resolution of 640 × 480 and 16 colors?
    a. CGA
    b. EGA
    c. MCGA
    d. VGA

22. Which of the following is best to use when cleaning a CRT monitor?
    a. hot water
    b. a damp cloth
    c. WD-40
    d. denatured alcohol
    e. Windex

23. Why do windows located near the PC need curtains?
    a. the sunlight can cause the phosphorous within the CRT to glow
    b. They prevent or reduce glare caused by the sunlight shining through the window
    c. They protect the video display from UV damage
    d. Sunlight can cause problems with fiber-optic cables connected to the back of the PC

24. The grid voltages of a color monitor are in the range of:
    a. 15,000 V
    b. 2,500 V
    c. 35,000 V
    d. 50,000 V

25. Which of the following procedures must be observed while working on a monitor? (Choose all that apply.)
    a. discharging the CRT anode
    b. removing all jewelry
    c. leaving the monitor plugged in to provide a ground
    d. wearing an ESD wrist strap

26. Which of the following may cause the monitor to emit a high-pitched sound?
    a. the video controller
    b. the hard drive controller
    c. the monitor power cable
    d. none of the above

27. When should you *not* wear an ESD wrist strap?
    a. when working on a disk drive
    b. when working on a CPU
    c. when working on memory
    d. when working on an exposed cathode-ray tube (CRT)

28. The presence of electromagnetic fields can result in which of the following problems? (Choose all that apply.)
    a. distortion of the video display
    b. shut-down of the PC
    c. RAM errors
    d. read/write errors on the disk

29. What is the first thing you should do when you discharge a CRT monitor?
    a. with the power turned off, disconnect all of the cables and let the monitor discharge for at least 15 minutes
    b. with the power turned off, disconnect all of the cables and let the monitor discharge for at least 5 seconds
    c. remove the outside cover
    d. remove the monitor's power supply

30. Which of the following components *cannot* cause a video problem?
    a. the microprocessor
    b. the video card
    c. the video signal cable between the monitor and the video card
    d. the monitor
    e. the video driver

31. Which would you do first when troubleshooting a faulty monitor?
    a. check its connections to the computer and power source
    b. use a meter to check the CRT and internal circuitry for continuity
    c. power down the monitor, then turn it on again to see if that corrects the problem
    d. power down the computer, then turn it on again to see if that corrects the problem

32. To reduce eyestrain and headaches, which of the following should you do? (Choose all that apply.)
    a. enable your screen saver
    b. keep your eyes level with the monitor or slightly above the monitor
    c. use a refresh rate of 60 Hz or more
    d. shut off all lights in the room
33. Which of the following standards are used in the United States to send television signals?
    a. NTSC
    b. PAL
    c. VHS
    d. Super VHS
    e. Beta

HANDS-ON EXERCISES

Exercise 1: Using the Monitor Controls

1. Find the controls for brightness. Adjust the brightness all the way up.
2. Find the controls for contrast. Adjust the contrast all the way up.
3. Adjust the brightness all the way down.
4. Adjust the contrast all the way down.
5. Adjust the brightness approximately halfway.
6. Adjust the contrast and brightness controls to their proper settings.
7. Find the controls for horizontal centering. Adjust the horizontal centering all the way to the right.
8. Adjust the horizontal centering to its proper setting.
9. Find the controls for vertical centering. Adjust the vertical centering all the way to the top.
10. Adjust the vertical centering to its proper setting.
11. Find the controls for horizontal size. Reduce the picture to its smallest setting.
12. Using the horizontal size controls, change the picture to its largest setting.
13. Adjust the horizontal size to its proper setting.
14. Find the controls for pincushioning. Adjust the pincushioning all the way in.
15. Adjust the pincushioning all the way outward.
16. Adjust the pincushioning to its proper setting.
17. Using the CMOS setup program, enable the Power Management feature within the program. Set the monitor so that it will power down after 5 to 10 minutes of nonuse.
18. Disable the Power Management feature.

Exercise 2: Testing the Video Card Using Software Diagnostics

Run a software diagnostic package to test the video card and monitor. Note: When you are running most of these tests, you must determine if the monitor and card passed or failed. Therefore, look for normal colors (pure white, red, blue, and yellow) and straight lines.

Exercise 3: Loading and Configuring Video Drivers

1. Using Windows 3.XX (the Setup icon in the Accessories group) or Windows 95 or 98 (Display icon or applet in the Control Panel), determine the video driver currently being used.
2. Change the video driver to standard VGA.
3. After restarting Windows 3.XX or Windows 95 or 98, select a Video 7 video card (or another one specified by your instructor).
4. If the computer did not boot properly, restart Windows 3.XX or Windows 95 or 98 in VGA mode. For Windows 3.XX, this can be done by running SETUP.EXE from the Windows directory. For Windows 95 and 98, this can be done by starting Windows in safe mode (press F4 when the "Starting Windows 95/98..." message appears on the screen).
5. Load the proper video drivers.

6. Using the Setup icon in the Accessories group (Windows 3.XX) or the Display icon or applet in the Control Panel (Windows 95 and 98), try to find out the maximum resolution and maximum number of colors your system can use.

7. If you have the video card setup disk or if the option is available in the display icon, try to change the refresh rate to a higher value.

8. If your monitor is using an 800×600 or higher resolution, try to use large fonts (if available).

9. If your monitor is using an 800×600 or higher resolution, adjust it to 640×480 and to the most colors that resolution will support. Note how the picture changes.

10. Activate a screen saver.

Exercise 4: Analyzing the Video Card and Connector

1. Shut off the computer.
2. If the video card is an expansion card, remove it. If the video card is on the motherboard, disable it using the motherboard documentation.
3. Turn on the computer. Note the error message, if any.
4. Turn off the computer.
5. Find the video RAM on the video card or motherboard. Try to determine the amount of RAM.
6. Replace the video card back in the system.
7. Test the system to make sure that it still works.
8. Look at the number of pins on the video card connector that plug into the VGA/SVGA port. Don't be alarmed if some pins are missing.

Exercise 5: Discharging the CRT Monitor

COMPLETE THIS EXERCISE UNDER THE SUPERVISION OF AN EXPERIENCED TECHNICIAN AND BE SURE TO WORK WITH A PARTNER. Do not wear an ESD wrist strap during this exercise. Remove any jewelry and wear rubber shoes. Lastly, if you have any questions about this procedure, ask your instructor.

1. Unplug the monitor and let it sit for at least 15 minutes.
2. Find the screws that hold the monitor case together and gently remove the back of the monitor. Note: Do not pull the back of the case hard. If you missed a screw, you could break the deflection yoke or CRT neck. Make sure not to touch any components in the monitor, including any wires.
3. Take an insulated screwdriver and connect a 1-megaohm resistor in series with ground.
4. While the screwdriver is still grounded, gently place it under the anode cap. You should hear a crackle. Discharge the monitor for a few seconds.
5. Look to see if there are any monitor controls inside the monitor.
6. Reassemble the monitor and test it to make sure that it works.

Exercise 6: Loading Video Drivers from the Internet

1. Find and download the drivers for the following video cards using the Internet:
   ATI Technologies—Graphics Ultra Pro (Windows 3.1X)
   Diamond Multimedia Systems, Inc.—Stealth 3D 4000 (Windows 95)
   the driver for your system
2. Install the driver for your system.

16

Input Devices

INTRODUCTION

Input devices move information into the computer. The keyboard (the primary input device) and the mouse (including trackballs and other pointing devices) are the two most common input devices, but there are also others. For the game enthusiast, the game port connects paddles, joysticks, flight sticks, and other types of game-related peripherals. For notebook and laptop computers, there are IrDA ports, which allow two devices to communicate without wires. Lastly, there is the scanner that can convert pictures into data that the computer can read.

OBJECTIVES

1. Know which computer devices are input devices.
2. Compare and contrast the XT and AT keyboards.
3. List and describe the three types of keys used in keyboards.
4. Test a keyboard port by measuring voltages.
5. Clean a keyboard.
6. Remove a key and replace it.

7. Determine and correct keyboard problems.
8. Describe the proper use of keyboards to minimize repetitive stress injuries.
9. Explain how the mouse works and how it interfaces with the operating system.
10. List and describe the different pointing devices.
11. Physically install and configure a pointing device and load the appropriate software and drivers.
12. Determine and correct a pointing device problem.
13. Install and configure a joystick using a game port.
14. List examples or uses of IrDA ports.
15. Describe how a scanner works.
16. Install a scanner, install any necessary scanner software, and scan a picture with text.
17. Explain the purpose of OCR software.
18. Explain how TWAIN relates to graphic software packages.
19. Determine and correct a scanner problem.

16.1 THE KEYBOARD

The computer **keyboard** is used to input, or enter, letters, numbers, symbols, punctuation, and commands into the computer. It includes the same keys as a typewriter and it also has a numeric keypad, cursor controls, and 10 or more function keys. The standard typewriter layout is called the **QWERTY layout** and is by far the most common. Over the years, there have been attempts to change the standard keyboard layout to improve typing speed and ergonomics. The other standard is the **Dvorak layout,** which has vowels in the home row under the left hand and the most commonly used consonants in the home row under the right hand. Although most tests of this layout show it produces a moderate speed increase, the public is resistant to the change.

16.1.1 TYPES OF KEYBOARDS

Many different keyboards are available and they offer many different features. They can be categorized into four main types:

1. the 83-key XT keyboard
2. the 84-key AT keyboard
3. the 101-key or 102-key enhanced keyboard
4. the 104-key enhanced Windows keyboard

The **83-key XT** and **84-key AT** keyboards have all of the standard typewriter keys and include 10 functions on the left-hand side. The XT keyboard was made to work with the IBM PC and IBM XT and will not work for a 286 or later computer. The AT keyboard was made for the IBM AT and will work on any 286 or later computer. The XT keyboard is unidirectional and the AT keyboard is bidirectional. Bidirectional keyboards can be programmed (such as for multinational operations) and controlled by the computer. Some keyboards include an XT/AT switch so that they can be used on both XT and AT computers.

Most keyboards today are the **101-key/102-key** or the **104-key enhanced keyboards.** In addition to the standard typewriter keys, they include separate cursor controls, a numeric keyboard, and 12 function keys. The 104-key Windows keyboard has a Windows key and an application key. The Windows key opens the start menu without using the mouse, and the application key simulates the right mouse button to access Windows 95 and 98 quick menus. Some keyboards also include built-in pointing devices.

16.1.2 HOW A KEYBOARD WORKS

The keyboard is a mechanical device consisting of many small mechanical parts (the keys). There are many different kinds of keys used within the keyboard; some are quiet, and others click. Most of the keys can be categorized as a mechanical, membrane, or capacitive key switch.

The mechanical key switch has two bronze contacts separated by a plastic actuator bar. The key is kept in the up position with a spring. When the key is pressed, the bar slides down, allowing the contacts to touch two gold-plated contacts. When the key is released, the spring pushes the key back into its normal position.

The membrane key switch is a plastic actuator that rests on top of a soft rubber boot coated with a conductive silver-carbon compound. When the key is pressed, the plastic actuator collapses the rubber boot, allowing the conductive material to make contact with two open PC board contacts. When the key is released, the compressed rubber boot returns to its original shape.

The capacitive key is different from the other keys because it is not a mechanical device. Instead of making contact between conductors, the capacitive key uses two plates to store electric changes in a switch matrix that is designed to detect changes in the capacitance of the circuit. When the key is pressed, the top plate moves toward the bottom plate. As a result, a change in capacitance occurs that is detected by a comparator circuit in the keyboard. While these keys are more durable and are almost immune to dirt and corrosion, they are more expensive.

The keys are arranged in rows and columns. When a key is pressed, a unique row-and-column signal is generated and sent to the keyboard interface IC on the keyboard. The keyboard interface then converts the row-and-column signal into a single-byte code called a *key code* or *scan code*. (see tables 16.1 and 16.2.) When the key is released, a second signal is sent to the keyboard interface IC, which generates a break code. This allows you to press several keys at the same time, such as Alt + Tab, Alt + Enter, or Ctrl + F. The keyboard interface IC then sends the scan codes by means of a serial connection through the keyboard interface to the computer. Unlike transfers from other serial devices, which send data asynchronously, the transfer from the keyboard occurs synchronously with a clock signal. The **keyboard controller,** located on the motherboard, converts the signals to parallel data and generates an interrupt so that the input can be serviced by the microprocessor.

The cable that connects the keyboard to the motherboard is a 5-pin DIN or 6-pin mini-DIN (PS/2 connector). The pinouts for the two connectors are shown in table 16.3.

16.1.3 TROUBLESHOOTING THE KEYBOARD

Keyboard problems are among the more common problems that occur with the PC because there are so many small mechanical components and keyboards sometimes are abused by users. Typically, the problem will be caused by a faulty keyboard, faulty keyboard connector, or faulty motherboard. In addition, if a different type of keyboard is added to a system, some operating systems may require a change in the keyboard driver.

Generally, keyboards are made to work with XT systems or AT systems. In this case, AT indicates a 286 or higher system. Unfortunately, an XT keyboard will not work with an AT system, and an AT keyboard won't work with an XT system. Some keyboards, however, can be configured to work with both the XT and AT systems with a set of DIP switches or a normal slider switch on the bottom of the keyboard. Therefore, when you encounter a keyboard error, check to see if the keyboard has these switches and that they are configured properly.

Assuming the keyboard is configured properly, the easiest way to verify a keyboard is faulty is to replace it with a known good keyboard. If the problem goes away, the original keyboard must be bad. If the keyboard is bad, check the cords. Some keyboard cords can be easily disconnected and replaced, which might make replacing the entire keyboard unnecessary. If the problem does not go away, check the motherboard.

To test the keyboard connector on the motherboard, measure the voltages of several pins of the keyboard connector. The keyboard clock pin should measure between +2.0 V and +5.5 V, the keyboard data pin should be between +4.8 V and +5.5 V, and the power pin should be between +2.0 V and +5.5 V. Some motherboards have a fuse to protect them from electrical surges that may come through the keyboard. If a sufficient surge causes the fuse to open, the keyboard will not function and the fuse will have to be replaced.

One of the best ways to keep a keyboard in good condition is to clean it periodically. This includes vacuuming between the keys or using a can of compressed air while the

TABLE 16.1   Scan codes for alphanumeric keys on PC keyboards

Key	Make Code	Break Code	Key	Make Code	Break Code
A	1E	9E	] or }	1B	9B
B	30	B0	; or :	27	A7
C	2E	AE	' or "	28	A8
D	20	A0	, or <	33	B3
E	12	92	/ or ?	35	B5
F	21	A1	Left Shift	2A	AA
G	22	A2	Left Control	1D	9D
H	23	A3	Left Alt	38	B8
I	17	97	Right Shift	36	B6
J	24	A4	Right Control	E0 1D	E0 9D
K	25	A5	Right Alt	E0 38	E0 B8
L	26	A6	Caps	3A	BA
M	32	B2	Backspace	0E	8E
N	31	B1	Tab	0F	8F
O	18	98	Space Bar	39	B9
P	19	99	Enter	1C	9C
Q	10	90	Escape	01	81
R	13	93	F1	3B	BB
S	1F	9F	F2	3C	BC
T	14	94	F3	3D	BD
U	16	96	F4	3E	BE
V	2F	AF	F5	3F	BF
W	11	91	F6	40	C0
X	2D	AD	F7	41	C1
Y	15	95	F8	42	C2
Z	2C	AC	F9	43	C3
0 or /	0B	8B	F10	44	C4
1 or !	02	82	F11	57	D7
2 or @	03	83	F12	58	D8
3 or #	04	84	Up Arrow	E0 48	E0 C8
4 or $	05	85	Down Arrow	E0 50	E0 D0
5 or %	06	86	Left Arrow	E0 4B	E0 CB
6 or ^	07	87	Right Arrow	E0 4D	E0 CD
7 or &	08	88	Insert	E0 52	E0 D2
8 or *	09	89	Delete	E0 53	E0 D3
9 or (	0A	8A	Home	E0 47	E0 C7
. or >	29	A9	End	E0 4F	E0 CF
- or _	0C	8C	Page Up	E0 49	E0 C9
= or +	0D	8D	Page Down	E0 51	E0 D1
[or {	1A	9A	Scroll Lock	46	C6

keyboard is upside down. This will remove dust and dirt before they cause a key to stick or not to function. If a key sticks, the keycap can be removed and cleaned. An excellent tool for removing keycaps on most keyboards is the U-shaped chip-puller tool found in most PC repair kits. After the keycap is removed, use a can of compressed air to remove dust and dirt. If this doesn't work, the best course of action is to replace the

TABLE 16.2 Numeric and cursor keypad scan codes

Key	Make Code	Break Code	Key	Make Code	Break Code
Num Lock	76	F0 76	**5**	73	F0 73
*	7E	F0 7E	**6**	74	F0 74
−	84	F0 84	**7**	6C	F0 C6
+	7C	F0 7C	**8**	75	F0 75
Enter	79	F0 79	**9**	7D	F0 7D
0	70	F0 70	**Home**	6C	F0 6C
1	69	F0 69	**End**	69	F0 69
2	72	F0 72	**Page Up**	7D	F0 7D
3	7A	F0 7A	**Page Down**	7A	F0 7A
4	6B	F0 6B	**Insert**	70	F0 70

TABLE 16.3 Typical keyboard ports

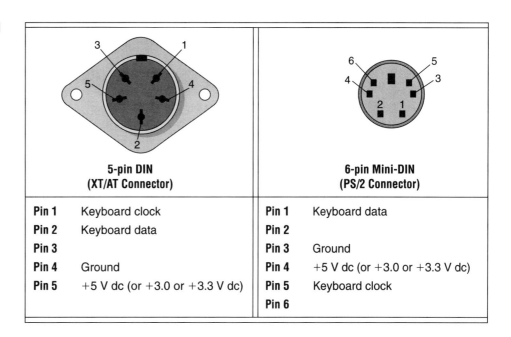

5-pin DIN (XT/AT Connector)		6-pin Mini-DIN (PS/2 Connector)	
Pin 1	Keyboard clock	**Pin 1**	Keyboard data
Pin 2	Keyboard data	**Pin 2**	
Pin 3		**Pin 3**	Ground
Pin 4	Ground	**Pin 4**	+5 V dc (or +3.0 or +3.3 V dc)
Pin 5	+5 V dc (or +3.0 or +3.3 V dc)	**Pin 5**	Keyboard clock
		Pin 6	

keyboard. Besides dust and dirt, a stuck key or keys can be caused by something spilled on the keyboard, such as coffee or soda. If this occurs, it is best to immediately flush out the keyboard with distilled water. Distilled water is best because it doesn't have any minerals that may corrode the contacts used in the keys. In addition, you can partially disassemble a keyboard and wash the components with water. If the spilled liquid has dried, soak the keyboard in water and then rinse it. Make sure the keyboard is dry before trying to use it.

If one or more keys wears out, keyboards can be taken apart and individual components replaced. However, some keyboards are made up of hundreds of little pieces and are sometimes impossible to reassemble if you go too far in taking them apart. It is sometimes easier and more cost efficient to replace the keyboard rather than spend a lot of time on it.

EXAMPLE 16.1 You turn on the computer and a "301" error message or "keyboard error" appears on the screen.

One of the most common error messages encountered on a PC is the "301" or "keyboard error" message. This usually happens when the keyboard is not connected to the computer, a common mistake for anyone, including experienced technicians. Of course, the experienced technician will check that the keyboard is connected before going any further. If the keyboard is plugged in and the system is still giving this error, there could be a stuck key on the keyboard. To unstick a key, try pressing each key on the keyboard. Also try cleaning under the keycaps. If the error still appears, the keyboard, keyboard cable, or motherboard will have to be replaced. The faulty component can be isolated by swapping one part at a time. The keyboard can be tested by trying it on another system. The motherboard can be tested by measuring the voltages of the keyboard connector.

EXAMPLE 16.2 You turn on the computer and the system indicates a "Gate A20 Failure."

This error message indicates that a 286 or higher machine must change to protected mode to utilize more than 1 MB of RAM. The first 1 MB of RAM is indicated with 20 address lines, identified as A0 to A19. Therefore, A20 is the 21st address line, which is the beginning of the extended memory. The gate A20 failure error indicates that the system, for some reason, could not activate the A20 line and change to protected mode. Since the A20 line is controlled by the keyboard controller, the gate A20 failure may be caused by either a faulty keyboard or a faulty motherboard.

To isolate the problem, check if the keyboard is configured correctly (XT vs. AT). Next, replace the keyboard with a known good one. If the problem still exists, replace the motherboard.

16.1.4 KEYBOARD ERGONOMICS

People who use the computer for long hours should be concerned with keyboard **ergonomics.** It is important that the wrists rest comfortably on the table in front of the keyboard and that the shoulders be relaxed. The wrists should not have to be bent to reach the keyboard. If they are, place a wrist pad in front of the keyboard to straighten them out. In addition, the chair should be adjusted so that elbows are at a 90-degree angle when the hands are on the keyboard. If these basic guidelines are not followed, the user may develop carpal tunnel syndrome. **Carpal tunnel syndrome** is a wrist and hand injury caused by holding the wrists stiff for long periods. This repetitive stress injury makes the nerves in the wrist swell, causing great pain.

To reduce the tension on the wrist, some companies have introduced ergonomically designed keyboards. Some are wedge shaped, allowing the shoulders to be straighter and the arms to be in a more relaxed position. Others have a built-in palm rest and a wrist-leveling device that allows the height of the front of the keyboard to be adjusted to help maintain a straight wrist.

16.2 POINTING DEVICES

The classic first pointing device is the **mouse,** which was invented in 1964 by Douglas Englebart. At that time, the mouse was called the X-Y Position Indicator for a Display System. Xerox later used the mouse with its experimental Alto computer in 1973. By 1979, Apple was using the mouse for the Lisa and later for the Macintosh computer. Today, the mouse and other pointing devices (trackballs, glide pads, and pointing sticks) are used to navigate most modern operating systems and environments, including Windows 3.XX, Windows 95 and 98, Windows NT, and System 7 and 8 (Macintosh's operating system). In addition, it is used in some DOS applications and a handful of CMOS setup programs.

16.2.1 HOW THE MOUSE WORKS

The mouse is a simple device consisting of a housing, a mouse ball, roller sensors, and a logic board. The mouse ball is a hard rubber ball located inside the mouse. When it is placed on a flat surface, the mouse ball protrudes from the bottom of the housing and makes contact with the surface. Inside the mouse, the mouse ball also makes contact with two rollers. One roller is for the X-direction (left and right) and the other is for the Y-direction (up and down). As the rollers are moved, sensors detect the motion and generate

FIGURE 16.1   Optomechanical
mouse

a series of electrical pulses. The pulses from both directions are amplified by the logic board contained within the mouse and sent to the computer. The signals are then interpreted by a software driver. The driver, which interacts with the operating system, generates the mouse pointer, reports its position, and moves the cursor on the screen.

Mice are mechanical or optomechanical. Early mice were mechanical. As the X and Y rollers were moved, they would move a shaft containing copper contacts. As the copper contacts moved and made contact with other metal contacts on the logic board, this would generate pulses of electricity. By counting the number of pulses in each direction, the computer could calculate the movement of the mouse. Unfortunately, the friction of metal on metal would cause the contacts to wear out, and the mouse was affected by dust, dirt, and hair interfering with the two contacts, causing the mouse to skip or not move. The mouse pad provided a clean surface for the mouse.

The newer optomechanical mice use light to detect motion. (See fig. 16.1.) As the mouse ball is rotated, the two X-Y rollers move and rotate slotted wheels. As the slotted wheels turn, light (generated by an LED) shines through the slots. A photodiode or phototransistor located on the other side of the wheel detects the alternating light signals and converts them to an electrical signal. As with the mechanical mouse, the electrical signal is then sent to the computer, causing the mouse pointer to move.

A special kind of mouse is the **trackball,** which is nothing more than an inverted mouse. Instead of physically moving the entire mouse, the hand or fingers moves the ball, which protrudes from the top. The advantage of the trackball over the mouse is that the trackball is stationary and doesn't require moving space, which is why some keyboards include trackballs.

No matter what the type of mouse (or trackball), they all have one, two, or three buttons. The primary button is used to perform a click (to select an option, such as a button or a menu) or double click (to start a process, such as starting a program icon). For Windows 95 and 98, Windows NT, and some Windows 3.XX applications, the secondary mouse pointer is used to access quick-access menus.

16.2.2   TRACKPOINT AND GLIDEPAD

In an attempt to keep the fingers on the home keys on the keyboard, IBM introduced the trackpoint. The **trackpoint** is a small rubber cap above the B key between the G and H keys that moves the mouse pointer by means of pressure transducers. The pressure transducers measure the amount of force being applied and the direction of the force. The more force, the faster the pointer moves. Consequently, a signal is sent to the rest of the computer and the mouse pointer moves.

The last pointing device is the **glidepad,** a flat square pad usually located below the keyboard. (See fig. 16.2.) As a finger touches the glide pad, transducers under the pad sense the body capacitance. As the finger moves, the pad generates electrical signals, which

FIGURE 16.2 Glidepad and trackpoint

move the mouse pointer. The glidepad is a small, stationary device, but its location allows it to be bumped easily, which can move the cursor to a different location.

16.2.3 INSTALLING A MOUSE

The first step in installing a mouse is physically connecting the mouse to the computer through a serial port, PS/2 mouse port, or bus port. The serial port is a 9-pin or 25-pin, two-row male connector. Most systems today come with two serial ports (COM1 and COM2). COM1 usually uses IRQ 4 and I/O addresses 3F8H-3FFH; COM2 usually uses IRQ 3 and I/O addresses 2F8H-2FFH.

The **PS/2 mouse port,** first introduced with the IBM PS/2, looks exactly like a PS/2 keyboard port, but even though they look alike, the PS/2 mouse can't be used in a PS/2 keyboard port and the PS/2 keyboard can't be used in a PS/2 mouse port. The advantage of the PS/2 mouse is that it doesn't take up a COM port. The standard resources for the PS/2 mouse port are IRQ 12 and I/O addresses 60H-64H. Because the mouse is controlled by the 8042-type keyboard controller chip located on the motherboard, it uses the same I/O address as the keyboard controller. (Note: Windows 3.XX can recognize mice only on COM1 and COM2, not COM3 or COM4.)

A third type of mouse connection is the bus port. A **bus mouse** connects to a special expansion card usually used when there are no serial ports available and the system does not have a PS/2 mouse port. A bus mouse should not be connected to a PS/2 mouse port. Since the bus mouse interface expansion card is an 8-bit card, which is extremely limited in its choice of IRQs, the bus mouse is not used very much.

Several years ago, the two mice standards were the Microsoft (MS) mouse and the PC (IBM) mouse. Therefore, some mice were manufactured to be configurable for either one by a slider switch located on the bottom of the mouse, although the most common interface used today is the Microsoft standard. If the mouse is not configured properly, it may not function.

After connecting the mouse, the correct software drivers must be loaded. DOS requires a file with a COM or EXE extension loaded in the AUTOEXEC.BAT file or a file with a SYS extension loaded in the CONFIG.SYS file with the DEVICE or DEVICEHIGH command. Windows 3.XX, Windows 95 and 98, and Windows NT have their own drivers built into the operating system and environment. If one manufacturer's mouse is replaced by one made by another manufacturer, the mouse may not work properly until the driver is changed to match the mouse. The mouse drivers in Windows 3.XX can be changed with the SETUP.EXE executed in the Windows directory or with the SETUP icon located in the MAIN group. Because Windows 3.XX has its own mouse driver, it does not need a mouse driver loaded in DOS. The mouse drivers in Windows 95 and 98 and Windows NT can be changed using the MOUSE icon or applet in the Control Panel. Lastly, the software being used must be written so as to accept a mouse. While all Windows programs use the mouse, many DOS programs do not. Some programs will automatically accept a mouse and others have to be configured to do so.

16.2.4 TROUBLESHOOTING POINTING DEVICES

One of the most common problems with mice is that dirt, dust, and hair that get inside the housing and cause the mouse to skip or not move. To check for and remove any foreign substance, mice and trackballs have a panel that opens so that the mouse ball can be removed. For mice, the panel is located on the bottom; on trackball housings, the panel is located on the top. These panels usually rotate in order to release but some may have to be pushed in one direction to release. The mouse ball falls out when the housing is then tipped. The ball should be washed thoroughly in warm soapy water or in an ammonia-water mix. After the ball is washed, it should be completely dried with a lint-free cloth or paper towel. Next, use a can of compressed air to blow out loose accumulations of dust and other foreign substances from the housing. Wipe each roller carefully with a cotton swab with isopropyl alcohol. Finally, check the LED and photodiode or phototransistor for dust and dirt to make sure that nothing is blocking the light pathway. (Note: Do not use harsh solvents or other cleaners unless they are specifically made to clean the mouse because some of these can melt the plastic or mouse ball and others may make surfaces too slippery.) Then reassemble the mouse or trackball.

EXAMPLE 16.3 The mouse is not recognized during boot-up.

Before disassembling the mouse and computer, check the obvious causes first. Make sure that the mouse is connected to the computer, and check under the mouse to see if there is an MS-PC configuration switch. If the mouse is connected and configured properly, the problem could be no software driver, an incorrect software driver, a faulty mouse, a resource conflict, or a faulty port.

The first thing to check is the driver. Make sure that the mouse was connected when the DOS driver was loaded or when Windows 3.XX, Windows 95 or 98, or Windows NT was starting. For DOS, the mouse driver can be verified with the MEM command and the TYPE or EDIT command (used to view the AUTOEXEC.BAT and CONFIG.SYS files). For Windows, the mouse driver can be loaded or changed using the SETUP.EXE located in the Windows directory or the SETUP icon located in the MAIN group. For Windows 95 and 98 and Windows NT, use the MOUSE icon or applet in the Control Panel.

If the driver appears to be loaded properly, swap the mouse with a known good mouse. You can also try the mouse in another system. If the mouse is bad, replace it. If there is no problem with the mouse, then the problem must be with the port. The port may be disabled or not working properly because of an IRQ or I/O address conflict or a COM conflict (two devices configured to the same COM port). To verify that the port is enabled, look at jumpers on the expansion card or motherboard or use the CMOS setup program. To look for resource conflicts, use a software diagnostic package (QAPlus, Checkit Pro, Micro 2000, Windows 95/98 Device Manager or Windows NT WINMSD). You can also verify the positioning of jumpers on the expansion card or motherboard or use the CMOS setup program. If no conflict is found, the port will have to be replaced or the mouse will have to be assigned to another port. (Note: Some serial and PS/2 mouse ports are part of the motherboard.)

FIGURE 16.3   Joystick

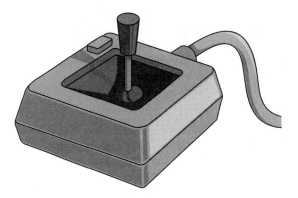

16.3   JOYSTICKS

The **game port** is a 2-row, 15-pin female port that allows up to four paddles or two joysticks to be attached to a PC. The paddle is a knob that can be rotated clockwise or counterclockwise to move an object on the screen. The joystick (including flight sticks and anything similar to a joystick) has a central stick that controls two variable resistors. (See fig. 16.3.) Much like the mouse, one resistor is for the X-axis and the other is for the Y-axis. As the stick is moved, the value of the variable resistor changes, causing a different analog electrical signal to go into the computer. The software then interprets the electrical signals.

The game port does not use an IRQ, DMA channel, or memory address. It needs only the single I/O address 201H. Because it doesn't use an interrupt, it has to be constantly scanned and requires a calibration program in most applications to interpret the variations in its variable resistance.

EXAMPLE 16.4   The joystick does not function.

A program must be able to use a joystick. Second, the software package must be configured to use the joystick. If there are two game ports (one on the I/O card and one on the sound card), there may be an I/O port address that must be set. If the joystick still does not function, either the joystick is faulty, the game port is faulty, or the game port is disabled (by jumpers or by software).

16.4   TOUCH SCREENS

A **touch screen** is a touch-sensitive transparent panel that covers a monitor screen. Instead of using a pointing device to select options, they can be selected by touching the screen. As the screen is touched, sensors detect a voltage change that is passed to the touch screen controller. The controller then processes the signal from the touch screen sensor and passes the data to the computer. Although touch screens seem like a neat concept, they are not widely used because the finger is a relatively large object compared to the objects displayed on the screen, which produces errors. And most people find that using touch screens causes the arms to tire after long periods.

16.5   IrDA

The **IrDA** port, sometimes known as the **Ir** port, was developed by the Infrared Developers Association (IrDA) to make use of wireless technology for the notebook and laptop computer. Some keyboards, serial port devices (mice and other pointing devices), and parallel port devices use IrDA. As the name indicates, IrDA ports use infrared light (like TV or VCR remote controls) to send data. Infrared light is an invisible electromagnetic radiation that has a wavelength longer than that of visible light. So far, the IrDA data rate is four megabits per second. Unlike other wireless technology, infrared does not use any radio waves. Therefore, it is not regulated by the FCC and will not cause interference on other electronic devices such as navigation and communication equipment, televisions, and radios.

Infrared signals are generated by a tiny light-emitting diode (LED) that focuses its beam into a 30-degree cone. To avoid interfering with other infrared devices, IrDA devices don't use much power. Consequently, the two communicating devices must be within a few feet

FIGURE 16.4   Flatbed scanner

of each other and must have a clear line of sight between them. In addition, bright sunlight may drown out the signal.

16.6   SCANNERS

A scanner (sometimes known as an optical scanner) is a device that can scan or digitize images on paper (much like a copy machine does) and convert them to data that the computer can use. They can then be stored in a file, displayed on the screen, added to documents, or manipulated.

16.6.1   CHARACTERISTICS OF SCANNERS

A scanner uses a series of charge-coupled devices (CCDs) mounted in a row. When a light source illuminates a piece of paper, the white spaces on the paper reflect more light than the dark areas. Some of the CCDs detect the presence or absence of light (black and white) while others detect the intensity of light (grayscale). Each CCD, at any moment, transmits its reading as a dot on the document being scanned. As the CCDs are moved from one edge to the other, the entire page is digitized row by row. Consequently, the document is made into a **bitmap.**

There are two types of scanners: flatbed and handheld. The **flatbed scanner** has a flat bed of glass on which the paper to be scanned is put face down. The CCDs are mounted on a moving arm, which moves from top to bottom. (See fig. 16.4.) A special type of flatbed scanner is the sheetfed scanner, which can be fed loose sheets of paper continuously, much like a copy machine.

The **handheld scanner** is much smaller than the flatbed scanner. (See fig. 16.5.) Instead of the CCDs being moved by the scanner, the handheld scanner is physically moved by the operator from one end to the other of a page. Although the handheld scanner is very portable, it can scan pictures and text only from two to five inches at a time. To keep the

FIGURE 16.5   Handheld scanner

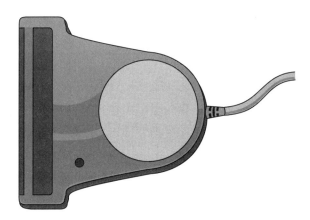

scanner moving straight and to help it differentiate among the rows to be scanned, the handheld scanner has small wheels.

The resolution of the scanner is the result of the number of CCDs and therefore the number of dots generated by the scanner. The denser the bitmap, the higher the resolution. Of course, higher resolution means that there is a lot more data to process and save. The number of CCDs and their density determine the horizontal resolution. The speed of the moving CCD and the focusing mirror determine the vertical resolution. Typical scanners support between 72 and 600 dots per inch (dpi).

Color scanners are enhanced grayscale scanners. Instead of scanning for one color, it scans for the three basic colors (red, green, and blue) by making multiple scans. Some scanners perform all three scans in one pass. The software then recombines the three colors to create a full color image.

Much like monitors, scanners have a bit depth, which is the number of bits used to represent each dot. If more bits are used to describe the color of the dot, the document scanned can be represented by more colors or grayscales. For example, a pure black-and-white image requires only 1 bit for each dot, while a 24-bit color scanner can represent 16.7 million colors.

16.6.2 INSTALLING AND USING THE SCANNER

Scanners can be connected to the computer using a SCSI interface, parallel port, USB interface, FireWire interface, or proprietary interface. Therefore, you might have to check for resource conflicts (I/O addresses, IRQ, DMA, and memory usage) when installing a scanner and install the appropriate drivers.

After the scanner is installed and configured, the scanner software which controls the scanner must be installed. This software allows you to choose when to scan, which areas to scan, brightness and other control settings, and to save the data into a bitmap (picture made of dots) graphics file, such as BMP or PCX. (Note: There are two types of graphic files, bitmap files and vector graphic files. **Vector graphic files** can save information as lines or circles instead of as individual dots. Bitmap graphics files can be modified with a paint program like Adobe Photoshop or Corel Photo-Paint, and vector graphic files can be modified with a draw program like Adobe Illustrator or Corel Draw. See table 16.4.) After the image is saved to file, it can then be modified with a paint program or other graphics package. Some of the changes possible are resizing, cropping (cutting off the sides of an image to make it the proper size or to remove unwanted parts), cutting, pasting and recoloring. Most graphics software can also save the file in a different format.

The de facto standard for scanners is **TWAIN**, which stands for "technology without an interesting name." TWAIN-compatible scanners include a TWAIN driver, which works with TWAIN-supported software like the common graphics programs (Adobe Photoshop and Corel Photo-Paint). Therefore, the scanner can be controlled with the normal graphics editing program and the image can be scanned into the program for immediate editing.

A scanned page of text is treated as an image made of dots. **Optical character recognition (OCR)** software converts the image of the text to actual text by analyzing the shape of each character and comparing its features against a set of rules that distinguishes each character and font. Most OCR software packages will then save the text into a Word, WordPerfect, RTF (rich text format), or ASCII text file.

SUMMARY

1. Input devices move information into the computer.
2. The keyboard is used to input (enter) letters, numbers, symbols, punctuation, and commands into the computer. It is the primary input device.
3. The standard typewriter layout is the QWERTY layout and is by far the most common one used today.
4. The XT keyboard was made to work with the XT computer; the AT keyboard was made for a 286 or later machine.
5. The keyboard is made up of many small mechanical parts (the keys).

TABLE 16.4 Common bitmap picture file formats

Bitmap Picture Format	Description
Paintbrush file format (PCX)	PCX files were originally developed in the early 1980s by ZSOFT for its PC Paintbrush program. It can support up to 24-bit color and uses run-length encoding (RLE) to compress the image data. Since it was one of the first graphic formats, it is supported by most optical scanners, desktop publishing systems, and most graphic software packages.
Bitmap (BMP)	The standard bitmapped graphics format used in Windows 3.XX, Windows 95 and 98, and Windows NT (such as wallpapers and boot-up screens). Windows bitmap files are stored in a device-independent bitmap format that allows Windows to display the bitmap on any type of display. BMP is the default filename extension but it may have others. The LOGO.SYS file (hidden file in the root directory of the C drive) in Windows 95 contains the bitmap image of the clouds and the Windows 95 logo shown during boot-up. Bitmap files can be stored in black-and-white, 4-bit, 8-bit, and 24-bit formats. In addition, bitmap files can be compressed by using run-length encoding (RLE). Another type of bitmap file is OS/2 BMP files. They are similar to Windows BMP files except for the way data is defined in the file.
Tagged image file format (TIFF)	TIFF files are one of the most widely supported file formats for storing bitmapped images for both the PC and Macintosh computers. TIFF files can be any resolution and any color level. They normally have a TIF filename extension.
Graphics interchange format (GIF)	A popular bitmap graphics file format used on the Internet because of its file compression. Although it does not compress as well as JPEG files, it does retain all of its detail. Animated GIF files are several individual GIF files combined into a single file. As each image is cycled through, the image is animated. Animated GIF files are also popular on the Internet because of their size as compared to Java applets and video formats (AVI or QuickTime files).
Joint photographic experts group (JPEG) format	A popular bitmap graphics file format used on the Internet because of its file compression. Although it can reduce files to about 5% of their size, some detail is lost in the compression. JPEG files will usually have a JPG filename extension.

6. Most keys are either mechanical switches, membrane switches, or capacitive switches.

7. The keyboard interface converts the row and column signal sent by the keys into a single-byte code called a *key code* or *scan code.*

8. One of the best ways to keep a keyboard in good condition is to clean it periodically.

9. To test the keyboard connector on the motherboard, measure the voltages of several pins of the keyboard connector.

10. The wrists should rest comfortably on the table in front of the keyboard, and the shoulders should be relaxed. Wrists should not have to bend to reach the keyboard.

11. The mouse and other pointing devices (trackballs, glidepads, and trackpoints) are used to navigate most modern operating systems and environments.

12. Newer mice are optomechanical devices that use light to detect motion.

13. The trackball is nothing more than an inverted mouse.

14. The first step in installing a mouse is physically connecting it through a serial port, PS/2 mouse port, or bus port.

15. After connecting the mouse, the next step in installation is loading the correct software drivers.

16. One of the most common problems with mice is that dirt, dust, and hair get inside the housing, causing the pointer to skip or not move.

17. The game port is a 2-row, 15-pin female port that allows up to four paddles or two joysticks to be attached to a PC.

18. A touch screen is a touch-sensitive transparent panel that covers a monitor screen.

19. The IrDA port, sometimes known as the Ir port, uses wireless technology (infrared light).

20. An optical scanner is a device that can scan, or digitize, images on paper (much like a copy machine does) and convert them to data that the computer can use.

21. The flatbed scanner has a flat bed of glass on which the document to be scanned is laid facing down.

22. Sheetfed scanners can be fed loose sheets of paper one after another, much like a copy machine.
23. The handheld scanner is much smaller than the flatbed scanner.
24. The de facto standard for scanners is TWAIN.
25. Optical character recognition (OCR) software converts images of text to actual text.

QUESTIONS

1. Which of the following are *not* input devices? (Choose two.)
   a. mouse
   b. keyboard
   c. printer
   d. monitor

2. Which of the following is the primary input device for the PC?
   a. keyboard
   b. mouse
   c. trackball
   d. scanner

3. Which of the following should be used to clean a keyboard?
   a. acetone
   b. clorox
   c. 409
   d. a wet cloth with a mild detergent

4. Which keyboard layout is most common?
   a. QWERTY
   b. Dvorak
   c. layman
   d. optomechanical

5. Which of the following statements is true?
   a. the AT keyboard is backward compatible with the XT system
   b. the AT system is backward compatible; therefore, an AT keyboard will work with an XT
   c. the XT keyboard will work only on an XT machine, and the AT keyboard will work only on a 286 machine
   d. the XT keyboard will work only on an XT machine, and the AT keyboard will work with a 286 or later machine.

6. Which of the following technologies are used in keyboard keys? (Choose three.)
   a. mechanical
   b. capacitors
   c. analog
   d. transistors
   e. membrane

7. A scan code is:
   a. a code use to control the scanner
   b. a code used to check for viruses
   c. a code that indentifies a key being pressed on the keyboard
   d. a code telling the computer to start polling the game port

8. Which of the following are types of keyboard connectors in use today?
   a. mini DIN-5
   b. mini DIN-6
   c. DIN-5
   d. DIN-6
   e. DB-15

9. In which of the following ways can you check the AT keyboard connector on the motherboard?
   a. putting one lead of an ohmmeter in socket 4 and checking the remaining socket for 2.5- to 5-ohm readings
   b. putting one lead of an ammeter in socket 4 and checking for a current of 250 to 500 milliamps
   c. putting one lead of a voltmeter in socket 4 and checking the remaining sockets for 2.5 to 5 volts
   d. putting one lead of a voltmeter in socket 1 and the other in socket 5 and looking for 3.5 volts

10. A 301 error code appears on an IBM Aptiva computer on boot-up. What is the problem?
    a. the keyboard
    b. the RAM
    c. the floppy disk drive
    d. the hard drive
    e. none of the above

11. When a key is no longer functioning, you should:
    a. throw the keyboard away immediately
    b. clean under the key (which may require removing the keycap); if this does not correct the problem, throw the keyboard away
    c. wash the keyboard in a sink of hot soapy water; if this does not correct the problem, throw the keyboard away
    d. desolder the bad key and solder a new one
12. What is the correct way to use a keyboard?
    a. bend the wrist up
    b. bend the wrist down
    c. use the mouse instead of the keyboard
    d. keep the wrist straight
13. An optomechanical mouse works on which of the following principles?
    a. mechanical-driven plastic slotted wheels break beams of light, generating pulses that may be counted
    b. data is transmitted using an infrared beam
    c. infrared light bounces off a reflective mouse pad
    d. location is calculated using simple trigonometry theories to calculate the position of two infrared light sources placed at 90 degrees to each other
14. Which of the following is not a pointing device?
    a. touch screen
    b. trackball
    c. mouse
    d. glidepoint
    e. trackpoint
15. The mouse can be connected using all of the following ports except:
    a. Ir
    b. PS/2
    c. bus
    d. serial
    e. parallel
16. Two common mouse drivers for DOS are:
    a. MOUSE.COM, which is normally loaded with a line in the AUTOEXEC.BAT file, and MOUSE.SYS, which is normally loaded with a line in the CONFIG.SYS file
    b. MOUSE.COM, which is normally loaded with a line in the CONFIG.SYS file, and MOUSE.SYS, which is normally loaded with a line in the AUTOEXEC.BAT file
    c. MOUSE.COM and MOUSE.SYS, both of which are normally loaded with lines in the AUTOEXEC.BAT file
    d. MOUSE.COM and MOUSE.SYS, both of which are normally loaded with lines in the CONFIG.SYS file
    e. MOUSE.COM, MOUSE.SYS, and MOUSE.DRV, which are normally loaded with lines in the CONFIG.SYS file
17. The mouse works in MS-DOS but not in Windows 95. What do you do?
    a. check for the proper mouse driver in the Mouse icon or applet in the Control Panel
    b. check jumpers on the motherboard
    c. check for the proper mouse driver in the AUTOEXEC.BAT and CONFIG.SYS files
    d. check the mouse cable and connector
18. The mouse pointer moves erratically on the screen. What is the most likely problem?
    a. ESD damage
    b. incompatible mouse
    c. dirty mouse
    d. bad cable
19. Which of the following describes a game port?
    a. female 2-row, 15-pin D connector
    b. female 3-row, 15-pin D connector
    c. male 2-row, 9-pin D connector
    d. male 2-row, 25-pin D connector
    e. female 2-row, 9-pin D connector

20. Which device allows the user to digitize information on a piece of paper?
    a. an optical mouse
    b. a glidepad
    c. a scanner
    d. a screen
21. The de facto standard for scanners is:
    a. HP
    b. Epson
    c. OCR
    d. TWAIN
22. Which of the following interfaces is best suited for receiving input from a scanner?
    a. the serial port
    b. the parallel port
    c. the IDE port
    d. the SCSI port
23. What software converts images of text to actual text?
    a. OCR
    b. drivers for the scanner
    c. computer reader
    d. glidepad
24. Which of the following is *not* a bitmap graphic format?
    a. BMP
    b. PCX
    c. GIF
    d. JPG
    e. DOC

HANDS-ON EXERCISES

Exercise 1: Taking a Keyboard Apart

1. Turn the keyboard over, and remove the screws that hold the keyboard together.
2. For each tab that holds the keyboard together, slide the blade of a flat-edge screwdriver between the cover (top part of the keyboard) and the base (bottom of the keyboard). Then pry them apart by twisting the screwdriver.
3. Hold the keyboard together and turn right side up. Then lift the cover free of the base and set the cover aside.
4. See how the cable is connected.
5. Identify the interface circuit board.
6. Hold the keyboard upside down and spray it with a can of compressed air.
7. Reassemble the keyboard.
8. Using a chip puller or similar tool, pull a keycap off.
9. Hold the keyboard upside down and spray it with a can of compressed air.
10. Put the keycap back on.

Exercise 2: Testing a Keyboard

1. Enter the CMOS setup program and make sure that the keyboard is enabled.
2. Shut off the computer, unplug the keyboard, and boot the computer. Notice any error messages.
3. Shut off the computer and plug in the keyboard. Next, enter the CMOS setup program and disable the keyboard. Save the changes.
4. Shut off the computer, unplug the keyboard, and boot the computer. Notice any error messages.
5. Shut off the computer and reconnect the keyboard. Enable the keyboard in the CMOS setup program.
6. Using the CMOS setup program, enable the Numlock setting and save the changes to CMOS.
7. After boot-up, observe whether the Numlock is on or off.
8. Using the CMOS setup program, disable the Numlock setting and save the changes to CMOS.
9. After boot-up, look to see if the Numlock is on or off.
10. Turn on the computer. During boot-up, press the Z key and keep it down. Notice the error message that appears on the screen.
11. Turn off the computer.
12. Determine whether there is an XT/AT switch underneath the keyboard. If there is, set the keyboard to XT and turn on the machine. Notice what happens.
13. Shut off the keyboard and set the keyboard back to AT.

Exercise 3: Disassembling and Cleaning the Mouse

1. Shut off the computer and disconnect the mouse or trackball.
2. Remove the mouse ball. This can be done by rotating the holding panel or by pushing the panel in one direction. Then tip the mouse so that the mouse ball falls out.
3. Find the X-axis and the Y-axis rollers. Use a cotton swab to clean any debris that is on the rollers.
4. Remove the screws on the bottom of the housing that hold the mouse together.
5. Gently separate the top and bottom halves and identify the buttons.
6. Look for the light source (LED), sensor, and slotted wheel on one end of the X-axis or Y-axis roller. Spin the roller.
7. Reassemble the mouse and test the mouse to make sure it is working properly.

Exercise 4: Testing the Input Devices

1. Make sure that the correct driver is loaded for the mouse.
2. Run the software diagnostic package for the keyboard, mouse, and game port.

Exercise 5: Installing a Mouse Driver in Windows.

1. In Windows 3.XX or Windows 95 or 98, change the mouse to a Genius mouse (or another one assigned by your instructor). Restart Windows.
2. Without using the mouse, install the correct mouse driver. For Windows 3.XX, run SETUP.EXE from the WINDOWS directory. For Windows 95 or 98, use the Mouse icon or applet in the Control Panel. Restart Windows.
3. Shut down Windows and unplug the mouse.
4. Start Windows and let it boot.

Exercise 6: Installing a Mouse Driver

1. Boot to DOS.
2. Find and install a mouse driver on the hard drive or on a floppy disk. The most common file names are MOUSE.COM, MOUSE.EXE, and MOUSE.SYS, often located in the MOUSE directory. If the mouse driver is a file with a COM or EXE filename extension, type in the filename to execute the driver. If the mouse driver is a file with a SYS filename extension, add the appropriate line in the CONFIG.SYS (located in the root directory of the boot device) and reboot the computer.
3. Test the mouse using EDIT.

Exercise 7: Configuring the Mouse and Keyboard in Windows

1. Using the Keyboard icon or applet in the Control Panel, set the repeat delay to long and the repeat rate to slow.
2. Start Microsoft Word, WordPad, or Write. Press the H key and keep it down. Notice how long it takes before it starts repeating and how fast the letters are repeating.
3. Using the Keyboard icon or applet in the Control Panel, set the repeat delay to short and the repeat rate to fast.
4. From Microsoft Word, WordPad, or Write, press the F key and keep it down. Notice how long it takes before it starts repeating and how fast the letters are repeating.
5. Change the repeat delay and repeat rate to settings that feel comfortable to you.
6. Using the Mouse icon or applet in the Control Panel, set the double-click speed to fast.
7. Go to the test area and try to perform a double-click.
8. Set the double-click speed to slow.
9. Go to the test area and try to perform a double-click.
10. Change the double-click speed to a setting that feels comfortable to you.
11. Adjust the pointer speed to fast. Move the mouse across the screen. Notice how far you have to move the mouse to move the mouse pointer across the screen.
12. Adjust the pointer speed to slow. Move the mouse across the screen. Notice how far you have to move the mouse to move the mouse pointer across the screen.
13. Change the pointer speed to a setting that feels comfortable to you.

Exercise 8: Installing a Scanner

1. If an expansion card is needed to connect the scanner, configure the resources (I/O addresses; IRQ, DMA, or memory addresses) and physically install the card.
2. Configure the scanner (if necessary).
3. Install any drivers (if necessary).
4. Install the scanner software.
5. Scan a picture.

17 Sound Cards

INTRODUCTION

Although sound cards were not used in early personal computers, they are considered standard in today's multimedia computer. They allow the computer to record sound from a microphone, manipulate sound files, and output sound through a set of speakers. This allows presentations to have music and special sound effects and moves games to a new level. Sound cards also allow the user to play audio compact disks, compose music, create special sound effects, and use voice recognition programs.

OBJECTIVES

1. Describe sound and its characteristics.
2. Explain how sound is converted to a sound file.
3. Explain how a sound is played through the sound card.
4. Describe Nyquist's sampling theorem.
5. Explain bit resolution as it relates to sound cards.
6. Define MIDI.
7. List the difference between FM synthesis and wavetable MIDI cards.
8. Install, configure, and connect a sound card.
9. Determine and correct problems with sound.

17.1 SOUND

To understand how sound cards work, you need to understand what sound is. **Sound** is produced by vibrations of compressed air. Sound travels in all directions away from the source. When the sound reaches the human ear, it causes the eardrum to vibrate, allowing you to hear the sound.

Sound is characterized by its amplitude and its frequency. The amplitude (loudness or intensity) is measured in **decibels (dB),** a unit of measurement based on a logarithmic curve. For example; a sound that is 100 times as intense as another is only 20 dB larger. A whisper measures 10 dB, normal conversation measures 65 dB, and a rock band with amplifiers can measure 110 dB of intensity. **Frequency** (pitch) is the rate of the vibration. It is measured in **hertz (Hz),** or cycles per second. Very few people can hear frequencies lower than 16 Hz or higher than 20 kHz. The lowest note on the piano has a frequency of 27 Hz while the highest note has a frequency of approximately 4 kHz.

17.2 THE SOUND CARD

Sound cards, which were not used in early personal computers, are considered standard in today's computer. (See fig. 17.1.) They allow the computer to record sound from a microphone, manipulate sound files, and output sound through a set of speakers. Sound can be saved to a file, so it can be used to improve presentations and make games more exciting. The de facto standard for sound cards are those developed by Creative Labs, such as their Sound Blaster cards.

17.2.1 RECORDING SOUND

The vibrations in the air that make up sound must be converted into electrical signals in order for them to be manipulated by the computer. A **microphone** is used to convert sound into analog electrical signals. (*Analog* means that the signal varies continuously without any discrete, or incremental, values. See fig. 17.2.)

FIGURE 17.1 Sound card

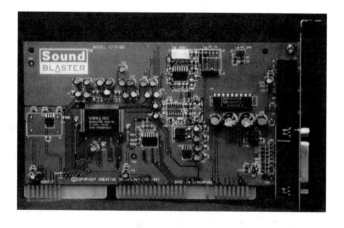

FIGURE 17.2 Original signal

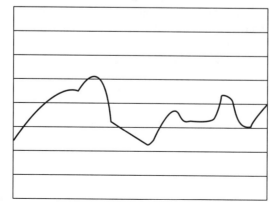

Most microphones used with the computer are either dynamic microphones or condenser microphones. Dynamic microphones have a diaphragm connected to a coil of wire (voice coil) that is wrapped around a permanent magnet. The diaphragm is usually a cone made of plastic. Sound causes the diaphragm to vibrate, which causes the voice coil to move. The voice coil thus generates a signal, which is sent into the sound card. Another type of microphone is the condenser microphone. The condenser microphone works by sending voltages through a capacitor. Instead of the diaphragm being wired in series with a magnet, it acts as one plate of a capacitor. As the diaphragm vibrates, the distance between the two plates changes, capacitance changes, and consequently the voltage is changed, causing different signals to be sent to the sound card.

The sound card amplifies and **digitizes** the signals; that is, it converts the signals into data that the computer can understand. The device that performs the analog-to-digital conversion is known as an analog-to-digital converter (ADC). Digitizing involves sampling the electrical signal and assigning a binary value to its amplitude. The larger the number of samples, the closer the recorded sound will be to the real sound. Unfortunately, sound files with a large number of samples are larger in size. (See fig. 17.3.) Recording should be done according to Nyquist's sampling theorem, which states that the sampling rate should be at least twice as fast as the highest frequency in the signal. The lowest standard sampling rate is 11 kHz, which is fine for normal speech. Since the human range of hearing does not go above about 22 kHz, audio compact disks use a 44 kHz sampling rate, which is often referred to as *CD-quality* sampling.

The number of bits that represent the binary number assigned to the signal sample is known as bit resolution. An 8-bit sound card (a card with a bit resolution of 8 bits, or 1 byte) can store one of 256 combinations of eight 0s and 1s. When amplitude is measured during a sample, it is assigned one of these specific binary values to indicate how loud the signal is. A 16-bit card allows greater accuracy because it can store one of 65,536 combinations of 16 0s and 1s. Most sound cards today are 16-bit cards. (See table 17.1.)

The core of the sound card is the **digital signal processor (DSP),** which is specifically designed to manipulate large volumes of digital data. The processor follows instructions provided by a ROM chip on the sound card that operate the DSP and direct the board's major operations. In addition to the ROM, the sound card has a small amount of RAM for calculations and for buffering information being sent to and from the expansion bus.

17.2.2 PLAYING BACK SOUND

The analog signals coming from the microphone are greatly amplified, sampled, and converted to a binary value by the analog-to-digital converter. (Note: Signals from a CD player or a stereo system don't require as much amplification.) Eventually the data is organized and stored in a file, the most common type of which is the **waveform audio (WAV)** file. (See table 17.2 for other common sound file formats.)

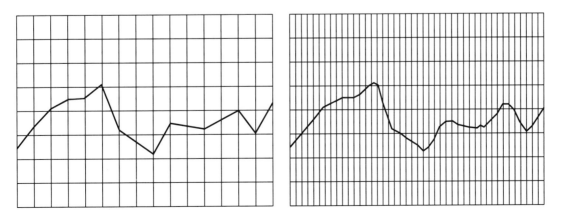

FIGURE 17.3 Two examples of sampling. The second one has more samples; therefore, the reconstructed signal is much closer to the original signal than the first one.

TABLE 17.1 Common sample rate and bit resolution comparisons

Sample Rate	Bits per Sample	Stereo/Mono	Size per Second
11,025 Hz	8 bits	Mono	11 KB
11,025 Hz	8 bits	Stereo	22 KB
11,025 Hz	16 bits	Mono	22 KB
11,025 Hz	16 bits	Stereo	43 KB
22,050 Hz	8 bits	Mono	22 KB
22,050 Hz	8 bits	Stereo	43 KB
22,050 Hz	16 bits	Mono	43 KB
22,050 Hz	16 bits	Stereo	86 KB
44,100 Hz	8 bits	Mono	43 KB
44,100 Hz	8 bits	Stereo	86 KB
44,100 Hz	16 bits	Mono	86 KB
44,100 Hz	16 bits	Stereo	172 KB

TABLE 17.2 Common sound file formats

WAV	*Short for waveform audio.* It was developed jointly by Microsoft and IBM. Since WAV support was built into Windows 95, WAV become the de facto standard for sound on the PC. Unfortunately, WAV files tend to be large. For example, a single minute of audio can require more than 1 MB of storage.
AU	*Short for audio.* A common format for sound files found on UNIX machines, on the Internet, and in the Java programming language.
AIF or IEF	*Short for audio interchange file format.* A common format for storing and transmitting sampled sound. The format was developed by Apple Computer and is the standard format for Macintosh computers. The format encodes audio data in 8-bit mono or stereo waveforms. AIF format does not support data compression, so AIF and IEF files tend to be large.
MP3	*Short for MPEG layer 3.* MP3 is a type of audio data compression that can reduce digital sound files by a 12:1 ratio with virtually no loss in quality.
RA	*Short for RealAudio.* RealAudio format was developed by RealNetworks and supports FM-stereo-quality sound. It is the de facto standard for streaming audio data over the Internet. Streaming allows the sound files to start playing while being transferred. To hear a web page that includes a RealAudio sound file, you need a RealAudio player or plug-in.

To play back sound, a software program reads the sound file and passes the data to the sound card. The sound card combines or mixes signals from the DSP, audio CD, and synthesizer into a single analog signal. If a sound card operates in stereo mode, it will have two mixers and amplifiers (one for the left side and one for the right side). The signal is then amplified and sent to a voice coil in the speaker. As the voltages change, the magnetic field changes, causing the voice coil to move. Sound is then generated by a diaphragm in the speaker connected to the voice coil.

Of course, any time analog signals are converted to digital signals and then back to analog signals, the sound is distorted. This is because samples are taken only at intervals, so changes in between samples are not taken into account. The sample is assigned a binary number based on increments—it can't be assigned a fraction of an increment. Therefore, the amount of distortion depends on the rate of sampling and the bit resolution. The distortion is called **aliasing.**

Sound cards have little or no power to drive a high-quality external speaker. Therefore, to get the best sound from a sound card, power must be supplied to the speakers, either through batteries or an ac outlet. Speakers can generate a magnetic field, so if they are placed near the monitor, that may distort the display, and if they are placed near a disk or other magnetic media, the data could be corrupted.

17.2.3 MIDI

Today, most sound cards have a **musical instrument digital interface (MIDI)** port (2-row, 15-pin female D connector). MIDI is an interface and protocol for connecting musical instruments to a PC and storing musical instrument data. Through the MIDI interface, several musical instruments can be daisy-chained together and played simultaneously. In addition, with sequencer software, the music can be captured, saved, edited, and played back.

A MIDI file and a sound file are quite different from each other. A sound file is made by sampling an analog signal; a MIDI file acts more like an enhanced music sheet. It contains information on each note, including its timing, volume, pitch, and instrument type (such as piano, guitar, drum, or flute). The MIDI file is processed by the DSP, but the sounds are actually generated by one of two types of synthesizer IC, FM or wavetable. FM synthesis mimics different musical instruments according to built-in mathematical formulas. Wavetable synthesis relies on recordings of actual instruments to produce sound, so it produces a more accurate sound than FM synthesis. Synthesizers have multiple channels, and several instruments can be played at the same time. In addition, the sounds from one instrument can be captured and played back as another instrument.

If people do not have musical instruments or do not want to connect them to the MIDI interface, most MIDI interfaces can be converted to a game port by changing a jumper on the sound card. Of course, if there is an existing game port, that may create an I/O address conflict.

17.2.4 COMPRESSION

When sound cards sample at 44 kHz using 16-bit resolution, the sound files can consume as much as 11 MB for every minute of recording. To reduce the disk space required, many sound cards have built-in data compression. File compression can also be done with software. The most efficient compression methods focus on compressing what a human can hear and ignore what a human can't hear.

17.2.5 SOUND CARD CONNECTORS

Sound cards typically have several ⅛″ minijack connectors. The audio-out connector is used to send sound signals from the sound card to a device (speakers, headphones, or a stereo system) outside of the computer. If the sound card supports stereo output, it may have two output connectors, one for the left channel and one for the right channel. An additional connector may be used specifically for a set of speakers or headphones. The line-in connector is used to record or mix sound signals on the computer's hard disks. There is also the microphone connector. (Note: The microphone connector records only in mono, not in stereo.) Lastly, most sound cards have a MIDI/joystick connector (2-row, 15-pin female).

17.3 INSTALLING A SOUND CARD

Sound cards are one of the more difficult expansion cards to install because they usually use one IRQ, two DMA channels, and up to four I/O addresses. These are set with jumpers, DIP switches, software, or by plug-and-play. Table 17.3 lists the default resources for a Sound Blaster card, which can, of course, be changed as needed.

Physically insert the sound card into an empty expansion slot and secure it with the holding screw. Next, attach speakers, the microphone, and other connectors to the appropriate

TABLE 17.3 Default resources for a Sound Blaster sound card

Device	Interrupt	I/O Port	16-bit DMA Channel	8-bit DMA Channel
Audio	IRQ 5	220H–233H	DMA 5	DMA 1
MIDI port		330H–331H		
FM synthesizer		388H–38BH		
Game port		200H–207H		

jacks. After the card is physically installed and configured, load the proper software drivers. For DOS, drivers are loaded in the AUTOEXEC.BAT and CONFIG.SYS files. For Windows 95 and 98 and Windows NT, the drivers are loaded directly into the operating system. If they don't load automatically, the drivers can be loaded using the ADD NEW HARDWARE icon or applet in the Control Panel.

After the installation is complete, you will usually notice an environmental variable in the AUTOEXEC.BAT file, for example:

```
SET BLASTER=A220 I5 D1
```

The A220 means the card is using I/O port address A220, the I5 indicates the card is using IRQ 5, and the D1 indicates the card is using DMA 1. The last step before using the sound card is installing an application that uses the sound card. Most sound cards come with bundled software, which includes a multimedia player, a sound recorder, sound control panel, and a mixer. Some sound card applications need to be configured with the I/O addresses, IRQ, and DMAs of the sound card.

17.4 TROUBLE-SHOOTING SOUND PROBLEMS

Most sound problems are often caused by a disconnected or improperly connected cable or a resource conflict (IRQ, DMA, or I/O address). Other problems could be caused by faulty speakers or a faulty sound card.

EXAMPLE 17.1 No sound is coming from new speakers or headphones.

Check the obvious first. Make sure that the speaker is turned on and that it has power. Check the volume control on the sound card, software mixer, and the speakers. In addition, make sure that the cables are connected properly to the speakers or headphones.

Before opening the computer, make sure that the drivers are installed properly, the environment is present (if needed), and the application software is configured for the sound card's resources. If the problem still exists, swap the cables, speaker or headphones, or sound card one at a time until you discover the problem.

EXAMPLE 17.2 One speaker or both produces a noticeable buzz or hum.

This problem is usually caused by a cable that isn't completely connected or by unshielded cables experiencing interference from an outside source. If the cable is experiencing interference, move the path of the cables or use better-shielded cables. If the problem still exists, swap the speakers and sound card one at a time until you discover the problem.

EXAMPLE 17.3 The volume is low.

First, check the volume control on the sound card, software mixers, and the speakers. In addition, make sure that the cables are connected properly. Next, make sure that the speakers are adequate and that they have enough power (from an ac outlet or batteries). Lastly, try using a stereo amplifier between the sound card and speakers.

EXAMPLE 17.4 Sound is coming from only one speaker.

First, make sure that cables are connected properly and that a mono plug is not inserted in the stereo jack. (Note: A mono connector has only one stripe, while a stereo connector has two stripes. See fig. 17.4.) Next, make sure that the correct driver is loaded and that the software mixer's balance control is set properly.

FIGURE 17.4 An audio connector with two bands

SUMMARY

1. Audible sound is produced by vibrations of compressed air.
2. Sound is characterized by its amplitude, or loudness (measured in decibels), and its frequency (measured in hertz).
3. Sounds cards are considered standard in today's computer. They allow the computer to record sound from a microphone, manipulate sound files, and output sound through a set of speakers.
4. The de facto standard for sound cards is the sound cards developed by Creative Labs (Sound Blaster).
5. A microphone is used to convert sound into analog electrical signals.
6. The sound card then amplifies and digitizes the sound.
7. Digitizing (also known as sampling) is done by taking samples of the electrical signal and assigning a binary value to the amplitude of the signal.
8. The core of the sound card is the digital signal processor (DSP), which is specifically designed to manipulate large volumes of digital data.
9. The amplitude is assigned a binary number depending on the resolution of the sound card (usually 8-bit or 16-bit).
10. To play back sound, a software program reads the sound file and passes the data to the sound card. The sound card combines, or mixes, signals from the DSP, audio CD, and synthesizer into a single analog signal, which it amplifies and sends to a set of speakers.
11. MIDI is an interface and protocol for connecting musical instruments to a microcomputer and storing musical instrument data.
12. A sound file contains samples of an analog signal;, a MIDI file contains instructions for playing specific notes.
13. FM synthesis mimics different musical instruments according to built-in mathematical formulas.
14. Wavetable synthesis relies on recordings of actual instruments to produce sound.
15. The sound card will usually use one IRQ, two DMA channels, and up to 4 base I/O addresses.
16. For sound cards to operate, they require the proper drivers.
17. Most sound problems are caused by disconnected or improperly connected cables, resource conflicts (IRQ, DMA, or I/O address), faulty speaker(s), or a faulty sound card.

QUESTIONS

1. Sound is measured in (choose two):
   a. amplitude
   b. frequency
   c. phase
   d. distortion
   e. distance
2. Which device allows you to record sounds?
   a. speakers
   b. keyboard
   c. capacitor
   d. microphone
3. Taking measurements at intervals of time is called:
   a. bit resolution
   b. amplifying
   c. sampling
   d. gain
4. How many tones can an eight-bit sound card produce?
   a. 16
   b. 256
   c. 512
   d. 1,024
   e. 4,096
   f. 65,536
5. Which of the following is a sound file?
   a. WAV
   b. MOV
   c. JPG
   d. AVI

6. The distortion caused by converting an analog signal to a digital signal and back to an analog signal is called:
   a. amplifying
   b. aliasing
   c. sensitivity
   d. harmonic
   e. modulation
7. An electromagnetic field caused by a set of speakers can result in which of the following problems? (Choose all that apply.)
   a. distortion of the video display
   b. total shutdown of the PC
   c. RAM errors
   d. read/write problem on magnetic disks and tapes
8. A MIDI interface is described as a:
   a. 2-row, 25-pin female D connector
   b. 3-row, 15-pin female D connector
   c. 2-row, 15-pin female D connector
   d. 2-row, 15-pin male D connector
   e. 2-row, 9-pin female D connector
9. Which form of synthesizer uses recordings of actual sounds?
   a. condenser
   b. FM synthesis
   c. wavetable
   d. amplifying
   e. dynamic
10. Which of the following is least likely to cause a sound problem?
    a. magnetic distortion
    b. IRQ conflict
    c. incorrect drivers
    d. improperly connected cable

HANDS-ON EXERCISE

Exercise 1: Installing a Sound Card

1. Using a sound card's documentation, configure it to use free resources (IRQ, I/O addresses, DMA, and memory addresses).
2. Install the sound card drivers. (If you are using DOS or Windows 3.XX, install the drivers using the disks or CD-ROM that came with the sound card. If you are using Windows 95 or 98 or Windows NT, install the drivers using the Add New Hardware icon or applet in the Control Panel. Note that you may still need to use the disks or CD-ROM that came with the sound card.)
3. Connect speakers or headphones to the sound card.

Exercise 2: Using a Sound Card

1. Install software that will use the sound card. (If you have DOS or Windows 3.XX, use the bundled software that came with the sound card. The resources used by the sound card may need to be entered into the software. If you have Windows 95 or 98 or Windows NT, make sure that the Media Player, Sound Recorder, Volume Control, CD-ROM Player, and Multimedia Sound Schemes are loaded. They are usually executed by using the Start button and Programs, Accessories, Multimedia menu. If they are not loaded, they can be loaded by using the Add or Remove Software icon or applet in the Control Panel. Note: If the sound card has bundled software, you may also want to install it so that you can compare it to programs that come with Windows 95 and 98 or Windows NT.)
2. Using Media Player or equivalent software, find, load, and play a file with a WAV filename extension. Windows 95 and 98 and NT will usually have WAV files in the WINDOWS\MEDIA directory.
3. Adjust the volume controls on the speaker and sound card. Play the WAV file.
4. Using the volume control or equivalent software, mute the volume. Play the WAV file.
5. Using the volume control, activate the sound and close the WAV file.
6. Connect a microphone to your sound card. Using the Sound Recorder or equivalent software, record a 5- to 10-second message using 8-bit resolution at 22,000 Hz mono settings. Save the file on the hard drive. (For Sound Recorder, the bit resolution, sample rate, and mono and stereo settings can be configured by using Properties under the File menu, and clicking on the Convert Now... button.)

7. Using the Sound Recorder or equivalent software, record the same message using 16-bit resolution at 44,000 Hz stereo settings. Save the file to the hard drive under a different name from the first file.
8. Look at the size of the two files.
9. Using Media Player, play one of your recordings.
10. If you have a CD-ROM drive and an audio CD, perform the following:
    a. Insert the audio CD in the CD-ROM drive.
    b. Using the Volume Control or equivalent software, mute the microphone recording. (When you first start Volume Control, it usually shows the controls for playback. To switch to the Volume Controls for recording, select Properties under the Options menu.)
    c. Load the CD Player and select the track that you want to record.
    d. Start the Sound Recorder and then the CD Player.
    e. Stop the recording after 30 seconds.
    f. Play the recorded sound using Sound Recorder.
    g. Save the file as a WAV file.
    h. Load and play the WAV file using Media Player.
11. If you have Windows 95 or 98 or Windows NT, open the Sounds icon or applet from the Control Panel. Change the Close a Program event to CHIMES.WAV.
12. Start a program and exit the program.
13. Change the Close a Program event back to the way it was.

18 Serial Ports and Modems

INTRODUCTION

The serial port interface is a general-purpose interface that can be used for almost any type of device. It is used mostly for mice and modems, but it can also be used for serial printers, plotters, label makers, bar code readers, scales, and device control circuits. In addition, the serial port can be used to talk to other computers. Today, all of the popular operating systems, including DOS with Windows 3.XX, Windows 95 and 98, and Windows NT, use a mouse to navigate. In addition, the Internet has made the modem (modulator-demodulator) more common than ever. Unfortunately, installing and configuring a modem can cause all kinds of headaches.

OBJECTIVES

1. Identify the serial port by looking at the back of a computer or an expansion card.
2. List the characteristics of a serial port.
3. Explain how the RS-232C and RS-422 standard relate to the serial port.
4. Determine how many serial ports a system can have.
5. Define a data frame and list and describe the components of a data frame.
6. Compare and contrast baud and bits per second.
7. Explain how the serial port communicates.
8. Define the purpose of a null modem cable and explain how it differs from a normal serial cable.
9. Install and configure a serial port.
10. Determine and correct a serial port problem.
11. Explain how a modem communicates with another computer using a standard phone line.
12. List the different methods by which data can be encoded in telephone transmissions.
13. Transfer a file using a modem.
14. Explain the AT command set.
15. Explain the process of using a fax/modem to send and receive fax documents.
16. Compare and contrast the differences between normal modems and ISDN modems.
17. Install and configure a modem.
18. Determine and correct a modem problem.

18.1 SERIAL PORTS

The **serial port interface** is a general-purpose interface that can be used for almost any type of device. It can be identified by its two-row male D port that has either 9 or 25 pins. (See fig. 18.1.) Serial ports are bidirectional asynchronous devices. They send data over a single wire as bits lined up single-file in series. The advantage of serial communications is that they are simple and are able to go long distances. As the name implies, the serial port is a **full-duplex** device, which means that data can travel in both directions at the same time and without synchronization or a timer (**asynchronous**).

The serial port on the PC conforms to the Electronics Industries Association (EIA) RS-232C standard (Recommended Standard Number 232; C is the latest revision of the standard). The full RS-232C standard specifies a 25-pin D connector, of which 22 pins are used; serial ports use only a few pins, so they follow a subset of the RS-232C standard. The RS-422 and RS-423 standards have since replaced the RS-232 standard because they support higher data rates and greater immunity to electrical interference. RS-422 supports multipoint connections; the RS-423 supports only point-to-point connections.

The typical computer can support up to four serial ports with an ISA bus or later standard. The IBM PS/2 supports eight serial ports. If more serial ports are needed, a multiport board, which has up to 128 serial ports, can be purchased. Of course, the operating system and application software must be able to recognize all of the ports. DOS 3.3 or higher only supports four serial ports; Windows 95 and 98 and Windows NT support up to 128 serial ports. Serial ports use reserved computer names such as COM1, COM2, COM3, and COM4 (COM stands for communication).

18.1.1 CHARACTERISTICS OF A SERIAL PORT

As a full-duplex device, the serial port uses separate lines for sending and receiving data and has a common signal ground wire. Not all of the devices that can be attached to a serial port require two-way communications, so these devices require only a transmit line and signal ground. The signals used by the serial ports are bipolar, which means they consist of positive and negative voltages. A value of 0 (space state) is represented with a positive value between +3 V dc and +15 V dc and a value of 1 (mark state) is represented by a negative voltage between −3 V dc and −15 V dc. These voltages differ, of course, from the voltages most commonly used by PCs, which are +5 V dc, −5 V dc, +12 V dc, and −12 V dc produced by the power supply. The advantage of a bipolar signal is that it sup-

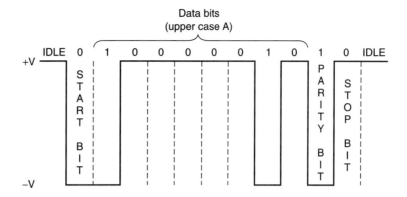

FIGURE 18.1 Serial port signal

ports very long cabling with minimum noise. In addition, the sending and receiving devices can distinguish between an idle state and a disconnected line.

Information sent through a serial port is sent as data frame. The data frame consists of a start bit, a number of data bits, one to two stop bits, and possibly some parity bits. Because the serial ports are asynchronous (no timer), they need some way to coordinate with each other. Therefore, whenever data is sent, a start bit is sent to notify the other end that data is coming. Since the serial line is kept positive when idle, the start bit (logical 1) drops the line to a negative voltage. After the start bit has been sent, the transmitting device sends the actual data bits. Most computers and computer devices use 5, 6, 7, or 8 bits to represent the data being sent, and both the receiving and transmitting devices must agree on the number of data bits transmitted. Seven data bits allow up to 128 different characters, and eight data bits allow up to 256 different characters (such as the ASCII characters). After the data has been transmitted, a stop bit is sent to indicate the end of the data frame. It can consist of 1, 1½, or 2 bits with a logical value of 1. Again, the sending and transmitting device must count the same number of stop bits.

To check for errors, serial devices will use parity checking or CRC checking. **Parity** error control could be odd parity, even parity, mark parity, or space parity. Mark parity will always have the parity bit set to a 1 and the space parity set to a 0. During parity checking, the 1s of the data bits are counted. If the data bits have an odd number, the parity bit is assigned a 0, keeping the data bits and parity bit an odd number. If the data bits have an even number, the parity is assigned a 1, keeping the data bits and parity bit an odd number. Therefore, when the data is sent to a receiving device, the receiving device counts the data bits and parity bit to make sure that the number is still odd. If the bit count is even, an error has occurred. Even parity is the opposite of odd parity. When the data bits and parity bit are counted, the total number should be even. Consequently, when the data is sent to a receiving device, the receiving device counts the data bits and parity bit to make sure that the number is still even. If the bit count is odd, an error has occurred. Unfortunately, if two or any even number of errors occur, the odd parity remains odd and the even parity remains even. Therefore, no error is detected. Of course, both the sending and the receiving device must use the same parity-checking scheme.

Another form of error checking is **CRC (cyclic redundancy check).** While parity checking monitors a group of 7 or 8 bits, CRC checks an entire block of data, such as 1,024 bytes. CRC performs a mathematical calculation (CRC value) on the data to be sent, and when the block of data is sent, this value is also sent. When the data reaches its destination, the same mathematical calculation is done and the result is compared to the CRC value sent. If the values are not the same, an error occurred during transmission.

18.1.2 UNIVERSAL ASYNCHRONOUS RECEIVER/TRANSMITTER (UART)

The central part of the serial port is the **universal asynchronous receiver/transmitter (UART),** which is a single IC chip located on the motherboard or on an I/O expansion card. It is the translator between the serial port and the system bus and is the component that processes, transmits, and receives data. For flexibility, the UART includes several registers that allow it to be programmed or configured. By using communications software, the number of data bits, the length of the stop bit, and the baud rate can be specified and modified as needed for each serial port.

Inside the computer, data is generated by the microprocessor and moved around in parallel format (system bus). This means that the several bits are being moved from one place to another simultaneously using several wires. Of course, the more wires there are, the more data can be transported. As the data comes from the system bus, the UART converts it to a serial signal (bits in a single file), adds the start and stop bits, and adds any error control (such as parity). Then the UART converts the digital signals (+5 V dc TTL) to a bipolar signal. The data is then sent through the serial port out to the serial cable. As data comes in from the serial port, the UART must reverse the process. First, the UART converts the bipolar signal to a +5 V dc TTL digital signal. It then strips the start and stop bits, checks for errors, and strips the error-control information. Finally, it converts the data back into parallel format through the system bus so that it can be processed by the computer.

Early UARTS (8250 and 16450) used a FIFO (first in, first out) buffer. If the computer did not retrieve the data fast enough, the data would be overwritten by new data coming in through the serial port. Newer systems use a 16-byte FIFO-buffered UART, like the 16550. Because the buffer is larger, the microprocessor only has to process the data every 16 bytes before any data is overwritten. Consequently, the serial communication is faster.

18.1.3 SERIAL PORT SIGNALS

Two terms are often used with reference to serial ports, **data terminal equipment (DTE)** and **data carrier equipment (DCE).** These terms indicate the pin-outs for the connector on the device and the direction of the signals on the pins. (See tables 18.1 and 18.2.) Typically, the computer is the DTE device, and the serial device connected to the computer is the DCE device. All of the signals sent through the serial port can be categorized as data lines, **handshaking** (flow control) lines, and ground lines. The data and handshaking signals are swapped at the DCE end.

When the computer (DTE) is turned on or initialized, it must initialize a serial device (DCE) and make a connection with it. This process begins when the computer sends a data terminal ready (DTR) signal to the serial device, telling it that the computer is ready to establish a connection. When the device is initialized and is ready for a connection, it will send a data set ready (DSR) signal back to the computer, establishing a connection. To maintain the connection, the DTR and DSR signals must remain on. If either stops, the connection is terminated. Before the two devices are ready to communicate, the request to send (RTS) signal is generated by the computer to tell the device that the computer wants to send data. When the device is ready, the device sends a clear to send (CTS) signal to the computer, telling it that it is ready to receive data. Together, these make up RTS/CTS, which is also known as hardware flow control. The data is then sent from the computer to the serial device using the transmit data (TD) wire, and data is sent from the serial device to the computer using the receive data (RD) wire.

Not all data sent by the serial port is controlled by hardware flow control (hardware handshaking); some is under software flow control (software handshaking), known as **Xon/Xoff,** which transmits special control characters from one device to another to tell it to stop or start sending data. To start sending data (Xon), the computer or device will send a Control-Q (ASCII value 17); to stop sending data (Xoff), the computer or device will send a Control-S (ASCII value 19). The last two signals are available only when communicating with a modem. The carrier detect (CD) signal is used by a modem to signal that it has made a connection with another modem or has detected a carrier tone. The ring indicator (RI) is used to tell the computer when a telephone ring is detected, such as when a remote user is trying to call in and access the computer.

18.1.4 SERIAL CONNECTORS AND CABLES

The first serial port used on the PC was the 25-pin male D connector, as specified by the RS-232 standard. The most basic full-duplex communication requires three lines (the

TABLE 18.1 25-pin serial port

Pin	Signal	Direction
1	Protective ground	
2	Transmit data (TD)	Output
3	Receive data (RD)	Input
4	Request to send (RTS)	Output
5	Clear to send (CTS)	Input
6	Data set ready (DSR)	Input
7	Signal ground (GND)	
8	Data carrier detect (DCD)	Input
9	+Transmit current loop	Output
11	−Transmit current loop	Output
18	+Receive current loop	Input
20	Data terminal ready (DTR)	Output
22	Ring indicator (RI)	Input
23	Data signal rate indicator (DSRD)	I/O
25	−Receive current loop	Input

TABLE 18.2 9-pin serial port

Pin	Signal	Direction
1	Data carrier detect (DCD)	Input
2	Receive data (RD)	Input
3	Transmit data (TD)	Output
4	Data terminal ready (DTR)	Output
5	Signal ground	
6	Data set ready (DSR)	Input
7	Request to send (RTS)	Output
8	Clear to send (CTS)	Input
9	Ring indicator (RI)	Input

FIGURE 18.2 Serial ports

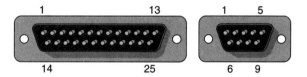

transmit line, the receive line and the signal ground), but other forms of serial communications use up to 10 different wires. (Note: Included in these 10 are the chassis ground and the signal ground. These two wires have different functions and should not be connected together.)

When multi-I/O cards were being developed, manufacturers found that they could not have a 25-pin parallel port and a 25-pin serial port on the same retaining bracket of an expansion card. To overcome the size restrictions, the 9-pin serial port (the 10 signals used in the 25-pin serial port minus the chassis ground) was introduced and has since become the standard serial port. A computer today usually has two serial ports. COM1 is usually a 9-pin serial port (most often used by mice and newer devices), and COM2 is usually a 25-pin serial port (most often used by serial plotters, printers, and modems). Of course, there may be times when two serial devices, both of which require the 9-pin connector or the 25-pin connector, are being used. To accommodate both devices, one is connected to the 25-pin connector using a 9-pin connector to a 25-pin port adapter. Table 18.3 shows the connections used by the standard 9-pin to 25-pin adapter.

TABLE 18.3 9-pin to 25-pin adapter

9-Pin Connector	25-Pin Connector
Pin 1 DCD	Pin 8 DCD
Pin 2 RD	Pin 3 RD
Pin 3 TD	Pin 2 TD
Pin 4 DTR	Pin 20 DTR
Pin 5 GND	Pin 7 GND
Pin 6 DSR	Pin 6 DSR
Pin 7 RTS	Pin 4 RTS
Pin 8 CTS	Pin 5 CTS
Pin 9 RI	Pin 22 RI

The RS-232C standard imposed a cable length limit of 50 feet. If a cable is in an electrically noisy environment, even very short cables can pick up stray signals. If the cable is well made and well shielded, the length can be increased significantly. A shielded cable has a wire braid or aluminum-coated plastic film wrapped around the wires to prevent signals from leaking in or out. In addition, the shielding of the cable is connected to the signal ground.

18.1.5 NULL MODEM CABLE

A normal serial cable is made to connect one computer (DTE) and one serial device (DCE). Therefore, if two computers (to transfer data or to play a game against an opponent) or other DTE devices were connected with a serial cable, the transmit line and receive line of one computer would be connected to the transmit and receive lines on the other computer, and the DTE devices would not be able to communicate with each other. Therefore, to make two computers communicate with each other, a **null modem cable** (sometimes known as a *crossover* cable) is used. The null modem cable crosses the receive and transmit wires—the DTR and RTS wires and the DSR and CTS wires. The reason that the cable is called a *null modem* cable is because it allows two computers to communicate with each other without a modem. Tables 18.4 and 18.5 illustrate how the null modem cable works and when it is used.

18.1.6 HIGH-SPEED SERIAL PORTS

Enhanced serial ports (ESP), or super high-speed serial ports, are ports that can communicate up to 921,600 bps using a 28,800-baud modem. The main reason for the speed increase is a faster UART (such as the 16550AF or 16550AFN) that has a 1,024-byte buffer and onboard data flow control. Of course, to use the faster speed, both the computer and the serial device must be able to communicate at that speed.

18.1.7 INSTALLING A SERIAL PORT

Installing a serial port requires choosing an available IRQ and a free COM designation or I/O address. Again, no two devices can use the same IRQ and no two devices can use the same I/O address.

As the computer is initializing, the following I/O addresses are checked in order for serial ports: 03F8H, 02F8H, 03E8H, 02E8H, 03E0H, 02E0H, 0338H, and 0238H. When a serial port is found, a COM designation is assigned. Typically, COM1 is set to 03F8H and COM2 is set to 02F8H. (See table 18.6.) The actual I/O addresses for each COM port are kept in the BIOS data area of RAM starting at 0400H. (Note: DOS recognizes only COM1 and COM2.) As table 18.6 indicates, COM1 typically uses IRQ4 and COM2 uses IRQ3. When the IBM AT computer was introduced, the BIOS was expanded to support up to four serial ports (COM1–COM4) but unfortunately there were no extra IRQ lines available.

TABLE 18.4 Null modem cable

	DCE #1			DCE #2		
Signal	DB-9	DB-25	←→	DB-25	DB-9	Signal
TD	3	2	←→	3	2	RD
RD	2	3	←→	2	3	TD
RTS	7	4	←→	5	8	CTS
CTS	8	5	←→	4	7	RTS
DSR	6	6	←→	20	4	DTR
DTR	4	20	←→	6	6	DSR

TABLE 18.5 Null Modem or Crossover Cable

Peripheral	Device Type	Cable Needed to Connect to PC
PC	DTE	Null modem cable
Modem	DCE	Straight-through cable
Mouse or trackball	DCE	Straight-through cable
Digitizer or scanner	DCE	Straight-through cable
Serial printer	DTE	Null modem cable
Serial plotter	DTE	Null modem cable

TABLE 18.6 Typical serial port resources

Bus Architecture	Port	Address	Alternative Addresses	IRQ
All systems	COM1	03F8H		IRQ4
All systems	COM2	02F8H		IRQ3
ISA	COM3	03E8H	03E0H, 0338H	IRQ4
ISA	COM4	02E8H	02E0H, 0238H	IRQ3
MCA	COM3	3220H		IRQ3
MCA	COM4	3228H		IRQ3
MCA	COM5	4220H		IRQ3
MCA	COM6	4228H		IRQ3
MCA	COM7	5220H		IRQ3
MCA	COM8	5228H		IRQ3

Therefore, COM1 and COM3 shared the same interrupt and COM2 and COM4 shared the same interrupt. This was possible as long as COM1 and COM3 were not being used at the same time and COM2 and COM4 were not being used at the same time. Today, with GUI interfaces requiring a mouse or some other pointing device, COM3 and COM4 can usually be assigned to other IRQs, such as IRQ5 (usually used by LTP2, which most people do not have). Of course, a PS/2 or bus mouse can free up one of the COM ports, and if more than four serial ports are needed, a multiport adapter can be purchased that can support up to 128 serial ports using one IRQ.

The serial port I/O address (which is assigned a COM designation) and IRQ can be configured in many ways. If the serial port is part of an expansion card, it can be configured with jumpers, DIP switches, or special software, or the card can automatically configure itself as a plug-and-play device. If the serial port is on the motherboard, it can be configured with jumpers or DIP switches, or it can be configured by using the CMOS setup program. (Note: Disconnecting the serial port cables will not disable the port, even if the cables are disconnected inside the computer.)

Question: Most expansion cards specify a COM designation instead of the I/O address. Therefore, what happens if you install a COM1, a COM2, and a COM4 in your system?

Answer: If you install a COM1, a COM2, and a COM4, you are really selecting the I/O address. During boot-up, the system checks the I/O addresses for serial ports and assigns the COM designation. Therefore, the three COM ports are assigned to be COM1, COM2, and COM3.

The last step before using the serial port is installing software drivers. You will rarely install software for the serial port (COM1, COM2, COM3, and COM4). However, many of the devices that connect to the serial port (such as the mouse or a label maker) may require drivers. Some of the drivers will automatically search for the appropriate serial port, while other drivers must be told which I/O address and COM port or IRQ the device is using. (Note: In Windows 3.XX, the COM port settings from within the Control Panel are often ignored except when using a serial printer or similar device that does not monitor its own speed.)

18.1.8 TROUBLESHOOTING SERIAL PORTS

A serial port problem can be caused by a disconnected cable, bad cable, resource conflict, invalid software configuration, bad or incorrect drivers, or the serial port itself. Cables to check would be the one that goes from the male D connector to the I/O expansion card or motherboard, and, for those serial devices that also have a power cable, make sure it is connected correctly. Much like hard drive and floppy drive cables, pin 1 is indicated with a red or blue stripe on the cable to match the small number 1 or 2 on the expansion card or motherboard.

Check that the resources used by the serial port, including the IRQ and I/O address and COM designation, are correct. Again, these are set with jumpers, DIP switches, the CMOS setup program, or configuration software, or by using plug-and-play. In addition, make sure that the software that is using the serial device is configured with the proper COM designation, I/O address, or IRQ. Also make sure that both the computer's serial port and the serial device are set to use the same baud rate, same number of data bits, same number of stop bits, and same parity method. If not, the data will be garbled at the end.

The device connected to the serial port will most likely need a driver. For example, if a mouse is running in DOS, a device driver (file with a SYS extension) is loaded in the CONFIG.SYS file or a TSR (file with a COM or EXE extension) is loaded in the AU-TOEXEC.BAT file. In Windows 3.XX, the mouse driver is loaded using the SETUP.EXE in the C:\WINDOWS directory or by using the SETUP icon in the Main group. (Note: When running Windows 3.XX, a driver loaded in DOS is not needed. In Windows 95 and 98 and Windows NT, the driver is loaded from the MOUSE icon or applet located in the Control Panel.)

A serial port can be tested by using a **serial port loopback plug.** The loopback plug is a special device that attaches to the serial port D connector and is nothing more than a cable that takes data being sent from the serial port and reroutes it back into the serial port. Therefore, the data received should be the same data that was sent out. A 25-pin serial loopback connector has the following pins connected together:

> 1 and 7
> 2 and 3
> 4, 5, and 8
> 6, 11, 20, and 22
> 15, 17, and 23
> 18 and 25

For a 9-pin serial loopback connector, the following pins are connected together:

> 1, 7, and 8
> 2 and 3
> 4, 6, and 9

Most software diagnostic packages also have serial port tests. Because of the variety of devices that can connect to the serial port, most software diagnostic packages offer a selection of device-specific tests (mouse, modem, loopback plug, or nothing). Of course, if you run a test for the wrong device, the test will most likely fail.

If the serial port is bad, it will have to be replaced. If the serial port is on the expansion card, replace the expansion card. If the serial port is on the motherboard, either replace the motherboard (sometimes a costly repair) or disable the serial port on the motherboard and install an expansion card that has a serial port.

EXAMPLE 18.1 Data is lost or corrupted.

Before opening the computer, make sure the cable is connected properly and that it is in good condition. Next, make sure that no devices are around that may generate large amounts of electromagnetic interference. If there are, either reroute the cable (or the device generating the electromagnetic interference) or try a well-shielded cable.

If the cable seems fine, check the software and hardware configurations to make sure that the serial port and device are set to the same baud rate, number of data bits, number of stop bits, and parity method. In addition, make sure that the correct driver is loaded and that the device is using the correct handshaking (software or hardware).

If all of these items are correct, then the problem has to be with the serial port or the device. To figure out which, try the serial device on another computer. If it works there, the problem must be the serial port; if it doesn't work, the problem must be the serial device.

18.2   MODEMS

A **modem (modulator-demodulator)** is a device that enables a computer to transmit data over telephone lines. Since computer information is stored and processed digitally and telephone lines transmit data using analog waves, the modem converts digital signals to analog signals (modulates) and analog signals to digital signals (demodulates).

Modems can be either internal or external. (See fig. 18.3.) The internal modem is an expansion card that is plugged into an expansion slot; the external modem can be attached to the computer using a serial port. In either case, the modem has at least one RJ-11 connector for the twisted-pair cable that connects the modem and the wall telephone jack. Some include a second RJ-11 jack to connect a phone. (See fig. 18.4.)

FIGURE 18.3   Hayes 56K internal and external modems (Courtesy of Hayes Microcomputer Products, Inc.)

FIGURE 18.4   RJ-11 connector

18.2.1   HOW A MODEM WORKS

When a computer wishes to call another computer, such as one used by an Internet provider or a Bulletin Board service (BBS), the calling computer activates the modem and dials the telephone number. The receiving computer will hear the ring and answer the call. As the receiving modem answers the call, it immediately puts out a guard tone, which is a certain frequency used to identify the device on the other end as a modem. This way, different tones can be used to distinguish between faxes, modems and voice (no tone). Next, the receiving modem sends an unmodulated carrier tone, which is used to inquire about the sending modem's capabilities, such as speed. The two modems also send several signals to measure the quality of the line. When both modems agree on a speed, they then determine the appropriate error control and compression. Finally, the modems turn on the carrier detect signal, which remains on throughout the modem connection. If the carrier signal stops, the connection is broken. (Note: The carrier signals use different frequencies so that they can exist at the same time.)

Sending data through the modem begins with the receipt of digital data from the computer. The modem then converts the digital signals into analog signals. The UART of the modem then adds the start and stop bits and any error control bits, such as parity. When the data reaches the other modem, the UART strips the start and stop bits, checks for errors, and converts the analog signal to a digital signal, which is then processed by the computer. As the modem is communicating, it is continuously monitoring the status of the line, the quality of the signals, and the number of errors encountered. When the modems register excessive problems, they interrupt the carries and reevaluate the line, thus reducing the speed of transmission. If the reduced speed decreases the number of errors, the line will be reevaluated again to see if the speed can then be increased. Of course, the two communicating computers must be set to the same number of bits used for data, the length of the stop bit, and the type of error control. If they are not, the receiving computer would misinterpret the data, resulting in errors or garbage. Usually, it is the calling computer that will be configured to the settings of the receiving computer.

EXAMPLE 18.2   You need to download some technical information that is not available on the Internet but is available on a BBS computer. You are given the phone number to the BBS computer and the following information: 9,600 baud at 7E1. The 9,600 baud is the speed of the modem on the other end, the 7 indicates 7 bits are used for data, and the E indicates that it uses even parity checking (a 0 would indicate odd parity). Lastly, the 1 indicates that the computer uses one stop bit.

18.2.2   BAUD RATE VERSUS BITS PER SECOND

Baud rate refers to the modulation rate, or the number of times per second that a line changes state. This is not always the same as bits per second (bps). When two serial devices are connected with direct cables, then the baud rate and the bps are the same. If the computer is running at 19,200 bps, then the line is also changing states 19,200 times per second to represent 19,200 logical 1s and 0s. As with the data and stop bits, the sending

FIGURE 18.5 Characteristics of a sine wave

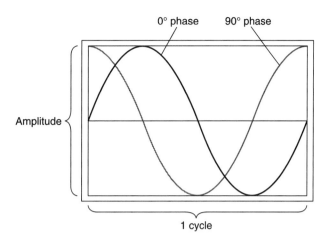

and receiving devices must agree on the baud rate. The speed of a normal serial port is 115.2 kilobits per second.

But when computers are communicating over telephone lines, the baud and bps rates differ. Telephone lines are limited to a maximum of 2,400 baud, but because they use analog and not digital signals, encoding can increase the bps by incorporating more bits into each signal change. The 9,600 bps rate is based on encoding 4 bits at the same time, the 14,400 rate encodes 6 bits, and the 28.8 rate encodes 12 bits. The bps can also be increased by using data compression. Although the speed of modems is usually expressed in bauds, the actual speed depends on how many bits per second they can transmit.

18.2.3 MODUALTION SCHEMES

The analog signals used to send data over telephone lines have sinusoidal waveforms. The sinusoidal waveform is characterized by its amplitude and frequency. (See fig. 18.5.) The **amplitude** represents the peak voltage of the sine wave; the **frequency** indicates the number of times that a single wave will repeat over specific period of time and is measured in hertz (Hz), or cycles per second. Another aspect of modulation is its time reference, or phase, which is measured in degrees as 0°, 90°, 180°, and 270° or 0°, 45°, 90°, 135°, 180°, 225°, 270°, 315°, and 360°.

Data is sent over the telephone lines by varying the amplitude, frequency, and phase of the signal. Frequency shift keying (FSK) was the earliest form of **encoding** data over telephone lines and is very similar to the frequency modulation used for FM radio signals. FSK sends a logical 1 at one particular frequency (usually 1,750 Hz) and a logical 0 at another frequency (often 1,080 Hz). FSK was usually used with 300 baud modems. Modulation also involves phase shift keying (PSK), which is the varying of the phase angle to represent data. Since a phase has four different values, it can represent two bits of data. Therefore, a 1,200-baud modem using PSK can transmit data at 2,400 bps. Quadrature amplitude modulation (QAM) combines phase and amplitude modulation to encode up to six bits for every baud (usually four bits). Therefore, a 2,400-baud signal can carry up to 9,600 bps. Trellis coded quadrature amplitude modulation (TCQAM or TCM) encodes 6 bits for every baud. Therefore, a 2,400-baud signal can carry 14,000 bps.

18.2.4 COMMUNICATION STANDARDS

There are a number of standards and protocols that specify how formatted data is to be transmitted over telephones lines. The International Telecommunications Union (ITU), formerly known as the Comité Consultatif International Téléphonique et Télégraphique (CCITT), has defined many important standards for data communications. Most modems have built-in support for the more common standards, which are listed in table 18.7. The most successful proprietary protocols are the Microcom networking protocols (MNP).

TABLE 18.7 Communications protocols

Protocol	Maximum Transmission Rate (bps)	Duplex Mode	Comments
Bell 103	300	Full	Used FSK. Bell 103 is the only standard in which the baud rate is equal to the data rate.
CCITT V.21	300	Full	
Bell 212A	1,200	Full	Uses quadrature modulation.
ITU V.22	1,200	Half	
ITU V.22bis	2,400	Full	Uses QAM (4 bits per baud) at 600 baud.
ITU V.29	9,600	Half	Data-transmission standard for Group III facsimile (fax) transmission.
ITU V.32	9,600	Full	Uses TCQAM (4 bits per baud) at 2,400 baud.
ITU V.32bis	14,400	Full	Uses TCQAM (6 bits per baud) at 2,400 baud.
ITU V.34	28,800	Full	Most reliable standard for 28,800 bps communication.
ITU V.34bis	33,600	Full	Enhanced V.34 standard.
ITU V.42	33,600	Full	An error-detection standard for high-speed modems.
ITU V.42bis	38,400	Full	Uses data compression protocol.
ITU V.90	56,600	Full	

During initilization, when the modems are exchanging operation parameters, they will first try to agree on the V.42 standard. If one of the modems cannot use that standard, it will try MNP 4, followed by MNP 3, MNP 2, and MNP 1. If the modems can't use any of these error control methods, then they will use none.

Some modems are able to identify errors during transmission by embedding an error-checking scheme into the data being sent. If the data seems to be corrupt, it is automatically corrected and resent. Of course, the error-correction information sent by one modem is to be interpreted by another modem, so both modems must agree on the same error-correction method. Although the error-detection technique is effective, it is still possible to experience data loss or corruption due to buffer overflow, interrupt conflicts, loose connectors, faulty cables, and faulty modems.

MNP Class 5 and the V.42bis standards support data compression. Data compression refers to the modem's ability to compress data as it is being sent. Because the data can be compressed to one-fourth its original size, the effective speed of the modem is quadrupled. A 28,000 modem, for example, can yield a transfer rate up to 115,200 bps. Some of the newer protocols, such as V.42 and MNP-4, use synchronization bits on the line to act as clock pulses. The data is then sent between the clock pulses, which enhances error control and leads to faster speeds. Of course, the modem on the other end must have a UART chip that can translate from synchronous to asynchronous. The 56K standard allows the fastest data transmission today. When possible, 56K modems do not translate information from a digital to an analog form, making maximum use of the digital circuits available in most of the Public Switched Telephone Network (PSTN).

18.2.5 DATA TRANSFER PROTOCOLS

Transferring files from one computer to another through a modem requires the use of a protocol, which establishes rules for uploading and downloading files. The most common transfer protocols are XMODEM, YMODEM, ZMODEM, and Kermit. (See table 18.8.)

TABLE 18.8   Data transfer protocols

Protocol	Description
XMODEM	A widely used file transfer protocol that uses 128-byte packets and a simple "checksum" method of error detection.
XMODEM-CRC	An XMODEM version that uses cyclic redundancy check (CRC) for error detection.
XMODEM-1K	XMODEM CRC with 1,024-byte packets.
YMODEM	Similar to XMODEM-1K but has a batch mode that allows multiple files to be transferred with a single command. It is sometimes called YMODEM Batch.
YMODEM-G	Designed for modems that already have error correction. It is similar to YMODEM except it does not provide software error correction. It is a streaming protocol that sends and receives a 1 KB continuous stream until instructed to stop. If any block is unsuccessful, the entire transfer is canceled.
ZMODEM	Like YMODEM-G, ZMODEM can restart a transfer from where it left off.
Kermit	Uses blocks (or packets) and checksum error detection but adjusts its packet size to accommodate the fixed packet sizes used by some computer systems and the condition of the lines. Like ZMODEM, it can recover from major line errors by resynchronizing the transmissions of modems after interruption.

Note that these protocols are not needed when connecting to the Internet, which is the main reason most people buy a modem. To connect to the Internet using a modem, arrangements must be made with an **internet service provider (ISP),** which provides either a **serial line internal protocol (SLIP)** or **point-to-point protocol (PPP)** software package to make the connection. The **TCP/IP protocol**—in reality, a complete set of protocols— is used for communicating with the Internet. The **terminal emulation (Telnet)** protocol allows using another computer as a terminal, the **file transfer protocol (FTP)** allows the transfer of files, and the **simple mail transfer protocol (SMTP)** allows the sending of electronic mail messages.

18.2.6   COMMAND SET

When the computer sends data using the modem, it sends a command to control the modem. The instructions the modem understands are referred to as the **Hayes command set** or the **AT commands.** Today, virtually all modems are Hayes compatible and follow the same set of basic commands. Most of the time, the user does not have to know these commands because most communications software packages know them. Some programs, however, require the user to enter these commands.

The AT commands that must sometimes be entered by the user can be divided into the basic command set, an extended command set, and register commands. (See table 18.9.) The basic commands begin with a capital character followed by a digit. The extended commands begin with an ampersand (&) and a capital letter followed by a digit. The register commands access small memory locations (registers) located within the modem. The order in which the commands are issued is important, and every command must begin with AT. In addition, there are no spaces between any of the commands or the numbers specified.

EXAMPLE 18.3   To make sure that the cables are connected properly and that the baud rate is set correctly, you would type in the AT command and press the Enter key. If everything is fine, an OK will be given.

To dial a number using a touch-tone telephone, you would type in the ATDT2633077 command and press the Enter key.

TABLE 18.9 Common AT command parameters

Parameter	Description
AT	The AT command tells the modem that it is going to receive a command. AT must be typed before any other command. AT as a command all by itself will elicit OK as a response from the modem. This indicates that the cables are connected correctly and the baud rate is set properly.
D	D tells the modem to dial the numbers following the D.
H	Hangs up the telephone.
P	P is a subcommand of the D command that tells the modem to dial in pulse mode. It is used if the phone line is not touch-tone.
Z	Resets the modem to default state.
~	Makes the software pause for half a second. More than one ~ can be used.
^M	Sends the terminating carriage return character to the modem.
AT$	Command quick reference.
&$	Help for ampersand commands.
D$	Help for dial commands.
S$	Help for S registers.

To dial a number using a pulse telephone, you would type in the ATDP2633077 command and press the Enter key.

To hang up the phone, you would type in the ATH command and press the Enter key.

To show all of the ampersand commands, you would type in the AT&$ command and press the Enter key.

To perform a hardware reset for the modem, you would type in the ATZ command and press the Enter key.

18.2.7 FAX/MODEMS

Fax is short for *facsimile transmission*. A fax machine scans a message written on a piece of paper, digitizes the text and pictures, and sends the data over a telephone line. A fax machine on the other end reassembles the text and images and prints them out on paper. Many computers today have a fax/modem, which can send a word-processed document (such as from Microsoft Word) directly to another computer. If the other machine has a fax/modem, the document can be displayed on the screen or printed to paper.

18.2.8 INTEGRATED SERVICES DIGITAL NETWORK (ISDN) MODEMS

Integrated services digital network (ISDN) lines allow voice, video, and data to be sent over digital telephone lines with an ISDN modem. Of course, an ISDN modem isn't really a modem because it does not modulate (convert digital signals to analog signals) or demodulate (convert analog signals to digital signals). Nevertheless, it acts very much like a modem. It responds to the AT commands, generates the same set of responses as a modem, and uses the same control signals (DTR, TRS, and CTS).

Basic ISDN (BRI) divides the telephone line into three digital channels: two B channels and one D channel. The B channels can transmit up to 64 kilobits per second of uncompressed data. The D channel, which can transmit 16 kilobits per second, does the administrative work, such as connecting and disconnecting the call and communicating with the telephone network, and it can also be used to carry data. Because there are three channels, the ISDN line can have three connections, such as a voice conversation, Internet access, and a credit card authorization line. In addition, the two B channels can be used together to deliver performance of up to 128 kilobits per second. This high bandwidth makes ISDN lines ideal for audio and video applications and any application that needs to move large amounts of data from one location to another.

The ISDN line can be set up by the phone company and can be installed and hooked up to the normal home or office phone cable. It uses the same four-wire (two pairs) twisted pair cable. If analog signals (such as voice, group 3 fax, and standard modem data) are also to be carried over ISDN lines, an ISDN terminator adapter (TA) must be used. In addition, if the ISDN line is to be used to communicate with an analog device, such as a standard modem or fax machine, special software or firmware, which emulates the analog-modulated waveforms of modems and fax machines, must be installed.

18.2.9 INSTALLING A MODEM

The first step in installing a modem, is to configure the resources. If it is an internal modem, you would usually choose a free IRQ, COM port, and I/O address. If it is an external modem, you must then configure the serial port. Even though the serial port is already assigned an IRQ, COM port, and I/O address, its speed usually has to be configured.

> **Question:** A computer running Windows 98 has two serial ports (COM1 and COM2). COM1 is being used by the mouse and COM2 is not being used at all. A proprietary communications software package needed for your business will use only COM1 and COM2. Therefore, you purchase an internal modem. How should you configure the modem?
>
> **Answer:** If you configure the modem to use COM3, the communications software package will not recognize the modem. If you configure the modem as COM1 or COM2, you have a resource conflict. Since you need the mouse (COM1) for Windows 98, you should configure the modem as COM2 and IRQ 3. Of course, for this to work, you will need to disable COM2 using either jumpers, DIP switches, configuration software, or the CMOS setup program.

The next step is to physically install and connect the modem. The modem is connected to the telephone wall jack with a twisted pair cable with RJ-11 connectors. You must then load the modem software drivers and install and configure the communications software. If you are using DOS or Windows 3.XX, the driver is loaded when the modem is selected in the communications software. (Note: When selecting the modem, you will have to specify its COM port and IRQ.) If you have Windows 95 or 98 or Windows NT, the driver is loaded by using the Add New Hardware icon or applet from the Control Panel.

The communications software package usually allows you to choose the baud rate (up to the speed of the modem), the number of data bits, the number of stop bits, and the parity method. In addition, many of these packages allow you to establish different parameters for different telephone numbers. When you call a particular telephone number, the software will automatically use the same parameters that were used for that number before.

When the driver is loaded, it will specify an **initialization string** for the chosen modem. The initialization string is the list of AT commands that the communications software will use to initialize and prepare the modem for connection. The string typically sets the speed, error correction, compression, various timeout values, and how the results will be displayed on the screen. Of course, if the modem is not listed in the software, you will have to choose a generic modem and specify the initialization string manually. The following are a few examples:

Generic 28.8 modem	AT&F&C1&D1&K3
Hayes Accura 144	AT&F
Hayes Optima 14400 V.32bis	AT&F&D0
Hayes V-Series/Ultra	AT&Q5S36=7&C1&D0&K3
US Robotics Courier HST Dual	AT&F&C1&D0
US Robotics Courier V.32bis/as	AT&F&D0&H1&K2
US Robotics Sportster 14.4	AT&F&H1&C1&D0
US Robotics Sportster 9600	AT&F&H1

Extra commands can be added to the setup string so that these commands are executed every time the modem is started. For example, an AT command can be added to the dial-up string that will deactivate call waiting (such as *70). Changing the command for a number dialed with the AT command ATDT9224225 to ATDT*70,92244225 will deactivate call waiting.

18.2.10 TROUBLESHOOTING A MODEM

Modem problems can be caused by bad or unconnected cable, bad or incorrect drivers, incorrectly configured software, a resource conflict, an incorrect setup string, a faulty serial port, or a faulty modem.

Cables to check are the serial port cable that goes from the D connector to the motherboard or I/O card and the twisted pair cable that goes from the phone jack to the modem. In addition, if it is an external modem, the power cable and the cable that connects the serial port to the modem must be checked.

Make sure that the modem is not experiencing a resource conflict (I/O address or COM designation and IRQ). The modem resources are usually set with jumpers or DIP switches or the modem is plug-and-play. If it is an external modem, make sure that the serial port is not experiencing a conflict and that the serial port is not disabled.

If there are no resource conflicts, make sure that correct modem has been selected in the operating system or communications software package and that the software is pointed to the correct resources. In DOS and Windows 3.XX, the modem is selected in the communications software. In Windows 95 and 98 and Windows NT, the driver can be loaded using the Add New Hardware icon or applet located in the Control Panel. Lastly, make sure that the modem and software are set to use the correct baud rate, number of data bits, number of stop bits, and parity method. If not, the data will end up garbled.

If you are dealing with an external modem connected to a serial port, the serial port can be tested with a loopback plug. If it is an internal modem, it can be tested with a software diagnostic package. If the serial port is bad, it will have to be replaced: If the serial port is on the expansion card, replace the expansion card; if the serial port is on the motherboard, replace the motherboard (sometimes a costly repair) or disable the serial port on the motherboard and install an expansion card that has a serial port. If the modem is bad, replace the modem.

EXAMPLE 18.4   There is no response from the modem.

When the modem does not respond, first make sure that it is connected properly. If it is an external modem, make sure that the modem has power and it is turned on. Next, make sure the operating system or communications software has the right driver installed and that the correct parameters (baud, data bits, stop bits, and parity) are set properly. In addition, if a setup string had to be entered, make sure that it is the correct one for the modem being used. If the modem is still not working, check it for resource conflicts. If the problem still exists, swap the modem with a known good modem. If the second modem works, then the problem is with the first modem. If the second modem doesn't work, the serial port or the motherboard is probably causing the problem.

EXAMPLE 18.5   The modem does not detect a dial tone.

If the modem does not detect a dial tone, make sure that the telephone cable is connected. Next, make sure that the telephone line is active. This can be done with a telephone line tester or by plugging a telephone into the jack and making sure that there is a dial tone. (Note: Most businesses have a switching telephone system. If this is the case, you may need to add a dial-out prefix to the telephone number.) Check for resource conflicts, operating parameters (baud, data bits, stop bits, and parity method), drivers, and setup strings. Lastly, swap the modem with a known good modem. If the second modem works, then the problem is with the first modem. If the second modem doesn't work, the serial port or the motherboard is probably causing the problem.

EXAMPLE 18.6   The modem outputs garbage.

Before opening the computer, make sure the cables are connected properly and are in good condition. Next, make sure that no devices are around that may generate large amounts of electromagnetic interference. If there are, either reroute the cable (or the device generating the electromagnetic interference) or try a well-shielded cable.

If the cable seems fine, check the software and hardware configurations to make sure that the serial port and device are set to the same baud rate, number of data bits, number of stop bits, and parity method. In addition, make sure that the correct driver is loaded and that the correct handshaking (hardware or software) has been used.

If all of these items are correct, then the problem has to be with the serial port, the modem, or the modem on the other end. To determine which you can try swapping out the modem and serial port. In addition, you can try calling another number or use another computer to call the same number.

EXAMPLE 18.7 The modem keeps hanging up.

Hanging up is caused by a bad telephone connection, a bad cable, interruption by call waiting, someone picking up the telephone at another extension, a bad modem, or a bad serial port. To determine whether it is a bad telephone connection, try another phone number; also try the same phone number from a different site. If the telephone connection is bad, the telephone company will probably have to be called in to repair it. To check the cable, replace it to see if the problem goes away. If the problem is call waiting, that can usually be disabled. Contact the telephone company (or look in the telephone book) to find out how to do this. To check the modem, swap it with a known good modem or try the modem in another system. Lastly, the serial port could be bad.

SUMMARY

1. The serial port interface (9-pin or 25-pin two-row D connector) is a general-purpose interface that can be used for almost any type of device (mice, external modems, serial printers, plotters, label makers, bar code readers, device control circuits, and other computers).
2. Serial ports are bidirectional asynchronous devices that send data over a single wire, each bit lined up single-file in series.
3. With an ISA or higher bus, the typical computer can support up to four serial ports (COM1, COM2, COM3, and COM4). COM stands for communication.
4. The serial port is a full-duplex device that uses separate lines for sending and receiving data and a line for a signal ground.
5. Information is sent through a serial port as a data frame. The data frame consists of a start bit, a number of data bits, one to two stop bits, and possibly some parity bits.
6. The baud rate is the modulation rate, or the number of times per second that a signal changes state, which is not necessarily the number of bits being sent per second.
7. The central part of the serial port is the universal asynchronous receiver and transmitter (UART), which acts as translator between the serial port and the system bus.
8. The RS-232C standard imposes a cable length limit of 50 feet.
9. The null modem cable is a special cable that crosses the receive and transmit wires. It allows two DTEs (such as computers) to communicate with each other.
10. The installation of a serial port requires choosing an available IRQ and a free COM designation and I/O address.
11. A serial port problem can be caused by a disconnected cable, bad cable, resource conflict, invalid software configuration, bad or incorrect drivers, or the serial port itself.
12. A serial port can be tested by using a serial port loopback plug.
13. A modem (modulator-demodulator) is a device that enables a computer to transmit data over telephone lines.
14. Modems encode bits by varying the signal amplitude, frequency, and phase of data sent over telephone lines.
15. The instructions the modem understands are referred to as the Hayes command set or the modem AT commands. Any modem that understands the Hayes modem commands is said to be Hayes compatible.
16. *Fax* is short for facsimile transmission. A fax machine scans messages written on paper, digitizes the text and pictures, and sends the data over a telephone line.

17. Integrated services digital network (ISDN) lines, which can transfer data at a rate of up to 128 kilobits per second, allow voice, video, and data to be sent over digital telephone lines.

18. The initialization string is the list of AT commands that the communications software will use to initialize and prepare the modem for connection.

19. Modem problems can be caused by bad or unconnected cables, bad or incorrect drivers, incorrectly configured software, resource conflicts, an incorrect setup string, a faulty serial port, or a faulty modem.

QUESTIONS

1. Which of the following has a 2-row, 9-pin male D connector?
   a. serial port
   b. parallel port
   c. game port
   d. VGA port
   e. EGA port

2. Which of the following devices are usually found connected to a serial port? (Choose two.)
   a. joystick
   b. modem
   c. printer
   d. mouse

3. How many bits of data can a serial port receive or transmit at a time?
   a. 1
   b. 8
   c. 16
   d. 32

4. What port takes eight bits as they come off the eight wires of the data bus and turns them on end so that they are on one wire in single file?
   a. serial
   b. parallel
   c. LPT1, LPT2, and LPT3
   d. SCSI
   e. IDE

5. In serial asynchronous transmissions, what bit is used to signal the beginning of a new data frame?
   a. start
   b. stop
   c. parity
   d. data

6. Which IRQ is usually assigned to COM1?
   a. IRQ 3
   b. IRQ 4
   c. IRQ 5
   d. IRQ 7

7. When installing an internal modem set to COM2, what should the interrupt be set to?
   a. IRQ 3
   b. IRQ 4
   c. IRQ 5
   d. IRQ 7

8. How many serial ports are supported by the PC?
   a. 2
   b. 4
   c. 8
   d. 32

9. Which of the following is the term for the number of signal changes per second?
   a. baud
   b. bits per second
   c. raw transfer speed
   d. bit speed

10. The central part of the serial port is the:
    a. microprocessor
    b. ADC
    c. DAC
    d. UART

11. Which hardware component controls serial port communications?
    a. ROM BIOS
    b. CPU
    c. DMA 8223
    d. UART 16550

12. What should the length limit (in feet) be for a serial cable?
    a. 6
    b. 10
    c. 12
    d. 50
    e. 100

13. A cable has a female DB-25 connector on each end. Pin 2 is crossed with pin 3, and pin 4 is crossed with pin 5. What is the most likely explanation?
    a. the cable was incorrectly made
    b. it is a proprietary cable
    c. it is a null modem cable
    d. the cable is a printer cable used to connect a parallel port to a switch box.

14. When is a null modem cable used?
    a. to exchange data between two DCE devices
    b. to exchange data between two DTE devices
    c. to send data from a DTE device to a DCE device
    d. to send data from a DCE device to a DTE device
15. A loopback plug tests which of the following?
    a. IDE hard drive cable   c. modem
    b. serial port   d. game port
16. Which of the following devices converts digital signals from the computer to analog signals to be used on the phone lines and converts analog signals back to digital signals?
    a. parallel port   c. modem
    b. serial port   d. ADC/DAC converter
17. A full-duplex device allows which of the following?
    a. transmitting and receiving data simultaneously
    b. transmitting or receiving data only at a specific time
    c. transmitting only
    d. receiving only
18. If you are transmitting the eight-bit binary number 11011000 and are using even parity, what would the parity bit be?
    a. 0   b. 1
19. Which of the following can be used to connect two computers together?
    a. null modem cable   c. VGA cable
    b. modem   d. SCSI connector
20. Which of the following signals must be present for a modem to receive data?
    a. high speed (HS)   c. transmit data (TD)
    b. carrier detect (CD)   d. receive data (RD)
21. In modem technology, CD stands for:
    a. change directory   d. carrier detect
    b. call data   e. comm detect
    c. change dial   f. cease deliver
22. What is the term used to refer to the process of two modems establishing communications with each other?
    a. interacting   d. linking
    b. connecting   e. pinging
    c. handshaking
23. Which of the following asynchronous lines does the terminal activate when it wants to send data to a modem?
    a. CTS   c. RTS
    b. DSR   d. DTR
24. Modems use what kind of transmission?
    a. synchronous   c. linking
    b. asynchronous   d. pinging
25. Which of the following is not a method of encoding data?
    a. PSK   c. QAM
    b. FSK   d. WRE
26. A modem that follows the AT command set is known as a(n):
    a. AT follower
    b. Hayes-compatible modem
    c. modem that can only work on a 286
    d. modem that can only work on a 286 and higher
27. Which AT command defines a hardware reset for a modem?
    a. ATF   c. ATE0
    b. ATZ   d. AT1
28. Which AT command is used for hang-up or disconnect?
    a. ATF   d. ATD
    b. ATZ   e. AT
    c. ATH

29. If a cable has two pairs of twisted wires inside a single jacket connected to a phone, what is it called?
   - a. unshielded twisted pair (UTP)
   - b. coaxial
   - c. power cable
   - d. fiber-optic cable

30. Which of the following parameters does not have to be specified when installing and configuring a modem?
   - a. number of data bits
   - b. number of stop bits
   - c. baud rate
   - d. type of parity
   - e. number of start bits

31. If a customer reports that he is unable to make a connection with his modem, which of the following should you check? (Choose all that apply.)
   - a. the jumpers or DIP switches on the modem
   - b. the telephone cable
   - c. the hard drive
   - d. the configuration of the communications software
   - e. the keyboard

32. What is the small plastic connector called that is on the end of an unshielded twisted pair wire such as the ones used on a telephone?
   - a. RJ-5
   - b. RJ-11
   - c. RJ-45
   - d. RJ-62

33. A new external modem does not work properly. Which of the following should be checked? (Choose all that apply.)
   - a. the modem cable and connector
   - b. the serial port settings
   - c. the communications parameters, such as speed, parity, data bits, and stop bits
   - d. the modem selected with the communications software

34. A modem cannot connect to another computer. The other computer indicates "no carrier detected." The problem is most likely:
   - a. the modem in the original computer
   - b. the phone lines
   - c. the original computer
   - d. the modem on the second computer
   - e. the second computer

35. If a high-speed internal modem is consistently not working at its full advertised speed, you may want to check (choose all that apply):
   - a. the other modem's maximum throughput speed
   - b. the maximum bus speed in the CMOS setup program
   - c. the version of the UART chip used by the serial port or modem
   - d. the version of the UART chip used by the parallel port

36. A customer complains that a modem is bad. It connects to another computer, but it transmits and receives garbage. What do you do? (Choose two answers.)
   - a. check the version of the software that it is using
   - b. check the version of the operating system that it is using
   - c. check the settings for the data bits, parity, and stop bits in both modems
   - d. check the driver

HANDS-ON EXERCISES

Exercise 1: Configuring a Serial Port

1. Disable all serial ports by using jumpers, DIP switches, configuring software, or the CMOS setup program.
2. Configure the 25-pin serial port as COM1 (IRQ 4 and I/O address 3F8H).
3. Boot the computer and perform the MODE command at the prompt.
4. Enable both of the serial ports. Set the 9-pin serial port to IRQ 4 (COM1) and I/O address 3F8H and the 25-pin serial port to IRQ 3 and I/O address 2F8H (COM2).
5. Run the MODE command to verify that both serial ports are active.
6. Where the serial ports connect to the motherboard or expansion card, disconnect the small ribbon cable.
7. Run the MODE command to verify that this did not deactivate the serial ports.

8. Reconnect the serial ports.

9. Using the Control Panel, record the baud rate, the number of data bits, the parity method, the number of stop bits, and the type of flow control. (If you have Windows 3.XX, use the Ports icon. If you have Windows 95 or 98, use the System icon or applet to find COM2 in the tree structure.)

10. Using the Control Panel, set COM2 to 9,600 baud, 7 data bits, even parity, 2 stop bits, and hardware flow control.

11. Close the Control Panel.

12. Go back into the Control Panel and change the COM2 parameters back to what they were before you changed them.

13. If you have Windows 95 or 98, verify that there are no resource conflicts with the serial port. (For Windows 95 or 98 use the System icon or applet in the Control Panel to find the serial port on the tree structure.)

Exercise 2: Testing the Serial Port

1. Using the MSD program, find the I/O address, baud rate, parity method, number of data bits, number of stop bits, and UART chip for both serial ports.

2. Connect a loopback plug to a serial port.

3. Using a software diagnostic package, test the serial port. (Note: You may need to tell the software diagnostic package that a loopback plug is installed.)

Exercise 3: Communicating with Another Computer Using the Serial Port and DOS

1. Connect a null modem cable from one computer to another using the second serial port.

2. On the client computer (the computer that will copy files from the server computer), add the following line to the CONFIG.SYS file in the C:\ directory and reboot the computer:

```
DEVICE = C:\DOS\INTERLNK.EXE /COM:2 /BAUD:19200
```

(Note: If the cable is connected to COM1, you will have to use /COM:1 instead of /COM:2.)

3. On the server computer (the computer that will provide files to the client computer), perform the following command at the C:\> prompt:

```
INTERSVR.EXE /COM:2 /BAUD:19200
```

4. At the client computer, perform the following command at the C:\> prompt:

```
INTERLNK
```

5. Under the Other Computer (Server) column, find the C drive. In the This Computer (Client) column find the drive letter that is opposite to the Server C drive.

6. Change to the drive letter that represents the server's C drive and perform a DIR command.

7. Find the README.TXT file in the server's DOS directory and copy it to the client's C:\ directory.

8. Disconnect the cable and reboot both systems.

9. Connect a normal serial cable to both COM2 ports.

10. Following the same procedures, try to get the two computers to talk to each other. Can you figure out why they did not connect?

11. Shut down both computers and disconnect the serial cable.

12. Put the null modem cable back on.

13. Boot the client computer.

14. On the client computer, perform the following command at the C:\> prompt:

```
MODE COM2:2400,O,7,2,
```

(Note: This will set the COM2 to a baud of 2,400, odd parity, seven data bits, and two stop bits.)

15. On the server computer, perform the following command at the C:\> prompt:

```
MODE COM2:9600,E,8,1
```

16. On the server computer, perform the following command at the C:\> prompt:

```
INTERSVR.EXE /COM:2 /BAUD:2400
```

17. At the client computer, perform the INTERLNK command to see if the computers connected. If they did not connect, can you figure out why? If you did get a connection, try to copy the README.TXT file again. After it is copied, view the contents of the file.

Exercise 4: Installing a Modem

1. Configure and install the modem. For an internal modem,
   a. If your system has a COM2, disable it.
   b. Configure your modem as a COM2 using IRQ 3 and I/O address 2F8H.
   c. Connect the twisted pair phone cable from the phone jack to the modem.
   For an external modem,
   a. Make sure that COM2 is active.
   b. Connect the twisted pair phone cable from the phone jack to the modem.
2. If you have an external modem, tell the operating system/environment the operating parameters of the serial port.
   a. If you have Windows 3.XX, use the Ports icon in the Control Panel to configure the serial port. In addition, use the Advanced... button to make sure that COM2 is set to the proper I/O address and IRQ for the modem.
   b. If you have Windows 95 or 98, use the device manager (System icon or applet in the Control Panel) to configure the operating parameters (baud rate, data bits, parity, stop bits, and flow control) of COM2.
3. If you have Windows 95 or 98, load the drivers for the modem. (This can be done with Add New Hardware applet from the Control Panel.)
4. Install the communications software package that comes with the modem or one that is provided by your instructor.
5. Look in the installation manual for the communications software to see if you need to select a modem for the communications software. This will usually need to be done in Windows 3.XX. In Windows 95 or 98, the software will usually use the driver that is already loaded into the operating system.
6. Use the communications software package to call a local BBS number with the modem. Most communications software packages allow you to enter a phone number and the operating parameters (baud rate, data bits, parity, stop bits, and flow control) for that phone number.
7. Disconnect from the local BBS number and exit the communications software.
8. Install the software provided by your instructor or Internet provider. Follow the directions that come with the software.
9. Load Internet Explorer or Netscape Navigator.
10. Connect to the Internet.
11. Start Internet Explorer or Netscape Navigator.
12. Find the web page for your school or business.
13. Disconnect from the Internet and close all programs.
14. Shut off the computer and remove the modem.

19

Parallel Ports and Printers

INTRODUCTION

The parallel port can be used to connect printers (common output devices that print text or pictures on paper) and other external devices, including external hard drives, tape drives, removable disk drives, scanners, and network cards. In addition, the parrallel port can be used with device control circuits and to transfer data between two computers.

OBJECTIVES

1. Identify the parallel port.
2. List the characteristics and uses of a parallel port.
3. Install and configure a parallel port.
4. Describe how a parallel port communicates with a printer.
5. Determine and correct parallel-port problems.
6. List the advantages and disadvantages of the main types of printers.
7. Describe the printing process.
8. Describe how page description languages speed up printing.
9. Describe the characteristics of paper and how they affect the reliability and quality of a printer.

10. Load paper and change the ribbon, ink, or toner cartridges on a typical printer.
11. Remove the print head from the dot-matrix printer, clean it, and reassemble it.
12. Determine and correct printer problems.
13. List and describe the steps of the EP process.
14. Perform preventive maintenance on a printer.
15. Install and configure a printer.

19.1   PARALLEL PORTS

The **parallel port,** sometimes referred to as the *printer port,* is a female, 2-row, 25 pin D connector. When the IBM PC was introduced, the parallel port was part of the monochrome display adapter (MDA) video card. Later, it was placed on its own expansion card or became part of a multifunction I/O expansion card. Today, many parallel ports are built into the motherboard. The typical PC can recognize up to three parallel ports (some computers can recognize four). The parallel ports are designated with the reserve names, LPT1, LPT2, and LPT3 (LPT stands for line printer). In addition, the LPT1 has an alias, PRN. This means that if you copy a text file to PRN, it will be sent to the device connected to LPT1.

The parallel port is much faster than the serial port. While the serial port can transfer only one bit at a time, the parallel port can transfer eight bits of data using eight different wires. In addition, parallel ports are synchronous devices that use a strobe signal as a clock signal. The maximum data transfer rate of a standard parallel port is 150 kilobytes per second.

19.1.1   STANDARD MODE

The standard for the parallel port interface is specified in the IEEE 1284 standard ("Standard Signaling Method for a Bidirectional Parallel Peripheral Interface for Personal Computers"), which was approved for final release in March of 1994. The first parallel port, standard parallel port (SPP), was designed by the Centronics Corporation and adapted for the PC by the Epson Corporation.

The parallel port consists of 17 signal lines (8 data lines, 4 control lines, and 5 status lines) and 8 ground lines. The data lines carry data from the computer to the parallel device (printer). The control lines are used for interface handshaking (control) signals from the PC to the printer. The status lines, which carry signals from the parallel device to the computer, are used for handshake signals and as status indicators (paper empty, busy, or peripheral error). (See table 19.1)

Like a serial port, the parallel port has a unique base I/O address. The I/O address is kept in the BIOS data area between 00408H and 0040FH. The data port, which includes the eight data lines, is accessed using the base address. The status port is accessed using the base address +1, and the control port is accessed using the base address +2. (See table 19.2.)

Before data can be sent to the printer, the printer has to be initialized. During normal operations, the computer puts out a constant +5 V dc charge on the initialize signal. If the voltage is removed, the printer resets. Therefore, every time the computer reboots or software switches the initialize signal to a low voltage, the printer resets. After the printer is initialized, it must be online to accept data. The device select signal is sent when the printer is online and is discontinued when it is offline. The select input signal indicates that the printer has been selected.

Data can be sent to the parallel port by using polling or interrupts. In **polling,** the most popular method, the BIOS polls, or checks, to see if the parallel port device is ready to accept another character. Interrupts are more efficient but can significantly slow down the computer while printing. To move data from the parallel port to the printer, the microprocessor writes it to the data register of the parallel port, which puts data on the data lines. Next, software reads the status register to make sure that the printer is not busy and that the printer is not signalling errors. If the printer is ready to accept data, the microprocessor activates the strobe signal, which is connected through the control register. When the strobe

TABLE 19.1 SPP signal definitions

TABLE 19.1 SPP signal definitions

Parallel Port (Type A)	Printer Port (Type B)	Printer Port (Type C)	Designation	Direction
1	1	15	-Strobe (-STR)	Port to printer
2	2	6	Data bit 0 (D0)	Port to printer
3	3	7	Data bit 1 (D1)	Port to printer
4	4	8	Data bit 2 (D2)	Port to printer
5	5	9	Data bit 3 (D3)	Port to printer
6	6	10	Data bit 4 (D4)	Port to printer
7	7	11	Data bit 5 (D5)	Port to printer
8	8	12	Data bit 6 (D6)	Port to printer
9	9	13	Data bit 7 (D7)	Port to printer
10	10	3	-Acknowledge (-ACK)	Printer to port
11	11	1	Busy (BSY)	Printer to port
12	12	5	Paper out (PAPER)	Printer to port
13	13	2	Select input (SEL)	Printer to port
14	14	17	-Auto feed (-AUTO)	Port to printer
15	32	4	-Error (-ERROR)	Printer to port
16	31	14	-Initialize (-INI)	Port to printer
17	36	16	-Device select (-DSL)	Port to printer
18		33	Strobe ground	Printer to port
19	20 and 21	24 and 25	Data 0 and 1 ground	Printer to port
20	22 and 23	26 and 27	Data 2 and 3 ground	Printer to port
21	24 and 25	28 and 29	Data 4 and 5 ground	Printer to port
22	26 and 27	30 and 31	Data 6 and 7 ground	Printer to port
23	29	19 and 22	Busy and faulty ground	Printer to port
24	28	20, 21, and 23	Paper out, select input, and acknowledge ground	Printer to port
25	30	32, 34, and 35	Auto feed, device select, and initialize ground	Printer to port
		16	Logic ground (0 V)	
		17	Chassis ground	
		18	Not used	
		34	Not used	
		35	Not used	

Parallel port   **Centronics port**

TABLE 19.2 Typical I/O addresses used by parallel ports

TABLE 19.2 Typical I/O addresses used by parallel ports

Parallel Port	Typical Data Port Address	Typical Status Port Address	Typical Control Port Address
LPT1	0378H	0379H	037AH
LPT2	0278H	0279H	027AH
LPT3	03BCH	03BDH	027AH

DATA
→ D0 (pin 2)
→ D1 (pin 3)
→ D2 (pin 4)
→ D3 (pin 5)
→ D4 (pin 6)
→ D5 (pin 7)
→ D6 (pin 8)
→ D7 (pin 9)

STATUS
— Reserved
— Reserved
← IRQ
← ERROR (pin 15)
← SEL (pin 13)
← PAPER (pin 12)
← ACK (pin 10)
← BUSY (pin 11)

CONTROL
→ STROBE (pin 1)
→ AUTO (pin 14)
→ INI (PIN 16)
→ DSL (pin 17)
→ IRQ enable
— Direction
— Reserved
— Reserved

signal is sent, the voltage of the strobe line, normally +5 V dc, is dropped to near zero for at least a half of a microsecond. The printer then activates the busy line so that no more information is sent until the current data is read and processed. It is the busy signal that is read during polling. After the character is processed, the printer then stops the busy signal and sends an acknowledge signal by dropping its normally high voltage to a low voltage.

The last control signal is the auto feed signal, which activates a line feed when the printer receives a carriage return signal. The status port also has an error signal and paper-out signal. The error signal tells the computer that there is some sort of problem with the printer. The paper out signal tells the computer when the printer is out of paper.

19.1.2 BIDIRECTIONAL MODES

In older PCs, the data register was designed only to send data, not receive it. Therefore, the port was unidirectional. However, most 386 machines and all machines since the 386 are bidirectional and half-duplex. *Half-duplex* means that data can travel in both directions, but only in one direction at a time.

Either the status signals (nibble mode) or the data signals (byte mode) can send data to the parallel port. The status signals, however, can send only four signals (bits) at a time. The byte mode requires the newer bidirectional port, which includes a direction bit. Many parallel ports can be reconfigured as bidirectional by setting jumpers or DIP switches, configuring the CMOS setup program, or running a software configuration program. In both modes interrupts are used to transfer data from the parallel device to the computer.

19.1.3 ENHANCED PARALLEL PORT MODE AND EXTENDED CAPABILITIES PORT MODE

Although parallel ports were much faster than serial ports, some parallel devices eventually required faster data tansfers than the standard parallel port could provide. Eventually, two standards for a faster parallel port emerged, the **enhanced parallel port (EPP)** and **extended capabilities port (ECP).** Both standards increased data transferral rates tenfold.

EPP achieves higher transfer speeds by moving the handshaking signals from the software to the hardware circuitry on the parallel port. In addition, the EPP standard uses additional registers beyond the status and control registers. ECP is similar to EPP but it can also use DMAs and data compression. Ports may need to be configured for EPP or ECP by setting jumpers or DIP switches or by using the CMOS setup program or a configuration program.

19.1.4 INSTALLING PARALLEL PORTS

When installing and configuring a parallel port, you must set the parallel port's resources, specifically I/O addresses and IRQs, with jumpers, DIP switches, setup software, or the CMOS setup program. LPT1 usually uses IRQ7 and I/O address 378H; LPT2 (if any) usually uses IRQ5 and 278H. If the parallel port is using polling (that is, it is not interrupt driven), it can share interrupts with other parallel ports.

19.1.5 CONNECTORS AND CABLES

The parallel port on the computer (type A) is a 2-row, 25-pin female D connector. The port on the printer (type B) is a 36-pin Centronics connector. A newer parallel port connector, introduced as part of the 1284 standard, is the type C connector, a high-density connector that uses all of the signals of the type B connector. The standard printer cable acts as an adapter between the connectors. (Note: parallel cables are more susceptible to noise and crosstalk, so they should be only between 6 and 10 feet long. If the cable is too long or is faulty, the data sent between the parallel port and the parallel device could become corrupted.)

**TABLE 19.3   Parallel Loopback
Plug Connection**

Pin 1	*connects to*	Pin 13
Pin 2	*connects to*	Pin 15
Pin 16	*connects to*	Pin 10
Pin 17	*connects to*	Pin 11

There are two ways of connecting one computer to another computer using the parallel ports. The first way is with a **lap link cable** (sometimes referred to as an *interlink cable*), which, unfortunately, transfers data only four bits at a time. The second way is with a universal connection module (UCM) cable made by Parallel Technologies, a cable that includes a special circuit on one of the wires that permits connecting PCs through two ECP ports.

> For more information on Parallel Technologies and their universal connection module, see the following website:
> **http://www.lpt.com/**

19.1.6   TROUBLESHOOTING PARALLEL PORTS

A parallel port that is not functioning or being recognized by the system can have one of the following problems:

1. A resource conflict (IRQ or I/O address–LPT designation)
2. Jumpers or DIP switches not set correctly or configuration software or CMOS setup program that has not been run
3. An unconnected cable (connecting the female 25-pin D connector to the I/O expansion card or motherboard)
4. A fault in the parallel port itself

These problems can also cause a device, such as a printer or a Zip drive, using the parallel port to not work. The device malfunction could also be caused by:

1. No driver loaded
2. Corrupt or improperly loaded driver
3. Faulty device

In either case, first check the obvious and then isolate. In addition, if the data is garbled, that is usually caused either by the cable being too long or by electromagnetic interference or an incorrect driver.

One tool that can be used to test the parallel port is the parallel loopback plug, similar to the serial loopback plug. The plug sends data out through the data port using a software diagnostic package and loops it back into the status port. Unfortunately, only a few bits can be tested in this way and therefore the test isn't a thorough one. Table 19.3 illustrates how the loopback plug is connected to the parallel port.

19.2   PRINTERS

A **printer** is a commonly used output device that prints text or pictures on paper. Today, most printers are connected through the parallel port (usually by a 36-pin Centronics port on the printer); a few older printers are connected through the serial port. Some printers can also be connected directly to the network and accessed through a network card. Newer interfaces such as USB and FireWire will also accommodate printers. As the computer age dawned, it was thought that computers would lead to a paperless office. However, the opposite has occurred and paper consumption has increased because it is so easy to print a document, proofread it and make changes, and print it again. More sophisticated software packages have also made it easy to produce stunning, professional-looking documents.

There are two major categories of printers: **impact printers,** which transfer ink onto the paper by pressing or striking against a ribbon, and **nonimpact printers,** which do not press or strike against a ribbon. The most common types of printers today are the dot-matrix printer, the ink-jet printer, and the laser printer. Other, less common printers are daisy wheel printers, thermal printers, LCD/LED printers, and electrosensitive printers.

Daisy wheel printers are impact printers that use a ball or wheel imprinted with characters. They can produce a clear image but are limited to the characters on the ball or wheel and cannot reproduce pictures or change fonts and styles or print unusual characters. **Thermal printers** are inexpensive printers that print by pressing heated pins onto a special heat-sensitive paper. The **LCD/LED printer** is similar to a laser printer except that it uses liquid crystal or light-emitting diodes instead of laser light. **Electrosensitive printers** use special colored paper that is coated with a thin layer of aluminum. Characters and images are formed by selectively removing the aluminum with electricity.

19.2.1 THE PRINTING PROCESS

In order to print, a software interface is needed to communicate the text and images to the printer. The simplest print systems use a few bitmapped fonts that are stored in ROM chips inside the printer or other fonts added by using font cartridges. When a print command is issued by the operating system or application software, a series of command codes is sent to the printer. Some of the commands define which bitmap font and style to use, and other codes indicate which characters are to be printed. The codes are matched against a font table in the printer ROM chips and the appropriate letters are printed to paper. Additional codes are paper movement commands, such as tabs and carriage returns. Another system specifies each dot that makes up a character, but this method takes a lot of PC processing. To alleviate some of the work done by the computer and to speed up the print process, most modern printers use a page description language. A **page description language** describes to the printer the whole page to be printed by using draw and position commands and mathematical formulas. The two most common page description languages, which are usually used in laser printers, are Adobe's **Postscript** and Hewlett Packard's **Printer Control Language (PCL).**

Normally, the user does not specify these printer codes and commands. Instead, the user creates the document and issues the print command. The print driver then translates the document into commands that the printer understands and sends them to the printer. Therefore, it is important to select the correct print driver. Otherwise, the incorrect codes would be sent and the printer would usually print garbage.

Many printers today are able to produce color, including some dot-matrix printers, many ink-jet printers, and some laser printers. The colors are usually based on the **CMYK color model,** which prints in four basic colors—cyan (greenish blue), magenta (deep purplish red), yellow, and black. By combining these colors, other colors can be produced. Some lower-quality printers use only three of these colors (cyan, magenta, and yellow) without the black. Although these printers cost less, they cannot print true black and their colors tend to be faded.

19.2.2 PAPER

Paper is usually characterized by its weight, thickness, texture, and finish. The type of paper used can affect the quality of a print job. The **weight** is the total weight of a **ream** (500 sheets) of 17″ × 22.5″ paper. The **caliper** is the thickness of the paper, which is usually expressed in thousandths of an inch. Generally, the greater the caliper, the greater the weight of the paper. The weight determines how well the paper will feed through the printer and how well the paper will accept the toner. Lightweight paper is not suitable for most printers and will usually cause frequent paper jams. Paper can be described by its **finish,** or the texture on the top surface of the paper. The smoothness or grain of the paper will affect how clearly the characters are formed. Depending on the type of printer being used, the smoothness will affect how well the image adheres to the surface. If the paper is not

FIGURE 19.1   Parts of a dot-matrix printer

smooth, the rollers can't grab it as well, causing paper jams. In addition, rough paper can put excess wear on paper-path components.

Paper must be kept dry. Damp paper does not feed well—the printer will grab multiple sheets, causing a paper jam—and may give the printed image a patchy appearance. In addition, paper being fed into the printer should be free of dust and dirt, which could contaminate the printer mechanism.

19.2.3   DOT-MATRIX PRINTERS

The **dot-matrix printer** is an impact printer that creates characters and images by striking tiny pins against an ink ribbon, paper, and platen. These printers are inexpensive, relatively fast (depending on their print mode), and very reliable. Unfortunately, they are also noisy and they do not produce high-quality output. One advantage of any kind of impact printer is that they can be used to print out multilayered forms (by using carbon or NCR paper) that require the same image on all layers. The two early standards for dot-matrix printers were Epson and IBM. Today, the most common dot-matrix printers are made by Epson and Panasonic.

The pins, or print wires, are part of the print head. (See fig. 19.1.) Behind the pins there is a permanent magnet that holds the pins back. When a pin is to strike the paper, electricity is sent through a coil wrapped around the pin. The electricity causes the coil to create an intense magnetic field that pushes the pin against the ribbon. After the current stops, the magnetic field collapses and the pin is pulled back to its resting position by the permanent magnet. The coils are not very efficient electrical devices and so they dissipate a lot of heat. The print heads therefore become hot, which can cause print wire jamming and coil burnout. The housing of the print head is shaped into a heat sink to dissipate heat faster.

Most print heads contain 9 or 24 pins. A 9-pin head that prints text and images with one pass is known as *draft mode*. In draft mode, the individual dots are very visible. For better quality, the 9-pin head could print in near-letter-quality mode, in which the print head prints an individual line twice (making it equivalent to 18 pins). The best quality from a dot-matrix printer is produced by the 24-pin print head. The 24-pin head has more than one column of pins and more pins, so it does a much better job of filling in the tiny gaps than a 9-pin print head. (See fig. 19.2.)

Most modern dot-matrix printers are bidirectional; that is, they can print right to left and left to right. Because the print head does not have to return to the beginning to print the next line, the printer is faster. The print head is moved back and forth on the paper by the carriage

FIGURE 19.2   Dot-matrix print head

transport unit (sometimes called the print head carriage assembly), which rides on one or two bars placed in front of the platen. The unit is moved back and forth with a timing belt (toothed belt), which is moved by the print head positioning motor. The print head must be stopped each time the print wires strike the paper. If it isn't, the dot could be smeared or the paper could be damaged. The print head is connected to a control board (the main circuit board, which acts almost like a motherboard) with a flexible cable. As the print head moves back and forth, the cable unfolds when it gets to the far end and folds up when it gets to the near end. Small optical sensors detect the current position of the print head.

The ribbon used in the dot-matrix printer is very similar to a typewriter ribbon. It is usually made of a continuous loop of nylon fabric contained in a cartridge. (See fig. 19.3.) Depending on the cartridge and the dot-matrix printer, the cartridge may remain stationary or move with the print head. To make sure that the print head does not use the same spot repeatedly, the ribbon is forwarded as the printer prints. If the ribbon did not forward, the spot on the ribbon that the printer is using would quickly run out of ink. If the ribbon moves forward erratically, the print image would be faded at certain places. Most ribbon cartridges have a tension knob used to keep the ribbon taut.

The paper is inserted into the printer as single sheets or as fanfold paper (also known as continuous form). Most printers can handle both types. The single sheets can be fed individually or by a paper feeder (the paper feeder can hold a stack of paper). Friction rollers or a tractor feed feeds the paper into the printer. Friction rollers wrap the paper halfway around the platen. To make sure that the paper does not slip, a set of rollers presses the

FIGURE 19.3   Common ribbons used in dot-matrix printers

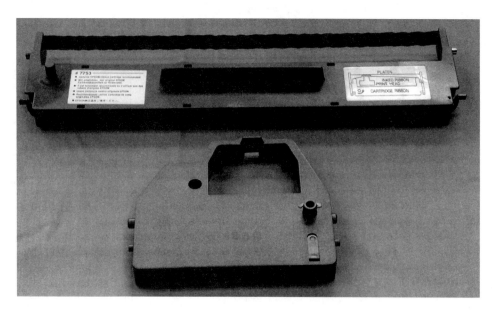

paper against the platen. Since paper comes in different thicknesses, the distance between the print head and the platen is adjustable, usually by means of a level on the top of the printer. If the print head is too far away from the paper, the text and images print lightly, and if it is too close, the text and images can become smudged. Fanfold paper, which is continuous paper divided by perforations into $8\frac{1}{2}'' \times 11''$ sheets and has small holes on the left and right sides, is fed into the printer by **tractor feed** (also known as pin-feed). Sprockets on a wheel or belt are placed in the holes of the fanfold paper. As the sprockets rotate around a wheel, the paper is pushed or pulled past the print head. The friction-feed rollers must be released when the tractor feed is used so that they don't interfere with the movement of the paper. It is best to remove paper from a dot-matrix printer by using the page feed or line feed controls on the printer. The paper should not be pulled out unless the friction-feed rollers are released and the paper is free of the tractor feed. In addition, the knobs on the side of the printer should be turned only when the printer is off. Turning the knobs when the printer is on will strip some of the gears inside the printer.

Most people don't realize that the printer has a microcontroller (microprocessor). As data is sent from the computer to the printer, the microcontroller receives it and the control signals and processes the information. It will then control the print head, the print head carriage unit, the paper-feed motors, and the ribbon. In addition, it monitors several optical sensors, including the paper-out sensor, print head position, and the home position sensor (so the sensor knows where to begin), and the control panel (form feed, line feed, online, and offline).

Some dot-matrix printers can print in color. Most of these use a multicolored ribbon with three or four bands corresponding to the primary colors (usually black, red, green, and blue). To print different colors, the ribbon is moved up and down so that the print head pin prints with the correct color. Other colors are formed by combining the primary colors on the ribbon. Because this requires printing the color images more than once in order to mix the colors, color printing is slower than printing in black and white.

The speed of the dot-matrix printer is usually expressed in characters per second (cps); a few line printers are measured in lines per minute. The speed, of course, will vary according to the print mode (draft mode or near-letter quality), whether it is printing color, and the complexity of the document.

19.2.4 INK-JET PRINTERS

The **ink-jet printer** works by spraying small droplets of ionized ink onto a sheet of paper. Modern ink-jet printers produce high-quality print (including color) that approaches the quality produced by laser printers, yet cost much less. And, because ink-jet printers are much smaller than laser printers, their portability has added to their popularity. The best-selling ink-jet printers are made by Hewlett Packard and, to a lesser extent, Canon. (See fig. 19.4.)

A typical ink-jet printer prints with a resolution of 300 dots per inch, although some newer models have higher resolutions. Since the droplets are smaller than the dot-matrix pins, the printer can achieve a better image. The ink comes from an ink reservoir stored in a removable ink cartridge and is sprayed through tiny nozzles located on the print head. (See fig. 19.5.) Each nozzle ejects ink droplets as they are formed by a piezoelectric pump or a bubble pump. The piezoelectric pump is a ring of piezoelectric ceramic material (a crystal that changes shape when subjected to electricity) placed in front of the print nozzle. As electricity flows through the ring, the piezoelectric material vibrates at approximately 100 kHz and constricts, squeezing the ink out through the nozzle. When the flow of current stops, the ring returns to its original size, forming a vacuum. The pressure of the vacuum causes fresh ink to replace the ink that was sprayed out. The bubble pump creates the droplets by heating a resistor at the bottom of the ink-jet nozzle. The ink boils and forms a bubble, pushing ink through the nozzle. When the droplet is large enough, it breaks away from the print head and attaches to the paper. As the resistor cools, the bubble collapses, causing a vacuum. The pressure of the vacuum causes fresh ink to replace the ink that was sprayed out.

The ink-jet cartridge can be easily replaced when it runs out of ink. It is important not to touch the print head when replacing the cartridge because the ink-jet holes are about half

FIGURE 19.4 Epson Stylus
Color 850 ink-jet printer
(courtesy of Epson America,
Inc.)

the diameter of a human hair and can clog easily with dirt or grease from fingers. Most ink-jet printers have a self-cleaning function that can unclog a nozzle, but the process does use a large amount of ink. Most ink-jet printers are also self-sealing so that air will not cause the ink to dry in the nozzle. The ink cartridge is designed to be used until the ink runs out and then thrown away. Unfortunately, there is no warning when the cartridges are running low. The page simply starts to fade as it is being printed. Today, many ink-jets can print in color. Like the dot-matrix printer, the ink-jet printer has three colors (cyan, magenta, and yellow), four colors (black, cyan, magenta, and yellow), or seven colors, which are mixed together to form other colors.

Question: Should an ink cartridge be refilled?

Answer: There are kits for refilling ink cartridges, which of course save money, but it is not usually a good idea. As ink passes through the nozzle, the nozzle wears down, and the nozzles are easily clogged with grease and dirt. Therefore, to improve poor print quality, first try a new ink cartridge.

As with a dot-matrix printer, the cartridge for an ink-jet printer is inserted into the print head assembly, which rides on one or two bars placed in front of the platen. The assembly is moved back and forth with a timing belt, which is moved by a print head positioning motor. The print head assembly is connected to a control board by a flexible cable. As the print head moves back and forth, the cable unfolds as it moves to the far end and folds up when it moves to the near end. Small optical sensors detect the current position of the print head.

FIGURE 19.5 Ink-jet cartridge

Paper is inserted into the printer as single sheets. The single sheets are usually fed by friction rollers that pin the paper against the platen. The paper is usually stored in a bin, often located at the bottom of the printer. When the ink hits the paper, it must dry before the paper can be handled. How well it dries depends on the type of paper and ink being used. If the paper absorbs too much of the ink, the image will be faded because there is not much ink on the surface. If the paper has a finish that causes the ink to bleed, the image will look blurry. If the paper doesn't absorb enough ink, such as with a glossy surface or plastic transparencies, for example, the ink will easily smear. The moisture of the ink may cause low-quality paper to become warped. Therefore, although the cost is a little more than regular copy paper, it is best to use special ink-jet paper.

19.2.5 LASER PRINTERS

Laser printers, like copy machines, use an **electrophoto (EP)** process to form images on paper with toner instead of ink. Consequently, laser printers produce very high-quality print and are capable of printing almost any text or image. They are also relatively fast—a typical laser printer is rated between 4 and 8 pages per minute (ppm), and some network printers can print up to 20 pages per minute. Of course, this speed does not include the time needed for the processing done by the computer and the printer.

Operation

The central part of the laser printer is a **photosensitive drum,** an aluminum cylinder coated with a nontoxic organic material that reacts to light. In darkness, the material can hold an electrical charge. As light is exposed to the drum, the drum discharges electricity. **Toner** is the material that is transferred onto the paper. It is an extremely fine powder made of plastic resin bonded to iron particles. The iron particles react to electrical charges and the plastic resin has a low melting temperature.

> **NOTE** With these characteristics, toner spills cannot be cleaned up by normal means. The best way to clean a toner spill is to use a vacuum cleaner with special filter bags, required because the toner is so fine that it would be sucked through a normal vacuum bag back into the air. A moist cloth can be used to wipe some toner up, but a dry cloth should be used to wipe toner off clothing. Toner has a low melting point, so only cold water should be used to wash hands, clothing, and carpets.

There are six basic steps to transferring the image onto the paper: (See fig. 19.6.)

1. Cleaning
2. Conditioning
3. Writing
4. Developing
5. Transferring
6. Fusing

During the cleaning stage, the photosensitive drum is cleaned to remove any residual toner and residual electrical charge. The toner is removed with a soft rubber scraper so that it won't transfer to subsequent pages and appear as random black speckles. The rubber scraper is used to avoid scratching the delicate photosensitive material on the drum; any scratch would appear on every image printed. The residual electrical charge is removed by an eraser lamp, leaving the drum's surface with a neutral charge.

During the conditioning stage, the main **corona wire,** which has a charge of −6,000 V dc, is located near the drum's surface. Since the drum and corona wire share the same ground, an electrical field is established between the two that transfers between −600 V dc and −1,000 V dc. The voltage transfer is regulated by the primary grid. At this point, the drum is ready to receive the image to be printed. If there is any dirt or debris on the corona wire, it will generate an uneven charge on the drum, resulting in lines or streaks.

FIGURE 19.6 The six stages of laser printing. During the cleaning stage, a photosensitive drum is cleaned to remove any residual toner (rubber scraper) and residual charge (eraser lamp). During the conditioning stage, the main corona wire charges the drum with a negative voltage. During the writing state, the image is formed on the drum by the laser. The developing stage transfers toner to the drum, where it sticks on the areas that are still charged. The transferring stage transfers the toner to the positively charged paper, and the fusing stage melts the toner into the paper.

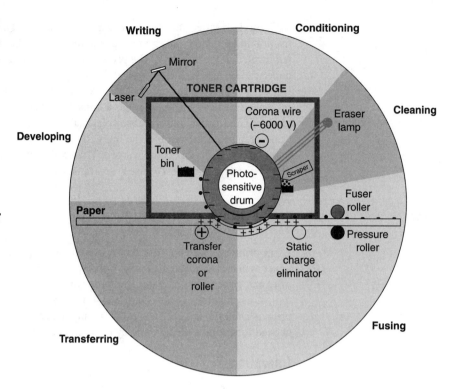

During the writing stage, the laser light (a class 1 laser), aimed by mirrors, sweeps along the drum line by line, selectively hitting parts of it. As the light touches areas of the drum, the photosensitive material it strikes grounds itself to the aluminum cylinder, reducing the charge to −100 V dc. Consequently, an electrostatic image is formed on the drum. Some faster laser printers have several laser beams working simultaneously.

In the developing stage, the toner, which has a negative charge, is applied to the drum by a developer roller (toner roller). The areas of the drum that were not hit by the light still have a strong negative charge, so the toner is repelled from them. The toner adheres to those areas of the drum that were struck by the light. The printer is now ready for the transferring stage. During this stage, paper is positively charged by a transfer roller (a black sponge-rubber roller) or a transfer corona wire. Because the paper is positively charged and the toner is negatively charged, the toner is attracted to the paper (opposites attract). (Note: Toner does not adhere to a rough surface as well, and a wrinkled or creased sheet of paper cannot be charged uniformly. If the print media is too thick, its attraction to a negative charge will not be as strong, and the toner may not adhere to the surface as well as it should.) To make sure that the paper is not attracted to the drum and does not wrap around it, it is discharged by a static charge eliminator (or eliminator comb) after the toner has been transferred. (Note: Transfer rollers should never be touched with the fingers. Skin oils on the roller can cause print quality problems.)

The last stage in the printing process is the fusing stage, in which the paper and fresh toner are pressed against each other and fused with two rollers, a fuser roller made of a Teflon-coated aluminum and a rubberized pressure roller. When paper emerges from the printer, the toner is permanently bonded to it. As the fuser roller rotates, excess toner is wiped off and silicon oil is added by a cleaning pad. The EP process then starts again with the cleaning stage.

> **NOTE** The fuser roller is heated to approximately 180° Celsius by a high-intensity quartz lamp. To prevent the toner from sticking to the roller, the roller is made of a nonstick substance such as Teflon. If work anywhere near the fusing area is being done, it is best to unplug the printer and wait at least 10 minutes so the fusing unit and lamp have a chance to cool. When performing periodic maintenance on a laser printer, clean the fuser assembly with a damp cloth.

Print Media

Because parts of the laser printer are extremely hot, it can accommodate only print media (paper, transparencies, and self-adhesive labels) designed for laser printers. Otherwise, transparencies may melt while in the printer and labels may become loose and get stuck in the printer or wrap around a roller. The component that moves the media through the laser printer is the **paper transport assembly,** which consists of a motor and several rubberized rollers. The first roller, known as the *feed* or *paper pickup* roller, is a D-shaped roller that pushes one sheet of paper into the printer. Then the registration rollers move the rollers through the EP cartridge. Most printers are **simplex** printers. This means that they can print on only one side of the paper. A few larger laser printers are duplex printers, which means they have a duplex tray that turns each sheet of paper over so that it can be printed on the other side. Of course, when duplex printing, the printer's output speed will be halved. Unfortunately, the duplex unit is mechanically complicated and the printer is more likely to jam.

Control

The large circuit board that converts signals from the computer into signals understood by the different components of the laser printer is the **printer controller circuitry.** It sends a signal through a cable to the printer controller assembly. The controller assembly formats a page of information into a series of commands for the different components and sends the signal through the appropriate cables to the appropriate components.

The power for the laser printer is supplied by the high-voltage power supply (HVPS) and the dc power supply (DCPS). The HVPS provides high-voltage electricity to energize the corona wire and transfer corona wire. The DCPS powers the logic circuitry with $+5$ V and -5 V and with $+24$ V for the paper transport motors. Because a laser printer consumes large amounts of power, it can cause power fluctuations, especially when warming up, which may affect the reliability of a computer on the same circuit. The corona wire (or wires) produce ozone as a result of the ionization of the surrounding air. Ozone is a corrosive gas that in large quantities can cause respiratory ailments, nausea, headaches, and premature aging of the skin. To reduce the amount of ozone released into the air, a laser printer will often have an ozone filter. If the filter becomes clogged, the ozone seeps undetected into a room in its pure form. Most **ozone filters** should, therefore, be replaced every 20,000 to 30,000 pages printed. The filter is usually accessible when the printer is opened for cleaning or it may be part of the toner cartridge.

Toner Cartridges

Most laser printers use replaceable **toner cartridges,** which simplify the adding of toner and help prevent many problems. A typical cartridge contains the toner, photosensitive drum, cleaning scraper blade, primary corona wire, developing roller, and a debris cavity that catches excess toner. (See fig. 19.7.) The photosensitive drum is very sensitive to light and so should not be exposed to any source of bright light, including sunlight, and it should not be exposed to extremes of temperature and humidity. (Note: When installing or replacing the toner cartridge, it is best to shake the toner cartridge so that the toner will be distributed evenly.) Because parts of the toner cartridge wear out, it is best to use a new toner cartridge instead of a refilled toner cartridge. If refilled toner cartridges are used (because they are cheaper), make sure that the company that refills the toner refills the cartridge only once, since the drum will eventually wear out.

Resolution

A typical laser printer will have a resolution of between 300 and 600 dots per inch (dpi); some high-end printers can achieve 1,200 dpi. Some laser printers can achieve an even higher resolution by using resolution enhancement and "microfine" toner. Hewlett Packard's **Resolution Enhancement Technology (RET)** prints like any other laser printer except it produces smaller dots. The smaller dots fill some of the gaps between two normal-size dots so that a line or curve appears smoother. Another advantage of RET is its

FIGURE 19.7 Laser toner cartridge and the photosensitive drum

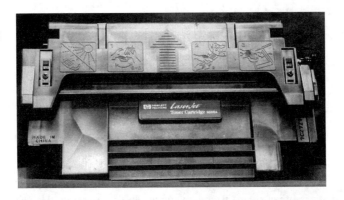

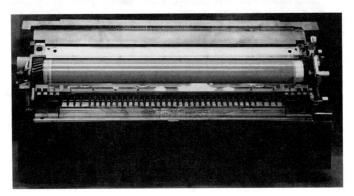

ability to reproduce more shades of gray. Laser printers can't print a true gray color. Instead, they use **halftones,** which simulate shades of gray by assembling patterns of black and white dots. Printers that have Resolution Enhancement Technology or the equivalent can generate more shades of gray because the dots are smaller than normal. Color laser printers are also available, and they work much like other printers in that they use four colors to create all of the other colors. Unfortunately, color laser printers tend to be about five to ten times as expensive as black-and-white printers.

Graphics are a particular challenge for all printers. Graphics are either bitmap graphic images or vector images. **Bitmap graphics** are sent to the printer as an array of dots. Because an image can contain many dots (a 300 dpi printer uses 90,000 dots per square inch), a bitmap graphic contains lots of information. The printer requires a lot of memory to store this information, and it also needs to do a lot of processing. **Vector graphics** use lines and curves to define an image. A line or curve is defined by mathematical equations, so they require a lot less printer RAM and processing and can be printed faster than bitmap images. Certain images, however, such as photographs (images made of dots), can be printed only as bitmap images. Laser printers were designed to print graphics. As with a PC, the complexity of the graphics that can be printed is partially determined by the amount of RAM the printer has. To print a full-page complex graphic document at 300 dots per inch (dpi), at least 1 MB of RAM (probably more) is needed. For a 600 dpi graphic document, at least 4 MB of RAM (probably more) is needed. Adding more RAM to some printers can increase performance, specifically the processing speed.

Maintenance

A good preventive maintenance and cleaning program will stop most laser-printer problems before they occur and will help ensure that the printer has the highest quality output possible. The program should include:

1. Cleaning the main and transfer corona wires with denatured alcohol
2. Cleaning the transfer guide and paper-feed guide with a lint-free cloth dampened with cold, demineralized water
3. Using the soft end of the corona cleaning brush to sweep away any paper dust or debris on the static eliminator

4. Cleaning the fuser separation pawls (claws) with a lint-free cloth dampened with cold, demineralized water
5. Replacing the ozone filter

19.2.6 INSTALLING A PRINTER

A printer is one of the easiest peripheral devices to install. The printer cable is connected from the PC's parallel port to the printer's Centronics connector, and then the printer's power cable is plugged in. (Note: New printers will usually have packing inside to prevent the print head and other internal devices from moving around during shipping. These must be removed from the system, of course, before the printer can be used.) The next step is installing the driver for the software that is using the printer. For Windows 3.XX, Windows 95 and 98, and Windows NT, only one driver has to be loaded for all Windows applications. For DOS programs, unless using "straight" text mode, a driver will have to be loaded for each DOS application. The driver is used to convert data from a document to commands that the printer understands. Although most of the alphanumeric data is standard for most printers, the control codes are not. Therefore, attempting to print a document using the wrong device driver will result in the wrong control codes being sent to the printer and it will print garbage (strange characters or many pages of programming code). A system may contain several print drivers for several different printers, so the correct one must be activated before printing. If it is not, the printer will usually output garbage.

Depending on the work environment, several people may share the same printer. This can be accomplished by installing a network or by means of a switch box. Most switch boxes have one port that connects to the printer using a normal printer cable and other connectors, anywhere from 2 to 16, that use 25-pin male to 25-pin male straight-through cables. Some switch boxes are manual and others are autoswitching. Manual switch boxes need to be manually set to the port (computer) before the printer can print. The autoswitching boxes automatically detect which printer is sending a print signal and switch to that port as needed. Autoswitching boxes should be used when connecting laser printers to a switch box because laser printers need a constant signal. If they don't get one, a printer error message will probably appear on the printer display.

19.2.7 TROUBLESHOOTING PRINTERS

Although printers are easy to install, they can cause all sorts of headaches. Any problem that occurs with a printer has one of four sources:

1. The printer (including cartridges and ribbons)
2. The print cable
3. The parallel port (or other interface)
4. The software (including drivers)

Most printers can perform a self-test that can be initiated by pressing one or more buttons (such as the online, form-feed, or line-feed buttons) while turning the printer on or by using the printer's control panel. Instructions on how to activate the print test are included in the printer documentation. The test will usually print all of the alphanumeric characters, and many of them will print the configuration for the printer, different types of fonts, or a graphic image.

A common problem that occurs is the paper jam—a sheet of paper catching or refusing to pass through the printer mechanism. A paper jam may be caused by using incorrect paper (the paper is too heavy or too light), damp paper, a wornout roller, or the buildup of paper fragments, toner, or other debris. Sometimes the printer may jam for no apparent reason. Of course, if the printer has regular maintenance performed on it, the jams will occur less frequently. Single-feed paper should be fanned before loading it into a holding tray with the paper curling downward. An important clue to what part of the printer is causing the jam is where the first part of the paper stopped. When removing the jam, be careful not to snatch the paper from the printer or pull fiercely, which is likely to rip the paper and leave a small piece behind, which may cause more paper jams. Many gears can turn only one way, so when turning knobs and pulling paper, make sure the knobs are being turned or the paper is being pulled in the right direction. If the rollers do not turn in the direction in which you are pulling, the paper will most likely tear. Lastly, make sure the printer is off and unplugged, that the dot-matrix print head and fuser assembly has had a chance to cool, and that the corona wire is not carrying an electrical charge. If you remove a paper jam from a laser printer and it says that there still is a jam, open and close the lid. Always refer to the printer manual for the proper way to remove a paper jam.

If the printer does not come on at all, that is probably a power supply problem. Make sure the power cord is plugged into both the ac wall jack and the printer, that the ac wall jack has power, and that the printer is turned on. If the printer still does not come on, open the housing and locate the printer's power supply. Before replacing the power supply, check the power supply fuse. If the fuse is blown, replace it. Of course, you should then be concerned with what blew the fuse to begin with. If the fuse is not blown, you will probably need to replace the power supply.

EXAMPLE 19.1 You give the print command and nothing happens.

As with any other problem, check the obvious first:

Check to see if the printer is plugged in
Check to see if the printer is on
Check to see if the printer is online
Check to see if the printer cable is connected properly
If a switch box is being used, make sure that all of the cables are connected properly and that the switch box is switched to the computer you are trying to print from.

If the problem still exists, you need to isolate it. The printer, the printer cable, the parallel port, or the software could be at fault. The easiest of these to check and one of the most common sources of problems is the software. Make sure that the correct driver is loaded and selected and that the software points to the correct printer port (LPT1, LPT2, or other).

If the computer is using Windows (Windows 3.XX, Windows 95 or 98, or Windows NT), print using another program. If the other program prints fine, then the first program has become corrupt and will probably have to be reinstalled. If the problem occurs in both applications, check the print manager to see if a particular print job is causing the problem or if the print manager or print spooler is stalled or having problems. If the print manager or print spooler is having problems, these can usually be corrected by rebooting the computer or restarting the print manager or spooler.

If the problem still exists, isolate it further as a hardware problem or software problem by booting the system to DOS or the command prompt (Windows 95 and 98 and Windows NT) and sending something to the printer. This can be done by sending a text file (such as AUTOEXEC.BAT) to the printer:

```
TYPE AUTOEXEC.BAT > LPT1
```

or

```
COPY AUTOEXEC.BAT LPT1
```

Of course, for these two commands to work, the printer must be connected to LPT1. (Note: Text files sent to a laser printer do not have a form-feed code. Therefore, you will usually have to perform a form-feed code manually using the control panel on the printer.) If the document prints, then you know that the hardware is working properly and that there is a software problem.

If the document does not print, then there is a hardware problem. The next step is having the printer perform a self-test. If the self-test fails, the problem is most likely caused by the printer. If the self-test works properly, the problem must be with the printer interface, the printer configuration, the parallel port, or the cable. If the self-test fails, the problem is most likely caused by the printer. To determine which component is causing the problem, start swapping them. The easiest one to swap is the printer cable. If there is a switch box, two cables and the switch box will have to be swapped. Swap one component at a time until you find which component is bad.

Next, try the printer on a different computer or try a different printer on the same computer. If the printer prints on another computer, the parallel port (or other interface) must be at fault. Make sure there is no resource conflict (IRQ or I/O address or LPT designation) and that the port is active (the jumpers, DIP switches, software, or CMOS setup program are correctly configured). If the parallel port uses a ribbon cable to connect the 25-pin D connector to the motherboard or expansion card, make sure that it is connected properly. If the printer is a serial printer, a null modem cable must be used and the serial port must be configured properly (baud rate, data bits, stop bits, and parity). If a different printer prints on the same computer, the problem must be with the printer configuration (DIP switches or Control Panel) or the printer interface. The printer configuration is the easiest and quickest to check, so this should be checked first. If the configuration seems fine, replace the printer or take the printer apart and diagnose the problem.

EXAMPLE 19.2 A document prints as garbage.

The most common cause of garbage (strange characters or many pages of what appears to be programming code) is the wrong driver being loaded or selected, but it could also be a software problem. Try printing from another application. If the printer prints in one application and not the other, the first application is causing the problem. Next, reboot the computer or restart the print manager or spooler so that the print manager or spooler has a chance to refresh itself. Finally, try reinstalling the driver, since the driver could have become corrupt.

If the problem still exists, make sure that the cable is connected properly and that it is no longer than 10 feet. A long cable is much more susceptible to electromagnetic interference. Also make sure the cable does not go near any device that generates a lot of electromagnetic interference (EMI). Before swapping any components, perform the printer's self-test. If the self-test fails, the problem is most likely being caused by the printer.

A faulty print cable, a faulty parallel port, or a faulty printer are the next likely causes of the problem. Swap the cable (or switch box and cables) first; then try the printer on a different computer or try a different printer on the same computer. If the same printer prints on another computer with no problems, the problem must lie with the parallel port (or other interface). If a different printer works on the same computer, the problem must be with the printer. The printer must be disassembled and fixed or it will have to be replaced. If the printer is a serial printer, make sure a null modem cable is being used and the serial port is configured properly (baud rate, data bits, stop bits, and parity).

Troubleshooting Dot-Matrix Printers

On occasion, the dot-matrix print head will have to be cleaned (pins become clogged with residual ink and dust) or replaced when some of the pins are not firing or they fire erratically. First, make sure that the printer is shut off and unplugged. Remove the print head (usually done by unsnapping plastic holding clips or removing some screws) and disconnect the ribbon cable leading to the print head, noting how the cable is oriented so that you can reconnect it properly. After the print head is removed, pour a small of amount of denatured alcohol into a cup or other container and insert the nose of the print head in the alcohol. Next, insert the part of the print head that contains the pins for two or three minutes. Do not submerse the print head. After the print head has had a chance to soak, dry it off, reinstall it, and reconnect the ribbon cable leading to the print head. Remove the ribbon, load the paper into the printer, and run the self-test a few times without the ribbon so that any ink inside the pins will be transferred to the paper. Depending on how dirty the print head was, this process may have to be repeated several times. When the print head is clean, apply one or two drops of light oil to the pins to lubricate them.

When performing periodic maintenance on a printer, make sure that you do not use harsh solvents, such as 409 all-purpose cleaner, since these will usually either soften parts of the printer or cause them to melt. Use a damp cloth or denatured alcohol instead. In addition, do not lubricate the gear trains or platen assembly of a dot-matrix printer.

EXAMPLE 19.3 Documents have light or uneven print.

The first thing to check on a dot-matrix printer is the distance between the print head and platen. If the distance is correct, replace the ribbon—it is most likely running out of ink. If the problem occurs again, make sure that the ribbon is advancing. If it is not, the problem is probably caused by a bad gear, the belt on the ribbon feed assembly, a bad ribbon, or incorrect insertion of the ribbon.

EXAMPLE 19.4 The print head does not print.

The first thing to check on a dot-matrix printer is the distance between the print head and platen. If the distance is correct, replace the ribbon—it is most likely running out of ink. If the problem occurs again, make sure that the ribbon is advancing. If it is not, the problem is probably caused by a bad gear, the belt on the ribbon feed assembly, a bad ribbon, or incorrect insertion of the ribbon. If the ribbon is advancing, the ribbon cable to the print head is not connected properly, the print head needs to be replaced, or the control board inside the printer needs to be replaced.

EXAMPLE 19.5 The print head does not move.

Make sure that nothing is jammed in the printer that may prevent the print head from moving back and forth. The problem could also be caused by the home position sensor, the print head position motor, the timing belt, or the control board.

EXAMPLE 19.6 The paper is not advancing.

First, check the paper-feed selector level to make sure that the correct type of paper feed (tractor feed or friction feed) is selected. Next, check for paper jams. If the problem still occurs, check the paper-feed motor.

Troubleshooting the Ink-Jet Printer

Most problems with an ink-jet printer occur because either the cartridge is empty (or low) or the nozzles on the print cartridge are clogged. In either case, it is usually best to replace the print cartridge. (Note: If you install a print cartridge and later remove it, it should not be reinstalled in the printer.) Most of the other problems encountered are very similar to those encountered with dot-matrix printers.

Troubleshooting the Laser Printer

Troubleshooting a laser printer is quite different from troubleshooting a dot-matrix or an ink-jet printer. Fortunately, many of the laser printer components are modular (such as the toner cartridge) and can therefore be replaced without too much difficulty.

> **NOTE** Consumers usually dispose of the toner cartridge by throwing it into the trash. Businesses, on the other hand, need to follow state and federal laws on the proper method of disposal. Recycling the print cartridge is always recommended.

EXAMPLE 19.7 Documents are light or have uneven print.

If the print image becomes faint or uneven, first attempt to change the printer contrast or density control. If this does not help, remove the toner cartridge and shake it so that the toner is distributed more evenly. If this does not correct the problem, replace the toner cartridge. If the cartridge is older than six months (the normal shelf life of a typical toner cartridge), it should be replaced. If replacing the toner cartridge does not fix the problem, then check the transfer corona wire and transfer roller, the high-voltage power supply assembly, and the drum ground contacts.

EXAMPLE 19.8 The printed documents are completely black.

If the pages coming from the laser printer are completely black, the problem is probably caused by a faulty main corona wire. If the corona wire cannot charge the entire drum, the drum will not hold a negative charge and no matter what image is drawn with the laser light, the toner will be attracted to the entire drum. Consequently, all of the toner will be transferred to the paper, making it completely black. Therefore, examine the corona wire. If it is broken, it will have to be replaced or the toner cartridge will have to be replaced. If the corona wire is dirty, a cleaning with alcohol should correct the problem. (Note: A dirty main corona wire can cause black streaks.)

EXAMPLE 19.9   The documents are completely white.

Try replacing the toner cartridge. If this doesn't fix the problem, look at the transfer corona wire. If it is broken or dirty, it will not attract the negatively charged toner from the drum. (Note: A dirty transfer corona wire may cause white streaks.)

EXAMPLE 19.10   The image smears on the paper.

If the image on the paper smears or the toner is not permanently fused to the paper, the fusing roller was not hot enough. If the problem occurs randomly—on one page the toner is fused properly, and on another the image smears—first clean the thermistor temperature sensor. If the problem still occurs, replace the thermistor temperature sensor and test it again. If the problem still exists, replace the fusing unit and cleaning pads.

EXAMPLE 19.11   Speckles appear on printed documents.

Speckles may be caused by loose toner caught inside the printer. Most of the time these speckles may be removed by running several pages through the printer. If the problem still occurs, try cleaning the corona wire or replacing the toner cartridge.

EXAMPLE 19.12   The paper in a laser printer is continuously jamming.

Determine first how far the paper gets before jamming. This will help you isolate the location of the jam. Although the most common area for paper jams is the pickup area, jams may also occur in the fusing area and registration area. Also make sure that the paper is dry. If the problem still occurs, check for worn rollers or for broken or missing teeth on the drive gear of the pickup roller.

SUMMARY

1. The parallel port, sometimes referred to as the printer port, is a female, 2-row, 25-pin D connector. Its primary function is to connect printers.
2. The serial port can transfer only one bit at a time, while the parallel port can transfer eight bits of data using eight different wires.
3. The PC can usually recognize up to three parallel ports.
4. Polling is the most popular method of sending data. The BIOS polls, or checks, to see if the parallel port device is ready to accept another character. Polling allows printer ports to share interrupts.
5. The interrupt method of sending data to the parallel port is efficient but can significantly slow the printing process.
6. Most parallel ports since the 386 are bidirectional.
7. LPT1 usually uses IRQ7 and the I/O address 378H; LPT2 (if any) usually uses IRQ5 and 278H.
8. The port on the printer (type B) is a 36-pin Centronics connector.
9. When a parallel port does not function or is not recognized by the system, the problem can be caused by a resource conflict, a disabled parallel port, an unconnected cable, or a faulty port.
10. A printer, the most commonly used output device, prints text or pictures on paper.
11. A page description language describes the whole page to be printed with draw and position commands and mathematical formulas.
12. Paper is usually characterized by its weight, thickness, texture, and finish.
13. Most print heads on dot-matrix printers contain 9 or 24 pins.
14. The ink-jet printer works by spraying small droplets of ionized ink onto a sheet of paper. Modern ink-jet printers produce high-quality print (including color printing) that approaches the quality produced by laser printers yet cost much less.
15. Replacing the ribbon or ink cartridge on a dot-matrix or ink-jet printer may solve a light print problem.
16. Laser printers, like copy machines, use an electrophoto (EP) process to form images with toner on paper.
17. The EP process has six basic stages: cleaning, conditioning, writing, developing, transferring, and fusing.
18. If the correct print driver is not loaded, the printed document will usually be garbage.

1. The parallel port is described as:
   a. a 2-row, 25-pin male D connector
   b. a 2-row, 25-pin female D connector
   c. a 2-row, 9-pin male D connector
   d. a 2-row, 9-pin female D connector
   e. a 2-row, 15-pin female D connector

2. Which of the following is a printer most likely connected to?
   a. serial port
   b. parallel port
   c. SCSI port
   d. keyboard port
   e. video port

3. How many bits does a parallel port send at one time?
   a. 1
   b. 4
   c. 8
   d. 16
   e. 32

4. Parallel cables use:
   a. one wire to transmit data with start and stop bits
   b. eight wires to transmit data
   c. eight wires to transmit data with start and stop bits
   d. two wires to send data
   e. two wires to send data with start and stop bits

5. What should the maximum length of a parallel cable be?
   a. 3 feet
   b. 6–10 feet
   c. 50 feet
   d. 100 feet

6. What happens if a parallel port is configured as LPT2 but there is no LPT1?
   a. it is used as LPT2
   b. it is converted to LPT1 during boot-up
   c. the port will not work
   d. it is converted to a serial port

7. What is the standard IRQ for LPT1?
   a. IRQ 2
   b. IRQ 3
   c. IRQ 4
   d. IRQ 5
   e. IRQ 7

8. What is the standard IRQ for LPT2?
   a. IRQ 2
   b. IRQ 3
   c. IRQ 4
   d. IRQ 5
   e. IRQ 7

9. If information is to be transferred between two computers using the parallel ports and a lap link (interlink) cable, which type of parallel port(s) does the computer need to have? (Choose all that apply.)
   a. standard
   b. bidirectional
   c. EPP
   d. ECP

10. The connector found on a printer is usually the:
    a. female 25-pin, 2-row D connector
    b. male 25-pin, 2-row D connector
    c. male 36-pin, 2-row D connector
    d. 36-pin Centronics connector

11. Which of the following is an output device?
    a. printer
    b. modem
    c. mouse
    d. touch screen

12. Two popular page description languages are:
    a. raster
    b. PostScript
    c. vector
    d. PCL
    e. QBASIC

13. When printing with a paper that has a surface other than that specified by the laser printer manufacturer, what is likely to happen?
    a. broken or missing parts of letters
    b. the top of each letter missing
    c. a faded appearance on the characters
    d. an outlined appearance of the uppercase letters

14. What is paper basis weight?
    a. the weight in pounds of an 8.5″ × 11″ single sheet of paper
    b. the weight in pounds of 1,000 sheets of 8.5″ × 11″ paper
    c. the weight in pounds of 500 sheets of 8.5″ × 11″ paper
    d. the weight in pounds of 500 sheets of 17″ × 22.5″ paper
    e. the weight in pounds of 1,000 sheets of 17″ × 22.5″ paper

15. Using paper with a surface roughness greater than the specifications of a laser printer manufacturer will:
    a. result in excess wear of paper path components
    b. void the printer's warranty
    c. cause the laser to concentrate, decreasing the image size
    d. cause paper jams at the start of each print cycle

16. In reference to types of paper, the term *finish* means:
    a. the texture or smoothness of both surfaces of the paper
    b. the quality of the edges of the paper
    c. the texture or smoothness of the front surface of the paper
    d. the distortion properties of the material used to make the paper

17. What product must be used to clean rubber rollers on a printer?
    a. denatured alcohol   c. soap and water
    b. 409 all-purpose cleaner   d. glass cleaner

18. Dot-matrix printers have how many pins in their print head? (Select two.)
    a. 5   d. 24
    b. 9   e. 32
    c. 16

19. What activates the print wire in a dot-matrix printer?
    a. power is applied to an electromagnet, forcing the print wire away from a permanent magnet in the print head
    b. a spring is released
    c. power is removed from an electromagnet, forcing the print wire forward by means of a spring
    d. the polarity of an electromagnet in the print head is reversed, moving the print wire forward
    e. a motor pushes the print wire forward

20. Which of the following should *not* be lubricated on a dot-matrix printer? (Choose two answers.)
    a. print head guide rail   d. paper advance motor
    b. platen assembly   e. print head pins
    c. paper feed gears

21. When a dot-matrix printer produces light or uneven print, what are the first two things that should be checked?
    a. the distance between the print head and platen
    b. the ribbon
    c. the printer cable
    d. power fluctuations
    e. the carriage assembly

22. Which of the following solutions should be tried first to fix light or uneven print on an ink-jet printer?
    a. adjusting the paper feed assembly
    b. using a paper that will absorb more ink
    c. replacing the print cartridge
    d. adjusting the print head closer to the paper

23. Which type(s) of printers can be used with multipart forms?
    a. dot-matrix printers   c. laser printers
    b. ink-jet printers   d. thermal printers

24. Why should ink cartridges in an ink-jet printer be replaced rather than refilled?
    a. the new nozzles on the ink cartridge print a sharper image
    b. refilling cartridges may void the warranty
    c. the ink may not be compatible with the paper

d. the ink may not be compatible with the printer

e. the nozzles may become corroded

25. What happens if the paper is too absorbent when printing with an ink-jet printer?

    a. the ink has a tendency to smear

    b. the ink will fade

    c. the ink will bleed, causing a blurry image

    d. the ink will dry too quickly

26. In laser printing, what occurs after the conditioning phase?

    a. the writing phase   d. the cleaning phase

    b. the fusing phase   e. the transferring phase

    d. the cleaning phase

27. In laser printing, what occurs after the fusing phase?

    a. the writing phase   d. the cleaning phase

    b. the conditioning phase   e. the transferring phase

    c. the developing phase

28. In laser printing, what occurs after the developing phase?

    a. the writing phase   d. the cleaning phase

    b. the fusing phase   e. the transferring phase

    c. the conditioning phase

29. In laser printing, what occurs during the developing phase?

    a. light is used to discharge an image on the drum

    b. toner is attracted to the drum

    c. toner is attracted to the paper

    d. toner is fixed to the paper

30. In laser printing, what occurs during the cleaning phase? (Choose two.)

    a. leftover toner is removed from the drum

    b. a uniform negative charge is applied to the drum

    c. light is used to discharge an image on the drum

    d. toner is attracted to the drum

    e. the drum is reheated

31. The function of the corona wire in a laser printer is to:

    a. apply a strong negative charge on the print media to attract toner

    b. apply a strong positive charge on the print media to attract toner

    c. apply a uniform negative charge to the photosensitive drum

    d. apply a uniform positive charge to the photosensitive drum

    e. to negate the charge on the photosensitive drum

32. Which of the following charges the paper with a uniform positive charge?

    a. primary corona   d. pressure roller

    b. laser   e. transfer corona or transfer roller

    c. fuser

33. The fuser assembly in a laser printer performs which of the following functions?

    a. presses toner particles into the print media using high-pitched sounds

    b. eliminates static electricity from the photosensitive drum

    c. places a positive charge on the print media to attract the toner

    d. presses toner particles into the print media while melting them

34. Which of the following is found in most laser toner cartridges?

    a. a drum, developing roller, corona wire, and scraper blade

    b. a drum, transfer roller, fusing roller, and transfer corona wire

    c. a main corona wire, transfer corona wire, drum, and pressure roller

    d. a fusing roller, drum, charging roller, and wiper blade

35. Which of the following should be part of any preventive maintenance routine for laser printers? (Choose two.)

    a. vacuuming the ozone filter   c. cleaning the fuser

    b. adjusting the paper tray   d. replacing the feed assembly

36. After cleaning a laser printer, the pages are speckled. How can this be corrected?

    a. by running several blank pages through the printer

    b. by installing another toner cartridge

c. by cleaning the print head

d. by resetting the printer

37. If after a paper jam is cleared from the tray in a laser printer, the printer still indicates a jam, what should be done?

    a. run the self-test

    b. turn the printer off to let it cool and then turn it on after approximately 10 minutes

    c. look for another jam in the paper tray

    d. open and close the top cover

38. Which of the following may cause light print from a laser printer? (Choose two.)

    a. rotating mirrors   d. the fuser unit

    b. the control board   e. the toner cartridge

    c. the transfer corona

39. Which of the following is the best way to remove toner?

    a. hot water   c. compressed air

    b. denatured alcohol   d. vacuuming

40. Which part of the laser printer should *not* be exposed to sunlight?

    a. the transfer corona assembly   c. the PC drum

    b. the toner cartridge   d. the transfer corona wire

41. To prevent toner from sticking to a laser printer's heat rollers, the cleaning pads apply which of the following?

    a. alcohol   c. ammonia

    b. oil   d. water

42. You are trying to determine why a printer cannot print. After checking the cable connections and making sure the printer is on and online, you decide to perform the printer's self-test. If the self-test works, which of the following is most likely the problem? (Choose two answers.)

    a. a bad toner cartridge

    b. an incorrectly inserted toner cartridge

    c. the cable

    d. the printer interface

43. The laser printer is on and the fan is running, but it won't print. What is the first thing to check?

    a. that the printer is online

    b. that all the cables are connected properly

    c. that the correct print driver is loaded

    d. that the printer has paper

    e. that the printer is not jammed

44. When trying to fix a paper jam, you should:

    a. note where in the paper path the paper stops

    b. check all voltages

    c. turn the printer off, then on again

    d. run a test page

    e. remove the paper jam

45. Which part of the printer is hot and can cause burns?

    a. the fuser   d. the dot-matrix print head

    b. the platen   e. the ink-jet cartridge

    c. the ribbon carriage

46. An HP LaserJet IV printer isn't printing at all. The computer indicates that the "device on LPT1 isn't ready." Therefore, you decide to do a printer self-test. The front panel test is unsuccessful, but the test print is successful. Which component do you suspect is causing the problem?

    a. the printer is not online   d. the coronoa wire

    b. the fuser   e. the formatter

    c. the power supply

47. After using a new laser printer for only two months, ghost images of previously printed documents appear on the new printouts. What will usually solve this problem?
   a. changing the transfer roller
   b. replacing the toner cartridge
   c. changing the fuser
   d. refilling the toner cartridge

HANDS-ON EXERCISES

Exercise 1: Configure and Test a Parallel Port

1. Disable the parallel port using jumpers, DIP switches, configuring software, or the CMOS setup program.
2. Configure the parallel port as LPT1 (IRQ 7 and I/O address 378H).
3. Boot the computer and perform the MODE command at the prompt.
4. Using the MSD program, find the I/O address and IRQ of LPT1.
5. Connect a loopback plug to a parallel port.
6. Using a software diagnostic package, test the parallel port. (Note: You may need to tell the software diagnostic package that you have a loopback plug.)
7. Determine whether your printer supports ECP or EPP using jumpers, DIP switches, configuring software, or the CMOS setup program.

Exercise 2: Install a Printer

1. Plug the power cable into the printer and the ac wall outlet.
2. Connect a printer cable from the parallel port to the printer.
3. Turn on the printer.
4. Turn on the computer and boot Windows 3.XX, Windows 95 or 98, or Windows NT.
5. Load the appropriate print driver and make it the default printer. (For Windows 3.XX, use the printer icon in the Control Panel. For Windows 95 or 98 or Windows NT, use the Add Printer icon (in the Printers folder in My Computer.)
6. Using Microsoft Word, WordPad, or Microsoft Write, create a document that uses at least three different fonts at two different sizes and includes at least one boldface word and one italic word.
7. Print the document to the printer using the Print option under the File menu. Make sure that the proper driver has been selected.
8. Install a second driver as designated by your instructor.
9. Using Microsoft Word, WordPad, or Microsoft Write, print the same document but use the second driver.
10. By using the printer's control panel, take the printer offline.
11. Print the document at least three more times with the correct driver.
12. Switch over to the print manager or print spooler to see the print jobs waiting for the printer to come back online. (In Windows 3.XX, the print manager can be accessed by using Alt+Tab, Alt+Esc, or the task manager. For Windows 95 and 98 and Windows NT, the print manager or print spooler can be accessed by double-clicking on the small printer icon in the task bar or by double-clicking on the printer driver in the Printer folder.)
13. Delete the last two print jobs.
14. By using the printer's control panel, put the printer back online and let the print job print.
15. Reboot the computer to DOS or another command prompt.
16. Send the AUTOEXEC.BAT (or another text file) to the printer. (Note: For laser printers, you usually need to perform a form feed after the text file has been sent to the printer.)
17. Delete the print driver and disconnect the printer.

Exercise 3: Take a Dot-Matrix Printer Apart

1. Remove the ribbon cartridge and paper.
2. Identify the print head, tension knob on the ribbon cartridge, guide rails, platen, and timing belt.

3. Reinstall the ribbon cartridge and the paper.
4. Turn on the dot-matrix printer and perform a self-test.
5. Using the control panel, take the printer offline.
6. Using the control panel, put the printer online.
7. Perform a line feed and a form feed.
8. Increase the distance between the platen and the print head and perform another self-test.
9. Change the distance between the platen and the print head back to the way it was.
10. Remove the ribbon cartridge and paper.
11. Remove the print head.
12. Take the top part of the printer off so that you can see inside.
13. Identify the power supply, power supply fuse, print head positioning motor, paper feed motor, and the main control board.
14. Reassemble the printer.
15. Perform another self-test.

Exercise 4: Take an Ink-Jet Printer Apart

1. Turn on the ink-jet printer and perform a self-test.
2. Perform a self-cleaning on the ink-jet printer.
3. Identify the print cartridge or print cartridges, guide rails, platen, timing belt, and drive assembly.
4. Take the top part of the printer off so that you can see inside. Don't remove the ink cartridge unless the ink cartridge is out of ink.
5. Identify the power supply, power supply fuse, print head positioning motor, paper feed motor, and the main control board.
6. Reassemble the printer.
7. Perform another self-test.

Exercise 5: Take a Laser Printer Apart

1. Remove the toner cartridge and the paper.
2. Reinstall the toner cartridge and the paper.
3. Turn on the laser printer and perform a self-test.
4. Using the control panel, take the printer offline.
5. Using the control panel, put the printer online.
6. Using the control panel, perform a form feed.
7. Remove the toner cartridge and the paper tray.
8. Locate and open the compartment that has the RAM for the printer.
9. Identify the corona wires, the fuser assembly, and the cleaning pads. (Note: These are usually found in the toner cartridge.)
10. Locate and identify the ozone filter (some ozone filters are part of the toner cartridge), the power supply and power supply fuse (if any), and the fuser and the pressure roller.
11. Reassemble the printer and install the toner cartridge and the paper.
12. Perform a self-test. During the self-test, turn the printer off while it is printing but before the paper comes out of the printer.
13. Remove the paper jam.
14. Perform another self-test.

20 MS-DOS

INTRODUCTION

MS-DOS stands for Microsoft Disk Operating System. It was the first operating system used on the original IBM PC. Because the IBM PC became the de facto standard for personal computers, DOS became the de facto standard for operating systems. The introduction of new operating systems (Windows 95 and 98 and Windows NT) is slowly phasing DOS out. But until the newer systems completely replace it, DOS will exist on many machines and the PC technician will be called on to fix those machines. In addition, fixing many of the problems in the newer operating systems requires booting to a command prompt and using DOS commands.

OBJECTIVES

1. List the DOS boot files in order of boot-up and define their function.
2. Differentiate between internal and external DOS commands.
3. Determine which command to use in a given situation and perform the common DOS commands (CD, CLS, COPY, DATE, DEL, DIR, MD, PATH, PROMPT, RD, REN, SET, TIME, TYPE, VER, VOL, ATTRIB, CHKDSK, DELTREE, DISKCOPY, EDIT, FDISK, HELP, FORMAT, LABEL, MEM, MOVE, MORE, SYS, TREE, UNDELETE, UNFORMAT, and XCOPY).
4. List the files or directory path of a given file or subdirectory location.
5. Define a batch file and list and define the commands that would go into a batch file.
6. Create a batch file.
7. Create an AUTOEXEC.BAT file with the appropriate commands, including the PATH, PROMPT, and SET commands.
8. Create a CONFIG.SYS file.
9. List and define the commands used in the CONFIG.SYS file.
10. Load the appropriate commands to enable the memory areas required.
11. List the differences between MS-DOS and PC-DOS.
12. Determine and correct a boot-up problem.
13. Install DOS and load the appropriate drivers.

20.1 WHAT IS MS-DOS?

DOS is a command-driven operating system, which means that all of the commands must be typed in the correct way (spelling and syntax). Compared to other operating systems, DOS is small and very simple—so small, in fact, that it can be booted from a floppy disk.

20.2 THE BOOT PROCESS

When booted, DOS reads and executes the following files in the order shown:

1. IO.SYS (IBMBIO.COM)
2. MSDOS.SYS (IBMDOS.COM)
3. CONFIG.SYS
4. COMMAND.COM
5. AUTOEXEC.BAT

To be read during boot-up, these files must be in the root directory of whatever disk the computer is being booted from (except for the COMMAND.COM or equivalent file, whose location can be specified from within the CONFIG.SYS file.) Of these five files, only IO.SYS, MSDOS.SYS, and COMMAND.COM are needed for boot-up. The

CONFIG.SYS and AUTOEXEC.BAT files are important configuration files that are usually needed to run most common applications.

20.2.1   IO.SYS AND MSDOS.SYS

Both IO.SYS and MSDOS.SYS are hidden (normally cannot be seen), read-only (normally cannot be deleted or changed) system files (files used by the operating system). For the disk to boot, IO.SYS must be the first directory entry in the root directory and MSDOS must be the second entry. In addition, IO.SYS must be the first physical file on the volume boot sector. (Note: Older versions of DOS and PC DOS [IBM's version of DOS] use IBMBIO.COM and IBMDOS.COM instead of IO.SYS and MSDOS.SYS.)

IO.SYS is the interface to the hardware, specifically the ROM BIOS chips. During boot-up, it loads a set of base device drivers, determines equipment status, and initializes attached devices, such as the printer. In addition, it loads and controls the device drivers loaded in the CONFIG.SYS and sets several system default parameters. MSDOS.SYS is the DOS kernel, or the central part of the operating system. It receives requests from software applications and translates them into commands that the IO.SYS can execute. In addition, it is the disk file manager, which allows the user to retrieve a file without worrying about where it is located on the disk.

If IO.SYS or MSDOS.SYS is corrupt or missing, a "Nonsystem Disk or Disk Error" error message usually appears. A "No Room for System on Destination Disk" error message appearing when attempting to create a bootable disk using the SYS command (or some other method) means there is not enough disk space to hold IO.SYS or MSDOS.SYS or that IO.SYS or MSDOS.SYS can't be placed properly in the root directory or the volume boot sector.

20.2.2   COMMAND.COM

COMMAND.COM, the command interpreter and command processor, is the user's interface to DOS. It reads commands that are executed at the keyboard and determines whether to execute them or pass them to the MSDOS.SYS. It also contains many of the DOS internal commands, like DIR, CD, VER, and COPY. Unlike the other boot files, COMMAND.COM is partly permanent and partly transient, which means that part of it can be removed from RAM to make room for something else and reloaded when needed. If COMMAND.COM is missing or corrupted, a "Bad or Missing Command Interpreter" error message usually appears.

20.2.3   CONFIG.SYS AND AUTOEXEC.BAT

The CONFIG.SYS and AUTOEXEC.BAT files are text files that can be changed with a text editor, like EDIT or Windows Notepad, or with a word processor if the file is first saved as a pure text file with no format codes. The CONFIG.SYS file is read three times during boot-up, executing certain commands each time that activate or manage the different memory areas and load device drivers. The AUTOEXEC.BAT file is a special batch file that can execute any command entered at the prompt. It typically loads TSRs and configures the DOS environment.

20.2.4   DBLSPACE.BIN/DRVSPACE.BIN

In DOS 6.0 and above, DBLSPACE.BIN or DRVSPACE.BIN is loaded so that DOS can use compressed drives. These files are located in the root directory and are hidden, system, and read-only. If disk compression is not being used, some RAM can be freed up by deleting the DBLSPACE.BIN or DRVSPACE.BIN file. In addition, DBLSPACE.BIN or DRVSPACE.BIN can usually be moved out of conventional memory by running MEMMAKER at the prompt. (We will talk more about MEMMAKER later.)

TABLE 20.1 Common internal DOS commands

Command	Description
CD (or CHDIR)	Displays the name of the current directory or changes the current directory.
CLS	Clears the screen, leaving the command prompt and cursor at the top left corner of the screen.
COPY	Copies one or more files to the location the user specifies. The COPY command will not copy hidden or system files.
DATE	Displays the date and prompts the user to change the date if necessary.
DEL (or ERASE)	Deletes the files specified.
DIR	Displays a list of the files and subdirectories that are in the directory specified. DIR is probably the most commonly used DOS command.
MD (or MKDIR)	Creates a directory.
PATH	Indicates which directories MS-DOS should search to execute executable files (files with a COM, EXE, or BAT filename extension).
PROMPT	Changes the appearance of the command prompt.
RD (or RMDIR)	Deletes an empty directory.
REN (or RENAME)	Changes the name of the file or files specified.
SET	Displays, sets, or removes MS-DOS environment variables.
TIME	Displays the system time or sets the computer's internal clock.
TYPE	Displays the contents of a text file.
VER	Displays the MS-DOS version number.
VOL	Displays the disk volume label and serial number (if the disk has them).

20.3 DOS COMMANDS AND FILENAMES

All DOS commands can be divided into two categories, internal DOS commands and external DOS commands. The instructions for the **internal DOS commands** are kept in the COMMAND.COM file loaded in the RAM. (See table 20.1.) Therefore, if booting to a prompt, any of the internal DOS commands can be executed. **External DOS commands** are commands for which instructions are not kept in the COMMAND.COM file. (See table 20.2.) Therefore, when executing these commands, DOS must search for a file with either a COM or EXE extension that contains the additional instructions. If the computer cannot find the file that has the instructions for the external DOS command, a "Bad Command or Filename" error message will appear.

Using most DOS commands requires an understanding of how to specify the path or location of a file or directory, a necessary skill because DOS assumes very little and must be told exactly what to do. To identify the location of a particular file or directory on a disk, start by designating the drive, followed by the root directory. Then each directory that leads to the file must be listed, followed by the filename and extension.

EXAMPLE 20.1 In fig. 20.1, the path of the COMMAND.COM file is C:\COMMAND. COM. The path of the README.TXT file is C:\DOS\README.TXT. The path of the DOS directory is C:\DOS.

Unlike today's newer operating systems, DOS can use only eight characters for a filename and three characters for a filename extension. The filename extension usually identifies the type of file. For example, files with a COM, EXE, or BAT extension are executable files, while files with the DOC extension are Microsoft Word files and files with the GIF extension are graphic files. In DOS, certain characters are reserved and can't be used for filenames and filename extensions. For example, the period (.) is used to divide the filename and filename extension, the backward slash (\) is used for dividing directories and

TABLE 20.2 Common external
DOS commands

Command	Description
ATTRIB	Displays or changes file and directory attributes.
CHKDSK	Checks the status of a disk and displays a status report. It can also fix disk errors.
DELTREE	Deletes a directory and all files and subdirectories that are in it. This command is available in DOS 6.0 and later.
DISKCOPY	Copies the entire contents of one floppy disk to another floppy disk. Since DISKCOPY performs a sector-by-sector copy, it overwrites the existing contents of the destination disk.
EDIT	Starts MS-DOS Editor, a text editor that can create and edit ASCII text files.
FDISK	Starts the Fix Disk program, which creates and deletes partitions on a hard drive.
HELP	Starts MS-DOS Help.
FORMAT	Creates a new root directory and file allocation table for the disk. It can also check for bad areas on the disk, delete all data on the disk, and make a disk bootable. All disks must be formatted to be used.
LABEL	Creates, changes, or deletes the volume label of a disk.
MEM	Displays the amount of used and free memory (RAM) on the computer.
MOVE	Moves one or more files to the location specified. The MOVE command can also be used to rename directories.
MORE	Displays one screen of output at a time. It is often used with the TREE and MEM commands.
SYS	Makes a disk bootable by copying IO.SYS, MSDOS.SYS, and COMMAND.COM to the disk without reformatting it.
TREE	Graphically displays the structure of a directory.
UNDELETE	Restores files that were previously deleted by using the DEL or ERASE command.
UNFORMAT	Restores a disk that was erased by using the FORMAT command as long as it wasn't unconditionally formatted.
XCOPY	Copies directories, their subdirectories, and files (except hidden and system files).

filenames, and the * is a wild-card character. The characters that can't be used in DOS file-names are: + = / [ ] " : ; , ? * \ < > |. In addition, spaces and ASCII control characters cannot be used.

Wild-card characters (* and ?) are used to specify groups of files. The asterisk (*) means any string of characters and the question mark (?) means any single character. For example, to specify all files that have a COM filename extension, you would use *.COM. To specify all files whose filename begins with MS, you would use MS*.*. To specify a filename that is four characters in length and ends in DOS, you would use ?DOS.*.

20.4 COMMANDS THAT EVERY PC TECHNICIAN SHOULD KNOW

No matter which operating system you are working on (DOS/Windows 3.XX, Windows 95 or 98, or Windows NT), there are certain DOS commands that you should know. If the GUI cannot boot for some reason, you will often need to fix the problem by booting with a bootable floppy disk and performing commands at the prompt.

When performing DOS commands, there is always confusion about when to use the backslash (\) and the forward slash (/). The backslash is always used to designate a location while the forward slash is used to designate a switch (nothing to do with location). Note that the backward slash is always the same as the backslash in the prompt shown on the

FIGURE 20.1 Sample of a disk
structure

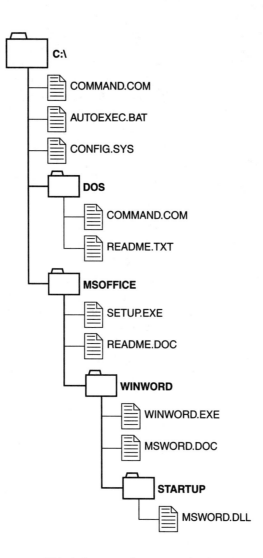

screen. This is because the prompt is showing the current drive and directory (location).
For example:

FORMAT A: /S   Makes a disk bootable (switch)
CD\DOS   Changes the current directory (location)
COPY C:\DOS\FORMAT.COM A:\DOS   Copy files from one location to another
XCOPY C:\DATA*.* C:\DOS /S   Copy files from one location to another,
                                        but also include subdirectories (switch)

20.4.1 THE DIR AND CD COMMANDS

The DIR command, which displays the list of the files and subdirectories, is probably the
most commonly used DOS command. (See fig. 20.2.) When the DIR command is used
without any parameters or switches, it displays the following:

1. The disk's volume label and serial number
2. The filename or directory name and the extension
3. The date and time the file was created or last modified and the data and time when a directory was made
4. The file size in bytes
5. The total number of files listed, their cumulative size, and the free space in bytes remaining on the disk

The DIR command has many switches. Some of the more common ones used by a technician are shown in table 20.3. Many of the DIR command switches can be combined.

FIGURE 20.2   The DIR
command

```
C:\>dir

Volume in drive D has no label
Volume Serial Number is 1CE8-1C7A
Directory of C:\

DOS               <DIR>              06-10-98    7:32p
WINDOWS           <DIR>              06-10-98    7:32p
COMMAND   COM             93,812    08-24-96   11:11a
CONFIG    SYS                 91    06-06-98   11:03a
AUTOEXEC  BAT                183    06-06-98   10:44a
DATA              <DIR>              06-10-98    7:33p
        3 file(s)          94,086 bytes
        3 dir(s)      179,634,176 bytes free
```

TABLE 20.3   Helpful DIR command switches

Switch	Description
/P	Displays one screen of the DIR listing at a time. This comes in handy when there are too many files to be shown on the screen at once.
/W	Displays the listing in wide format (five columns). This comes in handy when there are too many files to be shown on the screen at once. It does not show the dates, times, and byte size of the files. Note: Directories are indicated with brackets [ ].
/ON	O stands for order; N stands for name. Therefore, when this switch is used with the DIR command, the files will be listed in alphabetical order by filename. This comes in handy when looking for a certain file.
/AH	A stands for attribute; H stands for hidden. Therefore, when this switch is used with the DIR command, it will show all hidden files. This comes in handy when verifying the boot files on a disk.
/AD	A stands for attribute; D stands for directories. This command shows directories only.
/S	S stands for subdirectory. Therefore, when used, it will list every occurrence in the specified directory and all subdirectories. It comes in handy when looking for the location of a certain file or when trying to get the total byte size of a directory (including all subdirectories and files within the directory).

EXAMPLE 20.2   To show all files one screen at a time, perform the following command:

```
DIR /P
```

To show all files in alphabetical order, one screen at a time, perform the following command:

```
DIR /ON/P
```

To show the hidden files in the current directory, perform the following command:

```
DIR /AH
```

To show all files that have a GIF filename extension, perform the following command:

```
DIR *.GIF
```

To change the current drive, you would type in the drive letter followed by a colon (:) and press the Enter key. To change the current directory, you would use the CD command. To go up to the root directory, you would specify the backslash (\), and to go up to the parent directory (up one directory), you would specify the double dot (..).

EXAMPLE 20.3   To change to the TEST directory, which is located under the directory that you are currently in, perform the following command:

`CD TEST`

To change to the root directory no matter how many directories deep you are, perform the following command:

`CD\`

To change to the parent directory (one directory up), perform the following command:

`CD..`

To change to the SYSTEM directory under the WINDOWS directory (located off the root directory) no matter what directory that you are in, use the following command:

`CD\WINDOWS\SYSTEM`

The TREE command graphically displays the structure of a directory.

EXAMPLE 20.4   If you are in the root directory of the disk and perform the TREE command, it will show every directory on the disk.

`TREE`

If you also wish to show the files in the directory, add a /F (files) switch:

`TREE /F ¦MORE`

The ¦MORE pauses the TREE command one screen at a time. (Note: The ¦ is called a *pipe*.)

20.4.2   THE MD, RD, AND DEL/ERASE COMMANDS

The MD command is used to create directories, the RD command is used to delete empty subdirectories. DELTREE can delete files and directories (including those that have files and subdirectories) and files and directories that are hidden, system, and read-only. (Note: DELTREE is available only in DOS 6.0 and above.)

EXAMPLE 20.5   To create a TEST directory, type in the following command:

`MD TEST`

If the TEST directory is empty (no files or subdirectories), you would then use the following command to delete it:

`RD TEST`

To delete a TEST directory that has files or other subdirectories in it, you would perform the following command at the prompt:

`DELTREE TEST`

20.4.3   THE COPY COMMANDS (COPY, DISKCOPY, AND XCOPY)

The three primary copy commands used in DOS are COPY, DISKCOPY, and XCOPY. All of these commands have the same three parts: command, source, and target. The source is what is being copied and the target is the location where the copy is going.

The COPY command makes an exact duplicate of the file or files specified. It will not copy hidden or system files.

EXAMPLE 20.6 To make a copy of the RESUME.DOC file and call the copy JOB.DOC, use:

```
COPY RESUME.DOC JOB.DOC
```

To copy the AUTOEXEC.BAT file (located in the current directory) to the A drive, you would perform the following command at the prompt:

```
COPY AUTOEXEC.BAT A:
```

To copy the README.TXT file located in the C:\DOS directory to the A:\DOS directory while you are in another directory, you would type:

```
COPY C:\DOS\README.TXT A:\DOS
```

The command is COPY, the source is C:\DOS\README.TXT, and the target is A:\DOS. To copy the README.TXT file located in the C:\DOS directory to the A:\DOS directory while you are in another directory and to name the copy INFO.TXT, you would type:

```
COPY C:\DOS\README.TXT A:\DOS\INFO.TXT
```

Notice that all of the examples have three parts divided by single spaces.

The XCOPY command, like the COPY command, copies only the files specified and will not copy hidden or system files. The main difference between the commands is that if a /S is used with XCOPY, the command will also copy all the subdirectories that have files in them. If /E is used with the /S, it will copy the empty subdirectories.

EXAMPLE 20.7 To copy the data directory from the current directory to the F drive and all files and subdirectories (including empty subdirectories) in the current directory, you would use:

```
XCOPY *.* F: /S /E
```

To make an exact duplicate of a floppy disk, you would use the DISKCOPY command. Since the DISKCOPY command performs a sector-by-sector copy, the source disk and the target disk must be the same size and density. For example, to make a copy of DOS installation disk #1 (on a DS/HD 3½" 1.44 MB disk), you would need another DS/HD 3½" 1.44 MB disk. Because the DISKCOPY command does a sector-by-sector copy to the destination disk, any previous information on the destination disk will be lost. (Note: DISKCOPY is the only copy command that gives you the opportunity to switch disks back and forth when the same drive is the source and the target.) But because it does a sector-by-sector copy, it will copy directories, system files, and read-only files.

EXAMPLE 20.8 To make an exact duplicate of a disk using the A drive, you would perform the following command at the prompt:

```
DISKCOPY A: A:
```

The REN and MOVE commands are similar to the COPY command, yet they are not copy commands. The REN command allows you to rename a file, and the MOVE command allows you to move a file from one location to another or to rename a directory. Unlike the COPY command, which produces two files (the source and the target), the REN and MOVE commands leave only one.

EXAMPLE 20.9 To rename the README.TXT file to the INFO.TXT file, you would perform the following command:

```
REN README.TXT INFO.TXT
```

To move the README.TXT file (located in the C:\DOS directory) to the root directory of the C drive, you would perform the following command:

```
MOVE C:\DOS\README.TXT C:\
```

To rename the TEST directory to JOB directory:

```
MOVE TEST JOB
```

20.4.4   THE FORMAT AND SYS COMMANDS

The FORMAT command is used to prepare a disk for use or to erase everything on a disk. It creates the root directory (starting point on the disk) and the file allocation table (an index of files and directories on the disk and their location). In addition, if the /S parameter is used, it also makes the disk bootable. To perform an unconditional format when the disk can't be unformatted or if there have been read and write errors, you would use the /U switch.

EXAMPLE 20.10   To format the D drive, perform the following command:

```
FORMAT D:
```

To make a bootable floppy disk using drive A, perform the following command:

```
FORMAT A: /S
```

To perform an unconditional format on the floppy and make the disk bootable using drive A, perform the following command:

```
FORMAT A: /S /U
```

To format a DS/DD 5¼″ floppy disk in a DS/HD 5¼″ floppy drive using drive B, perform either of the following commands:

```
FORMAT B: /F:360  or  FORMAT B: /4
```

To make a disk bootable without reformatting it, use the SYS command. This will copy the IO.SYS, MSDOS.SYS, and COMMAND.COM files and place them in the correct place, assuming that there is enough room for them to fit on the disk.

EXAMPLE 20.11   To make an important software diagnostic disk bootable using drive A, you would perform the following command (assuming you are not in the A drive):

```
SYS A:
```

20.4.5   THE ATTRIB COMMAND

The ATTRIB command displays, sets, or removes the read-only (R), archive (A), system (S), and hidden (H) attributes assigned to a file or directory. (For more information on attributes, see chapter 13.) The archive attribute indicates whether a file has been backed up or not. To turn on an attribute, you use a plus sign (+), and to turn off an attribute, you use a minus sign (−).

EXAMPLE 20.12   To show all files and their attributes, you would perform the following command:

```
ATTRIB
```

To make the AUTOEXEC.BAT file read-only, you would perform either of the following commands:

```
ATTRIB +R AUTOEXEC.BAT  or  ATTRIB AUTOEXEC.BAT +R (only on recent ver-
```
sions of DOS)

To turn off the read-only, system, and hidden attributes of the BOOT.INI file, you would perform the following command at the prompt. Note that you must include spaces between each of the attributes.

```
ATTRIB -R -S -H BOOT.INI.
```

Question: What happens if you try to delete a file that is read-only?

Answer: If you try to delete a file that is read-only with the DEL command, DOS will respond with the "Access Denied" error message. DELTREE, on the other hand, can delete read-only files. In addition, if you are using File Manager (Windows 3.XX) or Explorer (Windows 95 and 98 or Windows NT), Windows will ask if you are sure that you want to delete a read-only file. If you say yes, the file is deleted. If you use DOS EDIT to modify a read-only file, EDIT will respond with a "Path/File Access Error" error message when you try to save it.

20.4.6 THE EDIT AND TYPE COMMANDS

Text files are files that contain only ASCII characters with no formatting codes. Common text files include batch files, the AUTOEXEC.BAT file, the CONFIG.SYS file, and Windows initialization files (files with an INI filename extension). To create a text file, you could use either the COPY command or the EDIT command.

To create a text file, you can use the COPY command with CON as the source. CON is short for Console, which indicates the keyboard when it is used as the source. Since the COPY command is an internal DOS command, you only have to boot the computer to a prompt to use the COPY CON command.

EXAMPLE 20.13 To create a text file called GO.TXT, perform the following command at the prompt:

```
COPY CON GO.TXT
```

Notice that the COPY command has three parts.

After starting the COPY CON command, you can then enter the content of the file. Unfortunately, if you press the Enter key to go to the next line, you can't go back to make changes. To save the file and return to the prompt, press the Ctrl+Z keys or the F6 key.

To display a text file, you would use the TYPE command. If the text file is too large to show on one screen, you can show it one screen at a time by adding the |MORE command.

EXAMPLE 20.14 To display the contents of the GO.BAT file, you would perform the following command at the prompt:

```
TYPE GO.BAT
```

To display the contents of the README.TXT file one screen at a time, you would perform the following command at the prompt:

```
TYPE README.BAT |MORE
```

To create long or complicated text files, it is best to use the DOS text editor, called EDIT. (See fig. 20.3.) EDIT, like many other text editors, is similar to a word processor. Of course, it does not support any formatting (fonts, font size, or styles) and it doesn't have word wrap. Therefore, to go to the next line, you must insert a hard return by pressing the Enter key. (Note: If you wish to copy EDIT to a floppy disk so that you can use it on any computer, you need to copy EDIT.COM and QBASIC.EXE.)

20.5 BATCH FILES

Batch files are text files that have a BAT filename extension. They contain commands that can be executed at the prompt. Therefore, a batch file can be used to group several commands into one command or to simplify the execution of complicated commands.

EXAMPLE 20.15 Let's take a look at an example of a simple batch file called M.BAT. M.BAT contains the following:

```
CD\ DOS
MSD.EXE
CD\
```

FIGURE 20.3   The MS-DOS editor program (EDIT)

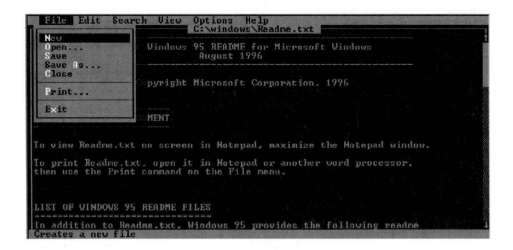

As you can see, it contains simple commands that can be executed at the prompt. Therefore, if you type in M followed by the Enter key or M.BAT followed by the Enter key, the batch file will change to the DOS directory (which is off the root directory) and execute the MSD.EXE file. When you exit from MSD, the batch file will continue by returning to the root directory.

EXAMPLE 20.16   Let's take a look at another example of a batch file called GO.BAT. GO.BAT contains the following:

```
FORMAT A: /S
COPY C:\DOS—SD.EXE A:
COPY C:\DOS\EDIT.COM A:
COPY C:\DOS\QBASIC.EXE A:
COPY C:\DOS\FORMAT.COM A:
COPY C:\DOS\FDISK.EXE A:
COPY C:\DOS\ATTRIB.EXE A:
```

Again, the batch file contains commands exactly as they would be typed at the prompt. Notice that the prompt is not included in the batch file.

There are certain internal commands made specifically for batch files. They are the CALL, ECHO, PAUSE, and REM commands. (See table 20.4.)

EXAMPLE 20.17   Let's take a look at a more complicated batch file called C.BAT:

```
@ECHO OFF
REM THE FOLLOWING COMMAND MAKES A COPY OF REM DOS'S TEXT FILES
CLS
ECHO INSERT A DISK IN DRIVE A
PAUSE
COPY C:\DOS\*.TXT A:
REM COPY A:\REDME.TXT A:\INFO.TXT
ECHO .
ECHO COPY IS DONE
ECHO .
ECHO YOU CAN NOW REMOVE THE DISK
PAUSE
```

The @ECHO OFF command, which should be placed on the first line, shuts off the prompt while the batch file is running. When the batch file is done, the prompt automatically comes back on. Although this is not necessary for the batch file to run, it can enhance its appearance. The ECHO INSERT A DISK IN DRIVE A, ECHO COPY IS DONE, and ECHO YOU CAN NOW REMOVE THE DISK commands leave messages telling the user

TABLE 20.4 Common commands used in batch files

Command	Description
CALL	Calls one batch program from another without causing the first batch program to stop.
ECHO	Displays messages for the user running the batch file or turns off the DOS prompt temporarily to give the batch file a cleaner appearance.
PAUSE	Suspends processing of a batch program and displays a message that prompts the user to press a key to continue.
REM	Enables the user to include comments in a batch or in the CONFIG.SYS file. The REM command is also useful for disabling commands without deleting the line.

what to do. The ECHO . skips a blank line. Much like the @ECHO OFF command, the ECHO . command is not needed for the program to run, but it does enhance the appearance as the batch file executes.

The PAUSE command is used to temporarily stop the batch file so that the user has a chance to read a message or to perform some action, such as insert a disk in a drive. The PAUSE command automatically generates a "Press Any Key to Continue" message.

Any text that is listed after the REM command is ignored by the batch file. The REM command is used to add comments or to disable a command within the batch file. If the batch file begins with an @ECHO OFF, the user will not see the REM statements on the screen. However, if the EDIT or TYPE command is used to view the text file, the REM statements can be seen. The first REM command is used to comment on what the batch file does. It should be used to comment on an uncommon command or to give warnings about the batch file that the user does not have to know about. A second REM statement disables the COPY command. If REM is inserted before a command, the command will be ignored when the batch file is executed.

The CALL command is used to run a batch file from within another batch file. If the command is not used when the first batch file is being executed, it will reach and execute the second batch file. Unfortunately, when it reaches the end of the second batch file, the system will not return to execute the rest of the first batch file.

EXAMPLE 20.18 To run the DOITNOW.BAT program from another batch program, you would include the following command:

```
CALL DOITNOW.BAT
```

20.6 AUTOEXEC.BAT

The AUTOEXEC.BAT file is a special batch file that automatically executes during boot-up. It has a BAT file extension and contains commands that you would normally perform at the prompt. In the AUTOEXEC.BAT files, you will usually find the PATH, PROMPT, and SET commands. An example of the AUTOEXEC.BAT file might be:

```
@ECHO OFF
PATH=C:\DOS;C:\WINDOWS
PROMPT $P$G
SET TEMP=C:\DOS
DEL C:\DOS\*.TMP
SET BLASTER=A220 I5 D1
WIN
```

The WIN command starts Windows 3.XX automatically. (Note: When loading Windows or a menu-type program, they should always be placed on the last line of the AUTO-EXEC.BAT file.)

20.6.1 THE PATH COMMAND

When any command is performed at the prompt, COMMAND.COM looks for instructions to perform those commands. The order in which DOS looks for instructions for commands is:

1. Look in COMMAND.COM in RAM to see if the command is an internal DOS command
2. Look in the current directory for a file that has a COM filename extension, followed by the EXE filename extension, followed by the BAT filename extension
3. Look in each directory in the order listed with the PATH statement in RAM. For each directory, look for the files with a COM, EXE, or BAT filename extension before going on to the next directory

If COMMAND.COM determines the command is an internal command or it finds an executable file, it will stop searching and execute those instructions. If COMMAND.COM finishes the search and has not found the instructions to execute, it will generate a "Bad Command or Filename" message.

EXAMPLE 20.19 To display the directories that DOS will search for executables files, you would perform the following command at the prompt:

```
PATH
```

To configure DOS to search the C:\WINDOWS and C:\WINDOWS\COMMAND directories for executable files, you would perform one of the following commands at the prompt:

```
PATH=C:\WINDOWS;C:\WINDOWS\COMMAND
PATH=C:\WINDOWS;C:\WINDOWS\COMMAND;
PATH C:\WINDOWS;C:\WINDOWS\COMMAND
PATH C:\WINDOWS;C:\WINDOWS\COMMAND;
```

The PATH command must use an equal sign (=) or a space and can end with a semicolon, though it doesn't have to. Semicolons are used to separate each directory to be searched. When listing each directory, be sure to include the entire path (location) of the directory, starting with the drive letter.

EXAMPLE 20.20 The following PATH command has been executed:

```
PATH=C:\DOS;C:\WINDOWS
```

Your current directory is the C:\DATA directory. You type in GO and press the Enter key. COMMAND.COM will first check in the RAM for an internal DOS command called GO. Since GO is not an internal DOS command, it will then look in the current directory, which is C:\DATA. It will first look for GO.COM in the directory. If it doesn't find it, it will then look for GO.EXE. If it doesn't find GO.EXE, it will then look for GO.BAT. (Note: If there were a GO.EXE listed before the GO.COM, it would still execute the GO.COM, not the GO.EXE.)

If COMMAND.COM still has not found the instructions for GO, it will then look at the PATH statement loaded in RAM. The PATH statement specifies two subdirectories, the C:\DOS directory and C:\WINDOWS directory. (Note: It will search only the directories that are specified. It will not search the subdirectories of the directories specified.) Therefore, COMMAND.COM will first look in the C:\DOS directory for GO.COM, GO.EXE, and GO.BAT. If it has still not found the file, it will then go to the C:\WINDOWS directory for GO.COM, GO.EXE, and GO.BAT. Lastly, if the file was not found after all of this, it will generate a "Bad Command or Filename" error message.

Note that because the root directory was not the current directory and is not listed specifically in the PATH statement, COMMAND.COM did not search the root directory. The C:\ in C:\DOS and C:\WINDOWS is telling only where these directories are located. If you want to specify the root directory of the C drive, you would use PATH=C:\;C:\DOS;C:\WINDOWS.

If you execute a command at the prompt and get a "Bad Command or Filename" error message, one of the following has happened:

1. The command was typed wrong
2. You are not in the directory of the executable file
3. You did not list the directory of the executable file in the PATH statement or there is an error in the PATH statement
4. The executable file is missing

Question: Which directories should you specify with the PATH statement?

Answer: You should specify only directories that have files with the COM, EXE, or BAT filename extensions that you use a lot. This should include DOS, so that you can always format or copy a disk no matter what the current drive and directory. (Note: Windows 95 DOS commands are located in the C:\WINDOWS command directory.) In addition, since most DOS computers have Windows 3.XX, you would usually include the C:\WINDOWS directory. You would not include directories that you rarely use. (Note: When running Windows 3.XX, the path is not needed for programs that you start by double-clicking on an icon.)

Question: At the C:\> prompt, you perform the following command:

```
COPY REDME.TXT A:
```

What error message would you get if the computer can find COPY but cannot find REDME.TXT?

Answer: COPY is an internal DOS command; therefore, when COMMAND.COM performs a search for the instruction on how to COPY, it will quickly find those instructions in RAM. Since COMMAND.COM knows now how to copy, it then looks to see what it was supposed to copy. Therefore, by looking at the command entered at the prompt, it knows it is supposed to find REDME.TXT. Since no path (location) was specified for REDME.TXT, COMMAND.COM assumes the REDME.TXT is in the current directory (C:\). It then searches the root directory of the C drive and does not find the file. Therefore, the error message that you get is "File Not Found." (Note: The PATH command is used only to find instructions to execute, not data.)

Question: During boot-up, you notice that you get several "Bad Command or Filename" error messages. When the computer has finished booting, you type in EDIT AUTOEXEC.BAT and press the Enter key at the C:\> command prompt. DOS responds back with a "Bad Command or Filename" error message. What is the problem?

Answer: The first thing to do is make sure that you typed the command correctly at the prompt. Next, check your PATH statement (by typing PATH and pressing the Enter key) and make sure that it includes the DOS directory. Check for spelling and semicolon placement. If there is an error in the PATH command, you must first provide a temporary solution and then a permanent one. To get access to the editor so that you can change the AUTOEXEC.BAT file, you must type the following command at the prompt:

```
PATH=C:\DOS
```

You can now execute the EDIT command to access the AUTOEXEC.BAT file. Of course, if you reboot the computer now, you will still have the same problem. Therefore, after correcting the PATH statement in the AUTOEXEC.BAT file, you would save the changes and then reboot the computer.

20.6.2 THE PROMPT COMMAND

The standard command prompt tells the user the location (current drive and directory) and prompts you for the next command. Examples of the prompt are C:\>, A:\>, C:\DOS,

TABLE 20.5   Metastrings used by the PROMPT command

Metastring	Display
$Q	Equal sign (=)
$$	Dollar sign ($)
$T	Current time
$D	Current date
$P	Current drive and directory
$V	MS-DOS version number
$N	Current drive
$G	Greater-than sign (>)
$L	Less-than sign (<)
$B	Pipe (¦)
$_	Carriage return and line feed
$E	ASCII escape code (code 27)
$H	Backspace to delete a character that has been written to the prompt command line

C:\DATA\LETTERS>, and F:\>. The PROMPT command changes the appearance of the command prompt. To help customize the prompt, the PROMPT command uses metastrings. A metastring is a group of characters that is transformed into another character or group of characters. The most common metastrings are the $P and $G. The $P shows the current drive and directory; the $G shows the greater-than sign (>). (See table 20.5.)

EXAMPLE 20.22   The following PROMPT command displays the standard prompt, including the current drive and directory and the greater-than sign (>).

```
PROMPT $P$G
```

The following PROMPT command makes the command prompt a little more user friendly:

```
PROMPT I am located at $P$_How may I help you?
```

20.6.3   THE SET COMMAND

The SET command is used to display, set, or remove MS-DOS environment variables, which are used to control the behavior of some batch files and programs and to control the way MS-DOS appears and works. A variable works much like variables in math. If you declare the value of X with the following command:

```
SET X=3
```

and you are given the following equation:

$$Y = X + 2$$

you know to substitute the 3 wherever you see X. Therefore, $Y = X + 2$ becomes $Y = 3 + 2$, which makes $Y = 5$. MS-DOS environment variables work the same way. When a program is running and it comes across an environment variable, it then looks in the RAM to find what the value is for the variable. When it finds it, it substitutes it into the program.

The most important environment variable is the TEMP variable, which defines where any temporary files (files whose filenames begin with a tilde (~) and have a TMP filename extension) are to be kept when they are created. Setting the TEMP variable does not create any temporary files; it only states a location. Some DOS commands (such as DISKCOPY),

Windows, and most Windows applications need to create temporary files to function. For example, if DISKCOPY could not make temporary files, you would have to insert the source disk and the target disk four times to copy a 1.44 MB floppy disk. In addition, many of the programs would generate errors and not function properly. (Note: For the TEMP variable to work, the directory specified must exist and there must be enough free disk space to create the temporary files.) The files so created are temporary; therefore, when the program that made the temporary files is exited, the temporary files are automatically deleted. DOS 6.22 will automatically add the SET TEMP=C:\DOS line. If there is no SET TEMP line in the AUTOEXEC.BAT file, Windows 3.XX will add the SET TEMP=C:\WINDOWS\TEMP line.

If your computer locks up to the point where you are forced to reboot or the computer reboots for whatever reason and you have not exited the program that created the temporary files, when you try to start the program again it may try to use the temporary files, which in turn will create other problems. Therefore, it is beneficial to have the temporary files automatically deleted during boot-up. Set the SET variable to the C:\DOS directory, then use DEL C:\DOS*.TMP to delete the files. (Note: If you get a "File not Found" when DOS tries to delete these files, it is not a bad thing—it just means that the DEL command tried to delete the temporary files but there were none to delete.)

If you find hundreds of temporary files in the temporary directory of a computer when no programs are running, it often indicates that the user has been shutting off the computer without properly exiting Windows. (Note: Another clue the computer has been shut off without exiting Windows is that the hard drive contains lost clusters—see chapter 13.)

Certain programs will add SET commands to the AUTOEXEC.BAT file on installation. The best advice to give you is that if you don't know what a command means, leave it alone. If you think that you have to delete a line, put a REM in front of the statement to disable it. Then, if you find that you need that line, you only have to remove REM.

EXAMPLE 20.23 To show the environment variables, perform the following command at the prompt:

```
SET
```

To set the TEMP variable to the C:\DOS directory, perform the following command at the prompt or list the following command in the AUTOEXEC.BAT file:

```
SET TEMP=C:\DOS
```

The next command is a common environment variable for the Sound Blaster sound card made by Creative Labs. It tells certain programs that the sound card is using the following resources: I/O address 220, IRQ 5, and DMA 1.

```
SET BLASTER=A220 I5 D1
```

A useful environment variable is the DIRCMD. To make the default DIR listing alphabetical, one screen at a time, you would use the following command:

```
SET DIRCMD=/ON/P
```

20.7   CONFIG.SYS

The CONFIG.SYS file is a special text file that executes special configuration commands that cannot be executed at the prompt. These commands configure your computer's hardware components so that MS-DOS and applications can use them and activate and manage the various memory areas.

EXAMPLE 20.24 A simple CONFIG.SYS might look like the following:

```
FILES=60
LASTDRIVE=Z
STACKS=9,256
```

20.7.1 THE FILES COMMAND

The FILES command defines the maximum number of file handles or files open in RAM. Each file handle uses a small amount of RAM to keep track of what files are in the RAM. If you have FILES=60, DOS can keep track of 60 files open at the same time. The maximum number of files allowed is 255. Although you could set the command to 255, the memory used to keep track of what files are in the RAM is kept in conventional memory (the first 640 KB of RAM), and because DOS has so little conventional memory (by today's standard), you don't want to waste it on something that you don't need. Windows 3.XX should be set to a minimum of 30 files. Of course, if multiple applications are to be run at the same time, such as a word processor, a spreadsheet, and a graphics package, you should increase this to a minimum of 50 or 60.

Another command, similar to the FILES command, is FCBS command. The FCBS command specifies the number of file control blocks (FCBs) that MS-DOS can have open at the same time. A file control block is a data structure that stores information about a file for programs that were written for DOS 1.0. Therefore, when you see this line and are not running any programs made for DOS 1.0, it can be deleted. (Note: The MEMMAKER program adds the FCBS line in the CONFIG.SYS file.)

20.7.2 THE LASTDRIVE COMMAND

The LASTDRIVE command specifies the maximum number of drives that can be accessed. If the LASTDRIVE command is not used, the default value is the letter following the last one in use. Therefore, if drives A and C are used, the default value is D. If the command is set to LASTDRIVE=Z, DOS reserves memory to keep track of all 26 drive letters. Using a command such as LASTDRIVE=Z does not mean that you have 26 drives; it only means that DOS will recognize all 26 logical drives (floppy drives, hard drives, logical drives or partitions, CD drives, network drives, and RAM drives).

20.7.3 THE STACKS COMMAND

The STACKS command creates stacks (an area of RAM to be used for hardware interrupts). When a hardware interrupt occurs, all current information in the microprocessor is stored into a stack. When the interrupt is done, the information is copied back into the microprocessor so that it can continue where it left off. An example of a STACK command is:

```
STACKS=9,256
```

which indicates 9 stacks of 256 bytes, not 9,256 stacks. Usually STACKS=9,256 is sufficient for most computers. If the number of stacks or the size of the stacks is not large enough, a "Internal Stack Overflow" error message will appear. To overcome the error, the number of stacks and the size of the stacks will have to be increased. For example, you could use STACKS=12,512.

20.7.4 THE SHELL COMMAND

During boot-up, DOS tries to load COMMAND.COM from the root directory of the boot device. The SHELL command specifies the name and location of the command interpreter (COMMAND.COM in another directory or another command interpreter from a third-party company such as 4DOS) that you want DOS to use. Since you must tell DOS which command interpreter to use before COMMAND.COM is loaded, the SHELL command is loaded in the CONFIG.SYS file.

To load COMMAND.COM in the DOS directory, you could add the following command in the CONFIG.SYS file:

```
SHELL=C:\DOS\COMMAND.COM
```

In addition, COMMAND.COM specified with the SHELL command can also be used to increase the size of the environment space used by the environment variables. By default, the environment is 256 bytes. This means that if you add all the characters established as environment variables (PATH, PROMPT, SET, and SHELL), the environment space cannot hold more than 256 characters. If the amount of environment space is exceeded, an "Out of Environment Space" error message will appear. To increase the environment space to 512 bytes and to make it permanent, you would use the following command in CONFIG.SYS:

```
SHELL=C:\COMMAND.COM /E:512 /P
```

20.8 MEMORY MANAGEMENT

When a computer is booted from a disk that has no CONFIG.SYS and AUTOEXEC.BAT files, DOS will recognize only the conventional memory (first 640 KB of RAM), and the hardware will use the reserve memory between 640 KB and 1 MB of RAM. To activate and manage the other memory areas, certain lines must be loaded in the CONFIG.SYS file.

EXAMPLE 20.25 A typical CONFIG.SYS file might contain the following:

```
FILES=60
LASTDRIVE=Z
STACKS=9,256
DEVICE=C:\DOS\HIMEM.SYS
DEVICE=C:\DOS\EMM386.EXE NOEMS
DOS=HIGH,UMB
```

To analyze how much memory is available and how it is being utilized, you would use the MEM command. To see what is loaded in the conventional memory and upper memory, you would perform the MEM /C |MORE or MEM /C /P. /P for the MEM command is available only in DOS 6.0 and above.

20.8.1 HIMEM.SYS

The HIMEM.SYS is the DOS extended memory manager (RAM above 1 MB found on any newer machine), which makes the extended memory available to DOS programs. It also prevents two programs from using the same memory area in the extended memory. The DEVICE command in the CONFIG.SYS file is used to load the HIMEM.SYS. Any time that the DEVICE command is used to load a driver, you should always include the entire path (location) of the file specified and its filename extension. (Note: Because Windows 3.XX requires extended memory to run, it requires HIMEM.SYS to be loaded.) In addition, if /TESTMEM:OFF is added to the end of the HIMEM.SYS line, DOS will activate the extended memory but will skip the memory test.

Question: HIMEM.SYS exists in DOS 4.0 and above and all Windows 3.XX. Therefore, if the hard drive has two HIMEM.SYS files, which one should you use?

Answer: You should use the one that is more recent. You can find out which is the more recent driver by using the DIR command and looking at the date of the file. Therefore, if you decide to use the file in Windows, the line in the CONFIG.SYS file would be DEVICE=C:\WINDOWS\HIMEM.SYS.

20.8.2 EMM386.EXE

The EMM386.EXE file uses extended memory to simulate expanded memory and to provide access to the upper memory area (unused portion of memory between 640 KB and 1 MB not being used by hardware). Like the HIMEM.SYS file, the EMM386.EXE file is loaded in CONFIG.SYS with the DEVICE command, although it has an EXE filename extension. The parameters used will determine if it simulates expanded memory or provides access to upper memory. (Note: EMM386.EXE requires HIMEM.SYS to be loaded and will work only on a 386 machine or higher.)

EXAMPLE 20.26 To specify that EMM386.EXE use extended memory to simulate expanded memory without enabling the upper memory, you would use:

```
DEVICE=C:\DOS\EMM386.EXE
```

To allow the EMM386.EXE to enable the upper memory without simulating expanded memory, you would use:

```
DEVICE=C:\DOS\EMM386.EXE NOEMS
```

(NOEMS means no expanded memory [EMS].) To allow EMM386.EXE to use extended memory to simulate expanded memory and to enable the upper memory, you would use:

```
DEVICE=C:\DOS\EMM386.EXE RAM
```

To make the best use of the system's memory, you should use the NOEMS option unless a program requires expanded memory. (Note: To fully enable the upper memory, you also need DOS=UMB.)

EXAMPLE 20.27 To specify that EMM386.EXE allocate a maximum of only 4,096 KB to simulate expanded memory, you would use:

```
DEVICE=C:\DOS\EMM386.EXE 4096
```

If there is a possible conflict between a device driver or TSR and hardware using the memory between 640 KB and 1 MB of RAM, you can exclude a memory range so that it will be used only by hardware devices. The following command will prevent EMM386 from using the memory between A000–BFFF of RAM for upper or expanded memory:

```
DEVICE=C:\DOS\EMM386.EXE RAM X=A000-BFFF
```

To find out if a device driver or TSR is conflicting with hardware using reserve memory, you can exclude all of the memory between 640 KB and 1 MB by using X=A000-FFFF. If the problem goes away, then you know it was a memory conflict. You would then use the hardware manual to determine the memory address that the hardware device is using so that you can exclude only the area being used.

20.8.3 DOS=HIGH AND DOS=UMB

When the DOS=HIGH command is used, DOS tries to load a large portion of itself in the high memory area (HMA) between 1 MB and 1 MB 64 KB, freeing conventional memory. Of course, this command requires HIMEM.SYS to be loaded first. When the DOS=UMB command is loaded in CONFIG.SYS, it does *not* try to load DOS into upper memory. Instead, DOS=UMB specifies that DOS should manage the upper memory blocks (UMB) created by the EMM386.EXE. Therefore, if you want to enable the upper memory, you must have HIMEM.SYS, EMM386 with the NOEMS or RAM option, and DOS=UMB loaded. (Note: The DOS=HIGH and DOS=UMB commands are often combined into one line: DOS=HIGH,UMB or DOS=UMB,HIGH.)

20.9 DEVICE DRIVERS AND TSRS

To enable hardware and to load useful utilities, you need to know how to load device drivers and TSRs. A **device driver** controls how DOS and applications interact with specific items of hardware. They can be identified with a SYS filename extension, which is loaded in the CONFIG.SYS file.

A **TSR,** which stands for terminate and stay resident, loads instructions into the RAM to control some hardware device or to provide some useful function while giving control back to the operating system. The TSR then performs its function quietly in the background while other programs are loaded. A program that is not a TSR (for example, EDIT or a word processing program) is loaded in the RAM but typically does not allow any other commands to be performed at the prompt until you exit the program. Since TSRs have a COM or EXE filename extension, they are loaded in AUTOEXEC.BAT. Remember that the AUTOEXEC.BAT file is a batch file that can contain commands that can be executed at the prompt.

EXAMPLE 20.28   CONFIG.SYS:

```
FILES=60
LASTDRIVE=Z
STACKS=9,256
DEVICE=C:\DOS\HIMEM.SYS
DEVICE=C:\EMM386.EXE NOEMS
DOS-HIGH,UMB
DEVICE=C:\SB16\SB16.SYS
DEVICE=c:\CDROM\ATAPI_CD.sys /D:CD0001
DEVICE=C:\ANSI.SYS
```

   AUTOEXEC.BAT:

```
@ECHO OFF
PATH=C:\DOS;C:\WINDOWS
PROMPT $P$G
SET TEMP=C:\DOS
DEL C:\DOS\*.TMP
SET BLASTER=A220 I5 D1
C:\MOUSE\MOUSE.COM
C:\DOS\MSCDEX /D:CD0001 /m:12 /L:E
DOSKEY.COM
WIN
```

20.9.1   MOUSE DRIVERS

A mouse purchased separately will come with a disk containing drivers. Some disks have installation programs for the drivers; otherwise, the drivers have to be loaded manually in AUTOEXEC.BAT or CONFIG.SYS. If the driver has a SYS file extension, it will always be loaded in the CONFIG.SYS file using the DEVICE command. If you create a mouse directory and copy a device driver called MOUSE.SYS to the MOUSE directory, it can then be loaded with the DEVICE command in the CONFIG.SYS file:

```
DEVICE=C:\MOUSE\MOUSE.SYS
```

As with the HIMEM.SYS, you must include the entire path (location) of the MOUSE file, including the drive letter and the filename extension. If the driver has a COM or EXE extension, the file is usually loaded in AUTOEXEC.BAT. Therefore, if you create a MOUSE directory on the C drive and copy a driver called MOUSE.COM into the MOUSE directory, it can be loaded in the AUTOEXEC.BAT file:

```
C:\MOUSE\MOUSE.COM   or   C:\MOUSE\MOUSE
```

Unless a PATH command that includes the MOUSE directory is executed before the mouse driver is loaded, you must specify where the MOUSE file is located: C:\MOUSE. Because DOS always looks for filenames with COM, EXE, and BAT extensions, you can omit the COM filename extension. Of course, the MOUSE directory and MOUSE.COM and MOUSE.SYS are only examples of actual names. The files could be named MOUSE.EXE, AMOUSE.COM, LMOUSE.EXE, or just about anything that follows the DOS naming scheme.

   If the disk that comes with the mouse has both the device driver and TSR, load only one of them, not both. If both are loaded, they may fight for control of the mouse, causing it to work improperly or not at all. In addition, loading both will use twice as much RAM.

Windows 3.XX has its own built-in mouse driver, so it does not require one to be loaded in the CONFIG.SYS or AUTOEXEC.BAT file.

20.9.2 CD-ROM DRIVERS

Most of the time when loading CD-ROM drivers, the floppy disk is inserted into a floppy drive and the SETUP.EXE, INSTALL.EXE, or similar file is executed to automatically install and configure the drivers. For DOS, the EIDE CD drives require a device driver to be loaded in the CONFIG.SYS; SCSI drives usually require a device driver for the controller card and a device driver for the CD-ROM drive. The driver for the Mitsumi IDE CD-ROM drive appears as:

```
DEVICE=c:\CDROM\ ATAPI_CD.sys /D:CD0001
```

The /D: is the drive signature to identify the drive. In addition to the driver, DOS requires the Microsoft compact disk extension (MSCDEX.EXE) file to be loaded in AUTOEXEC.BAT so that DOS can read the CD file system:

```
C:\DOS\MSCDEX /d:CD0001 /m:12 /L:E
```

The /D: indicates the drive signature, which must be the same as the one specified in the device driver loaded in CONFIG.SYS. The /M: specifies the number of sector buffers and the /L: specifies the drive letter assigned to the CD-ROM drive.

20.9.3 SOUND CARD DRIVERS

The software drivers for sound cards are loaded very much like the way the CD-ROM driver is loaded. The disk that comes with the sound card is loaded into the floppy drive and the SETUP.EXE, INSTALL.EXE, or equivalent file is executed and loads the appropriate driver in the CONFIG.SYS and any environment variables needed in the AUTOEXEC.BAT. For example, the installation disk that comes with the Sound Blaster sound card from Creative Labs automatically adds the DEVICE=C:\SB16\SB16.SYS line to the CONFIG.SYS file and the line SET BLASTER=A220 I5 D1 to the AUTOEXEC.BAT file.

20.9.4 ANSI.SYS

As already stated, if a driver has a SYS extension, it is loaded in the CONFIG.SYS file with the DEVICE command. Although there are many device drivers available to DOS, one DOS device driver, ANSI.SYS, is used most often. ANSI.SYS controls the video display and cursor movement and reassigns keys on the keyboard. For example, if you would like to change the DOS screen to a blue background with yellow letters or you are communicating with a BBS using a modem that supports text graphics and colors, you would have to load ANSI.SYS. (Note: After the ANSI.SYS file is loaded, you would then use the ECHO command or the PROMPT command to change the screen colors.)

20.9.5 DOSKEY.COM, GRAPHICS.COM, AND SHARE.EXE

When typing commands at the prompt, DOS remembers the last command entered so that it can be retrieved with the F1 or F3 key. The F3 key brings the entire command back, while the F1 key brings it back one character at a time. DOSKEY.COM is a TSR that allows DOS to recall commands executed at the prompt and to edit them. In addition, it enables the user you to create and run macros. DOSKEY.COM has a COM filename extension, so it can be loaded in the AUTOEXEC.BAT file.

GRAPHICS.COM is a TSR that enables the Print Screen key to send the information displayed on the screen to a printer. Like DOSKEY.COM, GRAPHICS.COM has a COM filename extension and so can be loaded in the AUTOEXEC.BAT file.

The SHARE.EXE program enables DOS to support file and record sharing. It should be used in network and multitasking environments (such as Windows) in which programs share files to make sure two people or two programs don't write to a file at the same time. SHARE.EXE does not have to be loaded if you are using Windows 3.11 for Workgroups.

20.9.6 SETVER.EXE AND POWER.EXE

As mentioned, a device driver that has a SYS filename extension is always loaded in the CONFIG.SYS file with the DEVICE command, and TSRs that have a COM or EXE filename extension are usually loaded in the AUTOEXEC.BAT file. There are no exceptions to this system for filenames with the SYS extension, but some EXE files are loaded in the CONFIG.SYS file, not the AUTOEXEC.BAT file. The most common examples are EMM386.EXE, SETVER.EXE, and POWER.EXE. EMM386.EXE has already been discussed.

EXAMPLE 20.29 CONFIG.SYS:

```
FILES=60
LASTDRIVE=Z
STACKS=9,256
DEVICE=C:\DOS\HIMEM.SYS
DEVICE=C:\EMM386.EXE NOEMS
DOS-HIGH,UMB
DEVICE=C:\SB16\SB16.SYS
DEVICE=c:\CDROM\ATAPI_CD.SYS /D:CD0001
DEVICE=C:\ANSI.SYS
DEVICE=C:\DOS\SETVER.EXE
DEVICE=C:\DOS\POWER.EXE
```

AUTOEXEC.BAT:

```
@ECHO OFF
PATH=C:\DOS;C:\WINDOWS
PROMPT $P$G
SET TEMP=C:\DOS
DEL C:\DOS\*.TMP
SET BLASTER=A220 I5 D1
C:\MOUSE\MOUSE.COM
C:\DOS\MSCDEX /D:CD0001 /M:12 /L:E
DOSKEY.COM
WIN
```

The loading of SETVER.EXE in the CONFIG.SYS file with the DEVICE command loads the MS-DOS version table into RAM. The MS-DOS version table lists names of programs and the versions of DOS they require that are supposed to be reported to the program when the program asks for the DOS version. For example, an old Novell utility used to connect to a File Server, called NETX.COM, was written to work with DOS 3.0 to 5.0. When NETX.COM is executed, it asks DOS what version it is to make sure that it can work with the version of DOS loaded into the RAM. If DOS 6.22 is running on a system, for example, NETX.COM asks what version is running. Of course, DOS replies with DOS 6.22. NETX.COM checks the DOS versions that it can work with and finds that it does not work with DOS 6.22. Therefore, an "Incorrect DOS Version" error message appears. To fix this problem, a command similar to the following one can be executed:

```
SETVER NETX.COM 5.00
```

Executing SETVER.EXE at the DOS prompt changes a table in the SETVER.EXE file. (Note: The DOS version number must have two decimal places.) After the SETVER command is executed at the prompt, the SETVER will display a lengthy message telling you to reboot the changes so that the changes to the table can be reloaded into RAM. When

NETX.COM is executed, NETX.COM asks DOS what version is running. Instead of giving NETX.COM a straight answer, DOS searches the MS-DOS version table and finds that it is supposed to lie to NETX.COM and report DOS 5.00. Therefore, NETX.COM assumes it is working with DOS 5.00 and loads itself into RAM.

Question: What happens if you boot from a DOS 6.22 floppy disk on a machine that has Windows 95 and you try to execute FORMAT.COM in the C:\WIN-DOWS\COMMAND directory?

Answer: Many DOS files verify the DOS version before they execute. Since you have booted with a DOS 6.22 floppy disk, DOS 6.22 is loaded in the computer's RAM. Therefore, when you try to use the FORMAT.COM from Windows 95, FOR-MAT.COM checks to see what DOS version is running and of course generates an "Incorrect DOS Version" message. To get around this problem, don't use the SETVER command to change the DOS version reported to FORMAT.COM. Instead, boot with a Windows 95 bootable disk.

The POWER.EXE is a file usually used on notebook and laptop computers. If the computer conforms to the advanced power management (APM) specification, the POWER.EXE reduces power consumption when applications and devices are idle. To activate the POWER.EXE, it must be loaded in the CONFIG.SYS with the DEVICE command. After the POWER.EXE is loaded in the CONFIG.SYS file, the POWER.EXE command at the command prompt turns the power management on and off, reports the status of the power management, and sets levels of power conservation.

20.10 LOADING DEVICE DRIVERS AND TSRS INTO UPPER MEMORY

By loading HIMEM.SYS, EMM386.EXE, and DOS=HIGH,UMB, all of the memory areas are active. But, although the upper memory has been created, it has not yet been used. To load a device driver into upper memory, you would use the DEVICEHIGH command. To load a TSR into upper memory, you would use the LH (or LOADHIGH) command. (Note: DEVICEHIGH and LH command loading the program into the upper memory, not the high memory area.)

EXAMPLE 20.30 CONFIG.SYS:

```
FILES=60
LASTDRIVE=Z
STACKS=9,256
DEVICE=C:\DOS\HIMEM.SYS
DEVICE=C:\EMM386.EXE NOEMS
DOS-HIGH,UMB
DEVICEHIGH=C:\SB16\SB16.SYS
DEVICEHIGH=C:\CDROM\ATAPI_CD.SYS /D:CD0001
DEVICEHIGH=C:\ANSI.SYS
DEVICEHIGH=C:\DOS\SETVER.EXE
DEVICEHIGH=C:\DOS\POWER.EXE
```

   AUTOEXEC.BAT:

```
@ECHO OFF
PATH=C:\DOS;C:\WINDOWS
PROMPT $P$G
SET TEMP=C:\DOS
DEL C:\DOS\*.TMP
SET BLASTER=A220 I5 D1
LH C:\MOUSE\MOUSE.COM
LH C:\DOS\MSCDEX /D:CD0001 /M:12 /L:E
LH DOSKEY.COM
WIN
```

To simplify the task of memory management, DOS 6.00 and above include the MemMaker program. The MemMaker program automatically optimizes the computer's memory by moving device drivers and TSR programs to upper memory.

20.11 DISK COMMANDS

Today's GUI and Windows applications require more memory and more disk space than ever before. Because the hard disk is a mechanical device, it is slow compared to the microprocessor and RAM. The BUFFERS and SMARTDRV commands can be used to increase the disk performance. In addition, you can create a drive made of RAM (RAM drive).

EXAMPLE 20.31   CONFIG.SYS:

```
FILES=60
BUFFERS=10,0
LASTDRIVE=Z
STACKS=9,256
DEVICE=C:\DOS\HIMEM.SYS
DEVICE=C:\EMM386.EXE NOEMS
DOS-HIGH,UMB
DEVICEHIGH=C:\SB16\SB16.SYS
DEVICEHIGH=C:\CDROM\ATAPI_CD.SYS /D:CD0001
DEVICEHIGH=C:\ANSI.SYS
DEVICEHIGH=C:\DOS\SETVER.EXE
DEVICEHIGH=C:\DOS\POWER.EXE
DEVICEHIGH=C:\DOS\RAMDRIVE.SYS 2048 /E
```

AUTOEXEC.BAT:

```
@ECHO OFF
PATH=C:\DOS;C:\WINDOWS
PROMPT $P$G
SET TEMP=C:\DOS
DEL C:\DOS\*.TMP
SET BLASTER=A220 I5 D1
LH C:\MOUSE\MOUSE.COM
LH C:\DOS\MSCDEX /D:CD0001 /M:12 /L:E
SMARTDRV 4096 128
LH DOSKEY.COM
WIN
```

20.11.1 SMARTDRV AND BUFFERS

The BUFFERS command, loaded in the CONFIG.SYS file, specifies the amount of memory for a disk buffer or buffer area. The buffer area is a block of memory used to collect data as it is being moved between the microprocessor and the controller card. Each buffer is 512 bytes. After the data is collected, the buffer tries to group data into larger chunks and move them all at once. Since the larger chunks fill the data transfer pathways more efficiently, the PC runs more efficiently. The buffer keeps the most recent information read to and from the disk. When it needs to make more room, it moves the oldest accessed information and copies it to disk.

The BUFFERS command can also specify the number of additional sectors DOS reads each time it is instructed to read a file. If the next sector needed on the disk is sequential to the one just read, it will already be loaded in the RAM. The maximum number of buffers is 99, and the maximum number of read-ahead buffers is 8. If a BUFFERS command is not loaded, DOS will assign 15 buffers and 1 look-ahead buffer for computers that have 640 KB of RAM. The syntax for the BUFFERS command is:

```
BUFFERS=nn   or   BUFFERS=nn,mm
```

where nn is the number of buffers and mm is the number of look-ahead buffers.

**TABLE 20.6   SMARTDRV
default values**

Extended Memory	Default Cache Size	Default Windows Cache Size
Up to 1 MB	All of the extended memory	0 KB
Up to 2 MB	1 MB	256 KB
Up to 4 MB	1 MB	512 KB
Up to 6 MB	2 MB	1 MB
6 MB or more	2 MB	2 MB

SMARTDRV.EXE, a software disk cache that caches, or buffers, between the hard drive and the RAM, creates a much larger buffer area, called a *cache area,* in the extended memory. (See table 20.6.) In contrast to the way the buffer area operates, the software controlling the cache area tries to anticipate what the microprocessor needs next. One way it does this is to keep a copy of information that has been recently accessed. If the information has already been accessed, there is a good chance that it will be accessed again. Another way is to read ahead an additional sector after the one that has been accessed. Whatever method or methods are used, when the disk needs to be accessed, the system will look in the cache area first. If it can't find what is needed, it will access the slower hard drive. The time it takes to search the cache area (RAM) is almost negligible compared to the time needed to access the hard drive. Therefore, if the needed information is in the RAM, the overall performance of the PC is increased. Another advantage that SMARTDRV.EXE has over BUFFERS is that when BUFFERS needs to make more room, it removes the oldest information accessed, while SMARTDRV removes the information that has been least accessed.

SMARTDRV.EXE has an EXE filename extension, so it is loaded in the AUTOEXEC.BAT file. SMARTDRV.EXE automatically loads into upper memory if available. (Note: For DOS versions 4.0 and 5.0, a disk cache is created by loading SMARTDRV.SYS in the CONFIG.SYS file using the DEVICE or DEVICEHIGH command.)

EXAMPLE 20.32   To create a disk cache with the default values, you would use the following command in the AUTOEXEC.BAT file:

```
SMARTDRV
```

To create a 4,096 KB cache area (overriding the default values), you would use the following command in the AUTOEXEC.BAT file:

```
SMARTDRV 4096
```

Since Windows for Workgroups 3.11 has its own built-in disk cache, you may want to reduce the disk cache when Windows is running. Therefore, to create a 4,096 KB cache area but reduce it to 128 KB when running Windows, you would use the following command in the AUTOEXEC.BAT:

```
SMARTDRV 4096 128
```

Some programs are written to access the disk, bypassing the cache area. If the disk has not been updated from the cache area, the program could encounter some problems. If you have such a program, you then need to disable the write-behind caching. This would be done with the following command:

```
SMARTDRV /X
```

If you are not loading SMARTDRV, you should use between 30 and 50 buffers. If you are using SMARTDRV, you should reduce the number of buffers to 10 or 15 and you should not use look-ahead buffers. To cache a CD-ROM, SMARTDRV must be loaded after MSCDEX.EXE. SMARTDRV does not cache network drives or compressed drives.

Some ESDI and SCSI hard drives need double buffering so that they can work with memory provided by EMM386 or Windows running in 386 enhanced mode. To fix this problem, you can enable double buffering using the SMARTDRV.EXE in the CONFIG.SYS file:

TABLE 20.7 Differences between DOS and PC-DOS

DOS	PC-DOS Equivalent
DoubleSpace	SuperStor
EDIT.COM	E.EXE
MEMMAKER.EXE	RAMBOOST.EXE
MSBACKUP.EXE	CPBACKUP.EXE

```
DEVICE=C:\DOS\SMARTDRV.EXE /DOUBLE_BUFFER
```

To determine if you need double buffering, add SMARTDRV.EXE to the CONFIG.SYS file. After rebooting the computer, execute SMARTDRV.EXE at the command prompt. If there is a "Yes" under the buffering column, double buffering is needed.

20.11.2 RAM DRIVES

The RAMDRIVE.SYS file creates a RAM drive. A RAM drive is a simulated hard disk drive consisting of RAM. After it is created during boot-up, the RAM drive will appear as a normal but extremely fast drive. Of course, when the computer is shut down, any information stored in it will disappear. To create a RAM drive, load the RAMDRIVE.SYS file in the CONFIG.SYS file using the DEVICE or DEVICEHIGH command.

EXAMPLE 20.24 To create a 64 KB (default size) RAM drive in conventional memory, perform the following command:

```
DEVICE=C:\DOS\RAMDRIVE.SYS
```

To create a 4,096 KB RAM drive in extended memory, perform the following command:

```
DEVICE=C:\DOS\RAMDRIVE.SYS 4096 /E
```

20.12 PC-DOS

PC-DOS is an MS-DOS-compatible version of DOS sold by IBM. PC-DOS uses IBM-BIO.COM and IBMDOS.COM instead of IO.SYS and MSDOS.SYS. Other differences are listed in table 20.7.

20.13 TROUBLESHOOTING CONFIG.SYS AND AUTOEXEC.BAT

Since the CONFIG.SYS and AUTOEXEC.BAT files are necessary to run Windows and other popular applications and to activate hardware, it is necessary to know how to troubleshoot them. Anytime you see "Bad Command or Filename" or "File Not Found" error messages during boot-up, the error is in the AUTOEXEC.BAT file. (Note: Files loaded with the LH [or LOADHIGH] command that can't be found will give a "File Not Found" error message.) There is not, however, a problem if a "File Not Found" error message appears when the system is deleting temporary files during boot-up.

If a file can't be executed in CONFIG.SYS, it will generate an error message similar to:

```
Unrecognized Command in CONFIG.SYS
Error in CONFIG.SYS line 6
```

This means that you must go to the CONFIG.SYS file and look to see what is causing problems in the sixth line.

If the machine is locking up during boot-up or a message is being displayed on the screen so fast that you can't see it, you need to isolate the problem. With DOS 6.00 or above, you can use the F5 key and F8 key during boot-up. If the F5 key is pressed when the computer first says "Starting MS-DOS...," the AUTOEXEC.BAT and CONFIG.SYS files will be skipped. If the F8 key is pressed instead of the F5 key, DOS will walk through those files one command at a time. Therefore, if a problem causes the computer to lock up, first use the F8 key to find out which line is causing the problem. Then reboot the computer and use the F5 key to bypass the AUTOEXEC.BAT and CONFIG.SYS files. You can then get to the AUTOEXEC.BAT, CONFIG.SYS, and other files to fix the problem.

If the machine uses an older version of DOS, you must then work with the REM statements. This means that you have to reboot the computer using a floppy disk, switch over to the hard drive, and add a REM statement on one of the lines in the AUTOEXEC.BAT and CONFIG.SYS files. You would then remove the floppy disk and reboot the computer. If the problem is fixed, then you know that the line with the REM statement was causing the problem. If not, you would reboot the computer, remove the REM statement, and try to put a REM statement on another line. You would continue to do this until the problem is found.

SUMMARY

1. DOS (disk operating system), created by Microsoft, was the first operating system used on the IBM PC.
2. DOS loads the IO.SYS, MSDOS.SYS, CONFIG.SYS, COMMAND.COM, and AUTOEXEC.BAT files during boot-up.
3. The instructions for the internal DOS commands are kept in the COMMAND.COM file loaded in the RAM.
4. External DOS commands are commands for which instructions are kept in files that have a COM or EXE filename extension.
5. The DIR command, which displays the list of the files and subdirectories, is probably the most commonly used DOS command.
6. The CD command changes the current directory.
7. Copy commands (COPY, DISKCOPY, and XCOPY) always have three parts: the command, the source, and the target.
8. The FORMAT command is used to prepare a disk for the first time.
9. The SYS command makes a disk bootable without reformatting.
10. The ATTRIB command displays, sets, or removes the read-only (R), archive (A), system (S), and hidden (H) attributes assigned to a file or directory.
11. Batch files are text files with a BAT filename extension containing commands that can be executed at the prompt.
12. The AUTOEXEC.BAT file is a special batch file that automatically executes during boot-up.
13. When a command is performed at the prompt, COMMAND.COM looks for instructions for the command in the RAM (internal command), the current directory, and the PATH statement.
14. If COMMAND.COM can't find the instructions for a command, it replies with a "Bad Command or Filename" error message.
15. The PROMPT command changes the appearance of the command prompt.
16. The SET command is used to display, set, or remove MS-DOS environment variables.
17. The TEMP variable defines where any temporary files (files whose filenames begin with a tilde [~] and have a TMP filename extension) are to be kept when they are created.
18. CONFIG.SYS is a special text file that executes special configuration commands (commands that cannot be executed at the prompt).
19. The FILES command defines the maximum number of file handles or files that can be open in RAM.
20. The LASTDRIVE command specifies the maximum number of drives that can be accessed.
21. The STACKS command creates stacks, an area of RAM to be used for hardware interrupts.
22. The HIMEM.SYS command is the DOS extended memory manager that prevents programs from using the same memory areas. It is needed to load any other memory command.
23. The EMM386.EXE command loaded in CONFIG.SYS uses extended memory to simulate expanded memory and provide access to the upper memory area.

24. When the DOS=HIGH command is used, DOS tries to load a large portion of itself in the high memory area (HMA).
25. The DOS=UMB command specifies that DOS should manage the upper memory blocks (UMB) created by EMM386.EXE.
26. Device drivers and TSRs enable hardware and useful utilities.
27. The DEVICEHIGH command is used to load a device driver into upper memory. The LH (or LOADHIGH) command is used to load a TSR into upper memory.
28. The BUFFERS command, loaded in the CONFIG.SYS, specifies the amount of memory for a disk buffer (each buffer is 512 bytes) or buffer area.
29. SMARTDRV.EXE is a software disk cache that creates a cache area in the extended memory.
30. The RAMDRIVE.SYS file uses part of the RAM to simulate a hard disk drive.

QUESTIONS

1. Which of the following files interprets the input entered at the DOS prompt?
   a. COMMAND.COM
   b. MSDOS.SYS
   c. IO.SYS
   d. AUTOEXEC.BAT
2. Which of the following files is the DOS kernel?
   a. COMMAND.COM
   b. MSDOS.SYS
   c. IO.SYS
   d. AUTOEXEC.BAT
3. What is the maximum allowable length of a DOS filename, including the extension? (Don't count the period.)
   a. 9 characters
   b. 10 characters
   c. 11 characters
   d. 13 characters
4. What is the correct boot sequence for DOS files?
   a. IO.SYS, MSDOS.SYS, COMMAND.COM, CONFIG.SYS, AUTOEXEC.BAT
   b. IO.SYS, MSDOS.SYS, CONFIG.SYS, COMMAND.COM, AUTOEXEC.BAT
   c. MSDOS.SYS, IO.SYS, COMMAND.COM, CONFIG.SYS, AUTOEXEC.BAT
   d. MSDOS.SYS, IO.SYS, CONFIG.SYS, COMMAND.COM, AUTOEXEC.BAT
5. The CD\ command has what effect?
   a. clears the disk
   b. changes to a new directory below the current one
   c. returns to the root directory
   d. goes to the parent directory
   e. goes to the child directory
6. What command shows all hidden files one screen at a time?
   a. DIR
   b. DIR /ON /W
   c. DIR /ON /P
   d. DIR /AH /W
   e. DIR /AH /P
7. Which of the following are external DOS commands? (Choose two.)
   a. FORMAT
   b. CLS
   c. VER
   d. COPY
   e. DISKCOPY
8. Identify the *incorrect* use of the COPY command:
   a. COPY A:RESUME.DOC A:
   b. COPY A:DATA.DAT A:DATA.TXT
   c. COPY A:*.* C:\DATA
   d. COPY A:??DOS.*
   e. none of the above
9. When using the XCOPY command, /S means:
   a. subdirectories
   b. search
   c. bootable
   d. system
   e. none of the above

10. You have a valuable disk that contains the QA Plus Diagnostic program, a diagnostic program used to test computer hardware. You need to make the diskette bootable using the A drive. What command would you use to make it bootable? Assume you are at the C:\ directory.

    a. SYS A:
    b. DISKCOPY A: A::
    c. FORMAT A: /S
    d. FORMAT A: /S /Q
    e. COPY SYS A:

11. How do you format a DS/HD 3½″ disk in a 1.44 MB floppy disk drive using the A drive?

    a. FORMAT A:
    b. FORMAT A: /F:360
    c. FORMAT A: /F:720
    d. FORMAT A: /4

12. How do you format the C drive and make it bootable?

    a. FORMAT C:
    b. FORMAT C: /S
    c. FORMAT C: /Q
    d. FORMAT C: /U
    e. none of the above

13. To make the README.TXT file read-only, you would enter:

    a. ATTRIB +H README.TXT
    b. ATTRIB README.TXT -H
    c. ATTRIB -R README.TXT
    d. ATTRIB +R README.TXT
    e. EDIT README.TXT
    f. DIR /AR

14. A user is in the A:\DATA directory, types C:, and is in the C:\ directory. Without changing directories, what is the shortest command to copy the entire contents of the A:\DATA directory to B:\?

    a. COPY A:\DATA B:\
    b. COPY A:\DATA*.* B:\
    c. COPY A:\DATA*.* B:*.*
    d. COPY A:*.* B:\
    e. none of the commands will copy the files to the B drive

15. Which command is *not* the proper use of switches?

    a. DEL C:\DATA*.* \P
    b. FORMAT A: /S/U
    c. DIR /AH /ON
    d. COPY C:*.DAT D:\DATA

16. Which statement about batch files is true?

    a. Batch files are executed only at system boot-up.
    b. Batch files can execute only .COM and .EXE files.
    c. Batch files can execute any combination of commands except those requiring parameter passing or variables.
    d. Batch files can execute any combination of commands performed at the command line prompt.

17. What is the effect of the DOS PAUSE command?

    a. The CPU is locked until CTRL-C is true
    b. The CPU is locked until the CONTINUE command is entered
    c. Program execution is suspended waiting for action by the user
    d. Program execution is suspended waiting for action by the user after a specified amount of time

18. Which of the following correctly identifies the DOS search order?

    a. floppy disk, hard disk
    b. search path
    c. internal command, current directory, search path
    d. current directory, search path
    e. internal command, current directory, root directory, search path

19. When the filename GO is typed at the DOS prompt, COMMAND.COM looks in the current directory for a filename in what order?

    a. GO.EXE, then GO.COM, then GO.BAT
    b. GO.BAT, then GO.COM, then GO.EXE
    c. GO.COM, then GO.EXE, then GO.BAT
    d. GO.EXE, then GO.BAT, then GO.COM

20. A user has the directory C:\LEDGER in the path. What would the shortest command be at the end of the AUTOEXEC.BAT file in order to execute the LG.EXE command found in the C:\LEDGER directory?

a. LG.EXE	d. LG
b. C:\LG.EXE	e. C:\LG
c. C:\LEDGER\LG	

21. What happens when DOS can't find instructions to follow?

    a. a "File Not Found" message appears

    b. a "Bad Command or Filename" message appears

    c. an "Invalid Command" message appears

    d. DOS will then go directly to the root directory and search all other directories not searched

22. The $P used with the PROMPT command means:

a. prompt	d. pink
b. paste	e. pin
c. path (current drive and location)	

23. Which of the following statements about where temporary files will be created is true?

    a. The SET TEMP line in the AUTOEXEC.BAT file determines where temporary files are stored.

    b. By default, TEMP files are stored in the DOS directory.

    c. By default, TEMP files are stored in the root directory.

    d. By default, TEMP files are stored in the C:\TEMP directory.

    e. By default, TEMP files are stored in a RAM drive.

    f. Temporary files must always be stored in the TEMP subdirectory under Windows.

24. The utility SMARTDRV.EXE found in MS-DOS:

    a. utilizes expanded memory to create a disk cache

    b. utilizes extended memory to create a disk cache

    c. creates a disk from RAM

    d. copies the ROM BIOS instructions into RAM

    e. is a hard drive utility that translates CMOS parameters

25. The upper memory manager provided by DOS is called:

a. MEMMAKER	d. HIMEM.SYS
b. UMM386.EXE	e. UMB386.EXE
c. EMM386.EXE	

26. By default, DOS is loaded into and runs in conventional memory. However, this can be changed with the following command in the CONFIG.SYS:

a. DOS=HIGH,UMB	c. RUNDOS, HIGH
b. HIMEM.SYS	d. DOS=XMS

27. Which parameter used with EMM386.EXE allows upper memory but no expanded memory?

a. EXPAND	d. DEVICEHIGH
b. RAM	e. EMS
c. NOEMS	f. no parameter is used

28. The extended memory manager for DOS is called:

a. MEMMAKER	d. HIMEM.SYS
b. UMM386.EXE	e. UMB386.EXE
c. EMM386.EXE	

29. Which DOS driver is used to emulate expanded memory?

a. HIMEM.SYS	c. RAMDRIVE.SYS
b. EMM386.EXE	d. SMARTDRV.EXE

30. Which of the following commands would be used to load programs (TSRs) into upper memory?

    a. DEVICEHIGH= in the CONFIG.SYS

    b. DEVICEHIGH= in the AUTOEXEC.BAT file

    c. LH in the CONFIG.SYS file

    d. LH in the AUTOEXEC.BAT file

31. Two common mouse drivers are:

    a. MOUSE.COM, which is normally loaded with a line in the AUTOEXEC.BAT file, and MOUSE.SYS, which is normally loaded with a line in the CONFIG.SYS file

b. MOUSE.COM, which is normally loaded with a line in the CONFIG.SYS file, and MOUSE.SYS, which is normally loaded with a line in the AUTO-EXEC.BAT file

c. MOUSE.COM and MOUSE.SYS, both of which are normally loaded with lines in the AUTOEXEC.BAT file

d. MOUSE.COM and MOUSE.SYS, both of which are normally loaded with lines in the CONFIG.SYS file

e. MOUSE.COM, MOUSE.SYS, and MOUSE.DRV, which are normally loaded with lines in the CONFIG.SYS file

32. For PC-DOS, what utility automatically optimizes the use of RAM?
   a. MEMMAKER
   b. RAMBOOST
   c. E.EXE
   d. MEM /D
   e. MEMCONFIG

33. Pressing the F8 key when the "Starting MS-DOS…" message appears:
   a. allows you to single-step through CONFIG.SYS and AUTOEXEC.BAT
   b. skips the loading of DoubleSpace
   c. causes DOS to skip CONFIG.SYS and AUTOEXEC.BAT
   d. allows you to choose among different boot sequences

34. What is wrong if a "Non-System Disk or Disk Error" message appears?
   a. COMMAND.COM has been deleted or corrupted
   b. IO.SYS and/or MSDOS.SYS are missing or corrupted
   c. CONFIG.SYS has an invalid command
   d. AUTOEXEC.BAT has an invalid command

35. What is wrong if a "Bad or Missing Command Interpreter" error message appears?
   a. COMMAND.COM has been deleted or corrupted
   b. IO.SYS and/or MSDOS.SYS are missing or corrupted
   c. CONFIG.SYS has an invalid command
   d. AUTOEXEC.BAT has an invalid command

36. Which of the following commands will prevent a TSR or device drive from using upper memory?
   a. DEVICE=C:\DOS\EMM386.EXE RAM
   b. DEVICE=C:\DOS\EMM386.EXE X=A000-AFFF
   c. DEVICE=C:\DOS\EMM386.EXE X=A000-EFFF
   d. DEVICE=C:\DOS\EMM386.EXE X=0000-FFFF

37. After upgrading to a new DOS version, an older application displays the error message "Incorrect DOS Version." What should be done to run this application?
   a. use the SETVER command
   b. restore the old DOS version
   c. contact the application's vendor support line
   d. run the SYS command on the drive with the correct DOS version

38. Which DOS command will send print jobs normally sent to the parallel port to the serial port? (You may need to research this question.)
   a. PARALLEL>SERIAL
   b. MODE LPT1=COM1
   c. DIRECT LPT1=COM1
   d. MODE PRINTER ()-SERIAL()

39. SMARTDRV.EXE can cache which of the following? (Select all that apply.)
   a. hard drives
   b. floppy drives
   c. CD-ROM drives
   d. network drives
   e. tape drives

40. Internal DOS commands are part of:
   a. IO.SYS
   b. MSDOS.SYS
   c. CONFIG.SYS
   d. COMMAND.COM
   e. AUTOEXEC.BAT

HANDS-ON EXERCISES

Exercise 1: Understanding Paths of Files and Directories

1. Using the accompanying figure, determine the path of the following files and directories:
   a. DOS
   b. MSOFFICE
   c. WINWORD
   d. STARTUP
   e. SETUP.EXE
   f. WINWORD.EXE
   g. MSWORD.DOC
   h. AUTOEXEC.BAT
   i. MSWORD.DLL

2. If you wanted to execute the SETUP.EXE file in the MSOFFICE directory, what would you type at the C:\> command prompt?

3. If you wanted to execute the SETUP.EXE file in the MSOFFICE directory, what would you type at the D:\> command prompt?

4. If you wanted to copy the CONFIG.SYS to the DOS directory, what would you type at the C:\> command prompt?

5. If you wanted to delete the MSWORD.DOC file, what would you type at the C:\> command prompt?

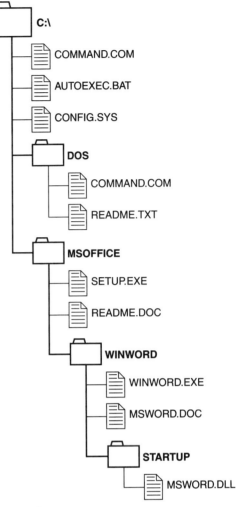

Exercise 2: Using Common DOS Commands

1. Format a floppy disk using drive A and make it bootable.

2. Create the directory structure shown in the accompanying figure on the A drive.

3. From the A:\ directory, show a graphical representation of the directory structure on the A drive.

4. From the C:\DOS directory, copy COUNTRY.TXT, EDIT.COM, FORMAT.COM, and LABEL.EXE to the DOS directory on the A drive.

5. Make the current directory A:\.

6. Without changing drives or directories, copy XCOPY.EXE from the C:\DOS directory to the A:\DOS directory.

7. Without changing drives or directories, copy COUNTRY.TXT to the JOB directory.

8. Change to the JOB directory.

9. Rename the COUNTRY.TXT file to TEXT.TXT.

10. Make a copy of the TEXT.TXT file and call it C.TXT.

11. Without changing directories, copy EDIT.COM from the A:\DOS directory to the JOB directory.

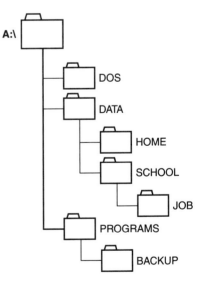

449

12. Move the EDIT.COM file from the JOB directory to the BACKUP directory.
13. Change to the DATA directory.
14. Change to the HOME directory.
15. Change back to the DATA directory.
16. Delete the HOME directory.
17. Delete the SCHOOL directory.
18. Change to the A:\DOS directory.
19. Using wild cards, delete the files that have an EXE filename extension.
20. Using wild cards, delete the files that have COM filename extension.
21. From the A:\ directory, show a graphical representation of the directory structure and its files on the A drive.
22. Perform a DIR /S.
23. Remove the first disk from drive A and insert a second floppy disk.
24. Format the disk using an unconditional format without making it bootable.
25. Copy the contents of the first disk to the second disk.
26. Format the second disk without making the disk bootable.
27. Without formatting the second disk, make the second disk bootable.
28. Create a TEST directory off of the C:\ directory.
29. Insert the first disk into drive A.
30. Copy the entire directory structure of the A drive, including the empty subdirectories, to the C:\TEST directory.
31. Delete the C:\TEST directory on the hard drive.
32. Change to the A:\ directory.
33. Perform a DIR command.
34. Show the hidden files using the DIR command.
35. Show the attributes of the files in the A:\ directory.
36. Using the COPY command, make a simple text file called NAME.TXT. In the text file, type your first name.
37. Display the contents of NAME.TXT without using EDIT.
38. Make the NAME.TXT file read-only.
39. Try to delete the NAME.TXT file using the DEL command.
40. Make the NAME.TXT file read/write (shut off the read-only attribute).
41. Make the NAME.TXT file hidden.
42. Use the DIR command to verify that the NAME.TXT file can't be seen.
43. Use the DIR command to display the NAME.TXT file.
44. Unhide the NAME.TXT file.
45. Make the NAME.TXT file read-only, hidden, and system.
46. Shut off the read-only, hidden, and system attributes of the NAME.TXT file.
47. Using EDIT, change the contents of the NAME.TXT file so that it contains your first name and your last name.
48. Load the README.TXT file that is located in the C:\DOS directory using EDIT.
49. Move to Section 5.1 of the README.TXT file, "Microsoft Antivirus." (Note: the beginning of the document is a chapter contents section followed by a table of contents and the information sections.) Read Section 5.1 to find out what you should do before cleaning a program with microsoft Antivirus.
50. Reformat both disks.

Exercise 3: Creating a Batch File

1. On the A drive, create an M.BAT batch file which does the following:

```
CD\ DOS
MSD.EXE
CD\
```

2. Test it by running the M.BAT file.
3. Create a batch file called C.BAT that will copy MSD.EXE, EDIT.COM, QBASIC.EXE, FORMAT.COM, FDISK.EXE, and ATTRIB.EXE to the A drive.
4. Test it by running the C.BAT file.

5. Create a batch file called GO.BAT with the following content:

```
@ECHO OFF
REM THE FOLLOWING COMMAND MAKES A COPY OF DOS'S TEXT FILES
CLS
ECHO INSERT A DISK IN DRIVE A
PAUSE
COPY C:\DOS\*.TXT A:
COPY A:\README.TXT A:\INFO.TXT
ECHO .
ECHO COPY IS DONE
ECHO .
ECHO YOU CAN NOW REMOVE THE DISK
PAUSE
```

6. Test the GO.BAT batch file.
7. Put a REM in front of the @ECHO OFF and save the changes.
8. Test GO.BAT. Notice the difference.
9. Edit GO.BAT and remove REM from the @ECHO OFF line.

Exercise 4: Using the PATH Command

1. Change to the C:\ directory.
2. Use the PATH command to display the current path.
3. To erase the path, perform the following command at the prompt:

```
PATH;
```

4. Perform the VER, DIR, DATE, TIME, and VOL commands.
5. Insert a formatted disk in drive A.
6. Perform the VER, DIR, DATE, TIME, and VOL commands. Try to figure out why these commands worked on the C drive and the A drive with no path.
7. Change back to the C:\ directory.
8. Try to run the LABEL.EXE and EDIT.COM files.
9. Change to the C:\DOS directory.
10. Try to run the LABEL.EXE and EDIT.COM files. Try to figure out why these commands did not work the first time but worked the second time.
11. Change back to the C:\ directory.
12. Use the PATH command to include the C:\DOS directory.
13. Try to run the LABEL.EXE and EDIT.COM files.
14. If your computer has Windows 3.XX, try to run Windows. (Hint: It is a WIN.COM file in the C:\WINDOWS directory.)
15. Use the PATH command to include the C:\DOS and the C:\WINDOWS directories.
16. If your computer has Windows 3.XX, try to run Windows. Start Windows.

Exercise 5: Creating AUTOEXEC.BAT and CONFIG.SYS Files

1. Format a disk using the A drive and make it bootable.
2. Create an AUTOEXEC.BAT file on the A drive that does the following:

   Gives the standard DOS prompt (path and greater-than sign)
   Has a search path including the DOS and Windows directories
   Stores the temporary files in the C:\DOS directory
   Deletes the temporary files stored in the C:\DOS directory
   Executes the SMARTDRV.EXE file in the C:\DOS directory

   If your computer has Windows 3.XX, start Windows.

3. Create a CONFIG.SYS file on the A drive that does the following:

   Has a maximum of 50 files open at the same time
   Sets 30 Buffers

Establishes 9 stacks, each stack being 256 bytes
Sets the last drive to Z
Loads the HIMEM.SYS (Hint: DEVICE=C:\DOS\HIMEM.SYS)

4. Reboot the computer to make sure there are no problems.

Exercise 6: Memory Management

1. Format a disk using the A drive and make it bootable.
2. Create an AUTOEXEC.BAT file on the A drive that does the following:

   Gives the standard DOS prompt (path and greater-than sign)
   Has a search path including the DOS and Windows directories
   Stores the temporary files in the C:\DOS directory
   Deletes the temporary files stored in the C:\DOS directory

3. Create a CONFIG.SYS file that allows 40 files to be open at the same time. Reboot the computer using the A drive.
4. Determine to see how much extended memory there is and how much is free using the MEM command.
5. Load the HIMEM.SYS in the CONFIG.SYS. Reboot the computer.
6. Determine how much extended memory there is and how much is free using the MEM command.
7. Load the EMM386.EXE with the RAM option in the CONFIG.SYS. Reboot the computer.
8. Determine how much expanded memory and how much upper memory there is and how much is free.
9. Have the EMM386.EXE use the NOEMS option instead. Reboot the computer.
10. Determine how much expanded memory and how much upper memory there is and how much is free.
11. Load DOS=UMB.
12. Determine how much upper memory there is and how much is free.
13. Put a REM in front of the EMM386.EXE line. Reboot the computer.
14. Determine how much upper memory there is and how much is free.
15. Remove the REM from the EMM386.EXE line. Reboot the computer.
16. Determine how much conventional memory there is and how much is free.
17. Add DOS=HIGH to the CONFIG.SYS file. Reboot the computer.
18. Determine how much conventional memory there is and how much is free.
19. Combine the DOS=HIGH and DOS=UMB into one line.
20. Put a REM in front of the HIMEM.SYS line. Reboot the computer.
21. Determine how much extended memory, upper memory, and conventional memory there is and how much is free.
22. Remove the REM from the HIMEM.SYS line. Reboot the computer.

Exercise 7: Loading Device Drivers and TSRs

1. Using the same disk from Exercise 6, find and load a mouse driver in the appropriate file.
2. Load DOSKEY.COM and ANSI.SYS in the appropriate file.
3. Create a 2,048 KB disk cache that reduces to 128 KB when running Windows.
4. Load SETVER.EXE in the appropriate file.
5. Reboot the computer.
6. Check to see how much conventional memory there is and how much is free.
7. Use the MEM/C command to see what is loaded in conventional memory and what is loaded in upper memory.
8. Load the mouse driver, DOSKEY.COM, ANSI.SYS, and SETVER.EXE into upper memory.

Exercise 8: Running MEMMAKER

Boot the computer using the C drive and run MEMMAKER.EXE to optimize memory usage.

Exercise 9: Boot Errors

1. Format a disk using the A drive and make it bootable.
2. Delete COMMAND.COM from the A drive.
3. Reboot the computer using the A drive. Notice the error message.
4. Reboot the computer using the C drive.
5. Copy the COMMAND.COM file from the C drive to the A drive.
6. Delete the IO.SYS file from the A drive.
7. Reboot the computer using the A drive. Notice the error message.
8. Reboot the computer using the C drive.
9. Make the disk in the A drive bootable without reformatting the disk.
10. Reboot the computer using the bootable disk.
11. Remove the bootable disk and insert a formatted nonbootable disk in the A drive.
12. Execute MSD.EXE from the C:\DOS directory.
13. Exit MSD.EXE. Notice the error message.
14. Remove the non-bootable disk and insert the boot disk into the A drive.

Exercise 10: Troubleshooting the AUTOEXEC.BAT and CONFIG.SYS Files

1. Format the disk from Exercise 9 using drive A and make it bootable.
2. Create the following CONFIG.SYS file:

```
FILE=60
LASTDRIVE=Z
STACKS=9,256
DEVICE=C:\HIMEM.SYS
DEVICE=C:\EMM386.EXE NOEMS
DOS-HIGH
DEVICEHIGH=C:\ANSI.SYS
DEVICEHIGH=C:\DOS\SETVER.EXE
DEVICEHIGH=C:\DOS\DOSKEY.COM
```

3. Create the following AUTOEXEC.BAT file:

```
@ECHO OFF
PATH=C:\DOSC:\WINDOWS
PROMPT $P$G
SET TEMP=C:\DOS
DEL C:\DOS\*.TMP
```

4. Find and correct all of the errors.

Exercise 11: INSTALLING DOS

1. Reformat the hard drive.
2. Install DOS using the DOS installation disks.
3. Install the mouse driver.
4. Install the CD-ROM drivers and sound card drivers.
5. Modify the AUTOEXEC.BAT and CONFIG.SYS files to do the following:
    a. Load DOSKEY.COM in upper memory
    b. Set the standard DOS prompt (path and greater-than sign)
    c. Set the search path to include the DOS and Windows directories
    d. Store the temporary files in the C:\DOS directory
    e. Delete the temporary files stored in the C:\DOS directory
    f. If your computer has Windows 3.XX, start Windows
    g. Create a 2,048 KB disk cache that reduces to 128 KB when running Windows
    h. Load all device drivers needed for the mouse, CD-ROM, and sound card into upper memory

21

Windows 3.XX

INTRODUCTION

Windows 3.XX is a graphical user interface (GUI) that works on top of DOS. Although DOS and Windows 3.XX are being replaced by newer operating systems such as Windows 95 and 98 and Windows NT, there are many existing machines that cannot support Windows 95 or 98 or Windows NT. Therefore, you may be called on to configure or troubleshoot a system running Windows 3.XX.

OBJECTIVES

1. List and describe the characteristics of Windows 3.XX.
2. Describe cooperative multitasking.
3. List what is needed in the CONFIG.SYS and AUTOEXEC.BAT files so that Windows will run properly.
4. Start Windows and perform normal file, directory, and disk maintenance tasks.
5. Create, manage, and delete icons and groups in the Program Manager.
6. Use OLE and DDE between common Windows applications.
7. Describe and modify the REG.DAT file using REGEDIT.EXE.
8. Install and configure a DOS program so that it can run under Windows properly.
9. Configure Windows 3.XX using the Setup Program and the Control Panel.
10. List and describe the common initialization files used in Windows.
11. Modify the common initialization files.
12. Install Windows and common Windows applications.
13. Explain what a general protection fault is and how to isolate such a problem.
14. Explain how free system resources affect the performance and reliability of the system.
15. Determine and correct a problem in Windows 3.XX.

21.1 WHAT IS WINDOWS 3.XX?

As a **graphical user interface (GUI),** Windows 3.XX uses icons to represent programs. The keyboard can be used to navigate Windows, but it was made for a mouse. Windows 3.XX is loaded after DOS boots the computer. Although it has many of the features and characteristics of an operating system, Windows 3.XX is considered an operating environment, not an operating system, because it cannot boot by itself. Windows got its name because all applications and documents run inside a window on the screen. The windows can be resized by grabbing their borders and the entire window can be moved around the screen. (See fig. 21.1.)

21.1.1 ADVANTAGES OF WINDOWS 3.XX

Compared to DOS, Windows is easier and more intuitive to use. To start a program or to perform some file or disk management in DOS, a command has to be typed at the prompt. If the command is typed incorrectly, DOS will usually generate a somewhat cryptic error message. To perform the same functions in Windows 3.XX, the user would typically double-click on an icon with the mouse to start a program or use the File Manager to perform most of the file and directory management. In addition to ease of use, Windows has many other features, such as sharing a common interface, multitasking, and data sharing.

Most applications made for Windows share the same interface. Programs like Microsoft Word, Microsoft Excel, Adobe Photoshop, and Corel Draw all have a common look and feel to them. For example, you will usually find New, Save, Save As, Exit/Close, and Print

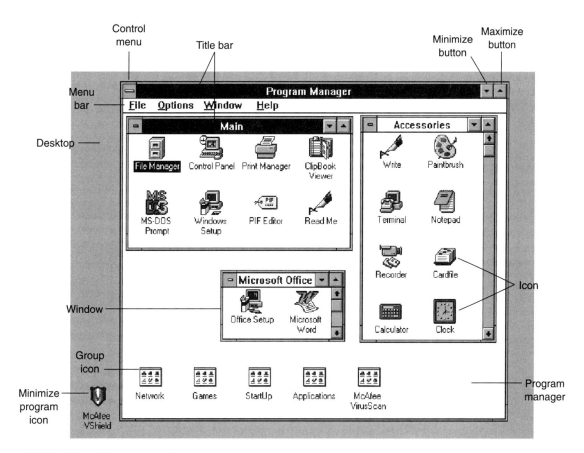

FIGURE 21.1   Windows 3.XX

options under the File menu, and you will usually find Cut, Copy, and Paste under the Edit menu. The Windows menu allows changing between different documents within the same application. Most applications also have minimize and maximize buttons in the top right corner and a control menu box (hyphen) in the top left corner of the program windows. Therefore, even if you start a program that you have never used before, there are certain things that you can expect.

Typically, DOS is a single-user, single-tasking operating system. If you wish to multi-task DOS applications, you would typically install software that supports task switching. Task switching allows loading multiple applications at the same time. Unfortunately, only one application can be active at a time, the other applications are suspended. Windows 3.XX uses **cooperative multitasking.** The user can start Microsoft Word to type a report, start Microsoft Excel to calculate some numbers, then switch back to Word to type those numbers, or cut or copy the numbers from Excel and paste them into the Word report. Again, the user doesn't have to save the information, exit Word, and then start Excel. In addition, while one application is active, the other applications can still perform assigned tasks in the background.

Cooperative multitasking is based on cooperation among applications. The microprocessor can run only one application at a time, and its quick switching back and forth between different applications makes it appear that they are all running at the same time. Cooperative multitasking in Windows 3.XX requires that the application using the microprocessor voluntarily give back control to other programs. If a software application were poorly written so that it does not give up control, that would cause problems for other applications.

21.1.2   HISTORY OF WINDOWS

The first version of Windows, Windows 1.0, appeared in 1985, followed by Windows 2.0 (Windows 286 and Windows 386). Unfortunately, the early Windows interface was not

TABLE 21.1 Specifications for running Windows 3.1

Standard Mode	Enhanced Mode
286 microprocessor or higher	386 microprocessor or higher
640 KB of conventional memory	640 KB of conventional memory
256 KB of extended memory	1,024 KB of extended memory
6 MB of free disk space (9 MB recommended)	8 MB of free disk space (10 MB recommended)
Floppy disk drive	Floppy disk drive
EGA monitor or better	EGA monitor or better
Mouse	Mouse
DOS 3.1 or higher (DOS 5.0 or higher recommended)	DOS 3.1 or higher (DOS 5.0 or higher recommended)

attractive to users and its performance was poor. In 1990, as Microsoft and IBM were introducing OS/2, Microsoft released Windows 3.0. Because this interface did not require massive upgrades to run on existing computers, it soon became the first popular icon-driven operating environment for Windows. It introduced the Program Manager and File Manager and could use more than 640 KB of RAM. In addition, it allowed virtual memory (disk space emulating RAM).

In 1992, Microsoft introduced Windows 3.1, which added newer drivers, better graphical display capability, and multimedia support. In addition, it had made Windows 3.1 more reliable than previous versions. The latest (and the last) version of Windows is Windows 3.11 for Workgroups (WFW). It offered support for both 16-bit and 32-bit applications, 32-bit file and disk access, larger resource heaps, and peer-to-peer networking.

21.2 STARTING WINDOWS 3.XX

The specifications in table 21.1 must be satisfied to run Windows 3.1 on a PC. As you can see from looking at the table, Windows requires extended memory. Therefore, HIMEM.SYS must be loaded in the CONFIG.SYS file. In addition, although not required to start Windows, EMM386.EXE and DOS=HIGH,UMB should be executed so that TSRs and device drivers can be moved into upper memory to free conventional memory and allow Windows to run more efficiently.

In the AUTOEXEC.BAT file, the Windows installation adds the Windows directory to the PATH statement, loads the SMARTDRV.EXE, and sets the TEMP environment variable (if one was not set) to the C:\WINDOWS\TEMP directory. The Windows directory listed in the PATH statement allows Windows to be started from any directory. SMART-DRV, a disk cache, increases Windows performance significantly. The TEMP variable is used to tell Windows and Windows applications where to store temporary files. If the variable is not set to an existing directory that has free disk space, there will be errors when running Windows and Windows applications. (Note: To start Windows automatically, the WIN command must be added to the end of the AUTOEXEC.BAT file.)

21.2.1 WIN.COM AND OPERATING MODES

The file used to start Windows is WIN.COM, which is located in the Windows directory. Because it is used to load Windows, it is sometimes referred to as the *loader file*. Its task is to check the machine type, memory configuration, and device drivers to determine which mode to operate (real mode, standard mode, or enhanced 386 mode). Table 21.2 describes the switches available to the WIN.COM file.

Real mode, mostly used on XT computers, was devised to run Windows applications created before Windows 3.0. It recognizes only the first 1 MB of RAM and is available only in Windows 3.0. To force Windows into real mode (assuming that the machine is capable of real mode), WIN /R is entered at the command prompt.

**TABLE 21.2   WIN.COM
Switches**

Available Switches	Function
WIN /?	Help for the WIN.COM command, showing all available switches.
WIN /R	Starts Windows in real mode.
WIN /S	Starts Windows in standard mode.
WIN /3	Starts Windows in enhanced mode.
WIN /B	Creates BOOTLOG.TXT, which records system messages generated during system start-up.
WIN /D:XXX	Used for troubleshooting.
	WIN /D:C Turns off 32-bit file access
	WIN /D:F Turns off 32-bit disk access
	WIN /D:S Specifies that Windows should not use ROM address space between F000:0000 and 1 MB for the breakpoint
	WIN /D:V Specifies that the ROM routine will handle interrupts from the hard disk controller
	WIN /D:X Excludes all of the adapter area from the range of memory that Windows scans to find unused space, which is equivalent to EMMExclude=A000–EFFF
WIN :	Starts Windows without showing the Windows start-up logo.
WIN /N	Starts Windows without starting the network.

Standard mode is the normal operating mode for a 286 computer. It allows multiple Windows programs to run at the same time and provides direct access to the extended memory. Therefore, Windows running in standard mode treats the total free conventional memory and extended memory as one contiguous memory block. Although standard mode does not use expanded memory, it can emulate expanded memory for DOS applications that require it. It will also run one DOS application under a full screen (not in a window). To force Windows into standard mode (assuming that the machine is capable of standard mode), WIN /S is entered at the command prompt.

The mode used most often is the **enhanced 386 mode,** which was made for the 386 computer. It allows multiple DOS and Windows applications to run at the same time and provides direct access to extended memory and virtual memory. Therefore, Windows running in enhanced 386 mode treats the total free conventional memory, extended memory, and virtual memory as one contiguous memory block. (**Virtual memory** is disk space that acts like RAM.) The more memory available, of course, the more applications can be run and the more documents can be opened. Like the standard mode, the enhanced 386 mode does not use expanded memory but can emulate expanded memory for DOS applications that require it. To force Windows into enhanced mode (if the machine is capable of enhanced 386 mode), WIN /3 is entered at the command prompt. (Note: Windows 3.11 for Workgroups runs only in enhanced 386 mode.)

21.2.2   IMPORTANT WINDOWS FILES

On start-up, Windows will eventually load the core files, the kernel file (KRNL286.EXE for standard mode or KRNL386.EXE for enhanced 386 mode), USER.EXE, and GDI.EXE. In addition, it will load the appropriate device drivers, font files (TTF, FON, or FOT filename extensions), dynamic link library files (DLL), and the support files for non-Windows (DOS) applications.

The **kernel** files control and allocate the machine resources, such as memory, and run and coordinate software applications. The User component manages input (from the keyboard and mouse) and output to the user interface (windows, icons, menus, and so on). The GDI.EXE controls the graphics device interface, which creates images on the video system, including windows, icons, and buttons on the screen. When you double-click on an icon, the USER.EXE interprets the double-click and tells the GDI.EXE to draw a window on the screen.

Unlike DOS, Windows uses one set of drivers to enable and control hardware devices. For example, only one mouse driver needs to be loaded and that mouse will be available for all Windows applications. The video drivers, printer drivers, keyboard drivers, sound drivers, network drivers, and system drivers operate in the same way.

Dynamic link library (DLL) files include sets of instructions and/or data that can be accessed at any time. They usually have a DLL filename extension. The purpose of DLL files is to modularize Windows—instead of one huge file containing all of the instructions needed for Windows, the instructions are broken down into smaller executable and DLL files. This allows the sharing of common code between executable files or breaking an application into separate components that can be easily upgraded.

PROGMAN.EXE is Windows' **Program Manager,** which is the core component of the graphical user interface. It usually fills most if not all of the desktop and contains the group windows and icons. The group windows contain the program applications, represented by icons. (Note: A program icon may appear in any or all program groups any number of times.)

21.2.3   WINDOWS 3.XX MEMORY MANAGEMENT

When running in enhanced 386 mode, Windows treats the conventional, extended, and virtual memory as one contiguous pool of memory and divides the memory into **heaps.** When a program is loaded into RAM, Windows takes memory from the heap and assigns it to the program. Theoretically, when the program is terminated, the memory used by the program goes back to the heap so that it can be reallocated to other programs. When a program does not return a portion of the memory to the heap this is known as a memory leak. The largest of the heaps is the system heap, the one used by the active programs and data. The remaining heaps are usually much smaller (64 KB): the GDI heap keeps track of fonts, icons, and mouse pointers, while the user heap keeps track of the windows and dialog boxes; the menu heap keeps track of menus, and the text string heap holds Windows text.

21.2.4   WINA20.386 AND IFSHLP.SYS

Windows 3.0 running in 386 enhanced mode requires the WINA20.386 file; Windows 3.1 or higher does not. The newer Windows versions running with a 3.0 driver may be unstable if the WINA20.386 file is missing. Of course, Windows 3.1 or higher running without a 3.0 driver does not need the WINA20.386 file, so it can be deleted. If you are unsure whether a 3.0 driver is loaded, it is best to keep the file.

The WINA20.386 file is usually kept in the root directory. If the file is moved to another directory, DOS and Windows must be alerted by adding SWITCHES=/W in the DOS CONFIG.SYS file and a DEVICE command in the [386Enh] section of the Windows SYSTEM.INI file. For example, if the WINA20.386 file is moved to the WINDOWS directory, the DEVICE command would appear as DEVICE=C:\WINDOWS\WINA20.386. Initialization files (files with an INI filename extension) will be discussed later in this chapter.

The IFSHLP.SYS is the installable file system helper driver that provides 32-bit file system access for Windows for Workgroups and is usually needed for 32-bit disk access, 32-bit file access, and network access. It is located in the WINDOWS directory and loaded in the CONFIG.SYS file with the DEVICE or DEVICEHIGH command.

21.3   FILE AND DISK MANAGEMENT

File Manager (WINFILE.EXE), located in the Main group, is an application included with Windows that manages disks, directories, and files. (See fig. 21.2.) It permits the user to:

1. Create and remove directories
2. Delete, copy, rename, and move files
3. Copy and format disks
4. View and change attributes

FIGURE 21.2 File Manager

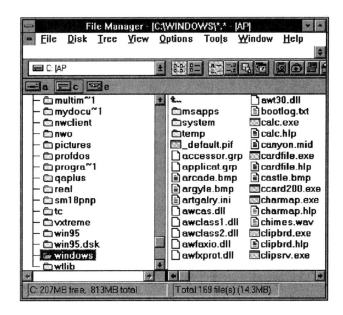

The Disk menu is used to perform disk commands (DISKCOPY, LABEL, FORMAT, and SYS). The File menu is used to perform file and directory commands (COPY, MOVE, DEL, REN, RD, and MD). Not all tasks require using the menus. A file or directory is moved to a different directory by simply dragging the item to the new location. A file or directory is moved to a different drive by pressing and holding down the Shift key and dragging the item to the drive. Copying an item to a different drive is accomplished by dragging the item to the appropriate drive icon. Copying to the same drive is done by pressing and holding down the Ctrl key and dragging the item to the drive. Any time that a file or directory is dragged to the drive icons under the menu bar, the file or directory will be copied or moved to the current directory of that drive.

A file or directory is deleted by selecting it and pressing the Del key on the keyboard or selecting the Delete... option from the File menu. A file or directory is renamed by selecting the file or directory and choosing the Rename... option from the File menu. The attributes of a file are shown or changed by selecting the file and the Properties... option from the File menu. In File Manager, the Ctrl or the Shift key can be pressed to select more than one file or directory. After the files are selected, they can then be copied, moved, or deleted all at the same time. Holding down the Ctrl key will select any file or subdirectory within the same directory. Holding down the Shift key while selecting two files or directories will select everything listed between the two. Again, after the file or directories have been selected, they can then be copied, deleted, or moved as one.

While running Windows, a DOS prompt (window or full screen) can always be started to perform DOS commands. This is done with the DOS Prompt icon in the Main group.

21.4 RUNNING WINDOWS PROGRAMS

The Program Manager is used to run and manage programs, including starting programs, opening documents, creating groups and icons, moving and deleting icons, and changing the properties of a group or icon.

21.4.1 STARTING A WINDOWS PROGRAM

There are several ways to run a Windows program. The easiest way to start a program is to double-click on its icon. Another way to start a Windows program is to use the Run... option under the File menu and then specify the path (location) of the executable file, including the filename, or use the Browse button to locate the executable file. (See fig. 21.3.) The third way is to double-click the executable file using File Manager.

FIGURE 21.3   Windows 3.XX
Run option

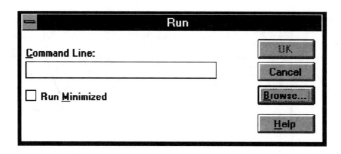

Because Windows is a multitasking environment, it allows the user to start one program and then switch back to the Program Manager or File Manager to start another program. When multiple applications are running, the user can then switch back and forth between the different applications. One way to do this is to press and hold down the Alt key and repeatedly press the Tab key until the application appears, or the Alt+Esc keys can be used to move to the next application. A third way to switch applications is to access the Task list with the Ctrl+Esc keys and double-click on the desired program or select the desired program and click on the Switch To button.

21.4.2   MANAGING GROUPS AND ICONS

By default, Windows has several existing groups of programs. They include the Main group, Accessories group, StartUp group, Games group, and Applications group. (See table 21.3.) The New... option under the File menu can be used to make a new program group or program item (icon). The Program group will ask for the description (name) of the new group and the group filename (a GRP file that stores information about the icons located in the group). If a group filename is not specified, it will select one based on the description of the group. The program item will ask for the description (name) of the icon, the command line (path of the file and any switches that are required), and a working directory. Again, the Browse... button can be used to select the location of the executable file. A quicker way to create a program item is to drag an executable file from the File Manager to the Program Manager. To delete a group, it must first be closed and, while it is highlighted, the Del key on the keyboard is pressed or the Delete option from the File menu is selected. An icon is deleted by selecting it and pressing the Del key on the keyboard or selecting the Delete option from the File menu. The Properties... option from the File menu is used to rename a selected group, to change the description of an icon, or to change the command parameters.

TABLE 21.3   Default Windows groups

Group	Description	Application Icons
Main	Windows system applications	File Manager, Control Panel, Print Manager, MS-DOS prompt, Windows Setup, and PIF Editor
Accessories	Simple Windows-based applications	Microsoft Write, Notepad, Paintbrush, Clock, Calendar, and Calculator
Applications	Applications found on the hard disk during Setup	
Games	Games included with Windows designed to develop Windows skills, such as how to use the mouse	Solitaire and Minesweeper
StartUp	Applications that automatically start when Windows is started	

FIGURE 21.4 Paste Special option

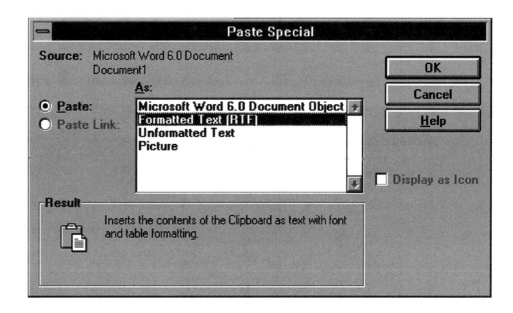

21.4.3 SHARING DATA

To share data between documents, Windows applications can use **dynamic data exchange (DDE)** or **object linking and embedding (OLE).**

DDE, introduced with Windows 3.0, allows users to copy data between applications while maintaining a link. Whenever data is changed at the source, it is also changed at the target. For example, an Excel chart could be inserted into a Word document, and as the spreadsheet data changes, the chart in the document changes. Although DDE is still used by many applications, it is slowly being replaced by OLE.

OLE (an enhanced version of DDE) is a compound document standard developed by Microsoft. It allows the user to create objects with one application and then link or embed them into another application. Embedded objects keep their original format and links to the application that created them. For example, an Excel chart inserted into a Word document can be changed by double-clicking on the chart from within the Word document. Excel would then run from within the Word document, allowing changes to be made without going to the Program Manager and starting Excel in its own window.

A common way to move data between applications or documents is to use the Clipboard. The Copy or Cut options from the Edit menu in the source application sends highlighted text or a selected picture into RAM, specifically to the Clipboard. The Paste option from the Edit menu then causes the source application to copy the data from the Clipboard into the target document using the first available format. The Paste Special option causes a dialog box to appear, listing the formats available for pasting the data. (See fig. 21.4.) The Paste Link option causes the application to make an OLE link to the source document. If the ObjectLink format isn't available, a DDE link is created instead.

In standard mode or 386 enhanced mode using an enhanced keyboard, the Print Screen option places a bitmap picture of the entire screen on the Clipboard. Pressing Alt+Print Screen places a bitmap picture on the Clipboard of the active window. (Note: When the computer is running in standard mode, graphics from an MS-DOS program cannot be copied onto the Clipboard.)

21.4.4 WINDOWS REGISTRY

The Windows registry (REG.DAT) is a special configuration database that is used by the File Manager to allow a selected document with a specific filename extension to be opened in the application in which it was created. (See fig. 21.5.) It is also used to identify what application an OLE object came from and allows the data document to be dragged to the Print Manager and be automatically printed without opening the application.

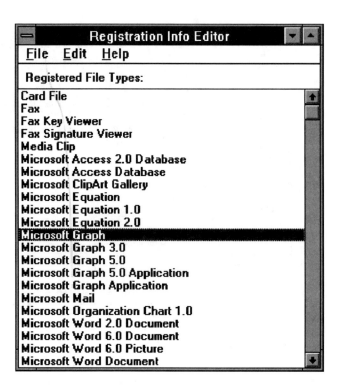

FIGURE 21.5   Windows 3.XX registry

The registration information editor (REGEDIT.EXE) allows the user to make changes to the REG.DAT file. If a Windows application has a registration file (file with a REG filename extension), the information can be installed or merged into the registration database. This is done by using the Merge Registration File option from the File menu. Double-clicking on the registration file in File Manager will automatically install the registration file. If there is no registration file or the user wishes to assign a filename extension to a particular program, the Add File Type option from the Edit menu in the registration information editor will accomplish these tasks.

Like any database, the REG.DAT file can become corrupt. Some of the symptoms of a corrupted registry are:

1. A file selected in the File Manager does not open
2. File Manager will not print a document
3. An error message appears indicating a problem with the registry, Windows registry database, or OLE
4. The REG.DAT file exceeds 65,536 bytes

To correct a corrupted registry, first back up the REG.DAT file to another directory or another name. Next, using the Run option under the File menu, perform the following command to rebuild the original registry:

```
REGEDIT /U C:\WINDOWS\SYSTEM\SETUP.REG
```

If the REG.DAT file does not exist in the C:\WINDOWS\SYSTEM directory, restart Windows. From the File Manager, select the REG.DAT file and choose the Associate option from the File menu and associate it with REGEDIT.EXE. Next, associate any file with a REG filename extension and restart Windows. Lastly, search for all files that have a REG filename extension on the system by merging them using REGEDIT or by double-clicking them in File Manager.

21.4.5   INSTALLING PROGRAMS

To install a Windows program, start the executable program that starts the installation process using the Run... option under the File menu or by using the File Manager. The most common installation files are INSTALL.EXE and SETUP.EXE.

464

FIGURE 21.6   DOS window

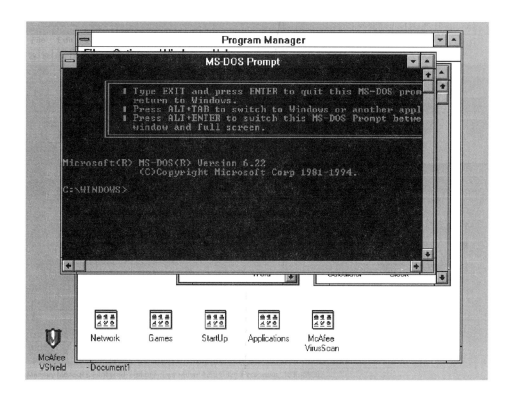

21.5   RUNNING DOS APPLICATIONS IN WINDOWS

Although Windows does a much better job running Windows applications, it can also run DOS programs (sometimes referred to as *non-Windows* programs). To start a DOS application, use File Manager or the Run… option in the File menu, or create an icon pointing to the executable file that starts the DOS program. A DOS session can also be started by using the MS-DOS prompt icon in the Main group and executing the executable file. (See fig. 21.6.)

After a DOS application is running, it can be run in a full screen or within a window (which can be moved and resized). When running a text-based DOS program in a window, Windows will show the DOS-based application in graphics mode. This allows cutting, copying, and pasting between the DOS application and other applications. Because Windows must convert the DOS text into a graphic image, DOS applications running in a DOS window are more resource intensive than a DOS program running in a full screen.

If an application needs expanded memory, an expanded memory board with the appropriate drivers must be loaded or EMM386.EXE (with the appropriate parameters) must be loaded in the CONFIG.SYS file so that extended memory can simulate expanded memory. In addition, even though Windows has its own built-in mouse driver, to use a mouse within a DOS application a mouse driver must be loaded in the AUTOEXEC.BAT or CONFIG.SYS file. After the expanded memory is active, a program information file (PIF) is used to specify the amount of expanded memory to be allotted to the program. (PIF is explained in section 21.5.3.)

21.5.1   DOS PROGRAMS IN STANDARD MODE

If Windows is running in standard mode, a DOS application cannot run as a window application, only as a full-screen application. If more than one DOS application is loaded at a time, each application will run in full screen. Unfortunately, only the current DOS application will be processed and all other DOS applications would be suspended (task switching).

When Windows is running a DOS application, it emulates a DOS real-mode environment out of extended memory and creates a temporary application swap file for that application. When the user switches away from the DOS application, Windows moves some or all of the application from memory to the application swap file. When the DOS program is ended, the application swap file is automatically deleted. Of course, the amount of hard

FIGURE 21.7   PIF Editor

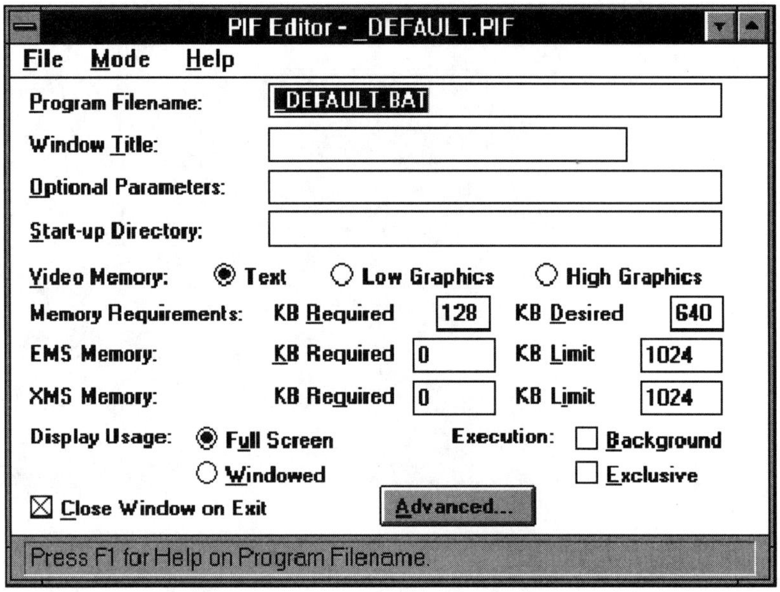

```
┌─────────────────────────────────────────────────────────────┐
│ ─          PIF Editor - _DEFAULT.PIF                  ▼ ▲    │
├─────────────────────────────────────────────────────────────┤
│  File   Mode   Help                                          │
│                                                               │
│  Program Filename:     │_DEFAULT.BAT                      │   │
│                                                               │
│  Window Title:         │                                 │   │
│                                                               │
│  Optional Parameters:  │                                 │   │
│                                                               │
│  Start-up Directory:   │                                 │   │
│                                                               │
│  Video Memory:      ⦿ Text    ○ Low Graphics   ○ High Graphics│
│  Memory Requirements:  KB Required │128│  KB Desired  │640│   │
│  EMS Memory:           KB Required │0│    KB Limit    │1024│  │
│  XMS Memory:           KB Required │0│    KB Limit    │1024│  │
│  Display Usage: ⦿ Full Screen   Execution: ☐ Background      │
│                 ○ Windowed                  ☐ Exclusive       │
│  ☒ Close Window on Exit    │ Advanced... │                   │
├─────────────────────────────────────────────────────────────┤
│ Press F1 for Help on Program Filename.                       │
└─────────────────────────────────────────────────────────────┘
```

disk space available determines how many application swap files Windows can create, which determines how many non-Windows applications can be started before running out of memory.

21.5.2   DOS PROGRAMS IN 386 ENHANCED MODE

In 386 enhanced mode, multiple DOS applications can be run at the same time, and most DOS applications can be run in a window. Each time a DOS application is run in 386 enhanced mode, Windows creates a virtual 8086 machine to run the application. The virtual 8086 machine emulates an 8086 microprocessor and RAM. To multitask DOS applications, the microprocessor switches back and forth between the different 8086 machines very rapidly, so it appears that all of the applications are running at the same time. The amount of processing done by the microprocessor is determined by the time slice value assigned to the DOS application. Therefore, Windows 3.XX uses preemptive scheduling with DOS applications and cooperative scheduling with Windows applications.

If a DOS application performs screen actions that are incompatible with Windows, the DOS application can't run in a window. However, most of these applications can run successfully at full screen. If the application uses a lot of graphic or memory resources, it should be run at full screen (exclusive) with high graphics that retain video memory. These settings are selected in the program information files.

21.5.3   PROGRAM INFORMATION FILES (PIF)

A **program information file (PIF)** contains information about a DOS program running in Windows. The file defines how much memory the program needs and how it uses various system components. Windows provides PIFs for many common MS-DOS-based applications; some companies will include their own PIFs. If PIFs have been provided by both Windows and a software manufacturer, use the PIF supplied by the manufacturer. An application that does not have a PIF will use the default PIF (_DEFAULT.PIF). Many DOS applications that do not work in Windows may work after a PIF has been created or modified using the PIF Editor located in the Main group. (See fig. 21.7.)

The PIF file for an application should be located in the application's directory or the Windows directory. An icon that points to the PIF, not the executable file, activates the PIF, which will specify the executable file and its operating parameters. (Note: Executing the MS-DOS prompt icon in the Main group executes a DOSPRMPT.PIF file.)

466

TABLE 21.4   Control Panel icons

Icon	Function
Color	Selects color schemes or customizes the colors used for the desktop, the area of the screen in which windows, icons, and dialog boxes appear
Date/Time	Changes the system date and time
Desktop	Changes the screen background and customizes the way windows and icons appear on the screen; selects and configures the screen saver
Drivers	Installs multimedia drivers
Enhanced 386	Changes virtual memory and 32-bit disk and file access
Fax	Configures the fax
Fonts	Manages the fonts on the system, including adding and deleting fonts
International	Configures international settings
Keyboard	Adjusts how the keyboard responds under Windows
Mouse	Adjusts how the mouse responds under Windows
ODBC	Configures the programming interface that enables applications to access data in a database management system that uses SQL as a data access standard
Ports	Configures the serial ports
Printers	Adds, deletes, and configures printers
Sound	Assigns different sounds to system and application events or specifies MIDI settings

FIGURE 21.8   Windows 3.XX Control Panel

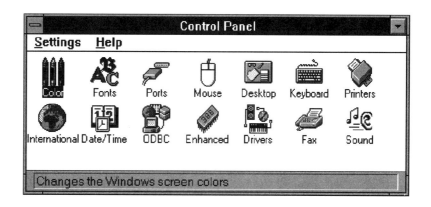

21.6 CONFIGURING WINDOWS

Windows is usually configured with the Control Panel and the Windows Setup program, both of which are located in the Main group. The **Control Panel** is a graphical tool for configuring the Windows environment and hardware devices. The Windows Setup program changes the video, keyboard, and mouse drivers.

21.6.1   THE CONTROL PANEL

The Control Panel (CONTROL.EXE) contains the icons listed in table 21.4 and shown in fig. 21.8. To make the Control Panel more versatile, some programs add additional icons. Whenever a change is made in the Control Panel, it is usually written into the WIN.INI, SYSTEM.INI, or CONTROL.INI file so that the configuration will be remembered.

FIGURE 21.9   Windows Setup program

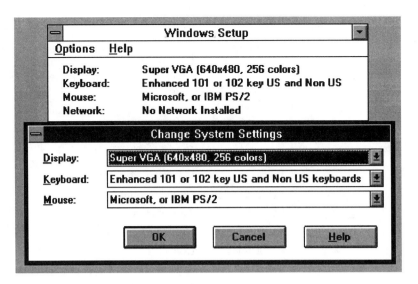

FIGURE 21.10   Using SETUP.EXE from the WINDOWS directory to change the video or mouse driver

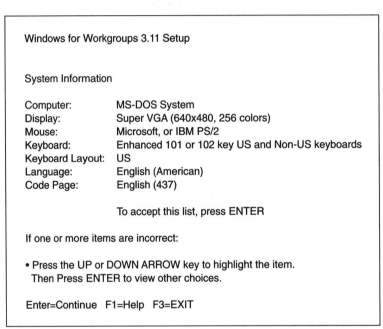

21.6.2   THE VIDEO SYSTEM, KEYBOARD, AND MOUSE

There are two ways to change the video, keyboard and mouse drivers: using the Windows Setup program (located in the Main group) or running the SETUP.EXE at the command prompt from within the Windows directory. (See figs. 21.9 and 21.10.)

Question: You change the video driver using the Windows Setup program. You then restart Windows and the screen is unreadable. You assume that the driver you selected is incompatible with your video system. What can you do?

Answer: Usually, you will have to reboot the computer. If Windows automatically starts during boot-up because it is listed in the AUTOEXEC.BAT file, you will have to use the F8 key or boot from a floppy disk so that Windows will not start. You then switch to the WINDOWS directory and execute the SETUP.EXE program. Because the SETUP.EXE executed at the command prompt from within the WINDOWS directory is a text-based program, you can then change to the correct driver.

If the wrong mouse driver is loaded, it is easiest to exit Windows and use the SETUP.EXE from the WINDOWS directory to change it. Another way is with keyboard commands. (Note: A serial mouse can be connected only to COM1 or COM2 in Windows 3.XX.) After

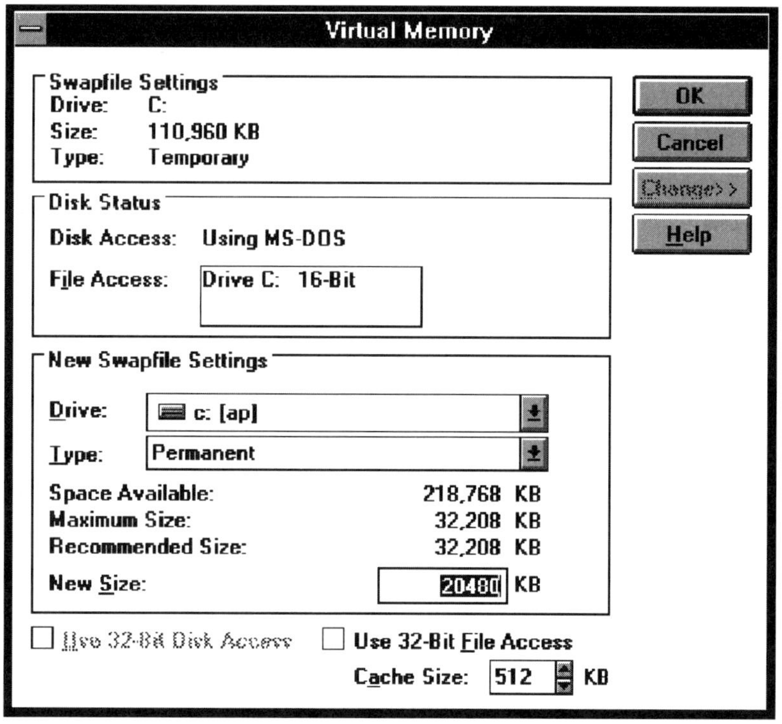

FIGURE 21.11 Configuring the virtual memory of Windows 3.XX

```
┌─────────────────────────────────────────────────────────────────┐
│ ─                        Virtual Memory                           │
│ ┌─ Swapfile Settings ──────────────────────────┐   ┌─────────┐  │
│ │  Drive:    C:                                 │   │   OK    │  │
│ │  Size:     110,960 KB                         │   └─────────┘  │
│ │  Type:     Temporary                          │   ┌─────────┐  │
│ └───────────────────────────────────────────────┘   │ Cancel  │  │
│ ┌─ Disk Status ─────────────────────────────────┐   └─────────┘  │
│ │  Disk Access:   Using MS-DOS                  │   ┌─────────┐  │
│ │                                               │   │ Change>>│  │
│ │  File Access:  │Drive C:  16-Bit           │  │   └─────────┘  │
│ │                └──────────────────────────┘  │   ┌─────────┐  │
│ └───────────────────────────────────────────────┘   │  Help   │  │
│                                                      └─────────┘  │
│ ┌─ New Swapfile Settings ──────────────────────────────────────┐ │
│ │  Drive:    │▭ c: [ap]                              │±│      │ │
│ │  Type:     │Permanent                              │±│      │ │
│ │  Space Available:           218,768  KB                      │ │
│ │  Maximum Size:               32,208  KB                      │ │
│ │  Recommended Size:           32,208  KB                      │ │
│ │  New Size:                  │ 20480 │ KB                     │ │
│ └──────────────────────────────────────────────────────────────┘ │
│   ☐ Use 32-Bit Disk Access    ☐ Use 32-Bit File Access          │
│                              Cache Size: │512│▲▼ KB              │
└─────────────────────────────────────────────────────────────────┘
```

the correct mouse and keyboard drivers are loaded, they can be configured using the Control Panel, specifically the mouse and keyboard icons. For example, the double-click speed of the mouse, the track speed of the mouse, and the amount of time it takes for the keyboard to start repeating after a letter is pressed and kept down can all be specified.

21.6.3 VIRTUAL MEMORY AND 32-BIT DISK AND FILE ACCESS

If Windows is running in 386 enhanced mode, it can use virtual memory—disk space simulating RAM that allows running more applications at one time than the system's physical memory would usually allow. Since a hard drive is slower than RAM, virtual memory is also considered slow. Therefore, some experts recommend using only small amounts of virtual memory (5 MB or less).

In Windows 3.XX, the virtual memory file is called a **swap file.** It is configured using the Virtual button in the 386 Enhanced icon in the Control Panel. (See fig. 21.11.) There are two types of swap files, the permanent swap file and the temporary swap file. A permanent swap file is a permanent contiguous file that always remains on the hard drive, even after exiting Windows. It consists of two files: SPART.PAR, which is a read-only file in the WINDOWS directory, and 386SPAR.PAR, which is a hidden file in the root directory of the drive specified for the swap file.

> **Question:** When using the Virtual button within the Enhanced 386 icon within the Control Panel, there is a recommended maximum size option when Permanent Swap File is selected. What does the recommended maximum size of the permanent swap file indicate?
>
> **Answer:** The recommended maximum size of the permanent swap file is the largest amount of contiguous (unfragmented) disk space available. Therefore, you cannot specify a larger swap file size than the recommended size because the permanent swap file must be one contiguous file.

Unlike the permanent swap file, the temporary swap file (WIN386.SWP) is created whenever Windows is started, and it will shrink and grow as the work is being done. Because it is temporary, the temporary swap file is deleted when the user quits Windows.

Of the two types of swap files, the permanent swap file offers the better performance. The default and recommended size should be ignored and the swap file should be restricted to 5 MB. The smaller swap file will force Windows not to use the swap file all of the time, thus improving performance. The command Set PageOverCommit=1 in the [386Enh] should also be added to the SYSTEM.INI file. (The SYSTEM.INI file is explained in section 21.10.2.) The temporary swap file should be used only when a permanent swap file is not possible, such as when the hard drive is too fragmented or the temporary files must be placed on a network drive. If either swap file becomes corrupt, select the Enhanced 386 button in the Control Panel, click on the Virtual Memory button, and specify no swap file. After Windows 3.XX is rebooted, the swap file can then be recreated.

If the computer has a Western Digital 1003 hard drive controller or equivalent and is running in 386 enhanced mode, 32-bit disk access can be enabled. The 32-bit disk access bypasses the ROM BIOS and uses 32-bit code to drive the disk controller and transfer data. Since Windows does not have to slow down by switching to real mode and communicating with the ROM BIOS chip, performance is improved. (Note: For hard drives larger than 528 MB, a driver is often needed to enable the 32-bit disk access.) 32-bit disk access can be unreliable on some battery-powered portable computers when the computer's power-saving features are enabled.

Windows for Workgroups 3.11 can use 16-bit file access (default) or 32-bit file access. When 16-bit file access is used, a 16-bit SMARTDRV cache is created. If the 32-bit file access is selected, a 32-bit cache is created for file management on the hard drives, and SMARTDRV cache is used only for the floppy disk drives. If the floppy disk drives are rarely or never used, the SMARTDRV Windows cache can be set to 0 KB to conserve memory. If the floppy disk drive is used occasionally, the size or the SMARTDRV Windows cache can be reduced (such as to 128 KB) to save memory.

21.7   FONTS

A **font,** or typeface, is a collection of characters (letters, numerals, symbols, and punctuation marks) that have common characteristics. Font sizes are usually expressed in points (a point is $1/_{72}$ of an inch), and fonts can have different styles (**bold,** *italics,* and underline). The font, the size of the font, and the style greatly affect the overall impact of a document.

A font can be described by its pitch, spacing, weight, and width. In a fixed font, such as Courier, every character occupies the same amount of space. In a proportional font, such as Arial or Times New Roman, the character width varies. The letter W is much wider than the letter i. The pitch, usually a characteristic of fixed-width fonts, is specified in characters per inch (CPI): 10 CPI = 12 points and 12 CPI = 10 points. The weight of a font refers to the heaviness of the strokes that make up a character; they can be designated light, regular, book, demi, heavy, black, and extra bold. The width refers to whether the standard font has been expanded or compressed horizontally. Fonts can also be described as serif and sans-serif. A serif font, such as Times New Roman and Courier, has projections that extend from the upper and lower strokes of the letters; sans-serif fonts, such as Arial, do not have serifs.

21.7.1   SCREEN AND PRINTER FONTS

Fonts used in computers can be classified depending on the output device. Screen fonts are used to represent characters on the monitor; printer fonts are used by the printer. The printer fonts can be further broken down into device fonts (fonts built into the printer), downloadable soft fonts (fonts downloaded into the printer), and printable screen fonts.

Windows uses special raster fonts as the system screen font for menus, window captions, messages, and other text. A set of system, fixed, and OEM terminal fonts are shipped with Windows 3.1 to match a system's display capabilities (CGA, EGA, VGA, or 8514 video displays). The default system screen font in Windows 3.1 is System, a proportionally spaced raster font.

FIGURE 21.12   Raster fonts

FIGURE 21.13   Symbol that indicates a font is a TrueType font

21.7.2   RASTER FONTS, VECTOR FONTS, AND TRUETYPE FONTS

Windows 3.XX, Windows 95, and Windows NT come with three categories of fonts: raster fonts, vector fonts, and TrueType fonts. **Raster fonts** are bitmap pictures made of dots of different sizes for specific video display resolutions. (See fig. 21.12.) For example, MS Serif comes in 8-, 10-, 12-, and 14-point sizes for CGA, EGA, VGA, and 8514 video systems. Raster fonts have a FON filename extension and typically cannot be scaled or rotated, although Windows can scale raster fonts to even multiples of their supplied sizes. For example, MS Serif can be scaled to 16, 20, 24, and 28 points. If the size selected is too large, the characters become jagged, which is referred to as the "bitmap effect."

Vector fonts are rendered using a mathematical model that defines each character as a set of lines drawn between points. Vector fonts can be scaled to any size but cannot be rotated. Because the font has to be mathematically generated, the vector font requires more processing than the raster font. Examples of Windows vector fonts include Roman, Modern, and Script. **Outline fonts** are vector fonts in which the outline of each character is geometrically defined. The most commonly used outline fonts are TrueType and PostScript.

The fonts most commonly used in Windows 3.XX, Windows 95 and 98, and Windows NT are **TrueType fonts.** (See fig. 21.13.) TrueType, introduced in 1991 by Microsoft and Apple, is used for both the screen and the printer and therefore allows Windows to be a **What You See Is What You Get (WYSIWYG)** interface. In addition, the TrueType fonts can be scaled and rotated without distortion. Each TrueType font requires a file with a FOT filename extension and one with a TTF filename extension. The TrueType fonts installed with Windows 3.1 are Arial, Courier New, Times New Roman, and Symbol.

Fonts are managed, added, and deleted with the Font icon in the Control Panel. Loading more fonts requires Windows to use more resources to keep track of the fonts. If you load too many fonts, that could lead to "Out of Memory" error messages.

21.8   COM PORTS

The Ports icon in the Control Panel configures the serial ports, which are used to connect mice and external modems. For example, double-clicking on a port such as COM1 allows the baud rate, data bits, parity, and stop bits to be configured. If the Advanced button is then clicked, the IRQ and I/O address of the serial port can be specified. For information on installing and configuring serial ports, see chapter 18.

> **NOTE**   In Windows 3.XX, the COM port settings from within the Control Panel are often ignored except when using a serial printer or similar device that does not monitor its own speed.

FIGURE 21.14   Installing a
print driver

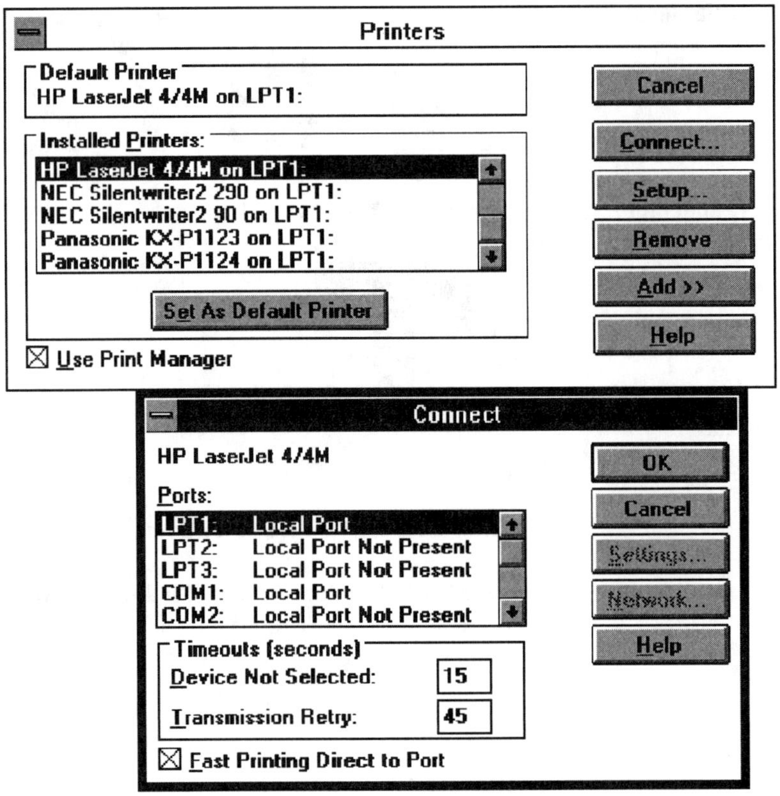

```
┌────────────────────────────────────────────────────────────┐
│ ▭                         Printers                          │
├────────────────────────────────────────────────────────────┤
│ ┌Default Printer────────────────────────┐    ┌──────────┐   │
│ │ HP LaserJet 4/4M on LPT1:              │    │  Cancel  │   │
│ └───────────────────────────────────────┘    └──────────┘   │
│ ┌Installed Printers:────────────────────┐    ┌──────────┐   │
│ │ HP LaserJet 4/4M on LPT1:          ▲  │    │ Connect… │   │
│ │ NEC Silentwriter2 290 on LPT1:     ▒  │    └──────────┘   │
│ │ NEC Silentwriter2 90 on LPT1:      ▒  │    ┌──────────┐   │
│ │ Panasonic KX-P1123 on LPT1:        ▒  │    │  Setup…  │   │
│ │ Panasonic KX-P1124 on LPT1:        ▼  │    └──────────┘   │
│ └───────────────────────────────────────┘    ┌──────────┐   │
│        ┌───────────────────────┐              │  Remove  │   │
│        │ Set As Default Printer│              └──────────┘   │
│        └───────────────────────┘              ┌──────────┐   │
│                                               │  Add >>  │   │
│ ☒ Use Print Manager                           └──────────┘   │
│                                               ┌──────────┐   │
│                                               │   Help   │   │
│                                               └──────────┘   │
└────────────────────────────────────────────────────────────┘

         ┌──────────────────────────────────────────────────┐
         │ ▭                   Connect                       │
         ├──────────────────────────────────────────────────┤
         │ HP LaserJet 4/4M                   ┌──────────┐   │
         │                                    │    OK    │   │
         │ Ports:                             └──────────┘   │
         │ ┌──────────────────────────────┐   ┌──────────┐  │
         │ │ LPT1:  Local Port          ▲ │   │  Cancel  │  │
         │ │ LPT2:  Local Port Not Present│   └──────────┘  │
         │ │ LPT3:  Local Port Not Present│   ┌──────────┐  │
         │ │ COM1:  Local Port            │   │ Settings…│  │
         │ │ COM2:  Local Port Not Present▼ │   └──────────┘  │
         │ └──────────────────────────────┘   ┌──────────┐  │
         │ ┌Timeouts (seconds)────────────┐   │ Network… │  │
         │ │ Device Not Selected:  [ 15 ] │   └──────────┘  │
         │ │                              │   ┌──────────┐  │
         │ │ Transmission Retry:   [ 45 ] │   │   Help   │  │
         │ └──────────────────────────────┘   └──────────┘  │
         │ ☒ Fast Printing Direct to Port                   │
         └──────────────────────────────────────────────────┘
```

21.9   PRINTERS

After the printer is installed and configured, the appropriate printer driver must be loaded and the printer's location (LPT1, LPT2, LPT3, COM1, or COM2) must be specified. (See fig. 21.14.) LPT1 is the printer's default location. The driver is used to convert data from a document to commands that the printer understands. If the wrong driver is used, the wrong control codes are sent to the printer and the printer will print garbage (strange characters or many pages of programming code). The proper printer driver is installed with the Printer icon in the Control Panel.

An application can access LPT ports in three ways. As a DOS application, the application can use the MS-DOS device names (LPT1, LPT2, LPT3, COM1, and COM2). Although this is the slowest method, it is the most compatible of the three. The second way to access the printer is by using the ROM BIOS Interrupt 17 printer-port service, which sends one character to the printer at a time. Although it is inefficient, it is better than using the MS-DOS device names. The last way, which is also the fastest way, is to address the LPT port directly.

To print, the Print… option on the File menu or a print button on a toolbar is usually used. The print button is the fastest method of printing a single document using the current printer driver and default printer options. The Print option from the File menu offers more control, such as the ability to change print drivers, the number of copies, and which pages to print. A third way to print is by dragging the file's icon (from the desktop or from File Manager) onto the Print Manager application icon or window.

When printing in Windows, the application usually creates a print file and sends it to the **Print Manager,** which manages the print queue or print spooler. The print queue is a holding area for the print jobs sent to the printer. The Print Manager works in the background, sending documents to the printer while the user continues to work. The Print Manager will appear as an icon on the desktop if it is not already running and can be used to check the status of the documents or change their status using the Print Manager window.

Question: A document does not print and the user decides to give the print command again. After several attempts, the user figures that there must be a problem with the printer and fixes it. Then all of the print jobs—the same document—sent to the printer start printing one by one. What can be done?

FIGURE 21.15 Using SYSEDIT to view and edit WIN.INI and SYSTEM.INI files

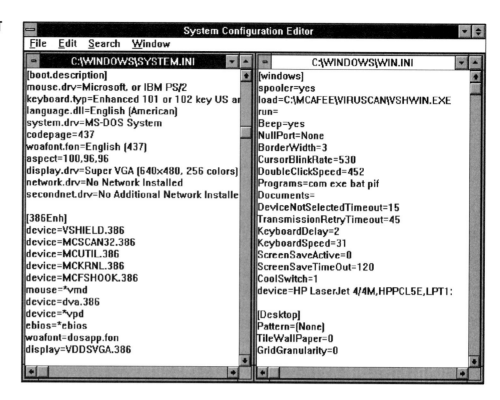

TABLE 21.5 Common initialization files

Filename	File Contents
WIN.INI	Entries that can be set to alter the Windows environment according to preferences, including the desktop appearance, colors, and automatic loading of programs and fonts
SYSTEM.INI	Entries that can be set to customize Windows to meet the system's hardware needs, including the shell in use, the mouse driver, and video drivers
CONTROL.INI	Entries that describe the color schemes and patterns used in Windows, the settings for printers and installable drivers, and the screen saver settings, including the screen saver password
PROGMAN.INI	Entries that define the groups in the Program Manager and the size and location of the Program Manager on the screen. Can be used to limit access to Windows resources
WINFILE.INI	Entries that define the appearance and behavior of items in the File Manager

Answer: Switch to the Print Manager to get a list of all of the printers and all of the print jobs. Then highlight the unneeded print jobs and click on the Delete button.

21.10 WINDOWS CONFIGURATION FILES

To hold configuration information, Windows uses **initialization files** (files with an INI filename extension), which typically are read when Windows is started. As changes are made in the Control Panel or Windows Setup, they are written to an initialization file kept in the WINDOWS directory. These files are text files that can be edited with any text editor, including Windows' Notepad and DOS's EDIT. In addition, Windows provides a utility called System Editor (SYSEDIT.EXE) located in the WINDOWS\SYSTEM directory that can edit the CONFIG.SYS, AUTOEXEC.BAT, SYSTEM.INI, and WIN.INI files. (See fig. 21.15.) (Note: SYSEDIT within Windows for Workgroups and Windows 95 will also display the PROTOCOL.INI file.) The most common initialization files are listed in table 21.5.

The initialization files are broken into logical groups called *sections.* The section names are recognized with a set of brackets ([ ]). The left bracket must be in the leftmost column on the screen. Each section consists of key names followed by an equals sign and its value. The value can be an integer or a string (group of characters). Initialization files are not case sensitive. For many entries, the value is shown as a Boolean expression. Therefore, the entry is enabled by entering True, Yes, On, or 1. The entry is disabled by entering False, No, Off, or 0. Comments, much like the REM statement in DOS, are lines that begin with a semicolon (;). A comment, ignored by Windows, is used to explain a line, provide a warning, or disable a command without removing the entire line. If a line is disabled by adding a semicolon or enabled by removing a semicolon, the changes will not be recognized until Windows restarts. The best resource for more detailed information about the entries in the initialization files is the Windows 3.1 Resource Kit, which can be downloaded from the Microsoft website.

21.10.1   WIN.INI FILE

The WIN.INI file is used to alter the Windows environment according to preference. For example, the Load= and the Run= commands will automatically load the program specified when Windows starts. This line is modified when a program is added to the StartUp group. The Load command will run the program as a minimized icon, while the Run command will not. (Note: Each of these lines can list several programs.)

21.10.2   SYSTEM.INI FILE

The SYSTEM.INI file customizes Windows to meet a system's hardware needs. It specifies which shell to use (usually PROGMAN.EXE) and specifies the mouse and video drivers. Because the SYSTEM.INI file contains the boot options for Windows, if it is missing or corrupt, Windows will not boot.

The most commonly modified section in this file is the [386Enh] section, which applies to settings for the 386 enhanced mode, including how Windows uses virtual memory, hard disk access, and virtual device drivers. Any item that contains an asterisk is a virtual device driver, which is a driver built into the WIN386.EXE file to provide basic Windows services. The three commands to know for modifying this section are EMMExclude, MaxBPs, and 32DiskAccess.

The EMMExclude specifies a range of memory that Windows will not scan when trying to find unused address space in upper memory (much like the X=mmmm-nnnnn in the EMM386.EXE command in the CONFIG.SYS). The range must contain two values between A000 and EFFF separated by a hyphen. The only way to change this line is to manually edit the SYSTEM.INI file. If Windows fails to boot into enhanced 386 mode after an expansion card has been added, the following line should be added to the [386Enh] section of the SYSTEM.INI file:

```
EMMExclude=A000-EFFF
```

If the problem goes away, then there is a conflict between hardware using the memory between 640 KB and 1 MB and Windows. Which memory area the card is using can be determined from the card's documentation, and that range only can then be specified.

The MaxBPs specifies the maximum number of breakpoints. A breakpoint is a method of transfer control for the Virtual Memory Manager (VMM) in 386 enhanced mode. If a third-party virtual device driver requires more breakpoints than the default value, the value will need to be increased. If a MaxBPs line is not stated, a value of 200 is used by default. It is recommended that the number of breakpoints be increased to 1,024 to make Windows more resistant to general protection faults. To set the maximum to 1,024, the following entry would be added to the [386Enh] section of the SYSTEM.INI file:

```
MaxBPs=1024
```

The 32BitDiskAccess command is used to turn the 32-bit disk access on or off. It is usually changed in the 386 Enhanced icon (Virtual Memory) of the Control Panel. If this feature is enabled and Windows will not start, an editor will have to be used to turn this to off.

21.10.3 PROGMAN.INI FILE

The PROGMAN.INI file contains the configuration information for the Program Manager. For example, it contains information about the size and location of the Program Manager window, whether the icons will automatically arrange themselves on the screen, and whether the group and icon settings will be saved upon exiting Windows. The PROGMAN.INI lists all the groups contained in the Program Manager and the associated group file. The group files, files with a GRP filename extension, contain information about the icons in the group. The group files are not text files and cannot be changed with a text editor.

Another section of the PROGMAN.INI file is the [restriction] section. It can be used to restrict certain options in the Program Manager—for example, changing or deleting groups and icons. Run Common on the File menu can be disabled by adding NoRun=0 to the restriction section, and EditLevel=1 can be inserted, which will prevent the creation, deletion, or renaming of groups.

An icon within a group is created by opening the File menu in Program Manager, selecting the New option, and selecting Program Item. The properties of an icon, such as the name and location of the executable file, are changed by selecting the icon, opening the File menu in Program Manager, and selecting the Properties option.

EXAMPLE 21.1 You click on an icon and receive an "Application Not Found" Error message.

You should first select the icon, open the File menu in Program Manager, select the Properties option, and make sure that the correct executable file and location are listed. Next, make sure that the executable file is actually in the directory located. If you still haven't found the problem, then it is best to delete the icon and reinstall the application.

21.10.4 OTHER INITIALIZATION FILES

Many Windows applications create their own initialization files to store configuration information. For example, Microsoft Word will create a WORD.INI file. Some applications will make changes to the current initialization files so that Windows and other applications know how to interface with the new application. Because the initialization files specify the programs' configurations, including the locations of needed files, a program directory cannot be copied from one computer to another and a program cannot be moved from one directory to another and always be expected to work. Programs need to be installed, not copied.

21.11 INSTALLING WINDOWS

To install Windows 3.XX, you insert Disk 1 into a floppy drive and execute the SETUP.EXE file. At the beginning of Setup, you are prompted to choose Express (offers fastest installation) or Custom (offers precise control). The Custom setup allows you to specify a Windows directory other than C:\WINDOWS and change the hardware selected by the autodetect routine, the preferred language, and network options and to specify which Windows components to install. (See table 21.6 and figs. 21.16 and 21.17.)

Most of the files on the installation disks are compressed, identified as such by the last character of the filename extension being an underscore (_). During the installation process, the Setup program uncompresses the file and renames it with the appropriate filename. If you need to expand and rename a specific file, you can use the EXPAND.EXE file located on the first installation disk.

TABLE 21.6   Windows SETUP.EXE options

Setup Options	Description
SETUP /?	Shows the Setup options.
SETUP /I	Ignores automatic hardware detection. Should be used if Windows freezes when SETUP.EXE is trying to identify the hardware. You will have to manually set the hardware settings.
SETUP /N	Sets up a shared copy of Windows from a network server.
SETUP /A	Begins Administrative Setup by expanding and copying all files from the Windows installation disks onto a network server and also marking the files as read-only.
SETUP /B	Sets up Windows with monochrome display attributes.
SETUP /T	Searches the drive for incompatible software that should not run at the same time as Setup or Windows 3.1 (for maintenance only).
SETUP /H:filename	Runs Batch Mode Setup to install Windows with little or no user interaction. The *filename* is the name of the system settings file that contains information about the user's configuration. Include the path if *filename* is not in the directory that contains the Windows Setup files.
SETUP /O:filename or SETUP /S:filename	Specifies the SETUP.INF file, including the path if necessary.

```
Windows Setup

=====================


   If your computer or network appears on the Hardware Compatibility List with an asterisk next to
it, press F1 before continuing.


        System Information
        Computer:        MS-DOS System
        Display:         Super VGA (800x600, 16 colors)
        Mouse:           Microsoft, or IBM PS/2
        Keyboard:        Enhanced 101 or 102 key US and Non-US keyboards
        Keyboard Layout: US
        Language:        English (American)
        Codepage:        English (437)
        Network:         No Network Installed

Complete Changes:        Accept the configuration shown above.

   To change a system setting, press the UP or DOWN ARROW key to move the highlight to the setting
you want to change. Then press ENTER to see alternatives for that item. When you have finished
changing your settings, select the "Complete Changes" option to quit Setup.

Enter=Continue  F1=Help  F3=EXIT
```

FIGURE 21.16   Windows Setup program (DOS mode)

FIGURE 21.17 Windows Setup program (GUI interface) that allows the user to choose which Windows components to install

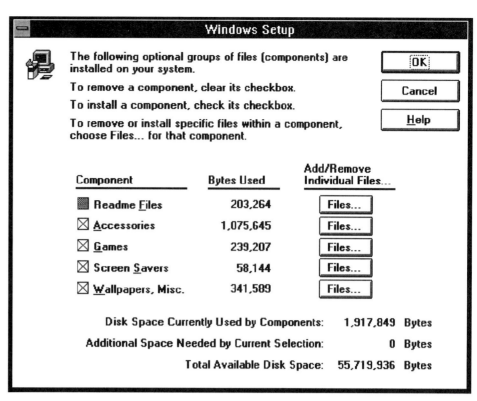

TABLE 21.7 Trouble-shooting Windows 3.XX web-sites

Website	Address
Microsoft Support Library	http://support.microsoft.com/support/downloads/PNP166.asp
Windows 3.1 Resource Kit	http://support.microsoft.com/support/kb/articles/Q124/4/35.asp
Common Questions in a Help File	http://support.microsoft.com/download/support/mslfiles/WINFAQ.EXE
Information on General Protection Faults	http://support.microsoft.com/support/kb/articles/q95/5/05.asp

21.12 TROUBLE-SHOOTING WINDOWS 3.XX

Windows is a complex operating environment consisting of many smaller programs working together as one. Therefore, as a technician, you will encounter problems from time to time. Table 21.7 shows where to find Microsoft's additional documentation, drivers, updates, and utilities on the Internet.

To help troubleshoot application problems, you can use a utility called Dr. Watson (DR-WATSON.EXE). If Dr. Watson is active and an application error occurs, Dr. Watson will create a text file called DRWATSON.LOG with information that may be used to correct the problem. It will also prompt you for details about the circumstances under which the application error occured and will sometimes detect a general protection fault problem before it becomes fatal, giving you the opportunity to save your work. GPF problems are discussed in section 21.12.2.

If Windows or Windows applications generate an unusual number of errors, reinstalling Windows and/or the application will fix many of these problems. Of course, you probably want to install Windows and the application into the same directory so that they will keep the same configuration.

> **NOTE** *Windows Magazine* offers WinTune 2.0 (freeware) to help test and optimize Windows 3.XX. It is available for download at:
> **http://winweb.winmag.com/software/wt20.htm**

21.12.1 MOUSE PROBLEMS

If the mouse is not working in Windows, first make sure that the mouse is connected properly and that the mouse was plugged in when you started Windows. If the mouse was plugged in after Windows was started, it won't work and you will have to restart Windows. Remember also that serial mice are recognized only on COM1 or COM2 in Windows 3.XX. And make sure that the proper driver is loaded using the Windows Setup program or the SETUP.EXE in the WINDOWS directory.

If the mouse still doesn't work, exit Windows, make sure that the DOS mouse driver is loaded, and test the mouse in EDIT or MSD. If the mouse works, the problem is a software problem. If it doesn't work, the problem is a hardware problem. If the problem is a hardware problem, you will need to test the mouse and the mouse port. Connect the mouse to a different computer or try a different mouse on the same computer to isolate the faulty component. In addition, make sure that there are no resource conflicts (I/O address and IRQ).

If a mouse is working but the mouse pointer jumps around the screen, that is usually caused by dirty rollers or dirty optical sensors. This problem can also be caused by an IRQ conflict with the mouse port.

21.12.2 APPLICATION PROBLEMS

You click on an icon and receive an "Application Not Found" error message. What can you do?

a. Delete the icon and reinstall the application.
b. Reinstall Windows 3.XX.
c. Check the PROGRAM.INI file.
d. Check the WIN.INI file.
e. Open the File menu and select the Properties option to check the path of the executable file.

21.12.3 GENERAL PROTECTION FAULTS

A common problem that occurs in Windows is the **general protection fault (GPF),** formerly called an **unrecoverable application error (UAE).** It signifies that something unexpected has happened within the Windows environment. Usually, a program has tried to access a memory area that belongs to another program or an application has tried to pass an invalid parameters to another program. A system integrity violation is a special form of a GPF. It indicates that a DOS application has caused the GPF, usually by trying to use a memory area belonging to another program.

Depending on the severity of the general protection fault, you may be able to save your work before restarting Windows. If the application is not responding, you may be able to perform a local reboot (Ctrl+Alt+Del) to terminate the frozen application. Unfortunately, most of the time, you will have to perform another Ctrl+Alt+Del to reboot the computer or you will have to use the reset button or on/off switch.

If a general protection fault occurs repeatedly, isolating it can be a long and lengthy process. If the general protection fault message indicates a GPF with the GDI.EXE, USER.EXE, or video driver, the problem is most likely caused by the video system and driver. Try to reload the driver or try to get newer drivers from the manufacturer. If the problem is with the kernel, then the problem is with memory settings. If the problem is with the printer driver, try to reload the printer driver or update the driver from the manufacturer.

If the general protection fault occurs with the same application, check for lost clusters with SCANDISK, check for viruses, and delete any temporary files from the temporary directory (defined with the SET TEMP line in the AUTOEXEC.BAT file). Remember that both lost clusters and many temporary files in the temporary directory often indicate that a user has been shutting off the computer without properly exiting Windows. You should also check if the software has a history of causing general protection faults and if there is a patch or fix that will correct the problem. After checking for lost clusters, viruses, and temporary files, try reinstalling the program so that any incomplete files will be restored. If the problem still exists, try reinstalling Windows. You should also make sure that the current DOS version supports the computer and that the latest versions of HIMEM.SYS, EMM386.EXE, MSCDEX.EXE, and SMARTDRV.EXE are used. If a Windows program was made for a version earlier than Windows 3.0, it is the program that has most likely caused the general protection fault.

Try to boot the computer with minimum CONFIG.SYS and AUTOEXEC.BAT files to see if the problem is with a device driver or TSR. If the problem still occurs, try to rename the WIN.INI file to WININI.OLD and restart Windows. If the problem goes away, the general protection fault was caused by a corrupted font, a corrupted printer driver, or software loaded with the RUN= or the LOAD= lines. You would then isolate each line by commenting out the lines one by one with a semicolon (;). Of course, if this turns out not to have been the problem or if it is and you correct the problem, don't forget to rename the file back to WIN.INI.

Another cause of a general protection fault could be a corrupted permanent swap file or a badly fragmented hard drive. Specify no swap file using the 386 Enhanced icon in the Control Panel window and run DEFRAG on the hard drive. When the DEFRAG is finished, you can recreate the permanent swap file. In addition, you could try turning off the 32-bit disk and file access.

If the general protection fault occurs in 386 enhanced mode but not in standard mode, the system is probably having a memory conflict in the upper memory blocks (UMBs). To eliminate the possibility of a UBM conflict, add the EMMExclude=A000-EFFF in the [386Enh] section of the SYSTEM.INI file. If EMM386.EXE is being used, you also need to exclude the A000-EFFF in the CONFIG.SYS file. If the problem goes away, you can then investigate which specific hardware memory areas need to be isolated.

Any time you install Windows, you should add the following two lines in the [386Enh] section of the SYSTEM.INI file:

```
SystemROMBreakPoint=On
MaxBPs=1024
```

Although these lines will not eliminate general protection faults, they will make Windows more resistant to GPFs. If you want more information on isolating GPFs, download Microsoft's Product Support Services Application Note WW0524: Troubleshooting GP Faults (WW0524.TXT), which can be found at http://support.microsoft.com/support/kb/articles/q95/5/05.asp.

21.12.4 WINDOWS RESOURCES

If you select the About Program Manager option in the Help menu of the Program Manager or the About File Manager option in the Help menu of the File Manager, Windows will display the amount of memory available to Windows and the percentage of free system resources (FSR). The amount of memory displayed will include virtual memory, if any is used. (See figs. 21.18 and 21.19.)

The kernel, GDI.EXE, and USER.EXE were discussed earlier in the chapter. The kernel loads and runs Windows applications and handles their memory management, the GDI manages graphics and printing, and USER controls user input and output, including the keyboard and the mouse. GDI uses a storage area limited to 64 KB, known as the *local heap*. USER has two storage areas, totaling 128 KB. The GDI heap contains information about graphical objects, such as pens, brushes, cursors, fonts, icons, buttons, scroll bars, and so on. The USER heap contains windows, icons, menus, and dialog boxes. The free system resources reflect the remaining free percentage of the USER or GDI local heap space, whichever is lower. As you run applications in Windows, more resources are used to keep track of what is going on in the Windows environment. Unfortunately, some Windows 3.XX applications do not release all of the system resources after the application has been closed. If either of the two heaps are used and filled, one or more of the following symptoms may occur:

1. An "Out of Memory" error message appears even if there is a lot of RAM and free disk space available

FIGURE 21.18 Using the About
Program Manager option within
the Help menu to show the
amount of free system memory

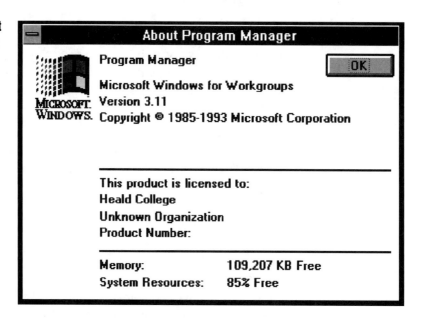

FIGURE 21.19 Using Microsoft
Word to view the system
information

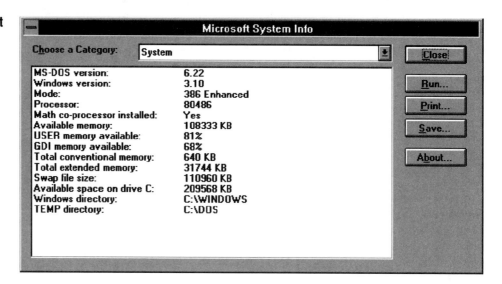

2. The screen takes a long time to redraw
3. Parts of the dialog boxes, warning messages, and graphics do not appear

If the system resources are low (30% or less), the system is about to run out of resources. To increase the amount of FSR, you can:

1. Minimize seldom-used groups
2. Not open groups with many icons
3. Reduce the number of application button bars
4. Not use wallpaper or use a small bitmap and tile it
5. Eliminate fonts that are not needed
6. Try to keep open an application that uses system resources every time it runs, instead of closing and reopening it many times
7. Clear the Clipboard
8. Disable the screen saver
9. Close any applications and documents that are not being used
10. Restart Windows to reclaim any resources that programs have not given back

If you still keep running out of system resources, you should consider upgrading to Windows 95 or 98 or Windows NT.

1. Windows 3.XX is a graphical user interface (GUI) that works on top of DOS.
2. Windows 3.XX uses cooperative multitasking, which is based on applications cooperating with each other.
3. Windows runs in three modes: real, standard, and enhanced 386.
4. Windows running in standard mode or enhanced 386 mode requires HIMEM.SYS to be loaded in the CONFIG.SYS file because Windows requires extended memory.
5. The WIN.COM file, located in the Windows directory, is sometimes called the *loader file* because it is used to load Windows.
6. File Manager (WINFILE.EXE), located in the Main group, is an application included with Windows that manages disks, directories, and files.
7. The Program Manager is used to run and manage programs (including starting them) opening documents, creating groups and icons, moving and deleting icons, and changing the properties of a group or icon.
8. To share data between documents, Windows applications can use dynamic data exchange (DDE) or object linking and embedding (OLE).
9. The Windows registry (REG.DAT) is a special configuration database used by the File Manager to bring up an application in which a document with a specific filename extension was created.
10. Windows can also run DOS programs (sometimes referred to as *non-Windows* programs), although Windows does a much better job at running Windows applications.
11. A program information file (PIF) contains information about a DOS program running in Windows.
12. Windows is usually configured with the Control Panel and the Windows Setup program, both of which are located in the Main group.
13. If Windows is running in 386 enhanced mode, it can use virtual memory—disk space simulating RAM that allows running more applications at one time than the system's physical memory would usually allow.
14. To hold configuration information, Windows uses initialization files (files with an INI filename extension), which typically are read when Windows is started.
15. The initialization files are broken into logical groups called *sections*. The section names are recognized with a set of brackets ([ ]).
16. To install Windows 3.XX, insert Disk 1 into a floppy drive and execute the SETUP.EXE file.
17. A general protection fault signifies that something unexpected has happened within the Windows environment. Usually a program has tried to access a memory area that belongs to another program or an application has tried to pass invalid parameters to another program.
18. If you select the About Program Manager option in the Help menu of the Program Manager or the About File Manager option in the Help menu of the File Manager, Windows will display the amount of memory available to Windows and the percentage of free system resources (FSR).

QUESTIONS

1. Of the following, which are *not* valid Windows system initialization filenames?
   a. WIN.INI
   b. PROGMAN.INI
   c. WINFILE.INI
   d. PROGRAM.INI
   e. SYSTEM.INI
   f. CONTROL.INI
2. Which of the following are required for Windows 32-bit disk access? (Choose all that apply.)
   a. the system must use a Western Digital 1003 controller or equivalent and run in 386 enhanced mode
   b. the system must use an Adaptec SCSI controller or equivalent and run in 386 enhanced mode
   c. the system must use an Adaptec SCSI controller or equivalent and run in standard mode
   d. the system must use a hard drive controller made for the VESA local bus or equivalent and run in enhanced 386 mode

3. When running Windows, what is the function of the CONTROL.INI file?
   a. contains color schemes, patterns, printer settings, and installation driver setting
   b. contains system hardware setting information
   c. controls Windows environmental settings
   d. installs screen drivers, printer fonts, and system hardware information
4. Which of the following defines Program Manager information, such as the size and location of Program Manager windows and GRP?
   a. WIN.INI
   b. SYSTEM.INI
   c. CONTROL.INI
   d. PROGMAN.INI
   e. WINFILE.INI
5. Under normal circumstances, which of the following INI files are most likely to be edited? (Choose two.)
   a. PIF.INI
   b. SETUP.INI
   c. SYSTEM.INI
   d. WIN.INI
6. Which of the following files is used to customize the Windows environment?
   a. WIN.INI
   b. SYSTEM.INI
   c. SETUP.INI
   d. CONFIG.SYS
7. Which Windows Control Panel icon allows you to change the swap file?
   a. system icon
   b. desktop icon
   c. drivers icon
   d. 386 enhanced icon
8. When running Windows in the 386 enhanced mode, what is the minimum amount of extended memory required?
   a. 256 KB
   b. 1 MB
   c. 128 KB
   d. 512 KB
9. If after adding an adapter, Windows will not run in enhanced mode, which of the following should you try?
   a. reinstalling Windows
   b. adding EMMEXCLUDE=A000-EFFF to the SYSTEM.INI file
   c. adding EMMINCLUDE=A000-EFFF to the SYSTEM.INI file
   d. replacing the adapter
   e. finding a newer driver
10. What type of multitasking does Windows 3.XX use?
    a. task switching
    b. preemptive
    c. cooperative
    d. sharing
11. To view the current Windows system resources, you would click on:
    a. Setup, then Resources
    b. Control Panel, then 386
    c. Help, then About Program Manager
    d. none of the above
12. The PIF extension is used for:
    a. print jobs
    b. font files
    c. printer drivers
    d. DOS applications
    e. PS/2 Applications
13. When running Windows, what is the purpose of a Program group file (a file with a GRP filename extension)?
    a. it contains the settings for the Program Manager
    b. it contains information about the icons contained in the Program group
    c. it sets the search path while running Windows
    d. it contains various operating mode parameters
14. What is the purpose of the Windows core file USER.EXE?
    a. manages printing and graphics
    b. coordinates and loads tasks and handles memory management in enhanced mode
    c. coordinates and loads tasks in standard mode
    d. controls input and output from the keyboard, mouse, and communication ports
    e. contains user configuration information
15. What is the function of the SYSTEM.INI file?
    a. controls Windows environmental settings
    b. contains color schemes, patterns, printer settings, and installable driver settings

c. contains system hardware setting information

d. installs screen drivers, printer fonts, and system hardware information

16. Which of the following is no longer supported by Windows 3.1?
    a. standard mode operations
    b. real mode operations
    c. 386 enhanced mode operations
    d. 286 enhanced mode operations

17. Which of the following is the correct procedure for installing a Windows program?
    a. type RUN from the DOS prompt, then enter the install program name
    b. click on the Start option from the File menu and enter the install program name
    c. click on the Run option from the File menu and enter the install program name
    d. click on the Start icon and enter the install program name
    e. none of the above

18. When creating a permanent swap file, which of the following are created? (Choose two answers.)
    a. 386SPART.PAR
    b. WIN386.SWP
    c. 386SPART.SWP
    d. SPART.PAR

19. A temporary swap file has what filename extension?
    a. PAR
    b. SWAP
    c. TXT
    d. TMP
    e. SWP

20. You get garbled output. The first thing to do is:
    a. see if the cable is plugged in
    b. replace the cable
    c. change the ribbon or cartridge
    d. see if the correct printer driver is installed and chosen

21. You get a general protection fault. Which would be the last thing to check?
    a. viruses
    b. faulty hardware
    c. that the temporary swap file exists and that there is free disk space on the drive of the temporary directory
    d. lost clusters

22. When reviewing files with an INI extension, what kind of information would you expect to find?
    a. setup information
    b. configuration information for DOS programs running under a Windows environment
    c. a sound file
    d. configuration information of a program

23. What file is used to start Windows?
    a. WIN.COM
    b. WIN.INI
    c. SYS.INI
    d. WIN.CNF
    e. WINDOWS.EXE

24. The best description of a temporary swap file is which of the following?
    a. a swap file that should be used when a permanent swap file cannot be because of a badly fragmented hard drive or network drive
    b. a swap file that has a TMP filename extension
    c. a file that is fixed in size and can't change
    d. a file where different versions of DOS can be stored

25. When using the Windows System Editor (SYSEDIT.EXE), which of the following files *cannot* be edited? (Choose two answers.)
    a. CONTROL.INI
    b. AUTOEXEC.BAT
    c. CONFIG.SYS
    d. SYSTEM.INI
    e. WIN.INI
    f. PROGRAM.INI

26. Which of the following will provide the best virtual memory performance?
    a. a temporary swap file
    b. a RAM drive
    c. configuring SMARTDRV.EXE so that it does not cache information when Windows is running
    d. a permanent swap file

27. What allows using specialized programs to create a document?
    a. OLE
    b. multitasking
    c. networks
    d. IFSHLP.SYS
28. Windows' Print Manager controls the:
    a. swap file
    b. print queue or spooler
    c. Clipboard
    d. printer fonts
29. The screen seems to take a long time to redraw. What is the most likely problem?
    a. GPF
    b. system integrity violation
    c. running out of system resources
    d. lost clusters on the hard drive or running out of hard disk space
30. A GPF is:
    a. something unexpected that has happened within the Windows environment, such as two programs using the same memory area or a program passing an invalid parameter
    b. the microprocessor not being able to switch to protected mode, causing Windows not to run in enhanced 386 mode.
    c. the microprocessor not being able to switch back to real mode to access DOS drivers
    d. not enough conventional memory
    e. not enough extended memory
    f. an undetectable virus
31. Most fonts used in Windows 3.11 and Windows 95 can be scaled and rotated. What are they called?
    a. Windows fonts
    b. raster fonts
    c. vector fonts
    d. TrueType fonts
32. *True or False*—You have closed all Windows applications (with the Program Manager). Therefore, it is OK to shut off the computer.
33. When running Windows, on which of the following ports can the serial mouse be installed?
    a. COM1 and COM2
    b. COM1 and COM3
    c. COM1 and COM4
    d. COM3 and COM4
    e. COM1, COM2, COM3, and COM4
34. Installation may fail if Windows detects a piece of hardware that it does not recognize during the DOS part of the installation. Which of the following commands allows Windows to perform the installation without detecting the hardware?
    a. SETUP /I
    b. SETUP /H
    c. SETUP /S
    d. SETUP /C
35. Which of the following files manages memory, loads applications, and schedules task executions?
    a. GDI.EXE
    b. USER.EXE
    c. KRNL286.EXE or KRNL386.EXE
    d. CONTROL.EXE
36. Which of the following checks the current hardware configuration and device drivers and determines whether Windows should run in standard or 386 enhanced mode?
    a. WIN386.EXE
    b. WIN.COM
    c. SYSTEM.INI
    d. WINDOWS.INI
37. When Windows needs more RAM than is installed in the computer, it moves 4 KB pages of data from RAM to the hard disk. This results in more memory than is physically available, which is called:
    a. extended memory
    b. expanded memory
    c. virtual memory
    d. HMA
38. Which of the following commands can be used to immediately activate the next application when you are running multiple applications in Windows?
    a. Ctrl+Tab
    b. Alt+Enter
    c. Alt+Esc
    d. Ctrl+Esc
39. Whenever a printer is first installed, Windows assigns it to which port?
    a. COM1
    b. EPT
    c. LPT1
    d. PRT1

40. You find that a customer's hard drive is filled up almost entirely with files that start with ~ and end with .TMP. This is an indication that:
   a. the hard drive is defective
   b. the hard drive is compressed
   c. the customer might be exiting Windows or Windows applications improperly
   d. the AUTOEXEC.BAT file needs a TEMP= line

41. In INI files, a remark is:
   a. [ ]
   b. ;
   c. *
   d. /*

42. You get an "Out of Memory" error message on a system with 32 MB of RAM. What is most likely the problem?
   a. GPF
   b. a system integrity violation
   c. running out of system resources
   d. running out of hard disk space
   e. running out of RAM

43. Within Windows, an icon:
   a. can exist in any or all program groups any number of times
   b. cannot exist more than once in a program group
   c. can exist only once regardless of which program group it is in
   d. can exist more than once if it doesn't call up the same program

44. Which of the following will cause a GPF?
   a. bad RAM
   b. bad or outdated video drivers
   c. stack overflow
   d. Improper use of the EMM386.EXE
   e. corrupted programs
   f. bad video card
   g. all of the above
   h. none of the above

45. Your mouse fails to operate in a DOS window. What is the solution?
   a. start the SETUP.EXE in the Windows directory or run the SetUp icon in the Main group and select the proper mouse driver
   b. load the mouse driver in the SYSTEM.INI
   c. load the mouse driver in the AUTOEXEC.BAT
   d. reboot the computer

46. You click on an icon and receive an "Application Not Found" error message. What do you do first?
   a. delete the icon and reinstall the application
   b. reinstall Windows 3.XX
   c. check the PROGRAM.INI file
   d. check the WIN.INI file
   e. open the File menu and select the Properties option to check the path of the executable file

47. Which of the following statements is true concerning 386 enhanced and standard modes in Windows 3.1? (Choose two.)
   a. In enhanced mode, multiple DOS and Windows applications can be run at the same time; standard mode can run multiple Windows applications but cannot run multiple DOS applications
   b. In enhanced mode, multiple Windows applications can be run at the same time; standard mode can run multiple DOS applications
   c. In enhanced mode, DOS programs are run in a window; standard mode runs DOS programs full screen
   d. In enhanced mode, DOS programs are run full screen; standard mode runs DOS programs in a window
   e. In enhanced mode, DOS programs can run in either a window or full screen; standard mode will only run in full screen

HANDS-ON EXERCISES   Exercise 1: Introduction to Program Manager

1. Start Windows. If Windows is already running, exit Windows and restart it.
2. Close all windows (except the Program Manager window).

3. In the About Program Manager option under the Help menu, record the percentage of free system resources.
4. Create a new group called COMMON APPS.
5. In the COMMON APPS group, create icons for the calculator (CALC.EXE), Notepad (NOTEPAD.EXE), File Manager (WINFILE.EXE), and Control Panel (CONTROL.EXE). (Hint: They are all located in the WINDOWS directory.)
6. In the COMMON APPS group, create an icon called System Editor that is linked to the SYSEDIT.EXE file in the C:\WINDOWS\SYSTEM directory.
7. Open the Main and Accessories groups.
8. In the About Program Manager option under the Help menu, record the percentage of free system resources.
9. Test each of the icons that you just created.
10. Close all of the programs that you just started.
11. Start the system editor (SYSEDIT.EXE located in the C:\WINDOWS\SYSTEM directory) with File Manager. Close the System Editor and File Manager.
12. Using the Run option under the File Menu of Program Manager, execute the System Editor by specifying the path (location) of the SYSEDIT.EXE file. Close the System Editor.
13. Using the Run option under the File Menu of Program Manager, execute the System Editor by using the Browse button. Close the System Editor.
14. Start Microsoft Write and Microsoft Paintbrush.
15. If you have Microsoft Word and Microsoft Excel, start them.
16. Check and record the free system resources.
17. Close Microsoft Write, Microsoft Paintbrush, Microsoft Word, and Microsoft Excel.
18. Check and record the free system resources.
19. Delete the icons in the COMMON APPS group.
20. Delete the COMMON APPS group.
21. Make sure that the Main and Accessories groups are still open.
22. Make sure that there are no checks for the Auto Arrange and Save Settings on Exit options under the Options menu.
23. Move at least five icons within the Main group on top of each other.
24. Enable the Auto Arrange icon under the Options menu.
25. Enable the Save Settings on Exit options under the Options menu.
26. Exit Windows.
27. Start Windows and observe that the Main and Accessories groups are still open.
28. Close the Main and Accessories groups.
29. Disable the Save Settings on Exit option under the Options menu.
30. Exit Windows.
31. Start Windows and observe the Main and Accessories groups.
32. Enable the Save Settings on Exit option under the Options menu.
33. Close the Main and Accessories groups.

Exercise 2: File Management

1. Start File Manager.
2. Format a disk using drive A. Do not make it bootable.
3. On the A drive, create a DOS directory.
4. Copy the FORMAT.COM, FDISK.EXE, ATTRIB.EXE, DISKCOPY.COM, RENAME.TXT, and DRVSPACE.TXT files from the C:\DOS directory to the A:\DOS directory.
5. Double-click on the DRVSPACE.TXT file on the A:\DOS directory.
6. Close Notepad.
7. Move the DRVSPACE.TXT from the A:\DOS to the A:\ directory.
8. Create an A:\DATA directory.
9. Under the DATA directory, create a TEXT directory.
10. Copy the DRVSPACE.TXT from the A:\ directory to the TEXT directory.
11. Perform a disk copy to another disk.
12. Keep the second disk in drive A and format the disk as a bootable disk.

13. Put the first disk into the drive.
14. Rename README.TXT in the A:\ directory to INFO.TXT.
15. Make the INFO.TXT file read-only.
16. Make the INFO.TXT file hidden.
17. If you can't see hidden files in File Manager, including the INFO.TXT file, enable Show Hidden/System files in the By File Type… under the View menu.
18. Click on the C drive icon.
19. Select New Window under the Window menu.
20. Minimize the content window, not the File Manager window. Notice that you have two windows that show contents.
21. Select the Cascade option under the Window menu.
22. Select the Tile Horizontally option under the Window menu.
23. Copy the DEBUG.EXE file from the C:\DOS directory in one window to the A:\DOS directory in the other window.
24. Close one of the windows.
25. Delete the FORMAT.COM file from the A:\DOS directory.
26. Delete the TEXT directory.
27. Delete the ATTRIB.EXE, DEBUG.EXE, and FDISK.EXE files all at the same time.
28. Delete the DATA directory.
29. Reformat the disk. Do not make it bootable.
30. Make the disk bootable without reformatting it.

Exercise 3: Object Linking and Embedding (OLE)

1. Start Microsoft Write. Type your name followed by a couple of lines of text.
2. Without closing Microsoft Write, switch over to the Program Manager and start Microsoft Paintbrush.
3. Draw some circles and squares.
4. Highlight the area with the circles and squares and copy it into the Clipboard using the Copy option in the Edit menu.
5. Without closing either program, switch over to the Program Manager and start the Clipboard in the clipbook viewer. Notice that the picture you copied is in the Clipboard.
6. Change back to Microsoft Write.
7. Paste the image into Microsoft Write using the Paste option under the Edit menu.
8. Switch over to Paintbrush and close the program without saving the image.
9. Save the current document in Microsoft Write with the TESTOLE.WRI filename.
10. Double-click on the picture in Microsoft Write.
11. Draw a line through the picture.
12. Close the Paintbrush program.
13. Save the Microsoft Write document.
14. Close the TESTOLE.WRI document.
15. Open a new document in Microsoft Write.
16. Using the Paste Special option under the Edit menu, paste the picture as a bitmap.
17. Close the Microsoft Write document.
18. Start the DOS prompt.
19. If the DOS prompt is not running in Windows, press the Alt+Enter keys.
20. Perform the following command at the prompt shown:

```
C:\WINDOWS>EDIT C:\DOS\README.TXT
```

21. Under the Control menu, there is a Mark option under the Edit option. Using the Mark option, highlight a paragraph.
22. Using the Copy option under the Edit option of the Control menu, copy the text into the Clipboard.
23. Switch to Microsoft Write and paste the text into the document.
24. Format the text as 18-point Arial using the Fonts… option under the Character menu. Highlight the text and copy it into the Clipboard.
25. Close the Microsoft Write document and start a new one. Don't save the current changes.

26. In the new document, select the Paste option. The paragraph that was copied onto the Clipboard will appear, even though the document it was copied from has been closed and was not saved.
27. Exit Microsoft Write without saving the files.
28. Delete the TESTOLE.WRI file.

Exercise 4: DOS Applications

1. Using Notepad, create a batch file called GO.BAT with the following content:

```
MEM
PAUSE
```

2. Save the batch file with a name of GO.BAT in the C:\DOS directory.
3. From the DOS prompt, test the GO.BAT batch file.
4. From the Run option in the File menu of Program Manager, execute the GO.BAT batch file.
5. Using the File Manager, execute the GO.BAT batch file.
6. Make an icon called Show Memory that points to the GO.BAT batch file.
7. Test the icon and record the amount of free extended memory.
8. Make a PIF file using the PIF Editor. The PIF should point to GO.BAT in the C:\DOS directory and should be called GO.PIF. Exit the PIF Editor.
9. Change the properties of the SHOW MEMORY icon so that it points to the GO.PIF file, not the GO.BAT file.
10. Test the icon and record the amount of extended memory and expanded memory.
11. Change the GO.PIF file so that you have 4,096 KB of extended memory. In addition, configure the PIF file to run in Windows.
12. Test the icon and record the amount of extended memory.
13. Change the properties of the icon to point to the GO.PIF file, not the GO.BAT file.
14. Test the icon and record the amount of extended memory.
15. Delete the GO.PIF and GO.BAT files and the GO icon.

Exercise 5: The Control Panel

1. Start the Control Panel.
2. Using the Date and Time icon, change the date to March 17, 1999.
3. Change the time to 3:00 A.M.
4. Change the date and time to the correct settings.
5. Start the Color icon from within the Control Panel.
6. Change the color scheme to the Arizona color scheme. Don't forget to click on the OK button so that the color scheme will go into effect.
7. Change to the Ocean color scheme.
8. Change the desktop to a dark blue.
9. Change the color scheme back to the Windows Default scheme. Note: The Windows default is not listed alphabetically.
10. Activate the Desktop icon located within the Control Panel.
11. Activate the Flying Windows screen saver. Set the screen saver so that it will activate after two minutes of inactivity.
12. Without moving the mouse or touching the keyboard, wait two minutes to see if the screen saver will come on by itself.
13. Change the distance between icons to 75 pixels. Don't forget to click on the OK button so that the changes will go into effect.
14. Change the distance between icons to 85 pixels.
15. From the 386 Enhanced icon, disable swap files.
16. After the computer reboots, use the About Program Manager under the Help menu of Program Manager to see how much free memory there is.
17. From the 386 Enhanced icon, set the virtual memory to be a 10,240 KB permanent swap file.
18. After the computer reboots, use the About Program Manager under the Help menu of Program Manager to see how much memory there is.

19. Using the DOS Prompt, show hidden files in the C:\ directory. Notice how big the swap file is.
20. If you can, enable the 32-bit file access and 32-bit disk access.
21. Place the disk provided by your instructor in the A drive. If you don't have a disk, find some fonts on the Internet and download them.
22. Using the DOS prompt, look for the font files on the A drive. Observe the extension.
23. Using Fonts in the Control Panel, install the fonts from the A drive.
24. Select the Ports icon in the Control Panel. Set the baud rate of COM2 to 19,200 baud, 7 data bits, 2 stop bits, and even parity.
25. Using the Advanced option, verify that COM2 is set to use IRQ 3 and I/O address 2F8.

Exercise 6: The Mouse, Keyboard, and Video

1. Start the Windows Setup icon in the Main group.
2. Record the current keyboard, mouse, and video drivers.
3. Change the current mouse driver to a Genius Serial Mouse driver and change the current video card to Video 7 (1 MB, 800 × 600, 256 colors).
4. Restart Windows. Notice any problems with Windows, including the mouse.
5. Since Windows probably did not start up properly, exit Windows (or reboot the computer if you have to).
6. Change to the C:\WINDOWS directory and execute the SETUP.EXE file.
7. Reset the mouse and video driver to the original settings.
8. Start and test Windows.
9. Within the Mouse icon of the Control Panel, there is small box diagram of a mouse with an L or R. Click on the left button of the mouse and then click on the right button. As you click them, the mouse buttons in the picture will turn black.
10. Maximize the mouse tracking speed. Test the mouse by moving it across the screen.
11. Minimize the mouse tracking speed. Test the mouse by moving it across the screen.
12. Maximize the mouse double-clicking speed. Test the mouse by clicking on the test area.
13. Adjust the mouse double-clicking speed back to its original setting.
14. Activate the mouse pointer trails and move the mouse. Mouse pointer trails are used on notebook and laptop computers with screens that cannot update fast enough to keep up with the mouse movements.
15. Deactivate the mouse pointer trails.
16. Start Microsoft Write.
17. Press the T key and keep it down. Notice how long it takes before the key starts repeating and how fast it repeats after it starts.
18. Using the Keyboard icon in the Control Panel, set the Repeat Delay to Short and the Repeat Rate to Fast.
19. Go back to Microsoft Write. Press the Y key and keep it down. Notice how long it takes before the key starts repeating and how fast it repeats after it starts.
20. Using the Keyboard icon in the Control Panel, set the Repeat Delay to Long and the Repeat Rate to Slow.
21. Go back to Microsoft Write. Press the Q key and keep it down. Notice how long it takes before the key starts repeating and how fast it repeats after it starts.
22. Place the Repeat Delay and the Repeat Rate to somewhere near the middle.

Exercise 7: Printers

1. Using the Printer icon in the Control Panel, delete all existing print drivers.
2. Install the LaserJet III printer driver. Assume that the printer will use LPT1.
3. If a printer is connected to the computer, unplug the printer cable.
4. Start Microsoft Write and load the PRINTERS.WRI file located in the C:\WINDOWS directory.
5. Use the Print option in the File menu. Make sure that the LaserJet III printer is selected.
6. Print the document three times.
7. Switch over to Print Manager. Because it is running as a minimized application icon,

489

you can use the Alt+Tab keys to switch to it. Notice the printer and its status are listed. In addition, notice that the three documents are listed under the printer.

8. Delete the three print jobs.
9. Close Print Manager.
10. Install the NEC Silentwriter 2 Model 90.
11. Install the correct print driver for the printer and make it the default printer.
12. Connect the printer cable to the printer.
13. Using the Print option in the File menu, print the first page of the document using the NEC Silentwriter 2 Model 90 printer. Notice what happens if you select the wrong driver.
14. If necessary, delete the print job from the Program Manager.
15. Print the first page of the document again but select the correct printer driver.
16. Delete the NEC printer driver and the HP LaserJet III print driver.

Exercise 8: Researching the Initialization Files

For this exercise, use SYSINI.WRI and WININI.WRI (located in the WINDOWS directory) and the Windows 3.XX Resource Kit (Microsoft Word format) from the Microsoft web site.

1. Load the WININI.WRI with Microsoft Write or the Resource Kit with Microsoft Word.
2. Scroll to the [desktop] section setting.
3. Find the IconVerticalSpacing and find out what it does. In addition, find out what unit it is measured in.
4. Find the following commands and find out what they do:

   ```
   IconTitleFaceName=
   IconTitleSize=
   IconTitleStyle=
   ```

5. Load the SYSINI.WRI with Microsoft Write or the Resource Kit with Microsoft Word.
6. Scroll through the document until you get to the [386Enh] section settings.
7. What is the 32BitDiskAccess command used for?
8. Scroll further into the document until you get to the EMMExclude= command. What does the EMMExclude= command do?
9. Scroll further into the document until you get to MaxBPs=⟨number⟩ setting. What does the MaxBPs setting do and what is the default setting for the MaxBPs?

Exercise 9: Initialization Files

For this exercise, use SYSINI.WRI and WININI.WRI (located in the WINDOWS directory) and the Windows 3.XX Resource Kit (Microsoft Word format) from the Microsoft web site.

1. Start the Control Panel icon within the Main group.
2. Double-click on the Desktop icon. Record the size of the border width.
3. Create an icon for System Editor.
4. Start System Editor.
5. Click on the WIN.INI edit window so that it becomes the active window.
6. From within the WIN.INI file, find the BorderWidth= keyname from within the [Windows] section. Compare the value assigned to the border width with the value that you recorded earlier.
7. Within the [Windows] section, record any lines which have the run= keyname.
8. Within the [Windows] section, record any lines which have the load= keyname.
9. Exit System Editor.
10. Go to the Program Manager and create a calculator icon in the Startup group.
11. Restart Windows and notice that the calculator automatically starts.
12. Start System Editor and look at the run= and load= commands and notice if any new commands have been added.
13. Find the ScreenSaverActive= keyname from within the [Windows] section. Can you figure out if the screen saver is on or off?

14. Add the following line to the WIN.INI file under the [desktop] section:

```
IconVerticalSpacing=100
```

15. Add the following lines to the WIN.INI file under the [desktop] section:

```
IconTitleFaceName=Arial
IconTitleSize=14
IconTitleStyle=1
```

16. Exit System Editor and save the changes. Restart Windows. Notice the text under the icons.
17. Using System Editor, load the WIN.INI file and put a semicolon (;) in front of IconTitleSize=14.
18. Exit System Editor and save the changes. Restart Windows. Notice the text under the icons.
19. Using System Editor, delete the following lines from the WIN.INI file under the [desktop] section.

```
IconVerticalSpacing=100
IconTitleFaceName=Arial
;IconTitleSize=14
IconTitleStyle=1
```

20. Switch to the SYSTEM.INI window. In the [boot] section, record the mouse driver and the current shell.
21. Add the following line within the [386Enh] section:

```
MaxBPs=1024
```

22. Exit System Editor and save the changes. Restart Windows.
23. Exit Windows. Using EDIT, delete the following line from the SYSTEM.INI under the [386Enh] section:

```
MaxBPS=1024
```

24. Exit EDIT and save the changes. Restart Windows.
25. Start the Notepad and load the PROGMAN.INI file. Notice the number of groups. Exit Notepad.
26. Go to the Program Manager and create a group called TEST.
27. Start Notepad and load the PROGMAN.INI file. Notice the number of groups. Try to figure out which file stores the icon information for the TEST group. Notice the filename extension.
28. Exit Notepad.
29. Delete the TEST group.
30. Open the PROGMAN.INI file with Notepad. Add the following command under the [settings] section:

```
NoRun=1
```

31. Exit Notepad and save the changes. Restart Windows. Open the file menu and notice the state of the Run option.
32. Add the following command under the [settings] section using Notepad:

```
EditLevel=2
```

33. Exit Notepad and save the changes. Restart Windows. Try to delete the System Editor icon.
34. Open the PROGMAN.INI file with Notepad. Put a semicolon before the EditLevel=2 command.
35. Exit Notepad and save the changes. Restart Windows.
36. Delete the System Editor icon.
37. Exit Windows.
38. Use EDIT to view the CONTROL.INI file.

39. Exit EDIT.
40. List all of the initialization files in the C:\WINDOWS directory and list all of the group files in the C:\WINDOWS directory.

Exercise 10: Installing Windows

1. Delete the C:\WINDOWS directory.
2. Insert Installation Disk 1 into drive A.
3. Install Windows. Use the Custom installation.
4. Add the MaxBPS=1024 line to the [Enh386] section of the SYSTEM.INI file.
5. If available, load Microsoft Office.

Exercise 11: Installing and Configuring Microsoft Office 4.3

1. Insert the MS-Office 4.3 disk 1 or CD-ROM into the compact disk drive and start the installation program (unless told otherwise). Install all of Office using the Custom installation except the WordArt (selected within Shared Applications).
2. After the installation is complete, double-click on the Microsoft Office Setup icon (located in the Microsoft Office Group). This will allow you to install or remove Office components.
3. Install WordArt.
4. When Word Art is installed, start Microsoft Word.
5. Type in your first name followed by your last name. On the next line, type in your address.
6. Select the Options... option located within the Tools menu. Click on the View tab.
7. To show the hardware returns, select the spaces and paragraph marks within the Non-printing characters section and click on the OK button. Notice the space and paragraph symbols.
8. Select the Options option located within the Tools menu and shut off the space and paragraph marks.
9. Click on the General tab. Notice the number of files on the recently used files list and the measurement units.
10. Select the Save tab. Make sure that the Save AutoRecover Info option is selected and notice the time of Autosave. Autosave allows Word to automatically save your document every so often.
11. Click on the Spelling tab. Make sure the Always Suggest option is selected.
12. Select the File location tab. Notice the default directory for Word documents.
13. Click on the Close button.
14. Go to any toolbar and click using the right (secondary) mouse button. Notice which toolbars are open. Select the Drawing toolbar.
15. Grab the Drawing toolbar without grabbing a button and drag it to the right of the screen until it becomes embedded.
16. Close the Wordart toolbar by click with the right (secondary) mouse button on any toolbar and deselect the Drawing toolbar.
17. To customize the toolbar, click on the Customize option located within the Tools menu.
18. Click on the Toolbars tab.
19. To modify the buttons on the Standard toolbar, drag the New button off the toolbar.
20. Within the File category, find the New... command and drag it to the beginning of the Standard toolbar. Click on the Close button.
21. Close Microsoft Word.

Exercise 12: Researching the Internet

1. Go to the Microsoft website (microsoft.com) and find and download the updates and patches for Windows 3.1 and Windows 3.11 for Workgroups.
2. Install the update and patches.
3. Find the 3.1 Resource Kit.

4. Find a document called WW0524.TXT (Troubleshooting the GP Faults) and download it.

5. Find and download the file Windows 3.XX Frequently Asked Questions and Answers (FAQ).

6. Using a popular search engine, perform a search for tips and hints to optimize or improve Windows 3.XX.

7. Find and download WinTune 2.0 from Windows Magazine.

8. Run WinTune 2.0 on your Windows 3.XX system.

22 Windows 95 and 98

INTRODUCTION

Windows 95, an innovative operating system for the PC, was designed to replace DOS and Windows 3.XX. It has a better, more intuitive user interface and it supports long file names (LFN). Behind the interface, Windows 95 is a preemptive, multithreading, multitasking environment. A mostly 32-bit operating system that is not limited by the conventional memory restrictions, it provides compatibility for most DOS and Windows 3.XX device drivers and applications. It supports plug-and-play technology and has built-in multimedia and network capability.

OBJECTIVES

1. List the minimum hardware and software requirements to run Windows 95.
2. List and explain the Windows 95 and 98 boot process.
3. Perform common file and disk management tasks.
4. Compare and contrast the FAT, VFAT, and FAT32 file systems.
5. Install and execute Win32-based, Win16-based, and DOS applications.
6. Explain how Win32-based, Win16-based, and DOS applications run in the Windows 95 and 98 environment.
7. Terminate a nonresponding application.
8. Share data between documents.
9. Remove a Windows application from Windows 95 or 98.
10. Print a document in Windows 95 or 98 and manage the print job.
11. Load the appropriate print driver.
12. Configure Windows using the Control Panel.
13. Use the Device Manager to find available resources, resource conflicts, and driver problems.
14. Create a Startup disk.
15. Configure the Desktop and Taskbar.
16. Make changes to the MSDOS.INI file when appropriate.
17. List and explain the six different keys found in the Windows 95 and 98 Registry.
18. Back up the Windows 95 and 98 Registry.
19. Use REGEDIT to make changes to the Registry when appropriate.
20. Install and configure Windows 95 and 98.
21. Determine and correct a problem in Windows 95 and 98.

22.1   WHAT IS WINDOWS 95?

Windows 95 is a complete operating system that was designed to replace DOS and Windows 3.XX. The most obvious difference between Windows 95 and Windows 3.XX is that Windows 95 has a better, more intuitive user interface that supports long file names.

22.1.1   THE DESKTOP

The Windows 95 interface is based on the desktop, where all of the work is done. On the desktop are the My Computer icon, the Recycle Bin, and the Taskbar (with the Start button). In addition, there may be a Network Neighborhood icon to access network resources (files, applications, and printers), an Inbox to receive electronic mail, and various folders (directories) and shortcuts to programs and documents. (See fig. 22.1.)

The My Computer icon includes all disk drives, the Control Panel, and the printer folder. From within the My Computer icon, all files on the drives can be accessed and managed.

FIGURE 22.1 Windows 95
interface

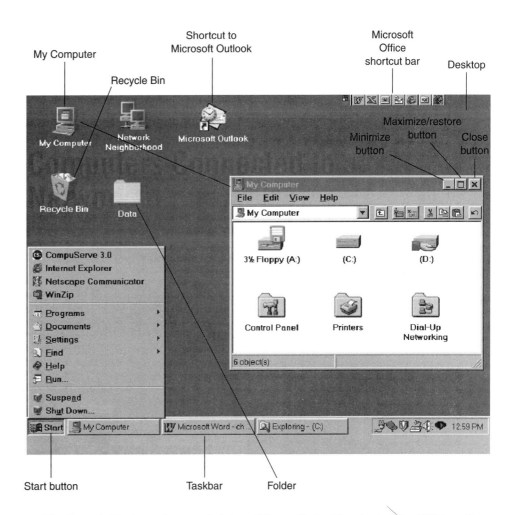

My Computer

Recycle Bin

Shortcut to
Microsoft Outlook

Microsoft
Office
shortcut bar

Desktop

Maximize/restore
button

Minimize
button

Close
button

Start button

Taskbar

Folder

The Recycle Bin is used as a safe delete. When a file is deleted using the GUI interface, Windows will store the file in the Recycle Bin, and it will remain there until the Recycle Bin is emptied or until the computer is running out of disk space (at which point Windows 95 will delete the oldest files first). If a file is deleted and the user later decides to undelete the file, he or she can open the Recycle Bin and drag the file to any location or choose the Restore option from the File menu.

The Taskbar is located at the bottom of the screen. Some taskbars are always visible; others are configured to auto-hide and reappear only when the mouse pointer is moved to the bottom of the screen. These taskbars are configured to auto-hide so that there is more free area on the desktop. The Taskbar is divided into three areas: the Start button, the notification area, and the active program buttons. (See fig. 22.2.) The Start button is used to start programs. In addition, it can open recently accessed documents and access the Control Panel and printer folder, find files, and get Help for Windows 95. (Note: The Start button is actually a series of shortcuts to programs.) The notification area, located on the right side of the Taskbar, is used for the clock and for any programs running in the background, such as printers and modems. The rest of the Taskbar is blank or holds the active program buttons, which can be used to switch between open programs.

When a window is open, the window will usually contain a minimize button, a maximize or restore button, and a close button in the top right corner and a control menu icon in

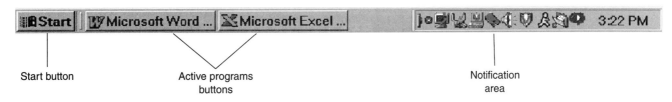

Start button

Active programs
buttons

Notification
area

FIGURE 22.2 The Taskbar

FIGURE 22.3 Windows
Explorer

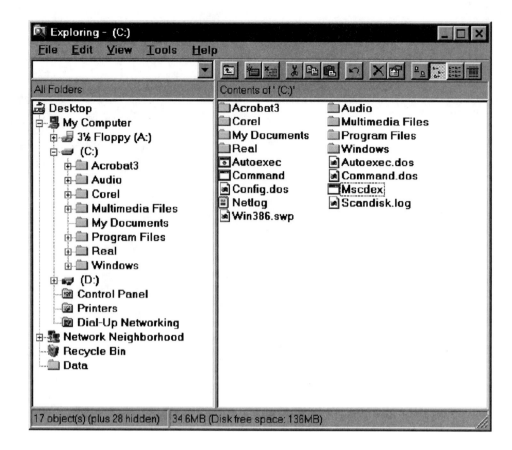

the top left corner. In addition, most program windows will include a menu and many will include one or more toolbars.

22.1.2 SHORTCUT MENUS

Shortcut menus have been added to Windows 95. They are accessed by clicking the secondary mouse button (usually the right mouse button) and contain common commands for the item selected. For example, if a file is clicked with the right mouse button, the user can choose to open the file, copy the file, delete the file, or show the properties of the file. If the disk drive in My Computer is clicked with the right mouse button, the user can open the disk, format the disk, or show the properties of the disk. If the user highlights some text in a word processing program such as Microsoft Word and clicks on the text with the right mouse button, the Cut, Copy and Paste options can be chosen or the formatting of the text can be changed.

22.2 DISK AND FILE MANAGEMENT

Disk and file management is usually done with My Computer or Windows Explorer (see fig. 22.3), which can be started by using the Programs option under the Start button. The most common disk and file management commands are shown in table 22.1. If several files or folders are to be moved, deleted, or copied at the same time, the Ctrl and Shift keys can be used to select multiple files. For example, pressing the Ctrl key and keeping it down will select any file or folder within the same drive or folder. Pressing the Shift key and keeping it down and selecting two files or folders will select everything listed between the two. After the file or directories have been selected, they can be copied, deleted, or moved as one.

Other ways to manage programs, disks, directories and files are to use:

- Program Manager (PROGMAN.EXE in the WINDOWS folder, which can be executed using Windows Explorer or by using the Run option under the Start button)

TABLE 22.1 Common disk and file management commands

To create a folder (directory) on the desktop, in the root directory or another folder	Select New from the File menu or New from the shortcut menu (right mouse button) and select the Folder option.
To delete a file or directory	Select the file or folder by clicking on it and drag it to the Recycle Bin, pick the Delete option from the shortcut or File menu, or press the Del key on the keyboard.
To format a disk	Select the Format... option from the drive's shortcut menu or select the Format... option from the My Computer File menu.
To copy a floppy disk	Select the Copy Disk... option from the drive's shortcut menu or from the My Computer File menu.
To copy a file or directory from one drive to another	Drag the file (click on the file and keep the left mouse button clicked while moving the mouse) to its new destination. Another way is to first select the file or directory and the Copy option from the shortcut menu or the Edit menu (Explorer or any disk or folder window). Then select the destination and the Paste option from the shortcut menu or Edit menu.
To move a file or directory to a different folder within the same drive	Press the Ctrl key while dragging the file to its new destination. Note: If the Ctrl key is not pressed, dragging will make a shortcut to the file or directory instead of moving the file. Another way is to first select the file or directory and select the Cut option from the shortcut menu or the Edit menu (Explorer or any disk or folder window). Then select the destination and the Paste option from the short cut menu or Edit menu.
To rename a file	Select the file and choose the Rename option in the File menu or in the shortcut menu. Another way is to click once on the filename.
To view or change the directory or file attributes (read-only, hidden, or system)	Select the folder or file and select the Properties option from the File menu or shortcut menu.

Note: Many 32-bit Windows applications also allow Cut, Copy, Delete, and Rename by using the shortcut menu from within some dialog boxes, including the Open and Save As dialog boxes.

- File Manager (WINFILE.EXE in the WINDOWS folder, which can be executed using Windows Explorer or by using the Run option under the Start button).
- MS-DOS Prompt (to start a DOS session to perform DOS commands, select the MS-DOS Prompt from the Programs option under the Start button or use the Run option and type in COMMAND and press the Enter key) Note: The standard external DOS commands are located in the WINDOWS\COMMAND directory.

22.3 WINDOWS 95 CHARACTERISTICS

Table 22.2 shows the requirements for installing and running Windows 95 and Windows 98. Although the requirements listed in the table for Windows 95 come from its documentation, they offer slow and sometimes unreliable operation. For acceptable performance and reliability, a 486DX microprocessor with a minimum of 16 MB of RAM is needed. Of course, with a faster microprocessor and additional RAM, Windows 95 will perform even better.

499

TABLE 22.2   Requirements for
Windows 95 and Windows 98

Requirements	Windows 95	Windows 98
Microprocessor	386DX microprocessor (or higher)	486DX/66 MHz microprocessor (or higher)
RAM	4 MB of RAM; 8 MB recommended to run multiple 32-bit applications	6 MB of memory; 16 MB recommended to run multiple 32-bit applications
Drives	A high-density floppy disk drive or CD-ROM drive (recommended); hard-disk drive with a minimum of 55 MB of free disk space	A high-density floppy disk drive or CD-ROM drive (recommended); hard-disk drive with a minimum of 195 MB of free disk space
Video System	VGA or better	VGA or better
Pointing Device	Not required, but highly recommended	Not required, but highly recommended
Software	MS-DOS 3.2 or later that supports partitions greater than 32 MB, or Windows 3.1 or later	MS-DOS 3.2 or later that supports partitions greater than 32 MB, or Windows 3.1 or later

22.3.1   WINDOWS 95 BOOT PROCESS

No matter which operating system is installed on a computer, when the computer is first turned on, the microprocessor starts in real mode (pretends to be an 8086). After the system does its POST, it searches for and loads the IO.SYS file, the real-mode configuration manager and operating system. The file contains enough information to start the computer, read the file system, and automatically load several files and commands that in DOS are loaded by the CONFIG.SYS and AUTOEXEC.BAT files. (See table 22.3.) (Note: The GUI includes its own software disk cache and a mouse driver for DOS programs, so loading a disk cache or a mouse driver is not necessary nor should it be done.)

The first configuration file processed by the IO.SYS file is the MSDOS.SYS file. Unlike the DOS MSDOS.SYS file, this is a text file that specifies the location of the necessary boot files, the location of the Registry (configuration database), and several start-up options. In addition to holding important configuration information, the MSDOS.SYS file is needed to provide backward compatibility with older software programs, as are the CONFIG.SYS, COMMAND.COM, and AUTOEXEC.BAT files, which provide backward compatibility for DOS drivers and applications. These files are used to load a DOS device driver (a file with a SYS filename extension loaded in the CONFIG.SYS) and a TSR (an executable file loaded in the AUTOEXEC.BAT) if there is no equivalent driver in Windows 95.

Next, WIN.COM is automatically executed and control is taken from the IO.SYS and given to the virtual memory manager (VMM32.VXD). The virtual memory manager then loads the Windows 3.XX device drivers, which have a DRV or a 386 (virtual mode driver) filename extension specified in the [ENH386] section of the SYSTEM.INI file. It then switches the microprocessor to protected mode and loads the protected mode operating system. The protected mode configuration manager is initialized and loads the 32-bit protected mode drivers (files with VxD), which are sometimes referred to as *virtual mode drivers*. As Windows 95 boots, it will scan the system for new devices. If one is found, the Hardware Configuration Wizard is executed. Sometimes, it will prompt the user to identify the hardware component so that it can load the appropriate drivers; otherwise, it will attempt to use the Add Hardware Wizard to automatically identify the hardware device and load the appropriate drivers.

After the device drivers are loaded, the Windows 95 core components are loaded, including the **kernel** (KERNL386.EXE and KERNEL32.DLL), GDI.EXE, GDI32.EXE, USER.EXE, and USER32.EXE files. The kernel file controls and allocates the machine

TABLE 22.3 Commands and files already loaded by the MSDOS.SYS file

Command/File	Function
HIMEM.SYS	Enables access to the extended memory and loads the Real Mode Memory Manager
DOS=HIGH,AUTO	Loads most of DOS into the high memory area (HMA)
IFSHLP.SYS	The Installable File System Helper loads device drivers that allow the system to make real file system calls
SETVER.EXE	Allows files that were made for an older version of DOS to work in Windows 95
FILES=60	Specifies the number of files that can be open at the same time. Unlike DOS, this command is not needed for Windows 95 and is included only for compatibility with older applications
LASTDRIVE=Z	Specifies the last drive letter available for assignment. Unlike DOS, this command is not needed for Windows 95 and is included only for compatibility with older applications
BUFFERS=30	Specifies the number of file buffers to create. Unlike DOS, this command is not needed for Windows 95 and is included only for compatibility with older applications
STACKS=9,256	Specifies 9 stacks of 256 bytes each to store information when interrupts occur. Unlike DOS, this command is not needed for Windows 95 and is included only for compatibility with older applications
SHELL=COMMAND.COM /P	Indicates which Command Interpreter should be used and that it cannot be unloaded
SET TEMP=C:\WINDOWS and SET TMP=C:\WINDOWS	Determines location of temporary files
PROMPT PG	Establishes standard DOS prompt at the command prompt
PATH=C:\WINDOWS; C:\WINDOWS\COMMAND	Sets the search path for executing files in the WINDOWS and COMMAND directories
COMSPEC=C:\WINDOWS\ COMMAND.COM	Specifies the Command Interpreter used
NET START	Starts the network connection

resources, such as memory, and runs and coordinates software applications, including loading the appropriate EXE and DLL files. In addition, it performs file I/O services and virtual memory management. Finally, Windows 95 loads the Windows environment and the fonts, checks for values in the WIN.INI file, and loads the Windows 95 shell (normally EXPLORER.EXE) and the appropriate desktop components. The User component (USER.EXE and USER32.DLL) manages input (from the keyboard and mouse) and output to the user interface (windows, icons, menus, and so on). It also interfaces with the sound driver, timer, and communication ports. The GDI (GDI.EXE and GDI32.DLL) controls the graphics device interface, which creates images on the video system, including windows, icons, and buttons, and interacts with the video drivers. The USER.EXE file interprets a double-click on an icon and tells the GDI.EXE to draw a window on the screen. The GDI also provides graphic support for printers and other output devices.

Dynamic link library (DLL) files are sets of instructions and/or data that can be accessed at any time and that are used to modularize Windows 95. This means that instead of there being one huge file containing all of the instructions needed for Windows, the instructions are broken down into smaller executable and DLL files. This allows executable files to share code and the division of applications into separate components that can be easily upgraded.

501

22.3.2 16-BIT AND 32-BIT PROGRAMMING

The IBM PC, which had the 8088 microprocessor, was a 16-bit computer because it could handle and process 16 bits of information at a time. Unfortunately, the 8088 data bus could bring in only 8 bits at a time. The later IBM AT, which included the 286 microprocessor, was a true 16-bit computer because it could process 16 bits of data at a time and had a 16-bit data bus. DOS, DOS programs, Windows 3.XX, and Windows 3.XX applications (Win16 applications) are 16-bit programs designed to work on 16-bit computers. When, a few years later, the 32-bit microprocessors (386 and 486) were introduced, DOS and Windows 3.XX could run on them and run faster because the microprocessor was faster, but the speed was not the fastest possible because the software was not written to use the entire microprocessor.

Windows 95 is mostly a 32-bit operating system so that it can take full advantage of 32-bit processing. Parts of it, however, are 16-bit so that it remains compatible with 16-bit applications, and also, since 32-bit code requires more memory, it reduces memory requirements. For example, the kernel is implemented as a 32-bit code to ensure high performance but runs older Windows applications (16-bit applications) by **thunking,** a process by which a 16-bit instruction is paired with the next instruction to make it a 32-bit instruction during execution. And while most of the GDI file consists of 32-bit code to improve performance, most of the User component remains 16-bit for application compatibility.

22.3.3 DRIVERS

As mentioned, Windows 95 can use DOS drivers and Windows 3.XX drivers as well as Windows 95 drivers. These drivers can be divided into two categories, real mode and virtual mode.

The real mode drivers are 16-bit drivers stored in conventional or upper memory. As the name implies, real mode drivers can be accessed only in the microprocessor's real mode. Therefore, when Windows 95 is running in protected mode, it must switch the microprocessor back to real mode, access the driver, and switch back to protected mode, which significantly slows the PC's performance. In addition, while in real mode, only one application or process can be run at time.

The virtual mode drivers are 32-bit drivers stored in extended memory. When the microprocessor is running in protected mode, it allows more than one application or process to run at a time, which means that more than one application can use the resource that the driver controls at the same time (multitasking). The virtual device driver keeps track of the state of the device for each application and ensures that the device is in the correct state whenever an application continues.

VxD files support all of the hardware devices for a typical computer, including disk controllers, serial and parallel ports, keyboard and display devices, and so on. The x in the VxD extension name represents the type of virtual device driver. For example, a virtual device driver for a display device is known as a VDD, a driver for a timer device is a VTD, a driver for a printer device is a VPD, and so forth. Windows 3.XX drivers were statically loaded (loaded at the beginning and remained in RAM the entire time) and took up a lot of memory. Windows 95 dynamically loads VxDs or loads them when they are needed. In addition, VxDs under Windows 95 don't require all of their memory to be page locked, thereby further increasing the available memory in the system. Some examples of virtual mode drivers are VFAT, VCACHE, and CDFS. VFAT, which is short for virtual file allocation table, is the virtual installable files system driver and acts as an interface between the applications and the file allocation table (FAT). The VCACHE is the disk cache system that replaces the SmartDrive system used in DOS and Windows 3.XX. VCACHE can dynamically change the size of the disk cache depending on available disk space, application requirements, and amount of RAM available. CDFS, short for CD-ROM file system, replaces MSCDEX.EXE used in DOS and Windows 3.XX. The CDFS uses the VCACHE driver to control the CD-ROM disk cache, allowing much smoother playback.

During boot-up, Windows 95 automatically unloads any real mode drivers for which it has protected mode drivers that provide the same functionality. For example, the real mode

DBLSPACE.BIN driver is unloaded and the protected mode DBLSPACE.VDX driver takes over. Real mode drivers that can be replaced safely are identified in the safe driver list (IOS.INI).

22.4 VFAT, FAT32, AND CDFS

By default, Windows 95 uses **VFAT,** an enhanced version of the FAT structure. VFAT is backward compatible to DOS's FAT file structure but supports long file names (up to 255 characters). Of course, in DOS or Windows 3.XX applications, only the eight-character filename and three-character extension will appear. (Note: Windows 95 can still access and use disks that have only a FAT file structure.)

FAT32 was introduced in the second major release of Windows 95 (OSR2/Windows 95B). An enhancement to the DOS FAT file system, FAT32 supported long filenames and used 32-bit FAT entries that supported hard drives up to two terabytes. In addition, it used disk space more efficiently because it had smaller clusters. The FDISK utility (from the Windows 95 OSR2/Windows 95B) must be used to install FAT32 on a volume on a hard drive over 512 MB. Unlike earlier versions of FDISK, FDISK will ask if you want to enable large disk support. If you answer yes, any partition you create that is greater than 512 MB will be marked as a FAT32 partition. At this time, Windows 95 OEM Service Release (2 and 2.5) and Windows 98 are the only operating systems capable of accessing FAT32 volumes. Therefore, DOS 6.22 or the retail version of Windows 95 (including Windows 95a) will not be able to access any files on a FAT32 volume. In addition, a drive with FAT32 cannot be compressed using Microsoft DriveSpace or DriveSpace 3.

CDFS is the virtual CD-ROM file system. It has the same responsiblities for a CD-ROM device as VFAT has for a standard hard disk. The CDFS driver is loaded dynamically as needed and is a protected-mode driver.

22.5 RUNNING PROGRAMS

Windows 95 will run Win16-based (Windows 3.XX) applications, Win32-based (Windows 95 and 98 and Windows NT) applications, and DOS applications. The program is selected by using the Program option in the Start button. An executable file can also be started by:

1. Clicking on the file (or data document) using Windows 95 Explorer or My Computer.
2. Creating a shortcut on the desktop or in any folder.
3. Using the Run option in the Start button. (See fig. 22.4.)
4. Typing the name of the executable file in an MS-DOS session

Windows 95 is a multitasking environment, so several programs can be run at the same time. The user can then change between different programs by:

- Pressing and holding down the Alt key and repeatedly pressing the Tab key until the desired application is reached
- Using the Alt+Esc keys to move to the next application
- Selecting the application button on the Taskbar

Windows 95 uses the Intel 386 microprocessor protection model. Processes (subprograms) running in Ring 0 are protected by the microprocessor, while processes running in

FIGURE 22.4   Run option under the Start Button

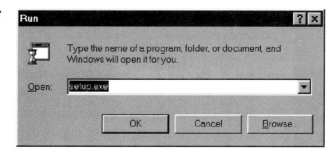

FIGURE 22.5 Programs under Windows 95

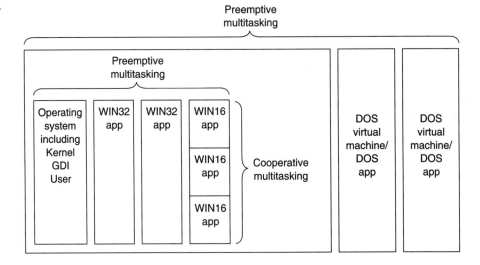

Ring 3 are protected by the operating system. Because programs running in ring 0 have full privileges over programs running in ring 3, and programs running in ring 3 have very little privilege over programs running in ring 0, the programs in ring 3 should not be able to cause problems for components in Ring 0. Therefore, Windows 95 runs the File Management subsystem and the Virtual Machine Manager (VMM) subsystem in ring 0 and the system VM (including the System Virtual Machine, or VM, and Virtual DOS Machines, or VDM, in ring 3. The VM is used to run Win16-based and Win32-based applications, and the VDM runs DOS applications.

When running programs, Windows 95 uses dynamic memory allocation so that it can use the RAM more efficiently. Dynamic memory allocation gives a program memory when it needs it and takes it away when the program is not using it.

22.5.1 WINDOWS APPLICATIONS

For Win32-based applications, Windows 95 uses preemptive multitasking. **Preemptive multitasking** is the process by which the operating system assigns time slices to tasks and applications. Tasks and applications with a higher priority get a larger time slice. In addition, Win32-based applications can take advantage of multithreading. Multithreading is the ability of an operating system to execute different parts of a program, called *threads,* simultaneously. This can enhance a program by improving throughput, responsiveness, and background processing. For example, Microsoft Word uses a thread to respond to keys typed on the keyboard by the user to place characters in a document. Other threads are used to check spelling and to paginate the document as the user types. If the user prints, another thread spools, or feeds, a document to the printer in the background. Of course, the programmer must carefully design the program in such a way that all the threads can run at the same time without interfering with each other.

Win16-based applications use cooperative multitasking, so in Windows 95 these applications cannot take advantage of preemptive multitasking. Instead, the Win16-based applications share the same memory area or **virtual machine (VM)** and are all assigned a single time slice. Unfortunately, if a program causes problems, all of the Win16-based applications can crash. All of the Win16-based applications are, however, run preemptive with Win32-based applications and other Windows 95 processes, which improves the performance of Win16-based applications. (See fig. 22.5)

22.5.2 DOS PROGRAMS

As mentioned each MS-DOS application executed is assigned its own virtual DOS machine (MS-DOS VM) with separate virtualized device access and addressable memory. The memory space created for an MS-DOS application mirrors that of a stand-alone DOS

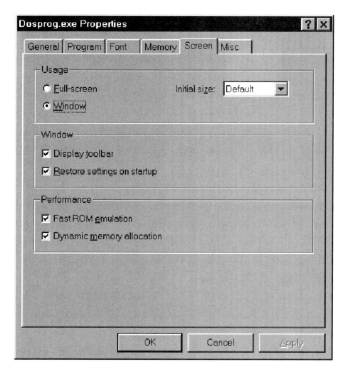

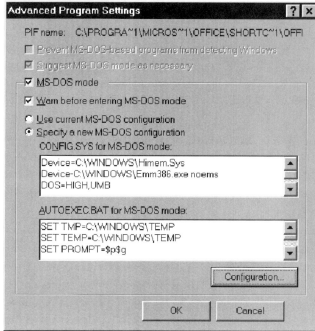

FIGURE 22.6   Memory settings for a DOS program. The picture on the left is the Memory tab within a DOS Properties option. The picture on the right is the Advanced button on the DOS Properties option.

environment with 640 KB of conventional memory, 384 KB of upper memory, and whatever extended or expanded memory is specified.

DOS applications can be executed in an MS-DOS VM or in MS-DOS mode. When running in an MS-DOS VM, the operating parameters for the DOS program can be specified by choosing the Properties option from the shortcut menu or from the File menu. This creates a program information file (PIF), which has a PIF filename extension in the directory of the executable file or in the WINDOWS\PIF file. Some of the available options include:

1. Running the program full screen or in a DOS window
2. The font used for text if it is running in a DOS window
3. The amount of memory for the program
4. Miscellaneous parameters, including interaction with screen savers and the mouse

Switching between full screen and a DOS window can be done by pressing the Alt + Enter keys. If an application cannot run in a DOS VM—for example, the application requires full access to the computer's resources or the application has video problems—the application would be run in DOS mode. To free up lots of lower memory for a DOS program, specify different AUTOEXEC.BAT and CONFIG.SYS commands for each application by using the Advanced button in the Program tab. (See fig. 22.6.)

As mentioned, DOS programs do not require a mouse driver to be loaded in the CONFIG.SYS or AUTOEXEC.BAT files because Windows has its own built-in driver. Some programs, however, may lose synchronization with the mouse when it leaves the application window. To correct this problem, select the Exclusive mode on the Misc tab in the Properties option (see fig. 22.7.), which will lock the mouse inside the MS-DOS window.

22.5.3   TERMINATING A PROGRAM

To close a program, do one of the following:

1. Choose the Exit option under the File menu
2. Click on the close button on the top right corner of the program window

505

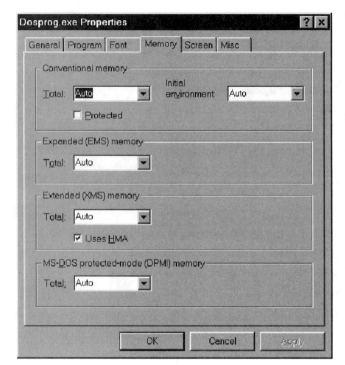
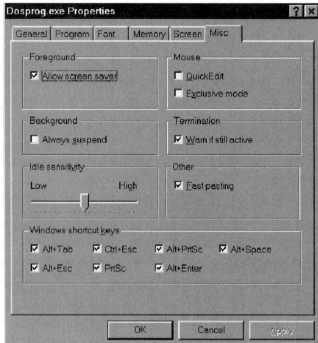

FIGURE 22.7   Screen and Misc tabs within the Properties option of a DOS program in Windows 95

3. Select Close from the Control menu icon
4. Use the shortcut menu on the application button running in the Taskbar and click on the Close button
5. Press the Ctrl+Alt+Del keys to display the Close Program dialog box and close the application. (See fig. 22.8.)

When a program locks up and does not respond, it can often be closed without affecting other programs by using the Close Program dialog box.

22.5.4   SHARING DATA

To share data between documents, Windows applications can use dynamic data exchange (DDE) or object linking and embedding (OLE).

FIGURE 22.8   Close Program dialog box after using the Ctrl+Alt+Del keys

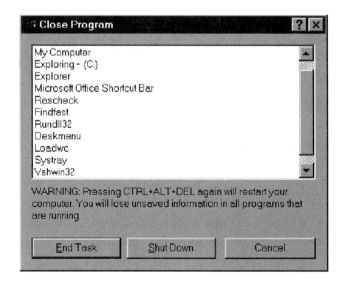

DDE was introduced with Windows 3.0 and allows users to copy data between applications while maintaining a link. Whenever data is changed at the source, it is also changed at the target. For example, an Excel chart in a Word document would change as the spreadsheet data changes. Although DDE is still used by many applications, it is slowly being replaced by OLE.

OLE (enhanced version of DDE) is a compound document standard developed by Microsoft. It allows objects created in one application to be linked or embedded in another application. Embedded objects keep their original format and links to the application that created them. For example, to make changes to an Excel chart in a Word document, you would double-click on the chart in the document and Excel would run from within the Word document. This allows changes to be made without going to the Program Manager and starting Excel in its own window.

A common way to move data between applications or documents is to use the Clipboard. By highlighting text or selecting a picture and using the Copy or Cut from the Edit menu in the source application, the text or picture goes into RAM, specifically to the Clipboard. Choosing Paste from the Edit menu when in the target document copies the data in the Clipboard into the current document using the first available format. If Paste Special is selected, the dialog box appears, listing the formats that can be chosen for pasting the data. With Paste Link, the application tries to make an OLE link to the source document. If the ObjectLink format isn't available, a DDE link is created instead. As with Windows 3.XX, the Print Screen option places a bitmap picture of the entire screen on the Clipboard. Alt+Print Screen places a bitmap picture of the active window on the Clipboard.

22.5.5   INSTALLING PROGRAMS

To install a Windows program, start the executable program that starts the installation process. The executable file is usually named INSTALL.EXE or SETUP.EXE. To find out the name of the executable file, it is best to look in the program documentation or at the first installation disk. To start the executable file, click on the file using Windows 95 Explorer or My Computer, use the Run option in the Start button, or type the name of the executable file in an MS-DOS session.

22.5.6   REMOVING A WINDOWS APPLICATION

When installed, a Windows program often adds information or modifies information in the Registry. To remove these entries and the program files on the hard drive, many programs include an Uninstall program or have an Uninstall option within the installation program. In addition, if the program follows the API (application programming interface) standard, it can be removed by using the Add/Remove Programs applet in the Control Panel. (Note: Although programs are uninstalled, some may still leave some files on the hard drive.)

22.5.7   WINDOWS ASSOCIATIONS

When a document in Windows 95 is double-clicked, Windows 95 will recognize the filename extension and start the appropriate program to open the file. This is known as *registering* a file. The information identifying the filename extensions is located in the Registry and can be accessed and modified by selecting Options… under the View menu in the My Computer, disk, or folder window and clicking on the File Type tab. (See fig. 22.9.)

22.6   PRINTING IN WINDOWS 95

After the printer is physically installed and configured, the appropriate printer driver must be loaded and the printer's location (LPT1, LPT2, LPT3, COM1, or COM2) specified. The driver is used to convert data from a document to commands that the printer understands. If the wrong driver is used when printing a document, the wrong control codes are sent to

FIGURE 22.9   Windows 95 file association

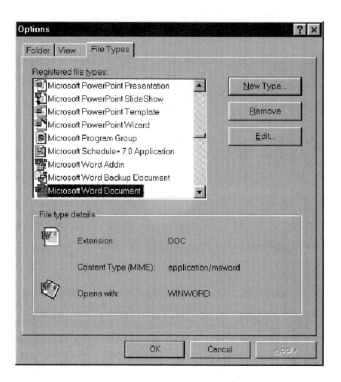

FIGURE 22.10   The Add Printer Wizard

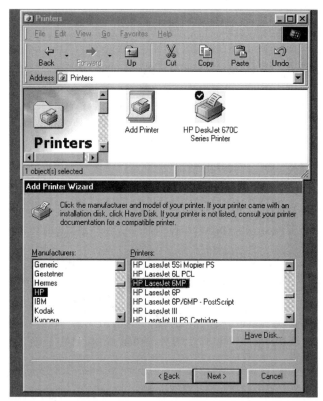

the printer and the printer will produce garbage (strange characters or many pages of programming code).

The printer driver can be loaded in one of two ways. One way is to start the Add Printer Wizard by double-clicking on the Add Printer icon in the Printers folder. (See fig. 22.10.) The Printers folder can be accessed using My Computer, the Control Panel, Explorer, or the Settings option in the Start button. The second way is by using the setup disks that come with the printer. (Note: Some printers, such as some newer Hewlett-Packard printers, are automatically detected and the drivers are automatically loaded from the Windows 95 or 98 CD-ROM.)

FIGURE 22.11 Print Manager. Notice the small printer icon located on the right side of the Taskbar.

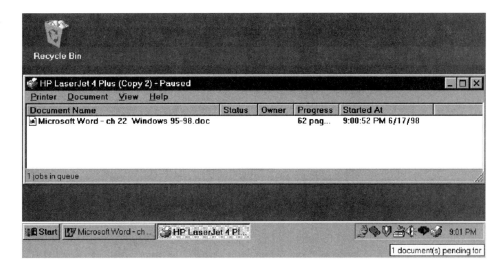

Printing is usually done by using the Print... option on the File menu or a Print button on a toolbar. The application then creates a print file and sends it to the Print Manager, which holds the print job until the printer becomes available. As the Print Manager holds the print job, a small printer icon will appear on the right side of the Taskbar. The status of a print job can be checked or changed by double-clicking on the printer icon on the Taskbar or by double-clicking on the printer icon in the Printers folder. (See fig. 22.11.) (Note: The Print Manager works in the background, so other tasks can be performed while printing.)

Question: A user decides to print, but the document does not print. Therefore, the user decides to print again. After several attempts, the user figures that there must be a problem with the printer and after the printer problem is fixed, all of the print jobs sent to the printer start printing one by one. What can you do?

Answer: Switch to the Print Manager, which will list all of the printers and all of the print jobs. The unneeded print jobs can be highlighted and deleted with a click on the Delete button.

> **NOTE** If the print icon is grayed out, Windows 95 and 98 cannot access the printer. This is usually caused by the printer being offline or the network connection not being up.

22.7 CONFIGURING WINDOWS 95

Windows 95 is a complex operating system consisting of many small programs. Because of its complexity, configuring Windows 95 can be done in several different ways. The most common is by using the Control Panel.

22.7.1 THE CONTROL PANEL

The **Control Panel** is a graphical tool used to configure the Windows environment and hardware devices. (See fig. 22.12.) It can be accessed from the Settings option in the Start button under My Computer. There are also various shortcuts to directly access certain Control Panel **applets** (icons). The default Control Panel applets are shown in table 22.4. The most commonly used applets are the System applet, the Display applet, the Add/Remove Programs applet, and the Add New Hardware applet.

The System applet can be accessed through the Control Panel or through the Properties option in the shortcut menu of My Computer. The General tab shows the version of Windows 95, the amount of physical RAM, and the OEM number of Windows 95. (See fig. 22.13.)

In the Device Manager tab, double-clicking on the computer on top of the tree structure or selecting the computer and clicking on the Properties button will reveal all the IRQ,

FIGURE 22.12   The Control Panel

FIGURE 22.13   System applet within the Control Panel

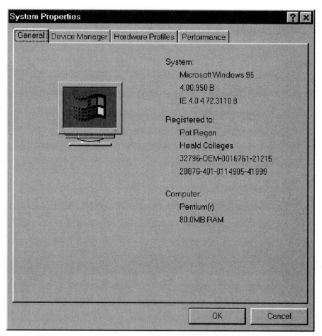

DMA, I/O address, and memory areas used by the different hardware components. (See fig. 22.14.) The rest of Device Manager shows all hardware devices organized in a tree structure. A red X through an icon means the hardware device has been disabled. A yellow circled exclamation point through the icon means that the hardware device has a problem. The problem could be a resource conflict (IRQ, DMA, I/O address, or memory address) or the drivers may not be loaded properly. (See figs. 22.15 and 22.16.) To see hardware in a category, click on the plus sign next to the hardware type. To see information about a piece of hardware, double-click on the hardware device icon or select the hardware device and click on the Properties button. The properties menu will usually contain several tabs that indicate if the device is working properly and what drivers are loaded, and options for updating them and viewing and changing the device resources.

The Performance tab of the System Properties dialog box shows the amount of physical RAM, percentage of free system resources, and the type of file system, virtual memory,

TABLE 22.4   Default Control Panel applets

Applet	Function
32-bit ODBC	Configures the programming interface that enables applications to access data in a database management system that uses SQL as a data access standard
Accessibility Options	Used for people who have physical disabilities
Add New Hardware	Starts the Add New Hardware Wizard, which can automatically detect new hardware devices and load the appropriate drivers or allows you to select the hardware component
Add/Remove Programs	Used to install and remove programs, add Windows 95 components, and create a start-up disk
Color	Used to select color schemes or customize the colors used for the desktop, the area of the screen in which windows, icons, and dialog boxes appear
Date/Time	Changes the system date and time
Display	Used to change the Windows environment, including menus, windows, and icons; controls the screen saver and allows you to install, change, or configure video drivers
Fonts	Used to manage the fonts on the system, including adding and deleting fonts
Joystick	Configures and calibrates joysticks and game paddles
Keyboard	Adjusts how the keyboard responds under Windows
Modems	Installs and configures modems
Mouse	Adjusts how the mouse responds under Windows
Multimedia	Used to configure audio, video, audio CD, and MIDI settings
Network	Installs and configures network cards and protocols
Passwords	Configures remote passwords and user profiles
PC Card (PCMCIA)	Installs and configures PC cards
Power	Enables and configures power-saving features so batteries used in notebook and laptop computers will last longer
Printers	Opens printer folder
Regional Settings	Configures international settings
Sounds	Assigns different sounds to system and application events or specifies MIDI settings
System	Shows version and OEM number and has the Device Manager, which allows you to configure all hardware devices and to resolve resource conflicts, set hardware profiles, and configure virtual memory

disk compression, and PC cards. (See fig. 22.17.) All of the settings displayed should be 32-bit; if one or more of them is not 32-bit, then an old DOS driver is probably loaded.

Virtual memory is disk pretending to be RAM. For Windows 95, virtual memory is known as a swap file. By default, the Windows 95 swap file is temporary and changeable. If hard disk space is running low, the size of the swap file is decreased. If hard disk space is available and more memory is required, the size of the swap file is increased. (See fig. 22.18.)

The Advanced settings (File System..., Graphics..., and Virtual Memory...) optimize Windows 95 and make troubleshooting certain problems possible. It is recommended that a system running Windows 95 have at least 10 MB of hard disk space left for file swapping. Less than this could cause numerous read/write errors, general protection faults, and drastically slow performance. Under the File System button, there is a setting labeled "Typical Role of This Machine." (See fig. 22.19.) This setting determines how much space is set aside in main memory to handle path and filename caching. The default, Desktop Computer, allocates space for 32 paths and 677 filenames, whereas the Network

FIGURE 22.14 Device Manager showing the hardware resources

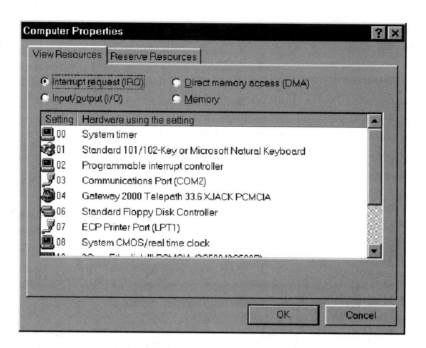

FIGURE 22.15 Windows 95 Device Manager. Notice that the 3Com Etherlink III card has a problem and that the Generic Ir Serial Port (COM1) is diabled.

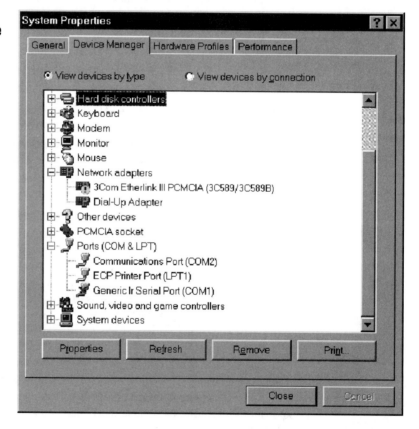

Server allocates space for 64 paths and 2,729 filenames. Even if the computer is not a network server, if there is more than 24 MB of RAM, it should set to Network Server for better performance. (Note: Network Server is not an available option on the original release of Windows 95. To make this option available to the original version, the changes to the Registry shown in table 22.5 would have to be made. The Registry and how to make the changes in the Registry will be explained later in this chapter.)

The Display applet configures the Windows environment, including menus, windows, icons, the desktop, and the screen saver. It also configures the video system, installs or upgrades video drivers, and sets the video resolution and number of colors. It can be accessed

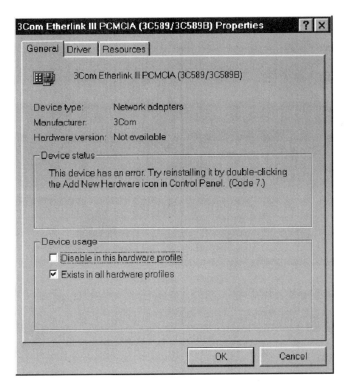
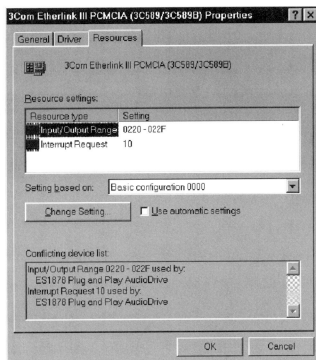

FIGURE 22.16 Properties of a device in Device Manager. Notice the resource conflict.

FIGURE 22.17 Performance
tab of the System applet of the
Control Panel

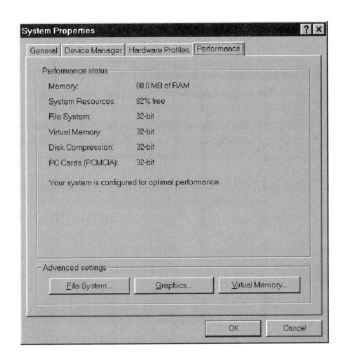

FIGURE 22.17 Performance
tab of the System applet of the
Control Panel

through the Control Panel or by choosing the Properties option on the shortcut menu of the
desktop. (See fig. 22.20.) The Add/Remove Programs applet installs and uninstalls programs, adds or removes Windows 95 components, and creates a start-up disk. The start-up
disk is used to start the computer to a command prompt to restart software programs that
will not run and to fix boot problems. When creating a start-up disk, you will be asked to
insert the Windows 95 installation disk or Windows 95 installation CD-ROM so that a
clean copy of all necessary files can be made. If you are working with systems that have
Windows 95a and Windows 95b versions, you will have to create a start-up disk for each
version. (See fig. 22.21.)

FIGURE 22.18 Virtual Memory settings from within the System applet of the Control Panel

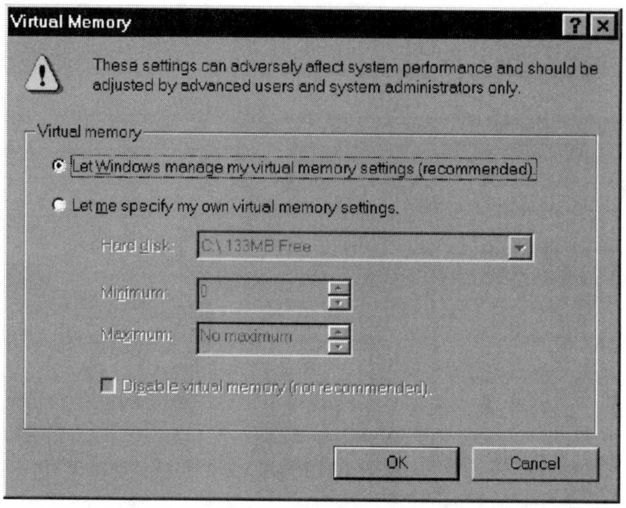

FIGURE 22.19 File System properties

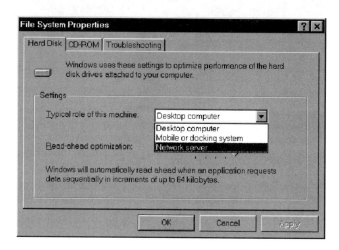

TABLE 22.5 Changes needed in the Registry to make the Network Server option available

Registry Setting	Value
HKEY_LOCAL_MACHINE\SOFTWARE \Microsoft\Windows\CurrentVersion\ FSTemplates\Server–ameCache	A9 0a 00 00
HKEY_LOCAL_MACHINE\SOFTWARE \Microsoft\Windows\CurrentVersion\ FSTemplates\Server\PathCache	40 00 00 00

22.7.2 THE DESKTOP AND THE TASKBAR

As already stated, the desktop contains the My Computer and Recycle Bin icons. In addition, it can hold folders, files, and shortcuts. A folder or a shortcut is created with the desktop's shortcut menu and the New option. The desktop folders, files, and shortcuts are stored in the WINDOWS\DESKTOP folder.

The Taskbar can be configured by using the Properties button (Taskbar Options) on the taskbar's shortcut menu or by using the Taskbar... option in the Settings option in the Start button menu. In the Taskbar Options tab, you can specify:

1. Whether the Taskbar auto-hides when it is not being used
2. Whether the taskbar will show the time
3. Whether the Start menu will use small icons or large icons

From the Start Menu Programs tab, programs listed under the Start button can be added, removed, or reorganized or the documents menu can be cleared. (See fig. 22.22.)

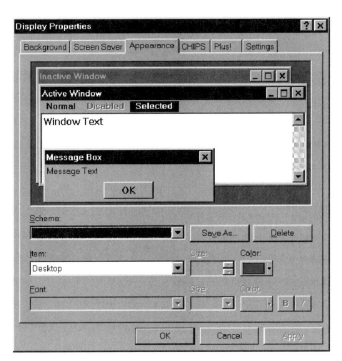

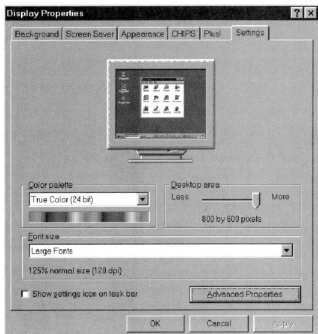

FIGURE 22.20   Display applet within the Control Panel

FIGURE 22.21   Add/Remove Programs applet within the Control Panel

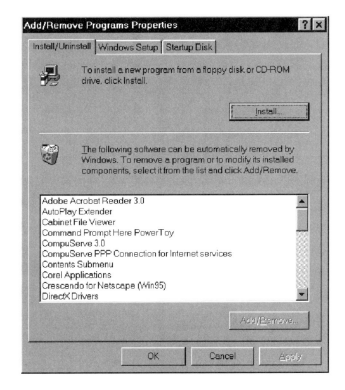

22.7.3   MSDOS.SYS FILE

As mentioned earlier in the chapter, the MSDOS.SYS file is an important configuration text file used during boot-up. MSDOS.SYS is located in the root directory and is a hidden, system, read-only file. It contains a [Paths] section that lists the locations for other Windows 95 files (such as the Registry file) and an [Options] section that can be used to personalize the boot process. Some of the file's contents are shown in table 22.6. To make MSDOS.SYS backward compatible to some older programs, it contains a large section of

FIGURE 22.22 Taskbar properties

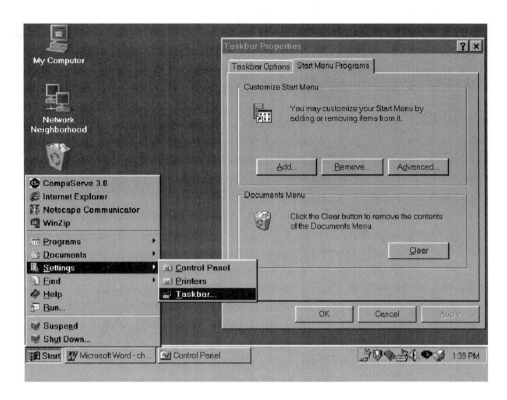

FIGURE 22.23 Windows 95 MSDOS.SYS file

```
[Paths]
WinDir=C: \WINDOWS
WinBootDir=C: \WINDOWS
HostWinBootDrv=C

[Options]
BootMulti=1
BootGUI=1
Network=1
;
;The following lines are required for compatibility with other programs.
;Do not remove them (MSDOS.SYS needs to be >1024 bytes).
;xxxxxxxxxxxxxxxxxxxxxxxxxxxxxxxxxxxxxxxxxa
;xxxxxxxxxxxxxxxxxxxxxxxxxxxxxxxxxxxxxxxxxb
;xxxxxxxxxxxxxxxxxxxxxxxxxxxxxxxxxxxxxxxxxc
;xxxxxxxxxxxxxxxxxxxxxxxxxxxxxxxxxxxxxxxxxd
;xxxxxxxxxxxxxxxxxxxxxxxxxxxxxxxxxxxxxxxxe
;xxxxxxxxxxxxxxxxxxxxxxxxxxxxxxxxxxxxxxxf
;xxxxxxxxxxxxxxxxxxxxxxxxxxxxxxxxxxxxxxxxg
;xxxxxxxxxxxxxxxxxxxxxxxxxxxxxxxxxxxxxxxxh
;xxxxxxxxxxxxxxxxxxxxxxxxxxxxxxxxxxxxxxxxxi
;xxxxxxxxxxxxxxxxxxxxxxxxxxxxxxxxxxxxxxxxxj
;xxxxxxxxxxxxxxxxxxxxxxxxxxxxxxxxxxxxxxxxxk
;xxxxxxxxxxxxxxxxxxxxxxxxxxxxxxxxxxxxxxxxxl
;xxxxxxxxxxxxxxxxxxxxxxxxxxxxxxxxxxxxxxxxxm
;xxxxxxxxxxxxxxxxxxxxxxxxxxxxxxxxxxxxxxxxxn
;xxxxxxxxxxxxxxxxxxxxxxxxxxxxxxxxxxxxxxxxxo
;xxxxxxxxxxxxxxxxxxxxxxxxxxxxxxxxxxxxxxxxxp
;xxxxxxxxxxxxxxxxxxxxxxxxxxxxxxxxxxxxxxxxxq
;xxxxxxxxxxxxxxxxxxxxxxxxxxxxxxxxxxxxxxxxxxxxr
;xxxxxxxxxxxxxxxxxxxxxxxxxxxxxxxxxxxxxxxxxs
```

X's to keep it at a minimum size of 1,024 bytes. For example, if an antivirus program detects that the MSDOS.SYS file is less than 1,024 bytes, it may assume that the MSDOS.SYS file is infected with a virus. Therefore, the X's should not be deleted. (See fig. 22.23.) A text editor (such as EDIT or Notepad) or TWEAK UI, which provides a graphical interface, can be used to change the contents of the MSDOS.SYS file. (Note: TWEAK UI can be downloaded from the Microsoft website.)

TABLE 22.6   MS.DOS.INI contents

[Paths] Section	
HostWinBootDrv=⟨Root of Boot Drive⟩ Default: C	Specifies the location for the root of the boot drive.
WinBootDir=⟨Windows Directory⟩ Default: Directory specified during setup (for example, C:\WINDOWS)	Lists the location of the necessary files for booting.
WinDir=⟨Windows Directory⟩ Default: Directory specified during setup (for example, C:\WINDOWS)	Lists the location of the Windows directory specified during setup.

[Options] Section	
BootDelay=⟨Seconds⟩ Default: 2	Sets the amount of time the "Starting Windows" message remains on the screen before Windows 95 continues to boot.
Purpose: BootFailSafe=⟨Boolean⟩ Default: 0	A setting of 1 forces the computer to boot in safe mode.
BootGUI=⟨Boolean⟩ Default: 1	A setting of 1 forces the loading of the GUI interface. A setting of 0 disables the loading of the GUI interface.
BootKeys=⟨Boolean⟩ Default: 1	A setting of 1 enables the use of the function key boot options (that is, F4, F5, F6, and F8). A setting of 0 disables the use of these function keys during the boot process. A setting of BootKeys=0 overrides the use of BootDelay=n.
BootMenu=⟨Boolean⟩ Default: 0	A setting of 1 enables the start-up menu. A setting of 0 requires pressing the F8 key when "Starting Windows" appears to invoke the start-up menu.
BootMenuDefault=⟨Number⟩ Default: 1 if the system is running correctly; 4 if the system hung in the previous instance	Sets the default menu item for start-up.
BootMenuDelay=⟨Number⟩ Default: 30	This setting is used to set the number of seconds the system will pause on the start-up menu. If the number of seconds counts down to 0 without intervention, the BootMenuDefault is activated.
BootMulti=⟨Boolean⟩ Default: 0	A setting of 0 disables the multiboot option. (for example, a setting of 0 prevents booting the previous operating system). A setting of 1 enables the F4 and F8 keys to boot the previous operating system. This setting is set to 0 by default to avoid the corruption of data by inadvertently booting MS-DOS and running a disk utility that does not recognize long filenames.
BootWarn=⟨Boolean⟩ Default: 1	A setting of 0 disables the safe mode boot warning message and the start-up menu.
BootWin=⟨Boolean⟩ Default: 1	A setting of 1 forces Windows 95 to load at start-up. A setting of 0 disables Windows 95 as the default operating system (this is useful only if MS-DOS version 5.X or 6.X is on the computer). Note: Pressing F4 inverts the default only if BootMulti=1. (For example, pressing the F4 key with a setting of 0 forces Windows 95 to load.)

continued

TABLE 22.6 *continued*

[Options] Section *continued*	
DRVSpace=⟨Boolean⟩ Default: 1	A setting of 1 allows the automatic loading of the DRVSPACE.BIN file. A setting of 0 prevents the automatic loading of this file.
LoadTop=⟨Boolean⟩ Default: 1	A setting of 0 does not let Windows 95 load COMMAND.COM, DRVSPACE.BIN, or DBLSPACE.BIN at the top of the 640 KB memory. If compatibility problems occur with software that makes assumptions about the available memory, try setting this to 0.
Logo=⟨Boolean⟩ Default: 1	A setting of 1 forces the default Windows 95 logo to appear. A setting of 0 prevents the animated logo from being displayed. A setting of 0 also avoids hooking a variety of interrupts that can create incompatibilities with certain third-party memory managers.

22.8 WINDOWS 95 REGISTRY

The Windows 95 **Registry** is the central information database for Windows 95 and is organized into a tree-structured hierarchy. It replaces the DOS AUTOEXEC.BAT, CONFIG.SYS, and initialization files (files with an INI filename extension, such as the SYSTEM.INI and WIN.INI) and includes hundreds of additional system settings. If you were able to print out the entire registry, it would fill several thousand pages. Initialization files, which are limited to 64 KB of text and support only two levels of information (section name and values), still exist in Windows 95 but only to provide backward compatibility to older Windows applications. Changes made using the Control Panel, such as installing or removing a program or adding or removing a printer, are automatically made in the Registry during boot-up. Changing the Registry manually (such as changing a value that cannot be modified by using the Control Panel or similar utility) requires using a program called Registry Editor (REGEDIT.EXE). (See fig. 22.24.)

The Registry is divided into six HKEYs, as shown in table 22.7. If any key is highlighted in REGEDIT.EXE, its contents appear in the Contents pane. An HKEY is divided into keys (similar to folders). H stands for handle, which contains thousands of text strings that can be configured. A boxed plus sign to the left of the Registry key indicates it contains one or more subkeys (similar to subfolders). Each subkey may contain its own subkey, and so on for several levels. In addition to the keys and subkeys, the Contents pane shows the Windows 95 configuration settings broken down into values. REGEDIT.EXE shows the data type icon (which represents the type of data that the value can store), the name of the value, and the value in the Contents pane. The data types are shown in table 22.8. The master HKEYs are the HKEY_LOCAL_MACHINE and HKEY_USERS, which contain 90% of the Registry's information. The master HKEYS are derived from Registry files (USER.DAT, which contains the user-specific settings, and SYSTEM.DAT, which contains the computer hardware configuration) hidden in the WINDOWS directory. The other HKEYs, sometimes referred to as the *virtual registry,* are a host of files created by Windows 95 at start-up.

The only time you should go into the Registry is at the direction of an article, book, product documentation, or support person. If you ever decide to change the values in the Registry, you should follow certain guidelines. First, back up the Registry (SYSTEM.DAT and USER.DAT) to a safe location, preferably to a floppy disk (if it fits on a floppy disk). If anything goes terribly wrong, you can restore the Registry. Next, make only one change at a time so that if there is a problem, you know which value is causing the problem.

FIGURE 22.24   REGEDIT.EXE showing the Windows 95 Registry

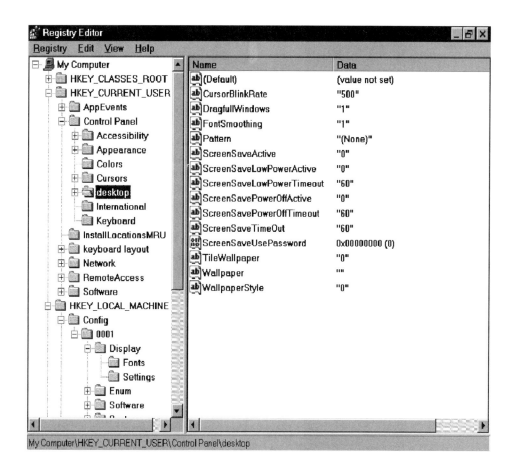

22.9   WINDOWS 95 UPDATES AND WINDOWS 98

Several months after the retail version of Windows 95 (version 4.00.950) was introduced, Microsoft issued Service Pack 1 (version 4.00.950a after installation). Some of the fixes done by Service Pack 1 included:

1. An OLE32 update
2. A Microsoft Windows 95 shell update that permitted browsing NetWare Directory Service printers from the Add Printer Wizard
3. Windows 95 Common Dialog update for Windows 3.1 Legacy printer drivers
4. The Windows 95 Password List update to protect the password file against potential security violations
5. An update of LPT.VXD to support ECP (enhanced communication parallel) port bi-directional communications
6. Several network updates

22.9.1   MICROSOFT PLUS! COMPANION FOR WINDOWS 95

The Microsoft Plus! Companion for Windows 95 is an add-on software package that includes several utilities and desktop enhancements left out of Windows 95. In addition, it includes System Agent, DriveSpace 3, Internet Explorer, the Dial-up Networking system, and a 3D pinball game. System Agent will schedule applications to automatically start at predefined times. DriveSpace 3 is an enhanced version of the disk compression software that comes with Windows 95. Internet Explorer 3.0 is a World Wide Web browser, and the Dial-up Networking server allows others to dial into a computer using a modem.

22.9.2   WINDOWS 95 OEM SERVICE RELEASES (OSR2)

OEM Service Release 2 (OSR2), released at the end of 1996, is an updated version of the retail version of Windows 95 and is sometimes referred to as Windows 95b. Unlike the retail

TABLE 22.7   Root keys of the Windows 95 Registry

Root Key	Description
HKEY_CLASSES_ROOT	Contains software settings for file associations and OLE information. This key points to a branch of HKEY_ LOCAL_MACHINE.
HKEY_CURRENT_USER	Contains settings for applications, desktop configurations, and user preferences for the user currently logged on. It points to a branch of HKEY_USERS for the user who is currently logged on. **AppEvents:** Contains the settings for which sounds to play for system sound events **Control Panel:** Stores Control Panel settings **InstallLocationsMRU:** MRU stands for "most recently used." It contains paths for StartUp folder programs. **Keyboard layout:** Specifies current keyboard layout **Network:** Contains network connection information **RemoteAccess:** Contains information about the current log-on location if using Dial-up Networking **Software:** Software configuration for the user currently logged on.
HKEY_LOCAL_MACHINE	Contains information about the type of hardware installed, drivers, and other system settings **Config:** Configuration information **Enum:** Hardware device information, such as monitor settings **Hardware:** Serial communication port information and settings **Network:** Information about networks for the user who is currently logged on **Security:** Network security settings **Software:** Software-specific information and settings **System:** System start-up and device driver information and operating system settings
HKEY_USERS	Contains information (such as desktop settings) about all users who log on to the computer (each user has a subkey) including the DEFAULT generic user settings. The DEFAULT user is used as a template for any new users.
HKEY_CURRENT_CONFIG	Contains information about the current running hardware configuration. The HKEY_CURRENT_CONFIG points to a branch of the HKEY_LOCAL_MACHINE\Config, which usually contains duplicate references to the same data. The duplicate references help prevent corruption in the Registry.
HKEY_DYN_DATA	Contains dynamic (continuously changing) status information for various devices as part of the plug-and-play configuration. It points to a branch of HKEY_ LOCAL_MACHINE.

version of Windows 95, OSR2 is available only to PC vendors and can be purchased only with a new computer, motherboard, or hard drive. Whereas the original version of Windows 95 was made to upgrade Windows 3.XX or to be installed on a new system, the OSR2 was made for new systems only. Therefore, the retail Windows 95 (version 950) cannot be upgraded with Windows 95 OSR2. The OSR2 provided a number of new features and bug fixes, including the fixes done with Service Pack 1. Some of the new features included:

- FAT32 file system
- DriveSpace 3 (disk compression)
- Online services software, including AOL, CompuServe, and MSN

TABLE 22.8   Types of data found in the Registry

Type of Data	Definition and Examples
String data	One or more alphanumeric values enclosed in quotation marks (except when a value is not set). Examples: "0" (Value not set) "" "vxdfile"
Binary data	A hexadecimal number. Examples: D8 08 00 00 60 0d 00 a0 01 04 ff ff ff 00
DWORD	A 4-byte hexadecimal number. Examples: 0x00000240 0x00000300 Note: Because the DWORD (double-word) format uses the same data-type icon as binary data, it is identified by 0x followed by an unspaced 4-byte (8-digit) hexadecimal number.

- Internet Explorer 3.0
- Microsoft Internet Mail and News, Internet Connect Wizard, NetMeeting, Microsoft and Peer Web Server
- Control Panel display tool enhancements
- OpenGL support and screen savers
- DirectX 2.0
- ActiveMovie
- Support for 32-bit PC cards
- Additional power management features
- Support for IrDa wireless communications
- Daylight Savings Time and time zone updates
- Updated user interface for hardware profiles

Microsoft OpenGL is a 3D graphics language designed to improve performance on hardware that supports the OpenGL standard. To demonstrate OpenGL, OSR2 includes 3D screen savers. (Note: When the OpenGL screen savers are active, they consume a large amount of processing.) DirectX is an application programming interface (API) developed by Microsoft that enables programs to access hardware features of a computer without knowing exactly what hardware is installed on the machine. DirectX was originally designed to allow Windows 95 to become a gaming platform but has grown into a multimedia platform. DirectX achieves this by translating generic hardware commands into specific commands for particular pieces of hardware. In particular, DirectX lets multimedia applications take advantage of hardware acceleration features supported by graphic accelerators. DirectX 2, released in 1996, supports the Direct3D architecture.

In February 1998, Microsoft released OEM Service Release 2.5 (OSR 2.5). Much like OSR2, OSR 2.5 can be sold only with a new computer, new motherboard, or hard drive. The new features include Microsoft Internet Explorer 4.01, updated online services, universal serial bus (USB) support, and a few minor fixes. In addition, it includes DirectX 5, which includes DirectDraw, DirectSound, DirectShow, and DirectAnimation to allow programs to manipulate multimedia objects and streams and supports universal serial bus (USB) and IEEE 1394 buses, accelerated graphics port (AGP), and multimedia extensions (MMX). The newest version of DirectX can be downloaded from the Microsoft website.

22.9.3   WINDOWS 98

Windows 98, released in June of 1998, is the newest version of Windows 95. The most obvious difference between Windows 95 and Windows 98 is the Active Desktop interface, which allows the operating system to use the same interface as Internet Explorer. (Note: the Active Desktop interface has been available with Internet Explorer 4.0.) (See fig. 22.25.) In addition, to the interface changes, Windows 98 offers the following:

- More stability—Microsoft fixed over 3,000 bugs
- Faster speed, particularly during boot-up and shutdown
- Advanced Power Management (APM) 1.2, allowing for a longer battery life on portable computers

FIGURE 22.25 Active Desktop interface

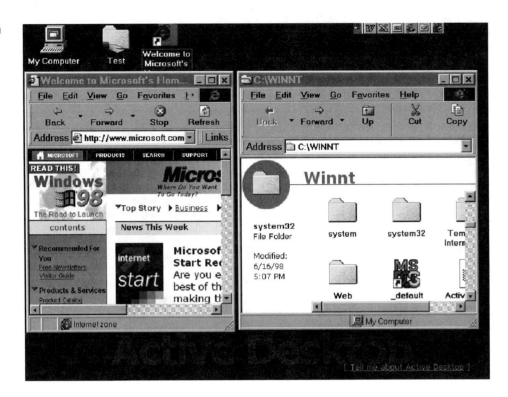

- Automatic performance of maintenance tasks, such as defragmenting the hard disk
- Better protection for the Registry by tracking changes to it with the last five copies of the Registry
- Improved system diagnostics, including a Registry checker, a version conflict manager, the Microsoft System Information program, and several troubleshooting wizards to help isolate problems
- Automatic downloading and updating of the operating system and drivers
- The ability to connect several monitors to a computer
- Integration of a multimedia architecture including broadcast architecture, which allows you to watch TV on your computer
- Support for a number of new technologies, including FAT32, accelerated graphics port (AGP), multimedia extensions (MMX), universal serial bus (USB), and digital versatile/video disk (DVD)
- A new unified driver model for Windows 98 and Windows NT called the Win32 Driver Model (WDM)

When Windows 98 ships, Microsoft also offers *Microsoft Plus! 98,* which contains several other utilities, including McAfee Viruscan, file cleaners, compressed folders, Deluxe CD Player (which can search the web for artists and songs), several new games, and shopping online.

22.10 INSTALLING WINDOWS 95

Windows 95 can be installed from floppy disk or CD-ROM or over a network. To start the Windows 95 installation, go to the first installation disk or CD-ROM and execute the SETUP.EXE file from within Windows 3.1 or later or at the DOS prompt (DOS 3.2 or latter). Table 22.9 lists the switches for the Setup program. In Windows 95 Setup, you can choose from the several types of installation shown in table 22.10.

22.10.1 RUNNING THE INSTALLATION PROGRAM

SETUP.EXE will first run SCANDISK to make sure that there are no problems with the disk. It will then check for other versions of Windows, for memory managers, and for a

TABLE 22.9 Setup switches

Switch	Function
SETUP /IS	Disables SCANDISK
SETUP /ID	Does not check for disk space
SETUP /IM	Ignores the conventional memory check
SETUP /IL	Installs the Logitech mouse driver, which is available only when installing from DOS
SETUP /IQ	Disables the crosslink hard disk check if /IS is used
SETUP /C	Does not load SMARTDRV; available only when installing from DOS
SETUP /IN	Does not run Network Setup; available only when installing from DOS
SETUP /T:<path>	Defines the location of temporary setup files; the directory specified must already exist and will be deleted when the setup is done
SETUP /<batchfilename>	Specifies the batch file that contains setup options so Windows can be installed as an unattended installation
SETUP /?	Displays the Help screen

TABLE 22.10 Types of Windows 95 setups

Setup	Description
Typical	Performs most installation steps automatically with minimal interaction from the user
Portable Setup	Performs an installation for users with notebook or laptop computers
Compact Setup	Performs a minimum installation for limited disk space
Custom Setup	Allows the most control of the installation process, including the location of the installation and which components to install

disk cache. If a cache is not loaded, it will load one. Next, it looks for TSR programs and device drivers that may be incompatible with the installation process and will either close them or ask the user to close them. If the installation is not run from Windows, the minimal Windows components are installed and started. If you are having problems with Windows 95 or 98 (such as GPFs or the computer locking up even after reinstalling Windows 95 and other applications), it is sometimes best to perform a clean installation—that is, remove everything from the hard drive before installing Windows 95.

The Setup program then switches the microprocessor into protected mode and attempts to detect the hardware installed in the system. If Setup cannot determine the hardware or its configuration settings, the user is prompted to provide the appropriate information. The boot files are copied onto the computer and the boot records are modified. When the system reboots, Windows will ask for the time zone and migrate any Windows 3.XX programs.

22.10.2 DUAL BOOTING DOS AND WINDOWS 95

If the retail version (or the retail version with service pack A) of Windows 95 or Windows 98 is being installed on a system that already has DOS and Windows 3.XX, Windows can be made to dual boot between DOS and Windows by using the Custom Installation option. When prompted, install Windows 95 or 98 into a directory other than the one that is holding Windows 3.XX—WIN95, for example. Before upgrading Windows 3.XX, make a copy of the necessary boot files, the CONFIG.SYS and AUTOEXEC.BAT files, Windows initialization (*.INI) and group files (*.GRP), dynamic link library files (*.DLL), and any other critical files, such as necessary drivers. Keep in mind also that since both operating systems and environments are being loaded, additional disk space will be required.

To start Windows 95, let the system boot normally. To start DOS (and Windows 3.XX), press the F4 key as soon as Starting Windows 95… appears during boot-up. Because Windows 95 does not have the initialization files for the WIN16-based applications, they will have to be installed a second time. Fortunately, the same installation directories used in Windows 3.XX can be specified. When Windows 95 is booted, the DOS boot files are renamed IO.DOS, MSDOS.DOS, CONFIG.DOS, COMMAND.DOS, and AUTOEXEC.DOS. When booting to DOS, the DOS boot files are renamed with their original names and the Windows 95 boot files are renamed WINBOOT.SYS (formerly IO.SYS), MSDOS.W40, CONFIG.W40, COMMAND.W40, and AUTOEXEC.W40.

Windows 95 OSR2 does not support dual booting with DOS/Windows 3.XX. Attempting to boot to a previous version of DOS will hang, or freeze, Windows 95 when rebooting to Windows 95. Therefore, if you still want to dual boot with the newer versions of Windows 95, you will have to use a third-party boot manager like Partition Magic 3.0 or Windows NT 4.0, or you can download Win95Boot from the following website:

http://www.tu-chemnitz.de/~jwes/win95boot.html

22.10.3 TROUBLESHOOTING THE SETUP

Problems with a Windows 95 installation can be caused by incompatible hardware, an incompatible TSR or device driver, faulty hardware, or viruses. SETUPLOG.TXT and DETLOG.TXT can help in the troubleshooting of a Windows 95 installation.

The SETUPLOG.TXT file is a hidden text file stored in the root directory that contains information written during a Windows 95 installation. Besides storing custom information, such as the user name and company, this file can be used to recover from a setup failure by recording any error conditions encountered during the installation. During a second installation attempt, Windows 95 will review the contents of the SETUPLOG.TXT file so that it can skip the steps that failed previously.

The DETLOG.TXT file is a hidden text file that contains a record of all devices found during the hardware detection phase of installation. If the hardware detection phase causes the computer to lock up or crash, a binary file named DETCRASH.LOG is created. The hardware problem can be viewed in the DETLOG.TXT file. Incompatible hardware is the number-one cause of Windows installation problems.

22.11 TROUBLE-SHOOTING WINDOWS 95 AND 98

When troubleshooting Windows 95 and 98 problems, there are several diagnostic tools that can help. If it is a hardware problem, a good place to start is with the device manager, which will show resource conflicts and improperly loaded drivers. If the problem seems to be low resources, you can look at the System properties (Control Panel System applet) to see the percentage of free system resources (FSR) or you can start Resource Meter. If you are installing Windows 95 for the first time, the SETUPLOG.TXT and DETLOG.TXT files will often indicate what is causing the problem. (See table 22.11 for a list of troubleshooting resources.)

22.11.1 BOOT PROBLEMS

If the computer locks up during boot-up, reboot the computer. When Windows does not complete a boot, it shows a boot menu on the next boot-up. The menu consists of the normal boot option, logged option, safe mode, step-by-step confirmation, command prompt, and safe mode command prompt only.

The logged option is used to create a BOOTLOG.TXT file located in the root directory of the boot startup drive during boot-up. The logged boot-up also occurs when pressing the

TABLE 22.11 Useful Windows 95 websites

Microsoft	**Microsoft Technical Support:** http://support.microsoft.com/support/c.asp **Windows 95 Download:** http://support.microsoft.com/support/downloads/PNP167.asp **Windows 95 Resource Kit:** http://www.microsoft.com/windows/downloads/contents/resource kits/w95 reskit/default.asp Note: The Windows 95/98 installation CD includes the electronic version of the Resource Kit. **Microsoft Office Resource Kit:** http://www.microsoft.com/office/ork/ **Power Toys (including Tweak UI) and Kernel Toys:** http://www.microsoft.com/windows/downloads/default.asp **RegClean:** http://support.microsoft.com/support/kb/articles/Q147/7/69.asp
WinTune 97 and 98	http://winweb.winmag.com/software/wt.htm
Windows 95 Support and Information Resources	http://www.compucall.com/tips.htm
Win95Boot	http://www.tu-chemnitz.de/~jwes/win95boot.html

FIGURE 22.26 Windows 95 Startup menu

```
Microsoft Windows 95 Startup Menu
==============================


 1. Normal
 2. Logged (\BOOTLOG.TXT)
 3. Safe mode
 4. Safe mode with network support
 5. Step-by-step confirmation
 6. Command prompt only
 7. Safe mode command prompt only
 8. Previous version of MS-DOS
Enter a choice: 1


F5=Safe mode   Shift+F5=Command prompt  Shift+F8=Step-by-step confirmation [N]
```

F8 key as soon as "Starting Windows 95..." appears on the screen during boot-up. The boot menu will then provide information about the specific steps in the startup sequence and any error conditions. (See fig. 22.26.)

Safe mode bypasses the startup files and uses only basic system drivers. The safe boot-up also occurs when pressing the F5 key as soon as the "Starting Windows 95..." message appears on the screen during boot-up or by typing WIN /D:M at the command prompt. The Step-By-Step Confirmation option starts Windows but asks Yes or No for each line in the startup files. The Command Prompt starts the operating system with startup files and registry but does not start the GUI. The Safe Mode Command Prompt Only option starts the system in safe mode but bypasses the startup files and does not load the GUI.

Some systems will also have a Previous Version of MS-DOS option. This will start the version of MS-DOS previously installed on the computer. The previous DOS version can also be loaded by pressing the F4 key as soon as the "Starting Windows 95..." message appears. This option is available only if BootMulti=1 is in the MSDOS.SYS file. If, however, this option appears on Windows 95 OSR2 versions or later, you do not want to choose it; if you do, you will go to DOS once but the system will not boot after that.

EXAMPLE 22.1 During boot-up, the following message appears on the screen:

"Missing or Corrupt HIMEM.SYS"

When this problem occurs, make sure that the HIMEM.SYS file is in the Windows folder and that it is the right version. If the correct HIMEM.SYS file is in the correct directory, make sure the CONFIG.SYS file does not have a line that specifies a different HIMEM.SYS file.

EXAMPLE 22.2 During boot-up, you receive the following message:"VFAT Device Initialization Failed. A device or resource required by VFAT is not present or is unavailable. VFAT cannot continue loading. System halted…" This error message occurs for one of the following reasons:

- The IFSHLP.SYS file is missing from the Windows folder.
- The CONFIG.SYS file contains a line (such as DEVICE=C:\WINDOWS\IFSHLP. SYS) pointing to a previous version of the IFSHLP.SYS file.
- The command to load the IFSHLP.SYS was deleted from the CONFIG.SYS file after re-installing Windows.
- The [Paths] section in the MSDOS.SYS file is incorrect.
- A WINBOOT.INI file from a previous incomplete installation is present in the root folder of the boot disk.

If the IFSHLP.SYS file is missing from the Windows folder, extract a new copy of the file from the original Windows installation disks or CD-ROM or copy it from another computer that is running the same version of Windows 95 or 98. If the CONFIG.SYS is in error, reboot the computer to the command prompt and use EDIT to make the appropriate changes to the CONFIG.SYS file. If the MSDOS.SYS file contains the incorrect path, reboot the computer to the command prompt and shut off the system, hidden, and read-only attributes of the MSDOS.SYS file. Then make the appropriate changes in the [Paths] section of the MSDOS.SYS file using EDIT. After saving the changes, turn the system, hidden, and read-only attributes on for the MSDOS.SYS file and reboot the computer. If the WINBOOT.INI file is present in the root folder of the boot drive, start the Windows 95 command prompt and delete the WINBOOT.INI file using the DELTREE command.

2.11.2 GENERAL PROTECTION FAULTS

Much like Windows 3.XX, Windows 95 may encounter a general protection fault. (See fig. 22.27.) It signifies that something unexpected has happened within the Windows environment—usually, a program has tried to access a memory area that belongs to another program or an application has tried to pass invalid parameters to another program. Other forms of general protection faults are exception errors and illegal errors. An exception error is a condition that causes the program or microprocessor to branch to a different routine. An illegal error occurs when an instruction is sent to the microprocessor that it cannot perform. (See fig. 22.28.)

If a general protection fault occurs repeatedly, isolating it can be a lengthy process. If the general protection fault message indicates a GPF with the GDI.EXE, USER.EXE, or video driver, the problem is most likely caused by the video system and driver. Try to use a new video driver from the manufacturer or try to use Windows 95 generic video drivers (the generic SVGA or VGA drivers). You can also use the Video Performance tab to move the slide bar a notch or two to the left. The Video Performance tab can be accessed by starting the Control Panel, double-clicking on the System applet, clicking on the Performance tab, followed by clicking on the Graphics button.

If the general protection fault occurs repeatedly while using a particular application, check for lost clusters with SCANDISK, check for viruses, and delete any temporary files from the temporary directory (defined with the SET TEMP line in the AUTOEXEC.BAT file). Remember that both lost clusters and many temporary files in the temporary directory

FIGURE 22.27 General protection fault (GPF), sometimes referred to as the "Blue Screen of Death"

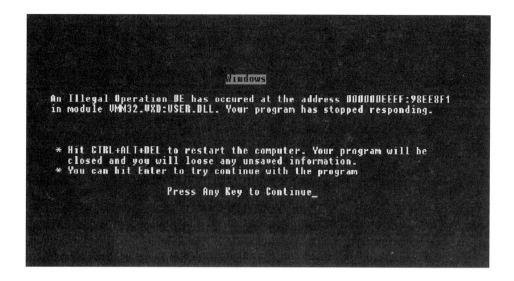

FIGURE 22.28 An illegal operation, which is a form of general protection fault (GPF)

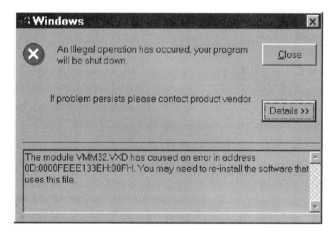

often indicate that a user has been shutting off the computer without properly exiting Windows. You should also check to see if the software has a history of causing general protection faults and if there is a patch or fix that will correct the problem. After checking for lost clusters, viruses, and temporary files, try to reinstall the program to restore any incomplete files. If the problem remains, try to reinstall Windows 95.

One cause of a general protection fault is an invalid page fault (PFE). An invalid page fault occurs when the operating system cannot find specific data that is stored in the RAM or virtual memory. It occurs more often when the system has little RAM or the hard drive is badly fragmented. Therefore, systems with more RAM and lots of free disk space on an unfragmented hard drive are more resistant to general protection faults.

Lastly, GPFs can be caused by a faulty RAM cache or faulty RAM chips. To determine if the RAM cache is faulty, disable it with the CMOS setup program or by using jumpers or DIP switches on the motherboard. If the problem goes away, you know it is the RAM cache. If the problem still exists, enable the RAM cache and check elsewhere. To isolate the RAM, remove a bank of RAM chips at a time (if there is a lot of RAM) or swap a bank with known good RAM chips.

22.11.3 WINDOWS 95 RESOURCES

The kernel, GDI.EXE, and USER.EXE files were discussed earlier in the chapter. The kernel loads and runs Windows applications and handles their memory management, the GDI manages graphics and printing, and USER controls user input and output devices, including the keyboard and the mouse.

**FIGURE 22.29   Windows 95
Resource Meter**

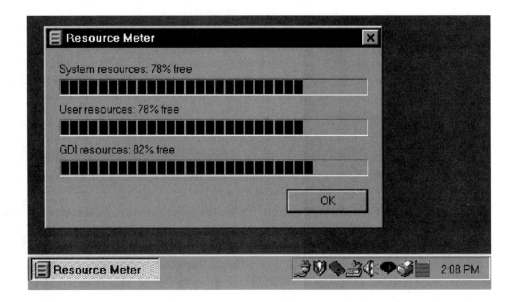

The GDI and USER use storage areas known as the *local heap.* The GDI heap contains information about graphical objects, such as pens, brushes, cursors, fonts, icons, buttons, scrollbars, and so on. The USER heap contains information about windows, icons, menus, and dialog boxes. Windows 95 has larger heaps than Windows 3.XX applications, including a larger 32-bit GDI heap, but it retains the same 16-bit GDI heap as Windows 3.XX so that it can support older programs. If any heap drops too low, the system can become unstable and cause problems even though there is a lot of free RAM. To view the amount of free system resources (the percentage of the heap that has the lowest amount of free memory), use the Performance tab in the System applet in the Control Panel. To see the amount of free system resources for the System, USER, and GDI, use a utility called Resource Meter. (See fig. 22.29.)

22.11.4   SYSTEM MONITOR

System Monitor is a useful tool to help measure the performance of hardware, software services, and applications to determine what is acting as a bottleneck and slowing the system. Running System Monitor before making a change to the system and then running it after making a change shows how much the change has affected performance. Four of the most useful items in System Monitor are the CPU usage, allocated memory, cache size, and swap files. (See fig. 22.30.)

22.11.5   DLL PROBLEMS

Because Windows 95 and 98 are a complicated multitasking environment with a shared interface, they have more application problems than there were with DOS. Some of these problems have an error message, such as "Missing DLL File, Illegal Operation," while others will not, such as when the computer locks up.

As a Windows application is installed, Windows will often do the following:

- Create a folder for the new program
- Copy the necessary files into the program folder
- Create shortcuts in the Start menu
- Make additions to the Registry or INI files
- Modify the AUTOEXEC.BAT or CONFIG.SYS file
- Copy DLL files into the WINDOWS or WINDOWS\SYSTEM directory

FIGURE 22.30   Windows 95 System Monitor

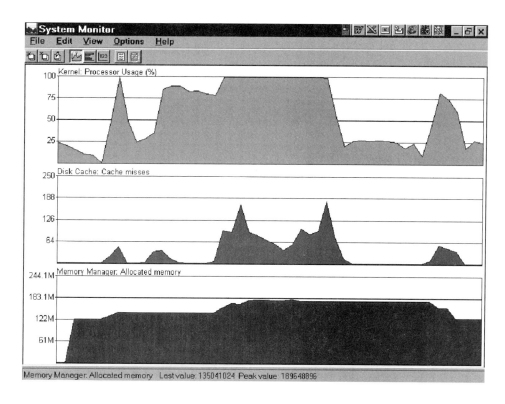

Many programs have an Uninstaller option (usually accessed through the Add/Remove Programs applet in the Control Panel) that can keep or remove these changes or additions.

As mentioned earlier in this chapter, DLL files (files with a DLL filename extension) are dynamic link libraries—libraries of program code sometimes shared by different programs. DLL files are used to modularize Windows and to allow other programs to share their resources. The DLL files for an application may be installed in the WINDOWS or WINDOWS\SYSTEM folder or stored in the individual program folder. Because several programs can use the DLL files with the same name and location, there can be version problems or missing DLL problems. For example, application A uses the shared DLL file called ABC.DLL. Application B uses the same ABC.DLL file but a later version. Because application B uses a newer version, it overwrites the existing ABC.DLL file. Depending on application A and the new ABC.DLL, application A may run with no problem, or problems such as locking up or general protection faults may occur. Unfortunately, you may not realize that the ABC.DLL file was changed, so you don't realize that the installation of application B caused the problem. To overcome this, check with the manufacturer for any updates for program A and reinstall application A and apply the updates.

Another problem occurs with DLL files when applications are removed using the Windows 95 and 98 Add/Remove Programs applet in the Control Panel. At some point during the uninstall, the program might ask if it is OK to remove any of the shared DLL files that are not being used by other applications. Unfortunately, if application B, which needs the shared DLL file, is started and the file isn't on the system, you will then get a missing DLL file error message. To fix this problem, you would reinstall application B to restore the DLL files.

22.11.6   WINDOWS 95 IS NOT RESPONDING

Sometimes in Windows 95 and applications loaded on Windows 95, a computer will stop responding. When this occurs, first try pressing the Ctrl+Alt+Del keys to bring up the Close Program dialog box. If the box appears, you can then see if one of the programs is not responding, select it, and click on the End Task button. If the problem still exists, press the Ctl+Alt+Del keys again and click on the Shut Down option. If problem still exists or if the Close Program dialog box does not appear, you will then be forced to reboot the computer by using the on/off switch or the reset button.

After rebooting the computer, you should check for viruses, run ScanDisk to clean up any lost clusters, and delete any temporary files that may be lingering from the previous

Windows 95 session. The temporary files will usually have to be deleted using the DOS mode. If the problem occurs again after loading the same application, reload the application and check with the manufacturer for any updates, patches, or fixes and to see if there are any known conflicts with other software applications. If after reloading the application the problem still exists, try reloading Windows. Lastly, check for power fluctuations and faulty hardware (RAM cache, RAM chips, microprocessor, motherboard, or any other device being accessed at the time that the problem occurs).

SUMMARY

1. Windows 95 is a complete operating system that was designed to replace DOS and Windows 3.XX.
2. The IO.SYS file, the real mode configuration manager and operating system, contains enough information to start the computer and automatically loads several files and commands that used to be loaded in the DOS CONFIG.SYS and AUTOEXEC.BAT files.
3. MSDOS.SYS is a text file that specifies the location of the necessary boot files, the location of the Registry (configuration database), and several start-up options.
4. To provide backward compatibility for DOS and Windows 3.XX drivers and applications, Windows 95 has CONFIG.SYS, COMMAND.COM, and AUTOEXEC.BAT files and initialization files (including the SYSTEM.INI).
5. After the device drivers are loaded, the Windows 95 core components are loaded, including the kernel (KERNL386.EXE and KERNEL32.DLL), GDI.EXE, GDI32.EXE, USER.EXE, and USER32.EXE files.
6. Dynamic link library (DLL) files are sets of instructions and/or data that can be shared by more than one application and accessed at any time and are used to modularize Windows 95.
7. The Windows 95 interface is based on the desktop, where all of the work is done. On the desktop are the My Computer icon, the Recycle Bin, and the Taskbar (with the Start button).
8. Disk and file management is usually done with My Computer or Windows Explorer.
9. By default, Windows 95 uses VFAT, an enhanced version of the FAT structure.
10. As an enhancement to the DOS's FAT file system, FAT32 supports long filenames, uses 32-bit FAT entries that support hard drives up to two terabytes, and uses disk space more efficiently by using smaller clusters.
11. For Win32-based and DOS applications, Windows 95 uses preemptive multitasking; for Win16-based applications, it uses cooperative multitasking.
12. When running in an MS-DOS VM, you can specify the operating parameters for the DOS program by choosing the Properties option from the shortcut menu or from the File menu.
13. To share data between documents, Windows applications can use dynamic data exchange (DDE) or object linking and embedding (OLE).
14. File association allows Windows 95 to recognize the filename extension of a document and start the appropriate program to open the file.
15. The print driver can be loaded by using the Add Printer Wizard (by double-clicking on the Add Printer icon in the Printers folder) or by using the setup disks that come with the printer.
16. The Print Manager will list all of the printers and all of the print jobs they hold.
17. The Control Panel is a graphical tool to configure the Windows environment and hardware devices.
18. The Device Manager shows all hardware devices and their resources organized in a tree structure.
19. The Display applet allows you to configure the Windows environment, including menus, windows, icons, the desktop, and the screen saver.
20. The Add/Remove Programs applet installs and uninstalls programs, adds or removes Windows 95 components, and creates a startup disk.
21. The Windows 95 Registry is the central information database for Windows 95 organized into a tree-structured hierarchical database.

22. Manually changing the Registry (such as changing a value that cannot be modified by using the Control Panel or similar utility) requires a program called Registry Editor (REGEDIT.EXE).
23. To start a Windows 95 installation, the SETUP.EXE file is executed from within Windows 3.1 or later or at the DOS prompt when it appears on the first installation disk or CD-ROM.

QUESTIONS

1. You just installed a Windows application in Windows 95. Typically, to start the program, you would:
   a. find the executable file using My Computer and double-click on it
   b. find the executable file using Windows Explorer and double-click on it
   c. click on the Start button, click on the Programs option, and click on the program in the appropriate folder
   d. click with the right mouse button on the desktop and select the program from the shortcut menu

2. When you delete a file by mistake, the file can be undeleted using the:
   a. Recycle Bin
   b. Trash Can
   c. Swap file
   d. paging file
   e. C drive

3. Which of the following will you *not* find in the My Computer icon?
   a. A drive
   b. C drive
   c. Control Panel
   d. Recycle Bin
   e. Printers folder

4. What section of the SYSTEM.INI file is always read by Windows 95 when it boots?
   a. [386Enh]
   b. [Standard]
   c. [boot]
   d. [Drivers32]

5. What is the minimum amount of RAM needed to install and run Windows 95?
   a. 2 MB
   b. 4 MB
   c. 8 MB
   d. 16 MB

6. A collection of files is grouped and stored in:
   a. folders
   b. icons
   c. applets
   d. windows

7. The three buttons on the right side of a window titlebar in Windows 95 are:
   a. minimize, maximize, close
   b. minimize, restore, close
   c. minimize, maximize/restore, close
   d. minimize, maximize, restore

8. How do you know whether an icon on the desktop of Windows 95 is a shortcut icon?
   a. it uses a special icon designated for shortcuts
   b. the icon is a different color
   c. the icon is smaller
   d. the icon has a little arrow in one corner

9. The F5 key does what? (Choose two answers.)
   a. if it is pressed during boot-up, it will start Windows 95 in safe mode
   b. if it is pressed during boot-up, it will start the Windows 95 boot menu
   c. if it is pressed during boot-up, it will start the previous operating system
   d. it is used to refresh a window
   e. it opens the context/shortcut menu

10. What are the programs found in the Control Panel of Windows 95 called?
    a. applications
    b. applets
    c. subprograms
    d. subicons

11. What Windows 95 Control Panel applet is used for removing the drivers for a hardware device?
    a. System applet
    b. Add/Remove Programs applet
    c. Add New Hardware applet
    d. Internet applet

12. You want to create a startup disk (a bootable disk used for troubleshooting Windows 95). Which applet would you use to create the disk?
    a. System applet
    b. Add/Remove Programs applet
    c. Add New Hardware applet
    d. Internet applet
13. You have a program that follows the API specification. While removing the program, you want to make sure that the Registry settings and program files are removed. Which applet would you use?
    a. System applet
    b. Add/Remove Programs applet
    c. Add New Hardware applet
    d. Internet applet
14. How do you modify the appearance of the Windows 95 desktop? (Choose all that apply.)
    a. double-click on the Display applet in the Control Panel
    b. double-click on the System applet in the Control Panel
    c. double-click on the Accessibility applet in the Control Panel
    d. right-click on the System applet and choose the Desktop option
    e. right-click on the desktop and choose the Properties option
15. To change the video card driver, you would:
    a. use the Add/Remove Programs applet in the Control Panel and select the Video tab
    b. use the Display applet in the Control Panel and select the Settings tab
    c. use the System applet in the Control Panel and select the video card in the Device Manager
    d. modify the SYSTEM.INI file using a text editor
16. Where do you find the Add a Printer applet in Windows 95?
    a. double-click on the Add/Remove Programs applet in the Control Panel
    b. double-click on the System applet in the Control Panel and select the Device Manager tab
    c. click on the Start button, select the Settings option, and click on the Printers option
    d. click on the Add New Hardware applet in the Control Panel
17. Which tool(s) can be used to install an updated driver for a Windows 95 device?
    a. the Registry Editor
    b. the SETUP.EXE program
    c. the Add/Remove Programs applet
    d. the Add New Hardware applet
    e. the Device Manager
18. What happens when you use your mouse to right-click on an object in Windows 95?
    a. the properties sheet for that object will open
    b. a special Windows 95 properties sheet will open that allows you configure the Windows 95 environment
    c. a shortcut menu pertaining to that object will open
    d. you copy the object onto the Clipboard
    e. you open the Explorer for that object
19. Which file systems does Windows 95 (OSR2) support?
    a. FAT, VFAT, and FAT32
    b. FAT, VFAT, and NTFS
    c. VFAT, FAT32, and NTFS
    d. FAT, NTFS, and HPFS
20. What does it mean when one of the devices shown in the Device Manager has a circled exclamation point?
    a. the hardware has a problem
    b. the hardware is disabled
    c. the device is a high-priority device
    d. the device is currently being used and cannot be removed at this time
    e. the hardware was never installed
21. What is the easiest way to get information about a document being printed on the printer?
    a. open the File menu and select the Properties option
    b. double-click on the small printer icon in the Taskbar
    c. double-click on the Print Manager icon in the Printers applet in the Control Panel
    d. double-click on the Print Manager icon in the Control Panel
22. You have an MS-DOS-based game that has to be run in a full screen. What do you need to do to make sure the program will always start in a full screen?
    a. use the PIF editor to create a PIF file for the game
    b. using the Shortcut menu of the DOS program, select the Properties shortcut

    c. press the Alt+Enter keys

    d. right-click the icon for the program and choose Full Screen.

23. You have an e-mail program installed on your computer. How can you start the program automatically when Windows 95 starts?

    a. by dragging the program file to the desktop

    b. by dragging the program file to the Start menu

    c. by creating a StartUp folder on the desktop and dragging the program file to the folder

    d. by choosing Settings from the Start menu, clicking Taskbar, clicking the Start Menu Programs tab, and dragging the program file to the StartUp folder

    e. by dragging the program to the Recycle Bin

24. Which Registry subkey stores hardware-related information?

    a. HKEY_SYSTEM   c. HKEY_USERS

    b. HKEY_HARDWARE_DATA   d. HKEY_LOCAL_MACHINE

25. You want to make sure deleted items are removed from the Recycle Bin immediately. What do you need to do to configure the Recycle Bin?

    a. select the Display applet in the Control Panel

    b. select the System applet in the Control Panel

    c. right-click the Recycle Bin and select the Properties option

    d. delete the Recycle Bin from the desktop

26. You have just purchased a new HP LaserJet printer. What do you need to do to install the printer? (Choose two.)

    a. double-click on the Add New Hardware applet in the Control Panel

    b. reexecute the SETUP.EXE icon on the Windows 95 installation CD and install the Add Printer button

    c. double-click on the System applet in the Control panel and select the Add Printer button

    d. insert the disk containing the HP printer drivers in the disk drive and start the installation executable file

    e. double-click the Add Printer icon in the Printers folder (Control Panel or My Computer)

    f. double-click on the Add New Hardware applet in the Control Panel

27. What files make up the Registry? (Choose all that apply.)

    a. USER.DAT   e. SYSTEM.INI

    b. REGISTRY.DAT   f. WIN.INI

    c. BOOT.INI   g. MSDOS.SYS

    d. SYSTEM.DAT   h. IO.SYS

28. How can you copy a file to a floppy disk from Windows Explorer? (Select two answers.)

    a. by right-clicking the filename and choosing Send To

    b. by dragging the file to the floppy disk drive icon on the Taskbar

    c. by dragging the file to the desktop

    d. by right-clicking the filename and choosing Copy To

    e. by dragging the file to the A drive icon within My Computer

29. You are installing Windows 95 on your computer. Your computer locks up during the hardware detection phase. Which file will provide you with information on the possible causes of the problem?

    a. SETUP.LOG   c. DETLOG.TXT

    b. DETECT.LOG   d. DETCRASH.LOG

30. You installed a modem on your computer but the system does not recognize the modem. What do you do next?

    a. run the Add New Hardware applet in the Control Panel and ask Windows 95 to search for new hardware

    b. run the Add/Remove Programs applet in the Control Panel

    c. reinstall Windows 95 and let Setup automatically install all necessary drivers

    d. copy the required driver from the installation CD to the hard drive

31. The new interface given to Windows 98 is:

    a. DirectX   c. Active Desktop

    b. ActiveX   d. OpenGL

32. Which mode would you use to start Windows 95 with the default settings to fix problems?
   a. standard mode
   b. enhanced mode
   c. safe mode
   d. real mode
   e. protected mode
   f. default mode

33. How can the Device Manager be found?
   a. by double-clicking the System applet in the Control Panel
   b. by clicking on the Start button and selecting the Settings option
   c. by double-clicking on the DEVMAN.EXE file
   d. by double-clicking on the Device Manager icon on the Taskbar

34. What command is used to install Windows 95?
   a. INSTALL
   b. SETUP
   c. SETVER
   d. START
   e. GO

35. What utility is used to perform common file and disk management functions?
   a. Explorer
   b. File Manager
   c. System Editor
   d. PIF Editor

36. Most of the Windows 95 configuration information is kept in:
   a. initialization files (*.INI)
   b. system files (*.SYS)
   c. the Windows Registry
   d. configuration files (*.CFG)
   e. dynamic link files (*.DLL)

37. What does it mean when one of the devices shown in the Device Manager has a red X?
   a. The hardware has a problem
   b. The hardware is disabled
   c. The device is currently being used and cannot be removed at this time
   d. The hardware was never installed
   e. The device is not on or does not have power

38. What program allows objects from one program to be inserted into another program?
   a. OLE
   b. multitasking
   c. networks
   d. IFSHLP.SYS

39. While running Windows 95, the performance of the computer declines drastically. What is the most likely problem?
   a. insufficient free disk space
   b. choosing the Non-Turbo option during boot-up
   c. a corrupted Registry
   d. a faulty microprocessor or RAM chip
   e. a deactivated RAM cache

40. What would you use to track the performance of key system components?
   a. the System Monitor
   b. the Resource Monitor
   c. the System applet within the Control Panel
   d. the Network Monitor
   e. Microsoft Diagnostic

41. What would you do to install a program in Windows 95?
   a. click on the Start button, choose the Run option, and specify the location and name of the executable file
   b. from the Start button, select the Find option
   c. from the desktop, select the Install option from the Shortcut menu
   d. from any window, select the View menu and select the Options option
   e. open the File menu, select the Run option, and specify the location and name of the executable file

42. When upgrading from Windows 3.XX to Windows 95, which of the following must you do to allow dual booting between DOS and Windows 95?
   a. install Windows 95 in a different directory from the directory used for Windows 3.XX
   b. install programs only on Windows 3.XX or Windows 95, but not both
   c. boot to safe mode
   d. boot to the command prompt
   e. purchase the Windows 95 Plus! package and install it on your system

43. Which of the following files are *not* used in Windows 95 to provide backward compatibility for older programs?
   a. SYSTEM.INI
   b. WIN.INI
   c. MSDOS.SYS
   d. COMMAND.COM
   e. EXPLORER.EXE

44. HIMEM.SYS and other common commands loaded in the CONFIG.SYS file are automatically loaded by:
   a. IO.SYS
   b. MSDOS.SYS
   c. COMMAND.COM
   d. VMM32.VXD
   e. the Device Manager
   f. DOS.INI

45. Which of the following describes an illegal operation?
   a. an instruction was sent to the microprocessor that the microprocessor could not do
   b. there is a sharing violation as two programs try to use the same file at the same time
   c. software piracy has been detected
   d. while connected to the Internet, it has been determined that you broke a federal, state, or local law

HANDS-ON EXERCISES

Exercise 1: Introduction to the Windows 95 Interface

1. If any windows are open, close them.
2. Open the System applet in the Control Panel. The Control Panel can be opened from within My Computer or the Settings option under the Start button.
3. Select the Performance tab and record the amount of free system resources.
4. Close the System Properties window.
5. Click with the right mouse button (secondary mouse button) on My Computer to access the shortcut menu. Select the Properties option. Again click on the Performance tab.
6. Start the Resource Meter. It can be started by clicking on the Start button, clicking on Programs, clicking on Accessories, clicking on System Tools, and clicking on Resource Meter. If the Resource Meter is not loaded, it can be loaded by opening the Control Panel, double-clicking on the Add/Remove Programs applet, clicking on the Windows Setup tab, clicking on Accessories, clicking on Details, and putting a check next to Resource Meter.
7. The Resource Meter is currently running and is currently minimized as a small icon with green strips on the right side of the Taskbar. Move the mouse pointer to the Resource Meter without clicking. Notice the message that appears.
8. Double-click on the Resource Meter.
9. Start the Calculator by clicking on the Start button, clicking on Programs, clicking on Accessories, and selecting the Calculator. Close the Calculator by clicking on the Close button at the top right corner of the Calculator.
10. Start the Calculator by double-clicking on My Computer, double-clicking on the Windows folder, and double-clicking on the CALC file.
11. Start the Calculator by using Windows Explorer. Close the Calculator by double-clicking on the small calculator icon at the top left of the Calculator.
12. Start the Calculator by using the Run option under the Start button and specifying the path of C:\WINDOWS\CALC.EXE. Close the Calculator.
13. Start the Calculator by using the Run option under the Start button and using the Browse button to find CALC.EXE. Close the Calculator.
14. Open a window for the C:\WINDOWS\DESKTOP directory and notice the contents of the DESKTOP directory.
15. Create a shortcut for the Windows 95 Calculator (C:\WINDOWS\CALC.EXE). You can do this by using the Shortcut menu and select the New option followed by the Shortcut option. Try to determine what distinguishes a shortcut.
16. Test the Calculator shortcut. Close the Calculator.

17. Use Notepad to create a text file called NAME.TXT located in the C:\ folder. Include your first and last name in the file. Close Notepad.

18. Double-click on the NAME file under the C drive. Notice that Notepad automatically started. Close Notepad.

19. On the desktop, make a shortcut to the NAME file. This can be done by accessing the Shortcut menu (clicking on the desktop with the right mouse button—secondary mouse button), clicking on the New option, and clicking on the Shortcut option.

20. Test the shortcut to the NAME.TXT file. Close Notepad.

21. Create a new folder called COMMON APPS.

22. In the COMMON APPS group, create icons for the Calculator (CALC.EXE), Notepad (NOTEPAD.EXE), and Paintbrush (PBRUSH.EXE). (Hint: They are all located in the WINDOWS directory.)

23. Test the newly created shortcuts.

24. Open a window for the C:\WINDOWS\DESKTOP directory. Notice the contents of the DESKTOP folder. Try to figure out what the purpose of the DESKTOP folder is.

25. Open windows for the C:\, C:\WINDOWS, C:\WINDOWS\COMMAND, and C:\WINDOWS\SYSTEM folders.

26. Check and record the amount of free system resources.

27. Close all the windows.

28. Close all the programs that you just started.

29. Start Microsoft Write and Microsoft Paintbrush.

30. If you have Microsoft Word and Microsoft Excel, start them.

31. If you have a browser installed, such as Microsoft Internet Explorer or Netscape Navigator, start your browser.

32. Check and record the free system resources.

33. Close all of the programs.

34. Check and record the free system resources.

35. Delete the COMMON APPS folder, the Calculator shortcut and the Names shortcut.

36. Open a window for the C:\WINDOWS directory.

37. Select the Large Icons option under the View menu.

38. Select the Small Icons option under the View menu.

39. Select the List option under the View menu.

40. Select the Details option under the View menu.

41. Select the Toolbars option in the View menu.

42. Find and click on the Large Icons button. You may need to increase the window size to show all the buttons of the Toolbar.

43. Open the View menu and click on the Arrange Icons option under the By Type option. By Type means that the icons will be sorted by filename extension.

44. In the Windows window, without clicking on an icon, open the Shortcut menu (click the right mouse button), click on the Arrange Icons option, and click on the By Name option.

45. Make sure the Windows window does not auto-arrange its icons. This can be done by opening the View menu and clicking on the Arrange Option menu. If there is a checkmark on the Auto Arrange option, click on it to shut it off. If there is no checkmark on the Auto Arrange option, click somewhere on the desktop to close the menu.

46. Move some of the icons around without putting one on top of another.

47. Enable the Auto Arrange feature for the Windows window.

48. Close all windows.

49. Double-click on the My Computer icon.

50. Double-click on the C drive.

51. Open windows for the C:\WINDOWS, C:\WINDOWS\COMMAND, and C:\WINDOWS\SYSTEM folders.

52. Close all windows.

53. Double-click on the My Computer icon.

54. Select Options… under the View menu.

55. Under the Folder tab, select Browse Folders by Using the Single Window That Changes as You Open Each Folder option and click on the OK button.

56. Double-click on the C drive, double-click on the WINDOWS folder, and double-click on the SYSTEM folder. Notice how many windows are open.

57. Activate the Toolbar for the SYSTEM folder.
58. Click on the Up One Level button. Keep clicking on the Up One Level button until you get back to the My Computer window.
59. Select Options… under the View menu. Under the Folder tab, select Browse Folders Using a Separate Window for Each Folder and click on the OK button.
60. Close all the windows.
61. Start Microsoft WordPad.
62. Type your name.
63. Highlight your name and change the font to Arial using the Font option under the Format menu.
64. Increase the Font size to 18 points and make the text bold.
65. While the name is highlighted, use the shortcut menu to change the font to Times Roman and change the color to blue.
66. Close WordPad without saving the file.

Exercise 2: File Management

1. Insert a disk in drive A. Under My Computer, use the Shortcut menu of the A drive and format the disk. Do not make it bootable.
2. Open a window for the A drive.
3. Create a folder called COMMAND on the A drive using the Shortcut menu.
4. Open the A:\COMMAND folder.
5. Open a window for C:\WINDOWS\COMMAND.
6. Close all windows except for the two COMMAND windows.
7. Copy the FORMAT.COM, FDISK.EXE, ATTRIB.EXE, and DISKCOPY.COM files from the C:\WINDOWS\COMMAND folder to the A:\COMMAND folder.
8. Create a DATA folder in the A:\ folder.
9. Move the FORMAT.COM file from the A:\COMMAND folder to the A:\DATA folder.
10. Copy the FORMAT.COM file from the A:\DATA folder to the A:\COMMAND directory.
11. Using the Shortcut menu of the A drive, perform a disk copy to another disk.
12. Keep the second disk in drive A and format the disk as a bootable disk.
13. Insert the first disk into drive A.
14. Rename the FORMAT.COM file to DESTROY.COM in the A:\ folder.
15. Make the DESTROY.COM file hidden by using the Shortcut menu of the DESTROY.COM file and selecting Properties.
16. If you can't see the hidden files, select Options under the View menu, click on the View menu, select Show All Files, and click on the OK button. (Note: If you are using Windows 98, select the Folder Options, click on the View tab, and select Show All files under the Hidden Files section.)
17. Use the COPY option from the Shortcut menu of DELTREE.EXE file in the C:\WINDOWS\COMMAND directory.
18. Make the A:\ window active. On the A:\ windows, select the Paste option from the Shortcut menu.
19. Delete the DESTROY.COM file.
20. Using the A:\ window, highlight both folders at the same time and delete them.
21. Start Windows Explorer.
22. Using the Shortcut menu of the A drive shown in Windows Explorer, format the first disk without making it bootable.
23. Using the Format option, make the disk bootable without reformatting it. (Hint: Do not do a Full or Quick format.)
24. Create a folder called DOS COMMAND on the C drive using the Shortcut menu of the C drive window.
25. Click on the DOS COMMAND folder. The right side of the window should show no files.
26. Click on the plus (+) next to the C:\WINDOWS folder in Explorer to show the subdirectories under Windows.
27. Click on the COMMAND folder under the WINDOWS directory.
28. Copy the FORMAT.COM, FDISK.EXE, ATTRIB.EXE, and DISKCOPY.COM files from the C:\WINDOWS\COMMAND folder to the C:\DOS COMMAND folder.

29. Delete the FORMAT.COM and ATTRIB.EXE files from the C drive.
30. Double-click on the Recycle Bin. These are the files that you deleted in the GUI.
31. Drag the FORMAT.COM file to the desktop.
32. Highlight the ATTRIB.EXE file and select Restore from the Shortcut menu.
33. Look in the DOS COMMAND folder and notice that the ATTRIB.EXE file is back.
34. Select the Empty Recycle Bin option from the File menu.
35. Close the Recycle Bin window.
36. Access the Shortcut menu of the Recycle Bin and select Properties. Notice the maximum size of the Recycle Bin.
37. Click on the OK button.

Exercise 3: OLE

1. Start Microsoft WordPad. Type your name and a couple of lines of text.
2. Without closing Microsoft Write, start Microsoft Paintbrush.
3. Draw some circles and squares.
4. Highlight the area with the circles and squares and copy them onto the clipboard using the Copy option in the Edit menu.
5. Change back to Microsoft WordPad. You can use the Taskbar or the Alt+Tab keys.
6. Paste the image into Microsoft Write using the Paste option under the Edit menu.
7. Switch over to Paintbrush and close the program without saving the image.
8. Save the current document in Microsoft WordPad with the TESTOLE.DOC filename.
9. Double-click on the picture in Microsoft WordPad.
10. Draw a line through the picture.
11. Close the Paintbrush program by double-clicking on the WordPad document.
12. Save the Microsoft WordPad document.
13. Close the TESTOLE.DOC document.
14. Open a new document in Microsoft WordPad.
15. Using the Paste Special option under the Edit menu, paste the picture as a bitmap.
16. Close the Microsoft WordPad document.
17. Change the text to 36-point Arial bold.
18. Highlight the text and copy the text onto the Clipboard.
19. Paste the text.
20. Using the Paste Special option under the Edit menu, paste the text as a picture.
21. Using the Paste Special option under the Edit menu, paste the text as unformatted text.
22. Start the DOS prompt.
23. If the DOS prompt is not running in Windows, press the Alt+Enter keys.
24. Perform the following command at the prompt:

```
C:\WINDOWS>EDIT C:\WINDOWS\FAQ.TXT
```

25. Using the Mark button on the Toolbar, highlight some text. If the Toolbar for the DOS window is not showing, use the Shortcut menu of the Titlebar to activate the Toolbar.
26. Using the Copy button on the Toolbar, not the Copy option under the Edit menu of EDIT, copy the text onto the Clipboard.
27. Switch to Microsoft WordPad and paste the text into the document.
28. Exit WordPad.
29. Delete the TESTOLE.DOC file.

Exercise 4: DOS Applications

1. Using Notepad, create a batch file called GO.BAT with the following content:

```
MEM
PAUSE
```

2. Save the batch file with the name GO.BAT in the C:\WINDOWS\COMMAND directory.
3. From the command prompt, test the GO.BAT batch file.

4. From the Run option under the Start button, execute the GO.BAT batch file.
5. Using Microsoft Explorer, execute the GO.BAT batch file.
6. Make a shortcut called SHOW MEMORY that points to the GO.BAT batch file.
7. Test the shortcut and record the amount of free extended memory. In addition, notice the prompt shown while the batch file is being executed.
8. Select the Properties option in the Shortcut menu of the SHOW MEMORY shortcut. Notice the extra tabs for a DOS program compared to a Windows program.
9. Change the properties so that you have 4,096 KB of extended memory and change the working directory to C:\WINDOWS\SYSTEM. In addition, configure the shortcut to run in Windows.
10. Test the shortcut and record the amount of extended memory. In addition, notice the prompt shown while the batch file is being executed.
11. Delete the SHOW MEMORY shortcut and the GO.BAT file.

Exercise 5: The Control Panel

1. Start the Control Panel.
2. Double-click on the System applet. Record the Windows 95 version, OEM number, and the amount of physical RAM.
3. Click on the Device Manager.
4. Double-click on the computer at the top of the device tree.
    Find what device is using IRQ 5.
    Find which IRQ is being used for COM2 and the hard drive.
    Find which IRQs are free.
    Find what device is using I/O address 300.
    Find what device is using DMA 2.
    Find what DMAs are being used by the sound card.
5. Click on the OK button.
6. On the device tree, find and double-click on COM2.
    Find and record the device status.
    Find and record the bits per second, the number of data bits and stop bits, the type of parity and the type of flow control.
    Find and record the resources used by COM2.
    Find and record the entries in the Conflicting Device List.
7. Disable COM2.
8. If you have a sound card loaded, find it and delete the sound card from the device tree.
9. Click on the Performance tab.
10. Record the amount of physical RAM and the percentage of free system resources.
11. Record the performance status of the file system, virtual memory, disk compression, and PC cards.
12. Click the File System button.
13. Change the Typical Role of This Machine to Network Server.
14. Click on the CD-ROM tab.
15. Click on the Troubleshooting tab.
16. It is recommended that only advanced users and system administrators change the settings in the Troubleshooting tab. Try to figure out when you would change these settings.
17. Click on the OK button.
18. Click on the Graphics button.
19. Try to figure out when you would move the Hardware acceleration slidebar to the left.
20. Click on the OK button.
21. Click on the Virtual Memory button.
22. Click on the OK button to exit the Virtual Memory settings and click OK to exit the System Properties dialog box.
23. In the Control Panel, double-click on the Add New Hardware applet. Run the Add New Hardware applet to automatically detect any hardware that your computer may have, including the sound card. If the system doesn't find the sound card, you will have to manually choose the sound card.
24. In the Control Panel, double-click on the Add/Remove Programs applet.

25. Within the Install/Uninstall tab, count the number of programs that are registered.
26. Ask your instructor if there is a program that he or she wants you to remove.
27. Using Windows Setup, make sure the following Windows components are installed:
    Accessibility Options
    Character Map
    Backup
28. Create a start-up disk using the Startup Disk tab.
29. Close the Add/Remove Programs Properties dialog box.
30. Using the Date/Time applet, change the date of the computer to March 17, 2001. Record the day of the week of March 17, 2001.
31. Change the time to 2:00 A.M.
32. Change the time zone to Greenwich Mean Time.
33. Change the date, time, and time zone back to their correct settings.
34. Using the Display applet, change the background pattern to brick.
35. Enable the Flying Windows screen saver and have it activate after two minutes of inactivity.
36. Load the High Contrast Black (Large) appearance schemes.
37. Load the Lilac appearance scheme.
38. Increase the horizontal icon spacing to 75 pixels.
39. Change the icon text to 15-point Arial bold.
40. Load the Windows default appearance scheme.
41. Click on the Settings tab.
42. Record the current resolution and number of colors.
43. Change the screen resolution to 640 $\times$ 480 and number of colors to 16. Click on the OK button.
44. Change the screen resolution to 800 $\times$ 600, number of colors to 256, and choose small fonts. Click on the OK button.
45. Change the screen resolution to 800 $\times$ 600, number of colors to high color, and choose large fonts. Click on the OK button.
46. Change the display back to the recorded resolution and number of colors.
47. Click on the Advanced Properties button.
48. Record the manufacturer and type of the video card and monitor.
49. Change the video card driver to Video 7 VRAM/VRAMII/1024i.
50. If the computer does not boot properly, press the F5 key as soon as the "Starting Windows 95…" message appears during boot-up.
51. Change the video driver back to the recorded video driver.
52. Using the Mouse applet, maximize the Mouse Tracking Speed. Test the mouse by moving it across the screen.
53. Minimize the Mouse Tracking Speed. Test the mouse by moving it across the screen.
54. Maximize the mouse double-clicking speed. Test the mouse by double-clicking in the test area.
55. Adjust the mouse double-clicking speed to your own preference.
56. Activate the Mouse Pointer Trails and move the mouse. (The Mouse Pointer Trails are used on notebook and laptop computers with screens that cannot update fast enough to keep up with the movements of the mouse.
57. Deactivate the Mouse Pointer Trails.
58. Start Microsoft WordPad.
59. Press the T key and keep it down. Notice how long it takes before the key starts repeating and how fast it repeats after it starts.
60. Using the Keyboard applet in the Control Panel, set the Repeat Delay to Short and the Repeat Rate to Fast.
61. Go back to Microsoft WordPad. Press the Y key and keep it down. Notice how long the key takes before it starts repeating and how fast it repeats after it starts.
62. Using the Keyboard icon in the Control Panel, set the Repeat Delay to Long and the Repeat Rate to Slow.
63. Go back to Microsoft WordPad. Press the Q key and keep it down. Notice how long the key takes before it starts repeating and how fast it repeats after it starts.
64. Place the Repeat Delay and the Repeat Rate to somewhere near the middle.

Exercise 6: Configuring the Taskbar

1. Start WordPad and then Microsoft Paint.
2. Using the Taskbar, switch back to WordPad.
3. Using the Shortcut menu of the WordPad button, close WordPad.
4. Select the Start button, select the Settings option, and select the Taskbar option.
5. Enable the Always on Top and the Auto Hide option and click the OK button.
6. Move the mouse pointer to the bottom of the screen to unhide the Taskbar and move the mouse pointer away from the Taskbar to make it hide.
7. Using the Shortcut menu of the Taskbar, select the Properties option.
8. Click on the Start Menu Programs tab. Click on the Advanced button.
9. Expand the Programs Folder. Compare that to the Programs option under the Start button.
10. Go back to the Explorer showing the Start menu programs. Expand the StartUp folder. These are the programs that automatically start during boot-up.
11. From the Accessories folder, copy the calculator into the StartUp folder.
12. Close all windows and the Taskbar Properties dialog box and restart Windows. Notice the calculator automatically started.
13. Go back into the Taskbar Properties option and remove the calculator from the StartUp folder.
14. From the Start button, look at the files listed in the Documents option.
15. In the Taskbar Properties dialog box, click on the Clear button.
16. From the Start button, look at the files listed in the Documents option.
17. Close the Taskbar Properties dialog box.

Exercise 7: Printing

1. In the Printers folder, delete all print drivers that already exist.
2. Install the Hewlett-Packard LaserJet III printer driver. Assume that the printer will use LPT1.
3. If a printer is connected to the computer, unplug the printer cable.
4. Using the Shortcut menu of the HP LaserJet III icon in the Printers folder, pause the printer.
5. Start Microsoft WordPad and load the README.TXT file located in the C:\WINDOWS directory.
6. Use the Print option in the File menu. Make sure that the LaserJet III printer is selected.
7. Print the document three times.
8. Switch over to Print Manager by double-clicking on the minimized printer icon in the Taskbar.
9. Delete the three print jobs.
10. Close Print Manager for the Laser Jet III.
11. Install the driver for the NEC Silentwriter 2 Model 90.
12. Install the correct print driver for your printer and make it the default printer.
13. Connect the printer cable to the printer.
14. Using the Print option in the File menu, print the first page of the document using the NEC Silentwriter 2 Model 90 printer. Notice what happens if you select the wrong driver.
15. If necessary, delete the print job from the Program Manager.
16. Install the correct printer driver.
17. Print the first page of the document again, but select the correct printer driver.
18. Using the Shortcut menu of the LaserJet III Printer in the Printers folder, select the Properties option.
19. Print by selecting Test Print Page.
20. Click on the Details tab.
21. Click on the Graphics tab. Record the resolution, form of dithering, and current intensity.
22. Close the Laser Jet III Properties dialog box.
23. Delete the NEC and the HP LaserJet III printer drivers.

Exercise 8: Booting Windows 95

1. Reboot Windows. When the "Starting Windows 95..." message appears, immediately press the F8 key to bring up a boot menu.
2. Choose Safe Mode.
3. Shut down Windows and reboot it by selecting Command Prompt from the boot menu.
4. Reboot the computer and select the Boot Log option from the Boot menu. (Note: If you have Windows 95b or Windows 95c, do not choose the Previous Operating System option in the Boot menu.)

Exercise 9: Backing up and Restoring the Windows 95 Registry

1. Press the F8 when the "Starting Windows 95..." message appears on the screen.
2. Choose the Command Prompt Only option.
3. Create a folder under the WINDOWS directory called REGISTRY.
4. Perform the following two commands at the C:\WINDOWS> prompt:

```
DIR SYSTEM.* /AH
DIR USER.* /AH
```

5. In the WINDOWS directory, shut off the hidden, system, and read-only attributes for the SYSTEM.DAT file by executing the following command:

```
ATTRIB -H -S -R SYSTEM.DAT
```

6. Shut off the hidden, system, and read-only attributes for the USER.DAT file.
7. Copy the SYSTEM.DAT file to the REGISTRY directory by performing the following command at the C:\WINDOWS> prompt:

```
COPY SYSTEM.DAT C:\WINDOWS\REGISTRY
```

8. Copy the USER.DAT file to the REGISTRY directory.
9. Turn on the hidden, system, and read-only attributes for the SYSTEM.DAT and USER.DAT files.
10. Typically, Windows 95 keeps an extra copy of the Registry (Registry files with a DA0 filename extension). Restore the backup Registry files that have a DA filename extension.
11. Start and test Windows 95. If Windows 95 is not working properly, restore the copy of the Windows 95 Registry kept in the REGISTRY directory.

Exercise 10: Working with REGEDIT.EXE.

1. Start the Display applet in the Control Panel.
2. Set the Wallpaper to Bubbles and tile it.
3. Set the screen saver to Flying Windows and set the wait time to three minutes.
4. Record the resolution.
5. Set the number of colors to 65,536 (16-bit). If necessary, reboot the computer.
6. Start REGEDIT.EXE.
7. Find the following value:

```
HKEY_CURRENT_USER\Control Panel\Desktop\ScreenSaveTimeOut
```

Notice the value and compare it to the wait time of the screen saver. Remember that one minute equals 60 seconds.

8. Change the ScreenSaveTimeOut value to 120 seconds.

9. Find the following value:

```
HKEY_CURRENT_USER\Control Panel\Desktop\TileWallPaper
```

Although the TileWallPaper value is a string, the TileWallPaper uses only a 1 or a 0 value. A 1 indicates to tile the wallpaper; a 0 indicates not to tile the wallpaper.

10. Find the following value:

    ```
    HKEY_CURRENT_USER\Control Panel\Desktop\WallPaper
    ```

11. Find the following value:

    ```
    HKEY_LOCAL_ MACHINE\Config\0001\Display\Settings\Resolution
    ```

12. Find the following value:

    ```
    HKEY_LOCAL_ MACHINE\Config\0001\Display\Settings\BitsPerPixel
    ```

13. Change the BitsPerPixel to 8.
14. Exit REGEDIT.EXE and reboot the computer.
15. Open the Display applet from the Control Panel and notice the number of colors.
16. Start the REGEDIT.EXE program.
17. Open the HKEY_USERS root key. Notice the number of users, including the Default User.
18. Open the Default key. Notice the similarity between the HKEY_USERS\DEFAULT key and the HKEY_CURRENT_ USERS key.
19. Open a window to show the large icons of the C:\WINDOWS directory.
20. Find the BUBBLES.BMP file and notice the icon.
21. Find the HKEY_CLASSES_ ROOT\Paint.Picture\DefaultIcon value and change it to %1.
22. Go back to the C:\WINDOWS window and notice the appearance of the BUB-BLES.BMP icon.
23. Exit REGEDIT.EXE.

Exercise 11: Installing and Configuring Microsoft Office 97

1. Insert the MS-Office 97 CD-ROM into the compact disk drive and start the installation program (unless told otherwise). Install all of Office using the Custom installation except the Microsoft Photo Editor (selected within Office Tools).
2. After the installation is complete, double-click on the Microsoft Office Setup icon (located in the C:\Program Files—Microsoft Office directory). This will allow you to install or remove Office components.
3. Install the Microsoft Photo Editor.
4. When Microsoft Photo Editor is installed, start Microsoft Word.
5. Type in your first name followed by your last name. On the next line, type in your address.
6. Select Options… located within the Tools menu. Click on the View tab.
7. To show the hardware returns, select the spaces and paragraph marks within the Nonprinting Characters section and click on the OK button.
8. Select Options… located within the Tools menu and shut off the space and paragraph marks.
9. Click on the General tab. Make sure that the Macro Virus protection option is selected. In addition, notice the number of recently used files and the measurement units.
10. Select the Save tab. Make sure that the Save AutoRecover Info option is selected and notice the time of Autosave. In addition, notice the default format that documents are saved as (Save Word Files As option).
11. Click on the Spelling and Grammar tab. Make sure that the Check Spelling as you type and Check Grammar as you type options are selected.
12. Select the File Location tab. Notice the default directory for Word documents.
13. Click on the OK button.
14. Go to any toolbar and click using the right (secondary) mouse button. Notice which toolbars are open. Select the WordArt toolbar.
15. Grab the titlebar of the WordArt toolbar and drag it to the right of the screen until it becomes embedded.
16. Grab the top of the WordArt toolbar and drag it back to the center of Microsoft Word window.
17. Close the WordArt toolbar.
18. Click on the Customize option located within the Tools menu.
19. Click on the Commands tab.

20. On the Standard toolbar, drag the New button off the toolbar.
21. Within the File category, find the New… command and drag it to the beginning of the Standard toolbar. Click on the Close button.
22. Select the AutoCorrect option within the Tools menu. Click on the Options button.
23. If you don't want automatic bullets and numbering, deselect the Automatic Bulleted Lists and Automatic Numbered Lists options located in the Apply As You Type section.
24. Click on the OK button.
25. Close the current document and don't save the changes.
26. Open a new document. Notice the default font and font size.
27. Close the document.
28. Open the C:\PROGRAM FILES\MICROSOFT OFFICE\TEMPLATES\ NORMAL.DOT template.
29. Change the font to 12-point Arial.
30. Save the changes and close the NORMAT.DOT template.
31. Open a new document. Notice the default font and font size.
32. Close Microsoft Word.

23

Windows NT

INTRODUCTION

Windows NT is an operating system that can function as a desktop operating system or as a file, print, or application server on a network. It offers higher performance, greater reliability, and better security than machines running DOS or Windows 3.XX and Windows 95 and 98. Unfortunately, Windows NT is not 100% backward compatible with all older hardware and software.

OBJECTIVES

1. List the minimum hardware and software requirements to run Windows NT 4.0.
2. Describe and explain the Windows NT boot process.
3. Compare and contrast FAT, VFAT, and NTFS file systems.
4. Configure Windows NT using the Control Panel.
5. Use the Windows NT Diagnostics to find available resources, resource conflicts, and driver problems.
6. Use Event Viewer and Windows Monitor to find problems in Windows NT.

7. Create a startup disk.
8. Make changes to the BOOT.INI file when appropriate.
9. List and explain the five different keys found in the Windows NT Registry.
10. Use REGEDIT to make changes to the Registry when appropriate.
11. Install and configure Windows NT.
12. Determine and correct a problem in Windows NT.

23.1 WHAT IS WINDOWS NT?

Windows NT is an operating system that can function as a desktop operating system or a network file, print, or application server. Earlier versions of Windows NT used the Windows 3.XX interface, while Windows NT 4.0 uses the Windows 95 interface (see fig. 23.1). Behind these popular interfaces, Windows NT uses a different architecture, that offers higher performance, greater reliability, and better security than DOS or Windows 3.XX and Windows 95 and 98.

Like Windows 95, Windows NT is a **preemptive multitasking** operating system in that it assigns time slices to tasks and applications. Tasks and applications with a higher priority get a larger time slice. Unlike Windows 3.XX and Windows 95 or 98, however, Windows NT can support multiple microprocessors, allowing it to do true multitasking. Windows NT supports most DOS, WIN16-based, WIN32-based, and OS/2 applications.

Windows NT, like Windows 95, is a multithreaded operating system that can execute different parts of a program, called *threads,* simultaneously. Programs that are multithreaded have an improved throughput and enhanced responsiveness and can perform background processing. For example, Microsoft Word uses a thread to respond to keys typed on the keyboard by the user to place characters in a document while other threads check spelling and paginate the document as the user types. If the user prints, another thread spools, or feeds, a document to the printer in the background. Of course, a program using multithreading must be carefully designed so that all the threads can run at the same time without interfering with each other.

FIGURE 23.1 Windows NT 4.0 desktop

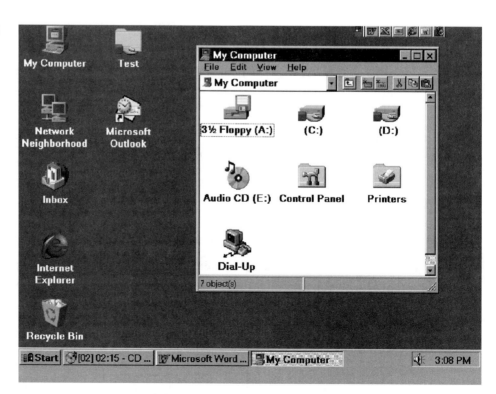

23.2 WINDOWS NT CHARACTERISTICS

The following are the requirements for installing and running Windows NT 4.0:

	Windows NT Workstation	Windows NT Server
Microprocessor	Intel 486DX/33 or higher	Intel 486DX/33 or higher
RAM	12 MB of RAM (16 MB recommended)	16 MB of RAM
Disk space	110 MB of free disk space	125 MB of free disk space
Display	VGA or higher	VGA or higher
Other	CD-ROM (or network card for installation over the network)	CD-ROM (or network card for installation over the network)

Even though these requirements are those listed in the Windows NT documentation, they will offer slow and sometimes unreliable operations. For acceptable performance and reliability, a Pentium with a minimum of 32 MB of RAM is needed. Of course, with a faster microprocessor and additional RAM, Windows NT will perform even better.

Microsoft has compiled a hardware compatibility list (HCL) of devices that have been tested and approved to work with Windows NT. The list is available on the Windows NT compact disk and at http://www.microsoft.com/hwtest. Before installing Windows NT or before purchasing a system, you should look at this list.

> **NOTE** Because the Windows NT architecture and Registry are different from the Windows 95 architecture and Registry, there is no method of upgrading Windows 95 to Windows NT. However, you can install Windows NT into a different directory (\WINNT directory is the default) and dual boot between the two operating systems. Unfortunately, you would have to reinstall your applications in Windows NT, and you would have to use the VFAT file system if you wish to use both operating systems.

23.2.1 WINDOWS NT BOOT SEQUENCE

During boot-up, the first Windows NT file read is NTLDR, which switches the microprocessor from real mode to protected mode and starts the appropriate minifile system drivers so that it can read the VFAT or NTFS file systems. Next, NTLDR reads the BOOT.INI (if one is available) and displays the Boot Loader Operating System Selection menu. (See fig. 23.2.) NTLDR then loads the operating system (such as Windows NT Server, Windows NT Workstation, Windows 95, or DOS) selected from the menu.

If Windows NT is selected from the boot menu, NTLDR runs NTDETECT to scan the system for hardware. Next, the NTLDR reads the SYSTEM hive from the HKEY_ LOCAL_MACHINE subtree in the Windows NT Registry. The SYSTEM hive specifies which device drivers to load during boot-up. When the device drivers are loaded, a hardware list is made and stored in the Registry. The Session Manager (SMSS.EXE) is then loaded, which loads the appropriate services needed for Windows NT to function. Lastly, the NTOSKRNL.EXE, the NT kernel, is executed. If DOS or Windows 95 or 98 was selected from the boot menu, the NTLDR loads BOOTSECT.DOS. The file contains the DOS or Windows 95 or 98 boot sector that was on the hard disk before Windows NT was installed. Another important boot file is the NTBOOTDD.SYS file. If the system has a SCSI hard disk, for which the BIOS on the SCSI adapter is disabled, the NTBOOTDD.SYS is needed to access the SCSI devices during boot-up.

The active partition that contains the NTLDR and BOOT.INI file is known as the *system partition*. The partition that contains the Windows NT operating system files (usually in the WINNT directory) is called the *boot partition*. If a system has only one partition containing

FIGURE 23.2 Windows NT Boot Loader Operating System Selection menu

```
OS Loader V4.00

Please select the operating system to start:

Windows NT Server Version 4.00
Windows NT Server Version 4.00 [VGA mode]
Windows NT Workstation Version 4.00
Windows NT Workstation Version 4.00 [VGA mode]
MS-DOS

Use ↑ and ↓ to move the highlight to your choice.

Press Enter to choose.
```

the initial boot files and the Windows NT directory, the partition is both the system partition and the boot partition.

23.2.2 WINDOWS NT ARCHITECTURE

Like Windows 95, Windows NT uses the Intel 386 microprocessor protection model. The kernel mode consists of processes (or subprograms) running in Ring 0 that are protected by the microprocessor. It has direct access to all hardware and all memory, including the address space of all user-mode processes. These subprograms include the Windows NT Executive, hardware abstraction layer (HAL), the microkernel, and the Windows NT executive services.

The user mode programs run in Ring 3 and are protected by the operating system. Ring 3 is a less privileged processor mode that has no direct access to hardware and can access only its own address space. Because programs running in Ring 3 have very little privilege over programs running in Ring 0, they can cause few problems for components of Ring 0, which is why most of the user's applications run in Ring 3. This arrangement allows for a secure and reliable platform and permits an application to be terminated (when, for example, it tries to access the hardware directly) without causing problems for the other applications running on the computer.

The hardware abstraction layer (HAL) is a library of hardware-manipulating routines. The microkernel, the central part of Windows NT, like the kernels in Windows 3.XX and Windows 95 and 98, determines what is to be performed and when it is to be performed while handling interrupts and exceptions. It is designed to keep the microprocessor or microprocessors busy at all times. The Windows NT executive services consist of managers and device drivers. They include the I/O Manager, Object Manager, Security Reference Manager, Local Procedure Call Facility, Virtual Memory Manager, Win32K Window Manager and GDI, hardware device drivers, and graphics device drivers.

Much like Windows 95 and 98, Windows NT has virtual memory (disk pretending to be RAM). Virtual memory allows more RAM, but because the disk is much slower than RAM, virtual memory is much slower than physical RAM. Windows NT maps physical and virtual memory addresses in 4 KB blocks called *pages*. The files that make up the virtual memory are called *paging files* (PAGEFILE.SYS). (Note: If a system has multiple hard disks, creating a paging file for each disk increases paging performance.)

23.3 MANAGING DISKS UNDER WINDOWS NT

By default, Windows NT uses **VFAT** (often referred to as just FAT), an enhanced version of the FAT structure that allowed operating environments beginning with Windows 95 to support long filenames (up to 255 characters). The VFAT structure is built on ordinary FAT, so each file has an eight-character name and three-character extension as well to be backward compatible to DOS and Windows 3.XX applications. Programs running in DOS and Windows 3.XX do not see the longer filenames. A WIN32 program (program made for Windows 95 or 98 or Windows NT) can see and make use of the longer names.

FIGURE 23.3   Disk
Administrator

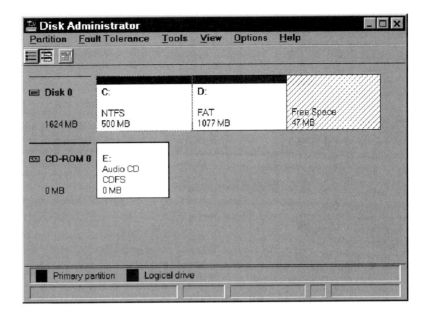

The Windows NT **NTFS** file system, designed for both the server and the workstation, supports long filenames, yet maintains an 8.3 name for DOS and Windows 3.XX programs. Created with security in mind, the system supports a variety of multiuser security models and allows several platforms to save files to the NTFS volume on the NT server, including DOS, Windows 3.XX, Windows 95, Windows NT Workstation, UNIX, POSIX, and even Macintosh computers. It does not, however, allow DOS to access an NTFS volume directly, only through the network (assuming the user has the proper permission or right to access the volume). It can compress individual files or directories, including those only infrequently used. (Note: Currently, Windows NT is the only operating system that can use NTFS partitions.) To make an NTFS volume more resistant to failure, NTFS writes updates to a log area. If a system crash occurs, the log area can be used to clean up problems quickly. In addition, the system tries to keep the hard drive unfragmented.

The following utilities are used to manage disks: FDISK, FORMAT, Disk Administrator, and CONVERT.EXE. The FDISK command, much like FDISK from DOS and Windows 95 and 98, allows partitions to be created and deleted at the command prompt.

The FORMAT command formats a disk at the command prompt. The syntax for this command is:

FORMAT drive: [/FS:file-system] [/V:label]

For example, to format the D drive as a NTFS partition, you would type the following command at the command prompt:

```
FORMAT D: /FS:NTFS
```

After Windows NT is installed, the Disk Administrator, a graphical menu-driver utility, can be used to create, format, and delete partitions and to create volume sets, stripe sets, mirror sets, and stripe sets with parity (see section 23.3.1). The Partition menu creates and deletes partitions. The Fault Tolerance menu creates and breaks mirror sets and creates or regenerates strip sets with parity. The Tools menu is used to format disks and to assign drive letters. (See fig. 23.3.)

The CONVERT.EXE utility can be used to convert a FAT partition to an NTFS partition. To convert the D drive, you would type the following command at the command prompt:

```
CONVERT D: /FS:NTFS
```

If a process is currently accessing the drive, a message will appear stating that the conversion will occur when the system is restarted. (Note: An NTFS partition cannot be converted into a FAT partition. The only way to transfer the data would be to back up the data on the NTFS partition, delete it, and create a FAT partition and restore the data.)

23.3.1 VOLUME SETS, STRIPE SETS, AND MIRROR SETS

Windows NT provides multiple configuration options that increase disk performance and/or fault tolerance. They include:

1. Volume sets
2. Stripe sets (RAID 0)
3. Mirror sets (RAID 1)
4. Stripe sets with parity (RAID 5)

A **volume set** combines 2 through 32 areas of unformatted free space (FAT or NTFS) on one or more physical drives to create a larger logical drive. If the volume set is using NTFS and becomes full, the volume set can be extended by adding another hard drive without rebuilding the entire set. In a volume set, data is written to one disk, and when the first disk becomes full, it is then written to the next disk. Therefore, although volume sets allow larger volumes, this does not increase disk performance and does not provide any fault tolerance. A **stripe set** functions like a volume set except the data is written evenly across all physical disks. Because all of the disks are being read from and written to concurrently, stripe sets provide much faster access. Like volume sets, stripe sets do not provide any fault tolerance.

RAID (redundant arrays of inexpensive disks) is a system of using two or more drives in combination as a fault tolerance system to protect against physical hard drive failure and to increase hard drive performance. RAID can be accomplished with either hardware or software and allows the system to keep on working during a hard drive failure without losing information. (Note: RAID does not replace a good backup and it does not protect against data corruption or viruses.) Windows NT can use RAID 1 (disk mirroring) and RAID 5 (disk striping with parity). **Disk mirroring** duplicates a partition onto two hard drives. Information is written to both hard drives simultaneously, which increases performance and gives fault tolerance if one of the hard drives fails. Disk duplexing is a form of disk mirroring. While disk mirroring uses two hard drives connected to the same card, **disk duplexing** uses two controller cards, two cables, and two hard drives. (Note: The system or boot partition cannot be mirrored.)

Disk striping with parity uses disk striping but includes a byte error correction on one of the disks. If one of the disks goes bad, the system will continue to function, and after the faulty disk is replaced, the information can be rebuilt on the replacement disk. Disk striping with parity requires at least three drives. It offers excellent performance and good fault tolerance. (Note: Neither the system nor the boot partition can be striped.)

23.3.2 BOOT.INI FILES

During boot-up, the BOOT.INI file provides a Boot Loader Operating System Selection menu that offers a choice among multiple operating systems. The BOOT.INI file is a read-only, hidden system text file located in the root directory of the system partition and is divided into two sections: [boot loader] and [operating system]. The entries in the [boot loader] section configure the number of seconds that the Boot Loader Operating System Selection menu appears on the screen and the default operating system loaded. (See fig. 23.4 and table 23.1). The [operating systems] section contains the list of available operating systems. Each entry includes an ARC path to the boot partition for the operating system, the string to display in the boot loader screen, and optional parameters. The optional parameters are shown in table 23.2.

An **ARC (advanced RISC computing) path** is used to specify the location (partition) of an operating system. It follows the format

multi(x)disk(y)rdisk(z)partition(a)

or

scsi(x)disk(y)rdisk(x)partition(a)

TABLE 23.1 The settings in the [boot loader] section of the BOOT.INI file	Timeout=XX	Specifies the number of seconds the user has to select an operating system from the boot loader screen before NTLDR loads the default operating system. If the value is 0, NTLDR immediately starts the default operating system without displaying the boot loader screen.
	Default=	The ARC path to the default operating system

TABLE 23.2 Optional parameters found in the BOOT.INI file	/BASEVIDEO	Specifies that Windows NT use the standard VGA video driver
	/DEBUG	Specifies to load the debugger. The debugger is useful when debugging problems that are regularly reproducible.
	/SOS	Displays the device driver names while they are being loaded

FIGURE 23.4   Typical BOOT.INI file

```
[boot loader]
timeout=30
default=multi(0)disk(0)rdisk(0)partition(1)\WINNT
[operating system]
multi(0)disk(0)rdisk()partition(1)\WINNT="Windows NT Workstation Version 4.0"
multi(0)disk(0)rdisk()partition(1)\WINNT="Windows NT Workstation Version 4.0
[VGA mode]"/basevideo /sos
C:\="Windows 95"
```

SCSI is used for a SCSI disk with its BIOS disabled. MULTI is used for disks other than SCSI or a SCSI disk with its BIOS enabled. The number after MULTI is the ordinal number of the hardware adapter card, starting from 0. The number after DISK is the SCSI bus number and will always be 0 for a non-SCSI disk or for a SCSI disk with its BIOS enabled. The number after RDISK is the ordinal number of the disk starting from 0. The number after PARTITION is the ordinal number of the partition, which, unlike the other values, starts at 1. If you boot from a computer that does not use the correct ARC path, you could get one of the following error messages:

"BOOT: Couldn't find NTLDR. Please insert another disk"

"NT could not start because the following file is missing or corrupt: \winntroot\ system32\ntoskrnl.exe"

"NTDETECT V1.0 Checking Hardware…"

"NTDETECT failed/missing"

23.4   THE CONTROL PANEL

The Windows NT Control Panel (similar to the Windows 95 Control Panel) is a graphical tool for configuring the Windows environment and hardware devices. (See fig. 23.5.) It can be accessed from the Settings option in the Start button under My Computer. Additionally, there are various shortcuts to directly access certain Control Panel applets (icons). The most commonly used applets are the System applet, the Display applet, the Add/Remove Programs applet, and the Add New Hardware applet.

The System applet has six tabs, including the Performance, Environment, and Startup/Shutdown tabs. (See fig. 23.6.) The Startup/Shutdown tab changes the default operating system and the timeout in the BOOT.INI file. (See fig. 23.7.) The Performance tab configures the paging file size (virtual memory). The minimum paging file is 2 MB, and for Windows NT Workstation, the default size of the file is equal to the total amount of RAM plus 12 MB, not to exceed the amount of available disk space. Usually, the size of the paging file can stay at the default value assigned during installation unless a large number of

FIGURE 23.5   Windows NT
Control Panel

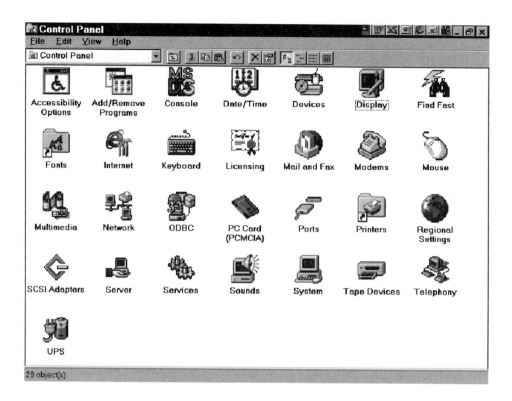

FIGURE 23.6   The System Properties tabs (accessed
through the System applet in the Windows NT Control
Panel)

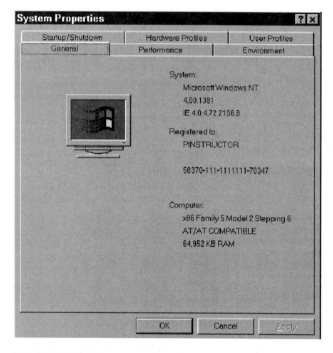

FIGURE 23.7   Startup/Shutdown options available in the
Control Panel's System applet.

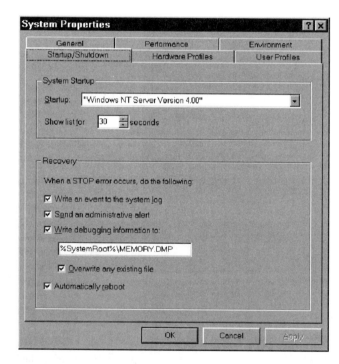

applications are being run, in which case you might want to increase the paging file size.
(See fig. 23.8.) The Environment tab changes system and user environment variables, such
as the TEMP and TMP variables. System environment variables are for all users, and user
environment variables are different for each user. (See fig. 23.9.)

Unlike Windows 95, the Windows NT System applet in the Control Panel does not include a device manager or an Add Hardware applet. And to view the use of I/O addresses,

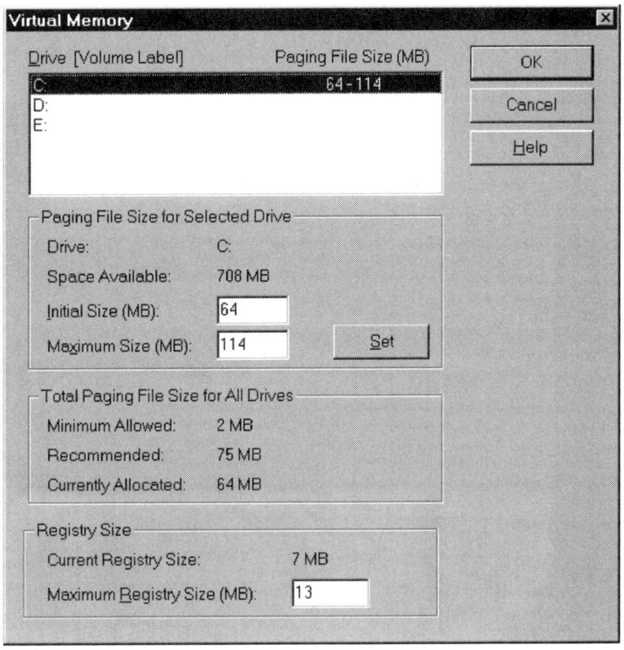

FIGURE 23.8 Page file in Windows NT configured within the System applet (Control Panel)

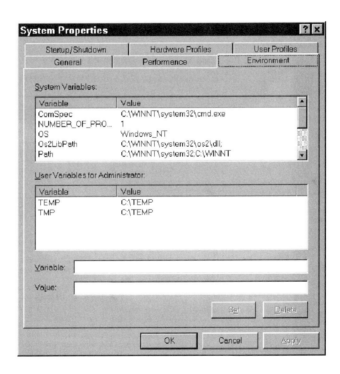

FIGURE 23.9 Environment tab accessed through the Control Panel's System applet

IRQs, DMAs, and memory addresses, you would have to use the Microsoft Windows NT Diagnostics program (discussed later in the chapter). Therefore, to load the various hardware device drivers, you have to use the other applets in the Control Panel. For example, to load the sound card drivers, you would use the Multimedia applet. Other device applets include the Keyboard, Mouse, Modem, Tape Devices, and SCSI Adapter applets.

> **NOTE** Windows NT does not support plug-and-play devices, but it can use them as long as the Windows NT device driver can activate the card and determine the card's resources.

TABLE 23.3 Windows NT registry subtrees

HKEY_CLASSES_ROOT	Contains file associations and OLE information
HKEY_CURRENT_USER	Contains settings for applications, desktop configurations, and user preferences for the user currently logged on
HKEY_LOCAL_MACHINE	Contains information about the type of hardware installed, drivers, and other system settings
HKEY_USERS	Contains information about all users who log on to the computer, including the .DEFAULT generic user settings. The DEFAULT user is used as a template for any new users.
HKEY_CURRENT_CONFIG	Contains information about the current running hardware configuration

FIGURE 23.10 REGEDIT32.EXE

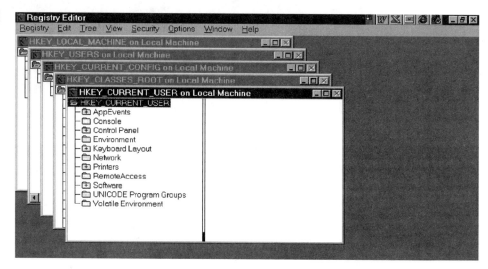

23.5 THE REGISTRY EDITOR

The Registry is a central database in which Windows NT stores all hardware and software configuration information. It controls the Windows NT operating system by providing appropriate initialization information to start applications and load components such as device drivers and network protocols.

The values in the registry are usually changed through the Control Panel when booting up, installing or removing a program, or adding or removing a printer. Once in a while, you may need to view or edit the Registry to change a value that cannot be changed in the Control Panel or other utility or to view and change hardware settings that cannot be done with Device Manager. Changes in the Registry should be made only when following directions from a professional magazine article, book, manual, or support person. If the wrong changes are made, Windows NT may not run properly or may not boot at all. To view and change the Registry, a utility called REGEDIT32.EXE is used. The Registry is divided into five subtrees, and like Windows 95 and 98, the root keys are then divided into subkeys, which may contain other subkeys or value names and data. (See table 23.3 and fig. 23.10.)

23.6 INSTALLING WINDOWS NT

To install Windows NT Workstation, go to the installation CD (or files if they are on the network) and use the WINNT.EXE file to start the installation process. If you are upgrading a computer that is already using Windows NT, use WINNT32.EXE. The WINNT.EXE will perform the following steps:

1. Create a set of setup boot disks for drive A on the computer
2. Create a WIN_NT.~LS temporary folder and then copy the Windows NT files

3. Prompt the user to restart the computer from the first Setup disk

The WINNT.EXE has the following parameters:

/X	Prevents Setup from creating Setup boot disks. Use /X when the Setup boot disks are already created.
/OX	Creates only boot disks
/B	Performs a floppyless installation

23.7 TROUBLE-SHOOTING WINDOWS NT

Much like other graphical operating systems, Windows NT can have a wide range of problems. To help isolate and diagnose these problems, Windows NT provides several programs and options.

23.7.1 GRAPHICAL UTILITIES

The are several tools that can help diagnose Windows NT problems include the Event Viewer, Windows NT Diagnostics, and Performance Monitor.

Event Viewer provides information on errors, warnings, and the success or failure of tasks. To start Event Viewer, click the Start button, select the Programs option, select Administrative Tools (Common), and click Event Viewer. (See fig. 23.11.) Double-clicking on an event shows details of the event. (See fig. 23.12.)

The Windows NT Diagnostics shows computer hardware and operating system data stored in the Windows NT Registry. Like the System applet in the Windows 95 Control Panel, it includes the system resources (IRQ, I/O addresses, DMA, memory usage, and device drivers). Performance Monitor is used to monitor real-time system performance, identify trends over time, and identify bottlenecks. Both of these programs are found under the Administrative Tools (Common) option under the Programs option (Start button). (See figs. 23.13 and fig. 23.14.)

The Windows NT Performance Monitor is a utility that measures and graphs performance characteristics and is useful in identifying bottlenecks. (See fig. 23.15.)

23.7.2 BOOT-UP OPTIONS

During boot-up, there are two options that can help troubleshoot and fix recently installed device drivers that are causing problems. The first one is used when, after installing a new

FIGURE 23.11 Windows NT Event Viewer is used to display an event and problem log.

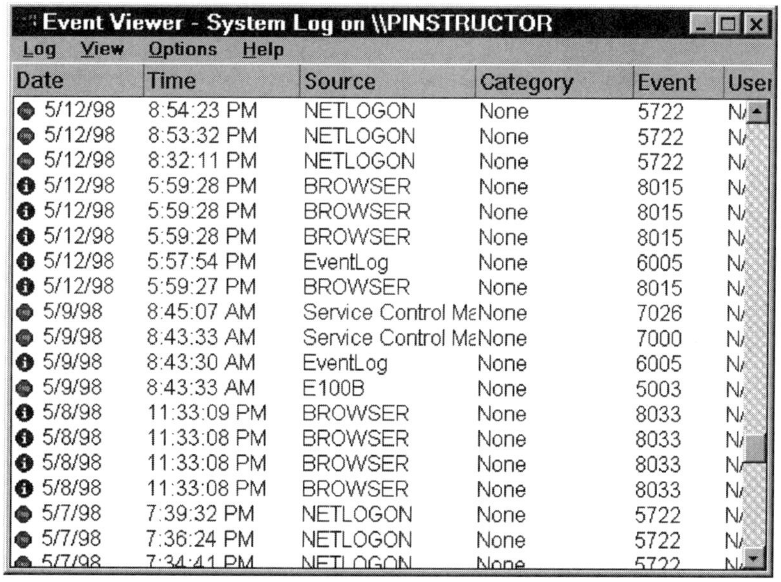

555

FIGURE 23.12   Details of an event shown with the Windows NT Event Viewer

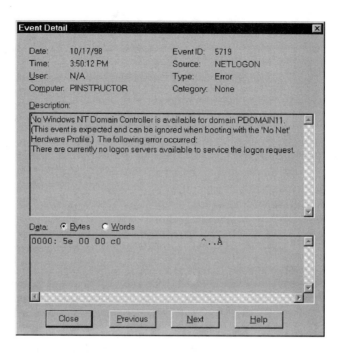

FIGURE 23.13   Windows NT Diagnostics program

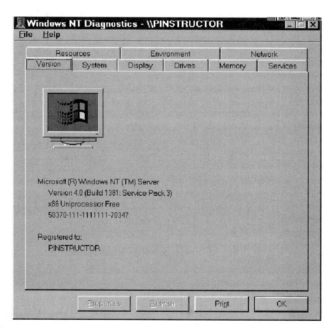

device driver in Windows NT, the system does not boot properly. When this happens, you can then invoke the Last Known Good configuration when prompted before logging on to Windows NT, which will restore the previous configuration settings at the last log-in. The second option is used if the wrong video driver has been selected and you can't see anything on the screen. When this happens, you can reboot the computer and select Windows NT [VGA mode], which will select the VGA driver (640 × 480 resolution with 16 colors). The 16 colors will not make for as attractive a screen as one with more colors, but the VGA mode will allow you to select the correct driver.

23.7.3   CREATING A WINDOWS NT BOOT DISK

A Windows NT Boot Disk enables you to start up Windows NT from a floppy disk so that you can troubleshoot and fix a problem or get a computer running again. To create a Windows NT Startup floppy disk, you must format it when running Windows NT so that it will

FIGURE 23.14 Windows NT
Diagnostics program showing
the IRQ usage

FIGURE 23.14 Windows NT Diagnostics program showing the IRQ usage

FIGURE 23.15 Windows NT Performance Monitor

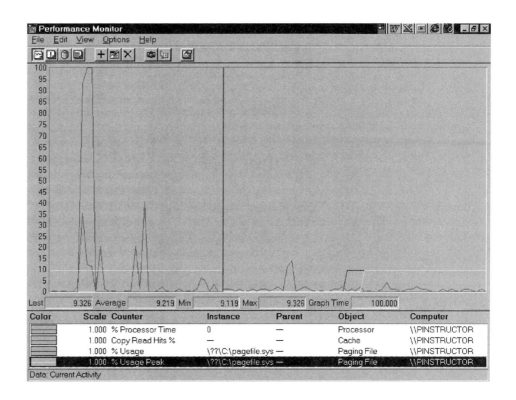

have the Windows NT Master Partition Boot Sector. You can use My Computer, Windows Explorer, or the FORMAT command at the prompt and copy the NTLDR, BOOT.INI, NTDETECT.COM, BOOTSECT.DOS, and NTBOOTDD.SYS (if you have SCSI devices with the BIOS disabled) files to the floppy disk.

23.7.4 EMERGENCY REPAIR DISK (ERD)

If a computer does not boot properly and the Last Known Good command does not fix the problem, you can use the Windows NT Setup disk and the **emergency repair disk (ERD)** to reconstruct the Windows NT system files and the Registry.

TABLE 23.4 Emergency repair disk options

Inspect Registry Files	You will be prompted for the replacement of each Registry file. Any changes to the Security and SAM registry hives are lost, and these files will be restored as they were at system installation. Changes to Software and System are restored to the last update of the emergency repair information.
Inspect Startup Environment	Verifies that NT is an option in the Operating System Select menu. If it is not listed in the BOOT.INI file, then the emergency repair process adds a Windows NT option for the next boot image.
Verify Windows NT System Files	This option identifies and offers to replace files that have been altered from their original state on the NT CD. This option verifies that the boot files, such as NTLDR and NTOSKRNL.EXE, are present and valid. If you have installed service packs on this machine, check Files on each service pack to see if they have to be reinstalled.
Inspect Boot Sector	Verifies that the primary boot sector still references NTLDR and updates the boot sector if it does not. This is useful if someone uses the MS-DOS SYS.COM utility or anything that destroys the NT boot sector.

To create an emergency repair disk, insert an empty, formatted disk in the A drive and execute RDISK.EXE in the SYSTEM32 folder (located in the WINNT folder). Click the Repair Disk button and select Update Repair Info. When the operation finishes, click on the Exit button. This disk will, of course, be good only for the computer that made it. (Note: To create an emergency repair disk that contains the most current Security Accounts Manager (SAM) database, you must use the /S option with the Repair Disk utility (RDISK).

To use the emergency repair disk, start the computer from the Windows NT Setup disk #1 (setup disks are made during installation or by using WINNT /OX). When requested, insert disk #2. When prompted, select the option to Repair by pressing the R key. Setup will then display options to inspect the Registry files, inspect the Startup environment, verify Windows NT System files, and inspect the boot sector. (See table 23.4.) You would then clear all sections that you do not want to use and click Continue to perform the selected tasks. After disk #3, you will be prompted for the emergency repair disk. You then remove the disk when prompted and reboot the computer.

SUMMARY

1. Windows NT is a preemptive multitasking operating system.
2. Windows NT is a multithreaded operating system that can execute different parts of a program, called *threads,* simultaneously.
3. Because the Windows NT architecture and Registry are different from the Windows 95 architecture and Registry, there is no way of upgrading Windows 95 to Windows NT.
4. During boot-up, the first Windows NT file read is NTLDR, which switches the microprocessor from real mode to protected mode, starts the appropriate minifile system drivers, and reads the BOOT.INI file to display the Boot Loader Operating System Selection menu.
5. The active partition that contains the NTLDR and BOOT.INI file is known as the *system partition.*
6. The partition that contains the Windows NT operating system files (usually in the WINNT directory) is called the *boot partition.*
7. The files that make up the virtual memory are called *paging files* (PAGEFILE.SYS).
8. Windows NT supports and uses the VFAT and NTFS file systems.
9. A volume set combines 2 through 32 areas of unformatted free space (FAT or NTFS) on one or more physical drives to create a larger logical drive.
10. A stripe set is similar to a volume set except the data is written evenly across all physical disks, which provides faster access.

11. Disk mirroring is duplicating a partition onto two hard drives. Information is written to both hard drives simultaneously, providing fault tolerance.
12. Disk striping with parity is disk striping that provides fault tolerance.
13. An ARC (advanced RISC computing) path is used to specify the location (partition) of an operating system.
14. The Windows NT Control Panel (similar to the Windows 95 Control Panel) is a graphical tool for configuring the Windows environment and hardware devices.
15. The Registry is a central database in which Windows NT stores all hardware and software configuration information.
16. The WINNT.EXE file from the installation CD (or the network) is used to install Windows NT Workstation.
17. The Event Viewer provides information on errors, warnings, and the success or failure of tasks.
18. The Windows NT Diagnostics shows computer hardware and operating system data stored in the Windows NT Registry.
19. The Windows NT Performance Monitor is a utility that provides graphical statistics that can be used to measure the performance of a computer and determine bottlenecks.
20. The Last Known Good configuration can be used to restore the previous configuration settings at the last log-in.
21. An emergency repair disk (ERD) can be used to reconstruct the Windows NT system files and the Registry.

QUESTIONS

1. *True or False*—Because Windows NT 4.0 uses the Windows 95 interface, any programs that will work on Windows 95 will work on Windows NT.
2. Which of the following does *not* describe Windows NT?
   a. Windows NT uses preemptive multitasking
   b. Windows NT uses cooperative multitasking
   c. Windows NT is multithreaded
   d. Windows NT supports multiple microprocessors
3. How would you upgrade Windows 95 or 98 to Windows NT?
   a. You would use the WINNT32.EXE utility
   b. You can install Windows NT into the same folder as Windows 95 if Windows 95 is using VFAT
   c. You would use the CONVERT.EXE utility
   d. You cannot upgrade Windows 95 or 98 to Windows NT
4. The file that contains the Boot Loader Operating System Selection menu is known as the:
   a. NTLDR   d. MSDOS.SYS
   b. NTDETECT.COM   e. NTOSKRNL
   c. BOOT.INI
5. For additional security, what file system in Windows NT would you use?
   a. FAT   d. NTFS
   b. VFAT   e. CDFS
   c. HPFS
6. Which of the following provides faster access and fault tolerance? (Choose all that apply.)
   a. volume set   c. stripe set with parity checking
   b. stripe set   d. mirroring
7. The location of a partition in the BOOT.INI file is known as the:
   a. search path   d. ARC path
   b. boot path   e. security path
   c. access path
8. In Windows NT, the virtual memory is called an:
   a. temporary swap file   c. expanded system file
   b. permanent swap file   d. paging file
9. *True or False*—Like Windows 95, Windows NT 4.0 supports plug-and-play devices.

10. Which utility allows you to see the log of problems encountered on a Windows NT machine?
    a. Performance Monitor   c. Event Viewer
    b. Network Monitor   d. Boot Viewer
11. The Registry is corrupted on a Windows NT machine. The best way to fix it is:
    a. reformat the hard drive and reinstall everything
    b. boot the computer using the NT Setup disks and use the ERD disk
    c. back up the hard drive, reinstall Windows NT, and restore the backup
    d. select Windows NT-VGA during boot-up

HANDS-ON EXERCISES

Exercise 1: Installing Windows NT

1. Create two partitions (a C drive and a D drive) on the hard drive.
2. Format the C drive as a bootable drive.
3. Format the D drive.
4. Install DOS.
5. Load the appropriate drivers to activate the CD-ROM drive.
6. Install Windows NT on drive D.
7. Run the Disk Administrator and notice the partitions on the hard drive.
8. Using the CONVERT command, convert the FAT file system to the NTFS file system on the D drive.
9. Run the Disk Administrator and notice the partitions on the hard drive.
10. Reboot the computer and study the Boot menu that appears on the screen. Boot to DOS.
11. Using the DOS ATTRIB command, shut off the read-only, system, and hidden file attributes for the BOOT.INI file.
12. Load the BOOT.INI file using EDIT.
13. Notice the menu items, the default menu item, and the boot time. DOS should boot from the C drive and Windows should boot from the second partition.
14. Change the partition number of the Windows NT workstation ARC path from 2 to 1. Save the changes and exit EDIT.
15. Reboot the computer and select the Windows NT workstation. Notice the error message.
16. Reboot the computer to DOS. Load the BOOT.INI file using EDIT and change the Windows NT workstation ARC path from 1 to 2. Save the changes and exit EDIT.
17. Reboot the computer to Windows NT.
18. Use the Windows NT Diagnostics utility to view the free IRQ, DMA, and I/O addresses.
19. If the computer has a sound card, use the Multimedia applet to install the appropriate drivers.
20. Test the sound card.
21. Start the Windows NT Diagnostics utility and view the IRQ, DMA, and I/O addresses used by the sound card.

24

Computers Connected to a Network

INTRODUCTION

As networks have become more popular, it has become evident that a PC technician must also be familiar with how to connect a PC to a network and to the Internet. In addition, the technician must be able to differentiate between problems caused by the computer and problems caused by the network.

OBJECTIVES

1. Define a network.
2. List the main components of a network.
3. List the common services provided by a network.
4. Compare and contrast client, server, and peer.
5. Compare and contrast LANs, MANs, and WANs.
6. Install and configure a network card.
7. Identify the different types of cables.
8. Describe the common types of cables used in local area networks.
9. Define a topology and list and describe the different types.
10. Compare and contrast between a hub, a bridge, and a router.
11. Define a protocol.
12. List the common protocols used in local area networks.
13. Install client software on a computer.
14. Install software to connect to the Internet.
15. Install a plug-in to a browser.
16. Share files and printers.
17. Access shared resources.

24.1   NETWORKS

A network is two or more computers connected together to share resources. (See fig. 24.1.) Most computers communicate with the network by a cable attached to the computer's network interface card (NIC), while a few computers can use some form of wireless technology (infrared, microwaves, or radio waves). Computers are networked according to certain protocols (TCP/IP, IPX, and NetBEUI), which are the rules or standards that allow computers to connect to one another. Currently, the benefits of a network include:

1. Sharing data or access to a program loaded on the network (file sharing)
2. Sharing printers (print sharing)
3. Sending messages back and forth (electronic mail, or e-mail)
4. Sending and receiving faxes
5. Accessing a modem or accessing the Internet directly
6. Accessing a centralized database
7. Scheduling appointments
8. Security for the network services and resources
9. A central location of data files so that it is easier to perform a backup of essential files

The two most common services provided by a network are file sharing and print sharing. File sharing allows files that are on another computer to be accessed without using a floppy disk or other form of removable media. To ensure that the file is secure, most networks can limit who has access to a directory or file and what kind of access (permission or rights) they have. For example, with full access to a home directory, the user can:

1. List, read, or execute the files in the home directory
2. Create files and directories within the home directory
3. Make changes to files in the home directory
4. Delete files or directories in the home directory

One group of people may be prevented from seeing or executing the files. A second group of people may be able to see or execute the files but cannot make any changes to the files and cannot delete them, while a third group can see, execute, and change the files.

Print sharing allows several people to send documents to a centrally located printer, eliminating the need for personal laser printers. As with files, networks can limit who has

FIGURE 24.1   Computers networked together

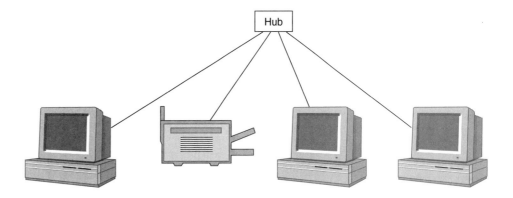

FIGURE 24.2   E-mail with Microsoft Outlook

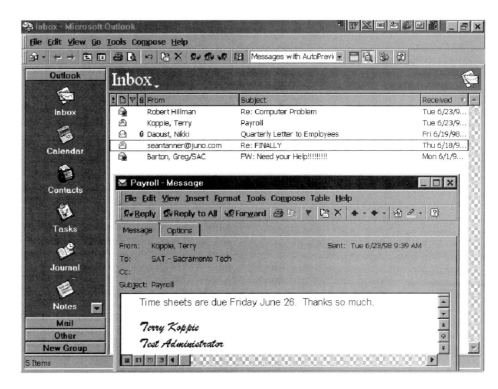

access to the printer. For example, if there are two laser printers, a standard laser printer and an expensive, high-resolution color laser printer, everyone can be assigned access to the standard laser printer, while only a handful of people can be allowed access to the expensive printer.

Two other popular network services include electronic mail (e-mail) and Internet access. Electronic mail, or e-mail, is a powerful, sophisticated tool that allows text messages and file attachments (documents, pictures, sound, and movies) to be sent to anyone with an e-mail address. In 1997, it was estimated that there were over 25 million e-mail users sending 15 billion messages per year. Much like mail handled by the post office, e-mail is delivered to a mailbox (delivery location or holding area for messages). An Internet mail address includes the user name followed by the @ symbol and the name of the mail server. When the addressee connects to the network, the e-mail message can be accessed. Other features of e-mail may include a return receipt so that the sender knows the e-mail was read or delivered, the ability to reply to the e-mail message by clicking on a reply button or option, sending an e-mail message to several people at the same time, or forwarding the message to someone else. (See fig. 24.2.)

Networks can also become part of the Internet or can make a common connection to the Internet possible for many users. The Internet itself is essentially a huge network that many people and organizations have used to post their own web pages or to exchange information and perform research.

24.2 NETWORK CHARACTERISTICS

All networks can be characterized by (1) a client/server or peer-to-peer network, and (2) a LAN, MAN, or WAN configuration.

24.2.1 SERVERS, CLIENTS, AND PEERS

Any computer on a network can provide services or request services depending on how the network is set up. A server is a computer that is a dedicated service provider, and a client is a computer that requests services. A network that is made up of dedicated servers and clients is known as a client/server network, a system designed for medium to large networks. Windows NT and Novell NetWare networks are primarily client/server networks. A peer-to-peer network has no dedicated servers. Instead, all computers can provide services and request services equally. Windows 95 and 98 and Windows for Workgroups can be used to form a peer-to-peer network.

24.2.2 LANS, MANS, AND WANS

There are currently three main categories of networks: local area networks (LANs), metropolitan area networks (MANs), and wide area networks (WANs). In LAN, computers within a close geographical area, such as a building or a campus, are connected. A MAN is a network designed for a town or city, usually with high-speed connections such as fiber optics. A WAN network uses long-range telecommunication links to connect the network over long distances and often consist of two or more smaller LANs. Typically, these LANs are connected through public networks, such as the telephone system. (See fig. 24.3.) A WAN can be either an enterprise WAN or a global WAN. An enterprise WAN is a WAN that is owned by one company or organization, while a global WAN is not owned by any one company and usually crosses national boundaries. The Internet is a global WAN that connects millions of computers. As of 1998, the Internet had more than 100 million users in over 100 countries, and the number is growing rapidly.

Another type of network is the intranet. An intranet is a network based on the TCP/IP, the same protocol the Internet uses, but unlike the Internet, the intranet belongs to a single organization and is accessible only by the organization's members. An intranet's websites look and act just like any other websites, but they are isolated by a firewall to stop illegal access. (Note: An intranet could have access to the Internet but does not require it.)

24.3 NETWORK INTERFACE CARDS (NICS)

The network interface card (NIC), sometimes referred to as the *network adapter card* or *network card,* is the physical interface, or connection, between the computer and the network cable. (See fig. 24.4.) The role of the network card is to prepare and send data to another computer, receive data from another computer, and control the flow of data between the computer and the cabling system.

Like any other expansion card, the network card must be configured (IRQ, I/O address, DMA, and memory address) and inserted into an expansion slot. If the network card and another device share the same resources, the network card and/or the other device will act erratically or not work at all. Network cards are configured with jumpers, DIP switches, or a software configuration program. If the cards are plug-and-play, they will configure automatically. After the network card is installed, a software driver will have to be loaded to activate the card; in many cases, the software driver must be told the resources the card is using.

To identify itself to the network, each network card has a network address, known as the media access control (MAC) address. No two network cards can have the same network address on a single local area network. If two network cards are on separate local area networks, they may have the same address—much like two identical street addresses that are located in two separate cities. Most of the addresses (ethernet and token ring cards) are burned into the ROM chips that come with the network card, while a few cards (such as ARCnet) use jumpers or DIP switches to determine the MAC address.

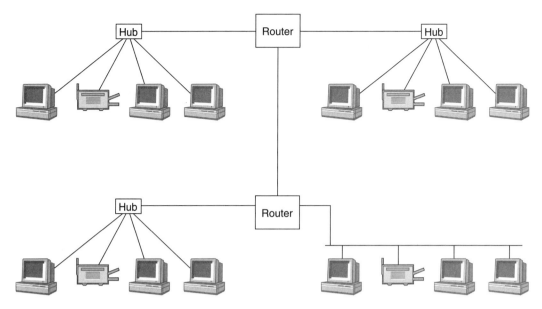

FIGURE 24.3   WAN

FIGURE 24.4   A network interface card (NIC) with a BNC and RJ-45 connectors

24.4   CABLE TYPES

The common cable types used in networks include unshielded twisted pair, shielded twisted pair, coaxial, and fiber-optic. These cables can be characterized by their cost, ease of use, length, and immunity to interference.

24.4.1   TWISTED PAIR CABLE

Twisted pair cable has two insulated strands of copper wire twisted around each other. The twist in the cable helps reduce crosstalk, that is, the overflow from an adjacent wire. Hearing someone else's faint conversation occurring in the background on your own telephone is an example of crosstalk.

Unshielded twisted pair (UTP) cable using the 10Base-T specification (ethernet and token ring networks) resembles telephone cable and is quickly becoming the most popular LAN cable in use. Whereas a telephone cable has two pairs of wires (four wires altogether) and uses an RJ-11 connector, a network cable typically will have four pairs of wires (eight wires altogether) and use an RJ-45 connector. (See fig. 24.5.) The UTP cable comes in five types, mostly depending on the number of twists per foot. (See table 24.1.) If a building is wired with extra twisted pair wire and the wires are of sufficient grade (usually category 3

FIGURE 24.5   Twisted pair cable with RJ-45 connector

FIGURE 24.6   IBM shielded twisted pair cable

FIGURE 24.7   Coaxial cable

TABLE 24.1   Types of unshielded twisted pair cable

Category 1	Traditional telephone cable made to carry voice but not data
Category 2	Made for data transmissions of 4 megabits per second
Category 3	Made for data transmissions of 10 megabits per second; has three twists per foot
Category 4	Made for data transmissions of 16 megabits per second
Category 5	Made for data transmissions of 100 megabits per second

or higher), the extra twisted pair cable can be used for a network. The maximum cable length is 100 meters, or 328 feet.

Shielded twisted pair (STP) cable is very similar to UTP cable except it uses a woven copper braid jacket and a foil wrap around both the individual wires and each pair of wires. The extra shielding makes the cable less susceptible to electrical interference and allows for higher transmission rates and longer distances. Shielded twisted pair cable is used mostly by IBM and Apple networks. (See fig. 24.6.)

24.4.2   COAXIAL CABLE

Coaxial cable has a solid copper core surrounded by insulation, braided metal shielding, and an outer cover. (See fig. 24.7.) It is called *coaxial* cable because the copper wire and the braided metal shielding share the same axis, or center. Because coaxial cable has more

FIGURE 24.8 BNC connector, T-connector, and terminating resistor

insulation, it can be used for longer distances than the twisted pair cable. When coaxial cable is used in a network, it forms the backbone to which all of the computers in the network connect. To prevent signals from bouncing back when they reach the end of the cable, coaxial cable has terminating resistors on both ends.

There are two types of coaxial cable: thin (referred to as *thinnet* or 10Base2) and thick (referred to as *thicknet* or 10Base5). Thinnet is a flexible cable resembling the type of cable used for cable TV. It connects to the network card by using BNC and T-connectors and can carry a signal up to approximately 185 meters (607 feet). (See fig. 24.8.) Ethernet networks use an RG-58 coaxial cable with 50-ohm terminating resistors; ARCnet networks use RG-62 cable with 93-ohm terminating resistors. (Note: A barrel connector is used to connect two cables.) The thicknet type of cable is a bit more difficult to work with than thinnet. Instead of using T-connectors to connect computers directly into the cable "backbone," thicknet cable connects with T-connectors to a drop cable that then connects to the network card. Because thicknet cable is thicker, lengths of up to 500 meters (1,640 feet) can be used.

24.4.3 FIBER-OPTIC CABLE

Fiber-optic cable is very different from the other types of cable. Instead of copper wire, it is made of glass or fiberglass so that it can transmit light instead of electricity. Fiber-optic cable is not susceptible to electromagnetic interference and is very difficult to tap or eavesdrop. It costs a lot more than the other types of cable, but it is capable of greater data transmission speeds and can transmit over greater distances. The disadvantages of the fiber-optic cable are that it is expensive to install, is more fragile than wire, and is difficult to split.

24.5 TOPOLOGIES

Network **topology** refers to the arrangement, or physical layout, of connected computers and cables. These arrangements are usually of the bus, star, or ring type.

24.5.1 BUS TOPOLOGY

The bus topology, known as *linear bus,* is the simplest network arrangement, in which a single cable (called a *backbone* or a *trunk* or *segment*) connects all of the computers in

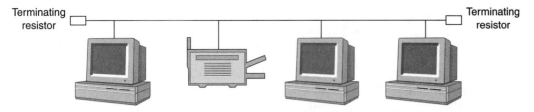

FIGURE 24.9   Bus topology

FIGURE 24.10   Ring topology

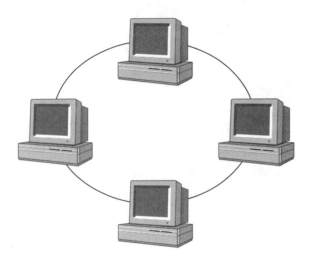

series. (See fig. 24.9.) Computers on the bus listen to the traffic on the network, and when a computer sees a message directed to it, it will then process the entire message. When a signal reaches the end of the cable on a bus network, the signal would typically bounce back if terminating resistors were not used on the two ends of the cable to drain the signal. If the backbone develops a break, the entire network would go down because the break would signify an end to the bus, which is not actually terminated. Typically, a bus network is connected by coaxial cable.

24.5.2   RING TOPOLOGY

A ring topology connects all of the computers in the network in a circle or loop with no ends. The signal travels around the loop in one direction. (See fig. 24.10.) As it enters a computer, the computer regenerates the signal and sends it to the next computer. If a computer fails or there is a cable break, the entire network goes down.

24.5.3   STAR TOPOLOGY

The star topology is probably the most common network configuration. All of the computers in the network are connected to a central device known as a *hub*. (See figs. 24.11 and 24.12.) Most hubs are active hubs (multiport repeaters), in which the hub regenerates the signal. Other hubs are passive in that they do not amplify or regenerate the signal. If a wire segment fails, the network is unaffected. Star networks usually use 10Base-T twisted pair cables.

24.6   BRIDGES, ROUTERS, AND GATEWAYS

A bridge is a device that connects two local area networks of similar topology or two segments of the same local area network and divides traffic on a network segment. A bridge will pass information for one particular workstation to that segment but will not pass broadcast traffic.

FIGURE 24.11   Star topology

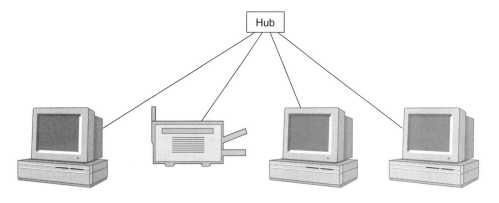

FIGURE 24.12   A hub

A **router** connects two local area networks (with similar or disassimilar topology). It is considered an intelligent device because it determines the best path to a destination computer or network. A **brouter** acts like a router for certain protocols and acts as a bridge for all others.

A **gateway** is a combination of hardware and software that links two different types of networks. Gateways can be used, for example, to connect a PC to a mainframe computer or to exchange messages between two different e-mail systems.

24.7   PROTOCOLS

A **protocol** is a set of rules or standards designed to enable computers to connect with one another and peripheral devices to exchange information with as little error as possible. Common protocol suites are TCP/IP, IPX, and NetBEUI. (A suite is a set of protocols that work together.)

Protocols are usually designed to fit a seven-layer model called the **open system interconnection (OSI) reference model.** (See table 24.2.) The network services in the application layer hand off information to the layer below until it gets to the physical layer. The physical layer than sends the data though the network medium, such as a cable or wireless technology. When the information gets to the intended computer, it is then sent up to the application layer and is processed by the computer. Almost all networks include the functionality of the OSI model, although two or three of the OSI layers may be combined in a protocol.

24.7.1   ETHERNET NETWORKS

Most local area networks are either ethernet, token ring, or ARCnet networks. Technically speaking, ethernet, token ring, and ARCnet are the protocols used to connect to the network.

Ethernet networks that follow the IEEE 802.3 standard use coaxial cable or the 10Base-T specification. Although the cable can be used for a bus or a star topology, the signal pathway is always a bus. Computers on an ethernet network use *carrier sense multiple access with collision detection (CSMA/CD)* to get access to the network. CSMA/CD is a

TABLE 24.2   OSI reference model

Layer	Name	Function
7	Application layer	Network services, including program-to-program communication.
6	Presentation layer	Manages data representation conversions; for example, the presentation layer would be responsible for converting from EBCDIC to ASCII
5	Session layer	Responsible for establishing and maintaining communications channels
4	Transport layer	Responsible for end-to-end integrity of data transmission; links the upper layers to the lower layers
3	Network layer	Routes data from one network to another
2	Data link layer	Responsible for physically passing data from one network connection to another
1	Physical layer	Manages putting data onto the network media (cable or wireless technology) and taking the data off

contention that listens for data transmission on the network lines and if nothing is happening, permits the computer to broadcast its data. If two computers broadcast at the same time, a collision occurs and the data from both computers becomes corrupted. Both computers will detect the collision, however, and will wait a different random amount of time and try to broadcast again. If the network is extremely busy, ethernet networks will have more collisions and the network will be slower because the computers often have to retransmit their data. Ethernet networks originally supported speeds of 10 megabits per second, but today a 100Base-T (or fast ethernet) network, which runs at 100 megabits per second, or a gigabit ethernet, which runs at one gigabit per second, is possible.

24.7.2   TOKEN RING NETWORKS

Token ring networks follow the IEEE 802.5 standard and use some type of twisted pair cable connected to a multiaccess unit (MAU). Although the token ring network uses a star topology, the signals follow a ring or loop. Token ring networks communicate at 4 or 16 megabits per second.

A computer accesses the network by means of a token that is passed from computer to computer. If a computer has data that has to be transmitted, it waits for the token before sending it. The advantage of the token ring network is that there are no collisions and so computers do not have to constantly rebroadcast on busy networks.

24.7.3   ARCNET NETWORKS

ARCnet (attached resource computer network) was developed as a simple, inexpensive, flexible configuration for small networks. ARCnet networks are connected in a star topology, usually by coaxial cable. ARCnet signals follow a bus design, whereas the computers use a token-passing scheme to access the network. ARCnet was designed for speeds of 2.5 megabits per second and up to 255 computers. An ARCnet plus network supports transmission rates of 20 megabits per second.

24.7.4   TCP/IP

TCP/IP (Transmission Control Protocol/Internet Protocol) is an industrial suite of protocols upon which the Internet is based. It is supported by Novell NetWare, Microsoft Windows NT, and other network operating systems.

TABLE 24.3 TCP/IP classes

Class	Network Identifier	Host Identifier*	Number of Hosts
Class A	First number defines network number	Last three numbers	16,000,000
Class B	First two numbers define network number	Last two numbers	65,000
Class C	First three numbers define network number	Last number	254

*A host is a computer or other device that acts as a computer (such as a network printer connected directly to the network).

Each TCP/IP address connects to a host (both server and client). The IP address is four 8-bit numbers divided by a period (.), with each number ranging from 0 to 255. For example, a TCP/IP address could be 131.107.3.1 or 2.0.0.1. Because the address is used to identify a single computer, no two connections can use the same IP address. Internet network numbers are assigned to a corporation or business by class. If the first number is between 1 and 127, the network is a class A. If the first number is between 128 and 191, the network is a class B. If the first number is between 192 and 223, the network is a class C. (See table 24.3.) In addition to the network number, the TCP/IP address has a host number. The network number identifies the entire network, and the host number identifies the computer on the network specified. (Note: The number of unassigned Internet addresses is running out, and a new classless scheme called CIDR, which is tied to the adoption of IPv6, is being developed.)

EXAMPLE 24.1   You have the network address 131.107.20.4. The 131 is between 128 and 191, which identifies the address as a class B network. Therefore, the 131.107 identifies the network and the 20.4 identifies the host or computer on the 131.107 network.

To make TCP/IP more flexible, a network can be subnetted into smaller networks. To identify which bits are used to define the network number and which bits are used to define the host address, a subnet mask must be assigned. The network number and the subnet mask must be the same for all computers on a network. The TCP/IP address and the subnet mask are assigned automatically when a computer connects to a network through a dynamic host configuration protocol (DHCP) server, or they are assigned by the network administrator. (See fig. 24.13.)

When a single local area network is connected to other networks, the computers need to know the default gateway, which specifies the local address of a router. If the default gateway is not specified, computers will not be able to communicate with computers on other networks.

24.7.5 IPX

IPX, which stands for **internetwork packet exchange,** is the networking protocol used by the Novell NetWare network operating system and Windows NT servers. The external network address identifies the network and the MAC address specifies the computer on the network.

24.7.6 NETBEUI

NetBEUI is short for **NetBIOS enhanced user interface.** It is an enhanced version of the NetBIOS protocol used by network operating systems such as LAN Manager, LAN Server, Windows for Workgroups, Windows 95 and 98, and Windows NT. Although the NetBEUI does not require much software, it is not routable, which means it cannot contact another network using NetBEUI.

FIGURE 24.13   TCP/IP dialog box for Windows 95

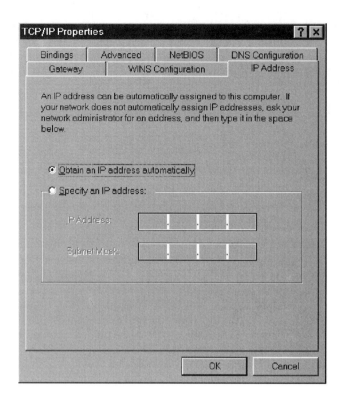

24.7.7   SLIP AND PPP

Two other protocols used to connect to a TCP/IP network such as the Internet using a modem are **serial line internet protocol (SLIP)** and **point-to-point protocol (PPP).** SLIP is an older and simpler protocol; PPP is more stable and has error-checking features.

24.8   WORKGROUPS AND DOMAINS

A **workgroup** is a group of computers that can send e-mail to one another, share data files, and schedule meetings. The computers in a workgroup keep track of their own user and group account information and do not share this information with other computers. A workgroup is a good network configuration for a small group of computers with not many user accounts or in an environment with a mix of Microsoft networks that does not include Windows NT server computers.

A **domain** is a group of computers and devices on a network that are administrated as a unit with common rules and procedures. For example, one Windows NT server computer acts as the primary domain controller (PDC) and maintains the centralized security databases for the domain. Other Windows NT server computers in the domain function as backup domain controllers and can authenticate log-on requests or act as stand-alone servers to provide network resources but only after authenticating access through the centralized security databases. Internet domains are defined by the IP address. All devices sharing the network part of the IP address are said to be in the same domain.

24.9   NETWORK SOFTWARE

A **network operating system (NOS)** includes special functions for connecting computers and devices into a local area network (LAN), managing the resources and services of the network, and providing network security for multiple users. The most common client/server network operating systems are Windows NT Server and Novell NetWare. (Note: Some operating systems, such as Windows for Workgroups, Windows 95 and 98, and Windows NT Workstation, can provide such network resources as file and printer access even though they are not servers.)

FIGURE 24.14   Windows 95 Network dialog box

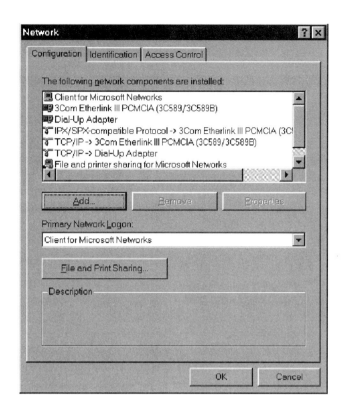

The workstations attached to the network communicate with the operating system through client software called *shells* or *requesters.* A network operating system (NOS) and the client software reside on top of the network protocols that enable data transmission across the LAN. In Windows 95 and 98 and Windows NT Workstation, the client software is installed and configured using the Network dialog box accessed by clicking on the Network applet in the Control Panel or by accessing the shortcut menu of Network Neighborhood and selecting the Properties option. (See fig. 24.14.)

The following network client software is needed to get full access to the network:

1. Client software such as *Client for Microsoft Networks* or *Client for NetWare Networks*
2. A network adapter driver or dial-adapter driver
3. A protocol stack such as TCP/IP or IPX/NWLINK
4. File and printer sharing for Microsoft Networks (optional)

Client for Microsoft Network connects a computer to other Microsoft Windows computers, and *Client for NetWare Networks* connects to other Novell NetWare servers and the files and printers shared through them. File and print sharing on Microsoft networks can share files or printers with Windows NT and Windows for Workgroups computers. (Note: Enabling File and Print Sharing on an individual computer still requires sharing a drive, directory, or printer before it can be accessed through the network.) Computers running Windows for Workgroups, Windows 95 or 98, or Windows NT Workstation, must be identified to the network with a NETBIOS computer name. As with TCP/IP addresses, no two computers can have the same name. Utilities such as Network Neighborhood are then used to access the computer and its network resources.

The identification tab in the dialog box is used almost exclusively by Microsoft Networking. (See fig. 24.15.) The computer name field should be unique—there should be no duplicate names within a workgroup. And in order to facilitate Microsoft Network services, the Windows 95 workstation should be in the same coworker workgroup. The computer description called for in the dialog box can be just a general description.

If file sharing is enabled on a Windows 95 or 98 or Windows NT computer, any drive or directory can be shared by clicking on the drive or directory and selecting the Sharing option from the File menu or by selecting the Sharing option from the shortcut menu of the drive or directory. The user would then provide a Share Name, the name seen by other clients, and the type of access that users can have. (See fig. 24.16.) A shared drive and directory will be

FIGURE 24.15   Network dialog
box

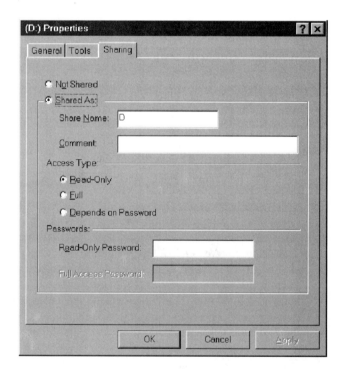

FIGURE 24.16   Sharing drive
directory

indicated by a hand icon under the drive or directory and can be accessed by using Network Neighborhood or by specifying the \\servername\sharename in the Run option under the Start button. (See fig 24.17.) A shared resource is accessed by using the universal naming convention (UNC), which starts as two backslashes followed by the name of the server where the shared resource resides followed by the name of the share. For example, to access the DOCS share on a server called FS1, you would use \\FS1\DOCS. To access the LET-TERS directory within the DOCS share on a server called FS1, you would use \\FS1\DOCS\LETTERS. To access a shared network printer called LJ4 on FS1, you would use \\FS1\LJ4.

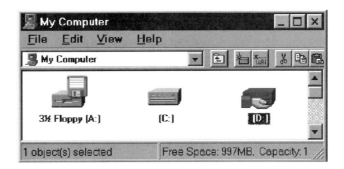

FIGURE 24.17 The hand indicates a shared drive or directory.

24.10 CONNECTING TO THE INTERNET

The Internet is a global network connecting millions of computers. As of 1998, the Internet had more than 100 million users in over 100 countries. Unlike online services such as American Online, Prodigy, and Compuserve, the Internet is decentralized by design. People can connect to the Internet through their employers who are part of the Internet or can gain access by using an online service, or **internet service provider (ISP).**

The main lines of the Internet, called the *Internet backbone,* are the biggest networks in the system and are owned by major Internet service providers such as GTE, MCI, Sprint, UUNet, and American Online's ANS. By connecting to each other, these networks have created a superfast pipeline that crisscrosses the United States and extends throughout the world. Because the U.S. backbone has many intersecting points, if one part fails or slows down, data can be rerouted over another part. In the United States, there are also five points—located in San Francisco, San Jose (California), Chicago, Pennsauken (New Jersey; near New York), and Washington, D.C.—that form networks owned by smaller regional and local ISPs, which, in turn, lease access to companies and individuals in the areas they serve.

TCP/IP is the primary protocol used on the Internet, which also uses **simple mail transfer protocol (SMTP), file transfer protocol (FTP),** and **terminal emulation (Telnet) protocol.** SMTP is a protocol for sending e-mail messages between servers that can be retrieved by an e-mail client using either post office protocol (POP) or Internet message access protocol (IMAP). The telnet program connects a computer to a server on the network and enters commands as though the user were entering them directly on the server console. The file transfer protocol is used to retrieve files from networked servers.

24.10.1 WEB PAGES

The **World Wide Web (WWW),** a subset of the Internet, is a huge collection of interlinked documents called *web pages* written in **hypertext markup language (HTML).** (See figs. 24.18 and 24.19.) HTML tells a web browser, such as Microsoft Internet Explorer or Netscape Navigator, how to display the page and its elements. Web pages are kept in web servers.

Locating an address on the Internet is usually done by typing in a domain name, such as http://www.microsoft.com, because it is difficult for most people to remember the TCP/IP addresses used by the Internet TCP/IP protocol. When the domain name is entered, a request is sent to a domain name system (DNS) server asking for the TCP/IP address. If the DNS server does not know the address, it will forward the request to another DNS server until it finds the address or it gets to the master DNS servers. A uniform resource locator (URL) is a global address of a document and other resources on the World Wide Web that includes a TCP/IP address or a domain name.

EXAMPLE 24.2 The parts of the address http://www.intel.com/home/buyers/index.htm have the following meanings:

http	Hypertext transfer protocol—the formatting language used to create World Wide Web documents
www	Word Wide Web—a part of the Internet that uses HTTP
intel	Domain name (combined by the domain function), which points to an organization. The organization must reserve this name or keyword so they have exclusive rights to it.
com	Domain function: .com—commercial .edu—education (school or university) .mil—military .gov—government .net—gateway or host .org—other organization, such as nonprofit organizations
Home/buyers	Name of the directories on the host (computer running TCP/IP)
Index.htm	Name of the file

FIGURE 24.18   Web page.

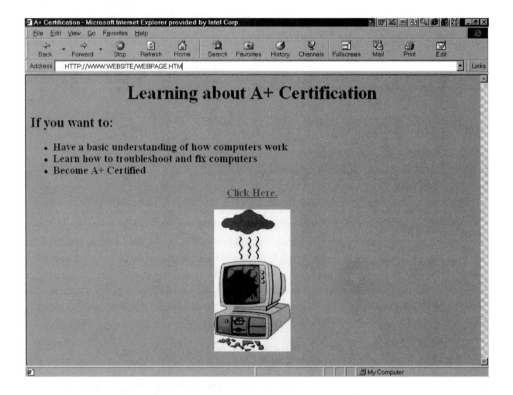

FIGURE 24.19   HTML code for the web page shown in fig. 24.18

TABLE 24.4   Popular browsers and plug-ins

Common Browsers, and Plug-ins	Website
Microsoft Internet Explorer and Add-Ons	http://www.microsoft.com/ie/download/
Netscape Communicator and Plug-Ins	http://www.netscape.com/download/index.html
Adobe Acrobat	http://www.adobe.com/supportservice/custsupport/download.html
RealPlayer Plug-In	http://www.real.com/products/playerplus/index.html
Shockwave Plug-In	http://www.macromedia.com/shockwave/download/

To extend the capabilities of a web browser so that it can play audio files or view movies or other multimedia files, browsers can accept plug-ins. Web browsers often come with a small suite of plug-ins. Additional plug-ins may be obtained at the browser's website, at special download sites on the web, or from the home pages of the companies that created the programs. Once a plug-in is configured to a browser, it will automatically launch when the user chooses to access that file type. Table 24.4 lists some browsers and websites from which plug-ins can be obtained.

24.10.2   COOKIES

A cookie is a small piece of information sent by a web server and stored on a PC so it can be used by a web browser in the future. This is useful when the browser is to remember some specific information, such as identifying a returning visitor or other previously selected information.

24.10.3   COMMON BROWSER ERRORS

The most common problems and error messages encountered when surfing the Internet are shown in table 24.5.

TABLE 24.5   Common errors displayed on an Internet browser

404	A host server responded to your browser but cannot find the web page on the server. This usually means that the web page was moved or deleted or that you typed in the wrong URL.
403	The requested resource is forbidden, which generally means you don't have the privileges needed to access that page.
503	The server is too busy to handle your request or there is some problem along the Internet. Try again later.
Unable to locate server. The server does not have a DNS entry.	The browser is unable to locate the server and cannot verify the domain name exists. Check to see if you typed in the wrong URL.
Host Unavailable	This means that the domain name exists but the server on the domain is not responding to the request because it is too busy or is offline. Try again later.

TABLE 24.6 Useful TCP/IP troubleshooting utilities

Utility	Purpose
WINIPCFG (Windows 95) **IPCONFIG (Windows NT)**	Shows the system's TCP/IP address, subnet mask, and gateway
PING address	Verifies a network connection with a particular TCP/IP host

24.11 TROUBLE-SHOOTING NETWORKS

Much like any other computer problem, a network problem can be caused by hardware or software. Some common problems are described in the following examples.

EXAMPLE 24.3 The computer cannot make a network connection after a network card has been connected.

First, make sure that the network cable is connected properly and that the network card connection light is on. If the problem still exists, make sure that the network driver, protocol, and network client software are installed and configured properly, including making sure that the proper protocol is loaded and the proper addresses are assigned. If all of the software seems to be configured properly, check the card for resource conflicts (I/O address, IRQ, DMA, and memory addresses). Lastly, suspect a faulty cable or card.

EXAMPLE 24.4 A modem is not making a network connection.

First, make sure that the modem is connected properly. If the modem seems to be working, make sure the software is configured properly, including the dial-up network software, the software driver for the modem, the protocol, and the proper phone number. (Note: Some telephone connections within a company require a 9 to be dialed to get an outside line.) If the problem still exists, check the modem for resource conflicts (I/O address, IRQ, DMA, and memory addresses).

EXAMPLE 24.5 The computer cannot communicate with a TCP/IP computer.

First, make sure that the network cable is connected properly and that the network card connection light is on. If the problem still exists, make sure that the network driver, protocol, and network client software are installed and configured properly. This includes making sure that the proper protocol is loaded and the proper addresses, subnet mask, and gateway are assigned. If all of the software seems to be configured properly, check the card for resource conflicts (I/O address, IRQ, DMA, and memory addresses). Lastly, suspect a faulty cable or card.

SUMMARY

1. A network is two or more computers connected together to share resources.
2. Most computers communicate with the network by a cable attached to the computer's network interface card (NIC); a few computer's can use some form of wireless technology (infrared, microwaves, or radio waves).
3. Protocols (TCP/IP, IPX, and NetBEUI) are the rules or standards that allow the computers to connect to one another.
4. The two most common services provided by a network are file and print sharing.
5. A server is a computer that is a dedicated service provider, and a client is a computer that requests services.
6. A network that is made up of dedicated servers and clients is known as a client/server network.
7. A peer-to-peer network has no dedicated servers. Instead, all computers provide services and request services equally.
8. A LAN connects computers within a close geographical network, such as in a building or on a campus.
9. The network interface card (NIC), sometimes referred to as the *network adapter card* or *network card,* is the physical interface, or connection, between the computer and the network cable.

10. The common cable types used in networks include unshielded twisted pair, shielded twisted pair, coaxial, and fiber-optic.

11. Twisted pair cable uses two insulated strands of copper wire twisted around each other. The twist in the cable helps reduce crosstalk.

12. The unshielded twisted pair (UTP) cable, which uses the 10BaseT specification, resembles telephone cable with an RJ-45 connector and is quickly becoming the most popular LAN cable.

13. Coaxial cable has a solid copper core surrounded by insulation, a braided metal shielding, and an outer cover.

14. To prevent signals from bouncing back when they reach the end of the cable, coaxial cable has terminating resistors on both ends.

15. The thinnet type of coaxial cable connects to the network card with BNC and T-connectors.

16. Fiber-optic cable is made of glass or fiberglass so that it can transmit light instead of electricity.

17. Network topology refers to the arrangement, or physical layout, of connected computers and cables.

18. The bus topology, known as linear bus, is the simplest network configuration in that a single cable (called a *backbone* or a *trunk* or *segment*) connects all of the computers in series.

19. A ring topology connects computers in a circle or loop with no ends.

20. The star topology, probably the most common network configuration, connects computers to a central device known as a *hub*.

21. A bridge is a device that connects two local area networks or two segments of the same local area network.

22. A router connects two local area networks and also filters for certain protocols.

23. A protocol is a set of rules or standards designed to enable computers and peripheral devices to connect to one another to exchange information with as little error as possible.

24. Most local area networks are described as ethernet, token ring or ARCnet networks.

25. The TCP/IP (transmission control protocol/internet protocol) is an industrial suite of protocols upon which the Internet is based.

26. IPX (internetwork packet exchange) is the networking protocol used by the Novell NetWare network operating system and Windows NT servers.

27. A workgroup is a group of computers that can send e-mail to one another, share data files, and schedule meetings.

28. A domain is a group of computers and devices on a network that are administrated as a unit with common rules and procedures.

29. A network operating system (NOS) includes special functions for connecting computers and devices into a local area network (LAN), to manage the resources and services of the network, and to provide network security for multiple users.

30. The Internet is a global network connecting millions of computers.

31. The World Wide Web (WWW), a subset of the Internet, is a huge collection of interlinked documents called *web pages* written in hypertext markup language (HTML).

QUESTIONS

1. Which of the following is *not* a network resource?
   a. e-mail
   b. file sharing
   c. print sharing
   d. IRQ sharing

2. Which of the following statements best describes a peer-to-peer network?
   a. A peer-to-peer network allows centralized administration of files and other network resources.
   b. A peer-to-peer network requires a centralized dedicated server.
   c. A peer-to-peer network provides the user the ability to manage his or her own shared resources.
   d. A peer-to-peer network requires at least one administrator to provide centralized resource administration.

3. Which of the follow is a computer that handles requests from client computers for data and processing resources?
   - a. a peer
   - b. a client
   - c. a server
   - d. a LAN
4. Which type of network is a small network that is usually confined to a building or campus?
   - a. LAN
   - b. MAN
   - c. enterprise WAN
   - d. global WAN
5. A client machine cannot connect to the network but all the other computers in the network can. Which of the following is the most likely cause of the problem?
   - a. a faulty coaxial cable on a bus topology
   - b. a faulty network adapter card on the server
   - c. a faulty network adapter card on the client computer
   - d. too much traffic on the network
6. Pat has just installed a network adapter card in his computer, but the operating system is unable to detect the network adapter card. Which of the following is the most likely cause of the problem?
   - a. the wrong protocol
   - b. a resource conflict, such as an IRQ or DMA conflict
   - c. a faulty cable
   - d. a faulty terminating resistor
7. An NE2000-compatible card is configured to use IRQ 3 and I/O address 0x300. Which device is the card conflicting with?
   - a. COM1
   - b. COM2
   - c. LPT1
   - d. LPT2
8. You connect the leads from a digital multimeter (DMM) to each of the conductors in a twisted pair cable. Which of the following settings should you use on the DMM to see if there is a short?
   - a. resistance
   - b. capacitance
   - c. dc voltage
   - d. ac voltage
   - e. current
9. What is the minimum category of UTP cable required for an ethernet network running at 10 megabits?
   - a. Category 1
   - b. Category 2
   - c. Category 3
   - d. Category 4
   - e. Category 5
10. Which of the following refers to signal overflow from an adjacent wire?
    - a. attenuation
    - b. crosstalk
    - c. beaconing
    - d. jitter
    - e. chattering
    - f. jabbering
11. A 10BaseT network uses what type of connector? (Choose all that apply.)
    - a. RJ-11 connectors
    - b. RJ-45 connectors
    - c. UTP cabling
    - d. BNC-T connectors
    - e. 50-ohm terminating resistors
12. Which of the following refers to an element of an ethernet 10Base2 network? (Choose all that apply.)
    - a. Category 3, 4, or 5 UTP cable
    - b. RJ-11 connectors
    - c. RJ-45 connectors
    - d. BNC connectors
    - e. 50-ohm terminating resistors
13. Which of the following access methods checks for network traffic before sending data?
    - a. CSMA/CD
    - b. testing
    - c. token passing
    - d. polling
14. Which of the following devices would you use to enable communications between dissimilar LANs that use different protocols?
    - a. bridges
    - b. routers
    - c. gateways
    - d. repeaters

15. The universal naming convention (UNC) provides a way for computers on the network to identify each other. Which of the following are included in a UNC string? (Select all that apply.)
    a. a domain name
    b. a computer name
    c. a workgroup name
    d. a share name
16. Which layer of the OSI model defines how cable is attached to a network adapter card?
    a. the cable layer
    b. the connection layer
    c. the hardware layer
    d. the physical layer
17. Which of the following uses 15-character names to identify computers on a network?
    a. TCP/IP
    b. IPX/SPX
    c. NetBIOS
    d. AppleTalk
18. Which of the following are dial-up communication protocols? (Choose two answers.)
    a. FTP
    b. PPP
    c. TCP
    d. SLIP
19. Pat is not able to access network resources from her computer. When she plugs her ethernet cable into a coworker's machine, she is able to access the network without difficulty. Which of the following network components is causing the problem?
    a. the server
    b. the router or gateway
    c. the cable
    d. the network adapter
20. You have just installed a 28,800 bps fax modem on a Windows 95 computer. What else do you need to do to connect to an Internet access provider? (Select two answers.)
    a. install TCP/IP
    b. install dial-up networking
    c. install remote access services
    d. install the Microsoft Network
21. When configuring a new network interface card for installation, which of the following would be a valid I/O address?
    a. 378
    b. 2F8
    c. 3F8
    d. 360
22. The Internet uses which network protocol?
    a. IPX
    b. TCP/IP
    c. NetBEUI
    d. token passing
23. A standard naming scheme used to identify web pages on the Internet is:
    a. TCP/IP
    b. NetBIOS
    c. URL
    d. naming
24. The language used to write web pages read by a browser is:
    a. HTML
    b. URL
    c. HTTP
    d. TCP/IP
    e. BASIC

HANDS-ON EXERCISES

Exercise 1: Create a Simple Network

This lab requires partners with two computers running Windows 95.

1. On both computers, install and configure a network card.
2. Install the cabling, hubs, and connectors.
3. Install and configure *Client for Microsoft Network* and the appropriate network driver.
4. Install and configure the TCP/IP protocol with following information (XXX is a number assigned by your instructor):
     Computer A: 131.107.XXX.1
     Computer B: 131.107.XXX.2
     Subnet mask: 255.255.0.0
5. Assign the following computer name under the Identification tab (XXX is a number assigned by your instructor):
     Computer A: COMPUTERXXX1
     Computer B: COMPUTERXXX2
6. Assign the following workgroup name under the Identification tab (XXX is a number assigned by your instructor):
     WORKGROUPXXX

7. Execute the following command at the Run option under the Start button:

```
WINIPCFG
```

Click on the OK button.

8. At the Windows 95 command prompt, execute the following command:

```
PING address_of_partner
```

Exercise 2: File and Print Sharing

Use the same network setup as in exercise 1.

1. Activate File and Print Sharing in the Network dialog box.
2. Share the C drive, the WINDOWS directory, and the WINDOWS\SYSTEM directory.
3. Install a local print driver on each of the computers.
4. Install a network print driver on each of the computers pointing to your partner's printer.
5. Using Network Neighborhood, find your partner's computer to access the shared resources.
6. Using the Run option under the Start button, type in the double backslash followed by the TCP/IP address of your partner's computer.
7. Using the Run option under the Start button, type in the UNC name (\\PARTNERS_ COMPUTER_NAME\SHARE_NAME), specifying one of the shared drives or directories.

Exercise 3: IPX and NetBIEU Protocols

Use the same network setup as in exercise 1.

1. Install the IPX/SPX protocol.
2. Remove the TCP/IP network.
3. Using the Run option, type in the UNC name specifying one of the shared drives or directories.
4. Install the NetBIEU protocol.
5. Remove the IPX/SPX protocol.
6. Using the Run option, type in the UNC name specifying one of the shared drives or directories.
7. Install the TCP/IP protocol.

Exercise 4: Connecting to the Internet

1. Install the appropriate software to connect to the Internet.
2. Install Microsoft Internet Explorer and Netscape Communicator.
3. Find and download the Adobe Acrobat Reader program and plug-in.
4. Access the iomega.com site and access one Adobe Acrobat Reader document.
5. Download the Adobe Acrobat Reader document.
6. Load the Adobe Acrobat Reader document.

Appendix A
A+ Certification

A+ Certification is a testing program sponsored by the Computing Technology Industry Association (CompTIA), that certifies that an individual possesses the knowledge, skills, and customer relations skills essential for a successful entry-level (6 months experience) computer service technician, as defined by experts from companies across the industry. The test covers a broad range of hardware and software technologies, but are not related to any vendor-specific products. To become certified, you must pass two parts—the Core and the DOS/Windows module portion.

To become certified, you must pass two test modules, the Core and the DOS/Windows modules (including Windows 3.x and Windows 95). Each exam will have approximately 75 questions with a sitting time of 1 hour and 15 minutes. The A+ Certification is open to anyone who wants to take the tests. No specific requirements are necessary, except the payment of the fee. Individuals may retake the test modules as often as they like, but the Core and the DOS/Windows modules must be passed within 90 calendar days of each other in order to become certified.

To schedule for the A+ test, you would call:

Sylvan Prometric at 1-800-776-4276

or

www.2test.com for CompTIA members

The following information is provided and copyrighted by CompTIA and used with their permission. To find the most update information, you can visit the CompTIA web site at:

http://www.comptia.org

Domain	% of Exam
1.0 Installation, configuration, and upgrading	30%
2.0 Diagnosing and troubleshooting	20%
3.0 Safety and preventive maintenance	10%
4.0 Motherboard/processors/memory	10%
5.0 Printers	10%
6.0 Portable systems	5%
7.0 Basic networking	5%
8.0 Customer satisfaction[1]	10%
Total	**100%**

[1]Note: These questions are not figured into your final score, but the scores from this section are reported at the bottom of your score report so that employers and clients know how you performed on this section.

Domain	% of Exam (Approximate)
1.0 Function, structure, operation, and file management	30%
2.0 Memory management	10%
3.0 Installation, configuration, and upgrading	30%
4.0 Diagnosing and troubleshooting	20%
5.0 Networks	10%
Total	**100%**

Approximately 75% of the test items will relate to Windows 95 and the remaining 25% will relate to DOS and Windows 3.x.

CORE OBJECTIVES

1.0 INSTALLATION, CONFIGURATION, AND UPGRADING

This domain requires the knowledge and skills to identify, install, configure, and upgrade microcomputer modules and peripherals, following establishing basic procedures for system assembly and disassembly of field replaceable modules. Elements include ability to identify and configure IRQs, DMAs, I/O addresses, and set switches and jumpers.

Content Limit

1.1 Identify basic terms, concepts, and functions of system modules, including how each module should work during normal operation.

Examples of concepts and modules:

- System board
- Power supply
- Processor/CPU
- Memory
- Storage devices
- Monitor
- Modem
- Firmware

- Boot process
- BIOS
- CMOS

1.2 Identify basic procedures for adding and removing field replaceable modules.

- System board
- Storage device
- Power supply
- Processor/CPU
- Memory
- Input devices

1.3 Identify available IRQs, DMAs, and I/O addresses and procedures for configuring them for device installation.

Contents may include the following:

- Standard IRQ settings
- Modems
- Floppy drive
- Hard drive

1.4 Identify common peripheral ports, associated cabling, and their connectors.

Contents may include the following:

- Cable types
- Cable orientation
- Serial versus parallel
- Pin connections

Examples of types of connectors:

- DB-9
- DB-25
- RJ-11
- RJ45
- BNC
- PS2/MINI-DIN

1.5 Identify proper procedures for installing and configuring IDE/EIDE devices.

Content may include the following:

- Master/slave
- Devices per channel

1.6 Identify proper procedures for installing and configuring SCSI devices.

Content may include the following:

- Address/Termination conflicts
- Cabling
- Types (example: regular, wide, ultra-wide)
- Internal versus external
- Switch and jumper settings

1.7 Identify proper procedures for installing and configuring peripheral devices.

Content may include the following:

- Monitor/Video Card
- Modem
- Storage devices

1.8 Identify concepts and procedures relating to BIOS.

- Methods for upgrading
- When to upgrade

1.9 Identify hardware methods of system optimization and when to use them.

   Content may include the following:

- Memory
- Hard Drives
- CPU
- Cache memory

2.0 DIAGNOSING AND TROUBLESHOOTING

This domain requires the ability to apply knowledge relating to diagnosing and troubleshooting common module problems and system malfunctions. This includes knowledge of the symptoms relating to common problems.

Content Limits

2.1 Identify common symptoms and problems associated with each module and how to troubleshoot and isolate the problems.

   Content may include the following:

- Processor/memory symptoms
- Mouse
- Floppy drive failures
- Parallel ports
- Hard drives
- Sound card/audio
- Monitor/video
- Motherboards
- Modems
- BIOS
- CMOS
- Power supply
- Slot covers
- POST audio/visual error codes
- Troubleshooting tools, e.g., multimeter

2.2 Identify basic troubleshooting procedures and good practices for eliciting problem symptoms from customers.

   Content may include the following:

- Troubleshooting/isolation/problem determination procedures
- Determine whether hardware or software problem
- Gather information from user regarding, e.g., multimeter
  - Customer Environment
  - Symptoms/Error Codes
  - Situation when the problem occurred

3.0 SAFETY AND PREVENTATIVE MAINTENANCE

This domain requires the knowledge of safety and preventive maintenance. With regard to safety, it includes the potential hazards to personnel and equipment when working with lasers, high-voltage equipment, ESD, and items that require special disposal procedures that comply with environmental guidelines. With regard to preventive maintenance, this includes knowledge of preventive maintenance products, procedures, environmental hazards, and precautions when working on microcomputer systems.

Content Limits

3.1 Identify the purpose of various types of preventative maintenance products and procedures and when to use/perform them.

Content may include the following:

- Liquid cleaning compounds
- Types of material to clean contacts and connections
- Vacuum out system, power supplies, fans

3.2 Identify procedures and devices for protecting against environmental hazards.

Contents may include the following:

- UPS (uninterruptible power supply) and suppressors
- Determine the signs of power issues
- Proper methods of storage of components for future use

3.3 Identify the potential hazards and proper safety procedures relating to lasers and high-voltage equipment.

- Lasers
- High-voltage equipment
- Power supply
- CRT

3.4 Identify items that require special disposal procedures that comply with environmental guidelines.

Contents may include the following:

- Batteries
- CRTs
- Toner kits/cartridges
- Chemical solvents and cans
- MSDS (Material Safety Data Sheet)

3.5 Identify ESD (Electrostatic Discharge) precautions and procedures, including the use of ESD protection devices.

Contents may include the following:

- What ESD can do, how it may be apparent, or hidden
- Common ESD protection devices
- Situations that could present a danger or hazard

4.0 MOTHERBOARD/PROCESSORS/MEMORY

This domain requires knowledge of specific terminology, facts, ways and means of dealing with classifications, categories and principles of motherboards, processors, and memory in microcomputer systems.

Content Limits

4.1 Distinguish between the popular CPU chips in terms of their basic characteristics.

Contents may include the following:

- Popular CPU chips
- Characteristics:
  - Physical size
  - Voltage
  - Speeds
  - On board cache or not
  - Sockets
  - Number of pins

4.2 Identify the categories of RAM (random access memory) terminology, their locations, and physical characteristics.

Content may include the following:

- Terminology:
  - EDO RAM (Extended Data Output RAM)
  - DRAM (Dynamic Random Access Memory)
  - SRAM (Static RAM)
  - VRAM (Video RAM)
  - WRAM (Windows Accelerator Card RAM)
- Locations and physical characteristics:
  - Memory bank
  - Memory chips (8-bit, 16-bit, and 32-bit)
  - SIMMS (Single In-line Memory Module)
  - DIMMS (Dual In-line Memory Module)
  - Parity chips versus non-parity chips

4.3 Identify the most popular types of motherboards, their components, and their architecture (for example, bus structures and power supplies).

Content may include the following:

- Types of motherboards:
  - AT (Full and Baby)
  - ATX
- Components:
  - Communication ports
  - SIMM AND DIMM
  - Processor sockets
  - External cache memory (Level 2)
- Bus Architecture
  - ISA
  - EISA
  - PCI
  - USB (Universal Serial Bus)
  - VESA local bus (VL-Bus)
  - PC Card (PCMCIA)
- Basic compatibility guidelines

4.4 Identify the purpose of CMOS (Complementary Metal-Oxide Semiconductor), what it contains and how to change its basic parameters.

Example Basic CMOS Settings

- Printer parallel port Uni., bi-directional, disable/enable, ECP, EPP
- COM/serial port memory address, interrupt request, disable
- Floppy drive enable/disable drive or boot, speed, density
- Hard drive size and drive type
- Memory parity, non-parity

- Boot sequence
- Date/Time
- Passwords

5.0 PRINTERS

This domain requires knowledge of basic types of printers, basic concepts, printer components, how they work, how they print onto a page, paper path, care and service techniques, and common problems.

Content Limits

5.1 Identify basic concepts, printer operations, and printer components.

  Contents may include the following:

- Types of printers:
  - Laser
  - Inkjet
  - Dot-matrix
- Paper feeder mechanisms

5.2 Identify care and service techniques and common problems with primary printer types.

  Content may include the following:

- Feed and output
- Errors
- Paper jam
- Print quality
- Safety precautions
- Preventative maintenance

5.3 Identify the types of printer connections and configurations.

  Contents may include the following:

- Parallel
- Serial
- Network

6.0 PORTABLE SYSTEMS

This domain requires knowledge of portable computers and their unique components and problems.

Content Limits

6.1 Identify the unique components of portable systems and their unique problems.

  Content may include the following:

- Battery
- LCD
- AC adapter
- Docking stations
- Hard Drive
- Types I, II, III cards
- Network cards
- Memory

7.0 BASIC NETWORKING

This domain requires knowledge of basic network concepts and terminology, ability to determine whether a computer is networked, knowledge of procedures for swapping and configuring network interface cards, and knowledge of the ramifications of repairs when a computer is networked.

Content Limits

7.1 Identify basic networking concepts including how a network works.

   Contents may include the following:

- Network access
- Protocol
- Network Interface Cards
- Full-duplex
- Cabling including Twisted pair, Coaxial and Fiber Optics
- Ways to network a PC

7.2 Identify procedures for swapping and configuring network interface cards.

7.3 Identify the ramification of repairs on the network.

   Contents may include the following:

- Reduced bandwidth
- Loss of data
- Network slowdown

8.0 CUSTOMER SATISFACTION

The domain requires knowledge of and sensitivity around those behaviors that contribute to satisfying customers. More specifically, these behaviors include such things as: the quality of technician–customer personal interactions; the way a technician conducts him or herself professionally within the customer's business setting; the credibility and confidence projected by the technician which, in turn, engenders customer confidence; the resilience, friendliness, and efficiency that can unexpectedly delight the customer above and beyond the solving of a technical problem. This domain is NOT a test of specific company policies or procedures.

Content Limits

8.1 Differentiate effective from ineffective behaviors as these contribute to the maintenance or achievement of customer satisfaction.

   Content may include the following:

- Communicating and listening (face-to-face or over the phone)
- Interpreting verbal and nonverbal cues
- Responding appropriately to the customer's technical level
- Establishing personal rapport with the customer
- Professional conduct, for example, punctuality and accountability
- Helping and guiding a customer with problem descriptions
- Responding to and closing a service call
- Handling complaints and upset customers, conflict avoidance, and resolution
- Showing empathy and flexibility
- Sharing the customer's sense of urgency

DOS/WINDOWS OBJECTIVES

1.0 FUNCTION, STRUCTURE, OPERATION, AND FILE MANAGEMENT

The domain requires knowledge of DOS, Windows 3.x, and Windows 95 operating system in terms of its functions and structure, for managing files and directories, and running programs. It also includes navigating through the operating system from DOS command line prompts and Windows procedures for accessing and retrieving information.

Content Limits

1.1. Identify the operating system's functions, structure, and major system files.

Contents may include the following:

- The functions of DOS, Windows 3.x and Windows 95
- Major components of DOS, Windows 3.x and Windows 95
- Contrasts between Windows 3.x and Windows 95
- Major system files: what they are, where they are located, how they are used, and what they contain
  - System, Configuration, and User Interface files
  - DOS
    - Autoexec.bat
    - Config.sys
    - Io.sys
    - Ansi.sys
    - Msdos.sys
    - Emm386.exe
    - HIMEM.SYS
    - Command.com (internal DOS commands)
  - Windows 3.x
    - Win.ini
    - System.ini
    - User.exe
    - Gdi.exe
    - Win.ini
    - Win.com
    - Progman.ini
    - ProgMAN.exe
    - Krnlxxx.exe
  - Windows 95
    - Io.sys
    - Msdos.sys
    - Command.com
    - regedit.exe
    - System.dat
    - User.dat

1.2 Identify ways to navigate the operating system and how to get to needed technical information.

Content may include the following:

- Procedures (e.g., menu or icon-driven) for navigating through DOS to perform such things as locating, accessing, and retrieving information.
- Procedures for navigating through the Windows 3.x/Windows 95 operating system, accessing, and retrieving information.

1.3 Identify basic concepts and procedures for creating, viewing, and managing files and directories, including procedures for changing file attributes and the ramifications of changes (for example, security issues).

Content may include the following:

- File attributes
- File naming conventions
- Command syntax
- Read-Only, Hidden, System and Archive attributes

1.4 Identify the procedures for basic disk management.

Content may include the following:

- Using disk management utilities
- Backing up
- Formatting
- Partitioning
- Defragmenting
- ScanDisk
- FAT32
- File Allocation Tables (FAT)
- Virtual File Allocation Tables (VFAT)

2.0 MEMORY MANAGEMENT

This domain requires knowledge of the types of memory used by DOS and Windows, and the potential for memory address conflicts.

Content Limits

2.1 Differentiate between types of memory.

- Conventional
- Extended/upper memory
- High memory
- Expanded memory
- Virtual memory

2.2 Identify typical memory conflict problems and how to optimize memory use.

Contents may include the following:

- What a memory conflict is
- How it happens
- When to employ utilities
- System Monitor
- General Protection Fault
- Illegal operations occurrences
- MemMaker or other optimization utilities
- Himem.sys
- SMARTDRV
- Use of expanded memory blocks using (Emm386.EXE)

3.0 INSTALLATION, CONFIGURATION AND UPGRADING

This domain requires knowledge of installing, configuring and upgrading DOS, Windows 3.x, and Windows 95. This includes knowledge of system boot sequences.

Content Limits

3.1 Identify the procedures for installing DOS, Windows 3.x, and Windows 95, and for bringing the software to a basic operational level.

Content may include the following:

- Partition
- Format drive
- Run appropriate set up utility
- Loading drivers

3.2 Identify steps to perform an operating system upgrade.

Content may include the following:

- Upgrading from DOS to Windows 95
- Upgrading from Windows 3.x to Windows 95

3.3 Identify the basic system boot sequences, and alternative ways to boot the system software, including the steps to create an emergency boot disk with utilities installed.

Contents may include the following:

- Files required to boot
- Creating emergency boot disk
- Startup disk
- Safe mode
- DOS mode

3.4 Identify procedures for loading/adding device drivers and the necessary software for certain devices.

Content may include the following:

- Windows 3.x procedures
- Windows 95 Plug and Play

3.5 Identify procedures for changing options, configuring, and using the Windows printing subsystem.

3.6 Identify the procedures for installing and launching typical Windows and non-Windows applications.

4.0 DIAGNOSING AND TROUBLESHOOTING

This domain requires the ability to apply knowledge to diagnose and troubleshoot common problems relating to DOS, Windows 3.x, and Windows 95. This includes understanding normal operation and symptoms relating to common problems.

Content Limits

4.1 Recognize and interpret the meaning of common error codes and startup messages from the boot sequence, and identify steps to correct the problems.

Contents may include the following:

- Safe Mode
- Incorrect DOS version
- No operating system found
- Error in CONFIG.SYS line XX
- Bad or missing Command.com
- Himem.sys not loaded
- Missing or corrupt Himem.sys
- Swap file
- A device referenced in SYSTEM.INI could not be found

4.2 Recognize Windows-specific printing problems and identify the procedures for correcting them.

Content may include the following:

- Print spool is stalled
- Incorrect/incompatible driver for print

4.3 Recognize common problems and determine how to resolve them.

Content may include the following problems:

- Common problems
  - General Protection Faults
  - Illegal operation
  - Invalid working directory
  - System lock up
  - Option will not function
  - Application will not start or load
  - Cannot log on to network
- DOS and Windows-based utilities
  - ScanDisk
  - Device manager
  - ATTRIB.EXE
  - EXTRACT.EXE
  - Defrag.exe
  - Edit.com
  - Fdisk.exe
  - MSD.EXE
  - Mem.exe
  - SYSEDIT.EXE

4.4 Identify concepts relating to viruses and virus types, their danger, their symptoms, sources of viruses, how they infect, how to protect against them, and how to identify and remove them.

Content may include the following:

- What they are
- Sources
- How to determine presence

5.0 NETWORKS

This domain requires knowledge of network capabilities of DOS and Windows, and how to connect to networks, including what the Internet is about, its capabilities, basic concepts relating to Internet access and generic procedures for system setup.

Content Limits

5.1 Identify the network capabilities of DOS and Windows, including procedures for connecting to the network.

Contents may include the following:

- Sharing disk drives
- Sharing print and file services
- Network type and network card

5.2 Identify concepts and capabilities relating to the Internet and basic procedures for setting up a system for Internet access.

Contents may include the following:

- TCP/IP
- E-mail
- HTML
- HTTP://
- FTP
- Domain names (Web sites)
- ISP
- Dial-up access

Appendix B
Useful Computer Tables

TABLE B.1 ASCII character set

DEC	BIN	HEX	ASCII	Ctrl	DEC	BIN	HEX	ASCII	DEC	BIN	HEX	ASCII
0	00000000	0	null	NUL	32	00100000	20	space	64	01000000	40	@
1	00000001	1	☎	SOH	33	00100001	21	!	65	01000001	41	A
2	00000010	2	☽	STX	34	00100010	22	"	66	01000010	42	B
3	00000011	3	♥	ETX	35	00100011	23	#	67	01000011	43	C
4	00000100	4	♦	EOT	36	00100100	24	$	68	01000100	44	D
5	00000101	5	♣	ENQ	37	00100101	25	%	69	01000101	45	E
6	00000110	6	♠	ACK	38	00100110	26	&	70	01000110	46	F
7	00000111	7	•	BEL	39	00100111	27	'	71	01000111	47	G
8	00001000	8	¬	BS	40	00101000	28	(	72	01001000	48	H
9	00001001	9	○	HT	41	00101001	29	)	73	01001001	49	I
10	00001010	A	♫	LF	42	00101010	2A	*	74	01001010	4A	J
11	00001011	B	♪	VT	43	00101011	2B	+	75	01001011	4B	K
12	00001100	C	▥	FF	44	00101100	2C	,	76	01001100	4C	L
13	00001101	D	✉	CR	45	00101101	2D	-	77	01001101	4D	M
14	00001110	E	▣	SO	46	00101110	2E	.	78	01001110	4E	N
15	00001111	F	♀	SI	47	00101111	2F	/	79	01001111	4F	O
16	00010000	10	⊜	DLE	48	00110000	30	0	80	01010000	50	P
17	00010001	11	⊜	DC1	49	00110001	31	1	81	01010001	51	Q
18	00010010	12	▫	DC2	50	00110010	32	2	82	01010010	52	R
19	00010011	13	‼	DC3	51	00110011	33	3	83	01010011	53	S
20	00010100	14	▥	DC4	52	00110100	34	4	84	01010100	54	T
21	00010101	15	♀	NAK	53	00110101	35	5	85	01010101	55	U
22	00010110	16	-	SYN	54	00110110	36	6	86	01010110	56	V
23	00010111	17	▭	ETB	55	00110111	37	7	87	01010111	57	W
24	00011000	18	↑	CAN	56	00111000	38	8	88	01011000	58	X
25	00011001	19	↓	EM	57	00111001	39	9	89	01011001	59	Y
26	00011010	1A	→	SUB	58	00111010	3A	:	90	01011010	5A	Z
27	00011011	1B	✧	ESC	59	00111011	3B	;	91	01011011	5B	[
28	00011100	1C		FS	60	00111100	3C	<	92	01011100	5C	\
29	00011101	1D	▫	GS	61	00111101	3D	=	93	01011101	5D	]
30	00011110	1E	◐	RS	62	00111110	3E	>	94	01011110	5E	ˆ
31	00011111	1F	∞	US	63	00111111	3F	?	95	01011111	5F	_

continued

DEC	BIN	HEX	ASCII	DEC	BIN	HEX	ASCII	DEC	BIN	HEX	ASCII
96	01100000	60	`	143	10001111	8F	Å	190	10111110	BE	+
97	01100001	61	a	144	10010000	90	É	191	10111111	BF	+
98	01100010	62	b	145	10010001	91	æ	192	11000000	C0	+
99	01100011	63	c	146	10010010	92	Æ	193	11000001	C1	−
100	01100100	64	d	147	10010011	93	ô	194	11000010	C2	−
101	01100101	65	e	148	10010100	94	ö	195	11000011	C3	+
102	01100110	66	f	149	10010101	95	ò	196	11000100	C4	−
103	01100111	67	g	150	10010110	96	û	197	11000101	C5	+
104	01101000	68	h	151	10010111	97	ù	198	11000110	C6	¬
105	01101001	69	i	152	10011000	98	ÿ	199	11000111	C7	¬
106	01101010	6A	j	153	10011001	99	Ö	200	11001000	C8	+
107	01101011	6B	k	154	10011010	9A	Ü	201	11001001	C9	+
108	01101100	6C	l	155	10011011	9B	¢	202	11001010	CA	−
109	01101101	6D	m	156	10011100	9C	£	203	11001011	CB	−
110	01101110	6E	n	157	10011101	9D	¥	204	11001100	CC	¬
111	01101111	6F	o	158	10011110	9E	P	205	11001101	CD	−
112	01110000	70	p	159	10011111	9F	ƒ	206	11001110	CE	+
113	01110001	71	q	160	10100000	A0	á	207	11001111	CF	−
114	01110010	72	r	161	10100001	A1	í	208	11010000	D0	−
115	01110011	73	s	162	10100010	A2	ó	209	11010001	D1	−
116	01110100	74	t	163	10100011	A3	ú	210	11010010	D2	−
117	01110101	75	u	164	10100100	A4	ñ	211	11010011	D3	+
118	01110110	76	v	165	10100101	A5	Ñ	212	11010100	D4	+
119	01110111	77	w	166	10100110	A6	ª	213	11010101	D5	+
120	01111000	78	x	167	10100111	A7	°	214	11010110	D6	+
121	01111001	79	y	168	10101000	A8	¿	215	11010111	D7	+
122	01111010	7A	z	169	10101001	A9	−	216	11011000	D8	+
123	01111011	7B	{	170	10101010	AA	¬	217	11011001	D9	+
124	01111100	7C	¦	171	10101011	AB	½	218	11011010	DA	+
125	01111101	7D	}	172	10101100	AC	¼	219	11011011	DB	¬
126	01111110	7E	~	173	10101101	AD	¡	220	11011100	DC	−
127	01111111	7F	Delete	174	10101110	AE	«	221	11011101	DD	¬
128	10000000	80	Ç	175	10101111	AF	»	222	11011110	DE	¬
129	10000001	81	ü	176	10110000	B0	¬	223	11011111	DF	−
130	10000010	82	é	177	10110001	B1	¬	224	11100000	E0	a
131	10000011	83	â	178	10110010	B2	¬	225	11100001	E1	
132	10000100	84	ä	179	10110011	B3	¬	226	11100010	E2	G
133	10000101	84	à	180	10110100	B4	¬	227	11100011	E3	p
134	10000110	86	å	181	10110101	B5	¬	228	11100100	E4	S
135	10000111	87	ç	182	10110110	B6	¬	229	11100101	E5	s
136	10001000	88	ê	183	10110111	B7	+	230	11100110	E6	
137	10001001	89	ë	184	10111000	B8	+	231	11100111	E7	t
138	10001010	8A	è	185	10111001	B9	¬	232	11101000	E8	F
139	10001011	8B	ï	186	10111010	BA	¬	233	11101001	E9	T
140	10001100	8C	î	187	10111011	BB	+	234	11101010	EA	O
141	10001101	8D	ì	188	10111100	BC	+	235	11101011	EB	d
142	10001110	8E	Ä	189	10111101	BD	+	236	11101100	EC	8

TABLE B.1 *continued*

DEC	BIN	HEX	ASCII	DEC	BIN	HEX	ASCII	DEC	BIN	HEX	ASCII
237	11101101	ED	f	244	11110100	F4	(	250	11111010	FA	
238	11101110	EE	e	245	11110101	F5	)	251	11111011	FB	v
239	11101111	EF	n	246	11110110	F6	Œ	252	11111100	FC	n
240	11110000	F0	=	247	11110111	F7	Â	253	11111101	FD	
241	11110001	F1		248	11111000	F8		254	11111110	FE	¬
242	11110010	F2	=	249	11111001	F9		255	11111111	FF	
243	11110011	F3	=								

TABLE B.2 Metric system prefixes

Multiplier	Exponent Form	Prefix	SI Symbol
1,000,000,000,000,000,000,000,000	10^{24}	yotta	Y
1,000,000,000,000,000,000,000	10^{21}	zetta	Z
1,000,000,000,000,000,000	10^{18}	exa	E
1,000,000,000,000,000	10^{15}	peta	P
1,000,000,000,000	10^{12}	tera	T
1,000,000,000	10^{9}	giga	G
1,000,000	10^{6}	mega	M
1,000	10^{3}	kilo	K
100	10^{2}	hecto	H
10	10^{1}	deca	Da
1	10^{0}		
.1	10^{-1}	deci	d
.01	10^{-2}	centi	c
.001	10^{-3}	milli	m
.000 001	10^{-6}	micro	μ
.000 000 001	10^{-9}	nano	n
.000 000 000 001	10^{-12}	pico	p
.000 000 000 000 001	10^{-15}	femto	f
.000 000 000 000 000 001	10^{-18}	atto	a
.000 000 000 000 000 000 001	10^{-21}	zepto	z
.000 000 000 000 000 000 000 001	10^{-24}	yocyo	y

TABLE B.3 Powers of two

n	2^n	Hexadecimal	Binary Number
0	1	1	1
1	2	2	10
2	4	4	100
3	8	8	1000
4	16	10	1 0000
5	32	20	10 0000
6	64	40	100 0000
7	128	80	1000 0000
8	256	100	1 0000 0000
9	512	200	10 0000 0000
10	1,024	400	100 0000 0000
11	2,048	800	1000 0000 0000
12	4,096	1000	1 0000 0000 0000
13	8,192	2000	10 0000 0000 0000
14	16,384	4000	100 0000 0000 0000
15	32,768	8000	1000 0000 0000 0000
16	65,536	10000	1 0000 0000 0000 0000
17	131,072	20000	10 0000 0000 0000 0000
18	262,144	40000	100 0000 0000 0000 0000
19	524,288	80000	1000 0000 0000 0000 0000
20	1,048,576	100000	1 0000 0000 0000 0000 0000
21	2,097,152	200000	10 0000 0000 0000 0000 0000
22	4,194,304	400000	100 0000 0000 0000 0000 0000
23	8,388,608	800000	1000 0000 0000 0000 0000 0000
24	16,777,216	1000000	1 0000 0000 0000 0000 0000 0000
25	33,554,432	2000000	10 0000 0000 0000 0000 0000 0000
26	67,108,864	4000000	100 0000 0000 0000 0000 0000 0000
27	134,217,728	8000000	1000 0000 0000 0000 0000 0000 0000
28	268,435,456	10000000	1 0000 0000 0000 0000 0000 0000 0000
29	536,870,912	20000000	10 0000 0000 0000 0000 0000 0000 0000
30	1,073,741,824	40000000	100 0000 0000 0000 0000 0000 0000 0000

TABLE B.3 *continued*

n	2^n	Hexadecimal	Binary Number
31	2,147,483,648	80000000	1000 0000 0000 0000 0000 0000 0000 0000
32	4,294,967,296	100000000	1 0000 0000 0000 0000 0000 0000 0000 0000
33	8,589,934,592	200000000	10 0000 0000 0000 0000 0000 0000 0000 0000
34	17,179,869,184	400000000	100 0000 0000 0000 0000 0000 0000 0000 0000
35	34,359,738,368	800000000	1000 0000 0000 0000 0000 0000 0000 0000 0000
36	68,719,476,736	1000000000	1 0000 0000 0000 0000 0000 0000 0000 0000 0000
37	137,438,953,472	2000000000	10 0000 0000 0000 0000 0000 0000 0000 0000 0000
38	274,877,906,944	4000000000	100 0000 0000 0000 0000 0000 0000 0000 0000 0000
39	549,755,813,888	8000000000	1000 0000 0000 0000 0000 0000 0000 0000 0000 0000
40	1,099,511,627,776	10000000000	1 0000 0000 0000 0000 0000 0000 0000 0000 0000 0000
41	2,199,023,255,552	20000000000	10 0000 0000 0000 0000 0000 0000 0000 0000 0000 0000
42	4,398,046,511,104	40000000000	100 0000 0000 0000 0000 0000 0000 0000 0000 0000 0000
43	8,796,093,022,208	80000000000	1000 0000 0000 0000 0000 0000 0000 0000 0000 0000 0000
44	17,592,186,044,416	100000000000	1 0000 0000 0000 0000 0000 0000 0000 0000 0000 0000 0000
45	35,184,372,088,832	200000000000	10 0000 0000 0000 0000 0000 0000 0000 0000 0000 0000 0000
46	70,368,744,177,664	400000000000	100 0000 0000 0000 0000 0000 0000 0000 0000 0000 0000 0000
47	140,737,488,355,328	800000000000	1000 0000 0000 0000 0000 0000 0000 0000 0000 0000 0000 0000
48	281,474,976,710,656	1000000000000	1 0000 0000 0000 0000 0000 0000 0000 0000 0000 0000 0000 0000
49	562,949,953,421,312	2000000000000	10 0000 0000 0000 0000 0000 0000 0000 0000 0000 0000 0000 0000
50	1,125,899,906,842,620	4000000000000	100 0000 0000 0000 0000 0000 0000 0000 0000 0000 0000 0000 0000
51	2,251,799,813,685,250	8000000000000	1000 0000 0000 0000 0000 0000 0000 0000 0000 0000 0000 0000 0000
52	4,503,599,627,370,500	10000000000000	1 0000 0000 0000 0000 0000 0000 0000 0000 0000 0000 0000 0000 0000
53	9,007,199,254,740,990	20000000000000	10 0000 0000 0000 0000 0000 0000 0000 0000 0000 0000 0000 0000 0000
54	18,014,398,509,482,000	40000000000000	100 0000 0000 0000 0000 0000 0000 0000 0000 0000 0000 0000 0000 0000
55	36,028,797,018,964,000	80000000000000	1000 0000 0000 0000 0000 0000 0000 0000 0000 0000 0000 0000 0000 0000
56	72,057,594,037,927,900	100000000000000	1 0000 0000 0000 0000 0000 0000 0000 0000 0000 0000 0000 0000 0000 0000
57	144,115,188,075,856,000	200000000000000	10 0000 0000 0000 0000 0000 0000 0000 0000 0000 0000 0000 0000 0000 0000
58	288,230,376,151,712,000	400000000000000	100 0000 0000 0000 0000 0000 0000 0000 0000 0000 0000 0000 0000 0000 0000
59	576,460,752,303,423,000	800000000000000	1000 0000 0000 0000 0000 0000 0000 0000 0000 0000 0000 0000 0000 0000 0000
60	1,152,921,504,606,850,000	1000000000000000	1 0000 0000 0000 0000 0000 0000 0000 0000 0000 0000 0000 0000 0000 0000 0000
61	2,305,843,009,213,690,000	2000000000000000	10 0000 0000 0000 0000 0000 0000 0000 0000 0000 0000 0000 0000 0000 0000 0000
62	4,611,686,018,427,390,000	4000000000000000	100 0000 0000 0000 0000 0000 0000 0000 0000 0000 0000 0000 0000 0000 0000 0000
63	9,223,372,036,854,780,000	8000000000000000	1000 0000 0000 0000 0000 0000 0000 0000 0000 0000 0000 0000 0000 0000 0000 0000
64	18,446,744,073,709,600,000	10000000000000000	1 0000 0000 0000 0000 0000 0000 0000 0000 0000 0000 0000 0000 0000 0000 0000 0000

Appendix C
POST Error Codes

TABLE C.1 AMI BIOS web sites

AMI Home Page	http://www.ami.com
How to identify your motherboard with AMI BIOS	http://www.ami.com/motherboards/support/identifying.html
AMIBIOS beep codes and recommended solutions	http://www.ami.com/amibios/support/beepcodes.html

TABLE C.2 AMI BIOS beep codes

Number of Beeps	Description	Recommended Solution
1	Refresh failure	Try reseating the memory first. If the error still occurs, replace the memory with known good chips. If the error still occurs, replace the motherboard.
2	Parity error	
3	Base 64K memory failure	
4	Timer not operational	The system board must be sent in for repair or replaced.
5	Processor error	
6	8042-gate A20 failure	Try reseating the keyboard controller chip. If the error still occurs, replace the keyboard chip. If the error persists, replace the keyboard and see if the system has a keyboard fuse.
7	Processor exception interrupt error	The system board must be sent in for repair or replaced.
8	Display memory read/write failure	Replace the video card or the memory on the video card.
9	ROM checksum error	Try reseating the system ROM BIOS chip. If the error still occurs, replace the system ROM BIOS chip or the motherboard.
10	CMOS shutdown register read/write error	The system board must be sent in for repair or replaced.
11	Cache memory bad	Make sure the system is configured properly (CMOS setup program and jumpers on the motherboard) for the RAM cache. If not, replace the RAM cache. (Note: Although the system will run slower, you could disable the RAM cache in the CMOS setup program or by jumpers on the motherboard.)

TABLE C.3   AMI POST error codes

POST Code	Description
01	Processor register test about to start, and NMI to be disabled.
02	NMI is disabled. Power on delay starting.
03	Power on delay complete. Any initialization before keyboard BAT is in progress.
04	Any initialization before keyboard BAT is complete. Reading keyboard SYS bit, to check soft reset/power-on.
05	Soft reset/power-on determined. Going to enable ROM, i.e., disable shadow RAM/cache if any.
06	ROM is enabled. Calculating ROM BIOS checksum and waiting for KB controller input buffer to be free.
07	ROM BIOS checksum passed, KB controller I/B free. Going to issue the BAT command to keyboard controller.
08	BAT command to keyboard controller is issued. Going to verify the BAT command.
09	Keyboard controller BAT result verified. Keyboard command byte to be written next.
0A	Keyboard command byte code is issued. Going to write command byte data.
0B	Keyboard controller command byte is written. Going to issue Pin-23, 24 blocking/unblocking command.
0C	Pin-23,24 of keyboard controller is blocked/unblocked. NOP command of keyboard controller to be issued next.
0D	NOP command processing is done. CMOS shutdown register test to be done next.
0E	CMOS shutdown register R/W test passed. Going to calculate CMOS checksum and update DIAG byte.
0F	CMOS checksum calculation is done; DIAG byte written. CMOS initialization to begin (if "INIT CMOS IN EVERY BOOT IS SET").
10	CMOS initialization done (if any). CMOS status register about to initialize for date and time.
11	CMOS Status register initialized. Going to disable DMA and interrupt controllers.
12	DMA controller #1,#2, interrupt controller #1,#2 disabled. About to disable video display and initialize port-B.
13	Video display is disabled and port-B is initialized. Chipset initialization/auto memory detection about to begin.
14	Chipset initialization/auto memory detection over. 8254 timer test about to start.
15	CH-2 timer test halfway. 8254 CH-2 timer test to be complete.
16	Ch-2 timer test over. 8254 CH-1 timer test to be complete.
17	CH-1 timer test over. 8254 CH-0 timer test to be complete.
18	CH-0 timer test over. About to start memory refresh.
19	Memory refresh started. Memory refresh test to be done next.
1A	Memory refresh line is toggling. Going to check 15 microsecond on/off time.
1B	Memory refresh period 30 microsecond test complete. Base 64 K memory test about to start.
20	Base 64 K memory test started. Address line test to be done next.
21	Address line test passed. Going to do toggle parity.
22	Toggle parity over. Going for sequential data R/W test.
23	Base 64 K sequential data R/W test passed. Any setup before interrupt vector initialization about to start.
24	Setup required before vector initialization complete. Interrupt vector initialization about to begin.
25	Interrupt vector initialization done. Going to read I/O port of 8042 for turbo switch (if any).

TABLE C.3 *continued*

POST Code	Description
26	I/O port of 8042 is read. Going to initialize global data for turbo switch.
27	Global data initialization is over. Any initialization after interrupt vector to be done next.
28	Initialization after interrupt vector is complete. Going for monochrome mode setting.
29	Monochrome mode setting is done. Going for color mode setting.
2A	Color mode setting is done. About to go for toggle parity before optional ROM test.
2B	Toggle parity over. About to give control for any setup required before optional video ROM check.
2C	Processing before video ROM control is done. About to look for optional video ROM and give control.
2D	Optional video ROM control is done. About to give control to do any processing after video ROM returns control.
2E	Return from processing after the video ROM control. If EGA/VGA not found, then do display memory R/W test.
2F	EGA/VGA not found. Display memory R/W test about to begin.
30	Display memory R/W test passed. About to look for the retrace checking.
31	Display memory R/W test or retrace checking failed. About to do alternate display memory R/W test.
32	Alternate display memory R/W test passed. About to look for the alternate display retrace checking.
33	Video display checking over. Verification of display type with switch setting and actual card to begin.
34	Verification of display adapter done. Display mode to be set next.
35	Display mode set complete. BIOS ROM data area about to be checked.
36	BIOS ROM data area check over. Going to set cursor for power-on message.
37	Cursor setting for power-on message is complete. Going to display the power-on message.
38	Power-on message display complete. Going to read new cursor positon.
39	New cursor position read and saved. Going to display the reference string.
3A	Reference string display is over. Going to display the Hit <ESC> message.
3B	Hit <ESC> message displayed. Virtual mode memory test about to start.
40	Preparation for virtual mode test started. Going to verify from video memory.
41	Returned after verifying from display memory. Going to prepare the descriptor tables.
42	Descriptor tables prepared. Going to enter in virtual mode for memory test.
43	Entered in the virtual mode. Going to enable interrupts for diagnostics mode.
44	Interrupts enabled (if diagnostics switch is on). Going to initialize data to check memory wraparound at 0:0.
45	Data initialized. Going to check for memory wraparound at 0:0 and find the total system memory size.
46	Memory wraparound test done. Memory size calculation over. About to go for writing patterns to test memory.
47	Pattern to be tested written in extended memory. Going to write patterns in Base 640 K memory.
48	Patterns written in base memory. Going to find out amount of memory below 1 M memory.
49	Amount of memory below 1 M found and verified. Going to find out amount of memory above 1 M memory.
4A	Amount of memory above 1 M found and verified. Going for BIOS ROM data area check.
4B	BIOS ROM data area check over. Going to check <ESC> and to clear memory below 1 M for soft reset.
4C	Memory below 1 M cleared (SOFT RESET). Going to clear memory above 1 M.
4D	Memory above 1 M cleared (SOFT RESET). Going to save the memory size.
4E	Memory test started (NO SOFT RESET). About to display the first 64 K memory test.
4F	Memory size display started. This will be updated during memory test. Going for sequential and random memory test.
50	Memory test below 1 M complete. Going to adjust memory size for relocation/shadow.
51	Memory size adjusted due to relocation/shadow. Memory test above 1 M to follow.
52	Memory test above 1 M complete. Going to prepare to go back to real mode.
53	CPU registers are saved, including memory size. Going to enter in real mode.
54	Shutdown successful; CPU in real mode. Going to restore registers saved during preparation for shutdown.
55	Registers restored. Going to disable gate A20 address line.

continued

TABLE C.3 *continued*

POST Code	Description
56	A20 address line disable successful. BIOS ROM data area about to be checked.
57	BIOS ROM data area check halfway. BIOS ROM data area check to be complete.
58	BIOS ROM data area check over. Going to clear Hit <ESC> message.
59	Hit <ESC> message cleared. <WAIT...> message displayed. About to start DMA and interrupt controller test.
60	DMA page register test passed. About to verify from display memory.
61	Display memory verification over. About to go for DMA #1 base register test.
62	DMA #1 base register test passed. About to go for DMA #2 base register test.
63	DMA #2 base register test passed. About to go for BIOS ROM data area check.
64	BIOS ROM data area check halfway. BIOS ROM data area check to be complete.
65	BIOS ROM data area check over. About to program DMA unit 1 and 2.
66	DMA unit 1 and 2 programming over. About to initialize 8259 interrupt controller.
67	8259 initialization over. About to start keyboard test.
80	Keyboard test started. Clearing output buffer, checking for stuck key, about to issue keyboard reset command.
81	Keyboard reset error/stuck key found. About to issue keyboard controller interface test command.
82	Keyboard controller interface test over. About to write command byte and initialize circular buffer.
83	Command byte written; global data initialization done. About to check for lock-key.
84	Lock-key checking over. About to check for memory size mismatch with CMOS.
85	Memory size check done. About to display soft error and check for password or bypass setup.
86	Password checked. About to do programming before setup.
87	Programming before setup complete. Going to CMOS setup program.
88	Returned from CMOS setup program and screen is cleared. About to do programming after setup.
89	Programming after setup complete. Going to display power-on screen message.
90	Floppy setup is over. Test for hard disk presence to be done.
91	Hard disk presence test over. Hard disk setup to follow.
92	Hard disk setup complete. About to go for BIOS ROM data area check.
93	BIOS ROM data area check halfway. BIOS ROM data area check to be complete.
94	BIOS ROM data area check over. Going to set base and extended memory size.
95	Memory size adjusted due to mouse support, hard disk type-47. Going to verify from display memory.
96	Returned after verifying from display memory. Going to do any initialization before C800 optional ROM control.
97	Any initialization before C800 optional ROM control is over. Optional ROM check and control will be done next.
98	Optional ROM control is done. About to give control to do any required processing after optional ROM returns control.
99	Any initialization required after optional ROM test over. Going to setup timer data area and printer base address.
9A	Return after setting timer and printer base address. Going to set the RS-232 base address.
9B	Returned after RS-232 base address. Going to do any initialization before coprocessor test.
9C	Required initialization before coprocessor is over. Going to initialize the coprocessor next.
9D	Coprocessor initialized. Going to do any initialization after coprocessor test.
9E	Initialization after coprocessor test is complete. Going to check extended keyboard, keyboard ID, and num-lock.
9F	Extended keyboard check is done, ID flag set, num-lock on/off. Keyboard ID command to be issued.
A0	Keyboard ID command issued. Keyboard ID flag to be reset.
A1	Keyboard ID flag reset. Cache memory test to follow.
A2	Cache memory test over. Going to display any soft errors.
A3	Soft error display complete. Going to set the keyboard typematic rate.
A4	Keyboard typematic rate set. Going to program memory wait states.

TABLE C.3 *continued*

POST Code	Description
A5	Memory wait states programming over. Screen to be cleared next.
A6	Screen cleared. Going to enable parity and NMI.
A7	NMI and parity enabled. Going to do any initialization required before giving control to optional ROM at E000.
A8	Initialization before E000 ROM control over. E000 ROM to get control next.
A9	Returned from E000 ROM control. Going to do any initialization required.
AA	Initialization after E000 optional ROM control is over. Going to display the system configuration.
0	System configuration is displayed. Going to give control to INT 19h boot loader.

TABLE C.4 **Award web pages**

Award Home Page	http://www.award.com/
Award's technical library, including setup utility configuration and POST codes and error messages	http://www.award.com/prodbrfs/prodbrf.htm

TABLE C.5 **Award BIOS beep codes**

Beeps	Error Description
One long and two short beeps	Video error
One long and three short beeps	Keyboard controller error
Two short beeps	Nonfatal error
One short beep	No error during POST

TABLE C.6 **Award POST codes**

POST Code	Description
01H	Processor Test 1—Processor status (1FLAGS) verification. Tests the following processor status flags: carry, zero, sign, overflow. The BIOS sets each flag, verifies they are set, then turns each flag off and verifies it is off.
02H	Determine POST type. This test determines whether the status of the system is manufacturing or normal. The status can be set by a physical jumper on some motherboards. If the status is normal, the POST continues through and, assuming no errors, boot is attempted. If manufacturing POST is installed, POST is run in continuous loop, and boot is not attempted.
03H	8042 keyboard controller. Tests controller by sending TEST_KBRD command (AAH) and verifying that controller reads commands.
04H	8042 keyboard controller. Verifies the keyboard controller returned AAH, sent in test 3.
05H	Get manufacturing status. The last test in the manufacturing cycle. If test 2 found the status to be manufacturing, this POST triggers a reset and POSTs 1 through 5 are repeated continuously.
06H	Initialize chips. POST 06H performs these functions: disables color and mono video, disables parity circuits, disables DMA (8237) chips, resets math coprocessor, initializes timer 1 (8255), clears DMA chip, clears all page registers, and clears CMOS shutdown byte.
07H	Processor test 2. Reads, writes, and verifies all CPU registers except SS, SP, and BP with data pattern FF and 00.
08H	Initialize CMOS timer. Updates timer cycle normally.

continued

TABLE C.6   *continued*

POST Code	Description
09H	EPROM checksum. Checksums EPROM; test failed if sum not equal to 0. Also checksums sign-on message.
0AH	Initialize video interface. Initializes video controller register 6845 to the following: 80 characters per row 25 rows per screen 8/14 scan lines per row for mono/color First scan line of cursor 6/11 Last scan line of cursor 7/12 Reset display offset to 0
0BH	Test timer (8254) channel 0. This and the next two timer tests verify that the 8254 timer chip is functioning properly.
0CH	Test timer (8254) channel 1.
0DH	Test timer (8254) channel 2.
0EH	Test CMOS shutdown byte. Uses a walking bit algorithm to check interface to CMOS circuit.
0FH	Test extended CMOS. On motherboards with chipsets that support extended information, this test is used to configure the chipset. These chipsets have an extended storage mechanism that enables the user to save a desired system configuration after the power is turned off. A checksum is used to verify the validity of the extended storage and, if valid, permit the information to be loaded into extended CMOS RAM.
10H	Test DMA channel 0. This and the next two functions initialize the DMA chip and then test the chip using an AA, 55, FF, 00 pattern. Part addresses are used to check the address circuit to DMA page registers.
11H	DMA channel 1.
12H	DMA page registers.
13H	Keyboard controller. Test keyboard controller interface.
14H	Test memory refresh. RAM must be refreshed periodically to keep the memory from decaying. This function ensures that the memory-refresh function is working properly.
15H	First 64 KB of system memory. An extensive parity test is performed on the first 64 KB of system memory. This memory is used by the BIOS.
16H	Interrupt vector table. Sets up and loads interrupt vector tables in memory for use by the 8259 PIC chip.
17H	Video I/O operations. This function initializes the video, either CGA, MDA, EGA, or VGA. If a CGA or MDA adapter is installed, the video is initialized by the system BIOS. If the system BIOS detects an EGA or VGA adapter, the option ROM BIOS installed on the video adapter is used to initialize and set up the video.
18H	Video memory. Tests memory for CGA and MDA video boards. This test is not performed by the system BIOS on EGA or VGA video adapters—the board's own EGA or VGA BIOS ensures that it is functioning properly.
19H	Test 8259 mask bits—channel 1. This and the next test verify 8259 masked interrupts by alternately turning the interrupt lines off and on. Unsuccessful completion generates a fatal error.
1AH	8259 mask bits—channel 2.
1BH	CMOS battery level. Verifies that the battery status bit is set to 1. A 0 value can indicate a bad battery or some other problem, such as bad CMOS.
1CH	CMOS checksum. This function tests the CMOS checksum data (located at 2EH and 2FH) and extended CMOS checksum, if present, to be sure that they are valid.
1DH	Configuration from CMOS. If the CMOS checksum is good, the values are used to configure the system.
1EH	System memory. The system memory size is determined by writing to addresses from 0 KB to 640 KB, starting at 0 and continuing until an address does not respond. Memory size value then is compared to the CMOS value to ensure that they are the same. If they are different, a flag is set and, at the end of POST, an error message is displayed.
1FH	Found system memory. Tests memory from 64 KB to the top of the memory found by writing the pattern FFAA and 5500 and then reading the pattern back, byte by byte, and verifying that it is correct.
20H	Stuck 8259 interrupt bits. This and the next two tests verify the functionality of the 8259 interrupt controller.
21H	Stuck NMI bits (parity or I/O channel check).
22H	8259 function.

TABLE C.6 *continued*

POST Code	Description
23H	Protected mode. Verifies protected mode, 8086 virtual mode as well as 8086 page mode. Protected mode ensures that any data about to be written to extended memory (above 1 MB) is checked to ensure that it is suitable for storage.
24H	Extended memory. This function sizes memory above 1 MB by writing to addresses starting at 1 MB and continuing to 16 MB on 286 and 86SX systems, and to 64 MB on 386 systems until there is no response. This process determines the total extended memory, which is compared with CMOS to ensure that the values are the same. If the values are different, a flag is set and, at the end of POST, an error message is displayed.
25H	Found extended memory. This function tests extended memory using virtual 8086 paging mode and writing an FFFF, AA55, 0000 pattern.
26H	Protected mode exceptions. This functions tests other aspects of protected mode operations.
27H	Cache control or shadow RAM. Tests for shadow RAM and cache controller (386 and 486 only) functionality. Systems with CGA and MDA adapters indicate that video shadow RAM is enabled, even though there is no BIOS ROM to shadow (this is normal).
28H	8242. Optional Intel 8242/8248 keyboard controller detection and support.
29H	Reserved.
2AH	Initialize keyboard. Initialize keyboard controller.
2BH	Floppy drive and controller. Initialize floppy disk drive controller and any drives present.
2CH	Detect and initialize serial ports. Initializes any serial ports presents.
2DH	Detect and initialize parallel ports. Initializes any parallel ports present.
2FH	Detect and initialize math coprocessor. Initializes any option ROMs present from C800 to EFFFH.
30H	Reserved.
31H	Detect and initialize math coprocessor. Initializes math coprocessors.
3BH	Initialize secondary cache with OPTi chipset. Initializes secondary cache controller for systems based on the OPTi chipset (486 only).
CAH	Micronics cache initialization. Detects and initializes Micronics cache controller if present.
CCH	NMI handler shutdown. Detects untrapped nonmaskable interrupt during boot.
EEH	Unexpected processor exception.
FFH	Boot attempt. When the POST is complete, if all the system components and peripherals are initialized and if no error flags were set (such as memory size error), then the system attempts to boot.

TABLE C.7 IBM BIOS beep codes

Beeps	Description
1 short	Normal POST—system OK
2 short	Initialization error, DMA, ROM, floppy, serial, or parallel
1 long, 1 short	System board
1 long, 2 short	Display adapter (MDA, CGA)
1 long, 3 short	Enhanced graphics (EGA)
None	Power supply, RAM, or motherboard
Continuous	Power supply or motherboard
Repeating short	Power supply or motherboard

TABLE C.8 IBM POST error codes

100-Series	System Board Errors	Recommended Solutions
101	Interrupt failure; general system board failure	Replace the motherboard.
102	System timer failed	Replace the motherboard.
103	System timer interrupt failed	Replace the motherboard.
104	Protected mode (AT)	Replace the keyboard. If the error still exists, replace the motherboard.
105	8042 command not accepted; keyboard communication failure	Replace the keyboard, keyboard controller chip, or motherboard.
106	POST logic test problem	Caused by a faulty expansion card or the motherboard.
107	NMI test failed	Replace the microprocessor or the motherboard.
108	Failed system timer test	Replace the motherboard.
109	Problem with first 64 KB RAM	Replace the memory. If the error still exists, replace the motherboard.
151	Real-time clock (or CMOS RAM)	Replace the CMOS battery. If the problem still exists, replace the motherboard.
152	System board circuitry	Replace the motherboard.
161	CMOS power failure	Replace the CMOS battery. If the problem still exists, replace the motherboard.
162	CMOS checksum error	Replace the CMOS battery. If the problem still exists,
163	Clock date error	replace the motherboard.
164	Memory size (POST finds value different from CMOS)	
165	Adapter added/removed (PS/2)	

200-Series	Memory	
201	Memory test failed	Replace the RAM. If the problem still exists, replace the motherboard. (Note: The address indicating which RAM chip is usually given.)

300-Series	Keyboard	
301	Stuck key or improper response	Make sure keyboard is plugged in and no keys are stuck. In addition, make sure nothing is resting on the keys.
302	Keyboard test error or keyboard is locked	The keyboard lock is on. If the keyboard lock is not on, you may have a faulty keylock switch or a keyboard key is stuck down.
303	Keyboard interface error (on system board)	Check the AT/XT switch on the keyboard. If the problem still exists, replace the keyboard cable or keyboard.
304	Nonspecific keyboard error	Check the AT/XT switch on the keyboard. If the problem still exists, replace the keyboard cable or keyboard.
365	Keyboard failure	
366	Keyboard cable failure	

400-Series	Monochrome Display	
401	Memory or sync test failure	Replace the monochrome video card.
432	Parallel port test failure	Replace the monochrome video card and/or parallel card.

500-Series	Color Graphics Adapter	
501	Memory or sync test failure	Replace the CGA card.

TABLE C.8 *continued*

600-Series	Floppy Disk System	
601	Drive or adapter test failure	Check floppy drive CMOS settings. If the problem still exists, check the floppy drive cable, drive power connector, floppy drive card, and floppy drive.
602	Drive failure	Check floppy drive CMOS settings. If the problem still exists, check the floppy drive cable, drive power connector, floppy drive card, and floppy drive.
603	Wrong drive capacity	
606	Disk verify function error	
607	Write-protected diskette	
608	Bad command	
610	Disk initialization error	
611	Timeout error	
612	Bad controller chip	
613	DMA failure	
614	DMA boundary error	
621	Seek error	
622	CRC error	
623	Record not found	
624	Bad address mark	
625	Controller seek failure	
626	Data compare error	
627	Change line error	
628	Disk removed	
700-Series	Floating-Point Unit	
900-Series	LPT1	
1000-Series	LPT2	
1100-Series	COM1	
1200-Series	COM2	
1300-Series	Game Control Adapter	
1301	Adapter failure	
1302	Joystick failure	
1400-Series	Printer	
1500-Series	SDLC Communications Adapter	
1600-Series	Display Station Emulation Adapter (DSEA)	
1700-Series	Hard Disk System	
1701	Drive not ready; disk or adapter test failure	Check hard drive CMOS settings and hard drive configuration. If the problem still exists, check the hard drive cable, drive power connector, hard drive card, and hard drive.
1702	Time out; disk or adapter error	
1703	Drive error	

continued

TABLE C.8   *continued*

1700-Series	Hard Disk System	
1704	Adapter or drive error	
1705	Record not found	
1706	Write fault	
1707	Track 0 error	
1708	Head select error	
1709	Bad error correction code	
1710	Read buffer overrun	
1711	Bad address mark	
1712	Nonspecific error	
1713	Data compare error	
1714	Drive not ready	
1730	Adapter error	
1731	Adapter error	
1732	Adapter error	
1780	Drive C: boot failure	Check floppy drive CMOS settings and partitions. If the problem still exists, check the floppy drive cable, floppy drive card, and floppy drive.
1781	Drive D: failure	Check floppy drive CMOS settings and partitions. If the problem still exists, check the floppy drive cable, floppy drive card, and floppy drive.
1782	Controller boot failure	Check hard drive controller configuration.
1790	Drive C: error	Check floppy drive CMOS settings and partitions. If the problem still exists, check the floppy drive cable, floppy drive card, and floppy drive.
1791	Drive D: error	
1800-Series	PC or XT Expansion Chassis	
2000-Series	First Bisynchronous (BSC) Adapter	
2100 Series	Second Bisynchronous (BSC) Adapter	
2200-Series	Cluster Adapter	
2400-Series	Enhanced Graphics Adapter	
2401	Adapter test failure	
2456	Light pen failure	
2500-Series	Second Enhanced Graphics Adapter	
2600-Series	PC/370-M Adapter	
2700-Series	PC/3277 Emulation Adapter	
2800-Series	3278/79 Emulator Adapter	
2900-Series	Printer	
3000-Series	Network Adapter	
3001	Adapter ROM test failure	
3002	Adapter RAM test failure	
3006	Interrupt conflict	

TABLE C.8 *continued*

3100-Series	**Second Network Adapter**	
3300-Series	**Compact Printer**	
3600-Series	**IEEE-488 (GPIB) Adapter**	
3800-Series	**Data Acquisition Adapter**	
3900-Series	**Professional Graphics Controller Adapter**	
4400-Series	**5278 Display Attachment Unit and 5279 Display**	
4500-Series	**IEEE-488 (GPIB) Adapter**	
4600-Series	**Artic Interface Adapter**	
4800-Series	**Internal Modem**	
4900-Series	**Second Internal Modem**	
5600-Series	**Financial Communication System**	
7000-Series	**Phoenix BIOS Chipset**	
7000	CMOS failure	
7001	Shadow memory	
7002	CMOS configuration error	
7100-Series	**Voice Communication Adapter**	
7300-Series	**3.5-Inch Floppy Disk Drive**	
7301	Drive or adapter test failure	Check floppy drive CMOS settings. If the problem still exists, check the floppy drive cable, drive power connector, floppy drive card, and floppy drive.
7307	Write-protected diskette	
7308	Bad command	
7310	Track zero error	
7311	Timeout	
7312	Bad controller or DMA	
7315	Bad index	
7316	Speed error	
7321	Bad seek	
7322	Bad CRC	
7323	Record not found	
7324	Bad address mark	
7325	Controller seek error	
7400-Series	**8514/A Display Adapter**	
7401	Test failure	
7426	Monitor failure	
7600-Series	**Page Printer**	
8400-Series	**Speech Adapter**	
8500-Series	**2 MB Memory Adapter**	

continued

TABLE C.8 *continued*

8600-Series	**Pointing Device**
8900-Series	**MIDI Adapter**
10000-Series	**Multiprotocol Communications Adapter**
10100-Series	**Modem and Communications Adapter**
10400-Series	**ESDI Disk Controller**
10450	Write/read test error
10451	Read verify test error
10452	Seek test error
10453	Device type mismatch
10454	Controller buffer failure
10455	Controller failure
10461	Format error
10463	Write/read sector error
10464	Drive map unreadable
10465	ECC error
10466	ECC error
10467	Soft seek error
10468	Hard seek error
10469	Soft seek error
10470	Controller diagnostic error
10499	Controller failure
10700-Series	**5.25-Inch External Floppy Disk Drive**
11200-Series	**SCSI Adapter**
12900-Series	**Processor Platform**
12901	Processor error
12902	Cache error
14900-Series	**PLASMA Display and Adapter**
16500-Series	**Streaming Tape Drive**
16520	Drive error
16540	Controller error
16600-Series	**First Token-Ring Network Adapter**
16700-Series	**Second Token-Ring Network Adapter**
19400-Series	**Adapter Memory Module**
21000-Series	**SCSI Hard Disk or Host Adapter**
21500-Series	**CD-ROM System**

612

TABLE C.9　Phoenix web sites

Phoenix Home Page	http://www.phoenix.com
Phoenix BIOS 4.0 setup guide and Phoenix POST and beep codes	http://www.phoenix.com/techs/techref.html

TABLE C.10　Phoenix beep codes—fatal system board errors

Beep Code	Code at Port 80H	Description	Recommended Solution
None	01H	CPU register test in progress	Replace the motherboard.
1-1-3	02H	CMOS write/read failure	Replace the motherboard.
1-1-4	03H	ROMBIOS checksum failure	The BIOS needs to be replaced or the motherboard needs to replaced.
1-2-1	04H	Programmable interval timer failure	Replace the motherboard.
1-2-2	05H	DMA initialization failure	Replace the motherboard.
1-2-3	06H	DMA page register write/read failure	Replace the motherboard.
1-3-1	08H	RAM refresh verification failure	Replace the RAM or motherboard.
None	09H	First 64 KB RAM test in progress	Replace the RAM or motherboard.
1-3-3	0AH	First 64 KB RAM chip or data line failure, multibit	Replace the RAM or motherboard.
1-3-4	0BH	First 64 KB RAM odd/even logic failure	Replace the motherboard.
1-4-1	0CH	Address line failure first 64 KB RAM	Replace the motherboard.
1-4-2	0DH	Parity failure first 64 KB	Replace the RAM or motherboard.
2-_-_	10H-1FH	First 64 KB RAM failure	Replace the RAM or motherboard.
3-1-1	20H	Slave DMA register failure	Replace the motherboard.
3-1-2	21H	Master DMA register failure	Replace the motherboard.
3-1-3	22H	Master interrupt mask register failure	Replace the motherboard.
3-1-4	23H	Slave interrupt mask register failure	Replace the motherboard.
None	25H	Interrupt vector loading in progress	Replace the RAM or motherboard.
3-2-4	27H	Keyboard controller test failure	Check keyboard XT/AT switch, keyboard cable, keyboard, or motherboard.
None	28H	CMOS power failure/checksum calculation in progress	Check CMOS battery. If CMOS battery is OK, replace the motherboard.
None	29H	Screen configuration validation in progress	
3-3-4	2BH	Screen initialization failure	There is no video card.
3-4-1	2CH	Screen retrace failure	Replace the video card.
3-4-2	2DH	Search for video ROM in progress	Replace the video card.
None	2EH	Screen running with video ROM	
None	30H	Screen operable	
None	31H	Monochrome monitor operable	
None	32H	Color monitor (40-column) operable	
None	33H	Color monitor (80-column) operable	

TABLE C.11 Phoenix BIOS codes—nonfatal system board errors

Beep Code	Code at Port 80H	Description	Recommended Solution
4-2-1	34H	Timer tick interrupt test in progress or failure	Replace the motherboard.
4-2-2	35H	Shutdown test in progress or failure	First check the keyboard for problems. If nothing, you have a bad motherboard.
4-2-3	36H	Gate A20 failure	First check the keyboard for problems. If nothing, you have a bad motherboard.
4-2-4	37H	Unexpected interrupt in protected mode	Check for a bad expansion card or bad motherboard.
4-3-1	38H	RAM test in progress or address failure >FFFFH	Replace the motherboard.
4-3-3	3AH	Interval timer channel 2 test or failure	Replace the motherboard.
4-3-4	3BH	Time-of-day clock test or failure	Try running the setup program that comes with the computer. Check the date and time. If that doesn't work, replace the battery or motherboard.
4-4-1	3CH	Serial port test or failure	Reseat, or replace, the I/O card. If the serial port is on the motherboard, disable.
4-4-2	3DH	Parallel port test or failure	Reseat, or replace, the I/O card. If the serial port is on the motherboard, disable.
4-4-3	3EH	Math coprocessor test or failure	Run a test program to doublecheck it. If the problem does exist, replace the math coprocessor (or CPU).
Low 1-1-2	41H	System board select failure	Replace the motherboard.
Low 1-1-3	42H	Extended CMOS RAM failure	Replace the motherboard.

TABLE C.12 Phoenix POST codes

POST Code	Description
02H	Verify real mode
03H	Disable nonmaskable interrupt (NMI)
04H	Get CPU type
06H	Initialize system hardware
08H	Initialize chipset with initial POST values
09H	Set IN POST flag
0AH	Initialize CPU registers
0BH	Enable CPU cache
0CH	Initialize caches to initial POST values
0EH	Initialize I/O component
0FH	Initialize the local bus IDE
10H	Initialize power management
11H	Load alternate registers with initial POST values
12H	Restore CPU control word during warm boot
13H	Initialize PCI bus mastering devices
14H	Initialize keyboard controller
16H	BIOS ROM checksum
17H	Initialize cache before memory autosize
18H	8254 timer initialization

TABLE C.12 *continued*

POST Code	Description
1AH	8237 DMA controller initialization
1CH	Reset programmable interrupt controller
20H	Test DRAM refresh
22H	Test 8742 keyboard controller
24H	Set ES segment register to 4 GB
26H	Enable A20 line
28H	Autosize DRAM
29H	Initialize POST memory manager
2AH	Clear 512 KB base RAM
2CH	RAM failure on address line *xxxx**
2EH	1- 3- 4- 3 RAM failure on data bits *xxxx** of low byte of memory bus
2FH	Enable cache before system BIOS shadow
30H	RAM failure on data bits *xxxx** of high byte of memory bus
32H	Test CPU bus-clock frequency
33H	Initialize Phoenix dispatch manager
36H	Warm start shut down
38H	Shadow system BIOS ROM
3AH	Autosize cache
3CH	Advanced configuration of chipset registers
3DH	Load alternate registers with CMOS values
42H	Initialize interrupt vectors
45H	POST device initialization
46H	Check ROM copyright notice
48H	Check video configuration against CMOS
49H	Initialize PCI bus and devices
4AH	Initialize all video adapters in system
4BH	QuietBoot start (optional)
4CH	Shadow video BIOS ROM
4EH	Display BIOS copyright notice
50H	Display CPU type and speed
51H	Initialize EISA board
52H	Test keyboard
54H	Set key click if enabled
58H	Test for unexpected interrupts
59H	Initialize POST display service
5AH	Display prompt "Press F2 to enter SETUP"
5BH	Disable CPU cache
5CH	Test RAM between 512 and 640 KB
60H	Test extended memory
62H	Test extended memory address lines
64H	Jump to UserPatch1
66H	Configure advanced cache registers
67H	Initialize multiprocessor APIC
68H	Enable external and CPU caches

*If BIOS detects 2CH, 2EH, or 30H, an additional word-bitmap (*xxxx*) is displayed indicating the address line or bits that failed.

continued

TABLE C.12 *continued*

POST Code	Description
69H	Setup system management mode (SMM) area
6AH	Display external L2 cache size
6BH	Load custom defaults (optional)
6CH	Display shadow-area message
6EH	Display possible high address for UMB recovery
70H	Display error messages
72H	Check for configuration errors
76H	Check for keyboard errors
7CH	Set up hardware interrupt vectors
7EH	Initialize coprocessor if present
80H	Disable onboard super I/O ports and IRQs
81H	Late POST device initialization
82H	Detect and install external RS232 ports
83H	Configure non-MCD IDE controllers
84H	Detect and install external parallel ports
85H	Initialize PC-compatible PnP ISA devices
86H	Reinitialize onboard I/O ports
87H	Configure motherboard configurable devices (optional)
88H	Initialize BIOS data area
89H	Enable nonmaskable interrupts (NMIs)
8AH	Initialize extended BIOS data area
8BH	Test and initialize PS/2 mouse
8CH	Initialize floppy controller
8FH	Determine number of ATA drives (optional)
90H	Initialize hard disk controllers
91H	Initialize local bus hard disk controllers
92H	Jump to UserPatch2
93H	Build MPTABLE for multiprocessor boards
95H	Install CD ROM for boot
96H	Clear huge ES segment register
97H	Fix up multiprocessor table
98H	Search for option ROMs. One long, two short beeps on checksum failure.
99H	Check for SMART drive (optional)
9AH	Shadow option ROMs
9CH	Set up power management
9DH	Initialize security engine (optional)
9EH	Enable hardware interrupts
9FH	Determine number of ATA and SCSI drives
A0H	Set time of day
A2H	Check key lock
A4H	Initialize typematic rate
A8H	Erase F2 prompt
AAH	Scan for F2 keystroke
ACH	Enter SETUP
AEH	Clear boot flag

TABLE C.12 *continued*

POST Code	Description
B0H	Check for errors
B2H	POST done—prepare to boot operating system
B4H	One short beep before boot
B5H	Terminate QuietBoot (optional)
B6H	Check password (optional)
B9H	Prepare boot
BAH	Initialize DMI parameters
BBH	Initialize PnP option ROMs
BCH	Clear parity checkers
BDH	Display MultiBoot menu
BEH	Clear screen (optional)
BFH	Check virus and backup reminders
C0H	Try to boot with INT 19
C1H	Initialize POST error manager (PEM)
C2H	Initialize error logging
C3H	Initialize error display function
C4H	Initialize system error handler
C5H	PnP and dual CMOS (optional)
C6H	Initialize notebook docking (optional)
C7H	Initialize notebook docking late
C8H	Force check (optional)
C9H	Extended checksum (optional)
D2H	Unknown interrupt

TABLE C.13 Phoenix POST code beeps for boot block in flash ROM

POST Code	Description
E0H	Initialize the chipset
E1H	Initialize the bridge
E2H	Initialize the CPU
E3H	Initialize system timer
E4H	Initialize system I/O
E5H	Check force recovery boot
E6H	Checksum BIOS ROM
E7H	Go to BIOS
E8H	Set huge segment
E9H	Initialize multiprocessor
EAH	Initialize OEM special code
EBH	Initialize PIC and DMA
ECH	Initialize memory type
EDH	Initialize memory size
EEH	Shadow boot block
EFH	System memory test
F0H	Initialize interrupt vectors
F1H	Initialize run time clock
F2H	Initialize video
F3H	Initialize system management mode
F4H	Output one beep before boot
F5H	Boot to mini DOS
F6H	Clear huge segment
F7H	Boot to full DOS

TABLE C.14 POST messages

128 KB Not OK, Parity Disabled	Replace the first bank of RAM or replace the motherboard.
8042 Gate-A20 Error	The Gate-A20 portion (21st address line used to access memory above 1 MB) of the keyboard controller has failed. Check XT/AT switch on keyboard and keyboard. Make sure the RAM chips are seated properly. Replace the keyboard controller or entire motherboard.
Address Line Short	There is a problem with the memory address decoding circuitry. Try rebooting (turn the system off and then on 10 seconds later). If the problem still exists, replace the motherboard.
Bad DMA Port=XX	Replace the motherboard.
Bad PnP Serial ID Checksum	The serial ID checksum of a plug-and-play card is invalid. Replace the expansion card.
BIOS ROM Checksum Error —System Halted	The checksum of the BIOS code in the BIOS chip is incorrect, indicating the BIOS code may have become corrupt. Replace the system ROM BIOS or the motherboard.
BUS Timeout NMI at Slot X	There was a bus timeout NMI at slot X.
C Drive Error	The system cannot get a response from drive C. Check the hard drive parameters in the CMOS parameter and make sure the disk is partitioned and formatted properly. Lastly, make sure that the hard drive is connected properly.
C: Drive Failure	The drive was detected but failed. Check hard drive CMOS settings and hard drive configuration. If the problem still exists, check the hard drive cable, drive power connector, hard drive card, and hard drive.
Cache Memory Bad	Make sure RAM cache is seated properly. Replace RAM cache or replace motherboard. (Note: You can also perform a temporary repair by disabling the RAM cache.)

TABLE C.14 *continued*

CH-2 Timer Error	Could be caused by a peripheral or motherboard.
CMOS Battery Failed or **CMOS Battery Has Failed**	CMOS battery is no longer functional. Replace the battery.
CMOS Battery State Low	Record your CMOS settings as soon as possible and replace the CMOS battery.
CMOS Checksum Error	Checksum of CMOS is incorrect. This can indicate that CMOS has become corrupt. This error may have been caused by a weak battery. Check the CMOS battery.
CMOS Display Mismatch	The video type indicated in the CMOS RAM is not the one detected by the BIOS. Check the CMOS setup program to make sure that the correct video type is selected. (Note: Most computers have it set to VGA or EGA/VGA.)
CMOS Memory Size Mismatch	Run the CMOS setup program. If the CMOS setup program does not show the correct amount of RAM on the motherboard, make sure the RAM is seated properly. If the problem still exists, replace the RAM and motherboard.
CMOS Memory Size Mismatch	Usually caused when memory is added or removed from the system but could be caused by memory that has failed. Run CMOS setup program.
CMOS System Options Not Set	CMOS values are either corrupt or do not exist. Run CMOS setup program. If the problem reoccurs, check the CMOS battery. If the problem still exists, replace the motherboard.
CMOS Time and Date Not Set	Run the CMOS setup program. If the problem reoccurs, check the CMOS battery. If the problem still exists, replace the motherboard.
Disk Boot Error, Replace and Strike Key to Retry.	If booting from the hard drive, take the disk out of the floppy drive and make sure that the hard drive is bootable. If booting from the floppy drive, make sure that the floppy disk is bootable.
Disk Boot Failure, Insert System Disk and Press Enter	No boot device was found. This could mean that either a boot drive was not detected or the drive does not contain proper system boot files. Insert a system disk into drive A and press Enter. If you assumed the system would boot from the hard drive, make sure the controller is inserted correctly and all cables are properly attached. Also be sure the disk is formatted as a boot device. Then reboot the system.
Diskette Boot Failure	The diskette in the specified boot-up drive is corrupt.
Diskette Drives or Types Mismatch Error—Run Setup	The type of diskette drive installed in the system is different from the CMOS definition. Run the CMOS setup program and enter the correct drive type.
Display Switch Is Set Incorrectly or **Display Switch Not Proper**	Many motherboards have a jumper or switch that specifies a monochrome or color video board. Check the jumper or switch and correct its position.
Display Type Has Changed Since Last Boot	Since the last system shutdown, the display has been changed. Run the CMOS setup program and reconfigure the display, if possible.
DMA Error or **DMA #1 Error** or **DMA #2 Error**	There is an error in the first DMA channel on the motherboard. This could be caused by a peripheral device. If the problem still exists, replace the motherboard.
DMA Bus Timeout	A device has driven the bus signal for more than 7.8 microseconds. Troubleshoot all expansion cards (remove them and try to isolate the failure).
DMA Error	There is an error within the DMA controller on the motherboard. Replace the motherboard.
EISA CMOS Checksum Failure	The checksum for EISA CMOS is bad, or the battery is bad.
EISA CMOS Inoperational	A read/write failure occurred in extended CMOS RAM. The battery may be bad.
EISA Configuration Checksum Error	The EISA nonvolatile RAM checksum is incorrect or cannot correctly read the EISA slot. Run the EISA Configuration utility. Either the EISA nonvolatile memory has become corrupt or the slot has been configured incorrectly. Also make sure the card is installed firmly in the slot. When this error appears, the system will boot in ISA mode, which allows you to run the EISA Configuration utility.

continued

TABLE C.14 *continued*

EISA Configuration Is Not Complete	The slot configuration information stored in the EISA nonvolatile memory is incomplete. When this error appears, the system will boot in ISA mode, which allows you to run the EISA Configuration utility. Run the EISA Configuration utility.
Error Encountered Initializing Hard Drive	The hard drive cannot be initialized. Be sure the adapter/controller is installed correctly and that all cables are correctly and firmly attached. Also make sure the correct hard drive type is selected in Setup.
Error Initializing Hard Drive Controller	Cannot initialize the controller card. Make sure the card is correctly and firmly seated in the system board. Be sure the correct hard drive type is selected in Setup. Also check to see if any jumpers need to be set on the hard drive.
Expansion Board Disabled at Slot X	The expansion board NMI was generated from slot X.
Expansion Board Not Ready at Slot X	AMI BIOS cannot find the expansion board in slot X. Verify that the board is in the correct slot and is seated properly.
Fail-Safe Timer NMI	A fail-safe timer NMI has been generated.
Fail-Safe Timer NMI Inoperational	Devices that depend on the fail-safe NMI timer are not operating correctly.
FDD Controller Failure	Check floppy drive CMOS settings. If the problem still exists, check the floppy drive cable, drive power connector, floppy drive card, and floppy drive.
Floppy Disk Controller Resource Conflict	The floppy disk controller has requested a resource (I/O address, IRQ, DMA, or memory address) that is already in use. Trying changing the resources used by the plug-and-play system.
Floppy Disk Cntrlr Error or No Cntrlr Present	Check floppy drive CMOS settings. If the problem still exists, check the floppy drive cable, drive power connector, floppy drive card, and floppy drive.
Floppy Disk(s) Fail	Check floppy drive CMOS settings. If the problem still exists, check the floppy drive cable, drive power connector, floppy drive card, and floppy drive.
Gate A20 Failure	The Gate-A20 portion (21st address line used to access memory above 1 MB) of the keyboard controller has failed. Check the XT/AT switch on the keyboard and keyboard. Make sure the RAM chips are seated properly. Replace the keyboard controller or entire motherboard.
Hard Disk Install Failure	Check hard drive CMOS settings and the hard drive configuration. If the problem still exists, check the hard drive cable, drive power connector, hard drive controller, and hard drive.
Hard Disk(s) Diagnosis Fail	The system may run specific disk diagnostic routines. This message appears if one or more hard disks returns an error when the diagnostics run.
HDD Controller Failure	Check hard drive CMOS settings and the hard drive configuration. If the problem still exists, check the hard drive cable, drive power connector, and hard drive.
ID Information Mismatch for Slot X	The ID of the EISA expansion board in slot X does not match the ID in CMOS RAM.
INTR #1 Error	Interrupt channel 1 has failed the POST test. Check expansion cards for IRQs 0–7.
INTR #2 Error	Interrupt channel 2 has failed the POST test. Check expansion cards for IRQs 8–15.
Invalid Boot Diskette	The BIOS can read the disk in floppy drive A but it cannot boot from it. Try another bootable floppy disk or check the floppy drive, cable, or controller card.
Invalid Configuration Information for Slot X	The configuration information for EISA board X is not correct. Run the ECU.
Invalid EISA Configuration	The nonvolatile memory containing EISA configuration information was programmed incorrectly or has become corrupt. Rerun the EISA Configuration utility to correctly program the memory. When this error occurs, the system will boot in ISA mode, which allows you to run the EISA Configuration utility.
K/B Interface Error	The keyboard is not plugged in correctly, the keyboard cable is bad, the keyboard is bad, or the motherboard has to be replaced.
Keyboard Error	The keyboard is not plugged in correctly, the keyboard cable is bad, the keyboard is bad, or the motherboard has to be replaced.
Keyboard Error or no Keyboard Present	The keyboard is not plugged in correctly, the keyboard cable is bad, the keyboard is bad, or the motherboard has to be replaced.

TABLE C.14   *continued*

Keyboard Is Locked...Unlock It	Unlock the keyboard. In addition, make sure there are no objects resting on the keyboard.
Memory Address Error at XXXX or **Memory Parity Error at XXXX**	Indicates a memory address error at XXXX location. Use the location along with the memory map for the system to find and replace the bad memory chips.
Memory Size Has Changed Since Last Boot	Memory has been added or removed since the last boot. In EISA mode, use the EISA Configuration utility to reconfigure the memory configuration. In ISA mode, enter Setup and enter the new memory size in the memory fields if possible.
Memory Test Fail	If POST detects an error during memory testing, additional information appears giving specifics about the type and location of the memory error.
Memory Verify Error at XXXX	Indicates an error verifying a value already written to memory. Use the location along with the system's memory map to locate the bad chip(s).
Non-System Disk or Disk Error. Replace and Strike Any Key When Ready.	If you are trying to boot from the hard drive, make sure there is no disk in drive A and make sure that drive C has the necessary boot files. If you are trying to boot from the floppy drive, make sure that the floppy drive has the necessary boot files.
No ROM Basic	There is nothing to boot from. (i.e., the system cannot find an operating system). Be certain that a bootable disk is defined in the CMOS setup program and that you have the correct CMOS parameters. In addition, make sure that you have an active partition.
NVRAM Checksum Error, NVRAM Cleared	The Extended System Configuration Data (ESCD), part of the plug-and-play system, was reinitialized because of a NVRAM checksum error. Try rerunning the ISA Configuration utility (ICU). If the problem still exists, replace the NVRAM IC or replace the motherboard.
NVRAM Data Invalid, NVRAM Cleared	Invalid data has been found in the ESCD, part of the plug-and-play system and has been automatically cleared. Try rebooting the system.
Off Board Parity Error	There is a parity error with memory installed in an expansion slot at address XXXX (hex). Make sure the RAM chip is seated properly. If the problem still exists, replace the RAM chip or motherboard.
Offending Address Not Found	This message is used in conjunction with the "I/O Channel Check" and "RAM Parity Error" messages when the segment that has caused the problem cannot be isolated.
Offending Segment	This message is used in conjunction with the "I/O Channel Check" and "RAM Parity Error" messages when the segment that has caused the problem cannot be isolated.
On Board Parity Error	There is a parity error with memory on the motherboard at address XXXX (hex). ("On Board" specifies that the memory is not on an expansion board, but rather is located on the motherboard physically). Possibly correctable with software from the motherboard manufacturer. In addition, check for viruses since some viruses cause parity errors.
Override Enabled—Defaults Loaded	If the system cannot boot using the current CMOS configuration, the BIOS can override the current configuration with a set of BIOS defaults designed for the most stable, minimal-performance system operations.
Parallel Port Resource Conflict	The parallel port has requested a resource (I/O address, IRQ, DMA, or memory address) that is already in use. Trying changing the resources used by the plug-and-play system.
Parity Error	There is a parity error with memory somewhere in the system. Make sure the RAM chip is seated properly. If the problem still exists, replace the RAM chip or motherboard.
PCI I/O Port Conflict	Two devices requested the same I/O address. Try changing the I/O address of one of the devices.
PCI IRQ Conflict	Two devices requested the same IRQ. Try changing the IRQ of one of the devices.
PCI Memory Conflict	Two devices requested the same memory resource. Try changing the memory required by one of the devices.
Press F1 to Disable NMI, F2 to Reboot	When BIOS detects a nonmaskable interrupt condition during boot, this will allow you to disable the NMI and continue to boot, or you can reboot the system with the NMI enabled.
Primary Boot Device Not Found	The designated primary boot device (hard drive, floppy drive, CD-ROM, Zip drive, or LS-120 drive) could not be found. Check the installation and configuration of each boot device.

TABLE C.14 *continued*

Primary IDE-Controller Resource Conflict	The primary IDE controller has requested a resource (I/O address, IRQ, DMA, or memory address) that is already in use. Try to free the resource.
Primary Input Device Not Found	The primary input device (usually the keyboard) could not be found. Check the installation and configuration of the input device, including making sure the input device is enabled in the CMOS setup program.
Primary Master Hard Disk Fail	Check the hard drive CMOS settings and hard drive configuration. If the problem still exists, check the hard drive cable, drive power connector, and hard drive.
Primary Slave Hard Disk Fail	Check the hard drive CMOS settings and hard drive configuration. If the problem still exists, check the hard drive cable, drive power connector, and hard drive.
RAM Parity Error—Checking for Segment	Indicates a parity error in Random Access Memory. Make sure the RAM chip is seated properly. If the problem still exists, replace the RAM chip or motherboard.
Secondary IDE-Controller Resource Conflict	The secondary IDE controller has requested a resource (I/O address, IRQ, DMA, or memory address) that is already in use. Try to free the resource.
Secondary Master Hard Disk Fail	Check the hard Drive CMOS settings and hard drive configuration. If the problem still exists, check the hard drive cable, drive power connector, hard drive.
Secondary Slave Hard Disk Fail	Check the hard drive CMOS settings and hard drive configuration. If the problem still exists, check the hard drive cable, drive power connector, and hard drive.
Should Be Empty but EISA Board Found	A valid board ID was found in a slot that was configured as having no board ID. Run the EISA Configuration utility.
Should Have EISA Board but Not Found	The board installed is not responding to the ID request, or no board ID has been found in the indicated slot. Run the EISA Configuration utility.
Static Device Resource Conflict or **System Board Device Resource Conflict**	A legacy card has requested a resource (I/O address, IRQ, DMA, or memory address) that is already in use. Try reconfiguring the expansion card or try freeing the resources needed by the card.

Appendix D
Operating System Error Codes

TABLE D.1   DOS/Command line error messages

Access denied	You or a program are trying to change a file that is read-only or is already in use by another program. If the file is read-only, you can shut off the read-only attribute by using the ATTRIB command.
Bad command or file name	You entered an invalid command at the command prompt or within a batch file. Make sure the command is spelled correctly, the executable file is present, and that you are in the directory of the executable file or that you have a correct path to the directory of the executable file.
Bad or missing command interpreter	During boot-up, the command interpreter (usually COMMAND.COM) can't be found or is corrupted. Using another disk, copy a good current version of COMMAND.COM to the boot device.
Bad or missing filename	The device driver specified in the CONFIG.SYS file was not found. Check the path specified in the CONFIG.SYS file, make sure the filename was spelled correctly, and make sure that the file is in the specified directory.
Batch file missing	A batch file was running and was either deleted, renamed or moved.
Current drive is no longer valid	The system prompt, which includes the current drive or the current path, could not show the drive that you asked for. For example, if you changed to a floppy drive without a floppy disk, you would eventually get a "Current Drive Is No Longer Valid" error message. At this point, you can change to a valid drive letter.
Data error reading drive x:	DOS was unable to read some of the data on the disk. Run SCANDISK on the disk. If the problem cannot be corrected, try to copy the data to another disk and throw the disk away.
Disk boot failure	During boot-up, IO.SYS or MSDOS.SYS could not be loaded. Boot with another disk and use the SYS command to recopy the files.
Disk unsuitable for system disk	When formatting a disk, FORMAT detected one or more bad sectors on the boot area of the disk.
Divide overflow	A program tried to divide by 0. This usually indicates a faulty software program. Contact the software manufacturer or programmer to load a fix or to find out if you have any other options.

continued

Drive types or diskette types not compatible	When using DISKCOMP and DISKCOPY, you are using two disks that have different sizes and/or different densities.
Duplicate filename or file not found	When using the RENAME command, you tried to change a file name to another filename that already existed for another file.
Error in EXE file	DOS detected an error while executing the instructions in a file with an EXE filename extension. Reboot the computer and try again. If the problem persists, use another copy of the program or reinstall the program.
Error loading operating systems	This error occurs during boot-up from a hard drive. It indicates that the operating system could not be loaded. Try rebooting the computer. If the problem still persists, replace the boot files using the SYS command from a bootable floppy. In addition, check the hard drive for viruses, run SCANDISK, and check for hard drive failure.
Error reading (or writing) partition table	DOS could not read a hard drive's partition because it is corrupt. Run FDISK on the disk and then reformat the drive.
Error reading directory	This error message occurs when using the FORMAT command. DOS was unable to read the directory because of a corrupt FAT or bad sectors. If the error occurs on a floppy disk, throw it away. If it occurs on a hard drive, check for viruses, run SCANDISK, and check for hard drive failure.
Extended error	COMMAND.COM has detected an error but cannot show you the error message because COMMAND.COM is missing from the disk.
FCB unavailable reading (writing) drive x:	A program using file control blocks (FCB) attempted to open more file control blocks than were specified with the FCBS= command. The FCBS= command is needed for programs made for DOS 1.0.
File allocation table bad, drive d—abort, retry, fail?	DOS cannot read part of the file allocation table. Run SCANDISK on the drive and check for viruses.
File creation error	DOS or a program could not create a file in the location specified. If a file already exists with the same name, the file may be read-only. If the problem still occurs, check for viruses and run SCANDISK on the drive.
File not found	A command was issued and DOS can find the instructions but could not find the file specified, meaning DOS cannot find the file in the current directory or the file has an invalid character in it.
General failure reading (writing) device	An error occurred when DOS tried to read or write to a device.
General failure reading (writing) drive x:	An error occurred when DOS tried to read or write to the disk drive.
Illegal device name	DOS does not recognize the device name specified when using the MODE command.
Incorrect DOS version	The program was not made to work with the current version of DOS in RAM loaded during boot-up. Boot with the correct DOS version, use the command made for the current DOS version, or use the SETVER command to change the DOS version table.
Insert disk with \COMMAND.COM in drive D and strike any key when ready	COMMAND.COM had to be temporarily unloaded from RAM. When DOS tried to reload it, COMMAND.COM was not on the floppy disk in the startup drive. Therefore, place a disk with COMMAND.COM in the boot drive.
Insert disk with batch file and strike any key when ready	You were running a batch file from a floppy disk and the floppy disk was removed. Reinsert the disk with the batch file

Insufficient disk space	The disk does not have enough free space to hold the file being written or copied.
Insufficient memory	The computer does not have enough free RAM, usually conventional memory, to execute the program or command.
Internal stack overflow, system halted	Your program used all of the stacks assigned or exceeded the size of the stacks. If this problem keeps recurring, increase the number of stacks and the size of the stacks using the STACKS command in the CONFIG.SYS file.
Invalid COMMAND.COM in drive D: or **Invalid COMMAND.COM, system halted**	DOS tried to reload COMMAND.COM from the disk in drive D and found that the file was from a different version of DOS. Insert a disk with the correct version of COMMAND.COM or copy the correct COMMAND.COM to the correct place.
Invalid directory	The directory that you are trying to go into does not exist.
Invalid disk change— abort, retry, fail?	A floppy disk was changed while a program had open files to be written to the floppy disk. Place the correct disk in the disk drive and press R to retry.
Invalid disk change reading (writing) drive x:	You have removed a disk that the operating system needs access to. This usually occurs with removable media, such as floppy disks.
Invalid drive in search path	You specified an invalid disk drive name in the PATH command, or a disk drive you named is nonexistent.
Invalid drive specification	DOS does not know what drive you are trying to go to, such as the Z: drive; if the drive does not exist, then you will get this error message.
Invalid media or track 0 bad—disk unusable	The disk that you are trying to format may be damaged. Try to perform an unconditional format. If the problem still exists, throw the disk away.
Invalid media type reading (writing) drive x:	The boot sector or the file allocation table (FAT) of the disk contains invalid information, making the disk unusable.
Invalid partition table	The operating system detected a problem in the hard drive's partition information. Try to correct the problem with FDISK.
Invalid path	The path contains illegal characters, the path name has more than 63 characters, or a directory name within the path is misspelled or does not exist.
Invalid path or file name	You gave a directory name or file name that does not exist, specified the wrong directory name, or mistyped a name.
Invalid STACK parameters	The STACK command in the CONFIG.SYS has the wrong syntax.
Lock violation reading (writing) drive x:	With a file-sharing program such as SHARE.EXE or network software loaded, a program attempted to access a locked file.
Memory allocation error. Cannot load COMMAND, system halted.	A program destroyed the area where DOS keeps track of memory. Restart DOS.
Missing operating system	The DOS hard disk partition entry is marked as active, but the DOS partition does not contain a copy of DOS. Try to use the SYS command on the drive or format the drive as a bootable drive.
No room for system on destination disk	There is not enough disk space to hold the system files, or the root directory is full.
No system on default drive	The SYS command cannot find the system files. Insert a bootable disk.

continued

Nonsystem disk or disk error. Replace and strike any key when ready.	Your disk does not contain IO.SYS and MSDOS.SYS or a read error occurred when you started the system. If you are trying to boot from the hard drive, make sure that there is no disk in drive A and make sure that drive C has the necessary boot files. If you are trying to boot from the floppy drive, make sure that the floppy drive has the necessary boot files.
Not enough memory	The computer does not have enough free RAM, usually conventional memory, to execute the program or command.
Not ready reading (or writing) drive x:	An error occurred when DOS tried to read or write to the disk drive.
Not ready reading (writing) drive x:	The disk isn't inserted properly, the floppy disk drive is not closed on 5¼″ disk drives, or there is a problem with the disk. If there is a problem with the disk, run SCANDISK on the disk or throw the disk away.
Out of environment space	There isn't enough room in the current environment to add the environment variables by using the PATH, PROMPT, and SET commands.
Out of memory	The computer does not have enough free RAM, usually conventional memory, to execute the program or command.
Parse error	COMMAND.COM has detected an error but cannot tell you the normal error message because the floppy disk containing COMMAND.COM is missing.
Path not found	A specified file or directory path does not exist. You may have misspelled the file name or directory name, or you may have omitted a path character (\) between directory names or between the final directory or the filename.
Path too long	You have given a path name that exceeds the DOS 64-character limit, or you omitted a space between a filename parameter.
Program too big to fit in memory	The computer does not have enough free RAM, usually conventional memory, to execute the program or command.
Read fault error reading drive x:	The disk isn't inserted properly, the floppy disk drive is not closed on 5¼″ disk drives, or there is a problem with the disk. If there is a problem with the disk, run SCANDISK on the disk or throw the disk away.
Sector not found reading (writing) drive x: **or** **Seek error reading (writing) drive x:**	The disk drive was unable to find the requested sector on the disk. This error is usually the result of a defective spot on the disk or a defective disk drive.
Sharing violation reading (writing) drive x:	With a file-sharing program such as SHARE.EXE or network software loaded, a program attempted to access a file that is in use by another program.
Source diskette bad or incompatible	The disk you attempted to read during a copy process was damaged or in the wrong format.
Syntax error	You phrased a command improperly by omitting needed information, giving extraneous information, inserting an extra space into a file or path name, or using an incorrect switch.
Target diskette bad or incompatible **or** **Target diskette may be unusable** **or** **Target diskette unusable**	A problem exists with the target disk. The disk is not formatted properly or is defective.

This program requires Microsoft Windows	You tried to run a program at the DOS prompt that needs Microsoft Windows to execute.
Trying to recover allocation unit nnn	A bad allocation unit was found when the FORMAT command executed.
Unable to create destination	The MOVE command was unable to create the destination file. Either the destination disk is too full or the destination in the root directory is full.
Unable to create directory	You or a program could not create a directory because a directory with the same name already exists, the root directory is full, or the directory name has illegal characters or is a device name, such as LPT or PRN.
Unrecognized command in CONFIG.SYS. Error in CONFIG.SYS line nnn	DOS cannot find the file specified in the CONFIG.SYS on line nnn. Check the spelling of the path and file and make sure the file is in the correct directory.
Unrecognized switch	You tried to use a switch that was illegal for the particular internal command.
Unrecoverable read error on drive x side n, track n	DOS was unable to read the data at the specified location on the disk. Try to copy the files to another disk and throw the disk away.
Unrecoverable write error on drive x side n, track n	DOS was unable to write the data at the specified location on the disk. Try to format the disk or throw the disk away.
Write failure, diskette unusable	The disk you are writing to has a bad sector in the boot sector or the FAT. Use SCANDISK to fix it or throw the disk away.
Write fault error writing drive x:	The operating system was unable to write data to the drive. Check to see if the disk is inserted properly in the drive. If the problem still exists, check the disk or the floppy disk drive.
Write fault writing device dev	The operating system could not write data to the device specified. The printer is turned on or online, an external modem is not on, or the cables are not connected properly.
Write protect error writing drive x:	The operating system attempted to write to a disk that is write-protected. If it is a floppy disk, open the write-protect hole or remove the write-protect tab.

Appendix E
Glossary

83-Key Keyboard. A keyboard with 83 keys. It was used with the IBM PC and XT and included 10 function keys on the left side of the keyboard.

101-Key Keyboard. A keyboard with 101 keys, including 12 function keys and separate cursor control keys.

104-Key Keyboard. A keyboard with 104 keys. It is similar to the 101-key keyboard but has a few extra keys used primarily in Windows operating systems.

3D Accelerator Video Cards. Video accelerator cards that can perform many of the complicated calculations associated with three-dimensional (3D) images.

3DNow! Technology. A set of 21 new instructions that use SIMD and other microprocessor enhancements to open the performance bottleneck in the 3D graphics pipeline between the microprocessor and the 3D graphics accelerator card.

80286 Microprocessor. A second-generation microprocessor used in the IBM AT computer. It has a 16-bit word size and 16-bit data bus.

80386DX Microprocessor. A third-generation microprocessor that was the first 32-bit microprocessor used in IBM PCs.

80386SX Microprocessor. A third-generation microprocessor that is a cut-down version of the 80836DX microprocessor. It uses a 32-bit word size and a 16-bit data bus.

80486DX Microprocessor. A fourth-generation microprocessor which is a 32-bit microprocessor with built-in RAM cache and math coprocessor.

80486SX Microprocessor. A fourth-generation microprocessor that is an 80486DX microprocessor without a math coprocessor.

8086 Microprocessor. A first-generation microprocessor. It has a 16-bit word size and 16-bit data bus.

8088 Microprocessor. A first-generation microprocessor used in the IBM PC and IBM XT computers. It has a 16-bit word size and 8-bit data bus.

A20. A microprocessor address line that gives access to the high memory area.

Accelerated Graphics Port (AGP). A spinoff of the PCI slot (based on the PCI 2.1 specification) made exclusively for video cards.

Access Time. The average amount of time it takes to move the read/write head to the requested sector. The sum of seek time and latency period, it is measured in milliseconds (ms).

Active Matrix Displays. A type of LCD display used in notebook computers.

Active Partition. A partition that is marked as the partition to boot from. Therefore, it is expected to have the necessary boot files.

Active Termination. A type of termination that acts as a voltage regulator to maintain a stable voltage through the chain by utilizing the termination power lines to compensate for voltage drops.

Address. A word or number that refers to a storage location or port.

Address bus. A bus that is used to define where the data bus signals are going to or coming from.

Advanced Power Management (APM). A standard that allows the system ROM BIOS (enabled in the CMOS setup program) or software to manage the power consumption of the system.

Aliasing. The distortion introduced when translating from an analog signal to a digital signal and back to an analog signal.

Alternating Current (AC). Current that reverses directions in cycles. Its polarity changes from positive to negative to positive again. The number of complete cycles per second is measured in hertz (Hz).

American Standard Code for Information Interchange (ASCII). An alphanumeric code/character set that represents 256 characters, digits, and symbols.

Amperes (Amps). The rate of current.

Amplitude. (1) The peak voltage of the sine wave. (2) Loudness or intensity.

Analog. Refers to a signal that can take any value within the overall allowable range.

Anode Cap. A flat, circular object resembling a suction cup located on the top of the CRT.

Antistatic Bag. A bag designed to keep electrostatic electricity away from the electronic components inside the bag.

Antivirus Program. A program that detects and/or eliminates computer viruses.

Aperture Grill. Hundreds of fine metal strips that run vertically from the top of a CRT monitor that are used to aim and focus the electron beams.

Applet. An icon.

Application Software. Software that allows a user to input, format, and organize data to create useable information. It is this type of software that allows the user to create a letter, report, budget, chart, graph, or database.

ARC (Advanced RISC Computing) Path. Used to specify the location (partition) of an operating system.

Architecture. The overall design and construction of a computer, software, or network.

ARCnet (Attached Resource Computer Network). A simple, inexpensive, flexible design for small networks. ARCnet networks are connected with a star topology and usually with coaxial cable. ARCnet signals follow a bus design, and the computers use a token-passing scheme to access the network.

Areal Density. A term that describes the physical amount of data that can be held on an area of a disk. It is expressed in bits per square inch and is calculated by multiplying the bit density (bits per inch, or bpi) and the track density (tracks per inch, or tpi).

Arithmetic/Logical Unit (ALU). The calculator part of the microprocessor that follows the instructions of the control unit. It performs mathematical operations such as adding, subtracting, multiplying, and dividing and logical comparisons such as NOT, AND, OR and exclusive-OR.

ASCII. Short for American Standard Code for Information Interchange. A standard that assigns a binary numeric value to letters, numbers, punctuation marks, and control characters.

ASCII Character Set. A character set that consists of the first 128 ASCII characters. The second group of characters (128–255) is known as the extended ASCII character set.

ASCII File. A simple text file that contains characters from only the ASCII character set.

Aspect Ratio. The ratio of the number of horizontal pixels and the number of vertical pixels.

Assembly Language. A low-level programming language that uses mnemonic abbreviations to represent machine operations and storage locations. It makes it possible to program the microprocessor directly without having to use machine language.

Asynchronous. A form of communication that has no synchronization or timer.

AT Attachment Packet Interface (ATAPI). A standard associated with the enhanced IDE standard that allows for CD drives, tape drives, and other storage devices.

AT Command Set. A set of standard instructions used to activate a modem.

AT Computer. (1) A computer with a 286 microprocessor. (2) A computer with a 286 or higher microprocessor.

Attenuation. Refers to loss in signal strength due to resistance, absorption, capacitance, or any characteristic of the transmitting medium.

Attribute. A characteristic or property.

ATX Motherboard. Similar to the Baby-AT motherboard, except the components are placed differently. The slots are parallel to the short side of the board, which allows more space for other components. The microprocessor and RAM are next to the power supply so that the airflow generated by the power supply runs over the microprocessor. Lastly, the ATX motherboard contains integrated I/O port connectors and an integrated PS/2 mouse connector and supports 3.3 volts coming from an ATX power supply.

ATX Power Supply. A type of power supply that blows air into the system directly over the microprocessor (to help cool the microprocessor) and pressurizes the inside of the case (keeping it clean). In addition, it contains software control of the power on/off signal so that it can shut down the system with software and always provides a 5-volt standby signal so that the system can be turned on with the keyboard.

Audio Video Interleave (AVI). A video standard that interleaves video and audio data. AVI files will have a AVI filename extension.

Baby-AT Motherboard. A motherboard that is the same size and has the same dimensions as the IBM XT motherboard.

Backbone. A portion of a network that handles the bulk of the traffic.

Backlit Light. A light used to illuminate LCD screens.

Backup *(noun)*. An extra copy of data. **Back up** *(verb)*. The process of creating a backup.

Backward Compatible. A computer, device, or software that is fully compatible with earlier versions.

Bad Sector. An area on a disk that cannot be used to read or store data.

Bandwidth. The capacity of a computer or communications channel.

Bank. A collection of memory chips that make up a block of memory readable by the processor in a single bus cycle.

Basic Input/Output System (BIOS). Instructions stored in ROM chips that control most of the computer's input/output functions, such as communicating with disks, RAM, and the monitor.

Battery. A device that supplies dc power, usually through chemical means.

Baud Rate. The modulation rate, or the number of times per second that a transmission line changes state.

BEDO RAM. Short for Burst Extended Data Output RAM. RAM faster than EDO RAM because it allows the page-access cycle to be divided into two components. To achieve faster access time, data is read from the memory array at the same time data is being transferred through the data bus. In addition, a counter on the chip is used to keep track of the next address so that sequential data can be accessed faster.

Benchmark. A test that attempts to measure hardware or software performance.

Beta Software. Software that has been released to selected users to test before its official release.

Binary Number System. A simple number system that has only two digits, a zero (0) and a one (1).

Bit. Stands for binary digit, the smallest unit of information on a computer. A single bit can hold only one of two values: 0 or 1.

Bitmap Graphics. A picture that uses dots to form graphic images.

Blackouts. Total power failures.

Boot Disk. A disk that can load the operating system using the A drive.

Boot Sector. A small program that is executed when a computer boots up. Typically, the MBR resides on the first sector of the hard disk.

Boot Sector Virus. A virus that hides or resides in the boot sector of a disk.

Bootstrap Loader. A small program located at the beginning of a disk that locates the first active or bootable partition.

Boot-Up. Also referred to as *booting,* the process of loading or copying the operating system into RAM.

Bridge. A device that connects two local area networks of similar topology or two segments of the same LAN and that divides traffic on a network segment. A bridge will pass information for one particular workstation to a segment but will not pass broadcast traffic.

Brouter. Acts like a router for certain protocols and acts as a bridge for all others.

Brownouts. A drop in power that lasts longer than a sag. A brownout can force the computer to shut down, introduce memory errors, and cause unsaved work to be lost.

Bug. A logical programming error or glitch in hardware or software that causes some sort of problem.

Bug Fix. A release of hardware or software that corrects one or more bugs.

Burndy Connector. The type of connector used in AT power supplies.

Burst Mode. A mode used by many RAM chips and buses by specifying the location of data using the address bus and accessing data sequentially without resetting the address bus, thereby increasing performance.

Bus. A collection of wires through which data or power is transmitted from one part of a computer to another.

Bus Controller. Device used to translate signals between the CPU and the expansion bus.

Bus Interface Unit (BIU). The part of the microprocessor that links it to the rest of the computer.

Bus Mastering. When an expansion card with its own processor takes temporary control of data and the address bus to move information from one point to another. Consequently, the PC is faster.

Bus Port. A port that connects a mouse to an expansion card specifically made for a mouse.

Byte. A unit of storage consisting of eight bits that can hold a single character.

Cache Hit. The finding of requested information in the cache.

Cache Memory. A special ultrafast area of memory, usually made up of SRAM, that acts as a buffer between the microprocessor and the slower RAM.

Cache Miss. The failure of the system to find the required data in the cache.

Caliper. The thickness of paper, which is usually expressed in thousandths of an inch.

Capacitor. A device that stores electric charge (electrons). The amount of charge that a capacitor can hold is measured in farads (F).

CardBus. A 32-bit PC card or slot running at 33 MHz used in notebook computers.

Carpal Tunnel Syndrome. A wrist or hand injury caused by a person holding his or her wrist stiff for long periods. This repetitive stress injury makes the nerves in the wrist swell, causing great pain.

Case. The box that most of the computer components rest in. It is designed to protect these components.

Cathode Ray Tube (CRT). A type of monitor that consists of an electronic screen lined with a phosphorescent material. When an electron gun shoots electrons at the phosphorescent material, the material glows as it is struck.

CD-Digital Audio (CD-DA). Standard audio compact disks.

CD-E (Erasable). A type of CD that can be written to more than once.

CD-ROM (Compact Disk Read-Only Memory). Similar to a floppy disk or hard drive, a CD-ROM stores large quantities of data. The contents of a CD-ROM cannot be changed or erased.

Central Processing Unit (CPU). *See* Microprocessor.

Centronics Connector. A standard interface for connecting printers and other parallel devices.

Checksum. A method of calculating a sum from a set of values that is used for error detection.

Chipset. Chips and other components on the motherboard that allow different PC components to communicate with each other, including the microprocessor. It consists of the bus controllers, peripheral controllers, memory controllers, cache controllers, clocks, and timers.

CHS Addressing. An addressing mode that uses the cylinders, heads, and sectors to define locations on a disk.

Circuit. The conductor, such as a wire or metal trace, that connects the voltage source (power supply or battery) and electronic components. Electrons leave the voltage source through the path of least resistance to a common return known as *ground.*

Clamping speed. The amount of time it takes for a surge protector to respond to overvoltages.

Clamping voltage. The voltage that causes a surge protector to react.

Client. A computer on a network that requests services.

Client Software. Software that allows communications with a network.

Client/Server Network. A network that has dedicated servers and clients.

Clipboard. In Windows, a temporary storage location in RAM that holds information so that it can be copied or moved (cut) from one place to another.

Clock Speed. The speed at which the microprocessor executes instructions.

Clone. Hardware that is identical to the original of which it is a copy.

Cluster. The smallest amount of disk space addressable on a disk. It is made up of one or more sectors.

CMOS Battery. The battery found on the motherboard that is used to maintain the CMOS RAM.

CMOS RAM. A special form of RAM that uses a battery to maintain power while the computer is off. The CMOS RAM is used to hold important hardware configuration information, such as the size of the hard drive and the amount of the RAM.

CMOS Setup Program. Software, usually kept in the system ROM BIOS, used to change the configuration options contained in the CMOS RAM.

CMYK Color Model. A method of printing in four basic colors; cyan (greenish blue), magenta (deep purplish red), yellow, and black.

Coaxial Cable (Coax). A wire that has a solid copper core surrounded by insulation, a braided metal shielding, and an outer cover. It is called *coaxial* cable because the copper wire and the braided metal shielding share the same axis, or center.

Coercitivity. A term that describes the strength of the magnetic field used to store data on platters. Its measurement is in oersteds.

Cold Boot. Reloading a computer's operating system by turning the power to the computer off and then back on.

Color Depth. The amount of information that determines the color of a pixel.

Color Graphics Adapter (CGA). The first color graphics video card. It supported several modes, including a 16-color 80 × 25 character text mode, and could display up to 16 colors in several resolutions (320 × 200, 640 × 200, and 160 × 200).

Compact Disk (CD). A 4.72-inch encoded platter written to and read by a laser provided by a CD drive and similar to a CD used in a stereo system. CDs can store large amounts of information.

Compiler. A program that translates source code written in a programming language into object code.

Complementary Metal-Oxide Semiconductor (CMOS). Widely used IC chips that require less power than TTL chips.

Complex Instruction Set Computer (CISC). A set of over 200 instructions used by many microprocessors.

Compressed Volume File (CVF). A hidden file that simulates a disk in compressed format.

Compression and Decompression (codec). A process that allows files to take up less space and perform better because there is less data to process.

Computer. A machine composed of electronic devices used to process data.

Conductor. A material in which current can flow easily. Most metals, including silver and copper, are good conductors.

Constant Angular Velocity (CAV). The spinning of a drive at the same rate. Therefore, when reading the outside of the disk, where there is more data, the drive will have a higher transfer rate than when it is reading the inside of the disk.

Constant Linear Velocity (CLV). A rate of speed used by compact disk drives. Because the outer tracks hold more information than the inner tracks, the platter spins faster on the inner tracks than it does on the outer tracks to keep a constant reading rate for data.

Continuity Check. The verifying by a measuring device that a conductor or similar device has no resistance (0 ohms).

Control Bus. A bus that coordinates the data transfer between the microprocessor and another device.

Control Panel. A graphical tool to configure the Windows environment and hardware devices.

Control Unit. A clocked logic circuit that is part of the microprocessor and that controls the entire chip, including the ALU. It translates and follows the instructions contained in an external program (such as the ROM BIOS, the operating system, or application software) and keeps track of which step of the program is being executed.

Controller. A device that controls the transfer of data from a computer to a peripheral device and vice versa.

Conventional Memory. The first 640 KB of RAM. It is also known as *lower memory* and *base memory*.

Convergence. A term used to describe the clarity and sharpness of each pixel. It is based on the color monitor's capability for focusing the three colored electron beams into a single point.

Cooperative Multitasking. A type of multitasking that is based on applications that cooperate with each other.

Corona Wire. A wire used to transfer a positive or negative charge. It is usually found in printers.

Cross-Link File. A cluster used by two or more files.

Current. The rate of flow of electrons (electricity), which is measured in amps (A).

Current Directory. The active directory currently being viewed.

Cyclic Redundancy Check (CRC). An error-checking method that checks an entire block of data by performing a mathematical calculation on the data to be sent before and after.

Cylinder. Tracks stacked on top of each other.

Daisy Chain. A hardware configuration in which devices are connected to one another in a series.

Daisy Wheel Printers. Impact printers that use a ball or wheel imprinted with predefined characters.

Data. The raw facts, numbers, letters, or symbols that the computer processes into meaningful information. Data is normally considered the most important part of the computer.

Data Bus. A bus that carries instructions and data into and out of the CPU and other components.

Data Carrier Equipment (DCE). A device that communicates with a data terminal equipment (DTE) device, usually through a serial port.

Data Terminal Equipment (DTE). A device that controls data flowing to or from a computer, usually through a serial port.

Database. A program that allows users to work with files of related data. The data can be organized and retrieved quickly.

Decibel (dB). A unit for measuring the loudness of sound.

De Facto Standard. A standard for hardware or software that has been accepted by the industry just because it is the most common.

De Jure Standard. A standard that has been dictated by an appointed committee.

Decimal Number System. The most commonly used numbering system, having 10 different possible digits (base 10).

Degausser. A special demagnetizing device that is moved over the outside surface of the CRT to eliminate magnetic fields.

Demand Paging. Information that is swapped between the RAM and disk (virtual memory) only on the demand of the microprocessor.

Desktop. The visible elements of Windows that defines the limits of the graphic environment.

Desktop Case. A case that lies flat on the desktop.

Desktop Computers. Computers that are small enough to fit on a desk but are too big to carry around.

Desktop Publishing. Software that allows the user to combine graphics and text to create newsletters, reports, and other documents.

Device Driver. Software that controls how an operating system and applications interact with specific items of hardware.

Differential Backup. A backup that copies only the files created since the last full backup.

Digital. A term used to describe any device that represents values in the form of binary digits.

Digital Audio Tape (DAT). A small tape that can store large amounts of data.

Digital Multimeter (DMM). A device that combines several measuring devices, including a voltmeter and an ohmmeter.

Digital Signal. A signal that consists of discrete (predetermined and constant) values.

Digital Signal Processor (DSP). A processor specifically designed to manipulate large volumes of digital data.

Digital Video Disk (DVD). The newest type of compact disk, having the capability of storing massive computer applications, such as a full multimedia encyclopedia or a feature-length movie, on one compact disk.

Digitizing. The process of converting a signal into data that the computer can understand.

DIP Switches. Small devices consisting of 4 to 12 on/off switches.

Direct Current (DC). Current that flows in only one direction and has a fixed polarity (positive or negative).

Direct Memory Address (DMA). Channels used to move large amounts of data into RAM without any direction from the microprocessor, which permits the CPU to keep working, making the system run faster.

Directory. A special kind of file used to organize other files into a hierarchical structure. It is sometimes referred to a *folder.*

DirectX. An application programming interface (API) developed by Microsoft that enables programs to write programs that access hardware features of a computer without knowing exactly what hardware is installed on the machine.

Disk Cache. A portion of RAM used to speed up access to data on a disk.

Disk Compression. A process that expands the amount of space on a disk.

Disk Drive. A device that reads and writes magnetic or optical disks.

Disk Duplexing. A hard drive duplicated on another hard drive that is connected to another controller card so that it can provide fault tolerance.

Disk Mirroring. A hard drive duplicated on another hard drive that is usually connected to the same controller card so that it can provide fault tolerance.

Display Power Management System (DPMS). A standard introduced by the Video Electronics Standard Association (VESA). DPMS allows the monitor to go into standby mode (which uses less power than the normal operational state) and suspend/shut down mode (which turns the monitor off) during periods of inactivity.

Divide Error. A software glitch when a program tries to divide a number by zero.

Domain. A group of computers and devices on a network that are administrated as a unit with common rules and procedures.

DOS. *See* Microsoft DOS.

Dot Pitch. The distance between pixels.

Dot-Matrix Printers. Impact printers that use a series of pins to form letters and images.

Downloading. A term that describes copying a file from a remote computer to one's own computer.

DRAM. Short for Dynamic RAM. The storage cells consist of a tiny solid-state capacitor and a MOS transistor.

Dual In-Line Memory Module (DIMM). A type of RAM closely resembling SIMMs. A small circuit board consisting of several soldered DIP chips. To connect to the motherboard, the SIMM has a row of tin or gold metal plates (contacts) along the bottom of the module.

Dual In-Line Package (DIP). Chips, resembling a bug with many legs, that lie horizontally with metal leads extending down from the two long sides. The metal leads are inserted directly into the circuit board's DIP sockets.

Dvorak Layout. A keyboard layout with vowels in the home row under the left hand and the most commonly used consonants in the home row under the right hand.

Dynamic Data Exchange (DDE). A method of data exchange that allows users to copy data between applications while maintaining a link. Whenever data is changed at the source, it is also changed at the target.

Dynamic Link Library (DLL). Files that include sets of instructions and/or data that can be accessed at any time used to modularize Windows.

EDO RAM. Short for Extended Data Output RAM. It uses a two-stage pipeline, which lets the memory controller read data off the chip while it is being reset for the next operation.

Electrically Erasable Programmable Read-Only Memory (EEPROM). Pronounced double-E PROM. A special type of programmable ROM chip that can be erased with higher voltage than normal. EEPROM chips can be erased only a set number of times.

Electricity. The flow of free electrons from one atom to another.

Electromagnetic Interference (EMI). Any electromagnetic signal released by an electronic device that may disrupt the operation and performance of another device.

Electronic mail (e-mail). Messages, pictures, and files sent over the Internet, network, or telephone system.

Electrophoto (EP) Process. The process used by laser printers to form images on paper.

Electrosensitive Printers. A printer that uses special color paper coated with a thin layer of aluminum. Characters and images are formed by selectively removing the aluminum using electricity.

Electrostatic Discharge (ESD). Electrostatic electricity easily generated by a person that could damage electronic components.

Electrostatic Electricity. An electrical charge at rest created by friction and separation.

Electrostatic Mat. A mat that absorbs static electricity, used while repairing a computer.

Emergency Repair Disk (ERD). A disk used to reconstruct the Windows NT system files and the Registry.

Encoding. The method or pattern used to represent bits.

Enhanced 386 mode. A Windows 3.XX operating mode made for the 386 computer. It allows multiple DOS and Windows applications to run at the same time and provides direct access to extended memory and virtual memory.

Enhanced Graphics Adapter (EGA). The first successful color video system. It included a 16-color 80 × 25 text mode and a 16-color 640 × 350 graphics mode.

Enhanced IDE. An enhanced version of the IDE interface allowing up to four devices to be connected, including hard drives, CD-ROM drives, and tape drives.

Enhanced Parallel Port (EPP). A fast parallel port.

Enterprise WAN. A WAN that is owned by one company or organization.

Erasable Programmable Read-Only Memory (EPROM). A special type of programmable ROM that can be erased by shining ultraviolet light through a clear window at the top of the chip. Once erased, it can be reprogrammed.

Ergonomics. The science concerned with designing safe and comfortable machines for humans.

Error Correction Code (ECC). A form of error control that uses extra bits to check the accuracy of the data bits. Different from parity, ECC can also correct some errors.

ESD Wrist Strap. A strap worn around the wrist to reduce electrostatic discharge by a person.

ESDI Interface. Short for Enhanced Small Drive Interface. An interface used by early hard drives that was designed to replace the ST-506 interface.

Ethernet. A network protocol that uses coaxial or 10Base-T cabling with carrier sense multiple access with collision detection (CSMA/CD) to connect a network. While the cable connects the computers in a bus or a star configuration, the signal pathway is always a bus.

Execution Unit. Part of the microprocessor that does the actual processing of data.

Expanded Memory (EMS). The first memory that allowed users to break the 1 MB boundary. The expanded memory specification is known as the LIM (Lotus/Intel/Microsoft) specification.

Expansion Card. Circuit board inserted into the motherboard to expand the PC. It is sometimes referred to as a *daughter board*.

Expansion Slot. Also known as the I/O bus, it is called an *expansion* slot because it expands the system by allowing circuit boards, called *expansion cards,* to be inserted. It extends the reach of the microprocessor so that it can communicate with peripheral devices.

Extended Capabilities Port (ECP). A fast parallel port.

Extended ISA (EISA). A 32-bit expansion slot introduced to compete with the MCA slot. The EISA slot is no longer produced.

Extended Memory (XMS). The memory above 1 MB (FFFFFH) found on today's newer machines (386 and above).

Extended Partition. A type of partition created after the primary partition and that can be divided into one or more logical drives.

External Cache. A form of RAM cache often found on the motherboard but sometimes found in the microprocessor. External cache is sometimes referred to as *secondary cache* or *level 2* (L2) cache.

External Commands. Commands executed at the prompt that reside in files on a disk.

Fast Page Mode RAM (FPM RAM). A special form of DRAM that tries to reduce the number of wait states by accessing data in the same row (sometimes referred to as a page) as the preceding data.

FAT32. An enhanced version of the FAT structure that allows for long filenames, drives up to two terabytes, and has the ability to use disk space more efficiently.

Fax. Short for facsimile transmission. A fax machine digitizes the text and pictures in a document and sends the data over a telephone line.

Field Replaceable Unit (FRU). Any PC component that can be replaced without any special skills or tools.

File Allocation Table (FAT). (1) An index used to list which file is located in which cluster. (2) A type of file system used primarily with DOS.

File Attribute. A characteristic or property of a file.

File Infector Virus. A virus that resides in or attaches to a file.

File Manager (WINFILE.EXE). A Windows 3.XX graphical utility used to manage disks, directories, and files.

File Transfer Protocol (FTP). A common protocol (part of the TCP/IP protocol suite) that specializes in transferring files from one computer to another. It is found on the Internet.

Filtering. The process that smoothes out the ripple of rectified voltage.

Finish. Texture on the front surface of paper.

FireWire. *See* IEEE 1394.

Flash RAM. A form of ROM chip that can be reprogrammed using the normal voltage found in the PC by running a BIOS update program.

Flatbed Scanner. A scanner that has a flat bed of glass. The paper to be scanned is laid face down on top of the glass.

Floating-Point Number. A number with a decimal point or a number that includes exponents.

Floppy Disk Controller. Electronic interface used to connect the floppy drives to the rest of the computer.

Floppy Disk Drive. A drive that reads floppy disks.

Floppy Disks. Small, thin, plastic disks that are used to store files for long-term usage. They are inserted into floppy disk drives. The storage capacity of a floppy disk is very limited but it can be easily transported to another computer.

Font. A collection of characters (letters, numerals, symbols, and punctuation marks) that have common characteristics.

Forced Perfect Terminator (FPT). A form of terminating resistor that attempts to remove reflections by automatically matching the line impedance, thus allowing "perfect" termination.

Form Factor. Physical dimensions and sizes, usually defined for motherboards, power supplies, and cases.

Frame Buffer. *See* Video Memory.

Free System Resources (FSR). The amount of memory available to Windows, usually expressed as a percentage.

Frequency. The rate of a vibration.

Full Backup. A backup that backs up all files on a disk.

Full Duplex. A form of data transfer in which data can travel in both directions at the same time.

Fuse. A protective device that melts when a circuit has too much current, causing an open in the circuit pathway.

Fuser. A device used in printers and copy machines to melt the toner into the paper.

Game Port. A port that is used to connect joysticks, paddles, and flight sticks.

Gateway. A combination of hardware and software that links two different types of networks.

General Protection Fault (GPF). a condition signifying that something unexpected has happened within a Windows environment. It is usually caused by a program that tried to access a memory area that belongs to another program or an application trying to pass an invalid parameter to another program.

Giga (G). A prefix indicating a billion (1,000,000,000). In computers, a giga indicates 1,024 megabytes, such as in a gigabyte (GB).

Glidepad. A pointing device in the form of a flat square pad. As a finger touches the glidepad, transducers under the pad sense the body capacitance. As the finger moves, the pad generates electrical signals, which move the mouse pointer.

Global WAN. A WAN that is not owned by any one company and usually crosses national boundaries.

Graphical User Interface (GUI). A program interface that takes advantage of the computer's graphics capabilities to make the program easier to use. It usually uses a mouse pointer and icons.

Green PC. A PC that is made to conserve power.

Ground. A reference point in electronic circuits.

Half Duplex. A form of communication in which data can travel in both directions, one direction at a time.

Halftones. In printing, a method of simulating shades of gray by assembling patterns of black and white dots.

Handheld scanner. A scanner that is held in the hand and is physically moved from one end of a document to the other.

Handshake. A form of control between two devices.

Hard Card. A hard disk drive and controller on a single expansion card.

Hard Disk/Hard Drive. The principal device for storing programs and data. It usually has a large capacity and is much quicker than a floppy disk drive. Because it usually cannot be removed from the computer, the hard disk is sometimes called *fixed disk.*

Hardware. The physical components that make up the personal computer. If an item can be touched and carried, it is hardware.

Hardware Interrupt (IRQ). A signal sent to the Interrupt Controller to signal that a device needs the attention of the microprocessor.

Hayes Command Set. *See* AT Commands.

Head Actuator. The component contained within a disk drive that moves the read-write heads back and forth.

Head Crash. The unexpected collision between the read/write head and the rotating platter that usually results in damage to the platter and/or the read/write head.

Head to Disk Interference (HDI). A small particle, such as dust or cigarette smoke, acting as a boulder between the read/write head and platter, causing physical damage to the read/write head and/or the platter and possibly a grinding noise.

Heap. An area of memory reserved for data that is created at run-time.

Heat Sink. A finned piece of metal clipped or glued to the top of the processor. Since it has more surface area than a flat piece of metal, it dissipates heat faster.

Helical Scan. A method used to record data on tapes. Much like a VCR read/write head, tape backup drives with helical scan use read/write heads mounted at an angle on a cylindrical drum. The tape is partially wrapped around the drum, and as the tape slides across the drum, the read/write heads rotate. As each head approaches the tape, the heads take swipes at the tape, reading or writing the data.

Hercules Graphics Card. A monochrome video card that uses the same monochrome monitor as the MDA video system. It can display in graphics mode with a resolution of 720×350.

Hertz. One clock cycle.

Hexadecimal Number System. A number system that has 16 digits.

High Color. A video system that displays 65,536 different colors. The 65,536 colors use 16 bits to define the color of the pixel.

High Memory Area (HMA). An area of memory that is 64 KB minus 16 bytes, starting at the 1 MB boundary. High memory can be used to access a small part of extended memory while being in real mode.

High Performance File System (HPFS). The file system made for OS/2 that supported long filenames.

High Sierra Standard. The proposed standard for CD-ROM disks from which the ISO-9660 Standard was derived.

High-Level Formatting. The process of writing the file system structure on the disk so that it can be used to store programs and data.

Host. A computer or other device that acts as a computer (such as a network printer connected directly to the network).

Hot-Swappable. A term describing a device that can be connected or disconnected or inserted or removed while the power is on.

HTML. Short for Hypertext Markup Language. A standardized hypertext language used to create a web page.

HTTP. Short for Hypertext Transfer Protocol. A protocol used to manage the links between one hypertext document and another.

Hypertext. A specially marked word or words used to move to another location within the same document or to another document.

I/O Address. An address used to identify an I/O device. The I/O address must be unique.

I/O Bus. *See* Expansion Slot.

IBM Compatible. A computer that is compatible with the IBM PC.

IBM PC. A personal computer made by IBM that set the standard for all personal computers. It consists of an 8088 microprocessor.

IDE. Short for Integrated Drive Electronics. An interface developed as a fast, low-cost hard drive interface.

IEEE 1394. Sometimes known as FireWire, an external port that can connect up to 63 external devices and made for devices that require large amounts of data transfer, such as those related to video devices.

Impact Printers. A printer that transfers ink onto the paper by pressing or striking movable parts against a ribbon and a sheet of paper. Impact printers include daisy wheel or ball printers and dot-matrix printers.

Incremental Backup. A backup that copies only the files that have changed since the last full or incremental backup.

Inductor. A coil of wire that can transfer voltage or current using magnetic fields (without physical contact). It resists the change of current.

Industry Standard Architecture (ISA). A 16-bit expansion first used in the IBM AT and still found on most PCs today. Also known as AT bus.

Initialization Files. A text file with an INI filename extension that contains configuration information for an operating system or an application.

Initialization String. A list of modem AT commands that the communication software will use to initialize and prepare the modem for connection.

Ink-Jet Printer. A nonimpact printer that works by spraying small droplets of ionized ink onto a sheet of paper though a small hole. It is superior to the dot-matrix printer in that it has a better print quality and is much quieter.

Insulator. A poor conductor of electric current used to prevent current where it is not wanted.

Integrated Circuit (IC). A device containing transistors, diodes, resistors, and capacitors in one miniaturized package.

Integrated Services Digital Network (ISDN). Special transmission lines that allow voice, video, and data to be sent using digital telephone lines.

Intel Comparative Microprocessor Performance Index (ICOMP). A test to measure the performance of a PC.

Interlaced Monitor. A screen that redraws in two sweeps as it refreshes every other line. During the first sweep, it refreshes the odd-numbered and lines and during the second sweep refreshes the even-numbered lines.

Interleaving. A process in which two banks work together. When one bank is getting ready for access, the other bank is being accessed.

Internal Cache. A form of RAM cache found inside the microprocessor. It is sometimes referred to as *primary cache* or *Level 1 (L1) cache*. Internal cache is faster than external RAM cache because it is a physical part of the microprocessor.

Internal Commands. Commands performed at the prompt that reside in the RAM (COMMAND.COM).

Internet Service Provider (ISP). A company that provides connection to the Internet.

Interpreter. A program that executes instructions written in a high-level language.

Interrupt. Something that causes the CPU to stop its current task so that it can do another task. Whenever the second task is completed, it will go back to the original task to continue where it left off. Interrupts can be divided into hardware interrupts and software interrupts.

Interrupt Controller. Device that coordinates hardware interrupts (IRQs) so that another device can get the attention of the CPU.

Interrupt Sharing. The ability of devices to share the same interrupt.

Interrupt Vector Table. A table of addresses for specific software routines (interrupt handlers) contained in the RAM or BIOS.

Interruptible Power Supply (UPS). A power supply that includes a battery to maintain power in the event of power fluctuations, including a power outage.

IPX (Internetwork Packet Exchange). A networking protocol suite usually used by the Novell NetWare network operating system.

IrDA Port. A port that connects to a device using infrared light waves (wireless technology). Keyboards, serial port devices (mice and other pointing devices), and parallel port devices have been designed to use IrDA.

ISA Slot. Short for Industry Standard Architecture. An ISA slot is a standardized 16-bit slot introduced with the IBM AT.

ISO-9660 Standard. The standard used for CD-ROM disks.

Joint Photographic Experts Group (JPEG). A picture and movie standard that compresses each frame by eliminating redundant data for each individual image. JPEG offers rates acceptable for nearly full-motion video (30 fps), a compression ratio of 30:1, and easy editing.

Jumper. Sometimes called a *shunt,* a small, plastic-covered metal clip that is used to connect two pins protruding from the motherboard. The jumper (same as an On switch) connects the pins, which closes the circuit and allows current to flow.

Kernel. The central part of an operating system that controls and allocates the machine resources, such as memory, and runs and coordinates software applications.

Keyboard. A device similar to a typewriter by which instructions and data are input to the computer. The keyboard is the main input device.

Keyboard Controller. A chip located on the motherboard that converts the parallel keyboard data and generates an interrupt so that the data can be serviced by the microprocessor.

Keyboard ROM BIOS. ROM BIOS chip located on the motherboard that contains instructions to control the keyboard.

Kilo (K). A prefix indicating a thousand (1,000). In computers, a kilo indicates 1,024, such as in a kilobyte (KB).

Lap Link Cable. A cable used to connect two computers through the computer's parallel port or serial port.

Laser Printer. A nonimpact printer that works like a photocopying machine. It transfers fine toner powder to paper and fixes it in place permanently by heating (fusing) the toner. The laser printer produces extremely high-quality print with a wide range of fonts and graphics. In addition, it is quiet and fast.

Latency Period. The time it takes after the read/write heads move to the requested track for the requested sector to spin underneath the head. The latency period is usually one-half the time of a single revolution of the disk platter. It is measured in milliseconds (ms).

LCD/LED Printer. A printer similar to a laser printer except that it uses liquid crystal or light-emitting diodes instead of laser light.

Legacy Cards. Expansion cards that are not plug and play.

Line Conditioner. A device used to filter out noise and to "fill in" brownouts.

Liquid Crystal (LC). An organic material that has the characteristics of both a liquid and a solid. Although it appears to be a liquid, it has the crystalline molecular structure usually found in solid objects. Essentially, the liquid crystal material is a vast array of rod-shaped molecules. In its normal state, LC is virtually clear, allowing light to pass through it.

Liquid Crystal Display (LCD). A type of monitor that uses liquid crystal. It is mostly used in notebook computers.

Load. (1) To install something, such as a program, from disk or CD-ROM. (2) To copy a program from a disk into RAM so that the program instructions can be executed. This is done by typing in or clicking on the name of an executable file or double-clicking on an icon. (3) In networking, *load* refers to the amount of data (traffic) being carried by the network. (4) In electronics, *load* refers to an element connected across the output terminals of a circuit that draws current from the circuit.

Local Area Network (LAN). A network connected within a close geographical network, such as a building or a campus.

Local Bus. A bus that has the same data path size as the microprocessor and connects directly to the microprocessor and runs at the same speed.

Log In. Also referred to as *login* or *logon.* A process that allows a computer system or network to recognize a user, often by means of a username or password.

Logical Block Addressing (LBA). An addressing mode that numbers each sector.

Lost Clusters. Clusters that get "lost" or detached from a file when a program unexpectedly stops running or isn't shut down properly or when power fluctuations or disk system problems occur.

Low-Level Formatting (LLF). The process that defines the tracks and sectors of the hard drive.

LPX Motherboards. A motherboard with expansion slots inserted into a riser card that protrudes from the motherboard. Consequently, these expansion boards are parallel to the motherboard rather than perpendicular, which permits cases to be smaller.

Macro. A formula language used in word processing, spreadsheets, and other application programs that is a set of instructions a program executes on command. Macros are used to group several keystrokes into one command or to perform complex menu selections. Therefore, they simplify redundant or complex tasks.

Macro Viruses. The newest strain of viruses and currently the most common. Unlike previous viruses, macro viruses are stored in a data document and spread when the infected documents are transferred.

Magneto-Optical Media Drives. Drives that use magnetic patterns to store data and a laser beam to read servo information on the platter that identifies the track.

Mainframe Computer. A very large and expensive computer capable of supporting hundreds or even thousands of users simultaneously.

Master Boot Record (MBR). The first sector of a disk, which contains a small program that reads the partition table, checks which partition is active (marked as bootable), and reads the first sector of the bootable partition.

Master Partition Table. A table listed in the Master Boot Record that lists all of the partitions on the hard drive.

Math Coprocessor. A chip that specializes in floating-point mathematical calculations.

Mega (M). A prefix indicating a million (1,000,000). In computers, mega indicates 1,024 kilobytes, such as in the megabyte (MB).

Megahertz. 1 million clock cycles per second; used to measure the operating speed of a microprocessor or other PC component.

Memory Addresses. 1) A range of locations of RAM. 2) A range of locations of RAM assigned to be used by a device.

Memory Controller. Device that translates signals between the RAM and microprocessor.

Metropolitan Area Network (MAN). A network designed for a town or city, usually using high-speed connections such as fiber optics.

Micro (μ). A prefix meaning one millionth.

Micro Channel Architecture (MCA). A 32-bit expansion slot introduced with the IBM PS/2. The MCA slot is no longer produced.

Micron. A millionth of a meter.

Microphone. A device used to convert sound into analog electrical signals.

Microprocessor. The primary integrated chip of the computer considered the brain of the computer because all of the instructions it performs are mathematical calculations and logical comparisons. It is sometimes referred to as the central processing unit (CPU).

Microsoft DOS (MS-DOS). The first operating system used in the IBM PC. It is a command-driven, single-tasking operating system. DOS stands for disk operating system.

MIDI. Musical instrument digital interface.

Milli (m). A prefix meaning one thousandth.

Minicomputer. A midsize computer that is between a personal computer and a mainframe computer in capacity. In general, it supports 4 to about 200 users simultaneously.

MIPS. Millions of instructions per second.

MMX Technology. MMX stands for multimedia extension and consists of 57 instructions that improve the performance of multimedia tasks.

Modem. Short for modulator/demodulator. This device enables transmission of data through telephone lines.

Modem AT Commands. A set of commands used by most modems.

Modified Frequency Modulation (MFM). Encoding method used on older disk drives.

Monitor. A device similar to a television. The monitor is the computer's main output device. It is also called a *display* or *video*.

Monochrome. A term describing a display or printer that displays two colors, one for the background and one for the foreground.

Monochrome Display Adapter (MDA). A monochrome video card used in the IBM PC and XT that could display 25 rows of 80 characters (80 × 25 characters).

Motherboard. The primary circuit board, known as the system board, which is expandable using expansion cards (daughter boards). The microprocessor is inserted into the motherboard.

Motion Pictures Expert Group (MPEG). A movie standard that can compress frames up to a 200:1 ratio at high quality levels because it only stores the incremental changes. Unfortunately, because it omits full information for every frame, it does not allow for easy editing.

Mouse. A pointing device that that can move the cursor back and forth on the screen (assuming the software supports pointing devices). These devices are easy to use and can improve productivity over a keyboard alone.

Multibank DRAM (MDRAM). A type of video RAM that breaks its memory into multiple 32 KB banks that can be accessed independently. This allows interleaving of the RAM.

Multipartite Virus. A virus that has the characteristics of both boot sector viruses and file viruses.

Multitasking. The ability to perform more than one task or application at the same time.

Musical Instrument Digital Interface (MIDI). An interface and protocol for connecting musical instruments to a PC and storing musical instrument data.

Nano (n). A prefix that means one-billionth.

National Television System Committee (NTSC). The color television signal standard used in the United States and Japan.

NetBEUI (NetBios Enhanced User Interface). An enhanced version of the NetBIOS protocol used by network operations. Although it does not require much software, it is not routable.

Network. Two or more computers connected together to share resources.

Network Interface Card (NIC). An expansion card that allows a computer to connect directly to a network.

Network Operating System (NOS). An operating system that includes special functions for connecting computers and devices into a local-area network (LAN), for managing the resources and services of the network, and for providing network security to multiple users.

NLX motherboard. A motherboard similar to the LPX motherboard but with several improvements. It supports larger memory modules and newer microprocessors and provides better access to motherboard components.

Noise. Radio frequency interference caused by telephones, motors, fluorescent lights, and radio transmitters that can introduce computer errors.

Nonimpact printers. Instead of striking the paper, nonimpact printers use other methods of printing. Ink-jet printers, laser printers, and thermal printers are all nonimpact printers.

Noninterlaced Monitor. A screen that redraws in one sweep. A noninterlace monitor is better than an interlaced monitor.

Nonmaskable interrupt (NMI). An interrupt that cannot be masked or switched off in the normal operation of the system through software. It is normally used to notify the microprocessor about parity errors.

Norton SI. A measurement system used to measure the performance of a PC relative to the original IBM PC.

NTFS. A new file system for Windows NT that supports long filenames and provides enhanced security.

Null Modem Cable. Sometimes known as a *crossover cable*. A cable used to connect two DTE devices together, such as two computers.

Object Linking and Embedding (OLE). An enhanced version of DDE that allows the user to create objects with one application and then link or embed them into another application. Embedded objects keep their original format and links to the application that created them.

OEM Service Release 2 (OSR2). An updated version of the retail version of Windows 95.

Oersted. A unit for measuring magnetic strength.

Ohmmeter. A device that measures resistance.

Open. A break in a conductor that prevents current from flowing.

Open Architecture. A hardware or software architecture, design, or specification that is public.

Open System Interconnection (OSI) Reference Model. A model used to categorize network technology.

OpenGL. A 3D graphics language designed to improve performance on hardware that supports the OpenGL standard.

Operating System (OS). The most important software in the computer. It coordinates the actions of the hardware, the software, and the user so that they can work as one.

Operating System/2 (OS/2). A graphical operating system begun by IBM and Microsoft to replace MS-DOS.

Optical Character Recognition (OCR). Software that converts the image of text to actual text.

Outline Fonts. Vector fonts that define the outlines of each character geometrically.

Overclocking. The process of running the microprocessor or bus speed at a clock speed faster than what the microprocessor or bus was designed for.

Ozone Filter. A filter used to absorb ozone gas, which causes various health problems.

Page Description Language. A programming language used by printers that describes the whole page being printed by using draw and position commands and mathematical formulas.

Page Fault. An error that occurs when the PC needs to access information that is stored in virtual memory or a program requests data that is not currently in RAM or virtual memory.

Pages. A fixed amount of data.

Paper Transport Assembly. A component that moves the paper through a laser printer.

Parallel Loop-Back Plug. A device used to test the parallel port by looping the parallel port's output back into the parallel port.

Parallel Port. A female, 2-row, 25-pin D connector that communicates with up to 8 bits at a time. Today's parallel port is used primarily for printers but can also be used for a wide array of external devices, such as external hard drives, tape drives, removable disk drives, scanners, and network cards.

Parallel Recording. A method used for recording data on tapes by spreading the data throughout the different tracks.

Parity. A form of error control that uses an extra bit to check the accuracy of the data bits.

Partition Table. An area of the hard drive that contains information on how the disk is organized.

Partitioning. The process of dividing a physical drive (hard drive) into one or more logical volumes called *partitions*. Each partition functions as if it were a separate hard disk.

Passive Matrix Display. A type of LCD display used in notebook computers. Passive matrix displays are not as bright as active matrix displays.

Passive Termination. The prevention by electrical resistors acting as voltage dividers of signals from reflecting or echoing when they reach the end of a chain. The resistors help ensure that the chain has the correct impedance load.

Path. (1) The location of a file. (2) A listing of directories at the command prompt used to look for files executed at the prompt.

PC Card. A small, flat expansion card typically used in notebook computers.

PC Slot. (1) The 8-bit slot (sometimes referred to as an 8-bit ISA slot) used in the IBM PC. (2) The slot used in notebook computers (formerly known as the PCMCIA slot).

Peer-to-Peer Network. A network that has no dedicated server. The computers on the network both provide network services and request network services.

Pentium II. A sixth-generation microprocessor that includes MMX technology and L2 RAM cache.

Pentium Microprocessor. A fifth-generation microprocessor that has two pipelines and an enhanced math coprocessor.

Pentium Pro Microprocessor. A Pentium microprocessor that includes L2 RAM cache.

Peripheral Component Interconnect (PCI) Local Bus. A 32-bit or 64-bit local bus developed by Intel to eventually replace older bus designs.

Peripherals. Any external devices attached to a computer. Examples include printers, external disk drives, monitors, keyboards, mice, and external modems.

Personal Computers. Computers that are meant to be used by one person.

Phase Alternate Line (PAL). The color television signal standard used in many parts of Europe.

Photosensitive Drum. A drum that is sensitive to light used in laser printers.

Physical Address. An address indicating a specific storage area in RAM.

Picture Element. *See* Pixel.

Pipeline. A term referring to how a microprocessor executes instructions. Each segment of the pipeline can execute its operation concurrently with the other segments.

Pipelined Burst Cache. A type of RAM cache that uses a register to hold the next piece of data to be read. Therefore, while reading one piece of data, the RAM cache is already accessing the next piece of data.

Pipelining. The process that allows the microprocessor or other components to start working on a new instruction before the current one has been completed.

Piracy. *See* Software Piracy.

Pixel. Short for picture element. The dots used in a display to generate text, lines, and pictures.

Platter. A round, rotating, magnetic plate on a hard drive that holds data.

Plug-and-Play (PnP). Describes a device that upon insertion into the computer is automatically configured and for which the appropriate drivers are automatically loaded.

Plug-In. Software added to a web browser so that it can play audio files and view movies or other multimedia files.

Pointing Device. A device such as a mouse or trackball that can move the cursor back and forth on the screen (assuming the software supports pointing devices). These devices are easy to use and can improve productivity over using a keyboard alone.

Point-to-Point Protocol (PPP). A protocol used to connect to a TCP/IP network such as the Internet using a modem.

Polling. A method by which the BIOS polls or checks to see if a device is ready to accept another character.

Polymorphic Virus. A virus that mutates or changes its code so that it cannot be as easily detected.

Portable Computers. Fully functional computers (laptops, notebooks, and subnotebooks) that can be carried about.

Ports. 1) Plug sockets that enable an external device. 2) An address or range of addresses that identify a device.

POST card. An expansion card used to diagnose computer problems by displaying a numeric code.

PostScript. A common page description language developed by Adobe.

Power (P). The rate of energy consumption or the amount of energy used in a certain length of time. In electronics, it is expressed in watts.

Power Good Signal. A signal sent to the computer from the power supply. When the signal is not being sent, the system is experiencing a short or overload, which causes the switching power supply to go into idle mode.

Power Supply. A device that converts AC into clean DC power.

Preemptive Multitasking. A form of multitasking that allows the operating system to assign time slices to tasks and applications. Tasks and applications with a higher priority get a larger time slice.

Print Manager. A program that manages the print queue or print spooler (a holding area for print jobs sent to the printer).

Print Queue. A holding area for print jobs sent to the printer. Also known as *print spooler.*

Print Spooler. A holding area for print jobs sent to the printer. Also known as a *print queue.*

Printed Circuit Boards. A flat board made of glass-epoxy in which thin metal traces are embedded to connect the different electronic components.

Printer. A common output device used with computers that produces images of text and graphics on paper. Some printers can also produce color images.

Printer Control Language (PCL). A common page description language developed by Hewlett-Packard.

Printer Controller Circuitry. The large circuit board in laser printers that converts signals from the computer into signals understood by the different components of the printer.

Processor Input/Output (PIO) Mode. The data transfer method used on most IDE drives, which use the microprocessor to handle data transfers.

Program Information File (PIF). A file that contains information about a DOS program running in Windows.

Program Manager. A core component of the graphical user interface in Windows 3.XX. It usually fills most if not all of the desktop and contains the group windows and icons.

Programmer. A person who creates software by specifying the instructions that the computer will follow in a programming language such as BASIC, C++, Visual Basic, or Java.

Prompt. Characters on the screen typically showing the current directory and prompting the user to type in a command.

Proprietary System. A hardware or software architecture, design, or specification that is privately owned and controlled by a company and whose specifications have not been divulged so that other companies cannot duplicate the product.

Protected Mode. A type of memory utilization available on 286 machines or later that recognizes extended memory and that protects programs from each other.

Protocol. A set of rules or standards designed to enable computers to connect with one another, and peripheral devices to exchange information with as little error as possible.

PS/2 Mouse. A mouse that doesn't use a serial port.

Quarter-Inch Tape Cartridge (QIC). A type of tape that measures one-quarter of an inch.

Quartz Crystal. A crystal made of piezoelectric material, which vibrates in the presence of electricity. The frequency is controlled by varying the size and shape of the piezoelectric material.

QuickTime. A movie standard developed by Apple Computer. QuickTime files have a MOV filename extension.

QWERTY Layout. The most common keyboard layout used in keyboards and typewriters.

Radio Frequency Interference (RFI). Electromagnetic signals that may interfere with other electronic devices.

RAM. *See* Random Access Memory.

RAM Cache. Ultrafast RAM used as a buffer between the microprocessor and the slower RAM.

RAM Drive. A simulated hard disk drive consisting of RAM.

RAM Shadowing. A process to speed up the computer by copying ROM instructions to the faster RAM.

RAMDAC. Short for RAM digital-analog converter. A chip located on the video card that translates the digital information into the analog information used by the monitor.

Random Access Memory. Integrated chips that are used for short-term memory. RAM holds instructions and data that the microprocessor accesses directly. When the computer is shut off, the contents of the RAM are lost.

Raster Fonts. Fonts made up of bitmap pictures in dots of different sizes for specific video display resolutions.

Read-Only Memory. An integrated chip that contains instructions and data that the microprocessor accesses directly. It is sometimes referred to as the "instincts" of the computer. Unlike RAM, ROM instructions are permanent and cannot be changed or erased by normal means.

Read/Write Head. Component within drives that reads and writes data to and from a platter.

Real Audio. A popular audio file format that supports streaming.

Real Mode. A Windows 3.XX operating mode used on XT computers to run old Windows applications written before Windows 3.0. It only recognizes the first 1 MB of RAM and is only available in Windows 3.0.

Real Video. A popular video file format that supports streaming.

Real-Time Clock. The PC component that keeps track of the time and date.

Ream. 500 sheets of paper.

Recordable CD. Also known as CD-WORM (write once read many) and CD-WO (write once). As the write-once name implies, the disks can be recorded only once and can't be changed after that.

Rectification. The process that turns AC current into DC.

Reduced Instruction Set Computer (RISC). A type of microprocessor that uses relatively small instructions, all of which are the same size.

Redundant Arrays of Inexpensive Disks (RAID). The combination of two or more drives to establish a fault tolerance system, to protect against physical hard drive failure, and to increase hard drive performance.

Refresh Rate. The number of times the screen is redrawn in a second. It is measured in hertz (Hz).

Refresh Routine. The routine that takes control of the data and address buses from the microprocessor and recharges all of the storage cells in the RAM.

Register. An internal storage area that acts as the microprocessor's short-term memory and work area.

Registry. A central information database for Windows 95 and 98 and Windows NT organized into a tree-structured, hierarchical database.

Regulated Power Supplies. A power supply whose output voltages are independent of line and load variations.

Reserve Memory. RAM between 640 KB and 1 MB reserved for hardware.

Reset Button. A pushbutton located in the front of the computer used to reboot the computer when the computer "freezes up" and a soft boot (Ctr-Alt-Del) does not work.

Resistance. Opposition to current flow, measured in ohms (Ω).

Resolution. The number of pixels (picture elements) that can be displayed on the screen at one time. Usually expressed as the number of dots going across and down the screen.

Resolution Enhancement Technology (RET). A method developed by Hewlett-Packard that produces smaller dots to fill some of the gaps between two normal-size dots so that a line or curve will be smoother.

Ribbon cable. A long, flat, gray cable.

Rich Text Format. A standard for formatting documents consisting of ASCII characters with special commands for such formatting information as fonts and margins.

RISC86 Instruction. CISC instructions rebuilt out of smaller and faster RISC instructions.

ROM BIOS Shadowing. The process of copying the contents of the ROM BIOS chips found on expansion cards into the RAM. System performance is increased by accessing the instructions in the faster RAM.

ROM Shadowing. A method where the contents of a slower ROM chip are copied into RAM. Since the information is accessed from the RAM, the PC has increased performance.

Root Directory. The starting point of any disk structure. It is considered the top of the tree structure.

Router. A router connects two local area networks (similar or dissimilar) and is considered an intelligent device because it can determine the best path to a destination computer or network.

Run Length Limited (RLL). Encoding method used on newer disk drives.

Sag. A very short drop in power lasting only a few milliseconds.

Scanner. A device that can scan or digitize images on paper (much like a copy machine does) and convert them to data that the computer can use. The data can then be stored in a file, displayed on the screen, added to documents, or manipulated.

Screen Saver. Software that is used to prevent burn-in of a screen. Today, screen savers also provide entertainment.

SCSI. Short for small computer system interface. A fast interface that can connect up to seven or more devices, including hard drives, CD-ROM drives, tape drives, and scanners.

SDRAM. Short for synchronous dynamic RAM. It is currently the fastest form of RAM and is synchronized to the external clock used on the motherboard.

Search Engine. An information search system for the Internet.

Sectors. 512 byte units, which make up a track.

Seek Time. The average time it takes the read/write heads to move to the requested track. Usually the time it takes the read/write heads to move one-third of the way across the platter. It is measured in milliseconds (ms).

Semiconductor. A material that is neither a good conductor of electricity nor a good insulator.

Serial Line Internet Protocol (SLIP). A protocol used to connect to a TCP/IP network such as the Internet using a modem.

Serial Loopback Plug. A device used to test serial ports that takes the output signal back into the serial port.

Serial Port Interface. A general-purpose interface that can be used for mice, external modems, and other devices. It is a two-row male D port with either 9 or 25 pins.

Serpentine Recording. A method used to record data on tapes, similar to parallel recording. Unlike parallel recording, serpentine recording writes the data onto one track and when the end of the track is reached, moves to the next track to write to the second track.

Server. A computer that is a dedicated service provider found on networks.

Shadow Mask. A fine metal mesh with openings that line up with the pixels and used to aim and focus the electron beams of the CRT monitor.

Short. A circuit with no or an abnormally low resistance path between two points, resulting in excessive current flow.

Simple Mail Transfer Protocol (SMTP). A protocol used in e-mail systems.

Simplex. (1) A form of communication in which data can travel in only one direction. (2) A term describing a printer that can only print on one side.

Single In-line Memory Module (SIMM). A type of RAM in the form of a small circuit board consisting of several soldered DIP chips. To connect to the motherboard, the SIMM has a row of tin or gold metal plates (contacts) along the bottom of the module.

Single In-line Pin Package (SIPP). A type of RAM in the form of a small circuit board that has several DIPs soldered onto it. The circuit board uses a single row of pins which are inserted into the motherboard.

Small-Outline DIMM (SODIMM). A form of RAM that is narrower and thinner than the full-size DIMMs and usually found in notebook computers. A small-outline DIMM is like a 72-pin SIMM in a reduced-size package.

Software. A series of instructions that are loaded into the computer's memory. Software is created by programmers.

Software Diagnostic Package. A software package that can report resources used by devices (I/O addresses, IRQs, DMAs, and memory addresses), perform hardware diagnostics, and troubleshoot and optimize software.

Software Piracy. The illegal copying, distribution, or installing of software (a theft of intellectual property).

Sound. Vibrations of compressed air. As sound starts out, it travels in all directions away from the source. When the sound reaches the human ear, it causes the eardrum to vibrate allowing the sound to be heard.

Sound Card. A device that adds music, speech, and sound effects to the PC.

Spare Sectoring. The process by which a drive has extra sectors set aside to replace sectors that are found to be unreliable.

Spike. Sometimes known as a *transient,* a quick overvoltage, which can damage the computer.

Spindle. The component found in disk drives around which the platter rotates.

Spreadsheet. A software package that works with tables of numbers and/or financial models.

SRAM. Short for static RAM. It consists of four transistors and two resistors that act as an electronic switch. SRAM is faster than DRAM chips and does not require refreshing. SRAM chips are typically used for RAM cache.

ST-506 Interface. An interface used by the hard drives in the IBM XT and early PCs.

Standard Mode. A Windows 3.XX operating mode normally used on 286 computers. It allows multiple Windows programs to run at the same time and provides direct access to the extended memory.

Standard. A definition or format approved by a recognized standards organization or accepted as a de facto standard by the industry.

Standing Power Supply (SPS). Device that uses a battery to power the computer during power fluctuations.

Standoff. A device that prevents the motherboard from shorting against the computer case.

Stealth Virus. A virus that tries to hide itself by monitoring and intercepting a system call.

Stepper Motors. Electrical motors that move from one position to another in steps.

Stripe Set. Similar to a volume set except the data is written evenly across all physical disks. Since all of the disks are being read from and written to concurrently, stripe sets provide much faster access.

Subdirectory. A directory below another directory. Every directory except the root directory is a subdirectory.

Super Computer. The fastest type of computer used for specialized applications that require immense amounts of mathematical calculations.

Surge. An overvoltage, which can stretch into milliseconds and can damage the computer.

Surge Protector. A device designed to prevent most short-duration, high-intensity spikes and surges from reaching a PC.

Swap File. A virtual memory file used in Windows 3.XX and Windows 95.

Switch. (1) An electrical or electronic device that opens and closes a current path. (2) A command line option to determine how the command will be executed or displayed.

Switching Power Supply. A power supply that switches on or off at very fast speeds. When the system needs more power, the switch stays on longer; when the system needs less power, the switch stays off longer. Small and efficient, the switching power supply has a unique overload characteristic that goes into idle mode when it detects a short or overload.

Symmetric Multiprocessing (SMP). A computer consisting of two or more microprocessors that share the same memory.

Synchronous Burst Cache. A type of RAM cache that accesses a memory area but then uses its own internal clock, which is in sync with the RAM, to count up and access sequential addresses. In addition, synchronous burst cache uses pipelining to access the next RAM address while transferring the current data.

Synchronous Graphics RAM (SGRAM). A form of video RAM that increases the speed at which memory transfers take place. In addition, it incorporates specific performance-enhancing features, specifically the acceleration features built into the video card.

System Board. *See* Motherboard.

System Clock. The PC component that acts as the heartbeat of the computer.

System ROM BIOS. The primary ROM BIOS chip found on the motherboard. It controls the boot-up procedures, performs a series of diagnostic tests known as the power-on self-test (POST) during boot-up, and generates hardware error codes (audio and video) if a problem is found during boot-up. In addition, the chip provides the most basic commands to control hardware and the compatibility between the operating system and the hardware. It contains the CMOS setup program.

System Routine. Many small individual programs found in ROM chips. They are low-level programs that directly manipulate the PC hardware.

System Software. Software (operating systems and compilers) that directs the entire system.

Tape Drive. A backup device that reads and stores data on tapes.

Tapes. A long polyester substrate coated with a layer of magnetic material that is used to store data. Unlike a floppy disk, a tape stores and retrieves data sequentially. Tapes are usually used to back up data.

TCP/IP (Transmission Control Protocol/Internet Protocol). An industrial suite of protocols on which the Internet is based.

Telnet. A common protocol (part of the TCP/IP suite) that allows the user to remotely log in to other machines on the Internet and work on the remote system or try software available there.

Tera (T). A prefix indicating a trillion (1,000,000,000,000). In computers, a tera indicates 1,024 gigabytes, such as in a terabyte (TB).

Termination. A method of using resistors to prevent signals from bouncing back when they reach the end of a wire.

Thermal printers. Inexpensive printers that press heated pins to a special heat-sensitive paper to form characters.

Thread. A part of a program that can execute independently of other parts.

Thunking. A process by which a 16-bit instruction is paired with the next instruction, making it 32-bit during execution.

Token Ring. A network protocol that uses some form of twisted pair cable connected to a multiaccess unit (MAU). Although the token ring network uses a star topology, the signals follow a ring or loop. Computers on a token ring only communicate when they possess a token that is passed from one computer to another.

Toner. An extremely fine powder made of plastic resin bonded to iron particles. The iron particles react to electrical charges and the plastic resin has a low melting temperature.

Toner Cartridge. A replaceable cartridge used in laser printers to hold toner.

Topology. The arrangement or physical layout of network computers and cables.

Touch Screen. A transparent panel that covers a monitor screen. Instead of using a pointing device to select options, they can be selected by touching the screen.

Tower Case. A case that stands erect.

Trackball. A pointing device that can move the cursor back and forth on the screen (assuming the software supports pointing devices). Unlike the mouse, the trackball protrudes from the top of its container. These devices are easy to use and can improve productivity over using a keyboard alone.

Trackpoint. A pointing device in the form of a small rubber cap found on keyboards that appears above the B key between the G and H keys. To move the mouse pointer, the rubber cap is connected to pressure transducers. The pressure transducers measure the amount of force being applied and the direction of the force. The harder it is pressed, the faster the pointer moves.

Tracks. Concentric circles that divide a platter.

Tractor Feed. A device with sprockets (placed on a wheel or belt) that are placed in the holes of fanfold paper. As the sprockets rotate around a wheel, the paper is pushed or pulled past the print head.

Transformer. A device with two or more coil windings used to step up or step down voltage.

Transistor. A device that can amplify signals or to be used as an electronic on/off switch.

Transistor-Transistor Logic (TTL) Chips. Standard IC chips based on two transistors, which run on $+5$ V dc power.

Trojan Horse Virus. A virus that appears to be legitimate software, such as a game or useful utility.

True Color. A video system that displays 16 million colors. The 16 million colors use 24 bits to define the colors of the pixel.

TrueType Fonts. An outline font commonly used in Windows 3.1X, Windows 95 and 98, and Windows NT. TrueType fonts can be scaled to any size and rotated.

TSR (Terminate and Stay Resident). A small program loaded into the RAM (typically with DOS) to control some hardware device or to provide some useful function. Unlike other programs, a TSR gives control back to the operating system while still functioning.

TWAIN. Short for technology without an interesting name. A standard that allows software to control scanners.

Twisted Pair. A cable made of two insulated strands of copper wire twisted around each other. The twist in the cable helps reduce crosstalk.

Underwriters Laboratories Inc. (UL). An independent, nonprofit organization that acts as a safety engineering consultant and certification body. UL's strict standards and solid reputation have led companies to pay UL to detect flaws and defects in their products before they hit the market.

Uninterruptible Power Supply (UPS). Device that protects the PC by using a battery to filter out power fluctuations.

Universal Asynchronous Receiver/Transmitter (UART). A single IC chip that acts as translator between the serial port and the system bus (parallel connection). In serial ports, it is the component that processes, transmits, and receives data.

Universal Serial Bus (USB). An external port that allows up to 127 external PC peripherals to be connected in series (daisy chain). The USB connector will accept any USB peripheral, including mice, keyboards, printers, modems, and external disk drives. The standard four-pin connector will connect seven devices directly, and these seven devices can be increased to 127 by connecting external hubs (each hub accommodates another seven devices) in a chain.

Upper Memory. Memory between 640 KB and 1 MB that is not used by hardware. It is used to load device drivers and TSRs to free conventional RAM.

Upper Memory Blocks (UMB). A division of upper memory.

UseNet Newsgroup. A set of bulletin boards on the Internet for conducting conversations on many different subjects, including computers.

User. The computer operator who is telling the computer what to do.

User-friendly. A term indicating that computer equipment or software is easy to understand and operate.

Vector Fonts. Fonts that are rendered using a mathematical model. Each character is defined as a set of lines drawn between points. Vector fonts can be scaled to any size but cannot be rotated.

Vector Graphics. A picture made up of lines and curves to define a graphic image.

Very Large-Scale Integration (VLSI). A type of IC chip that has between 100,000 and 1,000,000 components per chip.

VESA Local Bus (VL Bus). A form of local bus slot created by the Video Electronics Standards Association (VESA) originally to improve video performance.

VFAT. An enhanced version of the FAT structure that allows Windows 95 and Windows NT to support long filenames (up to 255 characters).

Video Accelerator. Video cards that include processors to help process video data.

Video Capture Card. An expansion card that can capture a still image from a television, camcorder, or VCR.

Video Card. The component that sends the visual output from the computer to the monitor. It tells the monitor which pixels to light up, what color the pixel should be, and what intensity. The video card is an expansion card or is built into the motherboard.

Video Chipset. The logic circuit that includes the video coprocessor that controls the video card. The chipset used is a major factor in determining overall video performance.

Video Electronics Standards Association (VESA). An organization formed by major computer, monitor, and video manufacturers. It is responsible for developing a Super VGA (SVGA) standard and created the VESA local bus.

Video Graphics Array (VGA). A video system considered the first modern monitor and from which all of today's monitors are derived. It supports a resolution of 640 × 480 at 16 colors or a resolution of 320 × 200 at 256 colors (chosen from a palette of 262,144 colors). It was also the first analog monitor used on the PC.

Video Memory. Memory found on video cards used to hold information to be displayed on the monitor.

Video RAM. *See* VRAM.

Video ROM BIOS. ROM BIOS chip located on the video card (or on the motherboard, if the video card is built into the motherboard) that contains instructions to control video systems.

Virtual 8086 mode. The operating mode of the microprocessor that divides the RAM into several pretend 8086 machines, each consisting of 1 MB of RAM. The microprocessor then switches rapidly between the different virtual (pretend) machines so that it appears that all of the machines are working at the same time (multitasking).

Virtual Machine (VM). A self-contained operating environment that behaves as if it were a separate computer.

Virtual Memory. Hard drive space pretending to be RAM.

Virus. A program, many with destructive tendencies, designed to replicate and spread, generally without the knowledge or permission of the user.

Virus Hoax. A letter or e-mail message warning you about a virus that does not exist.

Voice Coil Actuators. Head actuators that use electromagnetic force to move.

Voltage. The force that moves the electrons, measured in volts (V). Voltage is generated by the power supply or battery.

Voltmeter. A device that measures voltage.

Volume. A portion of a disk signified by a single drive letter. It can be a floppy disk, a partition, or several hard drives linked together (spanning).

Volume Boot Sector (VBS). the first sector of any partition or the first sector of a floppy disk. It is created by high-level formatting.

Volume Set. The combining of 2 through 32 areas of unformatted free space (FAT or NTFS) on one or more physical drives to create a larger logical drive.

VRAM. Short for video RAM. It is RAM typically used in video cards that is dual ported (read and written to at the same time).

Wait-State. A CPU clock cycle during which the microprocessor lies idle so that slower RAM and other components can catch up with it and function properly. The fastest setting would be no wait states.

Warm Boot. A type of booting that doesn't require the computer to perform all of the hardware and memory checks associated with a cold boot. A warm boot is usually done by pressing the Ctrl+Alt+Del keys.

Waveform Audio (WAV). A common sound file.

Weight. The total weight of a ream (500 sheets) of 17″ × 22.5″ paper.

Wide Area Network (WAN). A network that uses long-range telecommunication links to connect the network computers over long distances and that often consists of two or more smaller LANs. Typically, the LANs are connected through public networks, such as the telephone system.

Wild Card Characters. An asterisk (*) or question mark (?) used to indicate several files at the same time.

Window. A rectangular display area in which a particular program or utility can function.

Windows 3.XX. An operating environment that provides a GUI for DOS.

Windows 95. A popular graphical operating system that replaced DOS and Windows 3.XX.

Windows 98. An upgraded version of the Windows 95 operating system.

Windows NT. The most advanced version of the Windows operating system. It is a 32-bit operating system that supports preemptive multitasking.

Windows RAM (WRAM). A type of video RAM used by high-end video cards. It uses a dual-color block write to perform very fast pattern and text fills and can perform fast buffer-to-buffer transfers for video and double-buffered 3D animation.

WINSOCK. A DLL file that is responsible for providing Windows applications with the ability to communicate over a TCP/IP network.

Word Processor. Software that allows a document to be created much like it would be on a typewriter. Word processing software is the most common application software.

Workgroup. A group of computers connected together in which the computers keep track of their own user and group account information and do not share this information with other computers. A workgroup is a good network configuration for a small group of computers.

Workstation. A computer acting as a client and attached to a network. It communicates with the operating system by means of client software called *shells* or *requesters*.

World Wide Web (WWW). A subset of the Internet, the web is a huge collection of interlinked documents, called web pages, written in hypertext markup language (HTML).

WRAM. *See* Windows RAM.

Write Once Read Many (WORM). *See* Recordable CD.

WYSIWYG. An acronym for What You See Is What You Get.

Xon/Xoff. Software handshaking.

XT Computer. A computer with an 8088 or 8086 microprocessor. XT computers typically use DIP switches to configure the computer rather than a CMOS setup program.

Zero Insertion Force (ZIF) Sockets. A chip socket that allows a chip to be inserted and removed without special tools. It usually uses a handle to lock or unlock a chip in place.

Zip Drive. A drive that uses 100 MB removable disks.

Zoned Recordings. A scheme that divides the platter into zones. The outer zones have more sectors per track than the inner zones.

Zoomed Video (ZV). A direct connection used in notebook computers to the system's VGA controller.

Index